MEDIA AND POLITICS IN LATIN AMERICA

COMMUNICATION AND HUMAN VALUES

Series editors

Robert A. White, Editor, Centre for the Study of Communication and
  Culture, London, UK
Michael Traber, Associate Editor, World Association for Christian
  Communication, London, UK

International editorial advisory board

Binod C. Agrawal, Development and Educational Communication, Space
  Applications Centre, Ahmedabad, India
Luis Ramiro Beltrán, Unesco, Quito, Ecuador
James W. Carey, University of Illinois, USA
Marlene Cuthbert, University of Windsor, Canada
William F. Fore, Communication Commission, National Council of
  Churches of Christ, New York, USA
George Gerbner, University of Pennsylvania, USA
James D. Halloran, University of Leicester, UK
Cees Hamelink, Institute of Social Studies, The Hague, The Netherlands
Neville D. Jayaweera, World Association for Christian Communication,
  London, UK
Emile G. McAnany, University of Texas, USA
Walter J. Ong, St Louis University, USA
Breda Pavlic, Culture and Communication Sector, Unesco, Paris
Miquel de Moragas Spa, Autonomous University of Barcelona, Spain

Also in this series

Mass Media Religion: The Social Sources
of the Electronic Church
Stewart M. Hoover

The Mass Media and Village Life: An Indian Study
Paul Hartmann with B.R. Patil and Anita Dighe

World Families Watch Television
edited by James Lull

MEDIA AND POLITICS IN LATIN AMERICA

The Struggle for Democracy

edited by Elizabeth Fox

SAGE Publications

London · Newbury Park · Beverly Hills · New Delhi

First published 1988

SAGE Publications Ltd
28 Banner Street
London EC1Y 8QE

SAGE Publications Inc
2111 West Hillcrest Drive
Newbury Park, California 91320

SAGE Publications Inc
275 South Beverly Drive
Beverly Hills, California 90212

SAGE Publications India Pvt Ltd
32, M-Block Market
Greater Kailash - I
New Delhi 110 048

British Library Cataloguing in Publication data

Media and politics in Latin America: the
    struggle for democracy.—(Communication
    and human values).
    1. Latin America. Politics. Influence of
    mass media
    I. Fox, Elizabeth   II. Series
    320.98

    ISBN 0–8039–8164–3
    ISBN 0–8039–8165–1 Pbk

Library of Congress catalog card number 88–061485

Typeset by Photoprint, Torquay, Devon
Printed in Great Britain by J.W. Arrowsmith Ltd, Bristol

Contents

Preface

Latin America is one of the few regions of the world where privately controlled, commercially operated mass media predominate over any other form of media organization. Some of the Latin American private media empires compete successfully in the world market with US and European communications industries. Alongside the phenomenal growth of its private media, Latin America has experienced heated debates and controversial attempts to enact national communication policies to change media content and ownership. Latin American media have been the target of harsh censorship and virulent government repression. Finally, the region has originated much of the theory and action behind the New International Information Order and many of the most creative and varied grass-roots and 'alternative' media.

Media and Politics in Latin America: The Struggle for Democracy focuses on the fifty or so years of the Latin American media. The different chapters examine the many political and economic actors, the changing alliances and agreements and the impassioned debates and policies that forged the modern media.

In a region as complex and varied as Latin America, some limits were necessary to the scope of this book. For example, although the media in Cuba and Nicaragua are touched upon in the introductory overview chapter, an adequate study of the radical transformations of media institutions in these countries would be the subject of another book. Likewise, the new participatory uses of media in popular movements – increasingly widespread in Latin America – are not given the attention they deserve.

Media and Politics in Latin America focuses largely on broadcasting, although some chapters deal with the press as well as with films and video technologies. The focus on broadcasting is because it was more problematic. Historically, there has been less public debate concerning alternative models of newspaper ownership, management and financing than there has been concerning broadcasting. The liberal tradition of privately owned newspapers goes back much further in Latin American history than the relatively newer radio and television technologies.

Radio and television burst on the scene in Latin America in the twentieth century in a wide variety of forms and institutional arrangements. Their growth and penetration were rapid and far-reaching at a time of enormous economic and political transformations. In less than a generation, the mass media changed most people's way of receiving information and entertainment and of learning about the world. Sixty years after the first radio broadcast, by the early 1980s, the region had almost 120 million radios, one for every three inhabitants, and close to 50 million television sets, one for every seven inhabitants.

Radio and television have had far greater geographical, social and cultural penetration in Latin America than the press. Although the press is important in urban, middle-class sectors, the transistor radio is present in virtually every home.

The book begins with an historical overview of the growth of the mass media in Latin America. The following thirteen chapters are in-depth analyses covering roughly four crucial periods of media development and policy: (1) early commercialization and government intervention; (2) the media reform movements; (3) the dictatorships; and (4) the transition to democracy. No chapter is a complete history of media development or policy even in one country. Each is a vignette in considerable detail revealing a different aspect of the broader process of Latin American media politics. By and large, most of the chapters focus on the period between the late 1960s, when the movements towards media reform and national communication policies began, and the present.

Chapters 2 and 3 focus on the establishment of a commercial and transnational structure of the media in Argentina and Chile, showing how implicit *laissez-faire* policies and types of government intervention took shape. Chapters 4, 5 and 6 deal with media reform and efforts to introduce national communication policies in Peru, Mexico, and Colombia. Chapter 7 analyses the opposition role of the Church in alternative communication in El Salvador. Chapters 8 through 14 deal with media policies under dictatorships and in the transition to democracy in Chile, Argentina, Uruguay, Brazil and Bolivia.

Underlying all the chapters is a deeper question: given the realities of the political process, the conflicting interests of the actors, the weaknesses of the state and the political parties and the growth of the media conglomerates, are goals of social equality and participation possible in the Latin American media? The final chapter, which presents a synthetic analysis of the political process of media policy-making, returns to this basic question.

The contributors to this book are specialists in mass media history and policy. Their emphasis and bias, not surprisingly, are geared towards the examination of the history and development of communication policies in Latin America. This bias, however, should not be taken as a lack of recognition of the importance of other factors like overall technological change, the creative artistic processes and the wider social and economic context for the development of the media. Indeed, in the final analysis, these factors create the context in which media policies are conceptualized and implemented.

I began to put this book together a couple of years ago with the idea of evaluating the efforts towards democratization and redemocratization of communication taking place in Latin America. I asked my Latin American colleagues to contribute chapters focusing on what they considered the most significant aspects of the relationship between the mass media and the political changes that were occurring in their countries. This is the origin of the chapters by Patricia Anzola on Colombia, María de la Luz Hurtado on Chile, Heriberto Muraro and Oscar Landi on Argentina, Cesar Guimarães, Roberto Amaral and Ingrid Sarti on Brazil and Roque Faraone on Uruguay.

I asked other authors for contributions based on their ongoing research on key moments of communication policy-making in their countries. This was the case of the chapter by Carlos Catalán on Chile, Juan Gargúrevich on Peru, Rubén Sergio Caletti Kaplan on Mexico, Ricardo Sol Arriaza on El Salvador and Raúl Rivadeneira Prada on Bolivia.

When I began to work with the contributions, I felt the need for a chapter on the early development and precocious commercialization of the media in Latin America. Here I used the example of Argentina (Chapter 2).

My own Chapter 1 tries to fill in some of the gaps and provide a general historical review of the politics of mass media policy in the region. In Chapter 15 I bring together many of the conclusions from the different contributions and attempt to synthesize what I see as the four stages of mass media policy-making in Latin America.

In many ways, the idea behind the book was to collect and analyse some of the findings of what I considered a fresh approach in the literature and research on the mass media in Latin America. This approach, growing out of the experiences of a generation of Latin American researchers, is more nuanced and less polarized and ideological than the studies of the previous decade. It is based on a finer historical and political understanding of the phenomena of the mass media and their role in society. Given the towering problems involved in the construction of democracy in Latin America, I felt that a wider dissemination of these viewpoints might help foster dialogue and negotiation among the different national and transnational actors involved in mass media policy.

I would like to thank many people: the contributors for their confidence and patience; Bob White at the Centre for the Study of Communication and Culture in London for believing the book was possible and encouraging me to go ahead; Oscar Landi at the Centro de Estudios de Estado y Sociedad (CEDES) in Argentina for much invaluable input to the first drafts of my chapters; Rafael Roncagliolo at the Instituto para América Latina (IPAL) for providing me a steady and critical link with Latin America; Luis Ramiro Beltrán for my interest and work in mass media policy in the first place; and my husband Stanley Meisler for returning my love of language.

Elizabeth Fox
Paris

Acknowledgements

Longer versions of Chapters 9, 10 and 11 respectively have previously appeared in Spanish and Portuguese as:

Muraro, Heriberto, 'La comunicación masiva durante la dictadura militar y la transición democrática en la Argentina 1976–1986', pp. 13–57, in Oscar Landi (ed.), *Medios, Transformación Cultural y Política*. Buenos Aires: Legasa, 1986.

Guimarães, Cesar and Amaral Vieira, R.A., 'A televisão brasileira: um caso de conversão rápida à nova ordem', *Comunicação & Política*, 6–1 (1986).

Landi, Oscar, 'Medios, procesos culturales y sistema político', pp. 89–133, in Oscar Landi (ed.), *Medios, Transformación Cultural y Politica*. Buenos Aires: Legasa, 1986.

Glossary of Spanish Terms

Confederación Campesina de Perú   Peruvian Peasants' Confederation

Confederación Nacional Agraria   National Agrarian Confederation, Peru

Confederación de Trabajadores de la Revolución Peruana   Confederation of Workers of the Peruvian Revolution

Contras   counter-revolutionaries in Nicaragua

Corporación Financiera de Desarrollo   government development bank in Peru

Instituto Nacional de Cultura   National Institute of Culture

El Mago   'The Wizard', Carlos Gardel, the world's greatest tango singer

Pasquines   satirical, often political, newspapers

Plaza de Mayo   square in front of the presidential palace in Buenos Aires where the mothers of the disappeared demonstrated

Radios Mineras   radio stations owned by the Bolivian tin miners

Sindicato de Educadores de la Revolución Peruana   Teachers' Union of the Peruvian Revolution

Sindicato Unico de Trabajadores de la Educación del Peru   Sole Union of Peruvian Education Workers

Unidad Popular   Popular Unity, a coalition of leftist parties supporting Salvador Allende

Abbreviations

ALASEI Agencia Latinoamericana de Servicios Especiales de Información (Latin American feature news service)
ANEP National Association of Private Enterprise, El Salvador
APRA Alianza Popular Revolucionaria Americana (American Popular Revolutionary Alliance, Peru)
ASIN Acción de Sistemas de Información Nacional (association of national government information systems of various Latin American countries)
ATC Argentina Televisión Color (Argentine government television channel)
CIESPAL Centro Internacional de Estudios Superiores de Comunicación para América Latina (International Centré of Advanced Studies in Communication for Latin America)
COLCULTURA Colombian National Board of Culture
COMFER Federal Committee of Broadcasting, Argentina
CORA Corporación de la reforma agraria
EMBRATEL Brazilian public telecommunications company
ENRAD-PERU Peruvian national broadcasting company
ENTEL-PERU Peruvian public telecommunications company
ERP Revolutionary People's Army, El Salvador
ESI-PERU Peruvian government news agency
FARN Armed Forces of National Resistance, El Salvador
FARO Eastern Region Farmers' Front, El Salvador
FELLAS Federación Cristiana de Campesinos
ILET Instituto de Estudios Transnacionales (Institute of Transnational Studies)
INDAP Instituto de desarrollo agropecuario
INRAVISION Colombian public broadcasting institution
IPAL Instituto para América Latina (Institute for Latin America)
LEMEX company distributing Mexican films in Bolivia
OAS Organization of American States
PMDB Movimento Democrático Brasileiro
PUBLI-PERU Peruvian government advertising agency
RCTV Radio Caracas Televisión
SECOM Secretary of Communications, Argentina

SINADI   Sistema Nacional de Información (National Information System of Peru)
SINAMOS   Sistema Nacional de Apoyo a la Movilización Social (National System of Support to Social Movements, Peru)
SIP   Secretary of Public Information, Argentina
SODRE   Servicio Oficial de Difusión Radio Electrica, Uruguay
TELECOM   Colombian Public Telecommunications Institute
TELEVISA   Televisión Via Satélite (Mexican private communications company)
UNO   National Union of the Opposition, El Salvador
UTC   Unión de Trabajadores del Campo

Foreword

Luis Ramiro Beltrán

This book is about a dream. A dream of justice. The dream of democratizing communication in Latin America. An ideal, that is to say, of achieving egalitarian opportunities for truly free and balanced self-expression and cultural exchange.

Dreaming about social justice, especially in terms of a fair distribution of political and economic power, is an old and ingrained habit of many Latin Americans. It has relentlessly marked its presence, often underlined with bloodshed, from the rebellion of Tupac Amaru in colonial days, through Bolívar's Independence War, to the guerrilla war of Che Guevara in republican times.

Communication has always been a part of that dream. And dreaming of justice has also proved dangerous in this field. The egalitarian aspiration had already ignited the clandestine newspapers, the libertarian *pasquines* that defied Spanish and Portuguese oppression. And, from the outset of republican life to the present day, Latin Americans have often had to battle against censorship, seizure or destruction of media institutions by ruthless rulers. Imprisonment, exile and even assassination are frequently the price for defending freedom of information and the right to dissent in this part of the world.

However, the state is not the only enemy of democratic freedom in modern Latin America. Conservative and exploitative interests, native and from outside the region, have built a private and commercial mass communication system that, on several counts, falls short of being democratic. The realization of it, the perception of undemocratic elements in communication beyond government repression of non-compliant journalism, appears to have started only after the Second World War. Moving from realization to remedial action has proved a hard and slow undertaking fraught with frustrations. This book is a well-documented account of much of that process.

Ably put together by a US researcher who is deeply familiar with communications in Latin America, Elizabeth Fox, the book depicts the evolution of mass media from the days of the Mexican Revolution to the present. However, since it does not attempt to be all-inclusive, it concentrates on key developments recorded from the 1960s to the 1980s and gives preferential attention to the southernmost countries. The assessments contributed by fourteen highly qualified authors, including the editor herself, are conducted mainly in terms of public policies for the behaviour of private media, since these form the overwhelming majority in this region. The chapters refer only to cases where changes in the communication situation were sought within an overall environment of reform, mild or relatively radical but legal. Therefore, the book does not include chapters on the few countries that have undergone generalized and usually violent revolution; that is, Mexico (1910), Bolivia (1952), Cuba (1959) and Nicaragua (1979). The book emphasizes standard mass media against the 'mini-media' type of non-commercial alternative.

The book correctly notes that the quest for reforming communications took many years to develop into a significant and well-known movement. It was only in the mid-1960s that a few analysts – more lone snipers than company commanders – started articulating criticism of the powerful private media and the powerless public media. In the former case, they denounced tendencies towards oligopolistic and interlocking media ownership, biased distribution of access to messages for privileged urban minorities and the predominance of trivial, alienating and violent content; also the fostering of consumerism, racism and conservatism. In the latter, they found far more inclination to propagandistic concerns than to serving educational and cultural ends. And in both cases they identified indifference to development goals and tasks, except in terms of publicizing material works. The conclusion of those critics – scholars, politicians, media practitioners – was that the oligarchic élites subduing and exploiting the masses had also become dominant in the sphere of communication and culture, thus enhancing their power to favour the status quo.

Changing such a situation was attempted in only a very few cases during the course of the 1960s. The book refers to an effort by Chile's Christian Democrats to augment the state's communication capabilities while regulating private media activity. It also refers to the unusual instance of a military establishment conducting radical social transformation in favour of the majorities. This was the case of the Peruvian regime in 1968, which boosted and integrated state communication institutions and approved legislation imposing strong regulation on private mass media so as to modify their traditional orientations, which were deemed noxious. Meanwhile, commercial television spread triumphantly across the region, while the transistor allowed thousands of peasants to gain access to the world through portable radio receivers.

Another reform-minded movement gained power through elections in Chile at the outset of the 1970s: the Socialists of Salvador Allende. They too expressed a will for media reform but were unable to introduce changes as far-reaching as those being attempted in Peru. In fact, in 1974 the Peruvian military regime expropriated the Lima daily newspapers to try a new format of mass media ownership: social property instead of private or public. Each daily was to be delivered to a large social organization like peasant leagues or workers' unions. This innovative exercise did not work because the regime hesitated to surrender effective control of the press to groups it did not control. In the long run, the dailies had to be returned to their original owners. Also in 1974 a democratically elected government in Venezuela attempted to build a national council of culture and to bolster public radio and television to assist development efforts unsupported by commercial media. As in the cases of Chile and Peru, mercantile and conservative interests – national and foreign – reacted so harshly against the initiative that they soon managed to neutralize it.

In keeping with the book's central approach, Elizabeth Fox underlines the importance of a 1976 gathering in Costa Rica. This was the UNESCO-convened First Intergovernmental Conference on National Communication Policies which took place in spite of the virulent opposition of the international associations of media owners. The emphasis is important since this meeting marked the first time that a general proposal for communications reform reached the level of international consideration by high government officers. The action-oriented recommendations approved and the subsequent Declaration were a peak of the reform movement. Likewise, the conference crystallized and validated Latin American thinking about democratizing communication.

What, however, happened after the meeting? Very little, answers Fox, giving 'bad timing' as one explanation. In fact, by 1976, except for Mexico, Costa Rica, Venezuela and Colombia, the Latin American countries had once again been subdued by undemocratic government regimes. Thus, to discuss and apply pluralistic and consensual national communication policies was hardly viable. While the quest for the ideal was to move on to Africa and Asia, Latin Americans, pioneers in the quest, had to put it aside.

Sadly, the democratic environments in Latin America were unable to host transformation. Not even Venezuela, the outstanding originator and leader of many communication policy concerns, was able to implement any of the San José recommendations. Mexico became the only country to attempt major changes after the San José meeting.

Backed by two presidents of the republic, Luis Echeverría and José López Portillo, between 1970 and 1982, an overall reformulation of the communications rights of citizens was proposed which would democratize the entire communication system. In addition, reformers sought to make effective legal norms compelling commercial television to do educational and cultural programming. As in the case of Venezuela, the project was suddenly aborted under pressure from private interests, opposition and government politicians.

Will the dream of many never come true? Evidently and unsurprisingly, the story of communication reform through democratizing policies is so far one of failure in Latin America. And, with only a couple of relative exceptions, the chapters in this book testify convincingly to this deplorable fact. The explanations provided – in addition to government repression or private-enterprise opposition – are numerous. For instance:

First, recently restored democracies cannot afford to apply media-reforming policies. Burdened by a colossal foreign debt and haunted by excruciating demands resulting from the disastrous state of the economy, they have no resources to invest in such changes. On the other hand, they are so fragile that they cannot risk the anger of the private sector, to which some of them have even transferred state media. And obviously, if politicians are to get elected, they cannot be at odds with the media. In a few cases, some media empires have grown so huge and mighty, like Globo in Brazil or Televisa in Mexico, that governments – democratic or not – cannot survive in power without their sustained support. This has a price.

Secondly, many very important changes have taken place over the last ten years or so in terms of technologies, markets and audiences. This evolution has made the international communication industry so complex that to regulate it legally at national levels has become a most difficult undertaking. Even domestic control of cable, videotapes and direct foreign transmission aided by low-cost dish antennas has become hard and costly for governments.

Thirdly, international message-production and distribution patterns are changing rapidly and in many directions, some of them quite unexpected. These days, some Latin American television companies earn much of their income abroad and have become sizeable exporters of materials to Spanish-speaking territories in the United States. Inter-country television traffic is also on the increase within the region. US and European firms are sponsoring more co-production ventures which may blur the lines distinguishing foreign from native content. National production by independent video and TV groups is growing in spite of the economic crisis. Simplified and inexpensive technologies are granting measures of access and participation to popular-level audiences to a degree perhaps unthought of until recently. Some large television companies are beginning to find it profitable and convenient to mount educational and cultural productions which in the past they deemed the business of the state. Their flexibility to adapt to changing circumstances cannot be ignored. In view of such an emerging panorama, some reforms look impossible, while others may become unnecessary.

These thought-provoking observations have multiple implications. They cannot be discussed within the limits of this Foreword but should prove challenging for many an attentive reader of this book, especially in Latin America. Fox and her co-writers perform with skill a useful service to many in bringing such considerations to the foreground of public discussion. Few of the developments noted in this book are well known in a region still deficient in literature distribution and documentation exchange. Thus, politicians, planners, social scientists and communication specialists will undoubtedly profit from reading this volume.

However, acknowledging the evolution observed may not necessarily lead every reader to share all the conclusions extracted by the editor. Although many would easily adhere to the notion that radical communication reform in Latin America has become increasingly unviable and is probably undesirable too, Elizabeth Fox surely recalls Bolívar's lesson that there is nothing more practical than a good Utopia.

1
Media Policies in Latin America: an Overview

Elizabeth Fox

In July 1976 representatives of twenty Latin American and Caribbean governments met at a UNESCO-sponsored meeting in San José, Costa Rica, to discuss national communication policies. It was not an easy event to organize. The meeting had been in preparation since 1970 when the XVI General Conference of UNESCO authorized its director-general to help member states formulate policies for the mass media. National controversy over what was seen as potential government interference in broadcasting and the press had already made the governments of Ecuador and Venezuela withdraw offers to host the conference (Beltrán, 1982).

Latin America was the first Third World region as a whole to identify certain problems in its national media systems, propose national communications policies and in some cases carry out major structural reforms of broadcasting and the press. Reform-minded governments, media critics and intellectuals took part in the discussions and reforms. They criticized the huge import of news, recordings and television programmes, the lack of regional news exchange, the almost totally private control of the mass media and the absence of public services and channels of popular participation and access. They cited among other problems censorship of news and entertainment and a shortage of trained professionals, technological know-how and regional production facilities (UNESCO, 1976a).

Governments, planners, media critics and intellectuals in different countries aspired to remedy some of these problems with national communication policies. Policies would orient public investment in communication infrastructure and the adoption of new technologies, co-ordinate national communications and information systems with economic and social development goals and guide the training of new professionals. Policies would also ensure national content and strengthen national sovereignty particularly with regard to culture and trans-border information flows (UNESCO, 1976b).

Third World awareness about the media in general and especially about inequalities in the international flow of news and entertainment was on the rise in the late 1960s and early 1970s. This awareness permeated the statements and action programmes of the Non-Aligned Movement and fuelled the proposals for a New World Information and Communication Order.

In Asia and Africa radio and television were largely government-owned and operated. Leaders in these regions were mainly concerned with changes in the international flow of foreign news and entertainment. There was little discussion of internal reform of the media in these regions. Almost all Latin American broadcasting, however, as well as newspapers, was privately controlled and commercially operated. The participants in the San José conference were concerned with the internal reform of national media as well as with changes in the international flow of news and entertainment. Many saw the two problems as closely related.

Latin American broadcasters and newspaper owners, arguing freedom of expression, bitterly resisted what they considered the movement towards new government regulation. Their presence in San José gave the meeting a climate of potential confrontation. As a result, delicate diplomatic manoeuvring was needed to reach a consensus on many of the issues discussed. Before, during and after, the meeting received extensive and mainly negative publicity in the Latin American and world press.

The San José participants made thirty recommendations to UNESCO and to its member states. These recommendations proposed a series of measures to bring about a more balanced international exchange of news and entertainment. The measures would guarantee access and participation in the media to all members of society, protect individual rights and freedoms of communication and expression and assure the media's application to national and regional development goals. The meeting called on governments to enact explicit national communication policies and establish National Communication Policy Councils as advisory bodies. The councils would be composed of representatives of different groups and organizations including the private sector (UNESCO, 1976a).

In the years that followed, Latin American governments put into effect very few of the San José recommendations. Some exceptions were the eventual establishment of a regional Latin American Feature News Service (ALASEI) and an intergovernmental information service (ASIN). Practically none of the changes in the Latin American mass media after 1976, however, were the result of the San José recommendations or of the national communication policies they envisaged.

In part, what some analysts (Capriles, 1980; Motta, 1982) have called the failure of the San José meeting was the result of bad timing. By the time the intergovernmental conference on communication policies was held, the struggles to introduce policies to take into consideration the needs of the poor and disadvantaged sectors and the creative cultural traditions of the region were almost over. By 1976, the media in most Latin American countries had returned to the usual improvisation, the usual commercial exploitation and often abuse and the usual government neglect (except for censorship).

For the most part, governments and planners, out of political necessity or after losing power, had abandoned their search for a national communication policy. They no longer strove to attain a 'deliberately selected set of principles and standards to govern the functioning and use of the communications and information media in the service of objectives democratically chosen by national communities in accordance with criteria specific to each country' (UNESCO, 1976b: 7).

Chile, for example, experienced a period of intense public debate and transformation of its national broadcasting system beginning in the early 1960s. By 1976 the country was ruled by an authoritarian regime that had ended all debate and placed radio, television, newspapers and magazines under firm control (Munizaga, 1982).

Peruvian television, radio and press had undergone radical changes after 1968 including government expropriation of the Lima daily newspapers and of controlling stock in television channels and radio stations. By 1975 the government was on the road to dismantling state and collective ownership and returning to a *laissez-faire*, private commercial system (Gargúrevich, 1987).

Venezuela too had witnessed a period of heated public debate and criticism of its private and state broadcasting systems in the early 1970s co-ordinated by media policy experts with the support of the President. By 1976, faced with virulent opposition from private owners and advertisers, reformers had almost completely given up their struggles to implement national communication policies (Capriles, 1976).

The debate on communication policies and reform that began in Mexico in the late 1960s continued through the 1970s. It too, however, was dropped by the government in the early 1980s after failing to enact most major policy initiatives.

In many ways the San José meeting, coming at the end of a turbulent period of debate and reform, was a symbolic, ritual event summing up objectives and ideals long in formation in Latin America. Its call for an explicit, coherent and enforceable policy, for participation and access to the media and for cultural sovereignty and communication development was carried to other regions of the world. Long after it had been discarded by most Latin American governments, the debate on national communication policies and a New International Information Order continued to occupy the attention of international forums like UNESCO, the International Telecommunications Union and the United Nations.

The text and recommendations of San José, however, were not just historical documents. They held within them the seeds of future debates on the mass media. Beneath the central concern for national communication policies appeared new concerns like the rise of alternative communication, the lack of basic freedoms of expression under the military dictatorships, the enormous impact of new communication technologies and the vast transformations of the Latin American media empires.

More than anything, however, the San José recommendations (UNESCO, 1976a) were the product of the Latin American debates and reforms. They conveyed a critical sense that the mass media were by and large commercial enterprises run by small groups for personal gain that generally ignored larger development goals and social services. The recommendations made a strong case for a democratically co-ordinated and pluralistic effort by governments to remedy this situation. They also showed a constant concern with the government's obligation to guarantee freedom of expression and the right to communicate for all members of society.

By 1976, however, when the meeting finally took place, Brazil, Uruguay, Chile, Argentina, Bolivia, Peru, Ecuador, Paraguay and most of Central America were ruled by the military. Only Colombia, Venezuela, Costa Rica and Mexico had democratically elected governments. The rise of the authoritarian regimes raised grave doubts among even the most enthusiastic supporters of national communication policies. The military take-overs destroyed the democratic and representative institutions of policy-making and most channels of access and participation in government. Any new government responsibility in broadcasting or the press and any new public-service functions of the media became suspect.

The present chapter analyses the years leading up to and following the 1976 conference on communication policies. They describe the manoeuvring for power and control of the Latin American media that occurred after the establishment of the early commercial structure of the media.

The section on development, reform and revolution examines the roles of the different actors in the political processes within which the quest for reform gradually evolved. It then looks at the debates and implementation of the proposed policies. The section on dictatorship and democracy identifies some of the structural obstacles that accounted for the failures of reform and democratic communication policy formulation in Latin America. The conclusions point to some possible longer-term accomplishments of democratic media that seem to be emerging from within the broader socio-political and economic processes in the region.

The general historical framework of policy evolution provided by this chapter serves as an introduction to the thirteen chapters that follow. Roughly arranged in chronological order, these chapters each analyse the politics of mass media policies in a different country during certain key periods.

Taken as a whole, the volume gives a general idea of the main forces involved in the formulation of mass media policy in Latin America. It begins to grasp some of the different goals, strategies and achievements of these forces in relation to the democratization and development of the region.

The search for political, economic and cultural autonomy

Beginnings

The Latin American mass media were never perfect models of private ownership or public service, national expression or transnational culture. They were the product of many different interests: governments, political movements, artists, national and foreign capital, and publics. The character and roles of these interests shifted and changed from country to country and over the course of the last fifty years. As recent studies (Martin-Barbero, 1987: 95) have shown, the Latin American mass media and mass culture were never the mere popularization of a high culture but formed slowly with the gradual growth of a mass market, a central government, a national culture and an emerging complicity between traditional cultures and mass imagination.

Today almost all Latin American mass media, with the exception of Cuba and Nicaragua, are privately controlled and strikingly homogeneous commercial operations. In the 1920s and 1930s, however, governments, individuals and political movements in Mexico, Peru, Uruguay and other countries actively promoted different models of public-service and state-owned broadcasting structures. Many of these were non-commercial.

The Mexican Revolution (1910–17) ushered in a government committed to the private sector as well as to deep social reform. The revolution attempted to integrate new sectors of society – Indians, the rural poor – and forgotten regions of the country outside the capital city into the mainstream culture and politics of the country. The revolutionary government used and subsidized different forms of music, theatre, cinema and radio to promote a sense of national identity (Franco, 1985).

Under the Mexican government's principle of a mixed economy, privately owned commercial radio grew side by side with state-owned public-service radio. The Mexican state employed radio first as an instrument of information and propaganda and later as an instrument of culture and education. By the 1940s, however, pressure from the private sector both within and outside the ruling party succeeded in shifting the government away from state intervention in the economy and towards private and often transnational control. This shift affected many sectors of the economy including radio. By 1941 the Mexican government had almost entirely withdrawn from any role in media development and had sold state-owned stations to private investors. With the government's withdrawal from broadcasting, television began in the 1950s as an entirely private venture (Fernández, 1982; Esparza, 1984; García Canclini, 1986).

In some countries the possibility of a public or state-owned non-profit broadcasting system never got further than failed initiatives and political platforms. Peru, like Mexico with a large native Indian population, experienced social ferment and national cultural re-definition and reform in the 1920s and 1930s. The APRA party was born based on the rejection of foreign political, cultural and social models. The Peruvian Socialist Party founded soon after the APRA by José Carlos Mariátegui gave a central role in national development to indigenous cultures. These political movements, however, never achieved control of the government or succeeded in implementing their cultural policies.

Peruvian broadcasting was developed almost entirely by the private sector. Although the government set up the first Peruvian radio station in 1925, it soon went bankrupt and was sold to the Marconi Company. For the next forty or so years, the Peruvian state did not take an active role in national communication and cultural policy or in media development (Gargúrevich, 1987).

The early interest of the Uruguayan government in the introduction of broadcasting formed part of its larger national educational and cultural goals. Uruguay was a prosperous, politically stable country in the 1930s, and the state could afford to finance culture and the arts as well as other public services for its small, urban, middle-class population. In 1929 the Uruguayan government set up a non-commercial public broadcasting service with one publicly financed short-wave and two medium-wave frequencies. In addition to broadcasting the government subsidized the national symphony orchestra, the national ballet and a film club with its own theatre.

The Uruguayan government, however, did not limit the growth of private commercial radio. Economic prosperity and the high educational level of the population in the 1920s and 1930s made it possible for many small commercial radio stations as well as many newspapers to build up audiences attractive to advertisers and finance their operations with commercials. By the mid-1930s there were as many as twenty private radio stations in Montevideo supported solely by advertising.

In countries like Argentina and Chile, however, there was almost no public or government subsidy or ownership during the first decades of media development. By the turn of the century Argentina had one of the most developed systems per capita in Latin America of privately owned newspapers and magazines. This was the result of economic prosperity and the early growth of a literate urban middle class. In 1923 the Ministry of the Navy issued the first five radio licences to private radio stations. Fifteen years later there were forty-two radio stations spanning the country, many of them organized in two private radio networks (Ford and Rivera, 1985; Noguer, 1985).

A private broadcasting sector developed in Chile in the early 1930s. The Chilean government had already undertaken the expansion of the national education system and subsidized the arts and culture. Each national university had its own theatre and ballet company and symphony orchestra subsidized by state funds. The government, however, did not subsidize the nascent commercial radio stations. Nor did it attempt to develop a public or non-profit broadcasting system.

Early Brazilian broadcasting presented a unique model in Latin America. The first Brazilian radio stations, although privately owned, were not commercial. The first station was a cultural and education station set up in 1923 as a club and financed by its members. Other early radio stations took the form of associations or clubs financed by subscriptions. The Brazilian government taxed radio stations as well as the radio audience with taxes on receivers. Most of the first stations were cultural and educational and directed their broadcasts towards an élite audience. Brazilian radio was not allowed to use commercial advertising until after 1932, although it employed different forms of indirect commercial sponsorship (Sampaio, 1984; Federico, 1982).

Establishing the commercial structure of the media: 1930–60
By the mid-1930s commercial radio was well established in most

major Latin American cities. It had become the main vehicle for national musicians, comedians, journalists and entertainers. Radio carried the recordings of Mexican, Argentine and Caribbean artists and the wildly successful Latin American radio soap operas throughout the region.

In many countries, the early public-service goals and government ownership, subsidy and regulation of broadcasting inevitably clashed with powerful national and international forces behind commercial broadcasting. Politically powerful national and foreign industries were interested in the media as advertising vehicles. Latin America's struggle to develop its own industry and achieve economic independence had brought many new industrial workers into the urban markets. Commercial radio fulfilled industry's need for an advertising medium to reach the growing mass markets and provide information and amusement for the new urban work-force. The government-subsidized educational, cultural and, at times, élitist radios were unable to compete with the unregulated expansion of commercial broadcasting and were soon driven out of business or sold to the private sector.

US commercial radio networks and private media were also eager to invest in Latin American broadcasting and develop markets for their products. The Latin American public and state-owned non-commercial media needed government protection and subsidies to survive without advertising and finance national content. Without this protection, foreign capital and content – recordings, magazines, comics – began to pour into Latin America. The US-based Columbian Broadcasting Company set up the Cadena de las Americas, and the National Broadcasting Company operated the Cadena Panamerica, with affiliated radio stations in most countries of the region. In some countries private US companies purchased and operated their own commercial radio networks to advertise their products (Beltrán and Fox, 1980).

The 'good neighbour' policy, the consolidation of US investments and security-related ties with Latin America before and during the Second World War and the development of the Inter-American System eased the flow of private capital and US content into the Latin American media.

Pro-United States control of most Latin American broadcasting and newspapers was ensured by a co-ordinated US effort to gain support of Latin America for the Allied war effort during the Second World War. US companies received tax breaks on their advertising in pro-Allied Latin American media. Over 1,200 newspapers and 200 radio stations received a daily news service through the Office of Coordination of Inter-American Affairs under the direction of Nelson Rockefeller. The service was compiled from the US radio chains and news agencies. By the end of the war, over 75 percent of the world news that reached Latin America came from Washington, where it had been prepared by the State Department and the Office of Inter-American Affairs (Epstein, 1976).

As radio's economic strength and ability to reach larger and larger audiences grew, Latin American governments began to look at it in a new light. Some governments struggling to remain in power against growing popular demands became more concerned with radio's potential political impact than with its frequently neglected public-service cultural and educational roles.

Brazilian radio was subjected to government control and censorship early in its development. As a result of the events of the revolution of 1932, the federal government imposed censorship on all radio stations, allowing these to report only on the movements and advances of the pro-government Legalistas forces. From the first days of the Estado Novo until 1945 the Department of Press and Propaganda of the Vargas administration controlled and employed radio as a powerful political instrument of propaganda and public opinion (Federico, 1982).

Colombian broadcasting also experienced harsh government intervention in the 1940s. Private investors had by and large developed radio commercially, successfully resisting a brief threat of nationalization in 1936. In 1948 the Conservative government defeated a popular uprising sparked by the assassination of a Liberal political leader. Many of the radio stations had supported the uprising. After putting down the movement and establishing martial law, the government revoked all radio licences and modified the broadcasting laws strictly to limit news and political reporting. The new legislation, however, did not affect the commercial operations of the private stations, and they continued to prosper (Pareja, 1984).

Commercial expansion of private broadcasting in Peru and Venezuela was given a free hand in the 1940s and 1950s. Although there was political censorship, the media in these countries had no real public-service function or state protection, regulation or subsidy. The same was true for Mexico, where by the 1940s commercial broadcasting and the government were by and large in the same hands or shared the same economic and political interests.

The populist regimes of the 1940s and 1950s, like those of Perón in Argentina, Vargas in Brazil and Rojas Pinilla in Colombia, many times took an active interest in the growing mass media. Newspapers and radios frequently played an important role in their nationalist rhetoric and political strategies with the masses. These regimes supported the development of national film and publishing industries, imposed tariffs on imported series and music and limited foreign investment in broadcasting. They also exiled artists and journalists, censored films, radio, plays, books and magazines and, in the case of Perón, eventually nationalized many newspapers and radio chains by forcing their owners to sell to the government and to Peronist sympathizers at reduced prices.

In many Latin American countries government censorship of early broadcasting, magazines and newspapers limited their creativity and distorted their development as forms of national expression in ways that are impossible to measure. Censorship also established a bad precedent for future reforms and national communication policies. Other than the brief attempts at public-service broadcasting in various countries in the 1920s and 1930s, censorship provided the sole precedent of a public or state presence in the media. The Latin American private media carried out few public services like education or health information, and governments had rarely intervened in the media to impose these services. On the other hand, governments had engaged in media censorship and manipulation for political ends.

Television

When television arrived in the mid-1950s, privately owned, commercially operated broadcasting was the norm in Latin America. A politically docile commercial system satisfied the demands of the governments and the ruling parties and enabled national and foreign industries to reach mass markets to advertise their products.

In 1950 Mexico became the sixth country in the world to introduce television. During the presidency of Miguel Alemán Valdés (1946–52) the Mexican government rejected the idea of a publicly owned television system modelled on European broadcasting. The new private channels were owned by Mexican commercial radio stations affiliated with US radio and television networks NBC and CBS. Alemán himself developed personal ties with the private television industry.

Mexican television quickly became as dependent on US capital, content and advertising as was the rest of the Mexican economy. The government did not assign an educational television channel to the Ministry of Education until 1958. Ten years later, in 1968, the government made its first serious attempt to regulate television and introduce public-service functions (Fernández, 1982; de Noriega and Leach, 1979).

Brazilian television also began in 1950 with a small commercial station owned by Diarios e Emissoras, owners of newspapers and commercial radio stations. Television was virtually a monopoly of Diarios e Emissoras Associados until 1962. During the presidency of Juscelino Kubitschek (1956–61), Brazilian television benefited from the country's rapid economic growth and industrialization. In 1962 TV Globo, a newcomer in Brazilian television, signed an agreement with Time Inc. The injection of capital, technology and professional skills that came with TV Globo's agreement with Time spelled the end of Diarios Associados.

In 1964 the Brazilian military that toppled the civilian government gave special emphasis to the expansion of telecommunications for reasons of national security. Under the military, TV Globo, a private commercial company closely aligned with the political and economic interests of the military regime, grew to be the largest Brazilian television network and the fourth largest television network in the world (Amorim, 1982; Sarti, 1986; Lasagni and Richeri, 1986).

In Colombia, Argentina, Venezuela and Peru television was first set up by the government during military or authoritarian regimes. Colombian television continued under a mixed public–private regime, and Argentine television operated intermittently under private licences. The television systems in all four countries, however, soon developed the same characteristics of the politically conservative, private, commercial television systems of Mexico and Brazil. They all had large US investments, limited government regulation and mainly commercial goals.

Venezuelan state-owned television, for example, came on the air in 1952 during the dictatorship of Marcos Pérez Jimenez. Channel 4, a commercial station, began broadcasting six months later. Soon after, Channel 2 Radio Caracas Televisión founded by an American was on the air. Both were private commercial channels operating with licences of dubious legality. From 1953 on, the sorely underfinanced government channel existed on cheap imported and local cultural and educational programming, while commercial television, centralized in Caracas, rapidly expanded to cover the wealthy urban markets. By 1960 the three US television networks each had large investment in one of the three Venezuelan commercial channels (Pasquali, 1980).

The first Peruvian television broadcast in 1958 was the result of an agreement between the Peruvian Ministry of Education and UNESCO to set up an educational channel that could also be used for entertainment. Soon after the first broadcast, however, the government distributed licences for commercial TV channels to five private radio chains.

By 1960, in spite of attempts in many countries to set up small public-service educational or cultural television channels, commercial television modelled after television in the United States was firmly established in Latin America. Most channels had significant investments from the US media, the logical continuation of the US networks' earlier investments in Latin American commercial radio. ABC had a South American and a Central American television network, and both NBC and CBS – together with Time/Life and former Cuban television owner Goar Mestre – had investments in all the major commercial television systems in all the countries of Latin America (Beltrán and Fox, 1980).

Development, reform and revolution

In the late 1950s and early 1960s Latin American countries experienced severe economic problems, mounting social pressures and class struggles and growing revolutionary movements. Many governments, as well as the United States, perceived the success of the Cuban Revolution in 1959 as a threat to their own stability and to that of the region. Development planners in the United States and Latin America proposed state-led social and economic development as one possible solution to the growing political and economic instability of the region. Under the Alliance for Progress and justified by an expanded public role in Latin American development efforts, the United States government, until then the main promoter of US private investment in Latin America, demonstrated a new willingness to grant Latin American governments large amounts of direct economic aid (Mitchell, 1974: 178).

The rhetoric of the Alliance stressed the goals of social reform, but in fact this served to co-ordinate US economic, security and investment policies in Latin America. The Alliance was successful in several areas of social and economic reform like land reform and progressive taxation. Later, however, abandonment of social reform in favour of military and ideological security and economic development was clearly shown in the US policy towards Brazil and the landing of US troops in the Dominican Republic in 1965 (Mitchell, 1974: 186–97).

In some ways, however, the work of the Alliance for Progress through the public sector set the stage for the media reform movements in Latin America. The Alliance legitimized state investment and planning in the communications sector, until then almost exclusively controlled by private capital. Some of the public-service goals of the 1920s and 1930s like the use of broadcasting in education and culture resurfaced in the programmes of the

Alliance. This time the emphasis was on modern communication technologies.

National and international development programmes did not question the already established commercial broadcasters, newspapers and magazines. Instead these programmes poured enormous sums of money into communication equipment and projects to use radio, television and other media in health, education and rural development. These included educational radio and television systems, satellites and national agricultural extension programmes.

The United States involvement in development programmes using communication media had begun earlier when Nelson Rockefeller directed a wartime programme to improve food production in Latin America. After the war, the Organization of American States (OAS) launched massive efforts for research and training in agricultural extension methods. The agricultural diffusion studies and much of the development communication research in Latin America – initiated by the study carried out in Colombia in 1962 by Paul Deutschmann and Orlando Fals Borda – were conducted within this frame of reference (Beltrán, 1974).

Internal shifts in political and economic power during the 1960s and the emergence of new social groups and political actors, however, began to affect the until then fairly harmonious relationship between the commercial mass media and the political system. In some countries political parties, in others the military and in still others intellectuals began to criticize the traditional commercial and politically conservative role of the Latin American mass media. Development communication programmes and the relatively small, scattered public services did not satisfy the reformers' demands for a more representative public presence in the mass media and their application to larger social and cultural goals.

The work of Latin American scholars, some of whom had received their training in OAS development communication programmes, contributed to the reform movements. Studies by Bolivian researcher Luis Ramiro Beltrán and Paraguayan researcher Juan Díaz Bordenave argued that the uncontrolled growth of commercial media created problems for national development and political democracy. (Beltrán later worked closely with UNESCO in the design and organization of the meeting of Latin American governments on national communication policies in Costa Rica.)

Other researchers like Venezuelan professor Antonio Pasquali studied the harmful influence of mass culture in general on Latin American cultures and societies. Later, Pasquali worked with his government to plan institutional structures that would permit more diversified and representative national media. Brazilian educator

Paulo Freire's struggle to give a voice to the region's poor and oppressed, overwhelmed and suffocated by the mass culture of the commercial mass media, contributed to revolutionary educational and cultural programmes throughout Latin America.

The research of Armand Mattelart in the late 1960s and early 1970s on the transnational control of Latin American media, the class interests in their control and management and the role of popular movements supplied a theoretical framework and empirical evidence for debate and reform in Chile and elsewhere. And many more researchers throughout the region turned their attention to the critical analysis of the content, structure and function of the mass media in their societies.

The 'dependency' paradigm emphasizing the structural relationships of imperialist domination within which all other inter-American relationships must be located and understood provided a key component of the discussion of media reform. Calls for more national content and attacks on foreign (mainly US) films, TV series, wire services, magazines and comic books as forms of cultural imperialism were sounded in many countries throughout Latin America.

By the 1970s there was ample evidence to support the accusations of US domination of the Latin American media. Although direct US investment in television channels had decreased, US films and TV series accounted for about half of the content of Latin American television screens and movie theatres. Advertising by US companies prepared by US agencies led the lists of the top advertisers in most countries. Various studies had shown that the US wire services, the AP and the UPI, controlled between 60 percent and 83 percent of the international news, including news about other Latin American countries, of almost all national newspapers in the region (CIESPAL, 1967; Kaplún, 1973; Varis, 1973).

Change in Cuba, Peru and Chile

By this time, new political movements had come into power in Cuba, Peru and Chile respectively through revolution, military take-over and free elections. Their new leaders attempted to alter the distribution of wealth and power, including the media, in their societies. They gave access and participation in the media to their supporters and decreased the power of previous owners. The new regimes accused the private owners and commercial advertisers of ignoring the needs of the majorities and of propagating an alienating mass culture that benefited the economic and political interests of foreign and national élites.

Cuba experienced the earliest and most extreme form of long-lasting political change, reform and state intervention in almost all forms of expression. After the 1959 revolution, Fidel Castro took control of one of Latin America's most highly developed media systems with more television sets per capita than any other Latin American country. The Cuban government radically altered the country's dependent capitalist economy and eliminated private ownership.

Much of the private media's equipment and infrastructure was put at the service of government programmes of health, education and information. The Cuban Film and Art Institute founded in 1959 brought an end to the US domination of film distribution in the country and gave new life to the Cuban film industry. Studios and theatres were nationalized, as were private radio and six private television channels. Television was consolidated into two nation-wide channels on the country's only system. Channel 2 became the news and educational channel, while Channel 6 focused on culture and entertainment. Both became part of the Cuban Institute for Radio and Television (Hamelink, 1983).

The Cuban experience raised fears in the Latin American and US private media that similar processes of government expropriation and control could take place in other countries. These fears grew as ideology, a deteriorating economy and the hostile attitude of the United States pushed Cuba closer to the Soviet Union. Government campaigns in Cuba against most forms of independent cultural expression followed a period of relative cultural autonomy. The Castro regime began to demand ideological purity and attacked artists and intellectuals who supposedly had betrayed the revolution. *Granma*, the most important daily newspaper, practised an authoritarian style of journalism with strict government control of news and access. To some, these policies made Cuba a motivating symbol of the dangers of government control of communications. To others, however, Cuba represented the social and educational benefits of the reform of the private commercial mass media.

Governments in Peru and Chile attempted to set up less centralized and state-directed and more public and participatory national media systems than the classic Marxist-Leninist model of communication and information that developed in Cuba.

After toppling Fernando Belaúnde in October 1968, the Revolutionary Government of the Peruvian Armed Forces announced a new regime that would transform the economic, social and political structure of the country and free Peru from foreign investment and influence. The armed forces passed a new press law and set up a national telecommunication company, a national publishing house, a state-owned advertising agency, a government news agency and a national broadcasting company. The military expropriated controlling stock in the commercial radio and television stations. In 1974 it expropriated the Lima daily press and announced a plan to transfer management and ownership to representatives of different social organizations. The military appointed new directors to run the papers while the transfers could be completed.

The changes in the mass media were carried out in the face of strong opposition from the Peruvian private sector and from international associations of private broadcasters and newspaper owners. The reforms attempted, under the tutelage of the military, to integrate Peru's forgotten rural, mainly indigenous population and urban poor into the national economy and political system and restore their culture. In the case of the press, however, the government failed to build newspapers that either supported the regime's goals or allowed the genuine participation of the different sectors of Peruvian society in their management. In 1975 a slow return to civilian government and to a private commercial media system was signalled by a change in the direction of the military regime.

In Chile, the Christian Democrats were elected to office in 1964. They increased state ownership and subsidy of the mass media as part of their development programmes and longer-term political objectives of integrating new social sectors into the political system. The Christian Democrats' concept of integration, like that of the Peruvian military, emanated from the top and was carried out by means of different schemes of popular promotion like INDAP, CORA and Promoción Popular.

In part, the Christian Democrat administration hoped to achieve political support from the large mass of new voters – the number of voters increased by approximately 400 percent between 1958 and 1973 – through its use of communication. The Christian Democrats justified the increased role of the state in the mass media as a way to assure access to the media by all sectors of society, counteract foreign and national commercial abuse and achieve public-service educational and cultural development goals.

The relationship between the government and the mass media in Chile took on radically different characteristics when the left-wing coalition of Salvador Allende was elected to power in 1970. Before coming to power, Allende's Unidad Popular had denounced foreign influence in the national media and called for ending their capitalist monopolistic structure. Once in office, however, Unidad Popular did not immediately offer an alternative model of media ownership or financing. The coalition grouped together different political tendencies and lacked a unified concept of what to do with broadcasting, the press and traditional development communication programmes.

Furthermore, Allende's ability to modify the existing structure of the media was limited by a series of constitutional reforms that guaranteed private ownership of radio, newspapers and magazines. The reforms had been passed by the opposition-controlled Congress and negotiated with the Christian Democrats as a necessary condition in order for Allende to take office.

During the three years of Unidad Popular, the mass media were one of the main political battlegrounds of the different factions of Chilean society. Unidad Popular and its supporters struggled against an opposition press partially financed by the US government (United States Senate, 1975). The leftist coalition government tried unsuccessfully to maintain political control of the state-owned media set up by the Christian Democrats. Allende increased public ownership of publishing, films and recording companies, and under his government authentic grass-roots expression in other forms of communication increased greatly. By the 1973 coup, however, most newspapers, radio stations and television channels were under the control of the right-wing and Christian Democrat opposition.

Mexico and Venezuela

Media reforms proposed by the elected governments in Venezuela and Mexico occupied a great deal of public debate but were never implemented. The authors of the reforms were not new political groups representing radical departures from the previous regimes as was the case in Cuba, Peru or even Chile. In both countries the proposed reforms were practically the first attempt of any government to regulate or impose a public-service role on the mass media.

In the early 1970s the Mexican government undertook a series of political and social reforms that were necessary to accommodate new social and political groups in the system and to preserve the power of the ruling party. In order to carry out these reforms, the ruling party in Mexico found it needed to free itself from its past dependence on the private media and establish its own channels of communication.

The efforts of presidents Luis Echeverría (1970–6 and José López Portillo (1976–82) to make commercial television comply with government programmes and to regulate the new constitutional 'right to communicate' met with strong opposition from both private industry and factions within the ruling party. The opposition of the private sector, the personal links between members of the government and the private media and the basically functional role of the private mass media within the Mexican political system eventually outweighed the government's sentiments and need for reform. Government-owned media, however, were expanded (Fernández, 1982).

In Venezuela, partly in response to criticism from intellectuals and national cultural figures, Carlos Andrés Pérez, elected president in 1974, attempted to introduce a reform of the small publicly owned media. Pérez named a commission to reorganize state expenditures in advertising and reform the public administration of cultural institutions to meet the information, education and entertainment needs of the people. The commission recommended setting up an 'authentic mixed system' of public and private media that would allow wider geographic coverage, more development-oriented messages and greater public participation in the selection and elaboration of programmes. The commission also recommended changing the government's traditional *laissez-faire* policies and indirect subsidy to the private sector through government advertising.

The recommendations of the commission met with sharp opposition from advertisers, private broadcasters and newspaper owners, as well as from rival political parties. All questioned the government's right to place the media under a national cultural policy. The commission's recommendations were never enacted, although some of the reforms proposed under Pérez like regulations on advertising became law under President Luis Herrera Campíns in the early 1980s (Capriles, 1980, 1982).

The debate on media reforms
In spite of the great differences in the political philosophies that motivated them, the reforms and debates in Cuba, Peru, Chile, Venezuela and Mexico shared some common characteristics. All of the reforms were concerned in one way or another with introducing public-service functions in the media, preserving cultural and creative traditions and formulating policies for the large disadvantaged sectors of society. In their own way they were also concerned with devising democratic structures and financial and management arrangements that would be representative, participatory and workable. And none of them, with the exception of Cuba, proposed state or party control of the media as the only alternative to private entrepreneurial control.

These characteristics – concern for cultural autonomy and national content, a belief in the state's responsibility to formulate democratic national cultural and communication policies, a desire to break down traditional private control and increase the representation of wider social groups in the media – formed the framework of the 1976 intergovernmental conference in Costa Rica.

The reforms and debates on national communication policies in Latin America also shared the unanimous uncompromising opposition of private broadcasters, newspaper owners and advertisers. They vehemently opposed any public-service or new government role in the media like those that occurred in Cuba, Chile and Peru and those proposed in Venezuela and Mexico. The private owners and advertisers especially resisted expropriation and any interference in their operations, limitations on their earnings and regulation of their content.

A sharp ideological division resulted from the attempted and real reforms in the Latin American media. Left-wing and reform-minded governments supported a larger public role in broadcasting, although not necessarily in the press, under a mixed system of public and private management. They saw this as the only way to allow the media to fulfil their development potential, ensure democratic participation and national content and protect national culture and interests. Many Latin American and US private media owners, journalists and advertisers, however, considered state or public intervention in the media the beginning of totalitarianism and the end of freedom of expression.

The overthrow of the Somoza dictatorship by the Sandinistas in 1979 and the subsequent changes in the Nicaraguan media further increased the divisive experiences of the Latin American reforms. Although different from those that had occurred in Cuba twenty years earlier, the structural changes in Nicaragua were just as far reaching. While state and private radio continued to exist side by side, television became exclusively state-owned: Channel 6, belonging to President Somoza, became public property in 1979. Channel 2, belonging to private owners close to the Somoza family, was expropriated by the government a year later. The two channels were fused to form the Sandinista Television System. There was no Nicaraguan film industry before the revolution. The new government set up the Nicaraguan Institute of Cinema and greatly increased mass education and the participation of many new groups in other forms of communication (Mattelart, 1986).

La Prensa, founded in 1926, had been the symbol of resistance to the Somoza dictatorship. The assassination of *La Prensa*'s director, Pedro Joaquín Chamorro, by Somoza loyalists provoked the final stage of opposition to the dictatorship. Pedro Joaquín's widow, Violeta Chamorro, was a member of the first Sandinista junta. She later resigned, breaking with the Sandinistas. *La Prensa*, co-edited by Jaime Chamorro, brother of the slain journalist, became the main organ of opposition to the Sandinista government as well as the principal target of government censorship.

The Sandinista government faced internal opposition from political parties, the private media and some religious institutions and the growing hostility and aggression of the US government. It also faced anti-Sandinista broadcasts from Radio Impacto in Costa Rica and the Contras' September 15 radio station in Honduras. In March 1982 a state of emergency was declared citing as justification the state of war. The government initiated strict prior censorship especially in the press, involving closing down *La Prensa* from time to time. This infuriated private media owners throughout the Americas and further fuelled their arguments against any type of government intervention in private broadcasting or the press.

By 1976 most Latin American governments were retreating from their attempted national reforms. Governments continued, however, to take an active part in movements for international media reform through organizations like the Andean Pact, the Third World bloc at the UN, the Movement of Non-Aligned Countries, the MacBride Commission and UNESCO.

Many Latin American leaders joined the demands of African and Asian countries for political, economic and cultural sovereignty and a New International Information Order. Latin American intellectuals and political leaders, some exiled from their countries and working in regional centres like ILET in Mexico, continued to play a major role in the international debates on cultural imperialism and the growing role of the transnational corporations in the worldwide control of information and culture.

Dictatorship and democracy

In many Latin American countries the development programmes and social and economic reforms of the 1960s and 1970s did not achieve political democracy, economic growth and political security at the same time. The social inequalities and structural rigidities of the region seemed to be increasing. Critics from the right questioned the role of elected governments both as a source of economic leadership and planning and as a vehicle of assistance and redistribution of power and wealth. Revolutionary movements and pressure for wider political participation were growing, and the traditional social and political structures seemed incapable of containing them for much longer. To some, the military appeared to offer the only solution.

By the mid-1970s Argentina, Brazil, Chile and Uruguay were under military dictatorships. This new breed of military regimes pretended to obtain economic development by an autocratic state employing technocrats in increasingly close association with the transnational corporations. They ignored the political rights and the social and cultural needs of the majorities.

The authoritarian regimes manipulated formal education and symbols of nationalism and modernization. They used the mass media to control public and private information and communication. Through their control of the media the military regimes hoped to lower the level of political awareness of society and lessen the capacity of individuals to know their rights and responsibilities and exercise them socially and politically (O'Donnell, 1979).

The military placed private television and radio stations under tight political control, censored newspapers and magazines and arrested and killed many journalists. It found the modern media's monolithic organization of power, their sophisticated new technologies and their easy use of symbolism particularly well suited to achieve its goals of propaganda and information control.

At the same time, the new ideology of economic growth under political authoritarianism gave a free hand to the commercial and transnational development of the mass media. The military regimes' large investments in new communication technologies and extensive use of advertising gave a big boost to the commercial development of broadcasting and some newspapers. The level of government advertising increased by as much as 60 percent in the first year following the military coups in Chile and Argentina (Munizaga, 1982; Terrero, 1982).

Alternative media

People and organizations deprived of any access to the military-controlled mass media and often eager to keep alive a cultural and political resistance to the dictatorships began to use other media like community radio and newspapers, local video production and neighbourhood theatre. These experiences came to be known as 'alternative' media because they took the place of or supplanted information, opinion and entertainment functions of the mass media. The alternative media were also a form of expression or protest in a society where having an opinion or expressing an idea was dangerous.

Alternative media were not new to Latin America. Historically the region has harboured thousands of diverse and varied forms of cultural expression. Many used radio, cassette recorders, video cameras and recorders. They were the product of people or groups who were economically, ethnically, politically, geographically and culturally excluded from power. Much of the alternative media existed before the latest wave of dictatorships and some had their roots in the work of Paulo Freire in Brazil and Chile.

Some alternative uses of media, for example the Church-inspired radio schools for popular education operating throughout Latin America and the Radios Mineras of the Bolivian tin miners, had begun as early as 1947. The radio schools were a private initiative that employed radio broadcasts in combination with organized group reception for education and development programmes.

The miners' radio stations were owned by the miners and financed by their contributions. The number of radios mushroomed after the 1952 Bolivian Revolution when the government nationalized the mines, reformed land tenure and allowed universal suffrage. In the 1980 Bolivian military coup the twenty-three miners' stations formed a 'chain of democracy'. Five days after the army had taken over the rest of the country, the miners' stations continued on the air and broadcast against the coup until the military defeated the mining communities and captured their stations (Lozada and Kúncar, 1983).

Other alternative media were inspired and led by the Catholic Church. Vatican II had declared freedom of religious belief without interference from the state, the greater social concern of the Church and a greater involvement of the laity in church worship and work. In 1968 the Latin American Bishops' Conference in Medellín had declared the Church's 'preferential option for the poor' and provided many of the components of liberation theology. Based on the Medellín principles, the Catholic Church in Latin America developed many different types of group and popular communication as part of its pastoral action.

Other experiences of alternative communication outside the government-controlled mass media like those of the human rights groups and the Mothers of the Plaza de Mayo in Argentina were a direct result of the ravages of repression. These groups invented new forms of communication and new symbols and languages for a population bereft of other forms of expression.

In some cases the alternative media were both an authentic alternative to the government-controlled, alienating mass media and a form of democratic and participatory communication. In others, they served as filters that decoded, interpreted and helped people resist the monolithic messages of the mass media. In still others, the alternative media served a specific political role of popular organization and education.

Transition to democracy
By the 1980s with most of Latin America under military dictatorship, the democratization of communication structures, along with

reconstruction of other democratic and representative institutions of society, had become a central unifying concern of those who opposed the dictatorships. The new forms of popular expression, mobilization and participation present in the alternative media were a form of democratic communication. Eventually, once the military regimes were over, these experiences could be used to democratize and reform the mass media. The concept of reform beginning at the grass roots and developing new formats and new networks of communication became part of the general concern for the recovery of democracy in Latin America.

Yet, in spite of their strong ties with both rural and urban popular movements, the alternative media seldom became lasting substitutes for the usual fare of the mass media. In some cases, new types of programme and different mechanisms for popular participation in the traditional mass media were taken from the experiences of alternative communication. The democratization of the mass media, however, continued to be an elusive goal.

The dictatorships that had swept over Latin America in the mid-1970s slowly receded with the military, economic and political defeat of their authors. By 1986 only Paraguay and Chile still had military presidents, and 94 percent of the population of Latin America was living under civilian and constitutional regimes. The newly elected civilian regimes, however, found it as difficult to enact new communication policies and carry out reforms as their predecessors had ten and twenty years before.

The strong memories of control and censorship under the authoritarian regimes made new regulation or public-service functions of the media anathema to the private sector and to many political parties. Furthermore, in some cases the private commercial and often transnational mass media like TV Globo in Brazil had shown themselves better able to resist the censorship and manipulation of the military than the public-service or development-oriented programmes. The unexpected 'positive' achievements of the private commercially financed mass media under the dictatorships, like the growth of film production facilities in Argentina and Chile, threw a new light on some of the earlier criticism of their manipulative, undemocratic and politically conservative role.

Roncagliolo (1986) observed that much of the criticism of the private media had often been a simplified vision of the mass media as totally functional instruments of the given structure and not as spaces and stages for social struggle. The discovery of the contradictions in the private media, however, made it harder for the new civilian governments to propose reforms that increased state regulation or ownership. In any case, they did not have the necessary political or economic resources to undertake a major restructuring of the communications sector.

Most of Latin America emerged from the dictatorships in the worst depression since the 1930s. Per capita income had not grown in the last ten years and in some countries had declined to the levels of the 1960s. In some regions unemployment was over 50 percent. The economic hardships and the need to pay the staggering foreign debt had sharply reduced the size and activities of the public sector.

Even if the new democracies had the economic resources to implement communication policies and reforms, they did not have a clear idea of how to go about it. The leaders of the new democratic regimes had spent most of the last decade outside politics and removed from the daily exercise of government. They came to power without any new scheme to reorganize the mass media. Furthermore, they now depended on the same media to get elected. Many were used to the practices of small, alternative radios and newspapers – mainly concerned with survival and opposition. Once in office they were unprepared for the technological developments, political power and transnational expansion of the communications industry.

In Brazil, for example, the new civilian government was deeply indebted to TV Globo and *O Globo* for their political support during the transition to democracy and was hardly in a position to regulate TV Globo's vast operations. By then, giant TV Globo had seven fully owned stations, six partly owned stations, thirty-six affiliates, thirty radio stations, *O Globo* newspaper, a home video division and a record company. The network produced 90 percent of its own prime-time programming and earned $12 million dollars (only 2 percent of its overall revenue) yearly in foreign programming sales. New public-service obligations or economic regulations of TV Globo, if they occurred at all, would not come from the government. They would most likely be the result of pressure from independents in the television market to break up TV Globo's monopoly.

The administration of President Raúl Alfonsín in Argentina found itself the legal owner of television channels and radio stations it was unable to understand or regulate. It had inherited a bureaucratic nightmare riddled with corruption, contradictory laws and ubiquitous regulatory agencies. Alfonsín lifted censorship and transferred some government-owned stations to the private sector. In part, Argentina's new civilian government could not do much more. It had become the owner of television and radio stations it could neither provide programming for nor finance out of the public budget.

Moreover, the country had far more serious problems than media reform to face during the first difficult years of transition to democracy. The reorganization of the military, the trials of those officers responsible for human rights abuses and the towering foreign debt dominated the attention of most policy-makers and frequently made them more dependent on the private media for support.

The new Latin American democracies faced greatly changed national and international communications industries. The finances and technologies of the private media conglomerates were quantitatively and qualitatively different from the relatively simple communications industries of the early 1970s when national communication policies were first proposed.

The Latin American private communication conglomerates had grown and become more interconnected nationally and internationally as a result of sales and distribution opportunities made possible by cable, satellite and video combinations. Their size and international operations made the Latin American industries financially more complex and increasingly difficult to regulate under national laws. The global communications industries had achieved a progressive independence with regard to national borders (Roncagliolo, 1986: 86). Latin American researchers at ILET had identified this transnational phase as one that altered the nature and function of states by diminishing their erstwhile capacity to intervene in the economy and in their own historical development (Trajtenberg and Vigorito, 1981).

The distinction between foreign and national ownership, control and content had become blurred. US producers had increasing co-production and distribution arrangements among themselves and with European and Third World television and film producers. Many Latin American television companies had set up distribution companies and television networks for the large Spanish-speaking audience in the United States.

The changes in production, distribution and sales in the transnational communications industries affected all the countries of the region. In Mexico, for example, because of the country's severe economic difficulties, any real growth in the earnings of the gigantic private media empire Televisa was dependent on dollar-generated income brought in from outside the country. In 1986 the transnational operations of Televisa included Univision, a Spanish-language television network in the United States with close to $80 million in advertising billings and a US-based film distribution company that accounted for 70 percent of the total earnings of Televisa's films (Besas, 1987).

Like Televisa, faced with the worsening economies at home, other Latin American private media had found there was no longer any place to grow in their own countries. Radio Caracas Televisión (RCTV) in Venezuela, for example, one of the large private television networks, had become a major supplier of television programming throughout Latin America and the United States. RCTV had its own distribution company and two record companies in Miami and owned 20 percent each of two Puerto Rican television stations (Michie, 1986).

Changes had occurred before in the economic locus of the different actors in the Latin American communications industries. For example, the initial US direct investments in radio and television stations were progressively sold in the 1970s and replaced by US advertising and programming sales. During the early 1970s private investors in Argentina and Peru shifted their investments and control of television from channel ownership to production as a successful hedge against government expropriation. The latest series of developments, however, were more than a shift of economic control or financing of the media. They appeared to represent a qualitative restructuring of the world media markets that made any national regulation almost impossible under existing laws and definitions.

Mass media audiences had also changed since the 1970s. They had grown larger and more segmented by age and income. Different forms of user-active receivers as well as video production and viewing technologies had created new audiences and markets that bypassed traditional media structures and regulation. In 1985, for example, foreign television and film producers had sold 30 percent of their production in Latin America directly to the unregulated home video market. Foreign films and television now entered the home directly via satellite dishes or video cassettes (IPAL, 1986).

New policy implications

The changes in the Latin American media structures, markets and audiences had major implications for future national communication policies. In many instances the two main actors, the state and industry, appeared to have switched positions or joined forces. In Colombia, for example, private media owners seemed to be willing to focus on the export and higher-income national audiences reached by cable or satellite and to allow public regulation and new public services on some of their long-defended but less profitable national markets like over-the-air television.

In Brazil and Mexico, in another apparent switch, private

communications empires had grown so large that they found it both economically profitable and politically wise to undertake a series of activities traditionally financed by the public sector like educational television and cultural development. And in several countries the government and private sector working together had entered into an increasing number of joint schemes of production and distribution to finance national programmes that they later exported to Europe, the United States and other Latin American countries.

The increased availability of channels had made it in the financial interest of private media owners in some countries to relinquish traditional monopolies and provide access to different production groups and creative organizations. In Brazil, however, the small independent producers fought for constitutional reform and government regulation of the monopolistic control of the mass media by Globo.

In addition to the shifting positions of the main actors, superficially, the experiences of the Latin American media over the last decades seemed to defy much of the accepted theory that had motivated the reform movements. For example, in order to produce and finance national content the media had become transnational. In order to provide public services they had become vast private, commercial conglomerates.

At the same time, the changes of the last ten years had strengthened government and private-sector support for other concepts present in the 1976 conference on communication policies. For example, most countries had developed some sort of co-ordination between the private sector and the government for national production and for regional news and information exchange. Yet the search for an explicit set of principles and standards to govern the functions and use of the communication and information media in the service of objectives democratically chosen by national communities – one of the most controversial and cherished concepts of the conference and the media reforms of the 1970s – seemed to have been forgotten.

Technological changes and the economic success of the private sector had increased national production and public services as well as the access of different groups to the media. The objectives of the private sector, however, had always been profit-oriented. Without some sort of explicit public policy, there was no guarantee that the private sector would provide these same services in the future. Furthermore, there was no basic framework within which to address future problems when they arose.

One problem was that once the public-service functions of the mass media had been left to the initiative of the private sector there was no guarantee that these services would continue under different, less profitable economic conditions. A major economic setback or restructuring of the private communications industry could result in the disappearance of educational and cultural broadcasting in many Latin American countries.

Another problem had to do with the type of national content produced by the private media. For example, the tastes, values and needs of the US Hispanic population were not the same as those of Latin Americans living in Latin America. The use of export success as a major criterion to determine national production could create nationally produced content with as negative an impact on national culture as that of most foreign productions.

Finally, although the private sector could sometimes serve as a guarantee against government control and manipulation under dictatorial or authoritarian regimes it had neither the public accountability nor the mechanisms to enforce these freedoms for others, especially for the disadvantaged. The abandonment of communication rights to the exclusive criteria and responsibility of the private sector could leave important sectors of society unprotected and open to exploitation.

Latin America's recent and difficult option for democracy did not provide policies to resolve these or other future problems of the media. In a larger sense, however, it constituted a set of principles and standards to govern the functions and use of communications and information in society. A functioning democracy provided a minimum assurance that when new problems arose they would receive public debate. It also provided a representative structure for the different actors to negotiate their interests. These assurances have seldom been met in the past. In view of the rapid changes in the communications sector, it is perhaps not too late that they are met today.

References

Amorim, José Salomão (1982) *A Radio Difusão no Brasil 1974–1981.* Cadernos do Dept da Comunicação, 2. Brasília: Fundação Universidade de Brasília.

Beltrán, Luis Ramiro (1974) *Communication Research in Latin America: The Blindfolded Inquiry.* Leipzig: IAMCR Conference.

Beltrán, Luis Ramiro (1982) 'No Renunciemos Jamás a la Utopía', *Chasqui* (Quito), Apr.–June, pp. 6–13.

Beltrán, Luis Ramiro and Fox, Elizabeth (1980) *Comunicación Dominada: Estados Unidos en los Medios de América Latina.* Mexico: ILET/Nueva Imagen.

Besas, Peter (1987) 'Hispanic TV Giants Slug it Out: Reliance vs Univision for $100,000,000 Market', *Variety* (New York), 3(25), p. 1.

Capriles, Oswaldo (1976) *El Estado y los Medios de Comunicación en Venezuela.* Caracas: ININCO/UCV.

Capriles, Oswaldo (1980) *De las Políticas Nacionales de Comunicación al Nuevo Orden Internacional de la Información: Algunas Lecciones para la Investigación.* Caracas: IAMCR Conference.

Capriles, Oswaldo (1982) 'Las Enseñanzas del Proyecto RATELVE', pp. 117–52 in E. Fox (ed.), *Comunicación y Democracia.* Lima: DESCO.

CIESPAL (1967) *Dos Semanas de la Prensa en América Latina.* Quito: CIESPAL.

Epstein, Edward Jay (1976) 'Los Rockefeller: La Familia y el Imperio', *El Tiempo* (Bogotá), 1(18), 1, 7.

Esparza, Luis (1984) *La Política Cultural del Estado Mexicano y el Desarrollo de la TV.* Cuadernos de TICOM, 35. México: UNAM/Xochililco.

Federico, Maria Elvira Bonavita (1982) *Historia da Comunicação Radio e TV no Brasil.* Petropolis: Vozes.

Fernández, Fatima (1982) *Los Medios de Difusión Masiva en México.* México: Juan Pablos.

Ford, Aníbal and Rivera, Jorge B. (1985) 'Los Medios Masivos de Comunicación en la Argentina', pp. 24–45 in A. Ford, J.B. Rivera and E. Romano, *Medios de Comunicación y Cultura Pópular.* Buenos Aires: Legasa.

Franco, Jean (1985) *La Cultura Moderna en América Latina.* México: Grijalbo.

García Canclini, Nestor (1986) 'Cultura para Todos: Hegemonía Política y Consumo Artístico en México'. Madrid: Seminario Iberoamericano sobre Políticas Culturales y Democracia.

Gargúrevich, Juan (1987) *Prensa, Radio y TV: Historia Crítica.* Lima: Editorial Horizonte.

Hamelink, Cees (1983) *Cultural Autonomy in Global Communication.* New York: Longman.

IPAL (1986) *NTC/NCT Newsletter, a Review for South–North Exchange on New Communication Technologies*, 1(3). Lima: Instituto para América Latina.

Kaplún, Mario (1973) 'La Comunicación de Masas en América Latina', *Educación Hoy* (Bogotá), 5.

Lasagni, Cristina and Richeri, Giuseppi (1986) *L'Altro Mondo Quotidiano: Telenovela TV Brasiliana e Dintori.* Torino: Edizioni RAI.

Lozada, Fernando and Kúncar, Gridvia (1983) 'Las Emisoras Mineras de Bolivia: Una Histórica Experiencia de Comunicación Autogestionaria', pp. 105–32 in R. Reyes Matta (comp.) *Comunicación Alternativa y Búsquedas Democráticas.* México: ILET.

Martin-Barbero, Jesús (1987) *De los Medios a las Mediaciones: Comunicación, Cultura, y Hegemonía.* México: G. Gili.

Mattelart, Armand (1986) 'Communication in Nicaragua, between War and Democracy', pp. 7–27 in A. Mattelart (ed.), *Communicating in Popular Nicaragua.* New York: International General.

Michie, Larry (1986) 'On the Cutting Edge of Latino TV, Radio Caracas Taking Lead into US'; *Variety* (New York), 3(12), p. 130.

Mitchell, Christopher (1974) 'Dominance and Fragmentation in US Latin American Policy', pp. 176–204 in J. Cotler and R.R. Fagen (eds), *Latin America and the United States: The Changing Political Realities.* Stanford: Stanford University Press.

Motta, Luiz Gonzaga (1982) 'Costa Rica: Seis Años Después', *Chasqui* (Quito), Apr.–June, pp. 14–18.

Munizaga, Giselle (1982) 'Políticas de Comunicación bajo Regímenes Autoritarios: el Caso de Chile', pp. 41–68 in E. Fox (ed.), *Comunicación y Democracia.* Lima: DESCO.

Noguer, Jorge (1985) *Radiodifusión en la Argentina*. Buenos Aires: Editorial Bien Común.

de Noriega, Luis Antonio and Leach, Frances (1979) *Broadcasting in Mexico*. London: International Institute of Communications.

O'Donnell, Guillermo (1979) *Modernization and Bureaucratic Authoritarian Politics*. Berkeley: University of California Institute of International Studies.

Pareja, Reynaldo (1984) *Historia de la Radio en Colombia 1929–1980*. Bogotá: Servicio Colombiano de Comunicación Social.

Pasquali, Antonio (1963, 1980) *Comunicación y Cultura de Masas*. Caracas: Monte Avila.

Roncagliolo, Rafael (1986) 'Transnational Communication and Culture', pp. 79–88 in Rita Atwood and Emile McAnany (eds), *Communication and Latin American Society*. Madison: University of Wisconsin Press.

Sampaio, Mario Ferraz (1984) *Historia do Radio e da Televisão no Brasil e no Mundo (Memoria de um Pioneiro)*. Rio de Janeiro: Achiame.

Sarti, Ingrid (1986) *Os Efectos da Tecnologia da Ponta na Televisão, a TV-Globo*. Lima: IPAL.

Terrero, Patricia (1982), 'Comunicación e Información por los Gobiernos Autoritarios', pp. 25–39 in E. Fox (ed.), *Comunicación y Democracia*. Lima: DESCO.

Trajtenberg, Raúl and Vigorito, Raúl (1981) *Economía y Política en la Fase Transnacional: Algunas Interrogantes*. Mexico City: ILET.

UNESCO (1976a) *INFORME FINAL, Conferencia Intergubernamental sobre Políticas de Comunicación en América Latina y el Caribe*. Paris: UNESCO, COM/MD/38.

UNESCO (1976b) *Conference Working Paper, Intergovernmental Conference on Communication Policies in Latin America and the Caribbean*. Paris: UNESCO, COM-76/LACCOM/3.

United States Senate (1975) *Covert Action in Chile 1963–1973*. Washington: US Government Printing Office.

Varis, Tapio (1973) *International Inventory of Television Programme Structure and the Flow of TV Programmes between Nations*. Tampere: Institute of Journalism and Mass Communication.

2

Nationalism, Censorship and Transnational Control

Elizabeth Fox

A half-century ago, when broadcasting began, Argentina's per capita GNP was the highest in South America and twice as high as Italy's; its total GNP was greater than that of Canada. In the early twentieth century, Argentina had one of the most developed systems of media consumption and production per capita in Latin America, the result of the relatively early growth of a literate, urban middle class.

Six million Europeans had immigrated to Argentina, a vast country five times the size of France, at the end of the nineteenth century and the beginning of the twentieth. Most of them had settled in and around Buenos Aires, the capital, where they received universal primary-school education under the Law of Common Education of 1884, only two years after the equivalent legislation had been put into effect in France.

Argentina's traditional Spanish heritage mixed with the cultures brought by the waves of immigration. Newspapers, magazines, books, circuses, popular music and other forms of expression multiplied to meet the cultural, information, entertainment and educational demands of the fledgling urban society. Argentina had 165 newspapers in 1880 and 345 by 1895. The Argentine film industry, glorifying national themes, produced some of the earliest Latin American movies, *El Fusilamiento de Dorrego* in 1908, and *Nobleza Gaucha* in 1915 (Ford and Rivera, 1985).

The fertile pampas around Buenos Aires produced the beef, hides, wool and grains that had made Argentina a rich country by the turn of the century. The port lived off the pampas, shipping these commodities to Britain in exchange for manufactured goods. Some analysts (Scobie, 1964) have blamed the strange political, economic and cultural *malaise* of modern Argentina on the hypertrophy of its capital. They claim Buenos Aires, the home of almost half the population, distorted the culture and economy of the rest of the country and helped create the deep divisions between the urban élite and the poor that later contributed to bringing Juan Perón and the military to power.

The supremacy of Buenos Aires was reflected in the country's communication infrastructure. The British had built the Argentine rail system in the form of a half-circle with Buenos Aires at the hub. This same pattern was mimicked by the telephone, telex and broadcasting systems. The spokes ran out from the capital to the provinces, with few lines running between the cities in the interior of the country.

The urban consolidation of Buenos Aires facilitated the relatively early growth of Argentine broadcasting. In August 1920 four young medical students built a radio transmitter out of pieces of war surplus. Their first radio broadcast was *Parsifal* from the roof of the Coliseo theatre where the opera was being performed. In 1923 the Ministry of the Navy issued the first five radio licences to stations operating in the capital. By then Argentines had 60,000 radio receivers. Fifteen years later there were forty-two radio stations, many of which were organized in two private radio networks (LaCroix and Russovich, 1984).

The Argentine film industry blossomed during the 1930s, jumping from four releases a year in 1931 to fifty releases a year in 1939. It would not reach this level of production again until almost thirty years later (Schnitman, 1981). Argentine poets and writers wrote directly for the movie industry, and many films were based on well-known works of national literature.

The complex and relatively affluent urban society of Buenos Aires witnessed the expansion of the press between 1880 and 1910, of magazines and the editorial industry between 1900 and 1930, of silent and later sound films between 1900 and 1920 and again between 1930 and 1945. Finally, in the 1930s, it was radio's turn.

The newspapers, magazines, pocket books, films, music and radio shows of the popular urban culture of Buenos Aires were different from the traditional folk culture of the interior of Argentina. They had not yet, however, formed a mass culture (Rivera, 1981).

By the 1940s the Argentine media had reached the zenith of their cultural and economic development. A series of problems, however, soon began to affect the national media. Some of these problems, like the pro-Axis stand of Argentina during the Second World War and the acute hypertrophy of Buenos Aires, were particular to Argentina. Other problems, like the political manipulation and control of the media under Perón in the 1940s and 1950s, were to a greater or lesser degree present in other countries of the region. Finally, problems created by high foreign investments and the distortion of the national media by advertisers eager to reach the urban middle-class markets for consumer goods were present in all the countries of Latin America.

Swayed by their Italian ancestry and loyal to the German officers who had trained their army, the Argentines remained neutral and at times pro-Axis until 1945. This stand enraged the United States, which cut economic and military assistance to Argentina. Cultural and economic exchange between the two countries dropped to almost nothing.

The pro-Axis stand of Argentina during the Second World War limited US investment in Argentine broadcasting and kept out the flow of Hollywood films, US comic books and popular music. In this way, it indirectly protected the national media. At the same time, however, Argentina's war record greatly damaged the national film industry.

During the war, the US State Department set up the Office of Coordination of Inter-American Affairs to combat pro-Axis sentiment in South America and distribute pro-Allies news and propaganda. Unable to produce all its own material, the Office of Coordination subsidized national media industries in countries that supported the Allies' war efforts. This was the case of the Mexican film industry.

Mexican film producers benefited from loans, equipment, technical advice and a practically unlimited supply of raw film, while the Argentine film industry was allocated a raw film quota from the United States insufficient to keep its production at previous levels (Schnitman, 1981: 271). As a result of these measures, the Argentine movie industry went into a decline, and Mexican films replaced Argentine films in many Latin American theatres.

The Second World War had encouraged the development of the Argentine economy, the reduction of imports of both consumer and capital goods and the steady expansion of local industry to take their place. During the 1940s Argentina emerged from its agricultural age and began to enter an industrial phase in spite of serious limitations like a run-down transportation infrastructure, insufficient capital goods and equipment and the absence of a steel industry and the energy resources to support national industrial development (Scobie, 1964: 185).

After the Second World War, Argentina gradually shifted much of its work-force from agriculture to industry. A subsequent drop in international prices for many of Argentina's agricultural exports that subsidized the national industrialization programme, however, brought about the growth of a class of urban poor. Sharp social and economic divisions led to the yearning for unity and redress of social injustice that, for the next four decades, helped make Argentina susceptible to the Fascist and nationalist rhetoric of Juan Perón.

Perón, elected president in 1946 in one of the cleanest elections in Argentine history, manipulated his people with charisma and authority and with the sainthood he created for his wife, Evita – as if those things could solve their growing economic problems. His was the first government that took into account the power of the mass media.

The intoxicating optimism of the Perón era deluded Argentines into believing that their country was significant on the world stage and that their leaders fought for justice. Much of the delusion and unrealism of this period was founded on Perón's manipulation of broadcasting and use of censorship.

Radio had played an important role in Perón's rapid rise to power between 1943 and 1945. In 1943 Perón advised the military government of which he formed part: 'We are being attacked on all sides. I suggest we try advertising. Propaganda is a powerful arm, especially when one has control of the media. It is the time to think how we are going to advertise' (Sebreli, 1983: 63).

In 1943, the military government from which Perón emerged had established a state monopoly of all radio stations under the Secretary of Press and Information of the Presidency, with 1,600 journalists and writers dedicated exclusively, it later turned out, to promoting Perón and his wife, Evita.

Under Perón's regime, the mass media had a high percentage of Argentine national production and a low level of foreign investment. There was a significant national telecommunications hardware industry and a large export industry, mainly of films and books. Perón provided many training opportunities for high-quality media professionals (most of whom were exiled throughout Latin America after Perón's fall; Ford and Rivera, 1985).

The impact of the war had brought a new sense of nationalism to Argentina. The country's economic losses had been attributed to Argentina's dependence on the foreign buyers who took its raw materials and on the foreign sellers who provided expensive consumer and capital goods in return. Partly as a result of this nationalist sentiment and partly as a result of Perón's economic policies, in contrast to many other countries of Latin America, the Argentine broadcasting industry did not receive any significant foreign investment or content until the late 1950s.

The Peronist broadcasting policies called for the protection of national production, the defence of the Argentine national culture and the political organization of media workers. Perón's policies also called for the political control of the media and the censorship of films, radio, plays, books, magazines and, later, television.

The Peronist government provided substantial loans to the national film industry. A protectionist decree, voted into law in 1947, gave Argentine films a minimum of 25 percent screen time in the first-run theatres of Buenos Aires and 40 percent of screen time in the rest of the country. For three years, between 1949 and 1951, the government kept Hollywood pictures out of Argentina by suspending the import permits of US pictures.

The government's decision was based on the refusal of the Motion Pictures Export Association of America to accept the Argentina policy of reciprocity. Under this policy, the countries that exported their films to Argentina were expected, in turn, to buy Argentine films. Perón's protectionist measures for the national film industry, however, were not sufficient to offset the crisis of an industry without a consistent external market and a supportive middle-class public (Schnitman, 1981).

The Peronist government nationalized the four main radio networks: Estado, Belgrano, Splendid and El Mundo. These networks had originally been privately owned. Radio Belgrano was owned by Jaime Yakelevich, one of the pioneers in radio and television in Argentina; Radio Splendid was owned by the Peralta Ramos family, owners of *La Razón*; and Radio El Mundo was linked to British interests in Argentina and the Haynes publishing house (Getino, 1978: 28). After nationalization, Radio Belgrano was then relicensed to its previous owner to be administered under commercially favourable conditions.

Various deals orchestrated by Perón concentrated ownership of a substantial segment of the Argentine press in the hands of people close to his government. In 1947 Evita purchased the daily newspaper *Democracia*, which soon became an unofficial organ of the Peronist movement. *Democracia* resorted to wide coverage of sports and crime to attract popular readership (Page, 1983: 211).

Another Peronist publishing company, Alea SA, controlled most newspapers, magazines and a radio network, leaving independent only the dailies *La Prensa* and *La Nación* and the afternoon paper, *Clarín*. Later, in 1951, Perón expropriated *La Prensa* after a long and bitter struggle with the newspaper's owners.

In 1951 Perón set up television as a state monopoly. The first regular television transmission had 5 kW and a potential of 43 kW, and a range of 85 kilometres. The equipment was installed by Standard Electric, imported from the United States. The equipment had to be modified to meet the Argentine European standards (Pasquini, 1981: 163).

The rich and diverse Argentine media of the 1920s, 1930s and 1940s like films and recordings were encouraged by Perón's support for and protection of national media development. On the other hand, Perón's political control and censorship suffocated the media's autonomous development and siphoned off their resources, as occurred in the case of the 'nationalized' radio stations.

The Peronist experience of political manipulation of the media left a strong imprint of state control, censorship and commercial corruption on Argentine broadcasting. Under Perón, large segments of Argentine society were denied access to broadcasting and to any other form of expression including the arts, theatre, the press or simply the public square.

In 1955, a military and civilian insurrection overturned the government of Perón – the traditional right wing found it easier to call on the army than to organize a conservative party for political influence. With the military in power the direct relationship between the leader and the masses, facilitated by Perón's use of broadcasting, ended. Perón and his followers – between one-third and one-half of the Argentine population – were denied any open form of political and cultural activity and any access to the mass media for the next eighteen years.

After ousting Perón, the military outlawed the Peronist party and all parties that claimed continuity with Peronism. Anyone who had held a leadership position during Perón's government or who claimed allegiance to Perón could not run for office, form a new political party or appear in the media as a producer, technician, writer or actor (O'Donnell, 1973: 171).

Military coups interrupted the brief terms in office of the two civilian presidents who followed Perón. Arturo Frondizi, elected with the support of the banned Peronists in 1958, was ousted in 1962; Arturo Illía, elected president with 22 percent of the vote in 1963; was toppled by the military in 1966.

The provisional military government that replaced Perón in 1955 began a programme of democratization that resulted in a drastic decrease in the share of wage income in the GNP, weak labour unions and a transfer of wealth away from those sectors of the society that had supported Perón. The military began to dismantle the tariffs and exchange controls that Perón had established to protect national industry including the mass media.

In 1955 the government lifted all restrictions on foreign films. This created an immediate abundance of foreign productions in the domestic market that proved overpowering for local film producers. New protectionist measures for the national film industry were not put into place until 1957 (Schnitman, 1981).

After the fall of Perón, the military returned newspapers to their former owners but kept the radio stations under its control. The government, however, licensed new commercial radio stations. Over the next twenty years, the number of radio stations grew to approximately 150: 30 state-owned and non-commercial stations, 48 state-owned and commercially operated stations and 76 privately owned and commercially operated. Both state and privately owned radio stations sold time to commercial advertisers. As a result of the influence of advertising on programme selection, state and private programming was frequently similar.

In order to attract foreign capital investment, the civilian government elected in 1958 authorized the free transfer of earnings and capital of the foreign companies operating in Argentina. In one year, between 1958 and 1959, new foreign investment in Argentina jumped from US$8,397,247 to $217,667,530. Between 1958 and 1965, 55 percent of the foreign investment in Argentina came from the United States (Rofman, 1973).

Foreign capital and the upsurge in new advertising investment it brought with it soon began to change the face of the Argentine media. New magazine formats developed that closely copied magazines of international commercial success. Other magazines began to focus on the markets for the consumer goods of the multinational corporations newly installed in Argentina. Imported US and Mexican comic books replaced the Argentine comic books, triggering an exodus of Argentine artists and writers (Ford and Rivera, 1985: 35).

The Argentine television system is made up of TV channels and TV producers. By law, the owners of TV channels must be Argentines, and the channels can have no foreign capital. These conditions, however, do not apply to TV producers. For this reason, foreign capital entered Argentine television through the television production companies.

After 1960 US capital from the three main television networks entered the newly formed private channels and production companies of Argentine television. By 1969, through their respective production companies, ABC had investments in Channel 11 and NBC in Channel 9, and CBS was a co-owner of Proartel, the TV production company of Channel 13, along with Time/Life.

Each of the three private television channels of Buenos Aires together with their production companies was the flagship channel of a national television network. This was the result of the financial weakness of the channels in the interior of the country that limited their ability to produce their own programming or to negotiate their own advertising. Before their expropriation by Perón in 1974, the three private networks received over half the total advertising in Argentine television and produced over 80 percent of the national programmes broadcast by the channels in the interior of the country.

The entrance of foreign capital had an enormous impact on Argentine national broadcasting. For the first time, Argentina was exposed to the massive investments in advertising and the rapid push for mass markets that helped shape commercial radio and television as they are known today throughout Latin America. By 1972 advertising investment in Argentina was almost sixty times what it had been in 1960 (Getino, 1978). The twenty leading advertising agencies in Argentina in 1971 billed $80 million; two were US agencies (J. Walter Thompson and McCann Ericksson), while others were US affiliates or advertising departments of US multinational corporations (Getino, 1978).

The successive military regimes that followed Perón strengthened political control of the media but reduced state support and protection to national productions. Their economic policies continued to allow the entrance of foreign capital and media.

Peronism, first under Perón and then under his vice-president and second wife, Isabelita, briefly returned to power in elections held in 1973. During his second period in office, Perón attempted once again to swing the Argentine media back to a situation of state control. The commercial television licences were not renewed, and members of the short-lived Peronist administration began to work towards a national communication policy. The new policy would include government support to the national cultural industries firmly under their political control.

In March 1976 the most brutal of the many military regimes that has ruled Argentina in the last fifty years ousted Isabelita Perón and took control of the government. The military junta immediately suspended all political parties, labour unions and the guarantees and rights of the National Constitution.

In 1979, after three years of repressive military rule and state-directed terror against the population, almost three-quarters of the television sets in Buenos Aires were turned off. Surveys found audiences had dropped sharply. The Argentine public had come to expect very little of their media as they had come to expect very little of their government. They had been fooled too many times.

The potentially highly creative and diverse forms of communication that marked the first decades of media growth in Argentina could not survive the chronic political instability of the country. The media reeled from one extreme to another, from economic protection to free market policies, from government ownership to transnational investors. And at each swing, larger and larger groups of the population and regions of the country were deprived of any access or participation.

References

Ford, Aníbal and Rivera, Jorge B. (1985) 'Los Medios Masivos de Comunicación en la Argentina', pp. 24–45 in A. Ford, J.B. Rivera and E. Romano, *Medios de Comunicación y Cultura Popular*. Buenos Aires: Legasa.

Getino, Octavio (1978) 'Medios de Comunicación y Dependencia El Caso Argentino' (mimeo). Lima.

LaCroix, María Luisa and Russovich, Rosa Maria (1984) 'Historia de la Radio en la Argentina' (mimeo). Buenos Aires.

O'Donnell, Guillermo (1973) *Modernization and Bureaucratic-Authoritarianism: Studies in South American Politics*, Berkeley: University of California Press.

Page, Joseph (1983) *Perón: A Biography*. New York: Random House.

Pasquini, José María (1981) 'Argentina', pp. 119–90 in P. Schenkel, J.M. Pasquini, C.A. Medina, E. Fox, E. Vera, R. Salinas, O. Reyes, C. Ortega and R. Agudo, *Políticas Nacionales de Comunicación*. Quito: Editorial Epoca.

Rivera, Jorge (1981) *El Auge de la Industrial Cultural (1930–1955)*. Historia de la Literatura Argentina, 95. Buenos Aires: Centro Editor de América Latina.

Rofman, Alejandro and Romero, Luis (1973) *Sistema Socioeconómico y Estructura Regional en la Argentina*. Buenos Aires: Amorrortu Editores.

Schnitman, Jorge (1981) 'Economic Protectionism and Mass Media Development: Film Industry in Argentina', pp. 263–86 in E. McAnany, J. Schnitman and N. Janus (eds), *Communication and Social Structure*. New York: Praeger.

Scobie, James (1964) *Argentina: A City and A Nation*. New York: Oxford University Press.

Sebreli, Juan José (1983) *Los Deseos Imaginarios del Peronismo*. Buenos Aires: Legasa.

3

Mass Media and the Collapse of a Democratic Tradition in Chile

Carlos Catalán

Chile entered a pluralist period of liberal democracy in the 1920s that was to last until 1973. For fifty years, the political system was able to hold together, with brief interruptions, a wide spectrum of ideologies and social groups representing almost the entire national society. Only the rural peasants and the urban poor partially escaped both the system's benefits and its responsibilities.

Within this basic consensus, competing political parties offered the Chilean voter a broad choice of alternative ideologies and different solutions to the country's economic and social problems. These problems – inflation, a low rate of growth, inefficient agriculture and foreign control of copper, Chile's main export – had always been considerable.

Many changes occurred in Chilean society over these fifty years of political stability. The country industrialized, urbanized and lost many of its traditional social and cultural patterns. By 1960 about 70 percent of the population was living in urban centres. The urban population of Chile was 90 percent literate, and the national literacy figure, including rural areas, had reached 84 percent.

Urbanization, universal education and new jobs in national industry and the public sector had created an urban middle class and a market for the new cultural industries. By the 1960s large parts of the Chilean population were exposed to films, radio and television, and popular newspapers and magazines had a wide circulation.

Until a military coup toppled President Salvador Allende in 1973, the struggles and alliances of the many different cultural and political forces within Chilean society gave form to the Chilean mass media. Governments, political parties, national and foreign industries, advertisers, media owners, artists, universities and consumers worked to achieve their own priorities within a basic democratic consensus.

The privately owned mass media flourished under the conservative presidents who governed Chile before 1964. Between 1964 and 1970 the Christian Democrats increased state ownership and control of radio and television and created schemes to ensure the participation of the poor and less privileged in their content and operations. The Socialists, between 1970 and 1973, attempted a policy of nationalization of the content and state ownership of some media.

Although each government presented different policies and models of media development, for almost fifty years the Chilean media moved smoothly enough between state control and private commercial development to avoid any major crisis. The balance between public and private media control fell apart when the national political consensus broke down.

The national consensus regarding media management began to dissipate when the Christian Democrats and later the Socialist administration went beyond state regulation and public subsidies for the media and began to own media and produce programmes directly. By the time this occurred, however, there were no neutral institutions left in Chilean society. Political polarization and social conflict had exhausted any possibility of agreement on media management, the democratic tradition had collapsed, and the media had become another of the many battlefields of Chilean society.

A democratic tradition

Since the early 1900s the Chilean government had supported 'high culture', the fine arts and universal education. It had built public primary and secondary schools and established national universities. The public and private universities, following a tradition of public support to culture, formed their own theatre and ballet companies as well as symphony orchestras. For the growing Chilean middle class, along with education, culture and the fine arts were a mechanism of social mobility. The middle class expected the government to provide these services and regulate their equal distribution among the different members of society.

Contrary to the tradition of government support and distribution of education and the arts, the Chilean state did not subsidize the nascent mass media when they appeared in the early 1910s and 1920s. This lack of subsidy and regulation was partially the result of the scant cultural legitimacy the media enjoyed among the Chilean middle class. Furthermore, there was a strong tradition of private newspapers.

Left on their own, the film makers, publishers and owners of radio stations catered to the demands and tastes of the new urban market as their sole means of economic survival. The small national market was not big enough to finance national production, and the

Chilean media got used to importing less expensive films, recordings, books and magazines. Right from the start, the Chilean film and editorial industries were no match for the subsidized industries of neighbouring Argentina and Mexico.

Radio was the first to receive government regulation. In the 1920s legislation gave the president the exclusive right to assign radio frequencies. Frequency assignment was based, for the most part, on technical requirements of both the government and the licensee. Other radio laws established percentages for live programmes, national programmes and advertising, thereby providing some protection to national artists. The law gave the government the right to employ all radio frequencies in an official network when necessary and the right to make all future decisions on communications technology. By 1958 there were eighty radio stations in Chile, twenty of which were in Santiago.

Until 1964 radio ownership was almost exclusively private. The privately owned copper-mining company and the national agricultural association owned the two largest radio chains. Radio's commercial development did not necessarily favour national talent. Radio listeners were first and foremost consumers, and most content was commercial and banal; serious news and opinion were expected from the national newspapers, not from radio.

Contrary to what occurred with radio, with the consent of all the political parties, television did not become privately owned. When television was introduced in the early 1960s Chilean society was not the same society that had passively allowed private radio to develop in the 1920s and 1930s. Urbanization and the growth of national industries, helped by radio advertising, had created mass markets and demonstrated the rapid and seemingly inevitable advance of national and foreign mass-produced commercial messages over national culture.

At the same time, the growing political struggles among the different parties for the control of the government had made the state appear less neutral and eliminated the alternative of government ownership. People feared the power of television both as a political tool and as an instrument of mass culture. Of all the public institutions of Chilean society, the universities alone were considered free from political manipulation and commercial exploitation.

Hence, by exclusion rather than any specific policy, television was assigned to the universities. In this way, television joined the tradition of university extension in the arts and music. By 1963, however, when television finished its experimental phase, the directors of the university channels found they were unable to fill all the available air-time with national cultural productions. In the absence of state subsidies or specific policy guidelines, universities, although maintaining ownership, soon gave in to the barrage of cheap foreign, mainly US imports and commercial advertising.

By the mid-1960s the Chilean political equilibrium of the centre based on negotiation and compromise was beginning to crumble. This was partly the result of agrarian reform, the growth of urban industry and the considerable expansion of electoral participation begun in the early 1950s. The new voters helped elect the Christian Democrats in 1964 and, in 1970, Unidad Popular.

As Chilean society became more and more divided, the different political parties attempted to lure new voters with promises of political and economic change. The power of the media, especially television, to reach voters and influence opinions had grown with technical innovations and the expanding market for consumer goods. Still operating within the democratic system, the three main political groups struggled to control and influence the mass media, especially television.

The conservative parties believed that a free press and an unregulated market for newspaper owners and broadcasters constituted the sole guarantees of objective information, pluralist opinions and an informed populace. They defended the need for media regulation only on issues of immorality and advertising abuses and never questioned the private ownership or the commercial programming of the mass media. After 1964, when the conservatives lost control of the government and entered the opposition, they defended the free market model against what they considered government interference in the media by the Christian Democrats.

Fearing the Christian Democrats would use the media to gain votes and control public opinion, the conservatives accused the Christian Democrats of pressuring advertising agencies, manipulating the distribution of radio licences, using state subsidies of radio and television for political ends, abusing the government's use of radio chains and co-opting journalists. In 1966 a prominent right-wing senator warned that the control of the mass media prepared the way for the irrational control of the masses that could easily be carried out by some expert propaganda minister.

The conservatives voted against various laws proposed by the Christian Democrats and the left-wing parties that would have guaranteed access to the mass media by different political parties during elections, a factor of growing importance in Chile. The conservatives' opposition to this measure was especially strong when it concerned the press.

The Christian Democrats had attracted many of the new social and political movements with their programme of agrarian and social reforms and modernization. Popular education, especially through radio, was an important part of their government's programme of grass-roots mobilization and integration of the new social actors into the political and economic life of the country. The cultural policy of the Christian Democrats organized the community as both consumer and producer of the media by creating institutions at community, factory and rural level to encourage popular cultural expression.

Modern communication technologies had expanded media coverage, especially radio, and helped the Christian Democrats reach their new constituencies in the rural areas. The transistor radio came to Chile in 1964 and multiplied the radio audience beyond the previous limits of rural electrification. The number of television sets in Chile jumped from 56,000 in 1966 to 300,000 in 1969. The government helped the rapid growth of television by introducing nationally assembled television receivers at controlled prices, distributing subsidized receivers and rejecting a direct tax on television.

The Christian Democrats changed the old relationship between political power, economic groups and the mass media. Their policies decreased the control of the economic and political right wing over the mass media. President Frei's Christian Democrat administration made wide use of the national radio chains and set up a national television network. It also facilitated the creation of a chain of pro-government radio stations, guaranteed the people's right of reply on the media and regulated the access of political parties to the privately owned mass media during elections.

Generally, the Christian Democrats worked within the existing structure of the media to diminish private control and guarantee the access of the different political parties and social groups to the media. The National Television Channel, set up at the end of the Christian Democratic administration, was an exception to this policy.

The National Television Channel was the first channel directly owned and operated by the government. The Christian Democrats, certain that they would remain in office, struggled successfully to establish a government television channel. The new National Television Channel caused enormous polemic. Conservative opposition to the Christian Democrats called the channel a government propaganda arm. The left-wing parties accused the government of using the media to proselytize and compete unfairly with the university channels, fast becoming another source of political conflict.

As the result of the university reform of 1967, the university television stations, although still commercially operated, were closer to the left-wing parties than to the Christian Democrats or the traditional right wing. Student and community participation in their management had increased. The new management generally supported the programmes of reform and change of the left-wing parties and of the most progressive sectors of the Christian Democrats.

The new management had inherited serious economic difficulties. It faced the choice of making its programming style more commercial and seeking financial support through more advertising, or using the channel to broadcast expensive cultural programmes and losing money. The university split between supporters and detractors of commercial or cultural television. Soon after the university reform, private advertisers began a boycott of the university channels, protesting against the excessive politicization of their content, especially during the pre-electoral period.

The advertising boycott put the university channels in greater economic difficulties. Station managers and university officials pressured the government to increase direct government funding and subsidies for the channels' operations.

In 1970 the Christian Democrat government presented a law to regulate television. University television was bankrupt, and there was no national legislation covering television. Nor was there any law regulating access to television by the different political parties during the upcoming election.

The Christian Democrats' new television law coincided with the 1970 presidential elections. The different political parties waited to see the outcome of the elections before defining their position on the new legislation. After the Socialists won the elections, the final negotiations on the new television law were held between the Christian Democrats and Unidad Popular as part of the general negotiations to achieve the support of the former for Socialist candidate Salvador Allende. (The support of the Christian Democrats was necessary because Allende had not received a majority of the votes in the presidential elections and he needed the Christian Democrat votes in Parliament in order to become president.)

In its final form the new television law awarded broadcasting licences to the National Television Channel and to the channels of the University of Chile and the Catholic universities of Santiago and Valparaíso. Any change in broadcasting capacity or licences for new channels would have to be approved by another law. The television law assigned 40 percent of the national television budget to the National Channel and 20 percent each to the three university channels. The law allowed all the channels to sell commercial advertising but limited this to six minutes for each hour of broadcasting time.

The new legislation set up a National Television Council charged with the general orientation, supervision and control of Chilean television. The council was composed of representatives of the president, the Senate, the House of Deputies, the Supreme Court, the presidents of the National Channel and the three universities' channels and representatives of the television employees.

A directory for the National Channel, under the law, was made up of representatives of the president, Parliament, the National Television Council and employees of the channel. The president of the channel would be named by the Chilean president and approved by the Senate.

Each political party had access to television time in proportion to the number of votes it had obtained in the last parliamentary elections. The law set aside one hour a week for each party for political broadcasts during election periods and half an hour during the rest of the year and gave the opposition parties the right to reply on the National Channel.

In addition to the television law, between 1970 and 1973 Chilean radio, newspapers and magazines came under the Statute of Constitutional Guarantees, the political agreement negotiated between the Christian Democrats and Unidad Popular in order for Allende to become president. The statute guaranteed the right of all individuals and political parties to publish newspapers and magazines and operate radio stations. A new law would have to be passed by Parliament in order for the government to expropriate any of the existing media. Under the statute, any discrimination by state-owned companies in imports, licensing or the distribution of papers, ink or printing equipment was unconstitutional.

The new legislation helped resolve the uncertainty about the development of television in the country and establish a balanced and pluralist system of media operations. The legislation gave Parliament the power to make any changes in ownership or in the legal framework of the media. However, it severely limited the power of the president to change media structures or ownership and to carry out media reform.

During their long struggle for political power between 1958 and 1970 the left-wing parties had often criticized the media and called for their democratization as a necessary condition for the global democratization of Chilean society. The left wing had denounced the links of the Chilean mass media with foreign capital, especially through advertising, and had claimed that freedom of expression applied only to those who controlled the media.

Shortly before the 1970 elections the left-wing parties developed a more global criticism of the mass media. Research centres in Chile and other countries were responsible, in part, for this wider criticism. Studies analysed the role of radio, television, newspapers, magazines and comic books in the formation of social consciousness and in the reproduction of cultural hegemony. The Communist and Socialist parties used the results of empirical research on content and the foreign and monopolistic ownership of the mass media in their platforms and speeches.

The Chilean left-wing parties considered the structure of the mass media an obstacle to electoral success. After the 1964 elections, in which he had been closely defeated by Eduardo Frei, presidential candidate Salvador Allende made a speech to the Senate in which he observed: 'The tremendous strength of the mass media in the hands of powerful national and international economic sectors hinders the electoral struggle of the popular movements, even when they are a majority.'

Voted into office in 1970 on a programme of anti-imperialism, anti-monopoly and land reform, Unidad Popular did not immediately present an alternative model of the mass media, although the radical change of media ownership had been among its objectives. Unidad Popular gave first priority to the rapid expansion of state control of industry and agriculture and an immediate increase in the living standards and political participation of low-income groups.

Unidad Popular was a coalition of various left-wing parties. The lack of consensus among the various members of the coalition, along with the constitutional limitations on media reform and opposition from the right wing and the Christian Democrats, slowed down any new media policy initiatives.

Members of the Unidad Popular coalition had different interpretations of the media and of culture. This resulted in diverse and often contradictory policies, implemented in accordance with the internal distribution of power among members of the coalition. Members of Unidad Popular shared a general notion of culture, however, as an instrument of transformation of popular political awareness within an overall framework of class conflict and revolutionary change. They criticized the traditional concepts of free press and objectivity and claimed that the structure of media ownership and content responded to the politics of their owners. A minimum objective of their programme was to redress the existing unbalanced ownership structure and replace the private owners with different social organizations.

Within the coalition the Communists supported a programme to develop the mass circulation of cultural goods. Some sectors of the

Socialist Party supported the creation of mechanisms for the expression of grass-roots culture. The extreme left-wing sectors stressed the instrumental nature of culture and favoured more centralized government policies to raise revolutionary awareness and militant political commitment among the people. The different tendencies within the Unidad Popular coalition resulted in the increase of state ownership of publishing, recording houses and film production and support to cultural activities of popular organizations.

In January 1971 the opposition-controlled Congress passed a Law of Constitutional Reform further limiting the power of Unidad Popular to regulate the media. This reform was necessary, in the opinion of the opposition, in order to preserve democracy.

Article 10, No. 3, of the Constitutional Reform gave both the government and the universities the right to set up and operate television channels. By writing the norms on the ownership of television channels into the Constitution the opposition broke the executive's monopoly over television and made it possible for the opposition to set up new channels in any university.

In addition to the Constitutional Reform, the Christian Democrats and the right-wing parties carried out a violent campaign against the government in their newspapers and radio stations in which they denounced the loss of political pluralism on the National Television Channel. The opposition concentrated its attacks on two public-opinion programmes where representatives of the right wing and the Christian Democrats exchanged views with members of the government.

The political struggle soon spread to the control of the university channels. The Student Federation of the Catholic University, controlled by the Christian Democrats, accused the news department of the university channel of bias in favour of the government. The university officials called elections for a new board of directors of the channel. The opposition and government supporters each elected three members. The tie was broken by the Church's appointment of a priest as the new director of the channel. Instead of acting as a mediator between the two sides, the new director fired the news director and shifted the orientation of the channel towards the opposition.

Once in control of one university channel, the opposition turned its attacks to the National Television Channel, taking advantage of its majority in Parliament to vote against the budget for the government network. At the same time, the opposition submitted a proposal to expand the university channels and to fund privately owned radio stations, for the most part opponents of the Socialist government.

The Association of Private Radio Broadcasters objected to the government's monopoly of radio broadcasting, and its members began leaving the official network. The government suspended their licences. The controller-general and Court of Appeals, however, upheld the actions of the private stations on the grounds that, in the absence of a new law, the compulsory network was a violation of the Statute of Constitutional Guarantees.

The opposition university authorities struggled with the pro-government director and employees of the Channel 9 of the University of Chile over the control of the station. Unable to gain control of the station, the university authorities illegally set up another channel, Channel 6. Litigation followed between the public services, the courts, the Association of Journalists and the Ministry of Justice. The National Council of Television, in which the opposition held a majority, suspended Channel 9 and recognized Channel 6 as the legal university channel. The court ordered the directors of Channel 9 to leave the premises and sent in the national guard to remove them.

Although the Socialist government was unable to enact any significant new legislation on the mass media, it did regulate the cultural industries indirectly through import and price controls and increased public ownership of some media. Unidad Popular took over the bankrupt publishing house Zig-Zag, renamed it Quimantú and published enormous cheap editions of universal literature, socialist philosophy and popular magazines. At the same time, the government allowed the opposition magazine *Ercilla* to continue publishing on the old Zig-Zag presses and respected its editorial independence. The Socialist administration also acquired the IRT record company from RCA and put out many inexpensive recordings. Government-owned Chile films made many documentaries. Grass-roots participation in the media and in other forms of expression increased under the Socialists with the influx of government resources to new institutions for greater popular participation in the media.

The Unidad Popular government did not regulate these new media acquisitions and activities, however, and there was no guarantee of a plurality of opinions in their editorial policy. This lack of guarantee provided further grounds for criticism by the opposition. The boards of directors of the new state-owned media were named by the president but reflected the same internal policy divisions that existed within the left-wing coalition.

The polarization of Chilean society which began under the Christian Democrats and continued under the Socialists slowly weakened and eventually eliminated all democratic regulation of social conflict, including the laws and agreements on the mass media. The legal framework of the media gradually eroded, not from its own limitations, but as a result of the general deterioration of the political consensus. In the period just before the 1973 military coup, Chilean society entered a warlike state in which the outcome of all conflict was the necessary elimination of the adversary.

In their struggle to defeat Unidad Popular, the opposition parties broke the democratic rules of their own making, including those regulating the media. The opposition chose an insurrectional strategy against the elected government using national and international funds. As later was shown by the investigations by the US Congress, much of their funding went to finance the opposition media.

In 1971 the US government appropriated $1,240,000 to buy radio time and newspaper space to support the opposition candidates in the municipal elections as well as other activities against Allende's government. Between 1971 and 1972 the US government authorized $1,665,000 to support the opposition newspaper *El Mercurio* and $1,500,000 to opposition parties and the opposition media for the 1973 congressional election.

In August 1973 the opposition-controlled Chamber of Deputies declared the collapse of democratic institutions as a product of the Socialist government's conquest of total power. This motion was used as legal justification for the military coup a month later. The media were among the democratic institutions that had collapsed. All the Utopias – the free press and objective journalism of the right wing, the public-service participatory broadcasting of the centre and the anti-monopoly, anti-capitalist, government-directed media structure of the left – had failed. None could withstand the pressures of the growing political conflicts or negotiate a compromise once again acceptable to the whole of Chilean society.

4

Revolution and the Press in Peru

Juan Gargúrevich and Elizabeth Fox

One of the unique experiences of mass media policies in Latin America began in October 1968 when the Peruvian army overthrew President Belaunde Terry and formed a Revolutionary Government of the Armed Forces. The new regime, calling itself neither capitalist nor communist, announced its intention to transform the economic and social structure of the country and liberate Peru from foreign investment and influence. The military proposed to change national values, create a new Peruvian culture and modernize the Peruvian state. The military regime would also attempt to restructure the mass media to match the goals of its administration and permit the participation of different sectors of Peruvian society in media management.

The new regime immediately ran into stiff opposition from the traditional media. Six days after taking power, the new president, General Velasco Alvarado, expropriated the US petroleum companies operating in Peru. The Peruvian Federation of Journalists and the Federated Centre of Journalists of Lima protested against the take-over of the refineries. Most newspaper owners joined the journalists in their disapproval of the new regime. The owner of *Expreso* and *Extra*, who had strong ties with the international petroleum companies, printed highly critical editorials against the military's first major step. As a result, he was arrested and soon after sent into exile in Argentina.

The owner of *La Prensa* and *Ultima Hora*, also a strong defender of the US petroleum interests, vigorously protested against the military take-over in a series of editorials in his two papers. The reactions of the papers *Correo* and *Ojo* were more neutral. Of all the papers only *El Comercio* confirmed its traditional support of the military by extending its greetings to the new government and congratulating the military on the speedy recovery of the nation's natural resources.

The new government responded to the newspapers' criticism by raiding and closing down *Expreso* and *Extra* as well as a radio station owned by the same company. All three stayed closed for sixteen days while the government drafted a new law that guaranteed the payment of salaries to the employees of the papers and the radio station even when closed. In this way the military attacked the two papers but did not lose the support of their employees.

The newspapers that could still publish strongly criticized the media policies of the new regime. Newspaper owners demanded that the government explain the motives behind its censorship and harassment of the mass media and warned their readers of the dangers a government monopoly of the media would bring under a totalitarian regime.

During the first year of the military regime, before the government enacted any specific new legislation on the media, it repeatedly raided and closed down newspapers and magazines, detained and deported journalists and used a series of administrative measures to control dissent in the press. Meanwhile, the government prepared what it considered a comprehensive solution to the problem of the opposition media within the context of its plan to transform Peruvian society and modify the relationship between the state, the media and the people.

During its first year, the Revolutionary Government of the Armed Forces released a package of new laws and decrees unprecedented in Peruvian history affecting all aspects of national life. The military set out to transform land tenure and water rights, labour–management relations, the educational system, the role of foreign enterprises and most of the traditional economic and political relationships in Peruvian society such as private ownership.

The military leaders' new form of economic organization moved the country away from capitalist principles by creating a sector of the economy denominated 'social property' based on collective ownership of the means of production. The military's reform of industry and commerce gave workers and employees a share of the company's profits and management. Workers of firms with over six employees received a fixed percentage of their company's profits, some distributed immediately in cash and the rest retained as commonly owned shares in the firm. Under this plan, half the firm would eventually be owned by the firm's workers. The community's representatives would have the right to participate in management decisions, audit company books and records and look after the workers' interests.

The Peruvian military expanded and fortified what had been one of South America's weakest states. The state took over the fishmeal industry; a major share of mining and metal refining; most petroleum refining, marketing and exploration; the railroad, airline, telephone and cable companies; cement companies and electric utilities; commodity and mineral exporting and importing; and the distribution and marketing of most key commodities. The government set up a legal and administrative structure in charge of the newly nationalized areas. This structure included the Ministry of Transport and Communications, established in 1968.

In all these measures, the military stressed the need for a drastic change in national values and the creation of a new Peruvian culture dedicated to solidarity rather than individualism. The mass media were one of its most important tools to achieve this aim. At first, however, the government did not own or control the necessary media.

The military reforms met with stiff opposition from labour unions, the business community, peasants, students and professionals. The national press, many times speaking for the groups and sectors affected by the reforms, were filled with debates between the government and the opposition. During these debates, the armed forces arrested and deported journalists and foreign correspondents critical of their policies and repeatedly closed down opposition magazines such as *Caretas*.

On 3 October 1969, the first anniversary of the Peruvian Revolution, General Velasco openly attacked the press:

> Some of our honest and objective native newspapers believe it is honest and objective to hide how well Peru is spoken of today in the world. It doesn't matter. The day will come when their malicious sensationalism will be known, and Peruvians will understand how the owners of the national newspapers perfidiously hid the truth under the pious cover of press freedom in order to defend their own interests. The Peruvian oligarchy defends its interests and those of its foreign accomplices in a synchronized campaign of propaganda with the foreign news agencies, the international magazines and the majority of the national newspapers. (Gargúrevich, 1987: 205)

A little over a year after taking control of the government, the military issued a Statute of Press Freedom. The statute restricted ownership, capital and the management of newspapers to native Peruvians; recognized journalism as a profession; regulated the right of reply; and identified and established penalties for the crimes of libel and slander. The law set limits on the press's right to criticize the government. These limits were respect for the law, truth and morality, the demands of national security and defence and personal and family honour and privacy.

As a result of the new press legislation, the Revolutionary Government lost the support of the owners of *El Comercio*, the only newspaper that until then had consistently supported its policies.

The Peruvian newspaper owners violently attacked the new press statute because of what they considered the limitations on their freedom of expression. Soon after, the government released another law regulating journalism as a profession. The law gave journalists many of the measures they had struggled for in vain over many years: job stability, overtime pay and the right to opinion columns in their papers. The support of newspapers' employees secured by this and other government measures would play an important role in the military's future media policy.

In 1970, with the support of the papers' employees, the government expropriated *Expreso* and *Extra*. The law expropriating the papers called for the formation of a union made up of the papers' employees. This union, together with the Peruvian government, would run the papers.

The Revolutionary Government never completed the legal expropriation of the papers, however, and the co-operative structure of management with the papers' employees was never set up. After their expropriation, in spite of *Expreso* and *Extra*'s support of the regime, bureaucratic infighting within the military government blocked the legalization of the expropriation and the recognition of the employees' union.

The Revolutionary Government acquired another newspaper in 1970 when it took over 85 percent of the stock of the bankrupt Banco Popular. The bank owned the publishing house that published *La Crónica*.

The first indication that the changes in the press would spread to radio and television came from the Ministry of Education soon after the expropriation of the first two newspapers. A report from the ministry observed that almost all the TV channels and radio stations in the country were privately owned and commercially operated and that national and international advertising on these channels was responsible for the deformed and alienating content of the mass media. The ministry urged government control over content in order to protect the achievements of the military's education reform.

In 1971, in spite of constant and forceful warnings by the private media against state interference in radio, television and newspapers, the government issued a new telecommunications law. The law introduced radical changes in the ownership structure of Peruvian broadcasting media and put these formally at the service of national social and economic development programmes.

The telecommunications law placed radio transmission and communication services under state control and gave the government the option to expropriate 51 percent of the equity of any television station and 25 percent of the equity of any radio station. The law required that radio and television dedicate 60 percent of their programming time to national productions and established a form of workers' participation in the ownership and management of radio stations.

The Revolutionary Government had already set up in 1969 a national telecommunications company, ENTEL-Peru, in charge of telephones, satellites and telex. ENTEL-Peru was now put in charge of those radio stations and television channels expropriated by the regime. By 1972 ENTEL-Peru had five radio stations and three television channels under its control and represented the government on the boards of twenty-one radio stations and four television channels.

By 1974 the Revolutionary Government directly owned two newspapers and indirectly controlled one. In addition, it controlled all the TV channels and most of the radio stations. The time had come to create a centralized institution for the administration of the government media. This was the National Information System, SINADI, and the Oficina Central de Información, OCI, its executive organ. With the status of a ministry, SINADI managed, supervised, controlled and advised the government on all matters relating to radio, film and printed publications.

The military created five public enterprises to carry out the mandate of SINADI/OCI. They were CINE-PERU, a national film company; Editora-PERU, a national publishing house; PUBLI-PERU, a state-owned advertising agency; ESI-PERU, a government news agency; and ENRAD-PERU, a national broadcasting company. SINAMOS, the National System of Support to Social Movements, together with SINADI and the Ministry of Education, co-ordinated the media and education policies of the regime. The Casa de la Cultura del Perú, later the Instituto Nacional de Cultura, was put in charge of the traditional areas of culture and later became the equivalent of a Ministry of Culture.

Under the military regime the Peruvian government was the chief protagonist in the field of communications and culture. It controlled all cultural activities under the central administration of SINADI, OCI and the Instituto Nacional de Cultura.

In spite of radio's and television's switch from private to government control, however, broadcasting content continued much the same. Radio and television owners adjusted to the new regulations and continued to use many of the same actors, programmes and schedules they had used before their partial expropriation. The government did not provide new public funds to finance the expropriated channels. Commercial advertising remained their main form of support. The government appeared more interested in the political control of the media than in its announced aims to modify content in line with national development and cultural goals.

Except for minor programming changes, Peruvian television kept its fare of canned US films and series. One year after the partial expropriation of the television channels, a Peruvian magazine observed that Peruvians continued to watch US television series, soap operas and advertisements that showed the capitalist mentality and life-styles that the revolution had promised to change.

One of the few but much publicized victories of the Ministry of Education over foreign influence on Peruvian television was the government's rejection of the Spanish version of the US children's programme *Sesame Street*. The ministry also succeeded in eliminating advertising that used Santa Claus and snow-covered trees with the argument that these were foreign-inspired symbols of Christmas.

Government control of radio and television, however, did affect news and opinion programmes. After 1971 one of the few independent news and commentary programmes on government-controlled television, *Quipu 73*, lasted less than a year before the Revolutionary Government cancelled its contract.

The expropriation of the remaining private newspapers in 1974 appeared to some to be another measure to quieten opposition, although the government justified the expropriation as part of its plan to give organs of expression to different sectors of Peruvian society. At the time of their expropriation, the Revolutionary Government hardly expected the nationalization of the Lima dailies to create more problems than it solved, or that it would become the rallying point of national and international opposition to the regime.

Before the final expropriation of the independent press in 1974, although the Peruvian newspapers had protested against the Statute of Press Freedom, many journalists and newspaper employees supported the military government as a result of new legislation that favoured the interests of their profession. At the same time, however, the government would not tolerate any opposition and jailed and deported many journalists.

The expropriation did not please all the journalists and employees of the newspapers. The hopes of *Extra* and *Expreso* workers to form a co-operative were dashed when the two were included in the list of expropriated newspapers. Instead of going to their employees, as the government had originally stated, the new law assigned *Extra* and *Expreso* to the education sector and to the members of the community education councils made up of teachers, parents'

associations, community organizations, students, education employees, universities and teacher colleges.

The government did not identify the representative institutions of
each sector chosen to manage the dailies until a year after their
expropriation. During this time, the military named the directors of
the expropriated papers. After a year, *El Comercio*, formerly
owned by the Miró Quesada family, which had a private fortune in
trading and commerce, was assigned to the Confederación Nacional
Agraria, the Federación Agraria, the Comunidades Campesinas,
the Asociaciones de Conductores Directos and the Indian communities.

La Prensa, formerly owned by the Beltrán group, a consortium of
agro-industry and foreign capital, was assigned to representatives of
the industrial, mining, fishing and telecommunication communities.
Beltrán's afternoon paper, *Ultima Hora*, went to representatives of
the social service organizations.

La Crónica and *La Tercera*, of the Prado family, a consortium of
banks, real estate and insurance companies, were assigned directly
to the Revolutionary Government. *Correo*, and *Ojo*, formerly
owned by the Banchero Group, a fishing and industrial consortium,
went to professional organizations and to representatives of the
handicrafts, literature and the arts.

It was not an easy task to organize the new owners of the national
newspapers. Some of the social organizations assigned newspapers
openly opposed the military regime. This was the case of the
Confederación Campesina del Perú and the Sindicato Unico de
Trabajadores en la Educación del Perú. Most of the professional
associations also opposed the military.

Since seizing power in 1968 the Peruvian armed forces had
systematically undercut almost all politically influential organizations
in the country except for the Church and themselves. The military
had severely restricted the activities of long-established political
parties, crippled different economic interest groups and dissolved
the once-powerful National Agrarian Society. It had stripped the
National Association of Industry of its legal standing and deported
its president. It had first tried to weaken the autonomous peasant
federations that had gained some strength in the 1960s. Later, it
banned these federations under a law establishing a new National
Agrarian Confederation.

With some exceptions, the Revolutionary Government wanted to
deal only with those organizations it had set up or recognized. For
example, the Confederación de Trabajadores de la Revolución
Peruana (CTRP), the Confederación Nacional Agraria (CNA) and
the Sindicato de Educadores de la Revolución Peruana (SERP)

were government-controlled organizations that competed with already existing independent national organizations that for the most part opposed the government. As the military's economic policies began to affect their interests, however, the Revolutionary Government slowly lost the support of the various social organizations it had set up.

Other administrative and financial problems soon appeared in addition to the problems involved in organizing the new owners of the expropriated newspapers. The expropriated papers depended on the participation of the different social organizations as well as on the capacity of their boards of directors to interpret the guidelines of the military regime. It was almost impossible to carry out an editorial policy under the joint demands of the organizations and the government. Furthermore, in order to keep running, it was necessary for the papers to maintain their share of readers in the urban Lima market as well as their regular advertisers. Many people gave up buying papers, and advertisers often shifted their investments to other media.

In spite of the radical nature of the expropriations, apparently no one imagined a different form of support for the papers or questioned their original advertising base. The government expected commercial advertising to continue in spite of the papers' many attacks on the abuses of advertising and on the interests of their former owners. This did not occur, however, and some papers experienced a shift in their advertising revenues from the private sector.

After almost seven years in office and a year after the expropriation of the papers, faced with growing opposition, General Morales Bermúdez replaced General Velasco Alvarado in a palace coup. By this time, the mass media were firmly under state control. OCI had appointed directors of the expropriated newspapers. The state operated radio stations through ENRAD-PERU and controlled 51 percent of the shares of Peruvian television stations and 25 percent of the shares of certain radio stations. Through PUBLI-PERU the state was the largest advertiser in the country and controlled much of the advertising in the Peruvian media.

In spite of the Revolutionary Government's sweeping control of the media, it was losing the support of many intellectuals working within the regime. Faced with mounting internal and external criticism of its measures, the regime itself soon lost interest in defending many of its new communication policies and institutions.

The change in direction within the armed forces led to the gradual removal of many of the revolutionary measures introduced in the first period. The consequences of the shift took about a year to be felt in the area of cultural policies. In 1976 General Morales Bermúdez named a new director of the Instituto Nacional de Cultura and announced that conditions were not ready to pass the direction of the expropriated dailies over to their new owners. OCI named new directors for the papers and allowed them to make changes in their staff. The new directors fired many of the journalists who had worked for the papers during the Velasco administration.

Between 1976 and 1978 the policies of the previous administration were slowly abandoned. In 1978 the government dismantled the National System of Support to Social Movements and named a member of APRA, an opposition political party, director of the Instituto Nacional de Cultura.

The government of General Morales Bermúdez could not, however, afford to revive a vigorous opposition press or dismantle the newly formed public media institutions even if it had wanted to. The workers' strikes and popular demonstrations that resulted from its necessary austerity programme made it more necessary than ever for the administration to control opinion and information.

The military found it more and more difficult to control political unrest, the growing economic crisis, the demands of the popular movements and the pressure to hold elections. The press began to be the focus of considerable political conflict, and the government's intolerance with any opposition became more acute. OCI announced a special commission to re-examine press legislation without the participation of the representative sectors. OCI and the official news agency ESI-PERU increasingly controlled the content of the papers. News became bland and uniform, and newspaper sales dropped sharply.

In 1978 the government issued a new press law replacing the law that had expropriated the national newspapers. Under the new law, the Corporación Financiera de Desarrollo bought all the stock of the papers, resold it to individual employees of the papers and former stockholders and placed the rest on the open market. No one individual could own more than 5 percent of the total stock. The newspapers praised the new law, most journalists protested, and the former owners of the papers rejected it completely. It was never put into effect.

A year later, in 1979, President Morales Bermúdez called the expropriation of the newspapers 'the biggest error the government had made and, therefore, the hardest to remedy'. After this confession, the military government made no further changes in the media, leaving these for the civilian government that was to follow in 1980.

The fate of the expropriated newspapers was the central topic of much of the political discussion during the transition to a civilian government. Many journalists and employees of the expropriated papers hoped in vain that the new civilian government would turn the expropriated papers over to their present employees rather than return them to their former owners. Their pleas were not heeded.

As soon as he took office, President Belaúnde Terry, the same president the military had toppled twelve years earlier, named the same newspaper directors the military had ousted when they expropriated the papers in 1974. In this way control of the papers reverted immediately to their former owners.

Soon after, President Belaúnde Terry signed into law a bill passed by Congress returning the newspapers of national circulation to their former owners. Once in charge of their old papers, the owners requested the government's permission to fire those employees considered supporters of the previous administration. Armed with the necessary legal powers, in a short period the newspapers fired approximately 300 journalists and employees, many of them union members.

The initially popular regime's attempt to restructure the media to support the goals of its administration and permit full participation by the different sectors of Peruvian society in their management had failed on both counts. The papers never freely supported the government – with the exception of *Extra* and *Expreso* when they were run by their employees – and the full participation of the different sectors of society never occurred. The government proved unable, unwilling or too slow to accept the existing representatives of Peruvian society and felt it had to form its own. The contradiction between democratic participation and government control of the media was impossible to resolve.

Abroad, the experience was hailed by some as an innovative and essentially democratic scheme to harness the media in the direction of national-development goals and popular participation. Many others, notably private Western newspaper owners, harshly criticized control by government and the lack of freedom it implied. At home, in spite of initial support from many intellectuals and journalists, the media policies of the Revolutionary Government were generally considered to be an innovative participatory experience carried out unsuccessfully by a basically undemocratic regime.

General Juan Velasco's attempt to integrate Peru's forgotten, indigenous, rural and urban poor into national life, restore their culture and give them a mouthpiece in the traditional press under close military tutelage did not work or was not allowed to work in the face of growing national and international opposition and animosity. It was, for the most part, too late, too expensive and too authoritarian, and the social and economic goals of the 1968 revolution failed, leaving behind the authoritarian political model.

References

Gargúrevich, Juan (1987) *Prensa, Radio y TV: Historia Crítica*. Lima: Editorial Horizonte.

5
Communication Policies in Mexico: an Historical Paradox of Words and Actions

Rubén Sergio Caletti Kaplan

Since the early 1970s, the ongoing discussion of the mass media and the government's role in communication has been one of the loudest and most extraordinary watersheds in Mexican politics. At its highest point in the late 1970s and early 1980s it attracted more attention and participation than any other debate in the last fifteen years. It was not, properly speaking, one debate, but many overlapping interrelated debates. The debates did not follow any particular internal order, and it was mainly opposition to the proposed policies that gave the debates any coherence at all.

It is perhaps too soon to say what was the outcome of the discussion. What is certain, however, is that the questions addressed, the areas mapped out and the practical solutions that ultimately prevailed constitute a lesson in communication policies without precedent in Latin America. The originality of the Mexican experience lies in its sweeping ambitions, its wide scope and its resounding failure.

The magnitude of the debates bore little proportion to the real changes and actions taken regarding the mass media. The failure, however, was not only a failure of words. In Mexican politics, where words tend to be liturgical, where ideology is rewritten on the rocky surfaces of rhetoric and where silence is often a testimony to civic life, this was a real failure.

In spite of its lack of results, the Mexican debate on the mass media is important because of the challenge the mass media and the telecommunications industry continue to represent for Latin American societies and their governments. The Mexican experience of communication policies provides insights into a certain way of facing this challenge. It is probably the only attempt in the region to generate a profound political response to the challenge of the mass media from within the traditional power structure. (This was not the case of Peru and Nicaragua, where changes in the communication system formed part of overall changes in the political systems.)

The Mexican debate on the mass media was more than a struggle between different economic and political groups and factions, or the traditional discussions among populists, authoritarians and conservatives, although it had some components of this as well. The Mexican experience was basically an attempt to come to grips with the impact of the communications revolution and recover the control of communication policies for society and its representative institutions.

Undoubtedly, the way the process occurred and its eventual frustrations were closely related to the particular characteristics of Mexican politics. The size of the mass media and the inertia of the political system, however, are not only Mexican phenomena, and the Mexican failures and successes are relevant far beyond the national borders.

The key moments

The debate on the mass media in Mexico took off slowly in 1971 with a series of small skirmishes between the government and the private sector that gradually established the conditions for a final battle. By the early 1980s, in the midst of the Mexican petroleum boom, the growing mobilization of public opinion and the increased attention of the government paid to the discussion had created the expectation that this time real changes were going to occur in the mass media.

This was not the case of simply another pilot programme in rural communication or the application of yet another new technology to underdevelopment. On the contrary, everything seemed to indicate that the Mexican government had taken the sweeping decision to redefine the structure and function of the private commercial mass media and shake an audience of millions out of their passivity. Congress held a series of public hearings to gather opinions on the subject from different social groups and analyse specific policy alternatives. The president himself spoke out in favour of major changes in the media.

At his annual dinner with Mexican newspaper owners President José López Portillo raised doubts if the Mexican mass media guaranteed equal access to all sectors of the population. He suggested that some media might encourage consumerism, social differences and information colonialism. The president then called for the creation of a new participatory, democratic and egalitarian philosophy of communication for the national media.

This was not the first time the government had spoken out strongly on the role of the mass media. Shortly before the president's speech, L.J. Solana, the first national co-ordinator of social communication, observed that information was a common good and the Mexican people had the right to receive objective information and to express their own points of view. Non-participatory, vertical communication should no longer be the predominant form of communication in Mexican society.

A few days later Solana observed that although new technology had made the mass media faster and more efficient, they had not improved the quality of their content. Solana declared that communication was not the private property of media owners, and the air waves were not the property of the government. The right to information, he said, is the right of the people as the creators of information and as the protagonists of their own history.

Solana called for a new order that would respect individual sovereignty. Communication, he said, is an important form of power, and in a democracy the power comes from the people. Let us, he suggested, democratize communication.

Judging from the strength of the government's declarations on the mass media, it appeared as if the traditionally aggressive private media, the logical opponents of any possible new measure, had withdrawn to defensive positions. Their strategy seemed to be to minimize the effects and restrict the scope of any new communication policy. It looked as if the government had won the battle and had a smooth road ahead.

At the same time that López Portillo, Solana and other members of the government were expounding the philosophy of the announced reforms, various opinion leaders debated the proposed reforms in congressional hearings and in the pages of the daily newspapers. The core of the discussions was the right to information.

The discussion of the 'right of information', a short phrase in the Mexican Constitutional Reform of 1977, covered everything from corruption in news gathering, union-owned newspapers, TV violence and children, information and the secrets of state, the transnationalization of culture, the technology gap, professional training, truth in advertising, and satellites.

The ubiquitous debate on the right of information did little to speed up the reforms or clarify the issues. Possible errors in the government's strategy of presentation and discussion of the reforms, however, were not the main causes of its failure. The opposition of the private sector, the historical links between members of the government and the private media and the otherwise functional role of the private mass media within the Mexican system of government proved to be stronger than the sentiments of reform.

A further cause of failure was the contradiction between the open participation of the Mexican population in the media proposed by the reforms and the traditionally low participation of the same population in many aspects of the state and the economy. It is possible that the Mexican government was in no condition to absorb this potential popular mobilization or direct it in its favour.

The sum of these factors eventually paralysed the policy initiatives. The supporters of the reforms still had some life left in them, but their efforts fell on deaf ears. Solana drew up a series of specific proposals in order to pull the discussion out of the legal quagmire in which it had fallen. These proposals, although feasible under the existing legal framework, were doomed to failure. By the end of 1980 the private media had taken the offensive, a position they were prepared to keep.

Beginning in 1968, for the next fifteen years the Mexican government tried to formulate a political response to the mass media. The chain of closely related events contained in these fifteen years appears to have reached its end. What will follow will be a new and different process.

The steady growth and expansion of the private commercial mass media, and the looming social unrest within the Mexican political system that eventually provoked the Mexican government to action regarding the media, began before 1968. Not until 1968, however, did these two phenomena come together with sufficient force to attract the attention of the government.

In 1968 a series of student strikes and marches against the government culminated, on 2 October, with the massacre of students in Tlatelolco by government forces. During the following six months President Gustavo Díaz Ordaz negotiated with private radio and television for free broadcasting time for his government in exchange for tax breaks. The private media were happy to indulge the government, which was in bad need of the support of the media and of some propaganda to improve its image. Mexican private broadcasters gladly exchanged free broadcasting time for a series of beneficial financial measures that in the long run would greatly strengthen the position of the private media in relation to the state.

The next three presidential administrations were marked by the restoration of the previous relationship of the government and the private sector between 1971 and 1974, an attempt to reform this relationship between 1975 and 1981 and an attempt to reduce the scope of the reform and return the relationship to one of *laissez-faire* between 1982 and 1985. Each of the stages consisted of different theories of the relationship between government and the media although none was mutually exclusive in its ideas or concepts. In each stage the main, although at times hesitant, actor was the government. Each administration, however, was egged on and eventually overpowered by technological developments in communications.

The restoration

The basic feature of the administration of Luis Echeverría (1970–6) was the permanent and frequently open struggle to limit the private sector and strengthen the state-owned mass media. The purpose of this struggle, following the ideals of the Mexican Revolution, was for the state to recover its rights of guardianship over the culture and ideology of the people. The modern cultural industries disputed this right of guardianship, and after 1968 Mexican society itself began to distrust it. Yet between 1971 and 1974 the words and deeds of the government pointed systematically in this direction.

One of the essential political concerns of Echeverría was to revitalize the social agreement on which the Mexican state was based and increase the role of the government. In this way, Echeverría hoped to overcome the bloody political inheritance of Díaz Ordaz that had continued into his own administration with new student protests.

Echeverría accused the media, especially television, of failing to use their potential educational capacity and abusing their power to form the beliefs and ideologies of the Mexican people. He called for changes in television content. Many members of his administration and political and social leaders close to his government gave their support to the president's requests.

The government's accusation of the 'contamination of Mexican youth' by television seemed to be paving the way for a new federal broadcasting law that would replace the 1960 law. The government, however, never passed a new broadcasting law and in 1973 presented a series of regulations on the existing law that contained no new educational obligations for the private media. The government was not going to resolve the conflict by setting standards and limitations on the private media. Instead, the government was preparing to strengthen its own communication resources.

In 1972, after months of negotiation, the federal government bought Channel 13, a station founded just four years earlier by a cabaret owner who had gone bankrupt trying to compete with Telesistema, the private television network.[1] Echeverría's pattern of expansion of the government-owned media when faced with the impossibility of imposing standards on the private media would repeat itself in later administrations.

Mexican state-owned media were in a curiously backward

position in relation to the other countries of Latin America. Most countries had at least one state-owned television channel. The only previous experience of state-owned television in Mexico was the semi-autonomous Channel 11, operated by the National Polytechnic Institute. Channel 11 lacked the resources to develop programmes or beam its signal beyond a limited radius.

The purchase of Channel 13 by the government had an immediate effect on private television. By the end of the year the owners of Channels 2, 4, 5 and 8 announced their merger to form TELEVISA. The text of the announcement stated: 'Televisión Independiente de México SA and Telesistema Mexicano SA share the concerns of the federal government for the improvement of the content of Mexican television and are pleased to announce that they have made a great effort to co-ordinate their programming. In order to assure that these ends are achieved they have created a new company, TELEVISA SA.'

TELEVISA announced it would continue to satisfy the demands for entertainment of its respective audiences and in addition it would add eleven hours daily of educational and cultural programming. Upon initiating this new period of Mexican television, TELEVISA explained that it would try to raise the level of its transmissions, in this way fulfilling its obligations to the country.

The birth of TELEVISA, today the largest communication empire in Latin America, has often been attributed to Echeverría's pressures on Mexican private television and his administration's purchase of Channel 13. This attribution is at the same time a simplification. The real problem was not the purchase of Channel 13 or the merger of the private channels, but the inability of the Echeverría administration to direct the private capitalist development of the communication industry and influence the cultural characteristics of what it produced. His administration was unable to perform this role in the communications industries in spite of the mixed nature of the Mexican economy and the government's important role in most other sectors.

In addition to the purchase of Channel 13, the Echeverría administration carried out other projects in order to organize the public-sector mass media better and provide the government with the minimum tools necessary to implement a cultural policy. In 1971 the Mexican government set up the Centre for the Study of the Media and Education, a decentralized organization that eventually ended up operating a cultural channel, Channel 8 of Monterrey, the third largest in the country and the most important channel along the US border.

In 1972 the Echeverría administration established Televisión

Rural Mexicana, a news and cultural production company for the isolated, marginal rural zones of the country. Televisión Rural later became Televisión de la República Mexicana, transmitting to the interior of the country from Mexico City. In 1985 it was the basis for the government-owned, commercially operated Channel 7. In 1973 the Mexican government set up a Sub-Secretary of Broadcasting, the first organization expressly concerned with co-ordination between the government and broadcasters and with government production.

In addition to these activities, the Echeverría administration gave new life to the feeble Mexican national news agency, NOTIMEX; set up Radio Mexico Internacional using the short-wave frequencies abandoned by the private sector; and, in 1976 when *Excelsior* began questioning the administration's policies and performance, used a combination of threats and bribes to orchestrate the rebellion among the members of the liberal daily co-operative that ousted its editor.

The government was unable to implement a policy on media content for private broadcasting and simply added more public media to counteract the private media. The state-owned media such as Channel 13 slowly came to resemble the private media on a smaller scale and generally with lower technical quality. By the end of his administration Echeverría had more or less given up trying to restore the traditional Mexican balance that operated in some sectors of the economy between a state that controlled and directed society, a private industry that carried out complementary functions and a society organized to defend its rights.

Mexico had changed. The last efforts of the Echeverría administration were directed towards the consolidation of state security. To compensate for its losing battle with the private media, the administration lashed out at critics like *Excelsior* and set up a public organization controlling government information and advertising to negotiate with the private media.

In 1974 the same Echeverría administration that had spread rumours of a possible new federal broadcasting law to stop the abuses of the electronic media awarded a licence to Cablevisión SA, an affiliate of TELEVISA, to develop cable television in Mexico City. The tension between the government and the private media continued, however, and was manifest in the government's role in setting up a labour union for commercial television workers and in the president's persistent attacks on the quality of television content.

The only media where the Echeverría administration was able to achieve its aims – although on a smaller scale and with many problems – was the national movie industry. Echeverría named his brother, a professional actor, to run the state-owned Cinematographic Bank and gave him ample resources. Under his direction, long-censored Mexican movies were released to the public, and a new generation of directors was permitted to work on sensitive political and social issues. The industry responded with enthusiasm and produced new movies on Mexican politics, society and social problems. Between 1970 and 1976 the state made serious critical movies that often became box-office hits.

The attempted reform

The next presidential period was one of classic reform. Echeverría's efforts to 'govern' the media were abandoned along with his struggles to develop and expand the state's role in the media. The new administration attempted a global reformulation of both the private and the public communication systems with the introduction of a 'right to information' and a plan to democratize communication through the active participation of the population in the media.

President López Portillo wanted to make social communication part of his political reform, together with the development of national oil resources, self-sufficiency in food and the increased participation of the opposition in the government. His communication proposal had its origin in a constitutional reform that added a new sentence to Article 6 concerning freedom of expression. The new phrase stated that the state would guarantee the right to information.

This short sentence was one of the most controversial phrases in modern Mexican political history. In December 1977 Congress approved the general reform with little discussion. However, the right to information quickly became the crux of a violent conflict between the government and the private media. The comprehensive concept of right to information brought together, for the first time, many different legal, operational and cultural aspects of the electronic and traditional media that were usually kept separate. Its focus, following the concomitant international discussion on the New International Information and Communication Order, was on the basic relationship of the people, the media and the government.

The concept of the right to information contained within it a potential communication policy that would address the phenomena of social communications in their entirety and in relation to a concept of democracy. Mexico had not witnessed a comprehensive vision of policy such as this since the 1930s when Lázaro Cárdenas oversaw the organization of Mexican society, the capitalist development of the country and the consolidation of the Mexican state and ruling party.

Since then, Mexican presidents had more or less let commercial and technological developments determine the organization of social communication. The Federal Broadcasting Law of 1960 under Adolfo López Mateos, for example, was a timid and unsuccessful attempt to orient the spontaneous development of radio and television and was unable to regulate even advertising. This began to change when Echeverría tried to confront television, by then an independent political, economic and cultural power. The pretensions of López Portillo went even further.

The controversy over the right to information was far greater than that over any other aspect of the general political reform of López Portillo including the legalization of the Communist Party and the participation of the opposition parties in the government. The purpose of the general political reform was to resolve the previous administrations' inability to deal with political opposition and to give new life to a bureaucratic political system that lacked vigorous opposition and any real escape-valves for social unrest.

The Constitutional Reform was intended to create new political institutions and forms of participation. The Mexican people, however, were far more interested in the democratization of the media, and in increasing their own participation in them, than in organizing a new political party. To most Mexicans, the democratization of the media was more important than the democratization of a political system that had long ago lost its relevance. The proposed communication reform had a direct appeal to the Mexican people, while the political reform appeared to benefit only certain sectors and specific groups.

The right to information as well as the general political reforms were part of the political platform of the ruling Institutional Revolutionary Party (PRI), for the period 1976–82. The platform stated that the right to information was a new dimension of democracy and an efficient way to respect ideological pluralism and the rich diversity of ideas, opinions and beliefs in society. The new right would permit Mexico to overcome the exclusively commercial mass media and include the receiver of information in the traditional freedom of expression – in this way allowing the country to continue along the path of the Mexican Revolution.

The PRI platform recommended that the government re-examine the social function of the press, radio, television and cinema and evaluate the process and forms of organizations of the public and private institutions of communication. The government should, according to the platform, guarantee freedom of expression for the communication professionals and, at the same time, strengthen the participation in the media of political parties, trade unions, professional and scientific associations, social groups and Mexicans in general.

López Portillo began talking about communication and the right to information before he took office. He repeated his reference to the problem again in his inaugural address, in the celebration of Freedom of the Press Day and in the report to Congress of his first year in office. On 4 October 1977 he included communications in the political reforms he sent to Congress.

In the report of his second year in office, López Portillo announced that he would soon send a bill to Congress on the right to information that would develop and regulate the final part of Article 6 of the Constitutional Reform and define the right to information as a fundamental human and civil right. Before sending Congress the bill, the secretary of the interior showed some of the contents of the proposed legislation to the Chamber of Commercial Broadcasters. The secretary's dialogue with the private sector could hardly be considered conciliatory. The secretary told the Chamber that it was not possible to confuse freedom of expression with the right to information – the former implies the absence of the state; the latter implies an obligation of the state to develop the necessary actions in order to satisfy the needs of its people.

Soon after, possibly as a result of criticism of the proposed bill, the government changed its tactics and announced that it would hold a series of public sessions in order to inform itself about the positions of the political parties and of Mexican society in general regarding the new right. The government observed that the right to information was a delicate balance between freedom of expression and the right to information. The new right did not mean, as some had mistakenly thought, new obligations for the media. Rather, the first obligation to inform correctly fell to the government itself.

The sessions were never held, and no bill was presented to Congress. Almost a year later, Congress called for open hearings in order for different representatives of Mexican society to give their opinions on the new right. In the meantime, the pages of the daily newspapers were filled with editorials against the right to information.

In February 1980 congressional hearings began on the new right. For the next six months representatives of different sectors of Mexican society spoke out on the right to information. Their opinions were mainly favourable.

In all there were twenty sessions: fourteen in Mexico City and the rest in San Luis Potosí, Guadalajara, Jalapa, Hermosillo, Merida and Monterrey. A total of 128 position papers were heard: half from individuals, the rest from political parties, universities, social organizations, the national labour union and private industry. TELEVISA presented seven papers, the national press (heavily subsidized by the government) none, although many small provincial papers participated in the hearings. The hearings received extensive press coverage and opinion pieces from political parties, industry, unions and professional associations.

The participants in the hearings presented four demands: the modification of the government's own use and practices of communication and information and increased public access to official information; the control and limitation of national and transnational private communication monopolies and the improvement of the cultural level of their content; the reorganization and updating of the obsolete, insufficient and ubiquitous laws governing communication, especially the protection of communication professionals and the control of corruption; and the participation of the different social sectors in the existing mass media and as owners of new media.

When López Portillo opened his fourth session of Congress soon after the hearings, he did not mention the right to information in spite of the widely held expectations that he would finally present the bill. Instead, the president raised new doubts concerning the possibility of regulating the right to information without limiting freedom of expression. No bill was ever presented. The government's discussion on the right to information took a new tack as a right within the traditional freedom of expression that applied only to official government information. The new approach eliminated participation and democracy from the discussion.

At the president's request, during his last year in office, the general co-ordinator of social communication carried out a new study of communication policy alternatives. Solana's analysis contained a series of ambitious legal, political and administrative proposals to promote diversity and competition, discourage monopolies and support new industries within the existing communication structures. It would open channels of social participation in the media, separate the state-owned media from the government in office, promote freedom of expression and eliminate corruption.

The new proposal recommended setting up a National Council of Social Communication representing a wide range of social groups as an advisory body to the government on the mass media. It also recommended eliminating a series of government subsidies to the press, providing support to national industries for the development of communication technologies, regulating advertising and strengthening the media on the Mexican borders. Finally, the measures included the establishment of a government office to verify audiences and circulation.

Solana's 6,000-page proposal was leaked to the press and it received wide public discussion and criticism. For example, Luis Marcelino Farías, the president of the Congress and a former broadcaster, called the regulation of the right to information an attempt to square a circle.

A month later López Portillo named Miguel de la Madrid the new presidential candidate of the ruling party. By the beginning of 1982 Solana had been fired and replaced by Francisco Galindo Ochoa, the former presidential press secretary under Gustavo Díaz Ordaz.

The administration of López Portillo had been a period of prolific and ubiquitous government action in social communications. For example, López Portillo strengthened the public communications sector with the extension of Televisión Rural de Mexico to become Televisión de la República Mexicana and inaugurated the small experimental Channel 22 in UHF. He also increased the transmission potential of Channel 11, supported the development of a national news and information network in XEEP Educational Radio and began negotiations for a Mexican satellite.

In other areas, his government carried out a massive production programme of commercially distributed comic books on different aspects of Mexican history, literature and national problems. His administration conducted a vast adult education campaign in the state-owned media and subsidized the bilingual radio stations operated by the National Institute of Indian Affairs.

The most characteristic aspects of the communication policy of the López Portillo administration, however, were less laudable. He named his sister, Margarita López Portillo, director-general of radio, television and cinema. She withdrew official support for movies she considered morally or politically dissolute. Under her six-year direction there were six different heads of the Cinematographic Bank, and the national film industry struck its lowest point. The traditional and banal commercial movie makers moved in to fill the void left by the government.

State-owned television administration and programming became a national scandal. The private media adhered to the law at their pleasure and convenience with the exception of the government's efforts to limit advertising of alcoholic beverages and eliminate advertising from cable TV. TELEVISA grew to be a giant conglomerate. Finally, the government press offices of the López Portillo administration were characterized by chaos, lack of consistency and a feudalistic structure of interests and resources.

The return to *laissez-faire*

The next administration was an attempt to cool passions and return a certain order to the daily management of social communications in Mexico. The administration of Miguel de la Madrid, however, maintained some of his predecessors' rhetoric. The fleeting yet spectacular moments of debate on the media under Miguel de la Madrid came directly from previous debates. The predominant tone, nevertheless, was similar to that assumed by López Portillo at the end of his administration – a reluctance to stir up a discussion in which the government was not prepared to assume the final consequences.

Rather than attempt any real change, the de la Madrid administration was concerned with achieving a certain level of efficiency within the public sector that would match ends with means in a non-conflictive manner. This new tone had begun under López Portillo when the Mexican economic and foreign debt crisis led to the decision to abandon sensitive issues that were secondary to the resolution of the crisis. The controversies over communication policies all but vanished with the new co-ordinator of social communications. The administration of Miguel de la Madrid tried to avoid the two errors of the previous administration: on the one hand the ambitious proposals for change and, on the other, the administrative chaos and bad management of the government media.

The initial display of rhetoric concerning the importance of communications in Mexican society was replaced by bureaucratic inertia. The first years of the de la Madrid administration almost completely passed over the role of the state, the industry and the public in the media, and ignored the responsibility of the government in the development of the media for the public good.

The de la Madrid administration set up a new National System of Social Communication that consisted of three decentralized institutions of radio, television and film. These institutions were in charge of the co-ordination and management of the state-owned industries in each of the respective media.

In May 1983 a government-organized forum on social communication briefly renewed interest in the debate; 1,800 participants presented 2,600 papers, and the proceedings mobilized enormous public opinion. Once again, the participants in the forum demanded that the government increase access and participation in mass media content and management, limit private monopoly, increase cultural and education programming, defend cultural sovereignty, support professional media training and decentralize the media.

In spite of the enormous number of papers discussed in the forum
– 174 from the communication industry, 131 from political parties,
123 from universities, 84 from professional associations and unions,
150 from social organizations – neither the forum nor the discussion
around the new institutes succeeded in sustaining interest in the
debate. Some vestiges of the previous discussion, however, could be
discerned in the Mexican government's support for UNESCO
initiatives in the area of communications such as ALASEI, a Latin
American feature news agency.

The new government organized its own offices of communication,
rationalized the operations of the state-owned media and made
peace with the private media. Some of its achievements were the
new state-owned Channel 7, the strengthening of NOTIMEX, the
rejuvenation of the daily *El Nacional* and new specialized state-
owned radio services.

De la Madrid was able to eliminate many of the former abuses of
the state information services including their use of personal
political advertising. The government's peace with private broadcasters went beyond the simple absence of conflict. It included new
co-productions between the government and the private sector. As
the state-owned media slowly became more and more like the
private media, the private media could hardly complain at competition that was much to their advantage as the stronger party.

The repertory of the de la Madrid administration was limited to
the traditional concepts of freedom of expression, nationalism, the
defence of national sovereignty and federalism. Federalism, an
often mentioned and seldom fulfilled aim of the Mexican government, was of particular importance during the first years of the
administration. Various states set up their own publicly owned
media that linked up the state radio stations and television channel.
Michoacán, Quintana Roo and Tabasco inaugurated their own
regional television channels.

In spite of the rhetoric about national sovereignty, the de la
Madrid government did little to remedy the saturation of the
Mexican north and cable television by US television signals. The
Mexican flag, the national anthem and heroes of the Mexican
Revolution, however, could be seen more often in state-produced
programming. His government also changed the original plan to
hand the Mexican satellite over to TELEVISA in exchange for
TELEVISA's construction of satellite ground stations. In this way
the satellite came under state administration. Yet the new president
soon abandoned a strong state role in the planning and development
of the mass media.

The cycle that began fifteen years ago with the government's purchase of Channel 13 ended in 1985 with the establishment of the official government television network and the successful launching of the Morelos telecommunications satellite. The mass media no longer constituted a problem for the Mexican state. It no longer mattered that the private media set the ideological agenda for Mexican society or that the private lives of TV stars were more important than the running of the Mexican state. All communication policy had been reduced to the question of freedom of expression – a situation then, and in the future, favoured by the private media.

Notes

1. Telesistema consisted of three channels, each aimed at a different economic and cultural group: Channel 4, opened in 1950 by the O'Farrill family which owned the Novedades newspaper group; Channel 2, founded in 1952 by the Azcárraga family, leaders in radio and cinema; and Channel 5, founded the same year by the Alemán family.

6

Politics and Regional Television in Colombia

Elizabeth Fox and Patricia Anzola

Colombian television experienced few real changes until 1984 when Conservative President Belisario Betancur moved television out from under the direct control of the executive, authorized regional channels and created a new administration for national television. For thirty years Colombian television had evolved gradually and almost without interruption from 100 percent government control to a mixed administration of public ownership and private commercial franchises. During this period, however, there was little real modification of television's content, financing and control.

Owners of commercial radio stations and advertising agencies began to enter the Colombian television market even before the fall of the Rojas Pinilla military dictatorship that had first set up television as a public service in 1954. Advertisers soon learned to use the new television technologies to reach a growing urban middle-class audience. Colombian politicians, in turn, developed lasting ties of ownership and influence over the private companies that grew to control television's commercial operations.

For thirty years Colombia maintained the legal fiction of a nationwide public-service television system administered by the Ministry of Communications through its decentralized institution, INRAVISION. For almost its entire life-span, however, private enterprise operated Colombian television for profit, and revenue from commercial advertising financed almost all programming and production.

The military government of Rojas Pinilla paid for the original television studios and broadcasting infrastructure, and the Office of Information and Press of the Presidency produced and controlled the first television transmissions. The government, however, soon turned to the private sector in order to finance the national development of television.

An early law barred the government from selling time on the state channels to commercial advertisers. Private programming companies formed that rented air-time on the two government-owned channels. (A third channel with limited coverage, wholly financed by the government, was reserved for educational television.) The private programming companies sold commercial time to national and international advertisers on the air-time they rented from the government.

Over the years, although 100 percent publicly owned, the programme content, audiences and advertising of Colombian television developed in much the same way as the privately owned commercial television systems of the rest of Latin America. For example, close to one-half the content of Colombian television has always been imported from the USA and Latin American countries. The rest has been the typical national fare found all over Latin America of variety shows, sports, soap operas and government-controlled news. Commercials produced by national and foreign advertising agencies have occupied about 20 percent of broadcasting time.

With the proceeds of the rent it charged the private programming companies, INRAVISION financed the production of some education and cultural programmes on the small third channel and on the few time-slots on the national channels it did not rent out for commercial exploitation. After the initial government investments for television transmission – antennas, microwave relays and satellite ground stations – INRAVISION received no additional government subsidy for television operations or productions.

The minister of communications presided over the board of directors of INRAVISION, made up of the minister of education and two representatives of the president. The Ministry of Communication laid down the general characteristics of the programmes and advertising to be shown on the two national channels. The bids for franchises were periodic, and INRAVISION wrote the guidelines for each time-slot it franchised, for example, variety shows, soap operas, children's programmes or documentaries. INRAVISION awarded the franchises to the commercial programming companies based on the quality of the proposed content and the professional and financial viability of the company. The contracts for the franchises generally ran between two and three years.

The private sector, the Colombian government and the Liberal and Conservative parties that had ruled the country since 1957, by alternating the presidency and equally dividing government jobs in the public sector, were, for the most part, pleased with the Colombian television system. The party out of power was assured a voice on television news and opinion shows, and its members were assured part of the profits to be made from commercial programming.

The presence of many programming companies vying with each other for television franchises did not allow any one commercial company to grow big enough to challenge government management of television or sustain an independent news line – even if they had wanted to. The number of independent commercial programming companies bidding for air-time on the government-owned channels varied over the years between thirty and seventy. Generally, contracts were awarded to between twenty and thirty companies. Of these, the three largest – Punch, RTI and Caracol – usually controlled about 50 percent of the total air-time in the most profitable time-slots. These three companies co-ordinated their efforts in programming and advertising sales, forming what came to be known as 'the Pool'.

Because of competition among programmers, advertisers and their clients had more or less a free rein on Colombian television and were able to impose many programming demands and play off one programmer against another for better rates. More important for the private commercial development of television, however, was the near perfect monopoly of television held by the three or four larger programming companies ensured by government ownership of the air waves. There were no other channels competing for the Colombian television audience, and the large companies could co-ordinate their programming schedules among themselves.

The long stability of the Colombian national television system, however, hid regional, political and private-sector movements for change. The different regions of the country were anxious for some share in production, programming content, profit and news control. Some Colombian politicians were irked by the executives' control of television. Finally, new programming companies were eager for a share in the profits and wanted access to television and a larger number of channels.

Until late 1984 the three most serious challenges to the hybrid organization of Colombian television came, first, from a small independent programmer linked to a dissident wing of one of the traditional political parties who was anxious to gain a larger share of the television market; secondly, from one of the traditional political parties concerned with distortion of the news by the other traditional party; and thirdly (the only successful challenge, linked with wider political reform), from the cities in the interior of the country resentful of the centralization of television administration, production and programming in Bogotá.

The most successful challenge by an independent programmer was that of Consuelo de Montejo. Air-time on Colombia's second national channel was not always franchised to many different programmers. In 1965, when it was originally opened for public bidding, the government awarded the channel in a single bloc to a woman, Consuelo de Montejo, who had previously worked in advertising. Her partnership with the US television network ABC permitted Sra de Montejo to present an attractive bid for the new channel in terms of payment to INRAVISION and programming content. Her channel, Teletigre, had its own production studios, purchased with ABC.

During its five-year contract, Teletigre's fare of imported US programming and soap operas received higher ratings than the first channel. But as a result of pressure from the other programming companies and her political independence (and, at times, opposition), after five years Sra de Montejo lost her franchise. Two years later, in 1972, she introduced a bill in Congress that would give the programming companies greater independence in content and more control of the air-time they rented from the government. Her bill was rewritten at the committee level and its original intent was reversed. The rewritten bill would have eliminated the programming companies altogether by permitting the government to sell commercial time on the publicly owned channels directly to advertisers.

Sra de Montejo's original bill was quashed because the government did not want to lose the political control it exercised over television. The committee bill or counterproposal failed as a result of opposition from private programmers and advertisers who feared the government's ability to sell advertising directly, thereby taking over their lucrative role as intermediaries.

Colombian television was not challenged again until five years later, this time by the Conservative Party. Meanwhile, all television production was centralized in Bogotá and transmitted to the rest of the country by INRAVISION. There was no local production, and with few exceptions all programmes originated in Bogotá.

In 1976 under a Liberal president forty private programming companies presented bids for the 131 weekly hours of broadcasting time on the two national channels. When the winners of the bids were announced, to the consternation of the Conservative Party, they included, for the first time, an official government news programme. They also included a news programme for a company owned by the son and the son-in-law of the main Liberal Party candidate for the next presidential period. (This period was the first time that the long-standing agreement between the Liberal and Conservative parties to alternate the presidency was no longer in force.)

The president justified the introduction of the official news programme with the argument that the presidency needed its own information organ to communicate with the government, Congress and the Colombian people. Soon after its initiation, however, the entire professional staff of the official news programme resigned, complaining of excessive government interference in its operations.

The political balance of Colombian television and the government's traditional alliance with the private news programmers were both beginning to show some cracks.

The controversy over the political management of television continued into 1977, when representatives of the Conservative Party published statistics demonstrating the unequal distribution of television news and opinion programmes among the different political parties that were soon to compete in national elections. These statistics compared the percentage of votes the parties had received in the last congressional elections with their percentage of television news and opinion shows. The figures showed that the Liberal Party with 52 percent of the votes had 70.6 percent of the air-time. The Conservative Party with 38 percent of the votes had only 22 percent of the air-time. (The smaller parties with 7.7 percent of the votes had less than 2.5 percent of the air-time.)

The Liberal minister of communications met the complaints of the Conservative Party with an offer to make more television channels available to the country. Soon after, the Liberal government presented a bill to Congress that would authorize regional channels. The government defended its bill with the argument that access to television was limited for both programming companies and advertisers. With the small number of channels centralized in Bogotá there could be no real competition among programming companies and no positive government control over television. Finally, the limited availability of television time discriminated against the smaller programmers and led to the formation of monopolies.

The bill's proponents claimed the regional channels would compete with the two national channels managed by INRAVISION and improve the quality of their programming. They would also generate new jobs, stimulate regional development and decentralize decision-making to the cities in the interior of the country. The government was prepared to allow the regional channels to transmit in colour, not yet the case with the two national channels. In this way, the government observed, the private sector would pay the costs of introducing colour television that would later be adopted by the national channels.

In response to the Conservative accusation of unequal news time, the Liberal government seemed prepared radically to rewrite the rules of the game and give the country an entirely new structure for public and private television.

The government presented its proposed decentralized, private, regional television structure as a more economically efficient and democratic organization. Its bill, however, was defeated at the committee level. The opponents of the bill argued against the privatization of television and the excessive commercialization of the medium this might cause, although Colombian television was already over 90 percent commercially operated. Furthermore, the bill's detractors observed, private television was more vulnerable than government-owned television to manipulation by international advertising and programming sales. Finally, they noted, the country had other priorities like rural schools and electrification that were more important than colour television.

In conceding the defeat of the government's bill, the minister of communications reminded Congress that her government had presented the bill in response to the Conservative Party's complaints about the government's mismanagement of television. She defended the principle of private television as part of the government's defence of freedom of expression and a free market economy.

The 1977 attempt to privatize television ownership and set up many small regional channels was probably a red herring on the part of the Liberal government to distract attention from their increasingly partisan management of television news. As it was presented, the bill would probably have changed little of the actual content of television. The only companies in any position to bid for the regional channel were the existing commercial programming companies, which would have bid for channels only in those cities where their operations would be profitable. Considering that television advertising is directed at the approximately 15 percent of the population economically able to afford its products, and that 90 percent of this population is concentrated in the three biggest cities in Colombia, there would probably have been very few new regional channels.

The bill was defeated. Many of the arguments in favour of modifying the Colombian television system and the initial complaint of the Conservative Party of excessive control by the current administration, however, continued to be valid. Programming content was poor. The different regions were not represented, and the government exercised little real control over the quality or direction of television.

As foreseen and feared by the Conservative Party before the elections, the Liberal administration that governed Colombia between 1978 and 1982 was marked by unusually pronounced and abusively partisan political manipulation of television, economic corruption and censorship. This legacy of manipulation and corruption made a strong impression on the Conservative candidates who won the elections in 1982.

In 1984 the discussion of regional channels once again surfaced, this time at the initiative of Antioquia, one of the most economically and politically powerful regions of the country. Based on feasibility studies carried out by the regional development corporation and the University of Antioquia, the state governor of Antioquia presented a proposal to the minister of communications of the Conservative administration to authorize a regional cultural television channel for his state. Authorization was conceded in December 1984 by a presidential accord citing the need to incorporate the mass media in the process of regional development, education, culture and recreation.

Tele-Antioquia, the new channel, financed equally by INRA-VISION and the regional development corporation of Antioquia, was on the air by August 1985. The government regulation for Tele-Antioquia prohibited the use of commercial advertising. The channel was permitted, however, to have commercial sponsorship for its programmes.

Tele-Antioquia soon ran into trouble. It received little commercial support in the form of sponsorships and was savagely attacked by the national press and the commercial television programmers in Bogotá. The new channel was accused of having ties with the Mafia, illegal and disloyal use of advertising and taxing the already depleted state budget. Tele-Antioquia soon found itself unable to produce cultural programming on its limited budget, and pressure mounted from local industries to accept their advertising.

Soon after the authorization of the first regional channel, the Conservative government turned its attention to another traditional complaint against television – its political control by the presidency. The Conservative government presented a bill in Congress that would move Colombian television out from under the direct control of the president and ensure 'public' as opposed to government control. Law 42 was passed with the support of both the Liberal and the Conservative members of Congress. The smaller programming companies and the labour unions working in the media also supported the government's proposal. The large private commercial programming companies, fearing increased control over their operations, were the sole opponents of the new law.

The new law set up an 'associated company' for the administration of television. The new company was made up of the Ministry of Communications through TELECOM (the national telecommunications company), and COLCULTURA (the National Board of Culture). The law maintained the public-service definition of television and public ownership of the national radio and television channels.

In addition to INRAVISION's two new partners, the main changes under the new legislation were in the management of the government-owned channels. Law 42 established three new levels of control and administration of television: the National Television Council, the Administrative Board and a Watchdog Commission.

The National Television Council became the highest authority for television in the country. It was charged with setting the overall policy of INRAVISION, awarding the franchises for commercial air-time, setting tariffs, establishing the norms for programming content and quality and regulating the regional channels.

The government was a minority in the new National Television Council. Of a total of eleven members, only three were representatives of the executive branch of government. The members were the minister of communications, a representative of the president, the director of COLCULTURA, two representatives of Congress, a representative of the Colombian journalists, a representative of the National Academy of History and Literature, a representative of the communication schools, a former director of INRAVISION and two members of the Watchdog Commission.

Under the previous law the executive branch of government had sole authority over television. The members of the new council came from the legislative branch and various national organizations. This switch of power away from the presidency – although the president still named the director of INRAVISION – was the main purpose of the new law.

The new Administrative Board was designed to facilitate the daily management of television operations. A representative of the commercial programming companies sat on this board, for the first time giving the private sector a say in the operations of INRA-VISION. Other members of the Administrative Board were the minister of communications, the legal representative of TELECOM and two members of the National Television Council.

The third new body established by Law 42 was the citizens' Watchdog Commission designed to defend the interests of the different audience groups on Colombian television and keep a watch on the quality of television content. The twelve members of the Watchdog Commission represented different groups in Colombian society: the Church, universities, community organizations, labour unions, consumers, parents, journalists, housewives, doctors, industry and advertising.

The Watchdog Commission was an advisory body. It had no real power other than that derived from its capacity to mobilize public opinion and air different issues on television and through the media.

Law 42 did not change the franchising arrangements between the government and the private programming companies that actually ran the day-to-day commercial operations of the two national television channels. It did, however, increase the scope of future government regulation of the media by giving the Ministry of Communications responsibility for regulating cable and other forms of pay television when these appeared.

The new television legislation formed part of the Betancur administration's objective of giving access to wider sectors of Colombian society – opposition political parties, local and regional levels of government, the guerrilla movements that divided Colombian society – in the representative institutions of government. The television reform, as well as the more sweeping social reforms of the Betancur administration, were carried out in the face of considerable opposition from sectors within the two traditional parties that had controlled Colombian politics since 1957.

In the years preceding the reform, most recently as a result of the excessive government and commercial abuses under the previous administration, there had been increasing calls for changes in INRAVISION. The mix of public and private control did not entirely satisfy either the government or the commercial companies. The Betancur reform changed the structure of INRAVISION but did not modify the relationship between INRAVISION and the commercial programming companies. Although initially opposed to the new legislation, the major private programming companies soon welcomed the new law. Perhaps they saw the opportunity for greater private control of television as a result of the diffusion of power within INRAVISION.

Opposition political parties also welcomed the television reform. They saw greater opportunities for political pluralism in the reduction of the president's control over television. The reform could also mean greater participation and access to national television administration and opinion and news programmes for the smaller parties.

In spite of the clearly laid out levels of authority and organization of the new administration of INRAVISION, however, little real change occurred in Colombian television. A year after the law was passed, several of the members of the new boards still had not yet been named. One reason for this delay was that a new president (Liberal) and Congress took office soon after the legislation went into effect. Another reason is that bids for commercially exploited air-time did not go out immediately under the new legislation. Whatever the case, it took all parties involved a while to get used to their new partners and the new distribution of power and decide on their future role in television.

At the government's initiative, Law 42 also contained an article giving INRAVISION the authority to establish new regional television channels. The new law assigned the National Television Council the task of regulating the regional channels to be set up by INRAVISION in partnership with decentralized public companies and institutions from the regions.

In the case of the first regional channel, Tele-Antioquia, set up by presidential accord prior to Law 42, the regional partners were the public utility companies. The board of directors of Tele-Antioquia was made up of the national minister of communication, the state governor, the director of INRAVISION, the state secretary of education, the director of the state public utility company, the president of the University of Antioquia, a communications scholar from Antioquia and a representative of the regional Watchdog Commission.

Law 42 had anticipated that national funds from INRAVISION as well as from other public entities such as the state universities, telephone companies and utilities would finance the new regional channels. Commercial sponsorship from local companies, not the same as commercial advertising, would complement public financing.

In the case of Tele-Antioquia, it soon became apparent that the regional channels could not survive on these sources of financing. In spite of earlier denials by the government, the Ministry of Communications soon authorized the use of commercial advertising on the regional channels under the same conditions as on the national channels.

The commercial programming companies on the national channels strongly opposed the authorization of the direct sale of commercial advertising by the regional channels. They argued that commercial advertising on the regional channels would further reduce the amount of funds for advertising investment available nationally, their sole source of support.

In other regions of the country, different public institutions grouped together to form other regional channels in association with INRAVISION. For example, the five states on the Caribbean coast became partners of INRAVISION in Tele-Caribe. The north-western coffee-growing regions formed Tele-Café, and the important agricultural valley around the city of Cali set up Tele-Valle.

The prospect of many new regional channels raised serious questions concerning their economic viability and their effect on the financial base of national commercial television. The regional channels could force the government and the commercial programmers to rethink the audience preference and participation, national and regional cultural production and the political control of television. On the other hand, they could become yet another example of Colombian television's ability to resist change by setting up new mini-hybrids in the regions.

At any rate, after seeing the impending loss of their captive markets, the large private programming companies switched their sights to the cable television market directed at high-income audiences.

The driving forces of Colombian television – economic profit and political power – often in tandem, seemed to be able, yet again, to keep one step ahead of reformist policies and rhetoric.

Communication, the Church and Social Conflict in El Salvador, 1970–80

Ricardo Sol Arriaza

Between 1970 and 1980 the Church of El Salvador played an important role in the political events of the country. The Church made an enormous effort to gather and share the concerns and achievements of the Salvadoran people, and different ecclesiastical acts revealed profound support for national dialogue. The Church's use of the mass media was a key element in its criticism of the traditional structures of social and political domination and in its promotion of political awareness and solidarity among the people.

Much of the Church's commitment to the process of social change that occurred in El Salvador in the 1970s was carried out through an intense use of its richly varied communication resources. These resources ranged from the traditional homily to sophisticated technologies of the mass media such as the newspaper *Orientación* and the YSAX radio station. The Church employed these and other media to support social change and report the many injustices of which Salvadoran society and members of the Church were victims.

Two-way communication between the Church and the people began to develop in the mid-1960s. New streams of thought present in events like Vatican II and the Bishops' Conference of Medellín began to permeate the traditional ecclesiastical structures. Vatican II ruled that the central act of worship, the Mass, could henceforth be celebrated in the language of the people rather than in Latin. It declared freedom of religious belief without interference from the state, the Church's greater social concern and greater involvement of the laity in church worship and work. The 1968 Bishops' Conference approved the Church's newly stated 'preferential option for the poor', denouncing institutionalized violence and other social ills, thus providing many of the components for liberation theology.

In El Salvador, the change in the Church's traditional forms and contents of communication and its new focus on social injustice were strengthened by the appointment of Monsignor Oscar Arnulfo Romero, Archbishop of San Salvador.

Archbishop Romero was a believer in the mass media's influence on society. He combined his belief in the media with a strongly held commitment to the poor. Romero used the Church's media to counteract the power of the traditionally conservative commercial mass media. His strong commitment to the poor and his creative and dynamic use of the mass media were constantly present in the communication practices of the Salvadoran Church.

The socially engaged Church of El Salvador in the 1970s was often criticized and attacked by conservative and established political and economic interests. The period in which Romero was Archbishop of San Salvador was one of intense persecution of the Church. It included the harassment of foreign and local priests, the expulsion of foreign priests and a virulent advertising campaign depicting the Church as the cause of social chaos. Father Rutilio Grande of the Parish of Aguilares was the first victim of this campaign (Rivera y Damas, 1977).

In 1977 the Salvadoran Church's Inter-Diocesan Social Secretariat published a report describing the last eighteen months of repression:

> Ten bomb explosions, two searches, one ransacking and desecration of the blessed Sacrament, one threat to close the church radio, seven refusals for priests wishing to enter El Salvador, three priests tortured and two mistreated, three priests arrested, two priests and four laypersons assassinated, three priests forced to leave the country due to death threats. A defamation campaign. Threats to expel an order of religious women. Fifteen parishes without priests. (Americas Watch, 1982: 111)

The progressive transformation of the Salvadoran Church had its roots in different ecclesiastical events and was linked to the country's sharpened social conflicts. These conflicts came to a head in the late 1960s. Until 1969 El Salvador had been for the most part under the political and ideological domination of a hard-line military rule that represented the interests of the landed oligarchy. This domination reached its high point in 1969 with the military's exploitation of nationalist sentiment during El Salvador's war with Honduras.

After the war, with the return of at least 80,000 Salvadoran peasants who had been living in Honduras, social frustrations, pressure for land distribution and high unemployment increased. The impact of the refugees on the economy threatened the tense social balance of this small agrarian country – approximately 4.8 million people in an area about the size of Massachusetts.

The government had to open an escape-valve for the mounting tensions. In January 1970, on the initiative of the National Legislative Assembly, the government organized a Congress on

Agrarian Reform. The Church authorities of San Salvador sent a delegation of priests to the congress. The recommendations of the Church's delegates were included in the conclusions of the congress. The congress had not finished, however, when a priest from the delegation was kidnapped. He was not released until the Church authorities had strongly protested to the Ministry of Defence, and the Church-owned radio station, YSAX, had broadcast a special programme denouncing the kidnapping. The next morning Father Alas was found in a coffee field, drugged, nude and severely beaten (Rivera y Damas, 1977).

The participation of the priests in the Congress on Agrarian Reform and the kidnapping of Father Alas were the first significant conflicts between the Church and the traditional power structure of El Salvador. These unprecedented conflicts took place at a time of profound social and political change in the country.

The Salvadoran government and the local oligarchy had declared the concept of agrarian reform to be subversive, along with any other concept that entailed any modification of landownership, the basis of wealth and power. Pressures for land reform, however, were enormous. El Salvador had an average of 500 people per square mile against an average of 94 per square mile in the rest of the isthmus. The fact that the government agreed to hold a congress on agrarian reform was an indication of the magnitude of social unrest in Salvadoran society.

The peasants and political opposition had begun to organize and confront the government on different issues. By 1970 El Salvador's first guerrilla group, the Popular Forces of Liberation (FLP), had appeared, followed in 1971 by the Revolutionary People's Army (ERP) and in 1975 by the Armed Forces of National Resistance (FARN).

In 1970 the Salvadoran government attempted to gain legitimacy by holding elections. The government candidates lost, however, and the government modified the election returns to stay in power. The fraudulent elections further polarized the country between supporters and opponents of the regime.

Election fraud was not new to El Salvador. The government persecuted the opposition parties that were beginning to attract popular support during the presidential elections of 1967 and the legislative and municipal elections of 1968. One form of persecution was the government's systematic exclusion of the opposition parties from the mass media.

The government tried to win the March 1970 elections with publicity about its declared military victory over Honduras. This didn't work. A few months after the war, voters in the principal cities of the country refused to vote for the military candidates of the official party and elected the Christian Democrat candidates to local offices.

Two years later the opposition parties presented themselves at the polls under the common banner of the National Union of the Opposition (UND). When it became clear that the opposition had won, the Central Council of Elections, totally controlled by the government National Conciliation Party (PCN), changed the election results under the protection of the national guard and announced the victory of the official candidates.

The Catholic radios refused to accept political advertising during the electoral campaign. Yet, notwithstanding their decision to stay out of politics, the Church radios clashed with an intransigent regime that resisted even the mildest criticism and the smallest change. The Church and many of its representatives grew closer and closer to the problems and struggles of the growing lower classes. The Church found the mass media especially appropriate for its messages and audiences. In March 1972 several fire bombs exploded in a Catholic radio station causing extensive damage. What probably provoked the attack was the news programme of the archbishop, *Presenciando los Acontecimientos* (Rivera y Damas, 1977).

In 1972, as a consequence of an attempted coup, the regime announced a national curfew and a state of emergency during which various members of the opposition parties were kidnapped, killed or exiled. The Episcopal Conference denounced these actions. The clergy felt the growing need to organize and inform themselves and others about what was going on in the country. As a result, the Church began to publish the newspapers *Carta de Noticias* and *Justicia y Paz* oriented towards church and peasant audiences (Rivera y Damas, 1977).

As social unrest grew, it became harder and harder for the regime to control the country. Peasants fled to the cities, and a new class of marginal slum dwellers, landless labourers, low-paid civil servants, teachers and students formed mass popular organizations outside the traditional party structures. Government repression expanded to levels never before seen in the country. Sectors of the Church joined grass-roots organizations and accompanied them in their growing politicization and dissatisfaction with the government.

On 30 July 1975 the combined forces of the army, the national guard and the police broke up a student demonstration. (After the demonstration, the government began the custom of hosing down the streets to remove all evidence of its bloody repression.) One of the few acknowledgements of the demonstration was a mass for a slain student celebrated in the Cathedral of San Salvador. After the mass, members of the congregation organized six days of mourning in the cathedral to protest against government repression.

A form of communication between the people and the Church had begun that turned the pulpit into a vehicle of reflection and dialogue. This continued for the next ten years, finding its maximum expression in the radio broadcasts of Monsignor Romero. The communication would become so strong that it could only be silenced by a national campaign of persecution and extermination of priests and nuns, culminating in the assassination of Archbishop Romero.[1]

The occupation and permanent meetings in the cathedral acquired a national dimension and were witnessed and felt by wide sectors of society. Other events of this type quickly spread beyond the capital to the rural areas where most of the Salvadoran people lived. The Church's social activities encouraged the growing awareness and organization of the Salvadoran peasant, silenced for over fifty years by the most absolute government prohibition against any type of social or political organization.

Between 1970 and 1975 the Church organized Christian grass-roots communities that gave peasants education and leadership training. Some communities were organized around co-operatives. The communities soon ran into difficulties – frequently in the form of crude repression – and the methods of pastoral reflection quickly gave the communities a political dimension. The war with Honduras, the impact of the refugees and the election frauds of 1970 and 1972 increased the political awareness of the communities and placed them in sharp confrontation with the government (Cáceres Prendes, 1982).

The communities could soon be heard throughout the country as a result of their large, active membership and their numerous religious activities, celebrations and processions. Their many actions in the area of legal rights and their efforts to secure higher salaries, social benefits and compensation for lost land gave the Christian communities a strong national presence.

Government repression against the peasant organizations, such as the massacre of La Cayetana in the Diocese of San Vicente on 29 November 1974 and the massacre of Tres Calles in the Diocese of Santiago María in June 1975, further politicized the Christian communities. Many of their members became members of political organizations of peasants like FECCAS and UTC, and some Christian communities developed into political organizations. Many of the types of social and political analysis, dynamics of interpersonal communications and forms of recruitment of the peasant organizations were taken from the teachings and experiences of the Christian communities.

In June 1976, a year before the end of the presidential period of Colonel Arturo Armando Molina, under pressure from the United States, the Legislative Assembly passed a law creating districts of irrigation as part of a limited agrarian reform. The law applied to 145,230 acres of land in a cattle-raising and cotton-farming zone. The Salvadoran oligarchy reacted immediately. The National Association of Private Enterprise (ANEP) and other business organizations mounted a costly advertising campaign against the reform. Almost daily, newspapers ran open threats of a military coup against a regime that had dared to question private property, the cornerstone of Salvadoran society.

A new organization of powerful private landowners formed the Eastern Region Farmers' Front (FARO) to put an end to what they considered the dangerous government initiatives. The positions of FARO were far more aggressive than those of the ANEP.

At first, the ANEP–FARO alliance attacked the government in paid announcements in the national newspapers and exerted economic pressures against the government. The duel between the government and the private sector lasted two and a half months. At the end, the government gave in, and the Assembly annulled the project. After this brief confrontation, the government and ANEP–FARO joined together in a common front against the Church (Rivera y Damas, 1977).

ANEP and FARO stepped up their attacks against the Church in the press. In December 1976 *Diario de Hoy* announced that 'hordes of peasants organized by third world priests and marxist leaders and protected by the tolerance of the government are blooding our soil'. The Archbishop of San Salvador replied that in an unjust situation the Church should fight against injustice; the responsibility lay with those who had created the injustice.

The real struggle of the traditional sectors of Salvadoran society, however, was not with the Church but with the new social organizations that questioned the established order. By this time, the popular organizations of peasants, workers, teachers, students and slum dwellers had demonstrated their political strength and ability to present their demands for better salaries and working conditions and their irreconcilable differences with the established order.

The dominant sectors, however, held the Church responsible for the social and political unrest in the country and used all the means and media at their disposal to attack the ties between the Church and the larger community. Monsignor Romero, the new Archbishop of San Salvador, quickly realized the potential of the media to multiply the pastoral experience and transmit the good tidings of Christianity to a people crushed by a regime that denied them the right to express themselves in their own media or in the media of others.

Romero had worked in the mass media before becoming archbishop and was familiar with modern communications technology. For many years he directed the newspaper *Chaparrastique* in the west of the country and a radio station in the Department of San Miguel. When he was the assistant bishop, he was responsible for the newspaper *Orientación*. As the Archbishop of San Salvador, Monsignor Romero rediscovered his true vocation as a journalist and communicator.

When Romero became archbishop, the changes in the Catholic Church had already produced a new structure of pastoral action that emphasized secular participation. Under the administration of the previous archbishop, the Salvadoran Church had developed a strong representative structure that guaranteed community participation in the Church directly without the need of a priest as an intermediary. This function was performed by the delegates of the community organizations. The organizations had their own organs of communication that assured that the opinions of their members reached their representatives.

The Pastoral Council was set up in the same way. Most of its members were lay members. The diocese of the archbishop was divided into vicarages. In each vicarage a lay member was elected to represent the community on the Pastoral Council. There were a majority of lay members in other Church organizations like the Secretary of Relations, the Secretary of Pastoral Activities and the Secretary of Social Communication.

This organization created an important and agile flow of communication between the base and the authorities of the Archdiocese of San Salvador. This 'Popular Church' with its democratic representative structure and wide popular base and organization was the target of escalating incidents of repression and a virulently critical advertising campaign.

The appointment of Monsignor Romero in 1977 came in the midst of hostility from the pro-government newspapers and followed the assassination of Father Rutilio Grande. The new archbishop's appointment marked the beginning of a series of major changes in the Salvadoran Church (Stein, 1981).

The mass media of the Church played an important role in these events. The day of the assassination of Father Grande, priests and members of the ecclesiastical communities took over YSAX, the

Catholic radio station. They transmitted three intense hours of special programming – reflections, music, readings from the Bible – that began a new style for the station (Richard and Meléndez, 1982).

The weekly *Orientación*, the YSAX radio station, the steady flow of press bulletins from the archdiocese and the newspaper *Justicia y Paz* continued to document and speak out against the abuses of the regime. The priests who did not agree with the new philosophy of the Catholic Church were removed from their posts and sent to places where their disagreement could not harm the work of the Church.

Monsignor Romero took a clear position regarding his role as a communicator. The assassination of Padre Grande was a crushing blow nationally and internationally. Its impact transcended the local sphere. In the fierce defamation campaign of slander and insults in the mass media that followed the assassination, Monsignor Romero maintained that the battle of communication was an unequal but key battle. He called to work with him a number of people who could provide the necessary technical expertise and administrative skills to strengthen the mass media of the archdiocese.

As a result of his activities in the mass media, Monsignor Romero came to be called 'the voice of those who have no voice'. His own homilies broadcast over the radio had wide repercussions on the Salvadorans.

The path taken by the mass media of the Salvadoran Church during the crucial decade of the 1970s was the product of the explosive social and political situation in the country and the lack of any mass media that could freely and openly discuss national issues. The commercial interests of the privately owned newspapers, the self-censorship of journalists and the violent repression against those journalists and newspapers that dared to print criticism of the government motivated the Church to turn its own media into instruments of service, dialogue and criticism.

Monsignor Romero often pointed to the undemocratic nature of the Salvadoran press, which became silent in the face of pressures from government and industry. He proclaimed the need to hear other voices. On 10 August 1979, less than a year before his assassination, he broadcast over the YSAX station his pity and contempt for the merchants of news, ideas and information.

> Pity because they sell something rotten and dirty like their articles on crime and sex with no respect for their public; pity because they must lie, slander and vilify in order to build their empires; pity because they have sold their souls to bad money and to the wrong powers in order to silence the voices of those who protest and of those who have just complaints.

Pity because they have left the people without a voice. Contempt because the merchants of news, printing lies in the editorials of the local papers, do not deserve to be compared with the lowliest street vendor.

Other Catholic radio stations picked up Romero's complaints against the mediocrity and low morals of the private press. These stations called the private media 'commercial catalogues' and servants of the regime that censored everything, even their advertising copy, in order to curry favour with the government.

Undoubtedly, government threats and bombings of private newspapers influenced the papers' decisions about what to print. In early 1976 *La Crónica* had been machine-gunned twice. On 5 June an anonymous telephone caller told the editor he had been judged, found guilty and sentenced to death. On 14 July 1979 the offices and printing plant of the newspaper were burnt to the ground by incendiary bombs.

In 1980 seventeen news offices and radio stations were bombed or machine-gunned, twelve journalists were killed and three disappeared. By the end of 1980 the last two independent newspapers, *El Independiente* and *La Crónica del Pueblo*, closed down after numerous bombings, threats, military interventions and assaults on employees. During the year the premises of *El Independiente* were destroyed, and its editor was the target of numerous attacks. *La Crónica del Pueblo* closed down permanently after its editor and a photographer were abducted and found dismembered on 11 July 1980 (Americas Watch, 1982).

The Church's mass media presented themselves as an alternative type of media, open to debate and the rational analysis of the problems that affected the country. The Church had put its communications resources at the disposal of a wide range of positions and sectors within Salvadoran society. Many well-known intellectuals contributed articles, commentaries and analysis to *Orientación* and YSAX radio. The public participated in the radio station with letters and telephone calls, turning radio into a dynamic new form of dialogue with the people. The Church's communication practices threatened a government that owed its existence to the negation of all criticism and dialogue.

The regime's attacks on YSAX and *Orientación* often went further than the violent diatribes against the Church in the pro-government media. Numerous dynamite explosions forced the station temporarily off the air. Its signals were frequently jammed, especially when Monsignor Romero spoke or during news broadcasts. YSAX denounced these attacks and other forms of government interference and accused the government of doing nothing to stop the attacks against the radio station by the extreme right wing.

The attacks on its media, however, did not force the Church to alter its support for popular movements. The Church did not make concessions to the government, nor did it directly give its support to any of the many opposition political organizations. The Church defined its role as a 'voice of reason' identified with democracy and social justice, but open to any point of view that broadened understanding of the problems facing the country.

In March 1979 a YSAX editorial explained how it saw its independent role although it was seen by some as a dangerous leftist programme and by others as a right-wing organization serving the regime. YSAX tried to serve the truth and help the people, the editorial continued, in spite of the fact that some minority groups of both extremes were bothered by this and did not agree. YSAX, however, sought a just and democratic solution to the problems of the country rather than dogmatic and ideological answers.

The methods, practices and experiences of the Church's use of communication media changed during the 1970s. These changes came from the Church's work with the people and its relationships with the newly emerging grass-roots organizations. In the words of one analyst (Stein, 1981), the Church 'lost its paternalist varnish and its zeal to convert and preach and found a new form of communication that allowed the people themselves to speak and to express themselves through the mass media with their own creative and critical abilities'.

Notes

1. On 24 March 1980 Archbishop Romero was shot to death while saying mass in the cathedral. Although there were many witnesses, the assassin was never apprehended. The day before his death, Archbishop Romero delivered an appeal to members of the army and the security forces to stop repression and slaughter in the countryside, Hundreds of thousands of Salvadorans heard his homily through the Church radio station. Three American nuns, a lay missionary and five other priests were murdered the same year (Americas Watch, 1982: 54–6).

References

Americas Watch Committee/American Civil Liberties Union (1982) *Report on Human Rights in El Salvador*. New York: Random House.
Cáceres Prendes, Jorge (1982) 'Radicalización de la Lucha Política y Surgimiento de la Iglesia Popular en El Salvador', *Estudios Sociales Centroamericanos*, 33.
Richard, Pablo and Meléndez, Guillermo (1982) *La Iglesia de los Pobres en América Central*. San José: DEI Editores.
Rivera y Damas, Mons. Arturo (1977) 'Labor Pastoral de la Arquidiócesis de San Salvador, Especialmente de las Comunidades Eclesiales de Base en su Proyección de Justicia', *Estudios Sociales Centroamericanos*, 348–9.
Stein, Eduardo (1981) 'La Experiencia Centroamericana en Comunicación y los Procesos Democráticos'. Paper presented at Consejo Latinoamericano de Ciencias Sociales (CLACSO) meeting on Communication and Democracy, Santa Marta.

8

Repression and Innovation under Authoritarianism

María de la Luz Hurtado

People take models for their lives and dreams for their futures from the movies. Films give people forms of expression and different images of the world with which to judge and understand themselves and their country. In an ideal democracy a national film industry as well as imported films should be able to employ many styles and portray a wide variety of different subjects. All sectors of society should have access to films and be able to criticize them freely. Under an authoritarian regime this is seldom the case.

In Western democracies economic constraints such as a lack of government subsidies, the monopolization of film production and distribution and various entrance barriers limit what films are produced, distributed and shown. Most dictatorships, however, control all the films that are produced nationally and the films that enter the country, restrict all criticism and destroy most forms of access to the film industry.

The film industry is a complex system of production, distribution and exhibition. It is shaped by artistic and technological developments and by its political, economic and cultural context. Governments, banks, producers, directors, actors, technicians and, finally, the public form part of the industry and are all in some way responsible for its final products.

In Chile, as in other Latin American countries, the film industry's relationship with government has always been crucial. The state built the first national film studios and later rented them out to private producers. Public funds for Chilean universities and intellectuals formed the artists and writers that made up the national film industry. Between 1967 and 1973, the heyday of Chilean film production, different tax breaks and indirect subsidies helped private investors and film producers.

The military dictatorship that ruled Chile after 1973 put into effect authoritarian and non-democratic measures that changed the course of the national movie industry. The military took away tax exemptions and other forms of subsidy. Between 1975 and 1978 no new national films were released to commercial theatres. In the years that followed, the industry began to forge a new independence from the state and develop different models of film production and distribution. At the same time, the concentration of companies that distributed and exhibited foreign films increased sharply, and the demographics of the film-going public shifted radically.

The Chilean film industry, although destroyed by the military during the first years of the dictatorship, slowly began to discover new forms of survival. Some independent film makers achieved minimum financial independence, pluralist content and democratic participation in an alternative circuit for their films. The government film production company also changed. For the first time it became involved in film distribution and exhibition, and its operations began to show a profit. Many of these changes have their roots in earlier developments of the Chilean film industry.

The first films in Chile were made in 1902. In 1925 Chile produced fifteen silent films. Between 1934 and 1944 Chile produced two 'talkies' a year. The Chilean movie audience grew rapidly and developed an appetite for national films as well as for films imported from Mexico, the United States and Argentina.

It soon became clear to local film distributors and theatre owners that more profit could be made from imported foreign films than from local productions. Movie theatres and film distribution had become a lucrative business. Warner Brothers, United Artists, Twentieth Century Fox, Columbia and other North American companies soon dominated film distribution in Chile.

In the 1940s the Chilean government included national film promotion in its general policy for the substitution of imports and the development of national industry. As part of its policy, in 1942 the National Investment Corporation set up a government film company, Chile Films and provided generous funding and installations for Hollywood-type productions. These extravaganzas failed both artistically and financially. In 1950 the government rented Chile Films to a private company, whereupon it turned out one or two mediocre films a year until the early 1960s.

The universities were more successful than the government in their efforts to stimulate the Chilean film industry and train national film makers. The universities trained a generation of Chilean film makers and produced an important series of documentaries. By the mid-1950s the universities had their own studios and equipment; in addition to classes in film making and actual film production, they carried out debates and analysis on Chilean and foreign films and developed a tradition of film criticism. Later, with the coming of television, the same professionals who had been trained in the university film classes worked closely with the university-owned television channels.

The first dark age of the Chilean film industry lasted for over a decade during which less than one film a year was produced. In 1967, however, the Christian Democrats passed a new law on national film production as part of their general policy of increased state participation in artistic production and distribution. The new law reduced the tariffs on imported raw film and movie equipment, cut taxes on laboratories and studios and turned over the proceeds of a tax on theatre tickets to national film makers.

As a result of these measures, commercial film production jumped to six movies a year in 1967, followed by another six in 1968 and ten in 1969. Some of the classics of the Chilean film industry were produced during this period: *Largo Viaje* by Patricio Kaulen in 1967; *Tres Tristes Tigres* by Raúl Ruiz in 1968; *Valparaíso mi Amor* by Aldo Francia in 1969; *Lunes Primero, Domingo Siete* by Helvio Soto in 1968; and *El Chacal de Nahueltoro* by Miguel Littin in 1969.

Strengthened by the new economic incentives and spurred on by the interest of different political parties and the government, Chilean film makers took part in numerous public debates and seminars on the role of film in national society. The work of the Chilean film makers in Chile Films and their participation in the national and university television channels brought national film makers in close contact with the social and political changes taking place in the country.

Many Chilean directors favoured a revolutionary, pro-socialist movie industry. Some of the documentary film makers were influenced by the theories of 'cine imperfecto' of the Cuban film maker García. His theories expounded the need for a less expensive and technically complex form of film production for countries that lacked the financial and technical means for a more lavish movie industry. Using these theories, the production of documentary films in Chile leapt.

In 1973 the military ousted the elected government of President Salvador Allende. For four years, during what were in many ways the most repressive years of the regime – the second dark age of Chilean film – the entire Chilean movie industry including feature films, documentaries and news almost completely disappeared.

The military government immediately put members of the armed forces in charge of Chile Films and the university film departments. The new directors fired the supporters of the Socialist government and left their posts vacant. During the first year of the dictatorship, the military closed the audiovisual department and film library of the University of Chile and the film school of the University of Valparaíso. After 1974 no new students entered the School of Communication Arts of the Catholic University, until then one of the main training centres for young film makers.

After gaining control of the university television channels, the military government turned over the equipment and studios of the university film schools to the tightly muzzled national and university television channels.

Under the military government, the traditional relationship between television and film was reversed. Television now controlled the film industry rather than the film industry controlling television. The National Television Channel that had been partially owned by Chile Films now owned 99 percent of the stock of Chile Films. The board of directors of Chile Films became the same board as that of the National Television Channel.

The new authorities of Chile Films fired most of the film makers employed by the previous administration and sent some of them to prison. In addition to losing their jobs, Chilean film makers also lost the tools of their trade. Most of their equipment had been government-owned. Chilean independent film makers were unable to pay the high rents for cameras and studios charged by Chile Films under military management, and there were no independent studios where they could work.

In 1975 the military regime abolished the 1967 law protecting national film production and did away with all other forms of state subsidy and tax exemptions for the movie industry. In this way the military destroyed the financial base of the national film industry, as it had already destroyed its human and technological base.

It was impossible to make films without some form of government subsidy. Besides the costs of promotion and advertising, the average budget for a feature film in Chile was $120,000. At a price of one dollar a ticket, this meant a film must first be accepted for distribution and then be seen by at least 120,000 people in order to break even. Because Chilean films were not distributed internationally, all their earnings had to come from the national market. Even if the producer was able eventually to recover the initial investment, the capital put into the production of the film was tied up for at least a year at a high cost.

At first, the military exercised no other formal censorship over national film production or distribution once it had cleaned out Chile Films and the university film schools. High production costs, however, made it necessary for national film makers to have before completion a minimum guarantee that their films could be exhibited in Chilean theatres. Chilean producers often voluntarily presented the scripts of their films to the military for approval before filming began in order to ensure they could be shown when finished.

The military, however, prohibited the distribution of many foreign films, among them *Last Tango in Paris* by Bertolucci, *Casanova* by Fellini, *Pantaleón y las Visitadoras* by Vargas Llosa, *Pixote* by Hector Babenco, and *La Chinoise* by Godard.

After more than ten years in power, in 1983, the military finally put into effect a law requiring all filmed material to be authorized by the office of film censorship before distribution, even if it was not to be shown commercially.

Censorship and financial difficulties made political and economic exiles of many of Chile's most famous film directors, actors and technicians. This exodus destroyed most training opportunities for young film makers and stopped any real debate and discussion on national films. Many of the films made before 1973 were no longer available in Chile, not even for private showings.

Within a few years of the military take-over, national film production had all but vanished along with the film-making schools and the traditional links between the movie industry and the performing arts. The military regime had absorbed what was left of the Chilean film industry within the government-owned and controlled commercial television. Politically and economically, the regime had destroyed independent production. The only alternative left for Chilean film makers who wanted to exercise their trade was to go into the advertising business and work for television.

This alternative, nevertheless, offered film makers some interesting opportunities. After 1978 the national movie industry entered a new phase in which, for the first time in its history, the private sector became more dynamic than the public sector. Its main productions, however, were neither documentaries nor feature films. They were TV advertisements.

The free market economic policies introduced by the military government brought with them an enormous demand for advertising and new marketing techniques. The percentage of total advertising investment directed towards television increased by a factor of 20 between 1975 and 1984. Advertising jumped from a little over $7 million in 1975 to almost $150 million in 1984. Chilean television captured over 50 percent of total advertising in 1984. This was twice the percentage captured by television in Canada or the United States and four times the percentage for television in most European countries.

Almost all the film makers who had remained in Chile earned their living producing advertisements for television. With the new video technologies and production techniques, it was possible for the film makers to make television ads with comparatively low overheads and few permanent employees.

Competition was stiff, and Brazilian, Argentine and US agencies captured a great deal of the Chilean advertising market. The Chilean producers, however, quickly acquired the necessary creative and administrative skills to compete with foreign agencies. After 1982, when foreign exchange became more expensive, Chilean producers moved in to replace the foreign advertising agencies operating in the country.

Advertising, initially a short-term survival strategy looked down upon by the Chilean film makers imbued with the university experience of high culture, soon became their principal form of subsistence. Working under conditions of heavy censorship and with no government subsidies, Chilean film makers, at first guiltily and later more openly, turned into Madison Avenue admen.

As a result of the symbiosis between the movie industry and advertising, Chilean movie makers began to make money. For the first time, the independent film producers acquired capital, studios and equipment. By 1984 there were fifty-seven independent laboratories and studios for film and video production operating in Santiago.

Considering the small size of the Chilean market, much of the equipment of the independent laboratories was excessive. It would doubtless have been cheaper to rent rather than own studios and equipment. Nevertheless, the owners of the laboratories justified their investment in infrastructure with the argument that it gave them the conditions to make their own movies.

Some of the independent film studios and laboratories lent their equipment to young film makers for non-commercial productions. Other new forms of organization developed like Valcine, owned by the film producer Valcecki. Valcine housed four independent producers who had exclusive contracts for the use of the Valcine cameras and laboratories. This arrangement was profitable for all involved and gave the producers the freedom and capital to undertake creative projects in films and documentaries.

The reawakening of the Chilean movie industry in the form of the small, privately owned studios stopped the flow of many Chilean film makers abroad and permitted the return of others. The influx of new technology forced technicians and specialists to retrain themselves to compete in the national and international advertising market that supported their operations.

The enormous growth of the Chilean advertising industry and its demands for professionals in film and video production, combined with the military's privatization of the education system, led to the establishment of various private educational institutions offering degrees in film making and audiovisual techniques. After completing these degrees, most new Chilean film makers got their on-the-job training in advertising.

Although the new Chilean movie industry under the military had apparently avoided its traditional dependence on government subsidies and university studios, it had not solved the problem of the commercial distribution of its products or the long-range financing of feature films and documentaries. Profits from the advertising business paid for studios and equipment. They were not enough, however, to underwrite the production of feature films.

Only three full-length commercial feature films – *Julio Comienza en Julio* by S. Caiozzi in 1979, *Como Aman los Chilenos* by A. Alvarez in 1984 and *Los Hijos de la Guerra Fría* by G. Lustiniano in 1985 – were produced by the independent private sector after the military took over in 1973. Chile Films financed *El Ultimo Gruente* by S. López in 1983. (Two films – *García y el Forastero* by S. Riensenberg and *Bajo la Sombra del Sol* by S. Caiozzi and P. Perelman – were released in 1974 but were made before the coup.)

Cine-art circuits exhibit many of the feature-length and medium-length films produced by Chilean film makers: *La Tranquila Muerte del Chico Ormeno* by I. Aliago; *Pepe Donoso* and *El Charles Bronson Chileno* by C. Flores; *Coplas de la Tierra* by E. Tironi; *El Zapato Chino* and *Los Deseos Concebidos* by C. Sanchez; *Domingo de Gloria* and *El Maule* by P. and J.C. Bustamante; and *Chile, no Invoco tu Nombre en Vano* by Colectivo Cine Ojo.

Some Chilean documentary film makers made testimonial documentaries of important events in Chile's recent history, for example, *No Olvidar* by Ignacio Aguero about people who had 'disappeared' and *Lonquen* about the burial spot of a group of peasants killed by the military. In other documentaries, like *El Willy y la Miriam* by David Benavente, Chilean film makers analysed the poverty and umemployment facing many Chileans. A great number of these documentaries were later transferred to video and shown on closed circuit television to small groups of students and workers and to other social organizations.

From 1980 on, film makers and people with no previous experience in film like sociologists and anthropologists began to use videotapes in their work. Many times producers and viewers selected together the subject of the films, usually some current social or economic issue affecting their lives.

After 1982 a reduction in government censorship along with diminished demand for advertising that freed much of the video equipment produced a quantitative jump in video production. Approximately 200 video films were made between 1980 and 1984, among them *Cualquier Día, Historia de un Roble Solo, Tiempo para un Líder, El 18 de los García, Carrete de Verano, Dolores* and *Hecho Pendiente* by ICTUS; *Margarita Acuña Trancoso* and *Quién es el Loco Chorito?* by I. Aliaga; *El Estado Soy Yo* by C. Flores; *Papá te Habla de Lejos* and *Gracias por un Favor Concedido* by J.E. Forch; and *Santiago Blues* by J. Francisco Vargas.

Individual film makers, private academic institutions and national and international development foundations were the main producers and users of the video documentary. Some video films were educational or testimonial and were produced in close collaboration with social, religious or human rights organizations, labour unions, community groups and students. These films were generally anti-authoritarian and critical of the model of society imposed on the country by the military.

Chilean video production continued to grow, although not always smoothly. Quality varied, and there was a high turnover and exchange of professionals in the field. Video films had no formal distribution network and were not allowed on the government-controlled television channels, their only possible source of revenue. Producers financed their work out of their own pockets or, in some cases, with funds from international development and human rights foundations.

In spite of financial and distribution limitations, video films permitted Chilean film makers to continue to work in their trade and to incorporate new colleagues. Because it operated outside commercial circuits, video production was less encumbered by censorship than television or other media and therefore freer to experiment with more creative forms of expression.

By 1985 the non-commercial video films had a larger audience in Santiago than that of some commercial films. Organized viewers of independently distributed video films in the Chilean capital numbered over 200,000.

One consequence of the reorganization of the Chilean film industry in independent video productions was the creation of two professional film associations: the Association of Producers of Advertising Films and the Association of Audiovisual Professionals and Technicians, both non-existent before 1973.

The professional associations lobbied the Chilean government to recognize the legal rights of the film industry guaranteed under national law. They fought for a new law to promote the national film industry and to give national films access to television and theatres. The organizations protested against government censorship and carried out training and educational activities in film making and criticism.

Yet, in spite of the new activities in film and video within the country, by far the greatest number of films in the history of Chilean cinema are those produced by exiled Chilean producers, directors and actors – 176 films in ten years. Almost a third of these films were feature length, and most were in colour. Of the total, 65 were fiction and 99 documentaries.

The Chilean film industry in exile operated in many countries and in many different languages. Films were exhibited in both commercial and specialized, private circuits. None of the films were ever shown publicly in Chile.

Chilean film makers in exile did not have any special network or organization. They were not a movement. They were linked by their nationality, their exile and their efforts to preserve what they consider the cultural identity of their country and share it with a wide audience.

During their first years of exile following the 1973 coup, many Chilean film makers produced works about the ongoing political resistance to the Chilean military regime. Later, some film makers widened the scope of their productions to include the political struggles going on in different countries of the region, especially Central America. Others moved on to topics related to problems and issues in their new countries of residence.

Many of the films of exiled Chilean film makers won international awards and were the subject of studies, commentaries and articles in the foreign press. Their producers and directors became well connected with national and international financing and distribution circuits, and their actors and technicians learned the latest techniques of film making.

During the years of rebirth and growth of the private film industry in Chile and abroad, the government film organizations under military control also changed. After the initial military intervention, the massive firing of employees and the production of direct government propaganda, Chile Films was placed under the National Television system of the National Direction of Social Communication. Its two enormous studios were put at the service of government-controlled television.

After 1976 Chile Films received no further funds from the government. Its budget cut was consistent with the military's policy of self-financing for public institutions. Burdened with a massive debt, for several years Chile Films could barely pay the upkeep of its enormous infrastructure or the salaries of its employees. After 1980, under a private-sector management style and riding the wave of an economic boom, Chile Films began to recover. Much of its recovery was a result of its links with National Television and the entrance of Chile Films into the film distribution and exhibition business.

Chile Films had the infrastructure and personnel for all the stages of film and video production. Taking advantage of existing capital investment, its new administration started an aggressive programme of services and production for government and private industries. Services included TV and film newsreels, special reports, advertising spots and TV previews for the films it distributed.

The new private-sector mentality of Chile Films shifted the organization away from the production of national films – its original objective when set up in the 1940s – towards the more lucrative areas of film services and distribution. Chile Films became a profit-oriented business no longer motivated by public-service objectives or by the propaganda needs of the military dictatorship.

When the military took over, Chile Films already owned three movie theatres that had been nationalized during the Socialist administration. It undertook an aggressive advertising campaign for its theatres using the television time on the national channel it received in exchange for the use of its studios. When the box-office returns for these three theatres tripled, Chile Films began to expand its distribution business and rented other movie theatres. By the end of 1983 the Chile Films exhibition network had ten theatres.

The vertical integration of Chile Films soon included film production, distribution, promotion and exhibition. By 1982 Chile Films was operating in the black, and by 1983 its profits had multiplied by a factor of ten. Chile Films modernized its studios, rolled over its debts, paid the salaries of its 146 employees and began to finance new productions.

Movie audiences in all national theatres increased as a result of the promotional campaign of Chile Films on National Television. The increase in their box-office returns, however, did not completely offset the fear of the Chilean private film industry that one day the military would use Chile Films' growing monopoly over film distribution and exhibition for the cultural and political control of the population.

The mechanisms for this type of control already existed. The government Film Board authorized the distribution and exhibition of all audiovisual material shown in the country on television, in theatres and in private showings, as well as the promotional material that accompanied it. The board was made up of nineteen members, over three-quarters representatives of the government.

Distributors and theatres thought twice about what material they presented to the Film Board. Many politically sensitive films were never presented at all. Still, the board rejected about 20 percent of the films on either political or moral grounds.

The military regime decided what should be seen by the population and prohibited the exhibition of those films it considered harmful to national security or to the essential values of Chilean society. The military's position on film censorship differed from that of many independent, often Church-connected organizations that had set up educational programmes for film viewers. The Church, for example, believed the selection of films should be the responsibility of the public rather than of the government.

Increasingly, however, it was the commercial criteria of the film distributors rather than the government that decided what the public saw. In addition to Chile Films and the US distributors operating in Chile in 1984 there were sixteen independent film distribution companies. Half of these owned chains of movie theatres. Many had agreements with the US distribution companies that did not operate in Chile. All the thirty-two first-run movie theatres in Santiago were owned by film distributors.

Almost 70 percent of the films shown in Chile came from the United States. All but one of the biggest box-office earners in the last six years were American: *Star Wars*, *Kramer vs Kramer*, *Where is the Pilot?*, *E.T.* and *Police Academy*. Other foreign films came from Europe and, occasionally, from other Latin American countries.

The pattern of film distribution under the military contrasted sharply with that in operation in the country between 1970 and 1973. Unidad Popular attempted to diversify the films that entered the country by assigning quotas to Europe, Latin America and the United States. The Socialist government restricted the foreign currency available for film imports, limited the profits that could be sent out of the country and made foreign distributors invest some of their earnings in Chile. As a result of these measures some US distributors stopped distributing films to Chile, others reduced their operations, and a few were taken over by the government.

Under the military regime, the patterns of film exhibition and audience distribution showed a marked reversal from the processes of decentralization, integration and democratization that characterized the 1960s and the beginning of the 1970s.

In 1964, at the beginning of the Christian Democrat administration, almost 57 million movie tickets were sold to a population of 8.5 million Chileans. This audience grew to 75 million tickets by 1967 but dropped to 47.25 million tickets in 1970 with competition from national television. The movie audience grew again under the Socialist administration, and by 1972, 51 million tickets were sold in the country.

During the administrations of the Christian Democrats and the Socialists, over half the movie tickets were sold in the provinces outside Santiago, the capital. This was the result of their policies of national integration and development as well as of price controls on movie tickets.

During the first years of the military government, the price of a movie ticket increased 800 percent in one year. Unemployment tripled to 30 percent of the population. The movie audience fell precipitously to 23.4 million spectators. By 1983, ten years after the military take-over, more than half the movie theatres had closed down, and the movie audience was slowly climbing up from its 1982 low of 11.5 million spectators.

In 1985 half the total number of movie tickets were sold in Santiago as a result of the increased concentration of wealth in the capital. In poorer southern Santiago, however, there were only two movie theatres for a population of over half a million people. Most of the small theatres had been sold or absorbed by the three or four larger theatre chains including the largest of all, Chile Films.

During no period in its life has the Chilean film industry been independent of government policy. Particularly under the military government, but also under the Christian Democrats and the Socialists, the national film industry developed and changed with government subsidies and protection, censorship and interference. The economic policies that modified the face of the country also modified its film industry.

Some of the most recent developments in the film industry are the expected results of larger political changes caused by the authoritarian regime and its free market economic policies. At first glance, other developments in the Chilean film industry are more difficult to understand.

It is logical that a large number of Chilean film makers would leave the country under the military dictatorship and that film censorship and repression of freedom of expression would increase. It is surprising that many film makers who remained in the country were able to develop their own means of financial support and build up an independent production capacity as a result of the free market policies of the military regime.

It is logical that an authoritarian state should control the government film institute. It is surprising that this institution should acquire an economic rationality and private-sector entrepreneurial style of its own, closely co-ordinated with national television.

It is to be expected that under harsh economic changes, the Chilean movie audience should fall drastically and half the theatres would shut down. It is surprising that under the dictatorship Chilean film and video producers were able to build up a genuine rapport with their audiences at all stages of production, from the selection of the subject to the language of the film, and that more Chileans were able to see their products than could see many commercial films.

It is paradoxical that although the military took over the universities and closed down the film schools, during the dictatorship the technical capabilities of many Chilean film makers actually increased.

When the military dictatorship ends and the country returns to democracy, the new actors and interests of the Chilean film industry will find themselves in a radically different and often paradoxical world from the one that was brutally destroyed in 1973.

9

Dictatorship and Transition to Democracy: Argentina 1973–86

Heriberto Muraro

Between 1973 and 1976 the civilian governments that ruled Argentina were unable to achieve political, economic and cultural stability. The country was trapped between an extreme left and an extreme right. Labour unions, political parties and other organizations appeared to be leading the country towards civil war. After the death of Perón in 1974 the country entered a period of anarchy that was used by the armed forces to justify a military coup in 1976.

During the three years of Peronist government, the internal warring strains of Peronism shared the belief that the mass media, especially radio, should be state-controlled. They pushed through Congress a series of changes in the ownership, control, financing and legal structure of the mass media. Under Perón, the licences of the three main private television channels in Buenos Aires and two in the interior of the country were cancelled. When the Peronist labour unions subsequently occupied the television production companies tied to the capital city stations, the government declared the companies in the public interest and expropriated them (Schmucler and Zires, 1978).

The Secretary of Commerce levied a tax on advertising that decreased the earnings of the private media and the advertising agencies and increased state control of the media. The Peronist government prohibited local newspapers from using the stories about the country from the international wire services or from the foreign correspondents based in Argentina.

One of the first measures of the military government that took power in 1976 was to lift the ban on the international wire services and remove the tax on advertising. The armed forces greatly increased government investment in advertising. The military used the media to carry out expensive publicity campaigns to defend its economic and social policies and attack its enemies. In 1976, according to the Argentine Chamber of Advertisers (1975–6) advertising revenues jumped by 60 percent.

The military voiced its belief in freedom of expression and in private ownership but obliged the media to adhere strictly to the Doctrine of National Security. The military junta established unlimited jail terms for the director of any newspaper, radio station or television programme that published or broadcast information on the guerrilla groups operating in the country. The regime decreed ten-year jail terms for anyone who published or broadcast information against the armed forces, including mention of the gross violations of human rights carried out by the military (Terrero, 1982).

During the long military dictatorship, the armed forces put into force a regime of terror for the media. The junta murdered journalists, closed newspapers and censored publications. The military services drew up black lists of journalists, artists and entertainers and prohibited many foreign and national films, books and magazines. During its reign, seventy-two journalists disappeared and were probably murdered, hundreds were jailed and many fled into exile. The military expropriated the newspaper *La Opinión* of Jacobo Timmerman and took over other publications. Soldiers frequently seized and burned whole editions of local magazines and threatened and kidnapped labour leaders from the media industries (Avejera, 1985).

With few exceptions like the *Buenos Aires Herald*, the media accepted these repressive measures passively. The media limited their criticism of the military to questions of economic policy or minor administrative points. Few newspapers or radio stations gave space or time to the leaders of the disbanded political parties, and even fewer accepted the paid announcements of the human rights groups. There were, however, large publishing houses like Editorial Atlantida that actively co-operated with the military government by attacking the international human rights organizations and supporting the military's socially regressive free market economic policies.

In spite of its own declared principles against state intervention in any sector of the economy, the military maintained tight control of the Buenos Aires television channels expropriated earlier by Perón. Of all the stations, the armed forces returned only Channel 9 to its former owners when they refused to accept the indemnities offered them and the courts ruled in their favour. The military administration of commercial television was conducted with the aid of private advertisers and economic groups who developed a corrupt and complex system. The military introduced no real changes in television content other than the iron censorship of TV news.

The military control of the media allowed it to censor the news and other information severely. It also gave the military access to the vast sums that passed daily through the media. The military considered these earnings the justly won spoils of its victory over the subversives and the previous government.

Censorship severely affected the growth of the national media during the military regime. The impact of the military's economic policies, however, had an even more disastrous effect on media development. Previous economic policies in the country had almost uniformly attempted to promote national industry in order to create employment opportunities and reduce the vulnerability of the local economy to international economic changes. The latest military regime, on the contrary, sought to gain economic stability by eliminating the tariffs and protectionist measures that blocked the free play of the market-place and, according to its views, were responsible for the lack of technological and economic development of the country. With the same mentality with which it had fought against the leftist guerrillas, the military disciplined labour unions, industrialists and consumers to conform to its new economic model.

The salary level of public-sector employees dropped by 40 percent during the first three months of the military regime. Under the military, national salaries never again reached the levels they had achieved in 1973. A drop in demand followed the drop in salaries, and the rate of unemployment in the country began slowly to rise.

In co-ordination with its economic policies, the military restricted the access of the lower stratas of the economy to public secondary and university education. The economic crisis soon began to take its toll on primary-school attendance as well. In spite of the many informal mechanisms by which the people attempted to continue their education and access to cultural opportunities, a process of educational regression resulted in the growing educational and cultural inequality of the Argentine population. In 1983 the new civilian administration found that Argentina, a country with a system of universal education since the beginning of the century, had close to 6.5 million illiterates out of a total population of 30 million.

The impact of these changes in the population and in the economy was disastrous for the cultural industries. Newspaper and magazine circulation dropped by almost half. Book publishing and film production registered similar falls.

The military introduced a series of technological innovations in the Argentine cultural industries the results of which were almost as dire as those of their regressive educational and cultural policies. One of the innovations was the development, together with two private papers, of a national newsprint industry. The new national industry strengthened its owners – *Clarín* and *La Nación* of Buenos Aires – but weakened the smaller papers of the interior and those papers such as *La Prensa* of Buenos Aires that had traditional ties with international newsprint distributors. The military regime set up protective tariffs for national production, in this way causing serious economic damage to the smaller papers that imported newsprint.

Another innovation under the military regime was the introduction of colour television in 1978 in time to broadcast the World Cup football matches held that year in Argentina. The military wanted to take advantage of this opportunity to show the world that Argentina was not the giant concentration camp often portrayed in the international press. The armed forces built an enormous studio and transmission facilities for colour television production which they later passed to one of the government television stations, Channel 7.

In 1980 regular transmissions in colour began in Buenos Aires. The first year, Buenos Aires had approximately 191,000 colour receivers. By 1985, according to a commercial rating company (Audits Survey Latinoamericana, 1985), this number had jumped to over 1.8 million out of the 2 million households with television in the metropolitan area.

Until 1980 approximately 45 percent of the television sets in the country had been produced nationally by about a dozen local factories using 90 percent locally produced parts. The prices of the local sets were higher than those on the international market. Following traditional Argentine economic policy, the government protected local industry with a high tariff on imported receivers. The military removed these protectionist measures, and the industry went into a decline. The military encouraged the import of semi-finished colour television sets that required little local labour or parts. The local electronics industry soon became distributors of imported sets rather than manufacturers (Lahera and Nochteff, 1982).

Similar problems occurred in the Argentine telephone system under the military. Argentina had one of the highest ratios of telephones per capita in Latin America. Nevertheless, the national telephone system grew at the very low rate of 3.8 percent yearly for the last decade compared to a growth rate of 13.3 percent in Brazil and 9.5 percent in Mexico. The national telephone company had never been able to install more than 200,000 new telephone lines a year, the minimum necessary to maintain existing coverage. Much of the switching equipment dated from the 1930s, and parts of the country were not connected by coaxial cables or radio hook-ups.

The military regime's programme of innovation in telecommunications was partly the result of the country's commitment to broadcast the World Cup matches from many different cities in the interior of the country. The prolonged tension with Chile over the islands of the Beagle Channel and the possibility of an armed conflict on their long stretch of shared border stimulated the development of telecommunication networks in these areas. At the same time, however, the military ignored the pressing needs for telephone services in other areas of the country. The military borrowed over half a billion dollars from international banks, 4.5 percent of the total foreign debt of the public sector, in order to finance the new investments in telecommunication.

The military never paid attention to problems of Argentine broadcasting like the concentration of media ownership or the financial system of sales, resales and discounts to major advertisers that was responsible for most programming decisions. The military's piecemeal approach to broadcasting legislation ignored the close ties between the social structure of the country and its broadcasting system and the close links among the different media. Regulation never took into account the dependence of the private commercial media on the public and on changing audience tastes or the basic economics of market competition and audience ratings.

For example, Channel 7 ATC in Buenos Aires, a state-owned channel, competed with the other private and government-owned channels in the capital for audience ratings and advertising. This competition limited the ability of the directors of Channel 7 to undertake long-term cultural or educational programmes. Furthermore, because of a lack of government subsidies, private production companies produced a significant portion of the prime-time programming of Channel 7.

Legislation also overlooked the differences among the different private media. A small privately owned provincial newspaper was hardly the same as a private television production company that controlled a network of ten stations and had direct ties with the US television industry. Nevertheless, they were both subject to the same legislation.

A major challenge of the Argentine policy-makers who won the elections in 1983 after the military defeat of the dictatorship in the Malvinas Islands was how to resolve the stalemate between state and private control of the mass media. This would mean limiting the almost monopolistic tendency of the private media and, at the same time, encouraging the development of a strong, culturally and technologically appropriate national media system.

All in all, however, the scope of the debate on the mass media under the democratic regime elected in 1983 was modest. Government officials, the state-owned media, the media-related unions and the political parties took positions on the role of the media and defended certain principles. The private media and the general public for the most part ignored the debate or contributed isolated sporadic comments. The Catholic Church confined itself to attacking the relaxed morality and the upsurge of pornography that occurred under the civilian government.

In spite of the apparent lack of public support, the debate on the future of the mass media was of considerable political and economic interest to the country. In the years following the fall of the military regime, politicians discovered the potential political impact of the media, especially television, on the outcome of elections. The private sector learned to fear the possible effects of a new broadcasting law or anti-monopoly measures on its future activities. The traditional right wing looked with horror on the rise of pornography and what it considered the 'destruction of the values of Western civilization'.

The political transition in Argentina after 1983 was different from those of the past. Politicians had different goals for the mass media during the transition to democracy in the early 1970s. Then, policy-makers wanted to break the media's dependence on the developed countries, create or restore national and grass-roots culture and employ the media as instruments of consciousness-raising and political organization against the forces of imperialism and its local allies. All these goals were state-oriented and considered the public sector the most suitable author of cultural policies. Most policy-makers excluded the private sector from their policies and plans because of the private sector's suspect ties with international markets and investors.

After 1983 the debate took place within a radically different context. The previous goals of cultural independence and national expression had lost force in the face of the enormous foreign debt and other economic problems of the country. These goals were replaced with a concern for pluralism and for the protection of both the media and their audiences from government interference. The new political and economic context hardly favoured the development of state-oriented cultural policies. Few politicians were convinced that the state had the means or the technical capability to co-ordinate its own cultural activities, let alone formulate and carry out a coherent and stable national cultural policy.

There remained, however, an enduring concern for the democratization of the cultural industry and for questions of how much concentration and monopolization was compatible with a liberal democracy and with rapid technological change. The elimination of censorship continued to cause conflicts between the civilian administration and certain sectors of the armed forces, the political parties and the Catholic Church.

Regional political leaders were concerned with the enormous centralization of communication and cultural resources in the capital, Buenos Aires, and their relative scarcity in the periphery. Two other subjects of considerable national debate were the incorporation of a new type of private non-profit broadcaster in commercial broadcasting and the role of Congress in the control of information flows.

In 1986 the amount of proposed media legislation in Argentina suddenly jumped to about twenty new projects. In response, the private sector stepped up its own defensive activities – advertising campaigns, conferences and meetings of the communication field – to protect the system of private media against possible government interference.

Generally, the private sector was able to work together to defend its interests, although under its consensus lay a great number of real differences. There were major differences between the large media owners of Buenos Aires and the smaller media owners of the interior of the country and between the established technologies and the newer arrivals such as cable television. The local media owners feared take-over by large multinational enterprises using new communication technologies. National radio and television owners were wary of the possible entrance into broadcasting of powerful newspaper interests like *Clarín*.

Most private media owners felt threatened by the new technologies. They defended the concept of private media although they did not want to compete openly on the international market with the new media technologies and corporate structures. The private media feared both government competition and an open market with no government protection or regulation. (In this respect, the Argentine cultural industries were similar to many other sectors of the Argentine economy that demanded protection from the government while at the same time objecting to government regulation of their commercial operations.)

The programme of the new civilian government regarding the media was not clear. The political platform of President Raúl Alfonsín included a number of measures affecting the media: the preservation of freedom of expression and the press, the defence of national culture and identity and the modernization of the communication system. His government fulfilled the first objection immediately by eliminating the censorship of the military regime. The second and third objectives, especially the modernization of the information system, would mean the renovation of much of the existing communication infrastructure in the country. The national economic crisis and the crushing foreign debt made it extremely difficult to do so. The same financial limitations forced the government to maintain commercial financing of the state-owned media through advertising, thereby severely limiting the development of educational or cultural programming.

Furthermore, not all the members of Alfonsín's administration were of one mind regarding the media. Some politicians strongly supported public access and the right to reply to the media; others held positions closer to those of the private media owners. This lack of consensus made it impossible for the Alfonsín government to get a law through Congress guaranteeing the right of reply.

The different factions that made up the governing party had soon become aware of the importance of the media in election campaigns. For example, the government delayed the debate on a new broadcasting law until after the first congressional elections for fear of losing the support of the private media.

The government continued to control a considerable portion of the country's mass media – sixty-seven radio stations and seventeen television channels, including three of the four capital city channels. Government control of the media played a crucial role in the government's management of the attempted military take-over in the spring of 1987.

The opposition parties, especially the Peronist parties, pushed to open up the congressional debate on the broadcasting law and held the president responsible for its delay. They were limited in their action, however, by their unwillingness to appear to support state control of the media while they were out of power. Furthermore, the opposition was almost entirely dependent on the private media for political advertising and did not want to lose the media's support by suggesting new legislation.

To a certain extent, the uncertain and timid role of the political parties in the discussion of the media was the result of the weaknesses of the parties themselves and their lack of experience in the exercise of government and in the use of the modern media. (Argentina had only ten years of civilian government in the fifty years before Alfonsín took office.) After many years of limited political activity, the parties were just beginning to renew their ties with grass-roots organizations, the Church, the unions and other sources of support. The parties were slowly developing their own means of communication with their members.

These grass-roots and community organizations and the public in general were enthusiastic participants in the various cultural activities that accompanied the demise of the military regime. During the early stages of the transition to a democratic administration, even before the elections, the public was an avid consumer of the opinion shows, radio talk shows, films, books, magazines and pamphlets about the excesses of the dictatorship and the political platforms of the contending political parties.

Surveys showed that most people expected important cultural benefits from the new civilian government. They looked forward to the reopening of public universities, the end of censorship, the authorization of many films and books prohibited by the military and significant changes in the content of television. (The brazen manipulation of television by the military during the invasion of the Malvinas Islands was still fresh in the minds of many people.)

The general opinion, however, did not favour radical change of the media, an immediate politicization of its content or an increase of state control. Surveys showed (Muraro and Landi, 1985–6) that few people wanted to return to the acute politicization of the media of the 1970s or the censorship and corruption of the military regime.

The Argentine public knew what kind of media it didn't want. The problem would be finding out what media it did want and developing the political parties and other representative organizations necessary to achieve them as part of the slow reconstruction of democratic institutions.

References

Argentine Chamber of Advertisers (information supplied 1975–6). Buenos Aires.

Audits Survey Latinoamericana (information supplied 1985). Buenos Aires.

Avejera, Pedro (1985) 'Prensa y Crisis Estructural en Argentina (1973–1983)', *UNDA-AL Comunicación, Estudios y Documentos*, 5(14), pp. 24–35.

Lahera, Eugenio and Nochteff, Hugo (1982) *Cuestiones Planteadas por la Microelectrónica al Desarrollo Latinoamericano*. Buenos Aires: FLACSO.

Muraro, Heriberto and Landi, Oscar (1985–6) *Recepción del Discurso Informativo*. Buenos Aires: CEDES.

Schmucler, Héctor and Zires, Margarita (1978) 'El Papel Ideológico de los Medios de Comunicación en Argentina 1975: La Crisis del Lopezreguismo', *Comunicación y Cultura*, 5, pp. 119–78.

Terrero, Patricia (1982) 'Comunicación e Información por los Gobiernos Autoritarios: el Caso de Argentina', pp. 23–39 in E. Fox (ed.) *Comunicación y Democracia*. Lima: DESCO.

10

Brazilian Television:
a Rapid Conversion to the New Order

Cesar Guimarães and Roberto Amaral

The Brazilian military dictatorship lasted over twenty years. Between 1964 and 1985 a handful of generals selected by their peers governed the country together with a mutilated Parliament that had no political force, legitimacy or constitutional powers. The military dictatorship consistently imposed a plan of forced and rapid national modernization despite small differences between each successive general. The military's major accomplishments were the growth of an urban industrial work-force and Brazil's complete integration into the international economy.

The Brazilian military was a new strain of the long series of military dictatorships, *caudillos* and oligarchical regimes that at one time or another had ruled most countries of Latin America. Political scientists have called this somewhat different type of dictatorship a bureaucratic authoritarian regime.

The bureaucratic authoritarian regime allied the military to civilian technocracy and big business. The regime's objective was state-directed capitalism. It eliminated the representative institutions – the traditional intermediaries between government and the people – and controlled the masses through state-directed violence.

Under the military, Brazil had periods of extraordinary economic development and restricted or non-existent civil liberties. The concentration of wealth in the national economy and the concentration of power in the central government increased. Brazil's economic dependence and the central government's control of economic planning grew. The consolidated military regime abused human rights and restricted labour unions and political parties. Finally, during almost all stages of the regime, the government imposed restrictions on every level of the mass media.

The last two presidents of the long military regime, between 1974 and 1985, considered themselves authors of a gradual easing of political tensions and an opening up of the political system. The real transition from authoritarianism to a new liberal order, however, began when the Electoral College created by the regime to guarantee legally the presidency of its chosen successor suddenly shifted its support away from the regime.

During the Figueiredo administration, between 1979 and 1985, the Brazilian economy began to show signs of exhaustion. By the end of Figueiredo's term, inflation had reached 200 percent, and recessive measures had increased unemployment. The Brazilian foreign debt was already close to $100 billion.

The regime was gradually falling apart. Large sectors of business and industry had begun to disassociate themselves from the government, and previously docile politicians had become rebellious. The unanimity of the military bloc that had sustained the regime was beginning to crumble. Furthermore, the united opposition was able to take advantage of the changing circumstances.

In the 1982 legislative elections, the opposition won control of the state governments of São Paulo, Rio de Janeiro, Minas Gerais and Paraná, along with many seats in the House of Deputies. These victories strengthened the opposition and encouraged them to take their political movement to the public streets. Social and labour organizations followed their lead.

Until 1982 the only proposals to contain the military regime were minority proposals from extreme left-wing politicians, intellectuals and jurists to elect a constitutional assembly. Moderate left-wing and centre politicians, including the largest opposition party, the Movimento Democrático Brasileiro (PMDB), had proposed bringing down the authoritarian regime by gradually accumulating power in successive parliamentary electoral victories.

The leaders of the military regime announced they would not allow direct presidential elections to be held until 1990. The moderate left-wing and centre political parties supported a campaign for immediate and direct presidential elections. The moderates ruled out the possibility of a National Constitutional Assembly that would first require the highly unlikely violent fall of the dictatorship.

Under the dictatorship the president was chosen by an Electoral College made up of members of parliament and representatives of the state legislative assemblies. For twenty years they had always chosen a general. The campaign for direct presidential elections was a widespread movement to pressure Parliament – where the military regime held a majority – to approve a constitutional amendment allowing the president to be elected by popular vote. The catalytic role played by the Brazilian mass media, until then a docile instrument dependent on the military regime, was an unexpected new element in the movement for direct presidential elections.

All the national media eventually supported the campaign for direct elections. Brazilian television, however, although highly dependent on the military regime, helped establish the national dimension of the movement by broadcasting the enormous demonstrations of over a million people in Rio de Janeiro and São Paulo. The radical and unexpected changes in the mass media, especially in television, were most striking in the Sistema Globo de Televisión.

TV Globo was the fourth largest television network in the world. Over 50 million people watched its nightly newscast, *Jornal Nacional*. TV Globo covered 3,050 of the 4,000 Brazilian municipalities and reached 95 percent of the 17 million households in the country with television. In addition to forty-three television channels, the Sistema Globo owned one of the most influential Brazilian newspapers, *O Globo*, as well as a large chain of radio stations. It also published books, magazines and comics.

Sistema Globo had been born with the dictatorship. In 1965 it entered the field of television. TV Globo consolidated its operations during the government of Garrastazu Medici between 1970 and 1974 when the government designated telecommunications an area of national security. TV Globo rapidly entered the era of new technology with the first reception of satellite signals and the first nationwide transmission of television.

EMBRATEL, the state-owned Brazilian telecommunications company, paid for and set up the infrastructure that made it possible for TV Globo, a private company, to reach an audience of close to 80 million people. TV Globo became the television version of state-directed capitalism.

TV Globo stuck close to its roots throughout most of the dictatorship. It gave good coverage to the accomplishments of the military regime like the disastrous programme to colonize the Amazon Region with the Trans-Amazonic Highway and the Brazilian victory in the 1970 World Cup in Mexico. TV Globo's transmission of these and other events and achievements of national pride was an important element in the military's ideological control and manipulation of Brazilian society.

TV Globo played up national sentiment in each match of the Brazilian national football team and carried out patriotic campaigns like 'Brazil, love it or leave it' to discourage criticism and encourage self-exile by dissidents. TV Globo's reporting exaggerated the existence of small groups of armed resistance in the country, in this way justifying the continuing exercise of state terrorism and repression.

The members of the military government closely identified with TV Globo. General Medici, who ruled over the most repressive phase of the dictatorship, once explained that he was happy every night when he watched the news on TV Globo because on television news Brazil was at peace while the newspapers reported strikes, protests, violence and conflicts in various parts of the world. TV Globo's *Jornal* was like taking a tranquillizer after a hard day's work.

There was less political tension in the administrations that followed that of President Medici, and the politically docile TV Globo network grew steadily. Its mother company became an enormous media conglomerate and entered new areas of the national economy and international markets. If indeed it does exist, TV Globo fitted Althusser's concept of an 'ideological apparatus of the state'.

The campaign for direct elections changed the usual Brazilian political practices and flew in the face of some of the better-known theories concerning the role of the mass media in the formation of political beliefs and behaviours. For once, politics was not just an exercise of the élites, and the streets were not just the scene of disorganized masses. The mass media captured and expressed this new vision of the political process and demonstrated their ability to influence public opinion. The media also revealed their less well-known ability to react to changes in public opinion and change their own behaviour accordingly.

It is hard to measure the capacity of public opinion to modify the conduct and programming of the mass media. At times, however, and for certain events content is determined by the people and not by the media. People who for twenty years had passively watched and listened to the mass media for once publicly expressed what they wanted to hear and see, and TV Globo responded to their demands.

The campaign for direct presidential elections was a series of rallies and enormous demonstrations held in all the state capitals and big cities of Brazil between February and June 1984. All sectors of the opposition and some factions of the government party in Parliament ended up supporting the campaign originally convoked by the largest opposition party. The media at first ignored the campaign and until May provided uneven coverage. By June, however, they were unanimous in their enthusiastic and often brilliant coverage of the campaign.

At the beginning of the campaign, TV Globo covered the demonstrations in São Paulo as if they were movements of artists and musicians with only slight political overtones. Their first broadcasts focused on the artists and minimized the political significance of the demonstrations. *O Globo* newspaper of Rio de Janeiro ran a 5 cm box on the first page of its 26 January edition which read: 'Famous artists take the crowd to the town square, see page 2.'

By the time the campaign closed in Rio, coverage filled the front pages of almost all the important Brazilian newspapers. TV Globo attracted one of its biggest audiences ever when it made the opposition state governors Tancredo Neves, Franco Montoro and Leonel Brizola the stars of its news show on the demonstrations.

After having ignored the first rally in São Paulo, the biggest city in the country, TV Globo dedicated almost its entire 8 p.m. news programme to the demonstrations that followed in the provinces of Curitíba, Goiania, Vitória, Campinas and Santos. TV Globo and EMBRATEL brought news of the rallies to the whole country.

The TV Globo network covered the rallies from noon on, before they had got into full swing. In this way television encouraged people who were still at home to come out and join the demonstrations. TV Globo interrupted its previously untouchable programming schedule of soap operas, the corner-stone of its audience strategy, to cover the demonstrations.

In spite of immense popular support, the constitutional amendment to re-establish direct presidential elections lost the parliamentary vote by a small margin. The government was able to hold its party in line, and only a few defected to the opposition. In order to impose this discipline, however, the government took measures it had not had to use for a long time. Under Draconian legislation, the military declared a state of emergency in Brasília, fenced off the Parliament Building with troops and closed the entrance to the city to stop the demonstrators who flooded in from all over the country. The government limited freedom of the press, censored all news coming from Brasília and, when the amendment came to a vote, did not allow the session to be broadcast.

In spite of government censorship, the country witnessed a revolt of professional journalists who backed the popular outcry and used the media as a form of protest, often with the support of their directors. Radio Jornal do Brasil of Rio de Janeiro suspended all news broadcasts from Brasília and repeatedly informed its audience of government censorship of the events occurring in the Brazilian capital. The audience of *Jornal da Noite* of TV Globo watched in surprise while actor Jo Soares sat in complete silence for one minute to protest against government censorship. Later that afternoon, the Globo network refused to provide the government censors with a room for their work. The military regime never dreamed that it could lose the support of the network that had been its official mouthpiece and one of the principal beneficiaries of the Brazilian miracle.

Public opinion sensed that TV Globo was changing sides and that the dictatorship was beginning to end. The Globo network had been born with the regime, had grown up with the regime, but would not go down with the regime.

In spite of the defeat of the constitutional amendment for direct elections, the opposition parties did not lose the momentum they had gathered with their nationwide campaign. Direct elections were impossible, but the opposition continued their struggle in the Electoral College where they had long been a minority.

The Electoral College was one of the most important instruments of political engineering of the dictatorship. When it seized power in 1964, the military fulfilled a long-standing conservative aspiration. The conservatives feared that direct presidential elections put the presidency in permanent danger of falling to the left-wing candidates. Parliament, however, was easier to control. Since 1964 the generals chose the military presidents, who were then ratified by the Electoral College. The College was made up of all the members of Parliament and the representatives of the state legislative assemblies.

After the victory of the opposition parties in the 1982 legislative elections, the government deftly altered the composition of the Electoral College to ensure its own succession. It changed the proportional representation of the state legislative assemblies in the Electoral College by giving each state five representatives regardless of the size of its population. The opposition controlled the legislative assemblies in the most populous states, but the numerous small states in the north-east were loyal to the government. The military, therefore, still had a majority. The military trusted the new members of the Electoral College to carry out their duties with the same docility as in the past; their job was to ratify decisions that had already been taken.

The president had always been chosen by the military high command before his name reached the Electoral College. Figueiredo, however, introduced an innovation in his succession. He decided to choose a civilian from the government's party, the Partido Demo-crático Social, who would be ratified at the party convention. The Electoral College, always obedient to the military high command, would then transfer its loyalty from the military to the government's party. In this way the tradition would continue under civilian leaders. To Figueiredo's surprise, things did not work out as he had planned. He faced insubordination from the party and sectors of the government and met with defeat in the Electoral College.

The campaign for direct elections had disrupted the traditional discipline of the government party. Prominent members like Figueiredo's vice-president, Aureliano Chaves, a civilian, were beginning to give serious attention to the proposals of the opposition parties. Figueiredo drove Aureliano into the opposition. He took with him influential political leaders of the liberal wing of the government party including ex-President Geisel and the Globo television network. The government party did not choose Figueiredo's candidate for president but settled instead on Paulo Maluf, a former governor of the state of São Paulo.

The opposition parties formed the Democratic Alliance to support their candidates for president and vice president, Tancredo Neves and Senator José Sarney.

Six months before the presidential elections, Tancredo Neves was trailing behind Paulo Maluf in the Electoral College by 148 votes. In the next six months, the mass media played a crucial role in transforming this initial disadvantage into a victory for Neves by a margin of 300 votes.

By the time the presidential elections took place, the government party had been severely weakened from within. The military was unable to prohibit the direct broadcast of its party's defeat in the Electoral College. The mass media and especially TV Globo played a decisive role in the military's demise.

TV Globo had been caught short by the changes in public opinion in the campaign for direct presidential elections. In the Neves campaign in the Electoral College, however, it took the initiative. TV Globo helped form public opinion and influence the political process as the mouthpiece of the immense coalition movement of the Democratic Alliance.

During the few months of the presidential campaign, in its new role as mouthpiece of the opposition, TV Globo succeeded in forming a public image of the government's presidential candidate, Paulo Maluf, as the 'absolute enemy' of the nation.

TV Globo depicted Maluf as a product of the Brazilian miracle, a self-made millionaire who aspired to reach the presidency by corrupting the electors of the Electoral College. Maluf, the synthesis of all the illegality of the military regime, promised an uncertain future. The media portrayed Maluf as a danger that had to be stopped. Television transformed his self-assurance into arrogance and disdain for the opinions of others. In the proverbial morality of the middle class, Maluf was seen as an opportunist.

Opposition candidate Tancredo Neves appeared on the screens of TV Globo as a likeable old man who was going to save the country. Television emphasized the political qualities and personal virtues of Neves, blending these in with the real or imaginary attributes of the Brazilian national character.

TV portrayed Neves as a wise and honest old politician who had held many political offices; an unbeatable negotiator and the son of a traditional but generous family from the interior of the country; and a lawyer formed on his own merits. According to television, Neves, a liberal, sensitive to social justice, marked by his struggle against the dictatorship of Vargas (1937–45), would be the best person to lead the country in its new chapter in democracy. Neves brought together the traditional conservative self-image of the élites with the strong popular appeal of a cordial and conciliatory man adverse to conflict.

To a great extent, TV Globo formed the images of Maluf and Neves on its 11 p.m. news show, *Jornal da Globo*. This programme presented a new type of television journalism. Until then, all news programmes presented the news in a neutral manner with few gestures or signs of emotion and no indication of any position on the issues discussed.

The new *Jornal da Globo* was an exercise in interpretative journalism. An anchor-man replaced the neutral announcer and developed a certain complicity with the audience through gestures, expressions and changes in voice. The news reporters shared a code with their viewers with which they showed their approval or disapproval for what they were reading.

The *Jornal* livened up its presentation with commentators on national politics, international politics, the economy and sports. Daily, *Jornal* presented a negative image of the presidential candidate Paulo Maluf, strengthened the positive image of Tancredo Neves, and brought closer the possibility of his electoral victory.

Paulo Maluf was skilled in the tactics of an indirect election and tried to shield his delegates from Tancredo Neves. Neves, however, moved away from the traditional political tactics of indirect elections and acted as if he were competing for the popular vote with direct appeals to the Brazilian population. In spite of threats from Figueiredo's government, TV Globo broadcast Neves's mass demonstrations all over the country on its *Jornal Nacional* at 8 p.m., although in this case maintaining its previous style of neutral reporting.

When the people began to anticipate the defeat of the military's candidate for president, the regime, following a tradition of authoritarian intervention in political affairs, came to the rescue of Paulo Maluf. The military accused the opposition of carrying out a campaign of defamation and slander against the government.

Roberto Marinho, the editor-in-chief of *O Globo* and owner of the Globo Communication System, came to the defence of the popular demonstrations. Writing on the front page of *O Globo*, Marinho, an eighty-year-old journalist, called for the politicians to respect honestly and serenely the will of the people, in other words, to elect Neves.

In spite of the network's opposition, General Geisel's faction of the military gave TV Globo sufficient support from the armed forces to guarantee its future under the administration of Tancredo Neves. This support allowed TV Globo to act with great independence. Through its coverage of the massive demonstrations, television transformed the indirect elections into direct elections and assured the victory of Tancredo Neves. For example, the leader of the women's movement for Maluf abandoned his campaign, alleging irresistible popular pressure from her remote voters in the Amazon region. Many others from her party followed her lead.

On 15 January 1985 all the Brazilian radio and television stations broadcast live the election of Neves in the Electoral College by voice vote. It was a day of celebration. TV Globo broadcast nationally through its forty-eight affiliates to television receivers set up in public squares. Crowds cheered the end of the military regime with an enormous carnival. In the outpouring of popular emotion the national anthem replaced the samba, and the Brazilian flag replaced the banners of the samba schools.

The victory of Neves was a national catharsis. It was as if Brazil had won the world soccer cup against a hated rival. People embraced in laughter and tears in the streets and drank and danced through the day and into the night.

From that day on, TV Globo was careful to consolidate the victory by providing daily coverage of Neves, who was not to be inaugurated until 15 March. Television accompanied the president-elect on his trip abroad. TV Globo broadcast with great detail and commentary Neves's meetings with the Pope, President Pertini of Italy, the King of Spain, President Mitterand of France, and President Reagan in Washington.

Television provided daily information on Neves's difficulties in forming a cabinet from the many groups that had supported his candidacy and broadcast the first live news conference with a Brazilian president since the 1964 coup.

Meanwhile, TV Globo maintained its distance from the military regime and its neutral and objective coverage of the national news that had begun with its coverage of the campaign for direct elections. Television had clearly chosen sides. It no longer had to pretend. The illness, agony and death of Tancredo Neves would only reinforce its new style.

The inauguration of President-elect Tancredo Neves was set for 10 a.m. All the hotels in Brasília were full. The evening before, the media urged the residents of Brasília to open their houses to the masses of people pouring in from all over Brazil. The mood of the city and of the rest of the country that accompanied the celebration on television was euphoric. Suddenly, television announced that Tancredo Neves had been hospitalized with appendicitis.

Frustration and fear followed the announcement. The administration of Figueiredo would end inexorably at 10 a.m. the next day when the president-elect, in the best of cases, would be recovering from general anaesthesia in an intensive-care ward. Even if Neves were conscious, he could not be inaugurated. Under the Brazilian Constitution the president must be inaugurated in person before a joint session of the two Houses of Parliament.

Fear of an institutional impasse replaced the initial frustration of not reaching the presidency. It was an old story, and everyone knew the ending. In successive crises since the redemocratization of 1945, power would return to the military, and a military coup, ratified by Parliament, would follow. Conservative judges were always prepared to find new legal formulas, and a docile Parliament was always prepared to accept them. This had been the case in 1954 with the suicide of Getulio Vargas, in 1955 with the obstruction of Cafe Filho and Carlos Luz and the possession of Nereu Ramos, in 1961 with the resignation of Janio Quadros, in 1964 with the military coup that overthrew João Goulart and in 1969 with the death of General President Costa e Silva.

Two factors made this crisis different: the decision would be taken by the legislative branch of government, and the mass media would make it a public process. This time the crisis would not be resolved secretly in the barracks or in the military high command. The television networks broadcast live throughout the whole night. The television audience was a guarantee.

The mass media were an interface between political leaders and public opinion. They placed an important role in the different decisions, always favouring civilian power and the new regime. Once again, TV Globo won the match.

Once Neves's initial surgery was over, the question was who would be inaugurated the next day. There were two alternatives: Ulysses Guimarães, the recently elected president of the Chamber of Deputies and first in the constitutional order of succession, or Vice-President-elect José Sarney.

Ulysses Guimarães, president of the PMDB, was the most popular leader of the opposition parties and one of those responsible for the candidacy of Tancredo Neves and his victory in the Electoral College. José Sarney was the president of the party of the military government, the PDS, and the leader of the campaign against direct presidential elections. Sarney had joined the opposition after a conflict with Paulo Maluf. Later, Tancredo Neves had chosen him as his vice-president. Guimarães made his political career as a representative of powerful São Paulo. Sarney came from the province of Maranhão, one of the poorest states of the north-east.

Ulysses Guimarães was the logical choice under the terms of the constitution. Moreover, he was the preferred candidate of the Bandeirantes television network of São Paulo. TV Bandeirantes, which was close to the leadership of the PMDB in São Paulo, brought legal specialists to its studios to defend the candidacy of Guimarães. Figueiredo's chief of staff also supported the choice of Guimarães because of Figueiredo's personal dislike for Sarney.

Globo Communications, however, opted for the candidacy of Sarney and brought in its own legal specialists to convince its nationwide audience. Afonso Arinos, a famous constitutional lawyer known for his heterodox interpretations of the Constitution in moments of crisis, argued before a television audience of millions for Sarney and for civilian strength against the military heritage. Within a few hours, Brazilian television had created a country of specialists in constitutional law and built up a consensus. In this process of consensus-building, Brazilian television was a protagonist and not merely a passive recorder of events.

During the night of political negotiation, television cameras broadcast direct from the hospital. A sudden change in the diagnosis turned the initial appendicitis into a more serious illness. The doubts and fears about the health of Neves produced an almost unanimous identification with the political leader and helped form a national consensus behind his government, until then thought almost impossible.

On 15 March, in an emotional ceremony marked by the absence of the rightful successor, Sarney was sworn in as President of Brazil. President Sarney then walked to the Palace Planalto to take office. President Sarney named the same cabinet that Neves had selected earlier, including a communication minister who was a close friend of Marinho, the owner of Globo Communications.

For the next thirty-eight days, until the funeral of Tancredo Neves, the administration of Sarney restricted itself to carrying out the minimum needs of the national bureaucracy. Along with the rest of the country, the Sarney government was wholly absorbed by the agony and death of Tancredo Neves. For thirty-eight days, Brazilian television radically altered its regular programming schedule to transmit twenty-four hours a day, first from Brasília and later in São Paulo, frequent and often contradictory hospital bulletins.

The official medical bulletins tried to calm the fears of the country. The public gathered some optimism from the spokesperson of the presidency, former TV Globo journalist Antonio Brito, broadcasting from the hospital. His broadcasts, however, were increasingly doubtful about Neves's recovery.

Television was caught in the middle. On the one hand, it encouraged its audience on the basis of the official medical bulletins. On the other, it began to make room for justified pessimism and legitimize a new regime without Neves under the leadership of a still provisional president.

Television broadcast pictures of the crowds in front of the hospital praying for the health of the president and singing music from his native province and the national anthem – patriotism and religion, hope and fear. Finally, EMBRATEL broadcast the announcement of Neves's death to the suffering and paralysed country. A feeling of impotence shadowed the earlier euphoria of the victory against the military. Brazilians began to doubt the popular saying that God was a Brazilian. Soon, however, this impotence would turn into civic spirit – without Tancredo Neves but with the New Republic. Once again, the mass media played a decisive role in this shift of emotions.

Neves died on 21 April, the date of the celebration of the hanging of Tiradentes, the martyr of Brazilian independence. The funeral cortège was drawn through the streets of São Paulo to the airport, and his body was flown to Brasília and displayed for a day in the Presidential Palace he never occupied. The next day his body was flown to Belo Horizonte, the capital of the state he had once governed, where it lay in state in the governor's palace. From there the coffin went to São João del Rey, Neves's birthplace, where he was buried.

Step by step, television broadcast the events of the three emotion-charged days, accompanied by documentaries of Neves's life and the appropriate musical background.

This time in sorrow, Brazilian cities filled with crowds reminiscent of the campaign for direct elections. The national symbols – Brazilian flag, the national anthem and the green and yellow colours of the country – first used by the people during the elections after many years of their exclusive identification with the military, returned to the streets. The multitude turned the cortège into a demonstration of patriotism and of support for the new order consolidated on the basis of a great personal tragedy.

Two million people took to the streets of São Paulo in a mixture of a political demonstration and a religious act. The crowds wept and applauded Neves's widow and sung the national anthem. Television broadcast the scenes direct. At times the announcers were carried away by their emotions and could not read their prepared texts. The events in São Paulo marked the pattern of what was going to occur in Brasília and Belo Horizonte. The funeral hypnotized the entire country, captivating a television audience that had been glued to its sets for many days.

The events in Brasília, a city of civil servants with an urban design uninviting for mass demonstrations, revealed the power of the crowds over the official ceremony. A group of motor cyclists draped in green and yellow mixed in with the military cars in the cortège. The crowds closed several of the wide avenues that led up to the ministries and delayed the procession. Television broadcast the events and encouraged the participation of the crowds in the next step of the funeral. That night, television news broadcast the official ceremonies along with the popular demonstrations.

As a result of the delays that took place in São Paulo and Brasília, the procession reached Belo Horizonte late. The officials decided to speed it up by limiting the access of the crowds to the procession. Frustrated by the measures, millions rushed to the governor's palace where Neves lay in state. Dozens were wounded and some were killed, trampled to death in the crowd as they paid their last respects to their president. The intervention of Neves's widow finally restored order.

Tancredo Neves was buried in São João del Rey, a small city in the interior of the country. Television broadcast the entire funeral oration of President Sarney. The sad days of agony ended, and television returned the country to its normal programming schedule.

Without being fully aware of its role, television had transferred the affection of the people from the dead leader to the New Republic. From February 1984, when the campaign for direct elections began, to April 1985, when Tancredo Neves died, the mass media and especially TV Globo had played an extraordinary role in the political process. TV Globo, created by the authoritarian regime and completely identified with the military, played a major part in the campaign for direct elections and later in the campaign of Tancredo Neves.

The mass media and especially TV Globo had given legitimacy to the new regime. At the same time, TV Globo had assured its own legitimacy in the eyes of public opinion. A new TV Globo was born with the New Republic. Its role under the dictatorship was forgotten. Now the only memories were of Tancredo Neves. In ironic homage to Althusser, the same TV Globo that had served the military so well would be the quasi-official network of the New Republic. The new leaders of Brazil had the media to thank for many things. However, they would now also have to deal with a powerful new independent political force.

11

Media, Cultural Processes and Political Systems

Oscar Landi

The collapse of the Argentine military regime as a result, among other factors, of the mismanaged invasion of the Malvinas Islands in April 1982 forced the national media to adjust to a radically different political environment. The growing liberalization of Argentine society, the increased demand for information and the emergence of voices silenced during the long dictatorship made it possible for the media to play an important role in informing society, legitimizing certain topics and organizing the newly awakening political scene. Gradually and often painfully, stories taboo under the military appeared in the newspapers. Politicians returned to the television screens, and new voices spoke on the radio.

Information, however, was not always readily available. Argentina had entered the 'information age' of satellites, data banks and computers during the long military dictatorship. The new communication technologies, combined with the traditional forms of censorship and concealment, made it difficult for the civilian government and for the media to put together a true picture of the state of the economy, the size of the national debt and the fate of the thousands of people kidnapped, tortured and murdered by the military. The evidence either had been destroyed or was stored in secret data banks and information systems well hidden within the military bureaucracy.

It was hard for the media to give a true picture of the country when the facts were simply not there or were concealed beneath a barrage of sensationalism. Furthermore, even when journalists were able to get the whole story, the public, used to years of official lies and censorship, were wary of being deceived again and distrusted what they were told.

During the transition to a democratic government, Argentine politicians who for years had seen the media as instruments of government propaganda began to use the media, particularly television, within a wider arena of political action. Argentine newspapers, magazines and radio and television programmes soon assumed an active role in many aspects of the political process: debating issues, covering rallies, identifying candidates. Broadcasters and the press, however, were more interested in politicians and the political parties than the political parties were in them. Political leaders rarely mentioned the media in their political platforms or announced plans to implement new communication policies. In fact, it would have been difficult to do so.

The new civilian government inherited a legal and administrative structure for the communications sector that was insufficient for any real control over its operations and development. This insufficiency showed, for example, in the unregulated growth of cable television, the habitual violation by commercial radio and television of the legal limit of advertising time and the traditional failure of the media to follow the national guidelines of decentralization and regionalization.

By the end of the military regime, the broadcasting law and its regulatory body, the Federal Committee of Broadcasting (COMFER), had lost their effectiveness and authority. The structure of COMFER was not appropriate for the new democratic spirit of the country. Its board consisted of a president, representatives of the three branches of the Argentine armed forces, the secretary of public information, the secretary of communications and a representative of the private radio and private television stations.

It is easy to understand why little could be done to restructure the media under COMFER. It is harder to understand why the situation remained basically the same three years after the return to an elected civilian government. Part of the answer lies in the weaknesses of the Argentine political parties.

The Argentine political parties played a major role in the transition to a civilian government. The traditional activities of the parties – voter registration, political rallies, marches – reaffirmed the will of the people to leave the military dictatorship behind. The victory of the Radical Party in the November 1983 elections indicated shifts in the historical political affiliations of the country and wider political and cultural changes in Argentine society. In spite of the clear margin of electoral victory, however, after so many years out of power the Radical Party suffered from the usual Argentine *malaise*. It was a strong party in elections but weak as an institution and little equipped for the actual practice of government.

The institutional weaknesses of the Argentine political parties were the result both of historical processes and of the precipitated crisis of the latest military regime. From the moment the military seized power in 1976 until the end of the decade the military governed the country as if it was there to stay and its policies would last for ever. With the exception of the opposition of some labour movements and the protests of the human rights groups, most of the traditional political parties became caught up in the military's own vision of the future. Some parties saw themselves as the inheritors of the military regime, and almost all parties contemplated some form of co-government with the military as the only viable alternative to the dictatorship.

The cracks in the military regime began to show in the early 1980s. They were the result of internal failures and the inability of the armed forces to carry out their programme of transforming the country. Many problems were the result of the military's unwieldy decision-making structure of shared power among the three branches of the armed forces. In the midst of an increasingly speculative economy, the regime found it was unable to maintain the support of the private sector or to form its own political successor.

By 1982 Argentine society was showing increasing opposition to the regime. General Galtieri, convinced that the military had certain goals to achieve before beginning negotiations with the civilian leaders, tried to pre-empt the growing social unrest by invading the Malvinas Islands. In his defeat, he dealt the death blow to the regime. The civilian opposition did not have a chance to grow and gather strength to bring down the regime from below. The regime collapsed on its own, following the military's defeat by the British.

The only common rallying point of Argentine society during the transition from the military to democratic government was a 'return to the Constitution', the basic document that in 1953 had established the procedures of political representation, the separation of powers and individual rights and guarantees. For a country of growing social and economic differences, emerging from a long political crisis with an uncomfortable past, the Constitution fulfilled a symbolic function; it was a symbol of an 'us' in a politically and economically shattered society.

The Argentine Constitution of 1853 understandably contained almost no reference to the media except for the fundamental right of all citizens to publish their ideas in the press without prior censorship. The Constitution gave Congress the responsibility of organizing and regulating media, a responsibility that at the time referred to the telegraph and postal system. In the year and a half between the invasion of the Malvinas Islands and the elections, the Argentine political parties reached no further agreements concerning the organization or regulation of the mass media under a democracy besides those already in the Constitution.

When the newly elected civilian government took office in 1984 it inherited a communications sector that consisted of a number of ubiquitous feudal fiefdoms: a Secretary of Communications (SECOM), a National Company of Telecommunications (ENTEL), a National Company of Telegraph and Postal Services, a colour television station, the Argentine Long Distance Telephone Company, the Provincial Office of Telecommunications of Entre Ríos and a number of telephone co-operatives, all under the Ministry of Works and Public Services. In addition, the new government inherited a Secretary of Public Information (SIP) and a Federal Committee of Broadcasting (COMFER), both under the presidency.

The mandates of these organizations were many times contradictory and impossible to carry out. For example, the Secretary of Communications was in charge of the organization, administration and operation of the Official Radio Service (SOR). The Secretary of Public Information, however, supervised all its programming under the direction of COMFER.

The public administration of the communications sector consisted of a series of geological layers from the many periods of political instability and changes in government. The communications sector had not evolved with the new technologies or the different demands of society but with the different political regimes. Much of the organization of the communications sector was the result of negotiations between civilian and military bureaucracies and the dividing up of the entire public sector by the army, navy and air force.

During the early stages of the new government it became clear that two changes had to be made in communications policy: a new broadcasting law had to be enacted, and the public administration of the communications sector had to be reorganized. Neither of the two occurred during the first years of the new democracy. Certain obstacles blocked the government's basic decisions in the definition of communications policy. Politicians, government administrators, industry and advertisers had converging and diverging interests combining cordiality with mutual distrust. They all, however, shared serious reservations about any possible new rules of the game as defined by Congress.

After 1984 the climate in which the redefinition of democratic institutions including the mass media was carried out was different from the climate of the previous decades. There were fewer Utopias of social and political change. The projects of the authoritarian military regimes, of development planning and of the state as an instrument of national liberation or revolutionary power had all failed. Much of the previous belief in state- or public-supported solutions to social and cultural problems, including communications, had dissipated.

During the transition to democracy, the policies in the Argentine communications sector consisted of informal agreements between different interests. These agreements were made outside the institutions of government and within a rapidly changing industrial and commercial structure in the communications field. There was a stalemate between Congress, the executive and private industry for the definition of communication and cultural policies in the country. Moreover, the cultural industry was showing signs of stagnation.

When the Alfonsín administration took office, Argentine radio and, to a certain extent, the television industry were showing signs of slowing down. In the last ten years the number of television stations had increased from 35 to 40, while the total number of radio stations (government and private) had grown from 148 to 155. This growth was very slow considering the size and population of Argentina and the fact that 84 percent of the people received television signals and the entire population had access to radio.

Services of cable television were increasing mainly in the interior of the country. The legal status of cable television as a complementary service, however, was unclear. The cable operators were demanding that cable be included in the regular broadcasting services and given permission to carry commercial advertising.

The national book-publishing industry had suffered the effects of the removal of import duties on books after 1979 and had experienced a sharp drop in production. More national magazines were being published, but the circulation of each individual magazine was declining. The output of the record industry had also fallen sharply under the military partly as a result of the massive import of cassette players and cassette tapes.

Although consumer demand and sales had increased in the consumer electronics industry especially for colour television sets, video recorders and cassette players, most of these were imported. The domestic electronics industry had actually shrunk during the military regime.

Many of the changes of the Argentine cultural industries were similar to those that had occurred in other countries of the world. Most countries shared some of the inability of the regulatory structure of the Argentine government to keep up with technological changes in telecommunications. Three factors, however, made the Argentine regulatory structure different. First, the unfathomable relationship between broadcasters, producers and advertising agencies; second, the tangle of private and state broadcasting; and third, the historical identification of the public sector with the government in power.

For example, in Argentina, although the television channels were owned by the government, there was no government-owned or subsidized television production facility. Television channels sold or rented air-time directly to advertising agencies or companies that wanted to advertise their products. The television stations set the price for the television time according to the volume of sales and the schedules of payment – an all important consideration in an economy that had three-digit inflation for the last decade. This system discriminated against the smaller buyers, who were forced to pay higher prices.

Under the military administration of television, a type of television broker emerged who would buy up a large amount of television time and resell it to different agencies. The military auditors and overseers of the stations developed close relationships with these brokers and, at times, became brokers themselves.

Under this system of sales and brokers, indirect advertising like the appearance of brand-name products in television series or the use of the records of big-name singers was more important and profitable to the military managers of the stations than the direct sale of advertising spots. The costs and earnings of the different television channels under the military were almost impossible to figure out. They added up, however, to a sizeable transfer of earnings from the government to the private sector.

The mix of the government and the private sector in the management of broadcasting included not only shared financial interests but also shared concerns of political propaganda and cultural orientation. Within this tangle of public and private interests, there was no distinction between what was in the public sector and what belonged to the regime currently in power.

The Argentine newspapers provide an example of the way in which the Argentine military entangled its interests with those of the private sector. The Argentine government was a partner with the three main newspapers of Papel Prensa, the company that controlled all of the newsprint in the country. Papel Prensa sold newsprint to its stockholders at a reduced price. The government through Papel Prensa was able to control approximately 50 percent of the finances of the smaller papers by manipulating the price of the newsprint they had to buy from Papel Prensa, a monopoly.

Even before the latest military regime came to power, another important characteristic of the Argentine media was its concentration in Buenos Aires. This concentration started with the Argentine rail system and was followed by the telegraph and telephone lines. It increased with the introduction of new communication technologies and commercial arrangements.

Each city further out from Buenos Aires had a progressively smaller selection of television programmes to choose from as it was limited by the selection made by the previous city. The telephone company that owned the microwave system set tariffs for television signals according to the number of television receivers at the receiving end. It was therefore more expensive to transmit from the provinces to Buenos Aires than from Buenos Aires to the provinces.

At first, the television stations in the interior of the country produced their own television programming with their own professional staff for news and entertainment. The lack of legal protection and the competition from Buenos Aires combined to make these operations unprofitable, and the stations had to use canned programming and programmes retransmitted from Buenos Aires. During the transition from the military government, the percentage of nationally produced content on television was 66 percent for Buenos Aires and 55 percent for the rest of the country. All but 4 percent of the national programmes were produced in Buenos Aires.

In spite of these limitations, changes did occur in the Argentine cultural industries during the transition to democracy. During the first stages, however, new cultural policies were hardly distinguishable from the overall political changes of the country. The process of democratization – the end of censorship, the end of blacklisting of artists, the flood of new information and even pornography – had an immediate effect on culture, although it was not an explicit cultural policy.

The surge of many forms of popular and public theatre, dance and music at the end of the dictatorship formed part of the reshaping of the public sphere of politics and of the generalized rejection of the military government. Cultural expression played an important role in the emergence and consolidation of the political socialization of the people during the transition to a democratically elected government.

Some political parties and intellectuals asked what were the necessary cultural conditions for the democratization of the institutions of government and what should be the role of the government in the field of culture. Cultural policies like those carried out by the national, state, municipal and neighbourhood secretaries of culture emerged as a specific realm of government action. At the same time, however, the public and private cultural plans and policies formed part of larger issues that affected the entire country such as the trials of the members of the military regime for violations of human rights, the peace treaty with Chile for the Beagle Channel, the new divorce law and the new rights of women, and the campaigns against inflation.

The first important cultural policy of the new government was to put the Argentine colour television company, ATC – built by the military to cover the 1978 World Cup matches in Argentina – under the National Secretary of Culture. With this innovative measure the scope of activities of the Secretary of Culture multiplied enormously. Previously the National Secretary was responsible for the national museums, anthropology and folklore, music, theatre, visual arts and community outreach programmes. It was a modest structure with a low budget. Approximately 90 percent of its activities were in Buenos Aires.

This first cultural policy of the new government, however, soon ran into trouble. In 1984 the Secretary of Culture released its National Cultural Plan for 1984–9 in which it expressed concern about its powerful new charge. Its first concern was the contradiction between being publicly owned and commercially financed. Its second concern was the limitations imposed by commercial sponsorship on the quality of ATC's content and the veracity of its news services. Its third concern was the small amount of programming from the interior of the country.

ATC was a novelty for the Secretary of Culture but not for the public sector. Under the military regime ATC had combined the worst elements of repression and corruption, but under the Secretary of Culture it began a policy of increased freedom of expression and aiming for a higher artistic level. Many of its programmes, however, were of low quality and often failed to attract audiences.

It soon became clear that the Secretary of Culture was unable to administer a television company where important programming decisions were made by the private sector. In August 1986 ATC was moved from under the Secretary of Culture and placed directly under the Secretary of Public Information of the Presidency.

As the new democracy matured, other specific areas of government policy emerged, like open-air concerts and plays, subsidies for the traditional arts and museums, support for the national film industry and community and municipal artistic activities. These actions were directed towards diversifying existing cultural installations and providing opportunities for new voices, artistic expressions and forms of local communication in the state-owned media.

These actions were minimal compared with the size and scope of the mass media, the information circuits of new communication technology and the grandiose paragraphs of some national cultural plans. Yet they were enormous efforts for a government plagued with economic deficiencies, an excruciating foreign debt and an obsolete communications and cultural infrastructure. They were also minimal in comparison with the enormous demands on the Argentine state in the field of culture and communication that were coming from the traditional cultural industries, artists and intellectuals, and entrepreneurs of the mass media.

The demands of the traditional cultural industries – book publishers, theatre owners, recording companies – were for subsidies, loans, tax breaks and other forms of legal and financial benefits. These measures were necessary to lighten their pressing economic problems and guarantee their future, badly eroded by high costs, lack of investment and competition from newer media such as television and cable.

The demands of groups of artists and intellectuals, for the most part semi-employed or unemployed actors, journalists and university professors, were for higher salaries and job stability. Their demands reflected the traditional Argentine policy of protection of employment in the arts. The National Cultural Plan contained a series of initiatives in this area: protectionist laws for traditional crafts, visual arts, publishing, records, music, theatre and film. The plan also contemplated the creation of a national ballet, measures to refinance the National Arts Funds and a law that would require that imported television programmes be dubbed by Argentine actors.

The demands of entrepreneurs of the mass media were channelled through a Commission of Independent Mass Media made up of the Argentine Association of Magazine Publishers, the Association of Provincial Newspapers, the Association of Publishers of Buenos Aires, the Association of Private Radio Stations and the Association of Broadcasters. The private broadcasters and publishers had a strong bargaining position with the government as a result of the new role of the media in politics, the new licensing opportunities (especially if the newspapers were permitted to own television channels) and a public sector that had to sell many state-owned companies to the private sector in order to survive.

The demands of the three areas came together in a series of changing alliances that made it difficult to formulate public policy or reach a consensus.

The private entrepreneurs proved to be the strongest of the three areas. They were able to stop the passage of a law that would have given individuals the right of reply to certain publications or broadcasts and to block a new dubbing law that would have raised the costs of television production. Private media owners successfully proposed a series of protectionist measures that prohibited direct satellite broadcasts from abroad.

It was not easy for the new Argentine democracy to form a policy in the field of communications and culture. Each policy initiative meant new winners and new losers and threatened the precarious status quo. Private media owners were reluctant to allow the entrance of new players in the field, for example, through radio licences to non-profit public organizations. The government was reluctant to allow part of the state-owned broadcasting facilities to be placed under the jurisdiction of a public, non-governmental organization.

The return to a constitutional regime, however, raised the possibility of the terms of the Constitution being amended to include new rights, new institutions and new forms of representation. Some of these new measures could redefine the relationship between the state and the mass media.

This was not a good time, however, for Argentina to reinvent all-embracing state planning or to strive for a government cultural policy. The long years of military dictatorship, censorship and persecution directed towards the destruction of intellectuals and culture were a permanent warning against state intervention and control of cultural production and information flow.

An important part of any new government policy in communication and culture, therefore, would have to be the recognition of its own limits. This did not mean that the state could have no role in cultural policy, especially in a country such as Argentina with growing social inequalities. Government policies in communication and culture could strengthen the policies of the different social organizations and create innovative participatory institutions. Policies could open opportunities for debate and participation, protect grass-roots cultural initiatives, better distribute the cultural and information capital of society and provide new spaces for individual and group creation. National, provincial and municipal policies, however, could no longer be based on any pre-established norms or contents for each cultural activity.

Communication and Politics in Uruguay

Roque Faraone and Elizabeth Fox

The first Uruguayan radio stations were neither state-owned nor public services, and the Uruguayan government took no part in the first broadcasting experiments in the country soon after the First World War. Without government supervision or initiative, many small private radio stations soon appeared throughout the country.

Liberal governments had adopted forms of state ownership as far back as 1911, and by the 1920s Uruguay already had many of the characteristics of a welfare state. The Uruguayan state employed a significant percentage of the work-force and owned the power, telephone, railroad, cement, oil-refining and other industries. The government gave broadcasting a lower priority, however, than it gave social services like education, health and housing that it already provided. In any case, the small Uruguayan state felt no need to use radio for national unification, as was the case in neighbouring Brazil.

Perhaps due to the lack of early state involvement in broadcasting, Uruguay never developed any real legislation regulating radio and television. The approximately fifty private radio stations on the air in 1986 had all obtained their precarious and easily revocable operating licences by executive decree (Faraone, 1969: 45).

In spite of the initial reluctance of the state to provide radio services, in 1929 the government allocated a budget and one short-wave and two medium-wave frequencies to a non-commercial public broadcasting service, Servicio Oficial de Difusión Radio Eléctrica (SODRE; Paris de Oddone *et al.*, 1969: 114). SODRE's activities rapidly spread into other cultural fields: a national symphony orchestra, a national ballet, a film club operating in its own theatre and in 1963 a public television channel.

Uruguay was a prosperous country in the 1930s with an active economy based on agricultural exports. Most of its population of 2 million lived in cities, 30 percent in the capital, Montevideo, and the rest in smaller cities of between 10,000 and 40,000 inhabitants. Only 20 percent of the Uruguayan population was rural, concentrated in the south and along some areas of the Atlantic coast (Paris de Oddone *et al.*, 1969).

After the First World War, Uruguay, 'the Switzerland of America', enjoyed political stability, a collective presidential regime, high levels of health and education and a developed welfare system. Uruguay had one of the highest rates of literacy in Latin America. More people were able to buy and read newspapers in Uruguay than in most of the neighbouring countries.

Economic prosperity and the high level of education of the population made it possible for small local radio stations – as well as newspapers – to establish audiences attractive to advertisers and operate at a profit without state subsidy. The stable political climate and the low level of social conflict in Uruguay made it possible for the government to refrain from open interference in the private media's content or operations.

The peaceful coexistence of the private media, the government and the political parties, however, hid growing sources of social conflict. For example, during the regime of Gabriel Terra (1933–8), although newspaper owners were divided between supporters and detractors of his regime, a strike by newspaper workers brought the owners together in their own defence.

The many small radio stations were modest operations. To set up a station it was enough to have a good record library that could be played again and again and seldom updated. The more than twenty radio stations in Montevideo had similar programming schedules, although the top three or four had a better selection of music than the rest. Advertising, without legal limits, was the only form of support for these stations, and they competed ruthlessly. Local radio stations were informative and always highly political.

Popular music took up most radio broadcasting time. Only the public radios, CX6 and CX26, played classical music. Folklore and tangos, especially the old tangos of Carlos Gardel, 'El Mago', by then highly successful throughout Latin America, monopolized the other stations. Football games were an important component of the leading radio stations. Announcers and commentators developed their own distinctive, inimitable styles and consolidated audiences and regular advertising clients.

On a smaller scale, local advertisers financed the commercial radio stations in the interior of the country. In addition to music and entertainment, these stations played an important role in social and family life. Local radio broadcast free of charge personal messages to friends or relatives. In this way radio often took the place of inadequate telephone services. Uruguayan radio also played a key role in national politics.

Uruguay had universal suffrage after 1938. It enjoyed a high literacy rate and widespread public education, a long secular tradition, a relatively weak Catholic Church and a low-profile military (until 1973). Uruguayans traditionally took an active role in the workings of the state and of the political parties. The high degree of political participation of the Uruguayan population partially accounts for radio's active role in politics.

It is likely that early radio's coverage of politics resembled the political coverage of the written press. The press's coverage had always been highly combative and closely tied to the main political parties. Through the press and later radio, many people participated in the political life of the country. In the 1920s, for example, the *Tribuna Popular*, a newspaper of the Blancos, one of the traditional political parties, filled its front page with the resolutions of the convention of the Colorado Batllista Party, the other traditional party. Another newspaper, *El Día*, owned by the leader of the Batllista party, José Batlle y Ordóñez, published its own version of this same convention.

Editorials were typical Uruguayan radio programmes. The four-minute editorial *Opina el Espectador* came just before the news on a radio station with a high audience rating. The editorial covered different topics: juvenile delinquency, terrorism, patriotic celebrations, Uruguay's low birth rate, violence and the United Nations. The editorial always supported one point of view and then presented the other side. Although seldom more than a collection of sterotypes, *Opina el Espectador* demonstrated the early political maturity of broadcasting and of the Uruguayan population (Faraone, 1972).

During the first government of Juan Perón in Argentina (1945–55) many Argentine politicians persecuted for their political views fled to Uruguay. The radio stations of Montevideo and Colonia, near the Argentine border, made broadcasting time available to political exiles like Agustín Rodríguez Araya and Alfredo Palacios. Uruguayan radio transmitted detailed news of Argentina to the neighbouring Argentine provinces.

In the 1950s Uruguayan radio carried out a long campaign in support of a Paraguayan station that had been shut down by the dictatorial government. Each day CX14 *El Espectador* ended its main news show with the announcement, 'Radio Excelsior of Paraguay is still off the air.'

The many private stations transmitting to a highly politicized, urban, largely middle-class population had a lasting effect on the political life of the country. Political leaders like Luis Batlle Berres, Benito Nardone and Germán Araújo were in part a product of radio. Much of their popularity was based on the charisma of their broadcasting styles.

Political battles were often waged over the mass media. Luis Batlle Berres, nephew of José Batlle y Ordóñez, the founder of 'Batllismo', the progressive wing of the Colorado Party, was a rival of his cousins, the sons of Batlle, who had inherited the powerful newspaper *El Dia* from their father (Lindahl, 1962). In the 1940s Luis Batlle Berres bought the radio station CX10 Ariel and turned it into a tool for politically organizing his wing of the party. Once he became president, he founded the newspaper *Acción* and used it to increase his political influence.

Benito Nardone, working outside the traditional political parties, aimed his programme, CX4 Radio Rural, at Uruguayan farmers. Nardone criticized the government and defended the interests of the farmers. His populist broadcasts about the conflicts between large and small farmers and between landowners and salaried workers won him many followers. He played an important role in the elections of 1958, allying himself with one of the wings of the National Party. He later became a member of the National Council of Government – the position of president had not existed since 1952 – and was president of the Council for one year.

Television began in Uruguay in 1955 when Uruguayan economic prosperity was beginning to wane. Three commercial channels organized by national capital in association with US television networks were followed by a fourth SODRE-owned station. SODRE's Channel 5 operated at a minimum level mainly showing old movies until after 1964 when new legislation permitted both public and private advertising on the government-owned channel.

The Uruguayan National Association of Broadcasters bitterly contested the legislation permitting SODRE to accept commercial advertising. A heated parliamentary debate followed on the merits of public versus private broadcasting. In spite of the Uruguayan tradition of public service in many areas of the economy, the supporters of public broadcasting lost the battle, and from then on Uruguayan private commercial television predominated over SODRE's public-service channel.

After 1955 the Uruguayan economy, chronically dependent on agricultural exports, began to weaken. Economic stagnation and inflation increased social conflict and brought with it the progressive privatization of the economy. In order to deal with growing social unrest, the executive branch of government began to concentrate more power and move towards an authoritarian and non-democratic regime.

The mass media soon began to feel the effects of this authoritar-

ianism. In 1967, beginning with *Epoca*, the government began to
censor and shut down newspapers and magazines, among these
Extra, Democracia, De Frente, Ya, La Idea and *El Eco*. The
government prohibited any news about labour strikes, political
violence or protests and police action against the Tupamaros, a
growing urban guerrilla movement. The media were not allowed to
use the terms 'commando', 'cells', 'terrorists', 'political criminals',
'ideological criminals', 'extremists' or 'subversives'.

The government also began to control the foreign press and
foreign correspondents. Finally, the Argentine newspapers no
longer sent editions to Uruguay because they had no assurance that
they would be delivered.

Government censorship extended to schools, books, the postal
system, popular music and theatre. Radio, television and the press
slowly adapted to the new situation, in many cases becoming silent
partners of the regime's authoritarianism by their docile obedience
to government censorship, manipulation of information and outright
distortion of the news.

Between 1969 and 1973 broadcasters were able to get around
some of the censors' limitations. For example, the government
ordered that the Tupamaros be referred to only as 'delinquents'.
They could not be called Tupamaros, revolutionaries, rebels or
insurgents. Broadcasters called them the unmentionables, yet
everyone knew who they were talking about. It was more difficult
for the broadcasters to escape the ban on reporting the frequent
labour strikes. For example, people had to know what transportation lines were running in order to get to work and return to their
homes. The media were not allowed to broadcast this information
or report the strike. Radio stations used the phrase, 'Tomorrow,
bus circulation in the city will be normal', to inform the population
that the strike that they had never acknowledged was over.

Once in power, the military dictatorship that ruled Uruguay
between 1973 and 1984 quickly moved to close down more
newspapers and magazines: *Ultima Hora, El Popular, Acción,
Ahora, Marcha* and *El Oriental* in 1973; *Marcha, 9 de Febrero,
Ahora, El Diario, El Heraldo, El Terruño, Nuevo Amenecer, El
País, Mensajero Valdense* and *La Unión* in 1974; and *Aquí Está,
Informaciones, Víspera, El Día, El Civismo, El Telégrafo, El
Noticiero* and *Perspectiva de Diálogo* in 1975 (Galliner, 1977;
Organización Internacional de Periodistas, 1974; UN Secretary-
General, 1977). The few newspapers that managed to survive did so
by buckling under to the regime's demands.

After July 1973 the military totally censored broadcasting, books,
records and plays, prohibited all political parties and labour unions

and controlled the meetings of athletic and social clubs. The military persecuted folk-singers and popular musicians. In 1973 Daniel Viglietti, a well-known Uruguayan composer and singer, was arrested and along with other singers went into exile. The military banned the songs of many Uruguayan composers – Viglietti, Alfredo Zitarrosa, Numa Moraes, Los Olimareños, Marcos Velázquez, Yamundu Palacios, Jose Carvajal and the 'Camerata' – and refused to allow well-known Argentine and Spanish entertainers to perform in the country.

In December 1976 the police chief of Montevideo informed radio stations that they could not play seven tangos by Carlos Gardel – dead for forty years – because the tangos represented a state of mind that had been totally conquered.[1] The military censored the *murgas*, the informal groups of satirical popular carnival singers and made them take the words 'freedom', 'justice', 'social justice', 'equality', 'workers' and 'working class' out of their songs.

Censorship of news was tougher than that of popular music and entertainment, and journalists faced enormous dangers in their work.[2] News censorship was not limited to the present but reached back into Uruguay's history. The public were denied access to newspaper editions of entire years of the country's history, stored in the national library.

The military regime shut down many radio stations: CX20 Radio Sur, CX4 Radio Rural, CW1 Radio Colonia, CX44 Radio Panamericana, CX42 Radio Vanguardia and CX30 La Radio. It censored programmes: CW45 on 14 May 1974 and the *Diario del Campo* by Eduardo J. Corso on 14 December 1976. The stations that remained open exercised enormous self-censorship.

In addition to censorship, the military regime organized its own propaganda campaigns under the National Office of Public Relations. This office was made up of three members representing the president, the commander-in-chief of the armed forces and the office of planning and the budget. The public relations office was charged with informing about the achievements of the regime, organizing public opinion in favour of the programmes of the military government and counteracting unfavourable international news about the dictatorship.

In 1977 the military moved the Office of Public Relations out from under the presidency and placed it within the Ministry of Planning, Co-ordination and Propaganda. The Office of Public Relations was responsible for the official news bulletins and for anti-protest songs such as 'Disculpe' and 'Yo creo en ti' released to Uruguayan radio and television.

After November 1980 the political situation in Uruguay began to change. In spite of election fraud, the military lost a referendum on a constitutional reform that would have placed the future civilian regime under permanent military tutelage. The country and the military itself began to recognize the widespread unpopularity of the regime. Spontaneous and organized civil protests began against the military. These protests had enormous political significance because government censorship had destroyed any other form of political protest.

After 1980 Uruguayan broadcasting began the slow, tortuous return to freedom. In some cases this struggle was directly linked to the struggle for general political freedom. Germán Araújo, a protagonist in the fight for broadcasting freedom, had continued to transmit during the dictatorship from Radio Nacional although he was not allowed to use the traditional name of the station and called his radio simply 'La Radio'. Araújo resisted the attempts of advertisers to strangle his station financially and had withstood threats and detentions from the military. In the process he gained international recognition and prestige for his cause. When elections were held in 1984 Araújo was elected senator as a member of the Frente Amplio, a left-wing coalition.

Under the moribund dictatorship, broadcasters slowly began to recover some indirect means of expression. Audience participation programmes alluded obliquely to political prisoners or exiles, for example, by discussing the problems of a mother who could not see her daughter. Listeners deciphered these and other references in hidden complicity with the media.

Timid opposition publications from the traditional political parties slowly began to appear, first *OPINAR*, followed by *Jaque* and *Búsqueda*.

The recovery of democracy was slow. In 1982 the three political parties authorized by the regime held internal elections under the tutelage of the military. The candidates in the parties that were supported by the military received less than 20 percent of the votes in spite of press censorship, restrictions on rights of assembly and bans on certain political leaders.

Uruguayans were tired of the years of repression and blamed the military regime for the economic recession that had begun in 1982. Broadcasters, sensitive to political pressure because of their dependence on advertising and their easily revocable licences, timidly sided with public opinion against the military.

The election campaign began in August 1984 when an agreement was finally reached with the military. Official propaganda was highly visible throughout the campaign. The military regime censored any news of banned or jailed candidates or of unauthorized political parties.

The newly elected civilian government that took office on 1 March 1985 quickly restored press freedom. New dailies and weeklies were soon on the news-stands, and many traditional newspapers made their reappearance.

The civilian government inherited a greatly changed country, economically, politically and institutionally. Twelve years of arbitrary, corrupt and violent rule, carried out in virtual silence, had almost destroyed the normal organizations of society: the family, the school, the club, the political party and the labour union. Furthermore, the military presence was still strong. The Uruguayan military had not been defeated, as had its colleagues in Argentina, and was still a strong institution. The threat of the military and the strength of the commercial broadcasters constituted the two main obstacles to the reconstruction of democratic media in Uruguay.

In April 1985 the president named a new board of directors of public broadcasting headed by Carlos Maggi, a member of the president's party. Maggi immediately presented a plan to modernize the state television Channel 5 that included a prime-time news programme with a well-known journalist. The plan intended to raise the audience level of the public channel to that of the private channels. Pressures from the owners of the private television channels forced Maggi to abandon the news programme and resign. Although his resignation and the future of Channel 5 both received parliamentary debate, it was twenty years too late; the tide had turned against public-service broadcasting in Uruguay long before.

A little over a year later, the private television channels refused to accept paid advertising from a human rights group protesting against a proposed amnesty bill for those military officers who had participated in the kidnapping, torture and murder of political prisoners during the dictatorship. Private television's continued self-imposed censorship, in spite of the return of a civilian regime, demonstrated a fear of free expression that would be hard to overcome.

Notes

1. The tango 'Al pie de la Santa Cruz' says: 'hoy le negó el aumento al pobre obrero que le pidó un pedazo de pan' ['Today the poor worker who asked for a piece of bread was denied a raise']. The tango 'Aguaforte' says: 'declaran la huelga / hay hambre en la casa / es mucho el trabajo y es poco el jornal' ['declare the strike / there is hunger in the house / the work is long and the pay is short'].

2. In 1974 the publication of a short story that had received a literary prize in the weekly *Marcha* caused the imprisonment of the author of the story, of the jury for the prize (among these, Juan Carlos Onetti) and of the directors of the weekly (Carlos Quijano, Julio Castro and Hugo Alfaro). Later, Quijano had to go into exile in Mexico at age seventy-eight and Julio Castro died under torture in prison.

References

Faraone, Roque (1969) *Medios Masivos de Comunicación.* Montevideo: Nuestra Tierra.

Faraone, Roque (1972) *Opina El Espectador: un Estudio sobre la Opinion Radiofónica.* Costa Rica: ILDIS (Instituto Latino-Americano de Investigaciones Sociales).

Galliner, Peter (1977) *Revue Annuelle de la Liberté de Presse Mondiale.* London: Institut International de Presse.

Lindahl,G. (1962) *Uruguay's New Path.* Stockholm: Institute of Ibero-American Studies.

Organización International de Periodistas (1974) 'Uruguay Mass Media Aujourd'hui', *Les Affaires des Journalistes* (Praga).

Paris de Oddone, B., Faraone, R. and Oddone, J.A. (1969) *Cronologia Comparada de la Historia del Uruguay (1930–1945).* Montevideo: Universidad de la República.

UN Secretary-General (1977) *Derechos Humanos en el Uruguay.* New York: United Nations.

13

Between Memory and Illusion: Independent Video in Brazil

Ingrid Sarti

One of the most controversial themes in recent history has been the effect of the extraordinary advances in communication technology on social relations. The controversy stems from the fact that the mass media, although appearing to bring about progress under all circumstances, cannot be judged outside a specific social context. The application of the media towards freedom and social progress is the result of many different media forms and contents acting on many specific social and political processes. At any one time, the new communication technologies act either for or against freedom of expression and economic and social progress depending on diverse and varied political options.

The history of the media in Brazil over the last twenty years offers a good example of the ambiguity and complexity of the relationship between the media and politics. During this period, government communication policies rationalized the production and circulation of the mass media as agents of the conservative modernization the country was undergoing. Later, when the political transition away from the military regime announced a democratic future, the media were expected to adapt to a more just, egalitarian and politically active society.

The military regime inaugurated the era of mass communications in Brazil at a time when repression and silence coexisted with the opulence of the Brazilian economic miracle. Although the economic statistics for this period revealed enormous differences in the buying power of the population for all the goods advertised on television, in the public mind Brazil was one big family under the protective arm of TV Globo.

As a leader in national cultural production, TV Globo was a perfect example of a modern technology that was able to adapt itself rapidly to the new period of civilian rule in Brazil. This chapter is not about TV Globo, however, but about video, a technology intimately related to television but with its own history.[1] The following pages explore the role of video production in the democratization of the social and political market of telecommunications in Brazil. They ask if independent video production can become an alternative to the cultural model introduced in Brazil by television and especially by TV Globo.

The introduction of video technologies in the 1960s changed the structure of Brazilian television. Video technologies made possible the centralization of programming and hence the national television networks.[2] The use of video economized programming time and introduced a new rhythm of production as well as numerous experiments in television language.

It is paradoxical to examine video technologies solely in relation to their contribution to the development of television or film. Initially, video was not meant to resolve technical problems in television or film. Film makers first used the new video technologies in alternative productions outside commercial television. As one author observed, the appropriation of video technologies by existing media probably limited the development of video's application to ideological and artistic experimentation on a visual plane and to the search for a new visual language (Mendes de Almeida, 1984: 58).

Video production was first conceived outside the commercial television system and oriented towards a limited market either as video art or as educational material. The movement of video art in the United States in the 1960s, for example, was not only outside the commercial television system but against it. Television was seen as an enemy of artistic creation. Video, armed with creativity and ideas, was a means of counter-attack (Mendes de Almeida, 1984: 45–6).

The first independent video producers in Brazil formed part of this movement against mass commercial television. Video producers criticized the commercial nature of television and its links with the Brazilian military regime. Independent video producers accused television of cultural alienation and political authoritarianism. The exploration of the artistic and technological possibilities of video technology by the independent producers and their attempt to integrate video in the plastic arts, however, were carried out under the most adverse political and economic conditions. Independent video production was always a marginal movement both politically and culturally.[3]

From the end of the 1960s video production received the full impact of the accelerated development of the modern electronics industry in the field of telecommunications. The rapid expansion of videotape cameras and recorders in the industrialized countries changed cultural patterns and modified the original concept of alternative or art video. Rather than a radically different language, video became part of the new culture of television. Video came to be seen as a transition or compromise between the artistic creation of film and the uncontrollable cultural homogenization of television (Mendes de Almeida, 1984: 13).

Nevertheless, Brazilian independent video producers never completely abandoned their criticism of television. They still considered video a possible instrument for the democratization of the relationships between the producers and consumers of television. Other producers, however, perceived a diminishing distance between video and television. Some independent producers were beginning to air their tapes on commercial television. Commercial television in turn was beginning to experiment with video in various experiences of community television.

Video was in the cultural vanguard. Video made possible new types of production and experimented with new uses of the media. Video could change the vertical relationship between producers and consumers of television. Some felt video would force the conventional institutions of television, limited by different interests, to change. According to one Brazilian critic (Machado, 1985), video technology challenged the cultural function of television by permitting different possibilities of electronic language and by expressing the feelings of the people.

In the Brazil of the 1980s the transition to democracy inspired the development of video's mediating function between producers and consumers of television. Video was no longer on the margins of television production but it was not yet entirely subordinated to the commercial interests that controlled television. The new political context permitted alternative forms of cultural creation. New slogans stressing the democratizing role of television in Brazilian cultural life began to replace the radical slogans of the 1970s condemning commercial television.

The principal aim of the independent video producers was to enter the national telecommunications market. Competition with commercial television became their main objective. In order to achieve their aim and compete with commercial television under more favourable conditions, the independent video producers focused on new content and technical innovations. At the same time they directed their efforts towards changing national communication policies and legislation regarding television.

The independent video producers of the 1980s worked individually or in small groups with few institutional ties with the commercial mass media. Independent video had little capital. It was a small business that had to apply originality and youth to the visual language of video and exploit the full potential of the technology before it became obsolete.

The financial limitations of the independent producers affected their style. Video production is closely linked to the latest developments of the modern electronics industry. All the technical resources of video – special effects, frozen images, slow and fast motion camera – are part of the language of video (Mendes de Almeida, 1984: 60). The imported equipment of the independent producers was expensive and plagued by rapid obsolescence and high import duties. It was hard for them to keep up with the state of the art in video technology.

Brazilian video producers were not deterred by these obstacles. They hung their hopes on the success of an original and decentralized type of production. By the early 1980s a young generation of producers with great creative force had emerged on the electronic media scene.

The young producers knew their works would be seen by a public addicted to the TV Globo model of great technical virtuosity.[4] They therefore tried to show what TV Globo hid from the population. According to Machado (1985), the aim of the video producers was to invert the model of commercial television reporting, which reduced the ideological, cultural, linguistic, ethnic and religious diversity of the population to a homogenized and standardized text. The first documentary productions of the independent video producers contrasted starkly with the official news of the commercial networks.

The diversity of subjects treated by the young video makers, especially during the second half of 1986 when the political parties occupied much of the commercial media with their election campaigns, increased to include national politics. Independent video, however, did not limit itself to political issues but covered a wide range of other topics.

There was an inverse relationship, however, between the increasing technical and visual sophistication of the productions and the importance of their subject-matter. Video makers became more concerned with the search for new languages and the development of the art of video than with the message. The technical experimentation and excellence of their productions had become their calling card for commercial television.

The independent video makers, in open competition with commercial television producers, used all the means they had at their disposal to enter the television market. In the process, they discarded some of their previous characteristics as 'independents'.

Their hope was to disseminate their productions on as many channels as possible. These channels included advertising as well as cultural programmes.

Anything went when the final objective was to compete with TV Globo for its nightly audience of close to 100 million viewers. One of the best ways to reach this audience was to get space on the other networks. For this purpose, the independent producers organized themselves to defend their interests. They developed the concept of horizontal production in telecommunications and struggled to have this concept included in the new Brazilian Constitution.

The foray of the independent producers into the national politics of television was potentially an important contribution to the democratization of Brazilian telecommunications policy. The independents proposed setting up an alternative television system better adjusted to the demands of decentralized production. Under the traditional model of centralized and authoritarian media that evolved during the military dictatorship, the official television networks had unlimited rights to produce their own programming and were not obliged to hire independent producers or production companies, as is the case in the United States and other countries. The television channels, formed under the dictatorship, opposed any change that threatened their profits or survival.

The proposal of the independent producers (to be discussed in the Constitutional Congress) defended a democratic system of station licensing, the decentralization and regionalization of television production and the participation of the community in the selection of cultural programming. The new system would legalize an alternative system of television production and limit network production. The independent producers proposed other, more ambitious proposals as well, for example, a high-quality subscriber-supported television system using UHF as in the United States.

The young video producers explored a series of alternatives for their productions taking into account most of the possible political and economic developments in the country. Their use of legal mechanisms such as the Constitutional Congress demonstrated their intention to compete in the cultural market by means of organized action bringing about institutional changes under a new democratic regime.

The new producers fought against the monopolistic television market with their economic diversification and their increased technical competence in the creative field. The struggle had just begun, and those who invested in video had to keep one eye on the rear-view mirror and the other on the future. Many, however, placed their bets on independent, original and decentralized

Brazilian video production competing in an open and free television market (Mendes de Almeida, 1984).

The efforts of the independent video producers to influence the revision of national telecommunications policy were a bold and solid strategy. The proposal of the independent producers, however, was marred by their excessive admiration for television technology and their lack of a critical perspective situating Brazilian telecommunications within their economic and social context. The absence of critical judgement darkened the possibilities of video production as a genuine alternative to the dominant pattern of culture. The seduction of the electronic technology has pushed video makers on a path of wishful thinking that exaggerated the democratizing function of video *per se* and ignored the weight of external social and economic factors.

One factor that was left out of the proposal of the independent producers was community participation in video production. The question of how the community would participate in the selection of the cultural goods it consumes was not mentioned in any of the possible alternatives for Brazilian television. Nor was the creation of any mechanism by which the community could take part in decisions about what is produced and what is consumed. The mechanisms that could guarantee community representation were important considerations in a country like Brazil with great poverty and where most cultural production was determined solely by the market.

Another important gap in the proposed legislation was any consideration of quality. The independent video makers were eager to conquer the commercial television market. Their insertion in the mass television market would break the present monopoly and enable them to disseminate their productions widely. This strategy would increase the consumption of all video productions, up to now restricted to the owners of video recorders and the theatre public.

The proposed modifications in the commercial television market for independent producers would benefit producers and consumers. Nothing was said, however, about the quality or the content of the new productions. Although desired by many, once accomplished, nothing assured that the conquest of commercial television by the independent producers would benefit the cultural democratization of Brazil.

Nothing was more representative of the status quo and of the large economic interests in Brazil than commercial television. It had shown itself able to swim masterfully in the new political currents of Brazil. Television's unmatched use of new communication technologies, however, could not hide the economic and political interests television served. Television, the seductive goddess of 100 million Brazilians, was the first lady of Brazilian modernization that rested on top of economic violence, social inequalities and political authoritarianism.

Cultural democracy will begin when the independent producers and Brazilian policy-makers wake up from their dreams of modernization and technological development as the answer to all problems and recognize the reality of a violently authoritarian and élitist society.

Notes

1. For further reading on TV Globo, see Sarti, 1985; Barbosa Lima and Priolli, 1985; Lins da Silva, 1985.

2. In the second half of the 1960s the military government invested in telecommunications infrastructure that linked Brazil from the north to the south with a microwave system, underground cables and eventually satellites. This infrastructure made possible live national broadcasts and the development of networks. It was an important part of the government's policy of national integration and centralization and the groundwork for the TV Globo system.

3. For further reading on video art in Brazil, see Mendes de Almeida, 1984; and Machado, 1985.

4. The Globo network reaches 100 million viewers over an area of 4,200 square kilometres. It is the fourth largest network in the world after the three US networks. It is reported to have the best team of computerized television graphics in the world under the technical direction of Hans Donner.

References

Barbosa Lima, Fernando and Priolli, Gabriel (1985) *Brasil, os Años de Autoritarismo*. Rio: Jorge Zahar.

Lins da Silva, Carlos Eduardo (1985) *Muito além do Jardim Botânico*. São Paulo: Summus Editorial.

Machado, Arlindo (1985) 'Notas sobre uma Televisão Secreta', in *Televisão e Vídeo no Brasil, os Anos de Autoritarismo*. Rio: Jorge Zahar.

Mendes de Almeida, Cândido José (1984) *O Que é Vídeo*, São Paulo: Brasiliense.

Sarti, Ingrid (1985) 'Os Efeitos da Tecnologia de Ponta na Televisão: a TV-Globo' (mimeo). Lima: IPAL.

14
Bolivian Television:
When Reality Surpasses Fiction

Raúl Rivadeneira Prada

The most notable characteristic of the last seventy years of Bolivian politics has been institutional chaos. Brief periods of constitutional rule have been interspersed between frequent military coups, uprisings and insurrections which bring to power strong-armed regimes and suspend most liberties.

Thirteen out of Bolivia's twenty presidents between 1964 and 1987 were unconstitutional. General René Barrientos seized power in 1964. General Alfredo Ovando Candia ousted a civilian regime in 1969. General Juan José Torres ruled the country between 1970 and 1971. Colonel Hugo Banzer Suárez overturned Torres in 1971 and remained in power until 1978 when he was toppled by General Juan Pereda Asbún. General David Padilla Arancibia threw out Pereda soon after. In 1979 three months of constitutional rule were abruptly brought to a halt by Colonel Alberto Natusch Busch.

The democratic government of Lidia Gueiler fell in the armed assault led by General Luis García Mesa and Colonel Luis Arce Gómez on 17 July 1980. In 1981 Generals Waldo Bernal and Celso Torrelio and Rear Admiral Oscar Pammo replaced Meza. Torrelio ruled on his own until July 1982 when he was ousted by General Guido Vildoso. Finally, in October 1982 a constitutionally elected government came to power.

Undemocratic rule, especially the iron hand of Banzer between 1971 and 1978, crushed the freedom of the mass media, particularly of the press. Government repression and hostility led to fear, self-censorship and, at times, compliance with the regime. After the fall of Banzer in 1978, however, the press showed a growing independence that contributed to the slow construction of democracy after the coup of 1 November 1979.

Resistance was more difficult for radio broadcasters. Between July 1980 and May 1981 the Ministry of the Interior and of Information imposed strict censorship of radio news. Three times a day, all radio stations had to transmit a news bulletin prepared by the ministry. No other news was allowed. Many listeners turned off their sets during the official broadcasts. The BBC, the Voice of America and Radio Moscow became the main sources of news about their country.

Bolivian television, however, perhaps more than any other medium, suffered the abrupt changes and institutional chaos of Bolivian politics. It began in 1969 as a state monopoly under the strict control of the presidency. The government's monopoly began to crack in 1973 when universities were authorized to operate channels. The university channels offered an alternative to the monolithic official government television channel although they suffered grave limitations in their own programming and technical capacities.

In 1979 General Padilla authorized the licensing of private television channels. Before licences could be allocated to private initiatives, however, his regime was overturned by García Meza. The new president immediately re-established the government's tenacious monopoly over television. García Meza's subsequent occupation of the universities and appointment of military rectors placed the university channels under the tight control of the Ministry of the Interior and greatly reduced their relative independence.

On 20 October 1984, five years after the short-lived authorization of private channels, Channel 9, a private channel, defied the law guaranteeing the government's monopoly and went on the air. Faced with such defiance, the government did almost nothing. It meekly accepted the illegality of the new channel set up in the flurry of an intense advertising campaign by the private sector. The campaign criticized the government's monopoly of television and presented among other reasons for the channel's abrupt appearance on the air the need for freedom of expression, free markets and the defence of regional interests of La Paz.

In the days that followed the arrival of Channel 9, supporters of private television used a similar pre-emptive strategy to set up new channels in other cities throughout the rest of the country.

In an interview printed in the magazine *Comunicación* (1985) in La Paz a year after the appearance of Channel 9, the director acknowledged the station's illegality. 'When we first went on the air,' he explained, 'our main objective was to defend the regional interests of La Paz without ignoring the interests of the country as a whole. We knew we would face problems, but, ten days after going on the air without authorization, the government granted us a ninety-day licence.'

The breach opened by Channel 9 soon widened. The rapid

propagation of forty-five private channels created a situation the government was unable to control. In less than a year the private sector had accomplished its goal of dominating Bolivian television and ending the government monopoly, begun in 1969.

The private sector's illegal introduction of new television channels was based on an argument that was difficult to refute. For fifteen years the government had mismanaged its monopoly of television, subjecting it to intolerable abuse, manipulation and censorship. The university channels had been the target of both sectarian ideologies and partisan politics.

It seemed to many that the government and the universities had lost their opportunity to put television at the service of culture, education and national development. The private sector took advantage of the government's failure and with an initially popular gesture broke into the television system in a virtual avalanche of new stations.

By 1987, three years after the appearance of the first private channel, however, the cure for government mismanagement and manipulation seemed to be worse than the initial disease. The majority of the new channels had become instruments of consumerism and fulfilled almost none of the needs of the national communities. Private television had come to serve almost exclusively the interests of a national political and economic system closely tied to transnational corporations and cultural industries. The percentages of national and foreign programming in the private television channels of La Paz during a week in 1987 illustrate the high transnational influence on the medium – Table 14.1.

Table 14.1 *National and foreign programming, private TV channels of La Paz, Bolivia, week of 28 June to 4 July 1987*

Channel	Hours	Foreign	National
7	88	71 (81%)	17 (19%)
9	95	67 (70%)	28 (30%)
2	119	91 (76%)	28 (24%)
6	81	70 (86%)	11 (14%)
4	70	55 (79%)	15 (21%)
11	60	49 (82%)	11 (18%)

The percentages of national programming should be even lower than those shown above. The private channels include in the category of national programmes news and sports shows that generally contain a considerable amount of imported filmed material. In truth, there is little nationally produced content.

Programs like *Jenecheru* and *Paraleb 18* of Channel 7, *Semana* of Channel 9, *De Cerca* of Channel 6, *Enlace* of Channel 2 and *Tribuna del Pueblo* of Channel 4 total only about ten hours of broadcasting a week. Moreover, their technical quality is low, and much of the material is improvised in the studio.

National programming is a poorly defined category that is interpreted by the owners of the private stations as anything ranging from a studio cooking class to the direct broadcasting of a football game. Within this category there is little effort to present artistically and technically careful productions that are rooted in the national reality and that give television audiences a fresh view of their country.

The legal framework of television

In May 1986 the explosion of illegal private television channels in Bolivia forced the government, pressured by the chaotic situation of national broadcasting, to pass a General Regulation for Television Services. The law granted licences to the private stations for ten years, to be renewed every five years. (The usual limit of television licences in Latin America is five years.) It did not allow the same company to own more than one channel in any single city but allowed the same company or individual to own licences in different cities. This soon led to networks of private stations like that of Channel 9 in La Paz, Channel 4 in Cochabamba and Channel 8 in Oruro and the proposed eighteen-channel NITELE network.

The new law established general and ambiguous norms for television content. For example, Article 31 states that the television stations should present programming with a social interest. Article 37 requires that the foreign productions shown on the national channels be devoid of alienating content. This is defined as content that shows no respect for the personality and social and cultural characteristics of the country and that gives undue attention to foreign values.

Article 44 obliges the television channels to transmit at least 25 percent nationally produced programming. This percentage should increase in the next four years until it reaches 40 percent. Enforcement of this requirement, however, is difficult and is not even followed by the government channel.

The law also regulates the use of advertising. Article 48 states that, when possible, television advertisements should be artistically presented. Another article prohibits television channels from producing their own advertising and reserves this activity exclusively for advertising agencies.

The main defect of the new law, however, is not its ambiguity but its liberality. The law favours the private sector by allowing private channels almost complete freedom of action. The prohibitions, limits and requirements of the law are meaningless because there are no organizations set up to enforce them. For example, there is no organization for the classification of programmes, the supervision of operations or the control of copyright violation, violence and pornography. The law establishes no institutional structure for the classification of advertisements or for the control of advertising time. In 1987 over 30 percent of television advertising was for alcohol, night-clubs or films of violence and sex.

The new law's glaring deficiencies and lack of enforcement have often led to excesses like the frequent transmission of pornographic programmes. The government itself, as well as the Church and other social organizations, has criticized the heavy use of pornography, especially in the morning and afternoon hours when children are watching television. The sub-secretary of communications, a year after telling journalists that it was impossible to impose any type of programming on the private channels, criticized serious violations by the private channels of the new law and promised a system to enforce the application of its norms.

Furthermore, almost all the private television channels are involved in what has been called 'broadcasting piracy'. The channels use parabolic antennas to pick up the satellite transmissions of foreign television networks. In spite of the loud protests of the Globo network of Brazil, Televisa of Mexico and Venevisión of Venezuela, and of the companies owning the distribution rights of the pirated material, it has not been possible to stop this violation of the airwaves.

In June 1986, for example, LEMEX, the company that distributed Mexican films in the country, accused Channel 4 of broadcasting in its regular Sunday schedule the film *La Niña de los Hoyitos*, the exclusive distribution rights of which were owned by LEMEX. On the same day, it claimed, Channel 9 had shown *North Sea Hijack*, a Universal film distributed exclusively in the country by LEMEX. The month before, Channel 2 had transmitted *King Kong contra Godzilla*; and the Sunday before, Channel 4 had illegally broadcast *Como México no Hay Dos*.

The companies that hold the rights to the distribution of foreign films in Bolivia have resorted to publishing warnings under the advertisements for coming attractions. The warnings state that the rights for the movie are protected by the law and that any unauthorized exhibition in any form will be punished.

Such warnings, however, have had little effect. In July 1987 a La

Paz newspaper reported the illegal showing on Channel 11 of the film *La Ley de la Calle*. The article announced the arrival of the piracy and copyright violation consultant of the Motion Picture Association of America to discuss with the Bolivian authorities protecting MPAA films from television piracy.

Another common practice of the private television channels is pirating foreign news broadcasts. These broadcasts are often transmitted as if they were national news services. The private television channels record the news programmes of Peruvian, Chilean, Brazilian, Venezuelan, Mexican and Argentine television. The programmes are re-edited with Bolivian voice-overs that often repeat the same text as the original broadcast. In this way the Bolivian public receives an Argentine or a Chilean vision of the international news that often goes against national interests.

For example, in May 1987 unsuccessful negotiations were held for the solution of the dispute between Bolivia and Chile over Bolivian maritime rights. During the negotiations, several of the Bolivian private channels transmitted the Chilean version of the dispute taken from Chilean television.

The coverage and penetration of Bolivian television are still limited by the poverty of the country and its lack of electricity in many rural areas. Foreign broadcasts from Brazil, Argentina, Chile and Peru invade most border zones: Pando, Santa Cruz, Beni, el Chaco, Norte de la Paz and Sur de Potosí. Parabolic antennas pick up transmissions from Puerto Rico, Venezuela and Mexico.

Some communities receive only foreign television. In 1986, in a report to Congress, representative Guillermo Mariaca Iturri said that TVB, the government channel, did not reach Copacabana. A survey in this city carried out by the Ministry of Information had shown that over 50 percent of the children and youth of the community thought that Alan García, President of Peru, was the president of Bolivia. In Riberalta, his report continued, you could watch only Mexican television; and every Sunday, Channel 5 of Santa Cruz transmitted ten hours of Brazilian television in Portuguese with Brazilian advertisements. Finally, the congressman explained, the miners of Consejo Central Sur watched the official television channel of the Chilean government all day long, and their children were beginning to believe that Facism is the eighth marvel of the world.

In April 1987 the journalist Jesús Urzagasti reported that a parabolic antenna had been installed on the roof of the Bolivian telephone company in Villamontes. The antenna picked up the signal of the Chilean government station for the zone and for part of El Chaco. He wrote: 'Chilean television appears on Bolivian screens with the same entertainment, advertisements and censored news that characterize any dictatorship' (Urzagasti, 1987). A minor scandal occurred, however, when television broadcast as a victory the anniversary of the war with Chile in which Bolivia had lost its access to the sea.

The breakdown of the mismanaged and misdirected government monopoly over Bolivian television has hardly resulted in the freedom of expression and defence of national and regional values announced by the private channels when they first appeared on the air as symbols of liberty. Institutional chaos and censorship have been replaced by commercial opportunism, transnational aggression and national irresponsibility.

References

Comunicación (1985) Interview, Nov., pp. 49–50.
Urzagasti, Jesús (1987) Article in *Presencia*, 15 April.

15
Conclusions
Elizabeth Fox

The history of media policy in various Latin American countries reveals a failure to attain most ideals. Dreams of cultural development and autonomy, equitable access and participation, and balanced international exchange have largely come to nothing. On the other hand, the Latin American mass media have suffered relentless commercialization, erratic government intervention and thoughtless exposure to foreign exploitation. Criteria of national development have seldom guided the growth of the Latin American mass media.

Why have policy-making processes on the whole failed in regard to the media? The chapters of this book do not provide definitive answers to this question. Certain patterns and certain central issues, however, begin to emerge from the overview of media policies in Latin America over the last fifty years.

In the background of all the historical accounts of media policies or lack of policies are the social rigidities and the concentration of social and political power that characterize most Latin American societies. The formation of the Latin American commercial media empires is closely linked with the region's dichotomous social structure of widespread poverty and enormous wealth. These basic obstacles to change and reform often block democratic media policies as they do other social and economic policies seeking greater social justice and a more equitable distribution of wealth and power.

Although they form part of the larger history of the region, the Latin American media also have their own history. Within this history it is possible to discern four distinctive patterns or stages in the political process of media policy-making. Different decisions taken at each stage probably account for the specific failure of the Latin American media to transcend an almost exclusively commercial, often transnational and for the most part non-developmental role.

The first stage in the process of media policy-making was the early failure to establish a public policy tradition of broadcasting. The second stage encompassed those decisions that led to the consolidation of the monopolistic media enterprises. The third stage comprised the flawed attempts to carry out national reforms of the mass media. The fourth stage circumscribed the media under the recent military dictatorships and the movements towards democracy in the region. Each stage had somewhat different patterns and contexts of policy-making. Common threads like commercial interest and government intervention, however, ran through all four.

The early failure to establish a tradition
of media policy

Radio began in most of Latin America in the early 1920s. By then the region already had a strong tradition of private newspapers. For example, between 1918 and 1928 the number of newspapers and magazines in Peru grew sharply from 167 to 473 (Gargúrevich, 1987). Many newspapers employed sophisticated printing technologies and had a significant number of readers. Latin American newspaper owners had important ties with newspaper editors and owners in Europe and North America.

In most countries 1920s and 1930s politics were a continuation of the nineteenth-century liberal and conservative factions usually represented by fiercely competitive political parties. Gargúrevich (1987) has argued that newspapers in Peru during this period had two main functions. The first was partisan political debate and struggle. The other, more subtle, was the support of the traditional oligarchy through the pages of political commentary.

The liberal 'free press' tradition of the early twentieth century provided a background for the conceptions of independence and public service of the Latin American mass media. At the same time, this tradition was the foundation of the eventual commercial organization of private broadcasting and mass advertising.

A fairly autonomous Latin American cultural and literary tradition with high esteem for the arts – culture more literary than 'technological' – also influenced the early years of development of the print media. For example, there were eighty-eight literary and artistic newspapers and magazines registered in Peru by 1928 (Gargúrevich, 1987).

The élitist and often oligarchic tradition of governments fed an initial tendency to see early radio and films as literary and cultural forums rather than as channels of information and certainly not as commercial vehicles for advertising.

In some countries the early periods of media development were times of strong nationalistic, populist, *indigenista* and even socialization movements. In Mexico, for example, radio grew during the full flower of cultural and political change in the aftermath of the Mexican Revolution when the Revolutionary Party dominated the government. There was interest in translating many of the revolutionary goals of social change and national development into cultural and broadcasting policy. In Peru radio's arrival coincided with the formation of the APRA and the Peruvian Socialist Party. These political movements, however, seldom proposed or succeeded in setting up lasting national public-service broadcasting structures.

Many of the pioneers of radio in Latin America were amateurs, and the new technology was treated more as a novelty than as a serious new cultural or economic force. There was a willingness, as in the case of the early Brazilian radio clubs, to entertain novel conceptions of the organization of broadcasting. Some governments set up small public-service radio stations generally under the executive. In Uruguay, for example, public-service radio was placed alongside the other arts under a decentralized public organization that received government subsidy.

A few of the initial public-service policies of the Latin American mass media like those in Uruguay followed a European conception of public subsidy and organization of the arts rather than the fast developing private commercial broadcasting structure of the United States. Governments in other countries like Chile, however, preferred to ignore the new technologies and left their development, if at all, to private initiative.

Very little is known about the early first stages of mass media policy in Latin America. Students of media policy have focused mainly on the press or have begun their analyses with those periods when the commercial structure of the media was firmly in place. There appears to have been, however, a wide variety of different models and experiments with policies and structures of broadcasting and cultural institutions, many of which were short-lived or rapidly absorbed into a commercial system.

For example, in 1936 a Liberal regime in Colombia attempted to pass a law nationalizing broadcasting. The initiative was blocked by private enterprises already worried about losing their source of advertising and by newspaper owners concerned with the wider implications of government control of information (Pareja, 1984). Early broadcasting in Cuba was essentially cultural and noncommercial until the regulations were changed in 1934 with the country's new trade agreements with the United States.

Notwithstanding the heterogeneity of policies and ubiquitous structures of early media, the Latin American tradition of a centralized state seems to have exerted a powerful attraction during the first experimental phase of broadcasting. Most scattered initiatives that remained outside a commercial sphere soon came under state control. Here they usually rested firmly under the executive rather than under some form of public control that could shield the media from political change and manipulation. Few if any early experiences of public or community media survived.

On the whole, during the early stage of media development the countries of Latin America failed to establish any significant tradition of media policy based on some form of public philosophy. No general normative theory underlying media policy evolved regarding the function of the media in social, political, economic and cultural development. No 'sacred' media institutions were formed that would be more or less respected by any government no matter how dictatorial or undemocratic. The early years of the media in Latin America saw little general public discussion of the basic guidelines for media policy.

The lack of an early public philosophy of media development became more accentuated with the rapid consolidation of the commercial media in the 1940s and 1950s.

Consolidation of the commercial media

A strong push towards industrialization, especially import substitution and consumer items, began in Latin America in the late 1920s and increased during the Second World War when Latin America could not depend on Europe and the United States for manufactured consumer items. The growth of national industry and advertising and the expansion of urban markets changed the environment of the early Latin American experiments with radio, films and magazines. The growing industrial work-force, often organized by populist movements and ruling parties, as in the case of Brazil, Argentina and Mexico, fitted well with the growing mass media and seldom pushed for structural changes in ownership or content.

During this period, the Latin American countries developed almost no tradition of media organizations outside the emerging commercial structure of broadcasting. No significant political actors pushed for a media policy that would serve wider goals of social and cultural development. Meanwhile, government policy towards the private media was both supportive and erratic.

The alliance between private media owners and strong centralist governments in Latin America created a favourable context for the commercial and frequently transnational expansion of the mass media. The politically conservative private media owners shared the aims of their governments and of US investors. The lack of government regulation of broadcasters' commercial operations permitted the formation of lucrative monopolies unfettered by public-service obligations. Government credits and investments in communications infrastructure and electrification as part of their policies of industrial development subsidized the private media's monopolistic national expansion. At times, when national politics became increasingly corrupt and undemocratic, the growing media monopolies in some countries responded by consolidating their autonomous entrepreneurial and often political power.

In spite of the rapid growth of the commercial mass media, there was scant public subsidy to finance national productions or regulations to protect local markets from imported films, recordings, television series, magazines and comics. The relatively heterogeneous and at times highly creative local radio stations, magazines and films were forced to appeal to larger and larger audiences with mass productions in order to survive.

The size of national markets, the level of industrial development and the availability of government subsidy and protection to the national media varied from country to country. Sooner or later, however, media owners and artists throughout the region faced the choice between local cultural productions and bankruptcy on the one hand, and imported and mass-oriented productions and financial survival on the other.

As advertising grew, Latin American radio licence holders, film producers, magazine publishers and newspaper owners usually found it more profitable to attract large audiences with bland, standardized and frequently imported content than to finance high-quality national cultural programming and news reporting. Except for the individual efforts and motivation of the Latin American creative and artistic communities, they had little stimulus to do much else. US light-comedy and action adventure programmes devoid of social criticism attracted audiences and seldom caused problems with the government.

The liberal democracies and conservative military and civilian regimes that ruled Latin America during the 1940s and 1950s rarely included the growing mass media in their programmes of support and protection for national culture and the arts. Subsidies and protection of national cultural productions existed only in those countries where nationalism provided support for personal political aspirations. Then support for national artists and media owners was generally tainted with political opportunism and government censorship.

Media policy at this stage was virtually no policy except to allow entrepreneurs and foreign investors a free hand and a general openness to the 'United States model' of mass media, popular entertainment and rapid technological development.

The influence of the United States in Latin America had been on the increase since the First World War. The 'good neighbour' policy and the Inter-American system carried with them the goals of supporting US commercial expansion and consolidating US international security. After the Second World War the influence of the United States in Latin America expanded with the growing concern with communism. Throughout the region ties between Latin America and the United States spread in military, commercial, labour and development efforts.

US investments in Latin American radio stations and the distribution of US magazines, comics and news services existed prior to 1939. A significant upsurge of US television series, films, magazines and recordings in the Latin American media, however, took place during and after the war. The growing US influence in Latin America, often sanctioned by official US policy, included the investments by US television networks in the commercial television systems of almost every country in the region.

Another important influence of the United States on the Latin America media was in the field of development communications. The new programmes were partially in response to the growing economic and social disparities of the region and a result of a general fascination with US technology and technological solutions to problems of development. Beginning in the late 1950s many Latin American governments set up and strengthened development programmes of agricultural extension, health and education. The goals of these programmes were to extend technology out in to the hinterlands, a policy based on the modernization and diffusion model of communication.

There was little involvement of the commercial mass media in the programmes that attempted to spread development information and educational messages through formal organizations to urban and rural audiences. The government-supported development communication efforts like educational radio and television, however, freed the commercial mass media from the wider public-service obligations they might have assumed under different circumstances.

The flawed search for reform

The modernization and industrialization of the post-war period brought increasing cultural and social disparities to the region and growing political unrest. The new urban populations were more volatile than in the past. Militant dissident groups dedicated to revolutionary change formed in countries throughout Latin America. The Cuban Revolution provided an ideal of radical structural change for the new forms of popular movement. The political movements based on alliances of urban dissidents and the urban–rural sub-proletariat presented challenges to the traditional political élites.

In response to many of these changes, and especially after the Cuban Revolution, the United States modified the Inter-American system to permit gradual structural change with programmes like the Alliance for Progress. Funds and political support became available for popular organizations, mass education, agrarian reform and other measures like a progressive income tax. Programmes were directed at decreasing the region's growing economic disparities and easing the pressures for radical change. National and international funds were also made available for central planning offices that gave social equity goals greater priority in national development planning.

The Church likewise responded to the growing pressures for change in Latin America. The influence of Christian social movements and new philosophies within the Catholic Church turned it away from its simple opposition to communism to theories and action programmes for popular participation in national decision-making. Beginning in the 1960s the Latin American Church moved towards greater social support for popular organizations and more radical conceptions of structural change. As the Church became more deeply identified with popular movements, the Church's radio stations and efforts in group communication became alternative media for rural and lower-status urban groups.

At this stage, political leaders and planners, for perhaps the first time, recognized the central role of the mass media in the economies, cultures and politics of their countries. This realization, often part of larger structural reforms, was partially the result of the significant growth of the media. It was aided by the work of Latin American intellectuals and analysts of the mass media. Many of the more vocal critics of the media were employed by universities or governments and frequently had worked in development communication programmes.

Some social movements, political parties and Church-led organizations incorporated media policies in their proposals for overall structural change. In many countries, media policy and reform became a heated political issue. In a few countries controversial national communication policies were eventually enacted.

In the early 1970s attempts to introduce national communication policies occurred in Peru, Chile, Venezuela, Mexico and to a lesser extent Colombia. In general, the reforms were presented as ways to introduce greater cultural diversity into the monolithic formats of the commercial media, provide wider access to different social groups, employ the media for education and development and reduce the media's dependence on foreign news and entertainment.

The reform attempts were mostly top-heavy and government-oriented. Policy-makers usually excluded the private sector from media policy discussions. Reformers, however, generally lacked a solid political support base in social organizations and political movements. As Muraro points out in Chapter 9 on Argentina, all the reforms considered the public sector the most suitable author of cultural policies. Some reforms were more the product of personal relations of communication experts as advisers to central executive powers than a response to demands from listeners, viewers and community organizations.

The communication policies carried out by the Peruvian military regime between 1968 and 1975 illustrated the top-heavy nature of the reforms. It proved impossible to make the media conform to a greater public interest without falling into authoritarian government manipulation of their content and management. The expropriation of the Lima dailies by the military regime in 1974 as part of a reform process that deeply affected all sectors of the Peruvian economic and social structure proved impossible to implement. As Gargúrevich observes in Chapter 4, the reform's authors were unable politically, technically and financially to put in place the proposed measures of social ownership.

The Peruvian regime introduced policies of public ownership of television, radio and the press but was unwilling to put the media in the hands of social and political groups with a grass-roots base and experience. The authors of the reforms failed to accept the final consequences of their express philosophy of social property.

In some reforms the financial, managerial and creative aspects of the media received no attention or were simply expected to come automatically with the change of ownership. For example, the owners of the expropriated Peruvian television stations were able successfully to shift their capital and control from station ownership to production and distribution and keep the profitable operations of the television industry under their control. The expropriated Peruvian television channels continued to employ much the same content and advertising that they had under private ownership.

In Chapter 3 on Chile, Catalán examines the media policies of the Christian Democrats after 1964 and their effect on the Chilean mass media. For the first time, a government in power turned its attention to the media. President Eduardo Frei made wide use of the national radio chains and set up a national television network. He also facilitated the creation of a chain of pro-government radio stations, guaranteed the people's right of reply and regulated the access of political parties to the privately owned mass media. In addition, the Christian Democrats organized the community as both consumer and producer of culture by creating institutions at community, factory and rural level.

The struggle for political control of the private and public media in Chile accentuated during the Socialist administration of President Salvador Allende (1970–3) – a struggle that ended with the breakdown of Chilean democracy in the military coup against Allende.

The Venezuelan experience of media reform during the mid-1970s came from within the established power structure. The reform was a response to the growing economic and political power of the private mass media. Although the reform's authors made a genuine effort to find a formula for a mixed public–private media structure, the controversial reform basically increased the role of the government as owner and regulator of the media. It was the responsibility of the government to create the necessary institutions to ensure the participation of different social groups in the media. Faced with growing criticism from the private sector and opposition political parties, however, the government eventually abandoned its proposal.

The focus of the Mexican reforms in the 1970s was on the government as well as on the people as creators of information and as protagonists of their own histories. The proposals of the Mexican government attempted to generate a profound political response from within the traditional power structure to the political challenge of the private media empires. For over a decade the Mexican government struggled to meet the challenge posed by the growing private mass media and telecommunications industry to its social and political aims. It tried to do this by setting up government-owned media and by introducing a constitutional right to information.

In Chapter 5 on communication policies in Mexico, Caletti Kaplan calls the debate an attempt to come to grips with the impact of the communication revolution and recover the control of communication policies for society and its representative institutions.

The failure to enact most of the Mexican policies was the result of opposition from the private media as well as from groups within the government. The reforms called for the participation of the people in the media. The Mexican population, however, enjoyed little participation in most aspects of government or the economy. Caletti

Kaplan suggests that the ruling party was in no condition to absorb the potential popular participation that would be created by the new media policies or to direct this participation in favour of its political and economic objectives.

In Chapter 6 on the later Colombian reforms Anzola shows how the legislation reorganizing the public administration of television and authorizing regional channels formed part of the general goals of the Betancur administration (1982–6). These goals were to give access to wider sectors of Colombian society – opposition political parties, local and regional levels of government, the guerrilla movements – in the representative institutions of government. The television reform, as well as the more sweeping social reforms of his administration, were carried out in the face of considerable opposition from sectors within the two parties traditionally controlling Colombian politics. In the end, she suggests, the reforms achieved little real change and were rapidly absorbed by the traditional political and commercial forces.

The Latin American search for radical changes in its private and government-owned media and for national communication policies collided with the national and transnational private media empires. The confrontation occurred at a time when the Latin American private media and advertising empires were most confident, strongest and at the high point of their economic expansion and consolidation. Furthermore, as a result of the growing reach and importance of the media in political campaigns, Latin American politicians and the authors of the reforms were increasingly beholden to the national and transnational media for their own survival and power. The growing political power of the media limited reformers' ability to carry out their programmes.

The policy proposals and critical analyses that came out of the media reform movements correctly identified the monopolistic power of the national media empires and their transnational allies as obstacles to more representative and democratic management and operation of the media. The authors of the initiatives, however, for the most part failed to transform this understanding into a broad-based political movement to influence public opinion and support for their policy proposals. Rarely was an effective linkage forged between popular movements and the national media reform movements.

In practice, this often meant that the media reforms were the most politically expendable on the government's agenda of reforms and the first to be sacrificed when faced with opposition. On the one hand, proposed policies lacked grass-roots support. On the other, they aroused strong opposition from privately controlled broadcasting and newspapers at a time when the regimes were the most vulnerable in their struggles to stay in power and implement other far-reaching structural changes.

In spite of the frustrations of the national reforms, leaders of many Latin American countries, especially those still under democratically elected regimes, continued to support the Third World movements for a New International Communication and Information Order. The Latin American participation in the UNESCO-organized San José meeting on National Communication Policies in 1976 was perhaps the best example of their support for international change.

By the time of the San José conference, however – when a public philosophy for guiding the development of the media was proposed and engaged many in a widespread public debate – the tradition of a haphazard commercial development was firmly entrenched and hard to change. Furthermore, few governments still had the legitimacy to try to do so.

Dictatorship and redemocratization

Almost without exception, attempts to formulate communication policy and reform the mass media were discarded by the military regimes that ruled most of Latin America from the mid-1970s. Under the military, communication policy became a combination of free market commercial expansion, technological innovation, corruption, political censorship, repression and government propaganda.

In Chapter 11 Landi describes the Argentine military's creation of an administrative structure for the communications sector that was insufficient for any real control over its operations and development. Much of the military's almost feudal organization of the communications sector was the result of the division of the entire public sector among the three branches of the armed forces. Cable television grew with no order or regulation; commercial broadcasters habitually violated the legal limits of advertising time and ignored the national guidelines of decentralization and regionalization.

Military censorship and the repression of journalists and the media in Uruguay are unequivocally reported on by Faraone in Chapter 12. Faraone examines another dimension of the dictatorships, their use of propaganda. The Uruguayan military set up a National Office of Public Relations charged with informing about its achievements, organizing public opinion in favour of its programmes and counteracting unfavourable international news about its dictatorship.

The relationship between the dictatorships and the media, however, was not always one of straight repression and censorship. In Chapter 8 Hurtado relates the various and often contradictory effects of the free market economic policies of the Chilean military on the national film industry. In Chapter 10 Guimarães and Amaral explore the changing and sometimes paradoxical relationship of the Brazilian military with the formation of the Globo communications conglomerate.

The authoritarian regimes exercised almost total control and censorship of radio, television, newspapers and magazines, as well as theatre, music and most forms of entertainment. At the same time, however, the free market policies and the growth of the private sector, especially advertising, allowed some independent national film producers to establish a financial and technical base for their work. This process is illustrated by Hurtado in Chile and picked up again in Chapter 13 by Sarti on Brazil.

The growth of what came to be known as the alternative media was another important side-effect of the military regimes. In spite of repression, groups and organizations outside the monolithic structure of the military-controlled media and in some cases in the cracks and crevices of this structure created numerous alternative conceptions and practices of the media. It is hard to overestimate the contribution to communication theory and practice of these alternative conceptions and uses of the media. Ricardo Sol Arriaza describes some of these in Chapter 7 on El Salvador.

With the return to democratically elected regimes, however, the contribution of the Latin American experiences of alternative and popular communication to communications policy were modest. When the military regimes slowly gave way to civilian government, the new leaders were rarely prepared to bring the practices of the alternative media into the fully institutionalized dimension of communication policy and media systems.

The early 1980s saw the political and cultural exhaustion of the authoritarian regimes and a growing repugnance with their policies on the part of most sectors of society. The free market economic policies carried out by the military regimes were in crisis, and the worldwide concern with the growing and unmanageable Third World debt had begun. A desire for reconstruction and restoration of pluralism and a return of the traditional political parties filled the agenda as countries slowly emerged from military rule.

The democratization of the mass media proved to be far more formidable a task than it had appeared during the long dictatorships. Then, government corruption, censorship and blacklisting looked like the most serious obstacles. These obstacles were removed relatively easily. Few of the new political leaders, however, were willing or able to take on the commercial media. As Landi points out in Chapter 11, during the Argentine transition to democracy political leaders rarely mentioned the media in their political platforms or announced plans to implement new communication policies.

In Chapter 9 Muraro explores the context of media policy-making that faced Alfonsín's government when he took office at the end of 1983. There was a new concern for pluralism, decentralization and the protection of both the media and their audiences from government interference. The Argentine policy-makers who had won the elections after the military's defeat in the Malvinas faced the challenge of resolving the stalemate between government and private control of the mass media. This challenge involved limiting the almost monopolistic tendencies of the private media and encouraging the development of a strong, culturally and technologically appropriate national media system without increasing government intervention.

Surveys carried out by Muraro and Landi showed that most people expected important cultural benefits from the new civilian government. They looked forward to the reopening of public universities, the end of censorship, the authorization of films and books prohibited by the military and changes in the content of television. The general opinion, however, did not favour radical change of the media, an immediate politicization of its content or an increase of government control.

Muraro's chapter on the transition to democracy describes how the Argentine private sector defended its interests against private non-profit broadcasters and increased congressional control of information flow. He analyses the different and conflicting demands on the government from small local and large capital-city media, established technologies and the newer arrivals, broadcasters and the press. His chapter also explores the demands of the private sector in favour of government protection yet against government regulation.

Landi also explores the many conflicting demands placed on the Argentine state in the field of culture and communications. Traditional cultural industries demanded economic support and protection. Artists and intellectuals demanded subsidies, employment and job protection. Private entrepreneurs demanded unregulated opportunities for commercial expansion and protection of their markets. The conflicting demands made it difficult to formulate public policy or reach a consensus.

Both Landi and Muraro stress the uncertain and timid role of the

Argentine political parties in the discussion about media policy during the return of democracy. They attribute the parties' uncertainty to their structural weaknesses and their lack of experience in the exercise of government and use of the modern mass media. The new leaders were limited in new policy initiatives by a lack of resources, a lack of consensus within the party and a lack of ties with grass-roots organizations, unions and other constituencies.

Landi shows how the first major cultural policy of the new Argentine government – the transfer of the ATC television channel to the National Secretary of Culture – soon ran into trouble. It proved impossible for the Secretary of Culture to administer a commercially-financed government television company where programming and news decisions were made by the private sector.

Faraone presents a similar analysis of the difficult prospects for democratic media policy in the newly elected civilian regime in Uruguay. The government swiftly restored press freedom, and many dailies and weeklies returned to the news-stands. The strength of the commercial broadcasters and the threat of the military's return, however, posed major obstacles to the reconstruction of democratic national media.

A government plan to modernize the small state television channel and introduce new services was dropped as a result of pressure from the private channels. More than a year after elections, the private TV channels refused to accept a paid announcement from a human rights group protesting the amnesty bill for the military officers who had kidnapped, tortured and murdered political prisoners during the dictatorship. Faraone concludes that self-censorship of the private media, so necessary for their survival under the military, was hard to overcome.

In addition to the internal obstacles to communication policies in the newly democratic countries described by the different authors, governments throughout the region faced another obstacle to national media policy – the greatly heightened political and economic independence of the private commercial media. Much of the private media's independence was the result of the sizeable expansion of the transnational operations of the communications conglomerates over the last ten years.

Foreign sales, production and ownership of the Latin American media had grown unmeasurably, and the Latin American private media empires had expanded their ties with international media conglomerates. A new generation of managers and owners – more concerned with economic efficiency and the national and international growth of their companies than with national politics or sometimes even national markets – controlled the communication industries in many countries.

Brazilian giant TV Globo had become the fourth largest television network in the world and was part of a media conglomerate that included the influential *O Globo* newspaper and a chain of radio stations and publishing houses. The Globo empire had been born with the military regime that ruled the country between 1964 and 1985 and had stuck close to its roots throughout most of the dictatorship. Guimarães and Amaral, however, describe the shift of the Globo empire away from the military towards the civilian political forces during the campaign for direct elections and the presidential election of Tancredo Neves.

As the Brazilian authors point out, the mass media and especially TV Globo gave legitimacy to the new civilian regime. At the same time, however, TV Globo assured its own legitimacy in the eyes of public opinion. A new TV Globo was born with the new republic. The new leaders of Brazil had the media to thank for many things. They also had a powerful independent political force on their hands.

Another Brazilian author, Sarti, follows up on some of the questions raised by the analysts of TV Globo's rapid conversion to the new order. She asks if independent video production can offer alternative policies to the cultural model introduced in Brazil by television and especially by TV Globo.

In Chapter 13 Sarti observes that in the 1980s the transition to democracy inspired the development of video's mediating function between producers and consumers of television. Video was no longer on the margins of television production as it had been in the 1970s when video producers criticized the commercialization of television and its links with the military.

Gradually, however, an emphasis on the democratizing role of television in Brazilian cultural life replaced video producers' radical slogans of the previous decades. Their main aim became entrance to the fabulous Brazilian television market. Producers focused on new content and technical innovations to compete with commercial television. They also directed their efforts towards changing national communication policies and television legislation to break up Globo's quasi-monopolistic control of the market.

Sarti recognizes the importance of the democratizing policy initiatives of the independent producers. At the same time, however, she voices concern over their excessive admiration for television technology and their apparent lack of a critical perspective on the social and economic context of Brazilian television.

The absence of critical judgement on the part of the producers, she points out, diminishes the possibilities of video production as a genuine alternative to the dominant pattern of culture. The seducton of the electronic technology, Sarti suggests, has pushed independent video makers on a path of wishful thinking that exaggerates the democratizing function of video, ignores community participation and representation and loses sight of the realities of a violently authoritarian and élitist society.

Raúl Rivadeneira Prada's closing Chapter 14 on the private sector's break-up of the government and university monopoly of television in Bolivia reaches a similar conclusion regarding the pitfalls of diversity without a guiding public broadcasting policy. The more than thirty new private television channels in Bolivia replaced institutional chaos and government censorship with commercial opportunism, transnational dependence and national irresponsibility.

Future directions

Media policy in Latin America has largely ignored most social-responsibility goals of equality and participation. The centralization and often authoritarian nature of the Latin American state has not permitted independent, participatory and representative communication structures to develop. The reaction to state centralization and authoritarianism has generated a strong and legitimate sentiment among media owners, journalists and many of the people against government regulation or ownership.

Besides the state, there are few other significant political actors pushing for a coherent, balanced media policy that would serve longer-range goals of social, cultural and political development. Profit-making has usually overpowered the public-service obligations of the owners of the Latin American commercial media. The importance of the media in political campaigns and survival has usually overpowered political reformers' ability and desire to impose regulations. The programmes of political parties, social organizations and popular movements have seldom contained comprehensive, viable demands for change or alternative policies and institutions for the mass media.

Furthermore, some of the recent developments of the private media seem to have taken the rhetoric of reform policies of the past like local content but emptied them of their substance. One example is the foreign export success of the Latin American media empires. For the first time, Latin America appears to be changing the direction of some of the traditional North–South flow of films and television series. The content of the Latin American exports, however, is often as standardized, bland and trivial as the amorphous foreign markets they are intended to attract. They are as far removed from national and grass-roots culture as the Hollywood products they replace.

Another example is the new public-service, educational and cultural programmes of the private media. Latin American private media enjoy significant national and international commercial success. TV Globo, Televisa and other large media corporations can now afford to finance museums, educational television and some community cultural activities. Mattelart and Schmucler (1983), however, have shown that these public–private services mainly serve their private owners by providing tax exemptions and opportunities to enter lucrative new areas of technological expansion. They also aid the long-term commercial growth of the private empires and their monopolization of the information and communications sector. In a region of growing cultural inequalities, these services, however commendable, are no substitute for genuine, publicly accountable, non-profit national services of education and culture.

The gradual integration of communication goals in the discussions within the different countries of regionalization and decentralization is a sign of the search for genuine public-service mass media policies. Regional political leaders are becoming increasingly well informed and sophisticated in the intricacies of modern telecommunications and the cultural industries. This development could lead to more representative participatory communication policies and institutions that escape the traditional Latin American centralization of both the commercial and government-owned media. They could also, however, fall into the same mode on a smaller scale as the national media empires.

In short, the economic stakes have probably become too high and the political interests too powerful to be able radically to reform existing structures and operations of the modern mass media without the application of force and undemocratic measures. The increasingly widespread awareness in Latin America of the importance of the mass media and information technologies in daily life, however, has put communications policy on the agenda of an expanding number of lobbies and public interest groups. In some cases, the mass media are being introduced as a subject in school curricula.

The growing linkages between communications researchers, grass-roots organizations, policy-makers and the private media industries in Latin America suggest that future policies might be based on compromise. The growing interest and specialization of political parties, social groups and other organizations in communications and information policy could come to constitute a new realism in communication policy formation and implementation.

This new realism recognizes the limits of any government policy in communication and culture but does not mean that the state should have no role in mass media policy. It implies a clear distinction, however, between the state as the sum of public interest and the foundation of a public philosophy of broadcasting and the passing interests of the government in power.

References

Gargúrevich, Juan (1987) *Prensa Radio y TV: Historia Crítica.* Lima: Editorial Horizonte.

Mattelart, Armand and Schmucler, Héctor (1983) *América Latina en la Encrucijada Telemática.* Buenos Aires: Paidós.

Pareja, Reynaldo (1984) *Historia de la Radio en Colombia 1929–1980.* Bogotá: Servicio Colombiano de Comunicación Social.

Index

(continued from front flap)

acting in the 18th century; the style of Edwin Forrest, America's first star performer, who initiated the strenuous realism of the heroic school of acting; the classic school of tragedians; the school of emotionalism; the personality school; and the school of psychological realism. Wilson presents each style in nearly first-hand detail and clarity. He writes, for example, of Edwin Forrest's realism, "When Forrest was playing Iago to Kean's Othello, a husky canalboatman was seated in the front row of the pit, so close to the stage that he leaned his elbows on it. He was absorbed in the machinations of Iago, and became so convinced of Forrest's villainy that when the actor passed close to him he glared savagely and hissed: 'You damned lying scoundrel, I would like to get hold of you after this show is over and wring your infernal neck'." Nearly all forms of acting are discussed, including the techniques of the motion picture; thus scope as well as depth is given to this study of acting in America. Concluding sections consider the 20th century outlook in the commercial theatre and the phenomenon of the rapidly growing campus and regional repertory theatres.

GARFF B. WILSON, Professor of Speech and Dramatic Art at the University of California, Berkeley, and Associate Editor of the *Educational Theatre Journal,* has taught almost every subject in the field of speech and drama and has contributed articles to *Quarterly Journal of Speech, Educational Theatre Journal, Speech Monographs, Western Speech, Journal of Higher Education,* and *Readers Digest.* He is also known for his play direction, acting, and play readings.

16 pages of illustrations

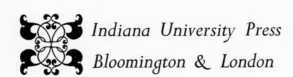

Indiana University Press
Bloomington & London

A HISTORY
OF AMERICAN
ACTING

by Garff B. Wilson

for

ANN V. CRAIG
Selfless Citizen, Faithful Friend

CONTENTS

ILLUSTRATIONS

following page 86

following page 214

Joseph Jefferson as Rip Van Winkle
Dion Boucicault in *The Colleen Bawn*
Scene from Thompson and Ryer's *The Old Homestead*
Thomas D. Rice as Jim Crow
Lydia Thompson as Robinson Crusoe
Lotta Crabtree
E. H. Sothern and Julia Marlowe as Romeo and Juliet
Richard Mansfield
William Gillette as Sherlock Holmes
Otis Skinner in *Kismet*
Minnie Maddern Fiske in her prime
Mrs. Minnie Maddern Fiske in *Tess of the D'Urbervilles*

GENERAL INTRODUCTION

WRITING A BOOK ON THE HISTORY OF AMERICAN ACTING IS A HAZARD-
ous project. It involves an imaginative re-creation of the personality
and performances of long dead actors. It also involves an evaluation
of their techniques and achievements on the basis of evidence which is
sometimes sketchy, usually subjective, and always second-hand. As the
late A. M. Drummond once said to me, "In evaluating a performer of
the past, you can study every critic, scan every photograph, read every
memoir, sift every shred of evidence, and still reach a conclusion which
is one hundred per cent wrong." True. But it is also true that there is
no living person who can prove that you are one hundred per cent
wrong. Moreover, anyone who challenges your judgment must base his
opinions on the same evidence that you have used.

Despite the hazards involved in analyzing the great performers of
the past, and despite the subjective nature of much of the evidence on
which a judgment is based, it is surprising how often one feels that he
has reached a reliable estimate. There are voluminous reviews of most
of the notable players of the nineteenth century. Critics may differ,
reports may vary, the taste of audiences may change, and yet a firm
outline and a clear image usually emerges from what may seem to be
confused or conflicting testimony. Over and over again I have been surprised and gratified to discover how frequently this happens. In the
pages which follow, I hope I have been able to convey this impression
of clear image and firm outline.

This book is not intended to be a general history of the American
theatre covering the development of playwriting, stagecraft, playhouses, finances, the influences of social, political, and economic
change, and all the other elements which contribute to the over-all history of the theatre. I am, instead, presenting a history of American
acting as recorded in the lives and achievements of the notable players

of the American stage. It will be necessary, of course, to sketch a background against which to view the performers. These "notes on the setting" will introduce elements of theatrical history other than acting, but the "notes" will be relatively brief and throughout the book the emphasis will be on acting and on the influences which shaped the styles of performance.

SCHOOLS OF ACTING

Previous records of American acting have been, for the most part, a series of unrelated critical reviews. Few attempts have been made to discern the similar methods and ideals of various performers or to group their styles into distinct schools. But an over-all survey of the history of American acting reveals a series of important relationships and discloses a significant pattern in the dramatic styles of American performers. Players can be grouped, at least loosely, into schools of acting to which their art belongs. Each of these schools has identifying characteristics: similar ideals and methods, similar approaches and practices, similar aims and results. The factors which determine the style of an individual performer often apply with equal strength to several performers and thus produce a group or school with a similar style. Often the group is shaped and influenced by the force of a dominating personality, like that of Edwin Forrest. Often the members of a school are contemporary, developed in response to the taste of a particular period. However, it must be noted that the various schools of acting which are discernible in an over-all view of the American theatre are not chronologically separate. In general, the schools do not succeed each other like links in a chain; that is, a school does not develop, flourish, decline, and then give way to a succeeding school— although sometimes this does happen. The various schools overlap and intermingle like the closely woven strands of a rope. During all of the nineteenth century and well into our own time, the cast of any single play represented several different types or styles of acting. Members of widely differing schools performed and competed with each other on the same stage. For example, Edwin Forrest, born in 1806 and chief representative of the heroic, muscular school, acted in the same production with a child named David Belasco, who became high priest of a sentimental, realistic style of acting which he taught until 1931. The

lives and careers of most of the notable performers in the American theatre are closely interrelated. Thus, in reading the following chapters one should bear in mind that although the players are discussed separately, and although they seem to move in separate worlds, they are, in fact, very close to each other—often exactly contemporary. Their styles of acting do not form a series of isolated, individual pictures; rather, they are the closely woven colors of a single rich tapestry.

It should be remembered that the grouping of performers into various "schools" of acting is not intended to be definitive or final. The grouping is done to reveal similarities and trends in the practice of acting, to show the relationship between individual players and groups of players, and to suggest a pattern for a large body of critical material which has hitherto been largely unorganized. There will be, of course, many admirers of the theatre who will resent my grouping of actors into schools and who will deplore my choice of labels to identify these schools. Some will feel that any attempts to classify or categorize the actors of the past is unnecessary and pedantic. Others will disagree with the categories or schools I have suggested and with the players I have assigned to them. Such disagreements are inevitable. How can it be otherwise in a subject which involves so many value judgments? But such disagreements can be useful, too, if they lead to a closer examination of the similarities and differences in the theory and practice of acting throughout the history of the American stage, and if they awaken an interest in an area of theatre which needs far more attention than it presently can claim.

EMPHASIS ON THE NINETEENTH CENTURY

Another aspect of this history which may raise a question is the emphasis on the nineteenth century and its now-legendary performers. There are a number of reasons for this emphasis, some objective and some purely sentimental.

The past exerts the fascination of legend and romance. At the same time, it can be viewed in perspective. The record is complete and can be studied more objectively than is possible in the case of contemporary acting. More than this, American acting was born in the nineteenth century; it developed, matured, and gained world attention during that period. It evolved styles and techniques which were stud-

ied then and can be re-studied profitably today. It laid the foundations for theatre practice in the twentieth century and thus has the interest of originality.

In the nineteenth century the figure of the actor towered over all other theatrical artists and artisans. During most of the century, the playwright, the company manager, the stage manager, the scene painter, the carpenter, and the stage hand were subordinate figures. There were no designers or directors as we know them today. Often the leading actor served as the company manager, the stage manager, the playwright, and even as the scene painter. The entire world of the theatre revolved around the actor, and so he was far more conspicuous than is his counterpart today.

In the nineteenth century the living stage was supported and enjoyed in American communities all over the nation. There were playhouses everywhere and, without the competition of movies, radio, and television, and without the ready availability of fast travel, thousands of citizens patronized the legitimate theatre. They knew the standard repertory of plays, and they knew all the traveling stars as well as the resident players of their own town. Their support and interest helped to stimulate fine acting by a host of talented players. Even discounting the glamor which history has given to actors of the "palmy" days, the record of their versatility and achievement is impressive. The greatest of them inspired admiration, emulation, and worship, and the impression remains that the nineteenth century might truthfully be called the golden age of American acting.

The performers of the past attract scrutiny for another reason. Surviving them are, very often, lengthy and careful analyses of their art by critics and observers who took the time to think about the craft of acting and to write about it with knowledge and affection. Today's review of a play is apt to be brief and succinct, composed under severe restrictions of time and space. The star of the performance may earn three or four lines of comment; supporting players are often dismissed with a phrase. There is no analysis of style or discussion of aesthetic principles or comparison with other performers of similar style or similar roles. Contrast such a modern review with one written by a leading critic of the nineteenth century, say William Winter or J. Ranken Towse or Henry Austin Clapp. Their reviews are detailed and thorough. Leading players are carefully evaluated aesthetically, theatrically, and often morally. The role under discussion is compared to the same

actor's performance of last week or last year and to the performances of the other stars who played the same parts. Whether one agrees or disagrees with the aesthetic principles or the moral judgments, one has a quantity of material to study and vivid descriptions to evaluate. Analyses of this kind are hard to find in the recent or contemporary theatre and so, again, one is tempted to linger in the nineteenth century.

In my descriptions of the notable players of the past century, I have drawn heavily upon the comments of the leading critics of the time. These men, of course, were products of their own age. They represent the principles and the prejudices of the nineteenth century. Their aesthetic, social, and moral ideals differ markedly from our own. In particular, they mix moral judgments with aesthetic criteria, which is usually repugnant to the critic of today. Although we often disagree with them, we must remember that they reflect the taste and standards of their time. They react as other intelligent playgoers of the nineteenth century must have reacted. Their evaluation of a player or of a performance reveals the effectiveness of that player or performance for the audiences of the period. When tastes and aesthetic principles change, style in acting changes too. But the critic of a later period cannot properly evaluate the art of an earlier actor by applying contemporary criteria to a past performance, just as it is unfair to denounce the costumes, makeup, and hairdo of a nineteenth century actor as ridiculous just because our tastes in these things have changed since then.

USE OF THE TERM "POPULAR THEATRE"

Although the actors of the legitimate theatre claim the lion's share of attention in this book, I have not ignored the influence of what I term "popular theatre": vaudeville, minstrelsy, burlesque, the circus, etc., in the nineteenth century; the movies, radio, and television in the twentieth century. My use of the term "popular theatre" will, no doubt, cause perplexity. The term is somewhat ambiguous because it suggests that the living stage was or is *un*popular compared to vaudeville, minstrelsy, or television. I do not intend such an interpretation. The term "popular theatre"—the least ambiguous one I can find—is intended to suggest that there are many forms of theatrical entertainment

different from the legitimate stage and that these forms have usually commanded greater attention from the masses of ordinary people than have the standard plays of the legitimate stage.

The popular theatre in its many sprightly forms has a fascinating history. Perhaps it deserves more attention and analysis than I have given it. Yet in the chapters I devote to it I hope it is clear that I recognize the importance of popular theatre, that I am aware of its continuing appeal to spectators in every period of our history, and that I do not underestimate its considerable contributions to acting in the American theatre.

STYLE AND ITS DETERMINANTS IN ACTING

Before the styles of acting evolved by the notable players of the American stage can be understood and before their careers and achievements can be evaluated, it is necessary to consider two basic questions: What is style in acting? and, What are the factors or influences which determine an actor's style? The history of American acting was written by the colorful personalities who dominated our stage and evolved unique manners of performance which made them stars. The basis for an appreciation of the ever-changing panorama of American acting is an understanding of the meaning and origins of style.

Style in acting, a term which is often misunderstood and misused, means the individual characteristics of appearance, voice, movement, and temperament which distinguish one actor from another; it is the distinctive mode of presentation used by an actor in the performance of a role. This distinctive mode or style is the result of at least seven determining factors, all of which must be recognized in evaluating style.

The first of these factors is the player's physical endowments. Nature gives to a performer a certain face, figure, and voice, and on these endowments he must build his art. For example, Edwin Forrest had a massive, muscular physique which gave him the strength and appearance of the Farnese Hercules. He chose roles which suited his physique—like Damon, Metamora, Jack Cade, and Coriolanus—and performed them with intensity and power. Edwin Booth, on the other hand, was graceful, slender, and of average height. He was not physically capable of the strenuous emotional displays of Forrest, so he

rejected them for an intellectual, spiritual quality which earned him praise as "the foremost poet of his profession." [1] That Booth was fully aware of the influence of his physical endowments on his style is revealed when he said, "It is rather safe to assume that actors establish their school upon their physique—for one must cover up what one cannot physically do." [2]

Like the male performers, the actresses of the American stage have also adapted their style to their physical endowments. The slight, boyish figure of Maude Adams impelled her to such boyish, whimsical roles as Peter Pan and L'Aiglon, while the strong, masculine physique of Charlotte Cushman made her an ideal Queen Katherine and (to her contemporaries) an acceptable performer in the roles of Romeo, Hamlet, and Cardinal Wolsey.

Facial characteristics and vocal endowments also influence style. Actors with droll or homely faces often become eccentric comedians so that they can capitalize on their facial peculiarities. Actresses with beautiful faces often rely on external charm alone and thus their style may remain cold and listless. Charlotte Cushman, who was *not* endowed with a beautiful face, developed an intense, restless manner of moving about the stage and, when asked to explain it, replied that if she were beautiful like Mrs. Siddons she could afford to stand still and be gazed at, but without beauty she had to occupy the eye of the spectator with action and movement or half her influence would be lost. [3]

The influence of Cushman's voice on her style is a further illustration of the effect of physical endowment on an actor's manner of performance. As will be related in a later section, Miss Cushman originally aspired to be a singer but after a successful debut in grand opera she ruined her singing voice by overstraining it in a large theatre. Her speaking voice was left with a husky, hollow quality, "a woody or veiled tone," as James Murdoch described it. This unique quality, plus wide range and unusual power, made Cushman's voice capable of expressing intense, sustained grief without loudness or sudden variations. These vocal characteristics became a noticeable feature of the actress's style, just as the thunderous tones of Forrest or the rich contralto of Mary Anderson identified and influenced their manner of performing.

The mental and spiritual attributes of an actor are also important determinants of style. The player with vivid imagination will tend to

act with intensity and insight. The actor with a nervous, high-strung temperament may develop a tense, explosive style of performing. The player with a scholarly mind may intellectualize his roles. Edwin Booth, who possessed a penetrating, poetical mind, endowed his roles with a spiritual quality which was unique. William Winter said of Booth that "the distinctive quality that illuminated his acting was the personal one of poetic individuality." [4] It is said that Henry Irving, the English actor, could neither walk nor talk but achieved success on the stage through "the character and quality of his intellect." [5] Likewise, Mrs. Fiske's keen mind and analytical approach gave her acting a subtle, intellectual quality which was praised by most critics.

The manners and customs of the period in which a player lives present a third and exceedingly influential factor in determining style. Just as styles of dress change with the years, so do fashions in etiquette and behavior fluctuate. A player automatically and unconsciously absorbs and incorporates these changing fashions in behavior. Where the Restoration gallant would bow and kiss a lady's hand with (to us) an exaggerated flourish, the modern gentleman will merely smile and give a barely perceptible nod of the head. Where the nineteenth-century heroine would blush and hide her face with a fan, the twentieth-century lady will raise an eyebrow and light a cigarette. In Mrs. Siddon's day a lady cultivated an erect carriage, a graceful walk, and elegance in all her movements. It was very natural, then, for Mrs. Siddons to stand, walk, and move in a stately fashion when she took the stage. Today the fashion in behavior dictates that a lady be casual, nonchalant, athletic—and so an audience shows no surprise when, in a modern play, Katharine Cornell slouches across the stage with hands in pockets, or when Katharine Hepburn, dressed in tennis shorts, lolls in a chair with one bare leg draped over the arm of the chair.

A fourth factor in determining style is the aesthetic ideals of a period. The formative effect of an aesthetic milieu is striking and pervasive not only in acting but in all the arts. For example, the eighteenth-century belief in balance, discipline, and good form—based on the ideals of classicism—produced the neat couplets of Alexander Pope, the precise, symmetrical paintings of David, and the restrained formal music of Handel and Thomas Arne. In the theatre, these ideals produced acting characterized by conventionalized tones and gestures

and by the acceptance of tradition in the interpretation of a role. When the aesthetic ideals of a period fluctuate, all the arts are affected—including the art of acting.

An additional factor is the force of training, example, and experience. The instructors who guide an apprentice actor, and the examples set by fellow players, inevitably exert an influence in developing an actor's style. When native Americans first began appearing on the stage, there were no schools of dramatic art to train them but there were the inspiring examples of many English players. A novice actor could study performances which illustrated any one of four distinct styles of acting, each of which had flourished in Great Britain in the eighteenth or early nineteenth century. A brief description of these styles will be useful in illustrating the influence of one actor upon another in the formulation of style, and it will also serve as a guide to those particular English styles which set an example for many early American players.

The first of the styles which dominated English acting in the early years of the eighteenth century can be called the neo-classical style. It was characterized by the following of certain traditions in acting a character, and by the acceptance of conventionalized tone and gesture in delivery. The author of a play taught the first actor of a part what characterization to use. "It was assumed that the author of plays knew how they should be acted, and that his interpretation of his own characters was not only the most accurate, but also the most effective interpretation." [6] This interpretation became fixed and was passed down from player to player. Critical judgment assumed that "the closer the imitation of the older actor by the younger, the better was the presentation of the play." [7]

In 1741 Charles Macklin appeared on the stage as Shylock, and David Garrick made his debut as Richard III. A second period, characterized by "realistic romanticism" was inaugurated. This was a period of revolt against the accepted traditions. Both Macklin and Garrick reinterpreted their characters. Their break with the past earned public acclaim, and thus they established the right "to go to nature herself, and to re-interpret a play in the light of life itself." [8] The Macklin-Garrick school rejected the conventionalized tone and gesture with which tragedy had been rendered and substituted a more easy, colloquial manner of speaking. In developing a characterization

they believed in a literal imitation of nature. Their creed was, "the closer the imitation of nature in art, the better the art."

A third style in English acting of the eighteenth century appeared in the late years of the century. During these years, Thomas Sheridan and John Walker stimulated a new interest in the propriety of pronunciation and in declamation as a separate art. Also, a new theory of art emerged, championed by Sir Joshua Reynolds. He said that the purpose of art, including the art of acting, was *not* to imitate the literal details of nature but to raise and elevate nature—to exclude the ugly and to exalt the ideal. John Philip Kemble and his sister, Sarah Kemble Siddons, the new leaders of the English stage, were deeply influenced by both the Sheridan-Walker theories of declamation and the Reynolds theory of art. Espousing both, they evolved a new style of acting in the practice of which there was no attempt to copy nature slavishly. Rather, nature was elevated and idealized. Grand declamation was substituted for the naturalistic diction of the Garrick school. Dignity and nobility took the place of true-to-life representations. So gifted were the Kembles that they made this style of performing acceptable and popular.

In 1814, Edmund Kean played Shylock at the Drury Lane Theatre, and his performance inaugurated a new period of tempestuous, passionate acting. The stateliness and elevation of the Kemble school gave way to fiery outbursts of emotion and dazzling displays of vocal pyrotechnics. Scenes in which the emotional intensity was low or the action was listlessly performed were alternated with tremendous, impassioned climaxes. Edmund Kean and Junius Brutus Booth both helped to popularize this style.

The period of great acting in America by native American players began shortly after the advent of Edmund Kean. It is not surprising that American performers were influenced by the several English styles which they observed around them. For example, Edwin Forrest modelled his early acting after the style of Thomas A. Cooper, a disciple of the Kemble school. Some time later, Edmund Kean visited the United States and Forrest was engaged to play second leads in Kean's troupe. Thereafter, Forrest altered his style to include the fiery, passionate displays which characterized Kean's performances.

Throughout the entire history of American acting, the factor of training and example has been influential in shaping an actor's style. Players in the early period studied their fellow performers—especially

the visiting stars—and adopted those methods and manners which seemed most effective. Actors in the later periods have come under the influence of dominating teachers or directors and have learned a style from them. In the later nineteenth and early twentieth centuries, for example, David Belasco molded many performers to fit his concepts of acting. Augustin Daly did the same. In our own day, the effect of the Group Theatre's instruction and training, as carried on by the Actors' Studio, can be seen in the performances of many players, and certainly the students of a great university teacher, like the late A. M. Drummond of Cornell, can recognize in each other the influence of the unique instruction they received.

The repertory popular in the early nineteenth century was a powerful factor in shaping the style of the first American actors. With few exceptions, this repertory came entirely from English and other European dramatists. Shakespeare provided the bulk of the plays, to which were added the tragedies of Dryden, Otway, and Rowe, and the comedies of such dramatists as Farquhar, Goldsmith, and Sheridan. The remainder of the plays consisted of the new successes which came year by year from the pens of contemporary dramatists. Among the most popular of these playwrights, as the century advanced, were Sheridan Knowles with such dramas as *Virginius* and *The Hunchback;* Edward Bulwer-Lytton with *The Lady of Lyons* and *Richelieu;* Dion Boucicault with *London Assurance* and dozens of others; Tom Taylor with *Still Water Runs Deep* and *Our American Cousin;* the German dramatist, Kotzebue, with *The Stranger, Pizarro in Peru,* and *The Virgin of the Sun;* and French playwrights, such as Sardou, whose tearful domestic melodramas were introduced to his fellow countrymen by the American actor and dramatist, John Howard Payne. In general, American playwrights in the nineteenth century were neither very popular nor very prolific, and what plays they did produce were largely imitative of foreign models.

It is evident that such a repertory, consisting largely of heroic tragedies in blank verse and sensational melodramas in turgid prose, would powerfully influence the style of the actors who performed them.

A final factor which influences the manner of performance of a player is the physical environment in which he performs, that is, the playhouse and the setting in which the play is produced. This can be

illustrated clearly if we contrast the environment which surrounded the early American actor with the settings and playhouses of today.

The first structures erected in the colonial period by Lewis Hallam and David Douglass were merely oblong wooden boxes filled with rough benches and embellished with a narrow stage at one end. In some of the larger buildings might be found a few stage boxes decorated and upholstered for the accommodation of distinguished patrons like George Washington. As American towns increased in population and wealth, more elaborate playhouses began to be constructed. All of them followed European models and featured a wide forestage, proscenium doors, pit or orchestra, boxes, and galleries. The lighting for both stage and auditorium was dim and crude. Until 1816, all illumination was furnished by candles or oil lamps. After 1816, gas lighting appeared but considerable time elapsed before its use became widespread. Electric lighting did not appear until the 1880's.

For many years, stage scenery was as crude as the lighting. Throughout the eighteenth and half of the nineteenth centuries it consisted of a series of wings and drops. The rear wall of the stage was hidden by a canvas curtain or drop and the sides were masked by canvas wings set parallel to the backdrop. The scenery—trees, waterfalls, rivers, meadows, and most of the furniture—were painted on the wings and drops. The floor was the bare wood of the stage.

The effect on acting of the dim lighting of the early playhouses is described by one historian of the drama as follows: "When the footlights consisted of half a dozen or more oil lamps, the point where their rays converged was properly known as the 'focus'. Here all important passages of the piece had to be delivered, since elsewhere a player was not clearly visible. It was not possible, of course, to develop naturalistic acting under the circumstances. . . ." [9]

On such a stage, so sparsely decorated and so dimly lighted, the player was the center of attention. If he expected to capture and hold the interest of his audience—most of them uncomfortably seated and often too hot or too cold—he had to project strong emotion and vivid action. The dimness of the lighting forced him to use broad, sweeping movements and exaggerated facial expressions. The size of the auditorium (in the nineteenth century many of them were huge) and the uncertainty of the acoustics forced him to use stentorian tones. His style of performance could not possibly duplicate the style of the modern player who appears, for example, in an arena theatre surrounded

closely by spectators and illuminated by powerful, flexibly controlled electric lights. In the modern setting, the player can perform with subtle, delicate art, both physically and vocally.

One can summarize the seven factors that determine style in acting by saying that nature supplies an actor with certain basic endowments of body and voice, mind and spirit. These are the raw materials out of which he shapes his art. His training and experience, molding his natural endowments, occurring in a particular social and aesthetic milieu, and applied to a particular role in a particular play presented in a particular playhouse, will determine his style. All of these influences must be kept in mind if one is to appreciate the history of American acting as recorded in the careers and achievements of its notable players.

IMPORTANCE OF A STUDY OF THE PAST

Historians often tell us that those who ignore history will sooner or later find themselves repeating the mistakes of history. This observation, while not entirely applicable to a study of the actors of the past, does have a certain relevance. Those who love and serve the theatre of today can learn much from the records of American acting. There is inspiration here and excitement and instruction, too. The problems faced by a contemporary actor or director are not entirely new. A host of gifted artists in the past have confronted and solved most of them with varying success in a great number of ways. Perhaps the old solutions can still offer comfort and guidance.

But a study of the development of American acting and of the notable performers who have contributed to it offers more than guidance and instruction. It offers enjoyment and delight. The magic of theatre is never-failing, and the fascination of studying that rare variety of human personality, the actor, is inexhaustible. Beyond enjoyment and delight there is another emotion: pride. The history of our stage is rich and colorful; the achievement of our native performers is notable; the theories, discoveries, and wisdom of American artists of the theatre have enriched the storehouse of world theatre and have touched the minds and hearts of men everywhere. A study of the history of American acting can give us pride in our past as well as hope and guidance for the future.

[NOTES ON THE SETTING]

The Early Years

THORNTON WILDER, IN ONE OF HIS FANCIFUL THREE-minute plays, introduces a background for the action which consists of an old-fashioned revolving cyclorama depicting Egypt and the Holy Land. A stage manager turns the scroll: the Tigris, the Euphrates, the Pyramids pass in swift review. In front of this moving background the characters of the play appear, speak their lines, act their roles, and then depart.

Such a device would be useful in presenting the history of American acting as it is reported in the careers of the notable players of the American stage. These players perform their roles, both as people and as actors, before a constantly shifting panorama: the social and political milieu changes from year to year; playhouses are built, they flourish, they decline, and new ones of altered form and machinery take their place; the scenery, lighting, and costuming change from decade to decade; dramatic literature varies in style and content; the public taste fluctuates and shifts; and the actor who appears before this moving background is shaped and molded in his manner of performance by the fluctuating influences around him. A glance at the ever-changing backdrop of the American actor is necessary for an understanding of his art and his achievement.

Theatrical activity in America, preceding 1752, was meagre. A few amateur dramatists had written plays; the newly founded colleges had presented dramatic dialogues; a couple of playhouses had been built;

a few amateur performances had been given. In 1752, a company of actors headed by Lewis Hallam arrived from England and produced a play in Williamsburg, Virginia. Three years before, a British troupe headed by the Messrs. Murray and Keane had performed in the colonies, and they continued to perform for some years. But it was the Hallam company, of 1752, consisting of twelve adults and three children, which introduced the first resident professional company in America. For several years this company, which was later reorganized and headed by David Douglass, traveled from town to town, giving plays wherever they could obtain permission. They built crude little theatres to house their productions or they performed in hotel dining rooms, warehouses, court houses, and even barns. Almost everywhere they fought the opposition of Puritans and Quakers and the legal bans against playacting. Often they resorted to amusing subterfuges in order to gain a hearing. When the Revolutionary War came, all forms of entertainment were forbidden in the colonies, so the Hallam company —which was now patriotically calling itself "The American Company" —retired to the West Indies. During the war the only playacting in the colonies was done by either British or American troops. But in 1784, the war being over, the American Company returned to the United States from Jamaica and professional theatre was re-established on American soil.

In the post-revolutionary era theatrical activity made progress. It was slow but steady. New companies were formed and more players arrived from England. New playhouses were constructed in such important towns as Charleston, Boston, Philadelphia, New York, and New Orleans. Most important, the anti-theatre laws were repealed in Philadelphia, Boston, and Rhode Island, and this established a pattern that was soon to be followed in other states and cities. In the post-war era the first comedy written by a native American was produced. Up until now, the repertory was made up almost exclusively of plays from Shakespeare, Restoration authors, and other English dramatists. In 1787, American audiences saw a play by a fellow countryman, Royall Tyler, entitled *The Contrast,* and in it the first stage Yankee made his appearance. About this time, America's first major playwright, William Dunlap, began writing and producing such dramas as *André,* and began introducing the works of the German dramatist, Kotzebue. The first of these adaptations from Kotzebue, entitled *The*

Stranger, was destined to become one of the most popular dramas of the nineteenth century.

The progress and development observable in the post-revolutionary period continued with increased momentum in the early years of the nineteenth century. By 1800, according to William Winter, there were one hundred and fifty professional actors in America, almost all of them British, of course, and their number was growing. More playhouses were built, more American plays were written. The towns and settlements along the Atlantic coast were organized into a regular theatrical circuit, and as the frontier was pushed westward, hardy pioneer actors followed. Amid astonishing hardships, they established theatrical activity in the wilderness.

In the early years of the nineteenth century, the leading theatrical cities were, of course, the centers of population on the Atlantic coast. Originally, Philadelphia was the most important town, but around the turn of the century New York began to surpass Philadelphia both in population and in importance as a seaport. Supremacy in theatrical affairs soon passed to New York, where it has remained ever since. But the theatre also flourished in other cities such as Boston, Charleston, Newport, Richmond, and New Orleans.

In 1810 occurred an event of major significance. George Frederick Cooke, a famous English tragedian, came to America and acted in the theatres of the leading towns. He was the first English star to deign to visit this country, and he set a precedent which was soon followed by most of the leading players of the English stage. In a few years, visiting stars—not only foreign but domestic—began to alter the character of the long-established resident stock companies. These companies were the only form of theatrical organization during the eighteenth century and during most of the nineteenth century. They consisted of a group of actors hired for the season to play a particular line of parts in one playhouse situated in one town. The company, which was supervised by a manager, presented a repertory of plays during the season and often the program was changed from night to night. The prosperity of the company depended, primarily, upon the strength of the group as a whole. The leading players remained unchanged throughout the season. When a visiting star like George Frederick Cooke appeared, he displaced the resident lead, and when the visitor departed the permanent company seemed to lose luster. As the century advanced, the resident companies came to depend more and more on visiting stars to

stimulate business, and more and more visiting stars appeared to fill the need. However, in the early years of the nineteenth century the resident companies were still strong and independent.

It was in such a company, having such a background as I have described, that the first native born American star, Edwin Forrest, made his debut in 1820.

I

THE HEROIC SCHOOL

EDWIN FORREST OCCUPIES A UNIQUE POSITION IN THE HISTORY OF American acting. He was the first player born in the United States to achieve great fame both at home and abroad. He represented a type of acting so vigorous that it created a host of imitators, yet so individual that many of the imitations were caricatures. His personal life and his professional life were filled with controversy. During his lifetime, his style was praised and ridiculed; for more than five decades his plays attracted hosts of enthusiastic admirers and earned him a vast fortune. Today the player and his plays are practically forgotten.

Forrest made his professional debut in 1820, at the age of fourteen. At that time, as we have noted, the American theatre was dominated by English actors, English managers, and English dramaturgy. Political independence had been won some forty years before, but culturally the United States was largely dependent upon Great Britain. With the advent of Edwin Forrest this situation began to change. Born and reared in Philadelphia and passionately American in his loyalties, Forrest achieved a reputation in the United States as dazzling as the fame of the English stars. He played great roles for more than fifty years, during which his personality and his style of acting remained as typical of the vigorous young American democracy in which he grew up as were the rowdy young fans, the "Bowery B'hoys," who idolized him.

Forrest's formal education, both general and dramatic, was slight. He attended a public school in Philadelphia for a short time, but be-

fore he was thirteen he had been apprenticed successively to a printer, a cooper, and a ship-chandler. His instruction in elocution came, principally, from a year's study with Lemuel G. White, whom Lawrence Barrett calls "a distinguished professor in that branch of dramatic art." [1] Very little is known of the theory or methods of Mr. White. Barrett mentions that White was a disciple of the Garrick and Kean schools, that is, the so-called natural schools as opposed to the artificial, declamatory school of the Kembles, and that among his more noted pupils were David Ingersoll and James E. Murdoch. In *The Stage* Murdoch has left a note concerning White's influence on Forrest: "Mr. White, who first formed Forrest's manner out of the usual schoolboy style of reading, was a man of great intelligence and culture in his art, but eccentric, enthusiastic, and very egotistical. In his idea of delivery the principal thing was *emphasis,* and at this he labored and pounded with every kind and degree of pressure and force. But this quality did not adhere to Forrest's mode of reading after he had once tested the practical method of dramatic action. White's influence was, however, observable in his articulation, which was always distinct." [2]

Forrest's smattering of formal education was a minor influence in shaping his career. His style of acting was largely the result of his own study, observation, and experience on the stage. Fortunately, his early acting was done in the company of excellent players. For example, the cast which supported him when he made his debut at the Walnut Street Theatre in Philadelphia included Frederick Wheatley, Willam B. Wood, the elder William Warren, Mrs. H. A. Williams, and the elder Mrs. Joseph Jefferson. James Rees characterizes this cast as one "which could not have been equaled in the country then, nor has it been since. . . ." [3]

Such companies of players were thoroughly familiar with the dramatic repertory. Substantially the same program of plays was given year after year, and the player thus had ample opportunity to become matured and seasoned in his roles. Each play was cast with the full strength of the company, and each part was considered of real importance.

Besides the veterans, with whom Forrest had the privilege of observing and working, there was a group of talented younger men who provided the stimulus of keen competition. John R. Scott, David Ingersoll, Augustus Addams, Charles Eaton, Charles Webb, and James

Murdoch were men who, in the early years of Forrest's career, enjoyed a reputation equal and in some cases superior to his own. Barrett, writing in 1881, observed that "To the actors of today, educated in the modern sensational dramas, the splendor of this company of tragedians seems unreal." [4]

From association with these players the alert and ambitious young Forrest learned much. He studied the performances of his fellow actors carefully, experimenting with the styles and techniques which seemed to him particularly effective. He eventually adopted those techniques which best suited his ideas and temperament. In the formation of his mature style two men exerted special influence on him: Thomas A. Cooper and Edmund Kean.

Cooper, although born and trained in England, was considered an American actor. He had come to the United States at the age of twenty, after he had failed to achieve any great success in London. His success here was prodigious. He became the idol of the American stage and held the top rank in public favor for many years. He relinquished it only when age and the popularity of Forrest compelled him to take a subordinate place.

As a neophyte actor, Forrest studied Cooper's style with care. From him Forrest learned the dignified posture, the formal movements, the measured, declamatory reading, and the ideal of poetic elevation and repose which were characteristic of the Kemble school.

But Forrest was soon to be subjected to another more powerful influence. In 1825 Edmund Kean visited the United States for the second time, again taking the country by storm with the tempestuousness of his genius. For Kean's performances in Albany, Forrest was engaged to play second leads. He enacted Iago to Kean's Othello, Richmond to his Richard, and Titus to his Brutus. This was one of the great experiences of Forrest's life, and it left an indelible stamp on his acting.

There are many records of Kean's acting and descriptions of his style. I shall quote only one, an analysis of Kean's technique as it was at the time Forrest played with him. Written by W. R. Alger, Forrest's official biographer, it outlines those traits of Kean which probably most impressed the young American tragedian. Alger says:

The essential peculiarity of Kean's greatness in his greatest effects was that his acting then was no effort of the will, no trick or art of calculation,

but nature itself uncovered and set free in its deepest intensity of power, just on the edge, sometimes quite over the edge of madness. He penetrated and incorporated himself with the characters he represented until he possessed them so completely that they possessed him, and their performance was no simulation, but revelation. He brought the truth and simplicity of nature to the stage, but nature in her most intensified degrees. His playing was the manifestation of inspired intuition, infallibly true and irresistibly sensational. It came not from the surface of his brain, but from the very centers of his nervous system, and suggested something portentous, preternatural, supernal, that blinded and stunned the beholders, appalled the imagination, and chilled their blood.[5]

Kean not only inspired Forrest by his example, but also encouraged him privately and complimented him publicly. He allowed Forrest to introduce new business and different readings into the part of Iago, and was so impressed with some of the innovations that he declared henceforth all Iagos would have to copy the young American. Later on, at a public banquet in Philadelphia, Kean said: "I have met one actor in this country, a young man named Edwin Forrest, who gave proofs of a decided genius for his profession, and will, I believe, rise to a great eminence." [6]

It is little wonder that after acting with Kean, Forrest's style underwent a great change. The natural, impulsive displays of passion, the fiery eloquence that "made the pit tremble," the realistic bursts of physical movement—all became incorporated in the young actor's technique.

The magnificent physique of Edwin Forrest is important to any analysis of his acting. Many critics believed that his physique was the greatest single factor in determining his style. Forrest was a handsome man. As a boy he had been frail, but through assiduous exercise he had developed an unusually powerful body. He was inordinately proud of it. The massiveness of his physique was doubly noticeable because he was not tall. His biceps bulged; his calves bulged. He never neglected an opportunity to demonstrate his strength on the stage.

Forrest believed intensely in the value of healthful food, fresh air, and, particularly, of physical exercise. He recommended physical culture to all his associates. As a young actor in New York, he took boxing and fencing lessons. Every morning he did strenuous exercises with dumbells and Indian clubs. He continued this until the very end of his life. It probably accounts for his excellent health; also, it may have

been the reason for his death. On the fatal morning his servant found him lying on his bed suffering from a stroke of apoplexy. Possibly the stroke had been brought about by his taking exercise which was much too violent for a man of sixty-six.

Forrest possessed a voice that was as powerful as his physique. No orator or actor of his day could equal it. We are told that it was great enough to shake the rafters of the largest amphitheatre, and yet capable of the softest, tenderest tones. "He could range from piano to forte, from lowest bass to highest treble with ease, and his vocal chords could withstand the most severe strain . . . he could play through two trage-dies in one evening and still deliver his final dying words as clear as a bell. . . . In the delicate and tender passages he could sing in a soft tremulo that would move the hardest heart." [7] It is certain that For-rest's physical and vocal make-up had real influence on his style of acting and on the way he interpreted his roles.

From this glance at Forrest's background and at the influences af-fecting him, a fair outline of his general style of acting is apparent. The primary characteristic of this style was a strenuous realism. Under the influence of Kean's example, as Forrest interpreted it, the American tragedian sought to portray nature as it existed around him in actual life. He aimed for complete, detailed character portrayals, unchanged by any idealization. Alger says he attempted "a living resurrection of the crude truth of nature in place of that idealized softening and tem-pered reflex which is the genuine province of art." [8]

Forrest's method of studying his roles reveals the aim of his style. In preparing for the part of Lear he visited many asylums and old men's homes. He studied various manifestations of insanity—its approach, its full expression, its decline. He observed the walk, the gestures, the movements of old men. He read the best scientific books on old age and insanity, and discussed his ideas with eminent physicians. "He often insisted that he had never met a doctor who knew as much about insanity as he did." [9] As a result, the following criticism of Forrest's Lear is typical. Douglass Jerrold in London said: "We never saw mad-ness so perfectly portrayed. It is true to nature—painfully so." [10] One is reminded of Forrest's remark when a young admirer praised his act-ing in *King Lear*. Forrest exclaimed, "By God, sir, I am King Lear."

Forrest's role of the Indian Chief in the famous American play *Metamora* was prepared with equal care. At one time in his life Forrest had been a close friend of Chief Push-ma-ta-ha and had lived with the

Chief and his tribe for several weeks. "He adopted their habits, shared their food, slept in their huts, . . . smoked the pipe of peace . . . left the print of his own moccasins on the hunting ground . . . and the crack of his rifle echoed along the rocky sides of the hills and lakes." [11] In preparing the role of Metamora, Forrest drew exhaustively on this experience. Apparently he achieved great success in the realism of his portrayal. Harrison writes: "So accurate had been his observations that he caught the very manner of their breathing. . . . Everything that could be absorbed by one nature from another was absorbed and represented. In *Metamora* he achieved a piece of acting that seemed to transcend all criticism." [12]

One evening a large delegation of Western Indians witnessed Forrest's performance of *Metamora*. They followed the play with rapt attention. In the closing scene they were so excited by the performance and so convinced of its reality that they rose and chanted a dirge in honor of the great chief who was dying on the stage.

On another occasion, when Forrest was playing Iago to Kean's Othello, a husky canal-boatman was seated in the front row of the pit, so close to the stage that he leaned his elbows on it. He was absorbed in the machinations of Iago, and became so convinced of Forrest's villainy that when the actor passed close to him he glared savagely and hissed: "You damned lying scoundrel, I would like to get hold of you after this show is over and wring your infernal neck." [13] When Kean met Forrest in the dressing room afterwards he generously said, "Young man, if my acting tonight had received as high a compliment as that brawny fellow in the pit bestowed on yours, I should feel very proud. You made the mimic show real to him, and I will tell you your acting merited the criticism." [14]

Many other instances show how realistically Forrest conceived and acted his roles. Scenes of combat in which he participated were always a terror to the other actors. There was no shamming the battle. Forrest became so excited that he fought and hacked with terrifying gusto. His opponents were always in real danger and had to defend themselves as best they could. Many were the cuts and bruises they received in these encounters.

Forrest was no less hard on himself. Rees relates that one night, while acting Lear, the tragedian worked himself into such a passion he almost had apoplexy. He fainted away, and had to be carried off the

the stage in an unconscious state. T. H. Morrell relates another striking instance. He says:

One night while performing the role of King Lear, . . . in the last scene of the second act, when depicting the frenzy of the old monarch, whose brain was overwrought with passion, and maddened by the injuries of his unnatural daughters, Goneril and Regan, in the excitement of the moment Mr. Forrest tore the wig of whitened hair from his head and hurled it twenty feet toward the footlights. The effect was a striking one, and the wig thus removed, revealed to the audience a head of glossy raven locks, forming a strange contrast to the hoary beard still appended and fastened by a white cord to the actor's chin.[15]

It might seem to a modern audience that such an incident would ruin the scene. Evidently it did not. Morrell says: "Among that vast audience not a single titter could be heard and scarce a smile was discernible"—surely a striking tribute to the illusion Forrest had been able to create.

The bulk of contemporary evidence seems to indicate that Forrest appeared convincingly real in his acting. Opinion, however, is not unanimous. Some critics felt that the tragedian enlarged his effects and "muscularized" them beyond the point of credibility. Others asserted that the "truth to nature" which the public professed to see in Forrest's acting was merely truth to a crude *stage* convention of reality and far removed from the realism of actual life. This is the opinion held by the editor of the *Easy Chair* of Harper's Magazine for December, 1863. After watching Forrest enact the role of Damon, the editor writes: "To criticise it as acting is as useless as to criticise the stories of Miss Braddon and Mr. Ainsworth as literature. That human beings, under any conceivable circumstance, should ever talk or act as they are represented in the Forrest drama and the Braddon novel, is beyond belief."

Forrest's brand of realism in acting included a great deal of detail. He presented all the movements, gestures, attitudes, postures, and expressions which he felt revealed the character. He chose to supply the details rather than leave them to the spectator's imagination. "The suggestive school of art expression was not of Forrest's belief," says Harrison. The great tragedian disliked the repressed type of acting introduced into "society plays." He felt it was suggestive only of the "dead body without the breath, the eye without light, words spoken without the detail of expression." Incidentally, Harrison—who was an

actor himself and had received some instruction and encouragement from Forrest—felt that Forrest's facial expressions were genuine and powerful. The tragedian modeled them "not on the Delsarte principle of facial expression, but on the soul's principle," says Harrison.

In his treatment of the details of stage business, Forrest seemed to change somewhat as he advanced in years. He eliminated many of the little naturalistic touches which at first had seemed effective to him. For example, in the part of Virginius, Forrest was for some years accustomed to using a knife with a hollow blade filled with red fluid. When he struck his daughter, the pressure of a spring released the fluid and it spurted out like blood from a wound. One evening a lady in the audience fainted at this spectacle. The incident made Forrest realize that such a device was a crude artifice and not art. He never afterwards repeated it.

In his readings, too, Forrest changed by omitting certain vocal tricks of imitation. We are told that in the famous lament of Othello, "Farewell the tranquil mind," he was accustomed to use a kind of musical recitative and to imitate the sounds mentioned in the passage. He uttered the words "neighing steed" in equine tones. He reproduced the shrillness of "the shrill trumpet." He gave a deep boom to the phrase "spirit stirring drum." And he swelled and rattled his throat to portray "the engines whose rude throats the immortal Jove's dread clamors counterfeit." Alger asserts that eventually "he learned to see that however effective this might be as elocution, it was neither nature nor art, but artificiality; and then he read the passage with consummate feeling and force, his voice broken with passionate emotion, but not moulded to any pedantic cadences or flourishes." [16]

Curiously enough, Forrest's desire for dramatic realism did not extend to the scenery of the play. He never cared a hang for the settings that surrounded him. They could be as tawdry and unconvincing as possible. He believed that *acting* should create the illusion of reality and not scene painting. In the latter part of Forrest's career, Edwin Booth appeared in a series of elaborately mounted Shakespearean revivals. Forrest witnessed some of these productions, but was not impressed by them. He called Booth's production of *Julius Caesar* the "scene painter's drama." He described the elaborate trappings as "gaudy kickshaws by which modern dramatic art is swaddled and smothered." [17]

Forrest had seen how Kean could electrify his audience with bursts

of passion. He felt this was immensely effective and also true to nature. And so whenever the occasion arose, he used his voice and body with great freedom. He could rage and thunder magnificently. "Give him a hero fired with democratic passions who slashed out at a tyrant, and he could arouse an audience to shouting." [18] He could also produce tears with his pathos and tenderness.

The detailed action and bursts of passion which Forrest presented through the medium of his powerful voice and body led some critics to assert, first, that he was a melodramatic ranter; and, second, that he never used his mind but only his muscles. He was called everything from a "bovine bellower" to "a bewildered animal with a little grain of genius." Charles T. Congdon said he could play only such roles as were "specially written for his private legs and larynx." Montrose Moses, writing in 1929, has concluded that he was "never able to exercise restraint" and that he was "an ungovernable man in all respects, as regards his personal behavior and his artistic methods." [19]

It cannot be denied that there is some truth in these charges. Even Alger, his loyal and worshipful biographer, admits two faults in his acting: one, an "excess . . . of physical and spiritual force in the expression of passion," and, two, a lack of *"souplesse,* of physical and spiritual mobility." James E. Murdoch acknowledges that Forrest "was often charged with rudeness and violence in his impersonations and even ridiculed for muscularity of manner." But he points out that he had never yet seen any tragedian who did not use all his physical powers in portraying passionate scenes. The actors of the day who followed the lead of Kean all used the utmost intensity and feeling which they could command. Forrest stirred up comment, not because he followed a different method from his rivals, but principally because he was a much stronger man. When he became excited, says Murdoch, "his passions appeared more extreme than those of one more delicately organized." [20]

Gabriel Harrison claims that he had seen Forrest act more than four hundred times. He asserts that even in Forrest's younger days, when he was most romantic and unrestrained—in roles like Damon, Rolla, the Gladiator, and Jack Cade—he was never melodramatic. "He had no tricks," writes Harrison, "and whatever the character he always invested it with the qualities of naturalness." [21]

The charge that Forrest never used his mind but only his muscles was ill founded. Most critics agree that he was one of the most careful

and analytic thinkers and analysers the stage has ever seen. He studied his author's text with scrupulous care. He investigated the background of the play, the customs and manners of the people represented. After research in all the pertinent fields, he built up a conception of his role, consistently and logically. No actor was more mental in his approach.

Forrest's analytical mind and careful habits of study were evidenced in the intelligibility of his reading. No actor could surpass him in the clearness with which he could convey the meaning of a line. This was admitted even by the newspaper which had always been most hostile to him—against which, in fact, he had once instituted proceedings for libel. The Philadelphia *Dispatch,* on December 17, 1872, said: ". . . Mr. Forrest had a strong analytical brain and habits of study which enabled him to grasp the meaning of a passage in Shakespeare more firmly than any actor we have ever heard. So far as interpretation of the sense was concerned, he was the greatest reader on the stage. . . . We despair of ever hearing such majestic delivery again." But, adds the *Dispatch,* "with unusual powers of comparison and analysis, he was deficient in imagination—a faculty essential to the actor of Shakespeare." [22]

The "deficiency in imagination" mentioned by the Philadelphia *Dispatch* names Forrest's greatest weakness as an actor: he lacked spiritual insight and the highest type of creative imagination. Whenever a character could be analyzed and grasped by *logic,* Forrest was able to achieve a convincing portrayal. He could understand figures like Damon, Metamora, Jack Cade, and Coriolanus, whose motives were uncomplicated and whose passions were strong and clear and physically demonstrable. King Lear, though one of the great and complicated characters of Shakespeare, was also within his grasp. In the actor's younger days, the strength of his mimic wrath and the realism of his mimic madness rendered his performance of Lear effective. In his later life, his sorrows—real or fancied—gave him a deep insight into the old king's character. However, in more subtle roles like Hamlet or Macbeth Forrest's deficiency was very clear. He could not logically understand these men. No amount of analyzing enabled him to feel the character of Hamlet. The prince's vivid imagination, the spiritual conflict which agonizes him and furnishes the key to much of his behavior, were quite beyond Forrest's comprehension. He read the lines with wonderful accuracy, says the Philadelphia *Dispatch,* but nothing could overcome his "want of appreciation" of the

character. In *Macbeth* the same lack of imagination and spiritual insight was apparent. Forrest did not seem to grasp how a strong man could be terrorized by imaginary horrors. He seemed to have no comprehension of that terrible vision-creating faculty which tortures Macbeth. Forrest's performance of the part offered isolated passages of beautiful reading but, according to the critics of the times, "the witches he could not see, the ghost of Banquo did not appall him, and the horrors of Macbeth's remorse he could not depict."

Nevertheless, his style of acting was immensely appealing to the majority of playgoers. They idolized this handsome, powerful man who handled his body like an athlete. They enjoyed watching his naturalistic movements and gestures, and especially the explosions of physical action in his portrayals. Despite traces of the formal grace of the Kemble school, Forrest's physical actions were broad, powerful, and often startling—effects which especially pleased the Bowery B'hoys. And his voice, as we have mentioned, had tremendous range and matched his physical activity in versatility and power. At the same time, his delivery never lost the clarity and precision which he had learned in his youth. Other features of his acting, which must be remembered in any summary of his style, were the detailed realism of his characterizations and mimic passions based upon a careful, analytical study of his roles, and the passionate conviction with which he lost himself in his portrayals. The heroic, strenuous style of acting he created was unique and exciting. In summarizing Forrest's appeal, Richard Moody writes: ". . . no native-born, native-trained actor climbed so high, summoned American writers to the drama with such fervor, spread the enduring glories of the mighty Shakespeare so widely, and carried the raging democratic fever to the stage with such fierce passion. And no actor compelled so many Americans to pay so much for a tempestuous evening in the theatre." [23] Perhaps Lawrence Barrett was right when he said ". . . take him all for all, we shall not look upon his like again." [24]

During his long and dazzling career, Forrest exerted considerable influence upon the actors of his time. The popularity of his style attracted a host of imitators. Some of these were gifted players who gained considerable success; others were hacks who, as W. R. Alger says, reflected discredit on Forrest "by imitating his faultiness instead of reproducing his excellence." [25] By far the most successful follower of Forrest was John Edward McCullough.

JOHN E. McCULLOUGH, CHIEF DISCIPLE
OF EDWIN FORREST

Born in Ireland, John Edward McCullough emigrated to the United States at the age of fifteen, arriving in the country unknown, destitute, and illiterate; he could not even write his own name. Yet before his death at the age of fifty-three, he was known and loved from New York to California as "genial John," and he was considered by his friends and fans to be second only to Edwin Booth in his eminence as a tragic actor.

The early struggles and ultimate success of John McCullough make a heart-warming story. His eventual collapse and death were tragic, yet before misfortune overtook him he had fulfilled the classic American ideal of winning fame and fortune through hard work and sterling character.

McCullough was born November 14, 1832, in the tiny village of Blakes near the northeast coast of Ireland. He was reared in ignorance and poverty. In 1847, he left his native land and journeyed to Philadelphia, where he searched out a cousin who had established himself as a chair maker. McCullough began learning the trade of chair making, and he also began teaching himself to read and write. He had a husky build, a handsome face, and ambition tempered by humility. A workman in his cousin's shop introduced him to the plays of Shakespeare. McCullough's interest in dramatics was aroused—and this led to membership in an amateur dramatic association and to elocution lessons from Lemuel White, the teacher of Edwin Forrest. One evening, the manager of Philadelphia's Arch Street Theatre saw McCullough perform in an amateur play and, impressed with the young man's looks and sincerity, hired him to play minor roles at $4 per week. McCullough's ambition to become an actor, born in a chair shop, was now confirmed; henceforth he was to devote his entire life to the theatre.

McCullough's professional development was slow. He had much to learn not only about acting but about art and education in general. He studied assiduously and read omnivorously. His progress was aided by his deep sincerity, his capacity for hard work, and his phenomenal memory. Two stories illustrative of the latter are featured in the accounts of his early life. One story records that in a single month's time, during the period he was employed as a chair maker, he read and absorbed the whole of Chambers' *Encyclopedia of English Literature*

digesting it so thoroughly that "he could quote from its data as reliably as if the volumes were open before him. . . ." [26] The other story records that when he was playing small parts for E. L. Davenport, in Boston in the season of 1860-61, the star was stricken with rheumatism and that McCullough, at eleven in the morning, had to be ready to read the star's role from a manuscript at the evening performance. The role was Robert Landry in Selby's play *The Dead Heart,* and was considered one of the longest parts in the whole range of romantic drama. McCullough determined to *act* the part that night without the manuscript. He spent the afternoon in intensive study memorizing both the lines and the business. When curtain time came, he astonished the company and the audience by a letter-perfect performance of the role.

After four years of apprenticeship, most of them spent in Philadelphia, McCullough's great opportunity came when Edwin Forrest hired him to play second leads to Forrest's starring roles. The choice of the younger actor by the older is easy to understand when the similarities between the two men are considered. Both were muscular, well built men; both had voices of great range and power; and both had physical strength and animal vitality which lent abundant force to their acting. According to one story, the first time McCullough acted with Forrest he engaged him in a vocal duel which enraged but also impressed the star. Forrest was playing an engagement in Philadelphia in the theatre where McCullough was employed, and one evening he had a scene with McCullough. The younger man determined to make an impression on Forrest and so, says McCullough, "I went after him in a vocal sense. He gave me one startled, savage look, and came right back at me with a volley of roars that rattled the big chandelier. We had it out then and all through the evening, and although Forrest was mad all over at the minute, he came around the next day." [27]

Although this story may be apocryphal, it is the kind of thing that could have happened, and it illustrates some of the qualities which Forrest found attractive in McCullough. The young actor, besides possessing ambition, physique, and vocal power, was intensely earnest, and hard working; he was a devoted student and planned his roles with meticulous care; he was vigorous, healthy, and handsome; and he had a genial warm-heartedness which lent charm to his acting and which won him the affection of all his associates. One critic describes him at this time as "a splendid type, beautiful in his modeling, handsome of face, free of movement, natural in grace with a rich, round, resonant

voice . . . ," [28] and Susie Clark, his adulatory biographer, adds that "His fine, frank face and grand head, with its wealth of brown hair, was illuminated by kindly soulful, blue eyes and one of the sweetest smiles . . . ever seen on the lips of man. . . ." [29]

McCullough remained with Forrest for five years playing such roles as Laertes, Macduff, Iago, Edgar, Richmond, Pythias, and Icilius, while Forrest played the starring parts. At this time, and for several years thereafter, McCullough style of acting was very similar to Forrest's. Both had studied under Lemuel White, who stressed vocal force and emphasis in his instruction, and they had similar physical endowments. Joseph I. C. Clarke, a prominent New York journalist and one-time dramatic editor of the *New York Tribune,* aptly describes McCullough's early style in these words: "My first impression was that his art was noisy, scorned repose, laughed at subtlety but hammered its points with a force that meant sincerity at least. It was virile without virtuosity. . . . It was, I take it, the 'Forrest school' going to seed, bold, noisy, direct to the audience, careless about settings, almost random as to costumes. The old triumphant carelessness that aimed at 'the gods' with a thunderclap speech, and if a 'hit' was scored, let that suffice." [30]

In 1866, McCullough and Forrest traveled to California and acted together at Maguire's Opera House. McCullough's performances received only luke-warm notices, the critics using such descriptions as "a fair piece of acting," "a decided improvement," "only fair to middling," etc. At the end of this engagement, Forrest and his protégé parted company, with the old actor delivering this farewell advice to McCullough: "Stay here. Leave off imitating me. . . . A lot of infernal fools are doing that, all over the country. Build yourself up here, and you will do well." [31]

McCullough followed Forrest's advice; he remained in San Francisco and prospered both financially and artistically. His desire to improve himself and to develop in his art were as strong as ever, and he began to free himself from the influence of his old master. He had often been criticized for his imitation of Forrest; now the critics began to notice a change and they praised him for it. They noticed also that McCullough improved steadily and perceptibly from season to season; in fact, a constant note in the critical reviews received by McCullough during his lifetime is a recognition of his growth and development as an actor. Year by year, until almost his final season, McCullough was congratulated for the steady improvement of his dramatic powers. Such

praise is tribute, not only to his acting, but to his basic sincerity, humility, and devotion of character.

McCullough was identified with the theatre of San Francisco for almost ten years. After his partnership with Forrest ended, he acted at various playhouses in the city and the surrounding area. In January of 1869, he began a partnership with Lawrence Barrett as co-manager of the beautiful new California Theatre, built by a group of San Francisco financiers to give the city a perfect theatre and a company superior to any in the nation. Barrett withdrew as co-manager in 1870, and for the next five years McCullough was sole manager and a leading actor of the company. As manager, he was energetic, resourceful, even-tempered, generous and helpful to all his company, and lavish in the care and money he spent on his productions. As an actor he continued to grow in polish and artistry and attracted a large group of admirers. When he retired as manager, after the theatre had encountered serious financial difficulties, his departure was universally regretted. Even his arch rival in management, Tom Maguire of Maguire's Opera House, said: "Mr. McCullough did a great deal for San Francisco. . . . A squarer man never lived. He was above doing anything mean, small or underhanded. . . ." [32]

Some years before relinquishing his position at the California Theatre, McCullough had begun a series of starring tours throughout the United States. After leaving San Francisco he continued these tours, and they constituted his major theatrical activity until his final illness and retirement.

After McCullough's return to the East, his consuming ambition for improvement led him to take dramatic lessons from Steele MacKaye, who was then spreading the gospel of François Delsarte on the American stage. MacKaye's instruction seems to have crystallized and harmonized the improvements which McCullough had been laboring to achieve since his separation from Forrest. Joseph I. C. Clarke, who had described McCullough's early style as one which was "noisy" and which "scorned repose" and "laughed at subtlety," now witnessed McCullough in his favorite role of Virginius and, looking back on the performance, said: ". . . this was a new McCullough indeed. Here was a chaste spirit, a sure, tempered emotion, utmost grace, restraint overlying power that only flashed out on the mountain tops." [33] A similar estimate of McCullough's improvement and change of style was made by A. C. Wheeler, the famous critic "Nym Crinkle," who wrote, in

1878, that when McCullough "played his last season at Booth's Theatre, everyone was amazed at the leap he had made in his art. His Othello and Richelieu astonished me by being entirely unlike his former impersonations of those characters. The native vigor, resonance, and fire were there, but they were disciplined and controlled. A nicer balance of faculty was apparent. The intelligibility of the subtler emotions had been made sharper and clearer. There were noble climaxes of passion, less waste of energy in making himself felt, a cleaner adaptation of tone and gesture to the exigent thought—more repose, more dignity, more grace." [34]

During the years from 1877 to 1883, McCullough's acting reached its highest level of achievement. The abilities which he had so earnestly cultivated through the years flowered and matured and won him a secure place in the estimation of both critics and the general public. However, it must be recognized that his reputation with the public was always higher than his standing with the critics. The warmth of his personality and his great sociability off the stage won him an unusual amount of personal popularity, and this popularity brought hundreds of customers to the theatres where he played. His multitude of admirers ignored such a critic as Alfred Ayres who said that McCullough was, at the best, "a tragedian of the third rate"; [35] so great was their esteem and affection for the man and so effectively did his acting appeal to them, that they hailed him uncritically as a "genius," a "great tragedian," and "second only to Booth." [36]

While McCullough's achievements in acting were impressive, it is doubtful if he belongs in the same class with Booth—or, indeed, with Forrest or Davenport or other eminent tragedians of the time. He lacked their versatility, their poetic fire, their power of imagination. William Winter, who was a devoted friend of McCullough's—but also an experienced critic—gives a fair judgement of McCullough when he says: "He was a tragic actor of fine natural talents, thoughtfully, carefully and thoroughly cultivated." [37]

McCullough had abilities and natural endowments which, utilized in the right roles, enabled him to achieve genuine excellence. His handsome build, his finely modeled head, and his rich, powerful voice have already been mentioned. These were real factors in his success for, it is said, no actor ever wore tights or a toga with more grace and authority and no actor was a more perfect embodiment of the ideal Roman

of such plays as *Virginius, Brutus, Damon and Pythias,* and *Julius Caesar.*

McCullough's great-hearted generosity, his manly sweetness, his simple dignity, and his deep sincerity—all of them qualities which characterized the actor when off the stage—were other factors in his success on the stage. McCullough was able to incorporate these qualities into his characterizations and, furthermore, he was able to project them successfully to an audience. Thus it followed that he excelled in roles "emblematic of noble manhood and lofty and tender feeling; parts that implicate splendid deeds, fidelity to duty, self sacrifice for love or honor; parts that move in the realm of the affections." [38] To act such parts required the ability to project manliness, dignity, pathos, tenderness, nobility, etc. McCullough was eminently successful in embodying such feelings, but he could also startle an audience with outbursts of anger, scorn, and tumultuous grief. He had reserves of passion which would erupt in the manner made popular by Edmund Kean and duplicated by Edwin Forrest. As a result, his portrayals of *King Lear* and *Othello* were magnificent in the scenes of rage or pathos but fell short in those scenes requiring subtlety of imagination. His Hamlet, says William Winter, "was little more than laboriously correct," [39] although the portrayal was often praised for being "human" and a "man of flesh and blood." His Macbeth was, in general, tame and uneven, rising to power and conviction only in the final scenes of action. However, in plays like *Virginius, Damon and Pythias,* and *The Gladiator,* McCullough was entirely at home and entirely successful. He looked the parts; he understood the parts; he embodied them convincingly and appealingly. The leading character in each of these plays is a man of strength, dignity, and simple passion. Virginius, for example, is the heroic Roman father who loves virtue and manliness, who serves his country loyally and unswervingly, who defends innocence and fights tyranny, and who, in the climax of the play, slays his adored only child to save her from dishonor. In this type of role, McCullough reached the zenith of his achievement. His success as Virginius is described by William Winter as follows: "It was a high, serious, noble work. . . . The sustained poetic exaltation of that embodiment, its unity as a grand and sympathetic personage, and its exquisite simplicity, were the qualities that gave it vitality in popular interest, and through those it possesses permanence in theatrical history. . . . The perfect finish of the performance, indeed, was little less than marvelous, when viewed

with reference to the ever-increasing volume of power and the evident reality of afflicting emotion with which the part was carried." [40]

McCullough's style of acting was never colloquial or realistic in the manner of the man-in-the-street. The traditions of his time and the plays in which he appeared demanded an elevation of manner which included graceful and dignified action and smooth, poetic elocution. Such a manner did not mean, however, that the actor appeared static, cold, or unreal. For example, in McCullough's performance of Virginius, according to Winter, "The intention to be real . . . was obvious, through its harmonious fulfillment; yet the realism was shorn of all triteness, all animal excess. . . . McCullough did not present *Virginius* brushing his hair or paying *Virginia's* school-bills; yet he suggested him clearly and beautifully. . . ." [41]

McCullough was able to portray the elemental passions of rage, grief, and despair with force and fire but without the effect of ranting. Explosive strength was a mark of the Forrest school and McCullough had it—and used it effectively—yet in his mature period he was generally praised for his freedom from extravagance. One critic, for example, in reviewing McCullough's performance of Lear said: "His appeal to the winds and the elements when he is wandering in the storm is all the more effective because its vehemence and terrible earnestness are unmarred by an extravagance in declamation or action," [42] and Henry A. Clapp, in the *Boston Advertiser* for February 26, 1878, said that McCullough's Virginius "has dignity without bombast, and immense force without violence."

In his portrayal of emotion, McCullough evidently shared the feelings he was projecting to his audience. There is evidence of this even though the actor has left no record of his theories of acting or of his methods of performing a part. For example, fellow players have reported that after the scene in *Virginius* when the Roman father kills his own daughter, McCullough would often be shaking with emotion, his face wet with tears; on these occasions his fellow actors were careful not to speak to him or intrude on his suffering. Furthermore, in an interview with a journalist of the period, McCullough was asked if he could easily put off his character with his costume. "Not at all," answered McCullough, "often when I play *Lear* I remain Lear half the night, and awake next morning weary and nervous and unrefreshed." The reporter then asked if this meant that McCullough really experienced the same emotions as those of the character he was acting, and

McCullough answered: "Exactly . . . sometimes when I act *Virginius* I feel at the moment I despatch *Virginia* as though I were killing my own child." [43]

The solid success McCullough achieved in the roles which especially suited him came to a tragic end in 1884. For more than a year preceding this date, his health had begun to fail and he had noticed a decline in his dramatic power. He took a vacation from the stage and tried to rebuild his strength but, though he refused to recognize it, his affliction was mortal. He returned to the stage in the fall of 1884, but on September 29, at McVicker's Theatre in Chicago, he suffered a mental and physical breakdown and had to be helped from the stage. Later, he revived somewhat, but his mental deterioration could not be arrested. In June of 1885 he was placed in the Bloomingdale Sanitarium in New York City, where he remained for four months. At the end of this time he was moved to his home in Philadelphia, and died two weeks later, on November 8, 1885. His family and friends tried to conceal the nature of his illness, but it is known that he died of paresis, the result of congenital syphillis.

Few actors have been mourned so deeply and universally as John McCullough, and few actors have received, both in life and in death, the demonstrations of affection received by this actor. During his active career he was the recipient of innumerable honors, banquets, and receptions; after his death, and after the impressive funeral services which attracted thousands of mourners, an ornate monument was erected to his memory in the Mount Moriah Cemetery in Philadelphia. He will be remembered as a personality who was sincerely loved and admired by many thousands throughout the country; he will also be remembered as an actor who, within his range and limitations, achieved a generous measure of success.

OTHER DISCIPLES OF THE HEROIC SCHOOL

Although John McCullough came closest to being the Elisha to Edwin Forrest's Elijah, there were other gifted players who can be considered disciples of the heroic school and who at one time provided keen competition for Forrest. Among the most notable of these were the following: Augustus A. Addams, David Ingersoll, John R. Scott, Charles H. Eaton, Joseph Proctor, and J. Hudson Kirby. All of

these men acted the leading roles in tragedy and melodrama, performing them in a robust, strenuous style. All of them, at some point in their careers, knew or acted with Edwin Forrest and thus had firsthand opportunity to observe the master and to learn from his success.

Addams, Ingersoll, Eaton, and Kirby must have been an unusually gifted and promising quartet. They all died before reaching the age of thirty, yet each, during his brief career, achieved national popularity. Augustus Addams, for example, "had every element physical and intellectual to place him in the highest niche of theatric fame." [44] He possessed a handsome, expressive face, a fine physique which he used with grace and confidence, and a voice of "great sweetness and power." Alfred Ayres thought he was superior to Edwin Booth as a tragedian [45] and many critics felt that he excelled Forrest in such heroic parts as Damon, Virginius, and Pierre, and would have eclipsed the old master if he had lived long enough.

David Ingersoll, who had barely reached the age of twenty-five when he died, was deemed a prodigy, according to William Winter, and was repeatedly described as "the silver tongued" by Lawrence Barrett. When Ingersoll was twenty-three years old he created the role of Jack Cade in the drama which was later to become a favorite of Edwin Forrest, and he too might have challenged Forrest's position had he lived longer.

Charles Eaton was called a "notable member of the Forrestian school" [46] and was said to have "few superiors in the histrionic arts." [47] Equal praise was given to J. Hudson Kirby, whose career lasted only ten years. He, too, was of the robustious, strenuous school of acting, although he did not possess the physical size or strength of other followers of the style. But the intensity of his emotional projection and the power of his voice were enough to win him a devoted following.

Joseph Proctor and John R. Scott both lived longer than the youthful quartet of Addams, Ingersoll, Eaton, and Kirby. For several years, John R. Scott was considered a dangerous rival to Forrest, although Wemyss asserts that "his reputation rested more upon the support he rendered Forrest, than any real merit of his own as a tragedian." [48] However, he was greatly admired for his commanding bearing and robust vigor and was a favorite with audiences of his time. When he appeared upon the British stage he displayed such power that, according to Lawrence Barrett, *The Times* of London said, "no actor pos-

sessing so many beauties and so many faults had ever been seen before upon the English stage." [49]

Joseph Proctor, although closely identified for many years with the leading role in *Nick of the Woods,* acted all the leading parts in tragedy and melodrama and developed a following in all the theatrical towns of the United States. He was by far the longest lived of Forrest's disciples, for his acting career covered almost sixty years, but even at the end of his career when Otis Skinner observed his acting, Proctor still exhibited the traits and methods of the heroic school.

It is interesting to note that all the performers of this school of acting achieved their greatest successes before so-called "popular" audiences. Forrest was the idol of the Bowery B'hoys and so were Scott, Kirby, Addams, and Proctor. All of them appeared repeatedly at the Bowery Theatre or the Chatham or the Franklin and less frequently, or never, at the more fashionable Park Theatre. When they visited London, they acted at such theatres as the Surrey more often than at Drury Lane or Covent Garden. Evidently their heroic, muscular style appealed strongly to the less sophisticated members of the public just as the muscular exploits of television's Western cowboys and gunmen appeal to the mass audiences of today.

Forrest and the style of acting he practiced had other followers, like J. A. Neafie, McKean Buchanan, and Daniel H. Harkins; in fact, Forrest's popularity begot what Alger calls "a whole brood of disciples." [50] Many of them, unfortunately, produced strange imitations or crude caricatures of the style and thus discredited it in the eyes of the public. Also, while Forrest and his disciples were still in their prime, the versatile tragedians of the classic school were developing a style of acting which was to become far more popular and influential than the heroic school. Nevertheless, the type of acting represented by certain aspects of the Forrest school has never completely disappeared. In the years which have followed the death of Forrest, occasional actors have appeared whose primary appeal has been their muscular physiques, manly bearing, and powerful voices. They have succeeded in heroic, masculine roles in which they were able to exploit their physical endowments in a realistic way. One of the best examples of this kind of actor was the New Jersey born Melbourne MacDowell, who flourished in the last quarter of the nineteenth century. His earliest role was that of Charles, the wrestler, in *As You Like It,* and his greatest success was achieved as Marc Antony in Sardou's *Cleopatra.* With his superb

physique and his sincere, forthright manner, MacDowell was considered the perfect embodiment of the Roman warrior—just as Forrest and McCullough had been before him. Other actors of the same mould have followed him, and in our own time the brawny heroes of Western melodrama all suggest the physical attributes of the Forrest school. In the stock characters they play, they are not called upon to read blank verse or to thunder the lines of a Metamora or a Spartacus, but they must excel in physical strength and agility and must exercise them realistically in defense of justice and virtue. As long as this type of hero holds the stage, we shall not lack a reminder of the heroic style of acting so successfully practiced by Edwin Forrest, the first great American star.

II

THE CLASSIC SCHOOL:
THE LADIES

WHILE EDWIN FORREST AND HIS DISCIPLES WERE EARNING THE plaudits of American and foreign audiences, "there was being nurtured," says Lewis Strang, ". . . a class of players destined in the end to outlive and to outact the school of heroic histrionism of which Forrest was the founder." [1] I shall call this school of acting the classic school, using the term "classic" to indicate a manner of performance "of the first rank, perfect in its way, a model of its kind."

These players, from whose ranks came some of our greatest performers, were close to the traditions of the European theatre. Like their predecessors, they benefited from rich and varied apprenticeships in stock or repertory companies in which they appeared in parts which ranged from low comedy to high tragedy. They prided themselves on their range and versatility, and in their maturity they played the great roles of the standard drama, usually specializing in Shakespearean drama. They revered the art of acting as a noble calling of great usefulness and benefit to society and, as a result of their long apprenticeships, they acquired a mastery of the techniques of their art. They learned to move with grace and dignity; they learned to execute their actions economically and effectively. They also trained their voices to be flexible, responsive, and varied, so that their elocution was characterized by correct pronunciation and skillful management of cadence and poetic rhythm. Like the members of the Heroic School, they valued the art of elocution and worked constantly to perfect the beauty and clarity of their speech.

The classic players aimed to be "natural," but their concept of naturalness was not the literal imitation-of-nature method practiced by Forrest; neither was it, of course, the suppressed, suggestive method of the modern school of psychological realism. They utilized a heightened, idealized treatment of speech and action which suited the greater elaborateness and elegance of the social manners of their time. They would have considered ludicrous, for example, the idea of giving Prince Hamlet or King Lear the speech and manners of a contemporary businessman or of reading the blank verse of Shakespeare or the rhetoric of Bulwer-Lytton in the tones and cadences used when gossiping at a tea party. Their type of idealized "naturalness" would undoubtedly appear artificial to a twentieth-century audience but it was both appropriate and convincing when it was used in the great roles of the standard drama of the nineteenth century.

These actors and actresses prepared their movements and delivery artfully and carefully with the result that their performances, at their best, appeared graceful and effortless; at their worst, they seemed studied and artificial. They studied the texts of their plays, analyzed the characters, and sought to create a consistent, unified delineation which fitted the design of the drama, and which was not a series of "points" but a portrayal of even texture and logical development. Edwin Forrest was a careful student who studied and analyzed his characters exhaustively, but the influence of Edmund Kean often led Forrest to play up the big scenes and to slight the other parts of the play.

The outstanding actresses of the classic school were Mary Ann Duff, Charlotte Cushman, Mary Anderson, Fanny Janauschek, and Helena Modjeska. The great male performers of the school were Edwin Booth, James Murdoch, Edwin L. Davenport, and Lawrence Barrett. In performance these players did not merely project their own personalities into their parts but sought to transform their personalities enough to project the illusion of separate dramatic characters. Like the players of the heroic school, they generally experienced a feeling of identity with the dramatic character and felt the emotions of the role—without, however, losing critical consciousness or control of body and voice. Unlike the players of the heroic school, they avoided tricks or mannerisms or exhibitionism of any kind in their effects. The art of these nine players, together with the achievements of their followers, exemplified the American stage during most of the

nineteenth century, for Mary Ann Duff began her American career in 1810, and Helena Modjeska made her farewell appearances in 1907.

MARY ANN DUFF

Many students of the theatre believe that Charlotte Cushman was the first great actress of the American stage. While it is true that she was the first native-born American woman to achieve top rank both at home and abroad, for twenty-five years preceding Miss Cushman's debut the stage of the United States was graced by a woman, English by birth but American by adoption, whom Joseph Ireland has called "the legitimate and undisputed Queen of the American stage." [2] She is the neglected and almost unknown tragedienne, Mrs. Mary Ann Duff.

Mrs. Duff, often called "the American Siddons," was born in London in 1794, the eldest child of an Englishman who served with the East India Company. Her maiden name was Dyke. In 1809, under her mother's tutelage and in the company of her two sisters, she made her stage debut as a dancer in Dublin, Ireland. The following year she married the actor, John R. Duff, and in the same year accompanied him to the United States and settled here. With the exception of a brief visit to England in 1827, she spent the remainder of her life in America and died in this country. It was in the United States that she learned the art of acting, built her career, and achieved her reputation as the foremost tragedienne of her time. Despite her foreign birth, she must be recognized as the first great actress of the American stage.

The records of Mrs. Duff's career are scanty. She left no diary or reminiscences. Only one brief biography has been written. Her active career extended from 1810 to 1838, a time when magazines and newspapers featuring dramatic criticism were relatively few. Her name has been forgotten and her achievements neglected, yet few actresses have ever received the amazing acclaim accorded Mrs. Duff by critics, public, and her great contemporaries. Fortunately, from the brief records which have survived it is possible to form a general idea of the style and effectiveness of her acting.

Beauty of face, grace of figure, and richness of voice were among Mrs. Duff's natural gifts. Joseph N. Ireland, her biographer, describes her thus:

She possessed a person of more than medium height, and of the most perfect symmetry,—not so commanding, perhaps, as that of Mrs. Siddons, but far more available, in her maturer years, for the youthful heroines of the drama, and far more graceful and pleasing to the eye than Miss Cushman ever possessed. Her face, called beautiful in her girlhood, throughout life was irradiated by eyes of the darkest hue and most speaking intelligence. The varying expression of her features has never been surpassed; while her voice was as soft and musical, in its quiet tones, as (we are told) was that of Mrs. Clibber,—wild and plaintive in its ejaculations of distraction and despair, yet resonant and thrilling in its forceful utterances.[3]

When Mrs. Duff arrived in the United States with her actor-husband, her only formal training had been in ballet. Her knowledge of acting, such as it was, had been learned from observation and a limited amount of practical experience. Physical appeal and personal charm were her principal assets. In her early appearances in Boston, where she and her husband had settled upon their arrival in America, she was praised for beauty, tenderness, and "expressive simplicity." She was frequently cast as a boy or a page so that she could exhibit her shapely figure. She was admired for the "unusual lustre" of her eyes. When she first acted Juliet, in 1810, she was complimented for *looking* the part, but was criticized for weakness of spirit. Critics said her style was indifferent and that she lacked both "conception and power."

For seven or eight years, Mrs. Duff's acting continued to be charming but weak. She was content to let her husband win the plaudits. Presently, however, John Duff began to lose his popularity. The support of the growing family of children rested more and more on Mrs. Duff. Apparently she decided she must exert herself to develop the latent talent which few people suspected she possessed. By 1817 her improvement was marked and caused favorable comment. In 1818 she played Juliet to the Romeo of the great English tragedian, Thomas A. Cooper, and this time it was said that in addition to youth and loveliness she had "the fervor and force of passion, the ecstasy of joy, and the agony of grief, terror, and despair combined in her most harmonious and powerfully developed personation." [4]

The Boston critics were astonished at her unexpected emergence as a powerful dramatic actress. W. W. Clapp said that suddenly, as if she were "touched by a magic wand" she discarded "the languor of indifference" and displayed "in vivid intensity the true fire of genius." [5]

Mrs. Duff's growing ambition received a powerful stimulus in 1821

when Edmund Kean visited Boston and she was assigned to act Ophelia to his Hamlet, Cordelia to his Lear, and Hermione to his Orestes. By this time Mrs. Duff had achieved a reputation for "passion and fire," but in her performances with Kean she outdid herself. In rehearsal Kean is said to have requested her to act with less force and intensity "as he merely desired his efforts seconded, not rivalled." [6] In performance, Mrs. Duff won applause equal to Kean's and so impressed the great tragedian that he declared she was superior to any actress on the British stage. It is said that he often repeated this opinion.

Mrs. Duff continued to demonstrate her newly developed powers and to win increased popularity and praise. The elder Booth, after acting with her in *Lear* and *Hamlet,* described her as the greatest actress in the world. Edwin Forrest, Thomas A. Cooper, and William Conway all spoke of her as the finest leading lady of their experience.

Mrs. Duff continued to act, chiefly in Boston and Philadelphia, until 1835. She also appeared in New York and won a host of admirers. However, her career in New York is peculiar. She played chiefly at the smaller theatres, like the Franklin and the Richmond Hill, and never filled an extended engagement at the larger, more fashionable playhouses. Her following among the press and the public was devoted and worshipful, but it did not include the "dilettanti" of the city, who seem to have ignored her because of her "provincial" background. This did not prevent the New York *Mirror* in 1826 from declaring: "The opinion lately expressed . . . that this lady is superior to any actress on the American or British stage, we think has every probability of being correct, and we are more and more inclined to believe in it every time we witness her performance." [7] Furthermore, it did not prevent the eminent Horace Greeley from visiting the Richmond Hill theatre, in 1832, and recording in his *Recollections of a Busy Life* that, ". . . I saw Mrs. Duff personate Lady Macbeth better than it has since been done in this city. . . . I doubt that any woman has since played in our city—and I am thinking of Fanny Kemble—who was the superior to Mrs. Duff in a wide range of tragic characters." [8]

In 1836, Mrs. Duff, who had been a widow for some years, married J. G. Seaver, an attorney. She accompanied him to New Orleans and became a permanent resident of that city. In 1837 and 1838 she played brief engagements in New Orleans and then, becoming deeply religious, she retired from the stage. She lived in self-imposed obscurity until her death, which occurred in New York in 1857.

The acting of Mrs. Duff in her maturity was very different from her early style. As she matured, she retained great personal magnetism and in addition she learned to project strong emotion and to stir her audiences by the controlled intensity of her feelings. She did not imitate the tempestuous outbursts of Kean, but developed a quiet, sustained force which was powerfully suggestive rather than openly exhibitionistic. The noted manager, N. M. Ludlow, described Mrs. Duff as "refined, quiet, yet powerful; not boisterous, yet forcible; graceful in all her motions, and dignified without stiffness." [9] Incidentally, he adds that she was "undoubtedly the best tragic actress of the United States."

Mrs. Duff was praised for her freedom from mannerisms and for her avoidance of tricks. She did not rely upon making "points," that is, she did not alternate startling dramatic flourishes with dull and careless scenes. She treated each line and each scene with thoughtful care and thus achieved a uniform excellence in her acting which created admiring comment. The New York *Mirror* of May 5, 1827, says:

Mrs. Duff has *one* great characteristic—one peculiarity that strikes all who see her, and this is uniformity of excellence. . . . From beginning to end you see before you only the character she is personating. The unity of her conception, the *oneness,* is remarkable. No temptation can induce her to break it. If a scene offers ever so much opportunity for display, and it is not authorized by the whole design and tenor of the part, she suffers it to pass unembraced. . . . Kean startled us with electric flashes—Mrs. Barnes occasionally shines with great vividness—but Mrs. Duff pours out one unceasing blaze during the whole time she occupies the stage. . . .

In her maturity, Mrs. Duff learned to identify herself with her characters and to lose herself in her parts. During the performance of great roles she became completely absorbed and seemed to forget both herself and her audience. One critic said: "She seems to have a separate existence during the continuance of the play, and to have lost all knowledge, and even all power of seeing the realities around her." [10] Despite such absorption there is no evidence that her control and self-discipline were ever relaxed.

In achieving her effects, Mrs. Duff had the assistance of an unusually affecting voice. It was variously described by critics as "full and mellow," "powerful and harmonious," "plaintively tender," and "thrillingly expressive." But the phrase most frequently applied to it was "soul subduing." Though this phrase was not explained, it evidently

meant that Mrs. Duff's voice had a quality which stirred the emotions of pity and tenderness very powerfully. Over and over the critics mention the "melting hearts" and the "streaming eyes" of Mrs. Duff's listeners.

The roles which Mrs. Duff acted most successfully and with the greatest popular appeal were those portraying grief, sacrifice, and noble suffering. She excelled in *The Distrest Mother* and *The Stranger,* in which she varied pathetic appeal with "lightening flashes of scorn and indignation." As Madame Clermont in *Adrian and Orilla* she achieved "the best sustained delineation of maternal affectation" which Edmund Kean had ever witnessed.[11] As Ophelia and Cordelia she was said to have no peer. Lewis Strang reports that: "Bathed in tears she was absolutely irresistible." [12]

Mrs. Duff's success as a generator of tears relates her to a long line of actresses who have excelled in this ability. But many of these belong to a school which can be described as "emotionalistic" because they confined themselves exclusively to tear-producing roles and to the limited techniques associated with these roles. Mrs. Duff played many other parts with eminent success. Ireland lists a minimum of 220 characters she acted during the twenty-eight years of her stage career. These parts included everything from farce to high tragedy and indicate a considerable degree of versatility. It was in the grand roles of Lady Macbeth and Queen Katherine that Mrs. Duff was supreme. In pathetic roles such as Hermione and Mrs. Haller she won a tremendous popular following. A fair percentage of comedy roles appear in the repertory, but in these roles, though Mrs. Duff acted with competence, she did not excel. Katherine, in *The Taming of the Shrew,* was her most successful comic character because, Ireland conjectures, little gaiety or joyousness is required in the portrayal. Her contributions to American acting, although now forgotten and ignored, were so impressive that they prompted the great comedian, John Gilbert, to declare more than twenty years after her death: "Mrs. Duff was the most exquisite tragic actress I ever saw, and I make no exceptions." [13]

CHARLOTTE CUSHMAN

In the same year (1835) that Mary Ann Duff was playing her farewell engagement in New York City, nineteen-year-old Charlotte Cush-

man, descendent of one of the Pilgrim Fathers, was making her debut in Boston. Miss Cushman's first appearance was not as an actress; it was as a singer in Mozart's *Marriage of Figaro*. She had been prepared for her debut by the coaching of James G. Maeder and the assistance of the celebrated vocalist, Mrs. Mary Ann Wood. She was successful enough to win favorable attention, and shortly after her Boston appearance she accepted an engagement in New Orleans, where she promptly ruined her singing voice by overstraining it in a large theatre. Since she was poor and burdened with the support of her mother, brothers, and sister, she desperately looked for some other employment, and was advised to try her luck as an actress. Without any professional dramatic training she launched a career which was eventually to win her great wealth and the topmost rank among American actresses.

After Miss Cushman's dramatic debut in New Orleans, she returned to the North and played in stock for eight years. Slowly and earnestly she learned the secrets of her profession. She had no formal instruction, but relied upon experience and observation to teach her. She was able to watch the work of many excellent players. The first of these to influence her were Thomas A. Cooper and Mrs. Powell. Both players were English by birth and training and they maintained the tradition of the stately Kembles. It is believed that the dignity and majesty of Cushman's manner were due, in part, to her admiration of the grand style of Cooper and Powell. Perhaps she received additional impetus toward this style from her early stage managers—Mr. Barton, of New Orleans, who was familiar with the acting of Sarah Siddons, and Peter Richings of New York, an English actor of the old school who was influential at the Park Theatre when Miss Cushman first acted there.

In 1843, the eminent tragedian William Macready played an engagement at the Park Theatre and Cushman supported him in several important roles. Macready was impressed by her ambition and undisciplined power, and took a sympathetic interest in her development. Cushman, in turn, was amazed at the polish and artistry of Macready's acting. In comparison, her own style was crude and uncontrolled. She resolved to discover his method and apply his techniques. From him she learned to study patiently, to examine the text and analyze the characters, and to search for the subtler meanings which might lie beneath the surface of a role. She also learned that all her efforts should be controlled; that both words and actions should be disciplined to

fulfill the overall design of the character and the play. "It must have been a curious fellowship," says Edward Robins, "with inspiration on the one side, and, on the other side, abundance of merit without one flash of inspiration." [14] But the association was most fruitful for Miss Cushman. She maintained she had "groped in the darkness until she met Mr. Macready and learned his method" and after learning it, her performances acquired "a harmony and completeness" which they had never before possessed.[15]

Macready urged the young actress to visit London and gain the experience of playing with an English company. Borrowing the necessary money for her passage, Miss Cushman made the trip and it proved to be a turning point in her career. Until this time her rise on the American stage had been steady but not spectacular. The box-office record of the plays in which she appeared shows receipts ranging from $100 to $250 per performance. Not until 1841, when she created the role of Lady Gay Spanker in *London Assurance,* did her appearances attract larger houses. *London Assurance* brought receipts which ranged from $418.50 to $848.00.[16] However, after her conspicuous success in England, where for almost five years her Bianca, her Rosalind, her Queen Katherine, and her Romeo were hailed as masterpieces, she returned in triumph to the United States. The actress had acquired the glamor of a foreign reputation, and her acting had gained authority and polish. Crowded houses and critical hosannas now greeted her appearances. She was judged to be the best American tragedienne, a reputation which she maintained until her final retirement in 1875.

Just as Edwin Forrest's physique and temperament exerted a powerful influence on his manner of acting, so did Cushman's appearance and personality affect her style. She was a tall woman, with square shoulders and a sturdy frame. Her forehead was high and broad, her nose retroussé, and her chin prominent. Her bluish-grey eyes, which were large and expressive, were by far her finest feature and "gave an air of refinement to an otherwise plain and unattractive face." [17] Though her movements were somewhat ungraceful and awkward, she gave the impression of strength and dignity. She was generally described as commanding, rather than handsome, and as masculine in appearance, rather than dainty or feminine.

There was a streak of masculinity in Miss Cushman's temperament, too. As a child she was a tomboy who smashed dolls, climbed trees, and tyrannized over her brothers and sister. As a woman she was hard-

headed and practical and enjoyed acting the masculine roles of Romeo, Cardinal Wolsey, Hamlet, and Claude Melnotte. Sometimes in her portrayals she exercised the same tyranny she had once used on her small brothers and sister. For example, George Vandenhoff said that in her early performances as Lady Macbeth she positively bullied the Thane. She "gets him into a corner . . . ," says Vandenhoff, and "as one sees her large clenched hand and muscular arm threatening him, in alarming proximity, one feels that if other arguments fail with her husband, she will have recourse to blows." [18]

It is not surprising that with her particular physical and mental endowments Cushman should have avoided the tender feminine roles and excelled in those parts which, when not completely masculine, showed the strength and audacity of a Lady Macbeth, or the majesty of a Queen Katherine, or the bizarre physical power of a Meg Merrilies. "Her true forte," said one critic, "is the character of a woman where most of the softer traits of womanhood are wanting . . . or in characters where, roused by passion or incited by some earnest and long-cherished determination, the woman, for the time being, assumes all the power and energy of manhood." [19]

If Miss Cushman's endowments hindered her assumption of certain roles, they were nevertheless her principal assets, for they enabled her to act great roles greatly and to project a stage magnetism which few players have ever equaled. "She was incarnate power:" says William Winter, "she dominated by intrinsic authority: she was a woman born to command: and of such minds as comprehend authentic leadership she achieved immediate, complete, and permanent conquest. There was, in her personality, a massive excellence that made admiration natural and entirely justified it." [20] Alfred Ayres felt that she could have ruled an empire and doubted if either Catherine of Russia or Elizabeth of England possessed her all-around mental gifts. Kate Reignolds said she did not woo her audience, she "seized upon them." This unusual power caused Lewis Strang to write: "As regards the potent spell of her personality, there can be no dispute, for scarcely a critic writes of her in cold blood and with satisfactory analysis." [21]

The unique power of Cushman's personality was enhanced by an unusual voice. Overstraining on the opera stage had left her speaking voice with a husky, hollow quality. Pure, ringing, elastic tones had given way to what Murdoch terms "a quality of aspiration and a woody or veiled tone." This unique quality, plus wide range and un-

usual power, made Miss Cushman's voice capable of effects which few players could duplicate. She was able to express intense, sustained grief without loudness or sudden variations. She could also rise to great vocal heights in scenes of anger or denunciation. Lawrence Barrett recounts that in her death scene as Nancy Sykes, when she called for Bill Fagin and begged him to kiss her, she sounded as if she "spoke through blood." Henry Austin Clapp reports that in her final scenes as Queen Katherine her use of the "sick" tone of voice surpassed anything of its kind he had ever heard. Adam Badeau declares that her superb vocal control enabled her "to break it with age, to thicken it with the choking sensation of death, to loosen it in the cry of agony, to repress it in the hollow murmur of despair." [22]

Not only was she great in coloring her voice with whatever emotion the scene demanded, Miss Cushman was also a superb elocutionist. In her reading, every syllable and every word were distinct, yet the full beauty of the rhythm and the balance of the lines were preserved. Intellectual content was not neglected; full expression was given to the significance of every phrase and every line. Alfred Ayres, who prized elocution above all dramatic virtues, said that Cushman and Forrest were the only great elocutionists this country has produced, and he approved the statement that in Miss Cushman's reading the meaning of the author was "as clear, as transparent, as if the thoughts themselves . . . were transfused through the senses." [23] James O'Neill, who acted Macbeth and Wolsey with her, declared that "she got more out of the language than anyone I have ever listened to." [24]

Miss Cushman believed that to project strong emotion a player must himself feel the emotion—especially if he is an English or American actor. The person of Anglo-Saxon blood, she explained, has too much self-consciousness to impress an audience if he does not lose himself in his part.[25] She testified that she felt the passion she assumed in her roles, and her fellow actors agreed that she indeed seemed to live everything that she did on the stage.

She saw to it that the painstaking care which Macready taught her to use in the study of a role was also applied to staging the plays in which she appeared. At rehearsals she was particular in the utmost detail. She insisted that every movement and gesture and piece of business be carefully worked out before a performance. Catherine Reignolds-Winslow recounts how Cushman rehearsed her for hours in a scene which took only thirty seconds to play—but the scene, when

perfected, earned "deafening applause" in performance. Clumsy or careless work was abhorred by Miss Cushman, and when she achieved stardom she desired only expert and experienced players around her. In 1851 she wrote to J. B. Wright, manager of the National Theatre, Boston, and begged him not to engage a certain aspiring but inexperienced young actress. "I really have not the courage to act with novices," she said.[26]

The high standards Miss Cushman demanded of herself and her associates grew out of the pride she took in her profession and the earnestness with which she pursued her career. She believed that acting was the greatest of the arts, and that a genuine actor was one of God's gifted creatures. In a letter to Miss Elizabeth Peabody of Boston, she wrote: "But no one knows better than myself after all my association with artists of sculpture or painting, how truly my art comprehends all the others and surpasses them, in so far as the study of mind is more than matter. Victor Hugo makes one of his heroines, an actress, say, 'My art endows me with a searching eye, a knowledge of the soul and the soul's workings. . . .' This is a truth more or less powerful as one is more or less truly gifted by the good God." [27]

The earnestness and sincerity of Miss Cushman's attitude toward the stage was evident in all her work, and it was the theme of her farewell address to the theatre-goers of New York. On the evening of November 7, 1874, after her final performance at Booth's Theatre, Miss Cushman told the huge assemblage which had gathered to honor her: "I found life sadly real and intensely earnest, and in my ignorance of other ways of study I resolved to take therefrom my test and my watchword—to be thoroughly in earnest, intensely in earnest, in all my thoughts and in all my actions, whether in my profession or out of it, became my one single idea. And I honestly believe that therein lies the secret of my success in life. I do not believe that any great success, in any art, can be achieved without it." [28]

With the aid of a strong body, a powerful personality, a keen intellect, an unusual voice, a lofty ambition, and a large measure of dramatic genius, Miss Cushman inevitably developed an impressive manner of acting. Her style, as it finally evolved, had sweep and power and majesty. She painted with bold strokes and unmixed colors. Her characters emerged in heroic outline. Subtlety of coloration and fineness of detail were sometimes added, but these, in general, were distinctly subordinate. Some observers felt the lack of poetic imagination

in her portrayals. Others believed that the poetry was present but it was epic rather than lyric in nature. James Murdoch says that she was "intensely prosaic" and although her understanding was keen and penetrating, "that glow of feeling which springs from the center of emotional elements was not a prominent constituent of her organization." [29] On the other hand, William Winter declared that "though she insisted on the basis of fact in acting, she was not mindless of the essential spirit of poetry. In each of her supreme performances—that spirit suffused the impersonation and made it radiant with intrinsic light." [30]

Miss Cushman's playing was sometimes sublime, but in the bold free style of her acting there lurked the danger of melodrama. At times, it is said, she was overly expressive and extravagant. Her Meg Merrilies was too wild and sensational for some tastes. Her Lady Macbeth occasionally exhibited an excess of physical energy. Often she was praised for the expressive force of her looks, gait, and gestures, but on one occasion an unkind critic described her movements as "a galvanized distortion of nature" and said that her constant activity conveyed the impression that she was "suffering under a violent attack of the colic." [31]

Another characteristic of Miss Cushman's style, at least in her later years, was a certain degree of "staginess." Her artful pauses seemed planned; her bold strokes seemed deliberate and calculated. A perceptive observer was conscious of the design and mechanism of her creations. A certain exaggeration of manner must have become habitual with Miss Cushman even when she was off the stage. She often visited the families of her friends, and Dr. S. R. Elliott, who enjoyed many of these visits, says: ". . . we grew to disregard the somewhat overexpressiveness with which she seemed freighted, and to regard, as evidences of genius, her reference to the weather in a hollow tone of voice, or her asking the hour with the solemn severity of a sibyl!" [32]

During Miss Cushman's career on the stage she acted at least 188 different roles. These covered every kind of character from low comedy to high tragedy. Such a wide variety of experience was not unusual for an actress in the mid-nineteenth century. Utility players in the stock companies of the time were required to act almost any part in any play at any time. Specialization did not come until the novice had served a thorough apprenticeship in all manner of roles. Charlotte Cushman was trained in this school, and the comedy parts in her record date

mostly from the early years. It is strange to imagine her acting Beatrice or Lady Teazle or Lady Gay Spanker, but she did perform these roles, often with genuine effectiveness. However, as she gained experience and prestige, she dropped the more uncongenial parts from her repertory and specialized in the characters of high tragedy. Within this field she demonstrated a remarkable degree of versatility. Her successful parts, in addition to Lady Macbeth, Queen Katherine, and Meg Merrilies, included such widely different characters as Mrs. Haller in *The Stranger,* Bianca in *Fazio* (the part in which she made her London debut), Rosalind in *As You Like It,* Pauline and the Widow Melnotte in *The Lady of Lyons,* Portia in *The Merchant of Venice,* Belvidera in *Venice Preserved,* and the male roles of Romeo, Cardinal Wolsey, Hamlet, and Claude Melnotte. Here is a range which must have been impressive even in an age of versatility!

It seems strange to playgoers of today that Charlotte Cushman could act masculine roles with considerable success. Her foremost achievement in this line was Romeo. She had acted the part with success in America, but it was in England that her portrayal of the role became a sensation. She staged it in London late in 1845 with her sister Susan as the Juliet. The play ran for eighty nights and received almost unanimous critical praise. The reviewers thought she looked the part very well, affirming that her voice, her walk, and her general deportment perfectly conveyed the illusion of a dashing young man.* Especially praised was her fresh interpretation which discarded the hackneyed conventions of the character and created a Romeo who was a living, breathing, ardent human being. An occasional critic was

* The following story, to illustrate Miss Cushman's nerve and manly temper as Romeo, is told by Clara E. Clement in her book *Charlotte Cushman* (Boston, 1882, pp. 67–68): "At the National Theatre, Boston, during the season of 1851–52, as she was playing Romeo to the Juliet of Miss Anderton, in the midst of one of the most romantic passages between the lovers, some person in the house sneezed in such a manner as to attract the attention of the whole audience, and everyone knew the sneeze was artificial and derisive. Miss Cushman immediately stopped the dialogue, and led Miss Anderton off the stage, as a cavalier might lead a lady from a place where an insult had been offered her. She then returned to the footlights and said in a clear, firm voice, 'Some man must put that person out, or I shall be obliged to do it myself.' The fellow was taken away; the audience rose *en masse* and gave three cheers for Miss Cushman, who recalled her companion and proceeded with the play as if nothing had happened. . . ."

shocked at the spectacle of a woman playing the part and at the "un-sexing of the mind and heart" which the actress underwent in assuming the role. The great majority, however, were lavish in their praise. The peak in enthusiasm was reached by the eminent dramatist and experienced man of the theatre, Sheridan Knowles, who exclaimed in a letter to a friend:

I witnessed on Wednesday night with astonishment the Romeo of Miss Cushman! Unanimous and lavish as were the encomiums of the London press, I was not prepared for such a triumph of pure genius. You recall, perhaps, Kean's third act of Othello? Did you ever expect to see anything like it again? I never did; and yet I saw as great a thing last Wednesday night in Romeo's scene with the Friar, after the sentence of banishment. . . . It was a scene of top-most passion!—not simulated passion—no such thing—real, palpably real! . . . I listened and gazed and held my breath, while my blood ran hot and cold. . . . I particularize this scene, because it is the most powerful; but every scene exhibited the same truthfulness. . . . My heart and mind are so full of this extraordinary—most extraordinary performance—that I declare I know not where to stop or how to go on! Throughout it was a triumph, equal to the proudest of those I used to witness years ago, and for a repetition of which I have looked in vain until now. There is no trick in Miss Cushman's performance. No thought, no interest, no feeling, seems to actuate her, except what might be looked for in Romeo himself, were Romeo reality.[33]

Upon Miss Cushman's return to the United States, she played Romeo many times for the American public. Her success in the part continued to be great in spite of the minority opinion which deprecated the unnatural spectacle of a woman, in male costume, making passionate love to another woman. A photograph of Miss Cushman as Romeo shows a large lady wearing a skirt-like costume of knee length, a fancy sword, white hose, black slippers, and a cap set rakishly on a rather thick head of hair. The figure is broad of hip and full of bosom and, to the modern eye, looks precisely like what it is: a large woman of middle age masquerading as a man. Such a photograph, lacking the living personality and genius of Charlotte Cushman, conveys an unhappy impression of the Romeo which so many people found stirring and convincing.

Little fault can be found with either the photographs or the records of Miss Cushman's acting in her three greatest roles: Lady Macbeth, Meg Merrilies, and Queen Katherine. In the first two characters Miss

Cushman was memorable, but to most observers Queen Katherine was her masterpiece.

Although many reviews of Miss Cushman's impersonation of Queen Katherine survive, no better description can be found, perhaps, than the one contained in Clapp's *Reminiscences*. He reports that Miss Cushman made Katherine "a document in human flesh, to show how a heavenly minded humility may be a wellspring of dignity. . . ." In the early scenes of the play, Miss Cushman emphasized the grandeur and simplicity of the Queen. In the second act, Katherine's appeal to the King was given with an "unstudied eloquence" which Clapp believed could not be surpassed by any player. In the fourth act, after Katherine is deposed, Miss Cushman's "genius and art found their loftiest and most exquisite expression." It was here that the homely, discarded wife used the "sick" tone of voice which was so unique and so profoundly moving. Miss Cushman "avoided excess with the nicest art, but quietly colored the whole scene with this natural factor of pathos." As the scene progressed, she portrayed nobility, pity, magnanimity, weariness, and unearthly sweetness. Clapp writes that after her vision of the "blessed troop, . . . Her cry, out of the depth of her great storm-beaten heart, of infinite longing for the rest of paradise . . . will be recalled today by thousands of men and women, and at this mere mention the lines will echo and reecho through the chambers of their memories." As the scene continues, Katherine is aroused to queenly anger for a moment, then she relaxes and in a broken voice delivers the final messages of meekness and affection which are to be given to her daughter and her false husband. In these words of farewell, says Clapp, "the supreme point of pathos was reached. The throb and thrill of her voice . . . deserve never to be forgotten. . . . Throughout the final fifty verses of the scene, Miss Cushman caused Katherine's voice to grow gradually thicker, as the night of death closed in upon sight and speech. But Katherine's last command, that she 'be used with honour' after her death . . . was superb and majestic." [34]

In the opinion of her admirers, the whole art of this unusual woman and consummate actress deserves this same description: superb and majestic.

HELENA MODJESKA AND FANNY JANAUSCHEK

The classic school of acting, brilliantly exemplified in the United States by the careers of such early tragediennes as Mary Ann Duff and Charlotte Cushman, was carried on by two foreign born actresses who adopted America as their native land and who enriched the American stage by the artistry of their acting. Fanny Janauschek (Franziska Magdalena Romance Janauschek) and Helena Modjeska (Helena Modjeska Chlapowski, Countess Bozenta) were both stars when they came to this country. Janauschek, born in Prague in 1830, had been educated for the stage in Germany where, at the age of eighteen, she became the leading actress in Frankfurt-am-Main. She remained in Germany for twenty years, winning adulation and renown as one of the greatest tragediennes of Europe. Decorations and honors were heaped upon her by the princes and rulers of many states, so when she made her American debut in 1867 it was as a star of the first magnitude. Helena Modjeska, although an actress of equal fame in Europe, came to the United States as an immigrant rather than as a star. She had been born in Cracow, Poland, in 1840, and had received her first theatrical training in a small provincial stock company organized and directed by her husband. At the age of twenty-five she returned to Cracow and made a successful debut. Three years later she was invited to appear at the Imperial Theatre in Warsaw where, it is said, her triumph was the greatest ever known in the annals of that theatre. She was engaged for life as the leading lady of the Imperial Theatre and for seven years was the reigning actress of the nation. In 1876, nine years after Janauschek made her debut, Modjeska traveled to California with a group of other Poles to establish an ideal colony where she could regain her health, which was failing, and where she could escape the oppressive Russian regime in Poland. It was only when the colony failed that Modjeska returned to the stage, making an unheralded debut at the California Theatre in San Francisco in the year 1877. Her genius was recognized instantly; she appeared in New York before the year was over, and was soon accepted as the great actress she was known to be in Europe.

Modjeska made her American debut in English, which she had learned in a period of six months after her resolve to become an American actress. She never lost her foreign accent but, although some

of the critics felt that it marred the beauty of her delivery and the meaning of her lines, the public as a whole accepted her accent and considered it "a piquant sauce to her acting." Janauschek, on the other hand, made her first American appearances in German, sometimes performing with German speaking actors and sometimes with an English speaking company. Persuaded by Augustin Daly to learn English, she retired from the stage for a year, and reappeared in 1870 as an English speaking actress. Like Modjeska, she never lost her accent —it always remained "noticeably marked"—but, as was the case with Modjeska, the defect of an accent "in no wise hindered or even marred the dramatic effect of her acting." [35]

In the first years after her debut as an English speaking actress, Janauschek achieved such popularity and success on the American stage that, following a return to Germany, she decided to make her home in the United States. For some time her career prospered, but presently the public taste for her style of acting began to decline and she slowly sank in popularity and fortune. When she died in Brooklyn in 1904, she was both impoverished and forgotten. Modjeska, on the other hand, maintained her hold on the public to the end of her career. She played almost continuously from the time of her American debut in 1877 until her last tour in 1907, which she was forced to cut short because of ill health. She died in California two years later, on April 8, 1909.

Although there are many similarities in the careers of Fanny Janauschek and Helena Modjeska, and although they both acted in the classic tradition, their styles of performance were markedly different. Janauschek's acting was intense, powerful, heroic. She was the ideal Brunhilde or Medea. Modjeska's acting, in contrast, was graceful, symmetrical, poetic. She excelled in such roles as Viola, Rosalind, and Adrienne Lecouvreur. The contrasting styles of the two actresses might be compared to the differences between Charlotte Cushman and Mary Ann Duff.

The contrasting physical attributes of Janauschek and Modjeska were powerful factors in shaping their respective styles. Janauschek was short and thick of stature, her figure being described as "majestic," "stately," or "massive." Her voice, which had been trained for grand opera, was deep, vibrant, and flexible, capable of great range and power. Her face, like Charlotte Cushman's, was not beautiful, but it was strong and expressive. "Nature planned her for heroic parts," [36]

says Philip Hale, who reviewed her acting for the Boston *Journal*. Modjeska, in contrast to Janauschek, was slender and graceful of figure; she had a finely moulded face with a well-shaped nose, a sensitive mouth, and large, dark, luminous eyes. Walter Prichard Eaton described her face as "interesting, expressive, and gracious rather than conventionally beautiful," [37] but the majority of critics seem to disagree with him because she is usually praised for possessing "a rich, sensuous beauty." [38] Modjeska's voice was well modulated, musical, and flexible —in many roles impressing the hearers with the qualities of sweetness and refinement. However, when the situation demanded it, Modjeska could produce deep, strong tones—an accomplishment which was the result of careful training. Early in her career, she tells us, she worked an hour or more a day on exercises designed to add deep tones and strength to her voice.[39] However, she never acquired the power and range which were Janauschek's by natural endowment.

Perhaps Janauschek's outstanding gift as an actress was her tragic intensity. She preferred the great roles where power and passion are required, and she had the requisite strength to embody these roles. Her playing always suggested reserves of power and emotion which she could unleash at the required times with startling effects. John R. Towse recalls that she endowed her Brunhilde "with a majestic dignity and thoroughly heroic passion" and that by means of her "imperious carriage, fiery declamation, noble gesture . . . she realized the grandeur of the mythical personage." [40] He described her Lady Macbeth as "murderous in her ambition and energetic in the prompting of her husband to murder, but she loved him passionately and in her own tigress fashion, tenderly." [41] Philip Hale, in reviewing her acting, characterized Janauschek as "An heroic woman, suggesting primeval emotions; titanic in outbursts of passion." [42]

Although Janauschek was great in the delineation of strong feeling, she was capable of a wide variety of subtler effects. Her Mary Stuart was praised for the "depths of pathos" which she sounded, and her dual role in *Chesney Wold,* an adaptation of Charles Dickens' *Bleak House,* was tremendously admired for the range of emotions exhibited by the actress: she played both the "coquettishly sensual, maliciously sly, vitriolically minded French maid" and the "cold, haughty, arrogant Lady Dedlock, who, in spite of her caste and pride, had known passion, and shame as the reward of passion." [43]

In all her portrayals, Janauschek was superb in her use of facial ex-

pression and meaningful gesture. Her face and eyes mirrored and reflected the emotions she was portraying, and her slightest movement
added to the effect. Otis Skinner, who once acted Seyton to Janauschek's Lady Macbeth, recounts that when she turned on him in an
early scene of the play and opened her eyes wide, "it was the unmask-
ing of a battery" and it gave him "a distinct electric shock." [44] Towse
recalls that one of the finest strokes of Janauschek's acting in the banquet scene of Macbeth was her shielding the face of her husband from
his own terrible visions "while she turned upon the audience a face
bloodless, drawn, and lined with despairing pity." [45] Otis Skinner also
affirms that Janauschek "could be almost as eloquent with scarves and
hangings as in her voice and gesture" [46] and he recalls that she could
stop in the middle of a sentence to rearrange her draperies and make
the action both eloquent and dramatic.

Janauschek conveyed the illusion of complete absorption in her
roles. Spectators forgot that she was assuming a part and identified her
with the dramatic character she was portraying. Janauschek sustained
this illusion through technical mastery of her art; in actual fact, she did
not allow herself to be swept away by the emotions she was projecting.
She never forgot to exercise conscious, artistic control of her effects.
Otis Skinner, recalling the days when he was a novice in her company,
says: "I have seen old Madame Janauschek, after a tragic scene, turn
up stage, carefully arranging her drapery, and speaking a flippant aside
to a supporting player, while the audience sat spellbound." [47] It was
from this example, and others like it, that Skinner learned the important lesson that an emotional debauch on the part of the player "is not
an expression of feeling in acting"; the spectators are the ones "to
supply the emotion," the actor "supplies the suggestion." [48] Janauschek, in her prime, could supply the suggestion so powerfully that
audiences accepted her as the living embodiment of the emotions she
portrayed, and her fellow artist, Helena Modjeska, was moved to ex-
claim of her, "what genius! I wish I possessed half her powers." [49]

The tragic intensity which Janauschek brought to her roles was
sometimes achieved by Modjeska, but tenderness, pathos, and lyrical
romance were more characteristic of her acting. Again and again, spectators and critics alike were impressed by her grace, her daintiness, her
innocence and joy, her womanly sweetness, her delicate pathos, her
tenderness, her dignity and refinement, and her irresistible personal
charm. William Winter says that "to think of her now is . . . to remem-

ber a presence of tender, poetic beauty, winning refinement, and perfect grace." [50] Added to these traits was an illusive, haunting quality which was difficult for a spectator to define, but which was vividly perceived by all who watched Modjeska's acting. John Creahan called it "that minor-like chord which seems to be a part of her being, which we have never discovered in any other actress. . . ." [51] Walter Prichard Eaton characterized the same quality as "an indefinable atmosphere of poetic elevation." [52] Jeanette Gilder called it a "charm so subtle, that we can find nothing to criticize"; while Otis Skinner, after describing Modjeska as "a wraith of a woman with a voice whose every cadence contained a caress" said "I know no better way to describe her Camille than to say it had fragrance." [53] Skinner further states that Modjeska's personal magic made the immoral *Camille* so captivating that "mamas were apprehensive of its effect upon their sons."

In creating a part, Modjeska always used the intellectual approach. She had to have a clear mental picture of her characters and to understand the workings of their minds before she could embody them. "I never undertake a role unless I can see it before me," she declared.[54] Her careful analysis of her parts was, unquestionably, one reason for the symmetry and balance of her conceptions and for the even texture of her acting. Perceptive spectators were always aware of a logic and consistency in her portrayals. The early scenes in her plays presaged the final scenes, and in the course of the action her characters progressively fulfilled a design which showed that the actress had firm grasp of a fully developed concept of the character. As the critic of the Brooklyn *Eagle* said, it was "the exquisite harmony, and proportion of all her scenes to each other" which placed her "upon a higher plane than actors who have more power in single moments." [55]

Another probable reason for the symmetry and even texture of Modjeska's acting was her practice of learning the words and actions of her roles at the same time. She did not memorize lines and then create the action to accompany the words but, as Mrs. Otis Skinner records after rehearsing with her in a new comedy, Modjeska "never learns [her part] by rote, but always goes through it, 'suiting the action to the word, the word to the action.' Only at the very last did she run through the lines without the business." [56]

Modjeska, like Janauschek, had mastered the techniques of her art through careful study and long apprenticeship and, in general, her technical skill was greatly admired. However, she was sometimes criti-

cized for permitting the mechanics of her art to show and for performing in a cold and studied manner. On certain occasions the critics were disturbed because they detected the careful planning behind every physical movement and every vocal inflection of the actress. Such a reaction seems to contradict Modjeska's own statement that ". . . I really passed through all the emotions of my heroines. I suffered with them, cried real tears . . . during my whole career I could not succeed in giving a performance without feeling the agonies of my heroines." [57] If Modjeska were able to identify herself so completely with her heroines that she always relived their agonies, how could she have appeared cold and studied on certain occasions? The answer seems to be that although she may have aimed at close identification with her characters during each performance, she sometimes failed of inspiration—as every actor does on occasion—and so had to rely on a studied technique for her effects. As William Winter remarked, ". . . Modjeska, like all great artists, was not invariably able to liberate all her facilities and rise to her loftiest height," [58] but these occasional lapses do not negate the impression that Modjeska's acting usually exhibited a beautiful balance of technique and inspiration.

Although Modjeska and Janauschek differed in temperament and in certain aspects of style, they both had undergone the rigorous training and apprenticeship of the classic European theatre, and they both held the same lofty concepts of the nature of dramatic art. Janauschek was fiercely loyal to such great roles as Medea, Brunhilde, Lady Macbeth, and Queen Katherine. She scorned the sentimental, tearful roles of French melodrama, which grew so popular during her later life, and she refused to play such roles or to change her style to fit them. Only in her last years, when she had fallen on evil days, did she stoop to play such a part as Mother Rosenbaum in *The Great Diamond Robbery,* but she was ashamed of it and said that she "hoped Booth wasn't looking down on her." Modjeska, likewise, believed in producing on the stage only the distinguished dramas of eminent dramatists. She was a priestess who worshipped at the altar of Shakespeare and served him faithfully during her entire career. If she occasionally played such roles as Camille, it was the exception rather than the rule, and even then she ennobled the part and made it almost acceptable to so stern a Puritan as William Winter.

Modjeska and Janauschek, although foreign born and foreign trained, adopted the American stage as their own and enriched the tra-

dition of classic acting in this country by their high ideals of dramatic art and by their superb performances of many celebrated roles.

MARY ANDERSON

Modjeska and Janauschek, Duff and Cushman, all clearly belong to the classic school of acting. They learned their art in the richly varied school of the stock or repertory company. They played with actors steeped in the tradition of the European theatre. They appeared in Old Comedy, in Shakespeare, and in all the plays of the classical repertory. Their most famous roles were the great characters of the standard drama.

Mary Anderson belongs to the classic tradition, but with her the old order weakens. Her training was different and her repertory was limited. She chose her roles from the standard drama, but they were roles that required womanly emotion rather than tragic power. Her appeal was based more on personal charm than on dramatic genius. She was not of the school of feminine emotionalism most notably illustrated by Clara Morris, but neither did she achieve the same high plane as Duff and Cushman or Modjeska and Janauschek.

In many respects the career of Mary Anderson is unique and puzzling. She began as a star, and never acted anything but leading roles. She was adored by the public, but condemned by most of the critics. She was almost entirely self-taught, and lamented her lack of training, but she did nothing to acquire the instruction she needed. She retired at the height of her popularity, after only thirteen and a half years on the stage, and never resumed her career although she was offered fabulous sums to do so. She is undoubtedly remembered as a far greater actress than she actually was.

Mary Anderson became stage struck very early in her life. At the age of twelve, she was given a volume of Shakespeare's dramas and immediately was entranced. Shortly thereafter, she witnessed her first play, *Richard III,* starring Edwin Adams, and her fascination with the drama increased. Some time later Edwin Booth played in Louisville, Kentucky, Miss Anderson's home town, and the young lady's future was decided. After seeing him as Richelieu, Mary was so transported that she sat up all night planning a stage career for herself. When Booth's engagement ended, the girl made her mother a proposition.

She promised that if she were allowed to leave school and study by herself, she would work harder than she had ever done before. Since Mary had always been an indifferent student, her mother agreed to give the new arrangement a trial. Arming herself with Shakespeare's plays, Murdoch on Elocution, Rush on the Voice, and several other volumes, Mary retired to an attic room and there began her training as an actress. She studied her regular school lessons, and in addition she memorized the leading parts in a number of plays, including several male roles. With the guidance of Murdoch and Rush, she conscientiously exercised her voice and claimed that at the end of six months it had become so much fuller and stronger it was hardly recognizable. The system of self-instruction was so successful that Mary's mother allowed her to continue. Presently, Mary had a chance to read for the leading actor of the Louisville theatre and impressed him so favorably that later on he arranged an interview for her with Charlotte Cushman. In 1873, Mary traveled to Cincinnati to read for Miss Cushman, and received the encouragement that confirmed her determination to become an actress. Miss Cushman told the young aspirant that she had all the attributes for success, although her force and power would have to be modified. She advised the girl to take lessons from the veteran George Vandenhoff, and she ended by offering the unusual recommendation that Mary begin *at the top* and avoid the drudgery of small parts in a stock company. Whether the latter advice was sound will always remain a matter of dispute.

Acting on Miss Cushman's suggestion, Mary went to New York and took ten lessons of an hour each from George Vandenhoff. These lessons were the only dramatic coaching she ever received. They gave her instruction in elocution and stage deportment and were thoroughly unpleasant and disheartening to the young actress. She confessed that she "chafed and champed under the curb," but when the experience was over she said that it "had tamed, clipped, and done me general good, and I shall always be grateful to that capital actor and teacher of declamation for showing me the folly of attempting male characters, and for suggesting Juliet, Julia, Pauline, and Evadne as better suited to my sex and youth." [59]

Returning to Louisville, Mary studied and trained herself intensively for several months. When John McCullough, the popular tragedian, came to town, he was rather unwillingly persuaded to listen to her reading, but he liked it so well he recommended the girl to Mr. Barney

Macauley, manager of the Louisville theatre. This led to Mary's debut as Juliet on the stage of Macauley's Theatre, November 27, 1875, when the young actress was sixteen years old. The playbill for the evening does not give her name but merely lists her as "a Louisville young lady." The young lady made a great hit. The indulgent home town audience was delighted, and showered her with praise and encouragement. Three months later she again acted at Macauley's Theatre, playing the leading roles of Bianca, Julia, Pauline, and Juliet. Then followed short engagements in St. Louis, New Orleans, and Owensboro, all of which were popular and successful. Later in the year, which was 1876, John McCullough invited her to appear at the California Theatre in San Francisco, and here she experienced what she termed "the most unhappy part of my professional life." The critics were violent in their dislike. They declared that she could not act and, furthermore, that she seemed devoid of the capability of learning. But Edwin Booth was in the city at the time and after witnessing two of her performances, he comforted her and encouraged her, predicting that she was sure to succeed if she continued to act. The young tragedienne was further encouraged by a highly successful starring tour of the South and of Canada. In 1877, she made her debut in Philadelphia, Boston, and New York, and in these cities she won tremendous popular acclaim. For the next twelve years, until her retirement in 1889, she acted throughout the United States and England, winning public adoration wherever she went.

In many places her appearance created an absolute furor. During her first tour of the South she drew larger houses than any previous player except Edwin Forrest. Seats which ordinarily were priced at 75 cents frequently sold for $25. In Boston she played to audiences numbering four thousand, and the receipts for one day's matinee and evening performance were as high as $7,000. When she played at the Fifth Avenue Theatre in New York, the average weekly receipts were $9,000. In the British Isles her popularity was equally great. Her London managers were forced to turn away hundreds nightly from the theatre in which she appeared. In Edinburgh, on one occasion, she played to a house of £450, the largest sum ever collected for a single performance at the Lyceum Theatre. In Manchester she broke all existing box office records.

America was intensely proud of its beautiful young actress and lovingly named her "Our Mary." Her hold over the public is indicated by

the newspaper headlines which heralded her return to the United States in 1899. In that year, after living abroad in retirement for almost ten years, she decided to pay a visit to her homeland. Excitedly and adoringly, the newspapers proclaimed: "OUR MARY IS COMING." Then followed the headlines: "OUR MARY HAS ARRIVED"; "OUR MARY IS IN OUR MIDST"; "AMERICA GREETS ITS FAVORITE DAUGHTER."

The qualities which won public affection for Mary Anderson were the same qualities which made her acting acceptable. They were: an attractive personality, a beautiful face and figure, a rich, melodious voice, a fair measure of dramatic instinct, and an admirable intellectual earnestness. On these endowments her acting was built, and it developed only so far as the limitation of these resources permitted.

Miss Anderson's physical endowments were outstanding. Her maidenly charm was hard to resist. She brought a purity and refinement to the theatre that were greatly admired, while the youth, the earnestness, and the virginal appeal of her personality touched many hearts and attracted huge audiences everywhere. "Singularly charming," "a vestal virgin," "the ideal of youthful womanhood," were typical of the comments she evoked. Personal magnetism of this sort has always been an important factor in success on the stage. With Mary Anderson, it was a factor of paramount importance.

In appearance, Miss Anderson had a classic kind of beauty. She was tall, with a sensuously curved figure and beautiful white arms. Her features were regular, her forehead smooth and high, and her eyes expressive. Many observers compared the purity and symmetry of her beauty to the goddesses of Greek sculpture.

Miss Anderson's voice was magnificent. Towse says: "It was a rich contralto, thoroughly feminine, but uncommonly full, deep, supple, and melodious." William Winter points out that it was clear and penetrating and yet possessed a velvety richness which "delighted every ear." The critic of *The Spirit of the Times,* after watching Miss Anderson's debut as Pauline in *The Lady of Lyons,* expressed distaste for her looks—he thought she was somewhat large and awkward—but he was captivated by her voice. He wrote: ". . . when she spoke a little thrill went through the assemblage. It was one of those low, round, sympathetic voices that stir you, and its articulation was so perfect that every shade of vocal meaning reached your ear. . . . I can only find one word to characterize her voice, and that word is rich. . . . It was warm, sensuous, and loaded with vitality. . . ." [60]

Another asset which Miss Anderson brought to her acting was intellectual earnestness. She trained herself for the stage with a youthful zeal and sincerity which she never lost in later years. She always studied her roles as carefully as she knew how, and if she failed in profundity of conception it was not from lack of effort. The Edinburgh *Scotsman* for April 28, 1884, compliments her on her "unmistakable capacity for grasping the essential significance of a character" and says that her delineation of character leaves the impression of "a thoughtful conception wrought out with consistency." Incidentally, Miss Anderson must have appreciated this compliment, for in her *Memories* she says that the chief difficulty in creating a character is to make it "harmonious from beginning to end." [61] This is one of the very few comments on the art of acting Miss Anderson has recorded.

Another comment on Miss Anderson's intellectual capacity and earnestness—and apparently a very penetrating comment—is contained in the Liverpool *Daily Post* for November 24, 1884. In reviewing a performance of *Romeo and Juliet,* the paper says: "Though Miss Anderson's personal charms are great, her intelligence is not less remarkable. She has thought the character out thoroughly and ably. Nothing has been taken for granted. The very faults of her execution show how elaborate has been her conception of the part, line by line. And, on the whole, her judgment is fairly sound. She makes the great points surely —some of them finely; and even if she were not at all beautiful, her impersonation would be acknowledged a thoughtful and intellectual one."

It is undeniable that Miss Anderson had a fair measure of dramatic talent. Cushman, McCullough, and the leading actors of the Louisville theatre all recognized the power in her schoolgirl elocution. Audiences who watched her first efforts on the stage felt a force and a magnetism which her lack of technique could not conceal. The young actress had an ear for the rhythm and sonorities of the language; she sensed the conflict and emotions in the scenes she enacted; and she was able to project much of her own sensibility to an audience. In her early years on the stage she was universally acclaimed for the promise of dramatic power which was a tantalizing concomitant of her opulent physical endowments.

Youth and beauty, charm and earnestness, refinement and talent, can win great personal popularity but they cannot create great acting. Miss Anderson's achievements, though always praiseworthy and popu-

lar, were strictly limited. Her playing never overcame certain defects which were partly due to her temperament and partly due to her lack of professional training.

The fact that she taught herself, and never enjoyed the experience of an apprenticeship on the stage, left her deficient in many theatrical techniques. She was criticized for not knowing how to make effective entrances and exits. She was not sure of her movements and so she often appeared awkward and self-conscious. When a situation did not call for specific action, she had little knowledge of the supplementary business and byplay which might be used. Some of her best vocal efforts were spoiled by crude or faulty delivery. The results of her deficient training are summarized by William Winter as follows:

With a superb voice, here is a defective elocution; with a magnificent figure, here is a self-conscious manner in the attitudes; with a noble freedom and suppleness of physical machinery, here is a capricious gesticulation; with a full and fine sense of opportunity for strong and shining points, here is but an incipient perception of the relative values surrounding characters . . . ; with a brilliant faculty for stormy and vehement declamation, here, as yet, is an imperfect idea of the loveliness of quiet touches, verbal shading, and suggestive strokes; with a vigorous and often grand manner of address, here is a frequent lack of concentration in listening. . . .

In short, says Winter, the achievement of Mary Anderson is, as yet, "the triumph of an exceptional personality shrined in a beautiful person." [62]

It appears that Miss Anderson was fully conscious of the handicap of her deficient training. At one point in her *Memories* she says: ". . . it was painfully disheartening to find myself stranded for lack of technical knowledge. . . ." At another point she confesses: ". . . most of my work was, to me, sadly immature and inartistic, and I felt it would take years of practical experience to remedy my lack of early training." [63]

As Miss Anderson continued her acting she naturally acquired polish and a more mature technique. After she returned from her first tour of England, many American critics noted her increased smoothness and conviction. However, these virtues seem to be confined to a limited range of effects. Long familiarity with a few roles had given her a mastery of certain techniques and these she repeated in all her delineations. Her competence had a narrow range. *The New York Times*

for September 7, 1878, described her situation in these terms: "Her art is a graceful club—covered, indeed, with velvet, but swung always in the same circles." John R. Towse, the eminent critic of the New York *Evening Post,* is more direct and devastating. He says: "She had certain formulas in which she was proficient, and she applied them to corresponding types of situation with a deadly and unmodified re-iteration. In the mechanism of her art she never advanced beyond a moderate proficiency. What she had learned to do, she did well, but her executive ability was rigidly limited. It ceased to expand." [64]

Another defect in Miss Anderson's acting was its artificiality. The actress was often criticized for lacking sincerity and warmth. She seemed cold and mechanical. Her movements appeared to many observers to be obviously statuesque and self-conscious.* Her delivery often sounded false and oratorical. Certain of the London critics, noting the studied effects of her playing, thought she had been influenced too much by the artificial grandeur of the Kemble school, and urged her to learn spontaneity and abandon. Others felt that she lacked sensibility and should learn to feel the words she spoke and the situations she depicted. Many American critics were less kind. One of them declared that her acting made the stage "a hawking wilderness" and that it was as "untrue to nature" as it was "inimical to art."

A clue to Miss Anderson's artificiality can be found in the authorities on which she based her self-training. She used the texts of Rush and Murdoch for her instruction in elocution, and these teachers, however sincere their intentions, were always criticized for the stilted and unnatural delivery which their methods produced. Another of Miss Anderson's authorities was François Delsarte. Early in her career she discovered his system of movement and gesture. In her *Memories* she declares: "Always on the alert for improvement, I determined to study

---

* Miss Anderson's overuse of arm movements is noted rather amusingly in the following comment from *The New York Times* for September 14, 1878: "I don't mind telling you, *sub rosa,* that I think a dress which covers Miss Anderson's arms hampers and muffles her. She acts more with her arms than any other actress I ever saw. She is almost oratorical. She manifests the slightest emotion by a curvilinear sweep. When she is sad, something long and white and round flashes in the air. Her action thus resolves itself into a sensuous telegraphic system.

"A whole essay might be written on arms in the air. We have had the leg drama, why may we not have the arm drama?"

it. As far as mechanical exercises were concerned, it seemed to me perfect, for it overlooks no muscle or tendon of the face or body, and gives strength, suppleness, and control over them all. The rest of the system I afterwards found it best to discard." [65] It is likely that the young actress' use of the Delsarte exercises contributed to the studied effects of her stage movements.

A final defect in the acting of Mary Anderson—and it would naturally follow from the others—was her failure at identification. She could not transform her own personality and create the illusion of character. She was always the charming and beautiful Mary Anderson. Thus, writes Towse, "she reached her artistic boundaries when she learned to express herself freely and fully . . . and was only fully successful when her part fitted her like a glove." [66]

Miss Anderson's repertory of parts, compared to those of Cushman and Duff, was very small. She acted no more than eighteen roles during her entire career. But neither this limitation, nor any other, seemed to matter to her adoring public. They ignored the carping of the critics and flocked to see her. Even her severest judges, who would never rank her as a great or finished artist, recognized that she was wholly delightful in certain roles. Galatea in Gilbert's *Pygmalion and Galatea,* Parthenia in Holm's *Ingomar,* and Perdita in Shakespeare's *Winter's Tale* were accounted her most successful parts. All of them suited her temperament and personality. In all of them she could exploit her youthful beauty and her feminine charm. In these and other roles she gave delight to thousands of playgoers, and when she retired, before the age of thirty and at the height of her popularity, she was loudly lamented by audiences in both the United States and Great Britain.[67] Towse justly estimates her place in the history of the American stage when he writes: "Her beauty, her spotless character, her graciousness, her intelligence, her refined manner, and her unquestionable dramatic instinct and ability contributed greatly to the honor and glory of the American stage while she adorned it; but for all that she was never a great actress or a great artist." [68]

III

THE CLASSIC SCHOOL:
THE GENTLEMEN

THE YEAR OF 1835, WHICH SAW THE DEBUT OF CHARLOTTE CUSH-
man, also marked the professional debut of Edward Loomis Davenport, one of the most gifted actors in a notable company of four versatile tragedians. The oldest member of this group, James Murdoch, was
already established as a rising young player in 1835; the youngest of
the company, Lawrence Barrett, was not yet born; and the greatest of
the company, Edwin Booth, was a mere infant two years old. Yet despite the differences in their ages, these four distinguished performers
became intimately acquainted; their careers and lives overlapped, and
their combined brilliance illuminated the American stage for many
years.

All four tragedians can be grouped with the classic school of Mary
Ann Duff and Charlotte Cushman. They underwent the same arduous
apprenticeship; they held the same splendid ideals of the art of acting;
and they followed similar methods and practices with similar outstanding results. Of all their talents, perhaps their versatility was the most
impressive. They became principally renowned for their acting in serious drama, but they also excelled in comedy, melodrama, and romance. In fact, says Lewis Strang, "whether they were best in tragedy,
in comedy, or in romance, no man had the hardihood to declare." [1]

Edwin Booth, the most eminent, will be considered first.

EDWIN BOOTH

Booth was once asked why he always looked "insulted" when taking his curtain calls at the end of a play. He replied: "I have given my life to these great roles. I do not consider myself an entertainer! I am an interpreter. I reveal the soul of masterpieces. . . . They (the spectators) should bow their heads reverently before these poems I reveal to them." [2] The loftiness of purpose which Booth reveals in this statement is characteristic of his attitude toward the drama he loved and the high art of acting he served. He believed that only the best plays in the language should be given, and these in the noblest style of acting which could be achieved.

Edwin Booth was born in Belair, Maryland, on November 13, 1833, the fourth son of a famous actor father, Junius Brutus Booth, who was considered to be an arch rival of Edmund Kean. As a boy, Edwin had little formal education. For several years he travelled throughout the country with his gifted but eccentric father, serving him as a friend, guardian, and valet. Naturally Edwin's first conceptions of acting were gathered from his illustrious parent. The elder Booth was a fiery, impulsive actor who dazzled his audiences with mighty outbursts of emotion and thrilling vocal displays. Like the acting of Edmund Kean, the playing of the elder Booth was "a manifestation of the inspired intuitions, infallibly true and irresistibly sensational." [3] Inevitably, Edwin was influenced by this style, but the influence did not persist for long. The elder Booth died when Edwin was nineteen, and thereafter the young actor began the cultivation of an individual style which was to win him world-wide acclaim.

Edwin's debut on the stage was almost accidental. In 1849, while his father was performing in Boston, Edwin assumed the bit part of Tressel in *Richard III* in order to relieve the burden of an overworked prompter. Thereafter, Edwin occasionally played minor roles in his father's company. His serious apprenticeship began in San Francisco, where he had gone with his father in 1852. The elder Booth died later in the same year, but Edwin remained in the west until 1856, playing a great variety of roles in both tragedy and comedy. On one occasion during this period, he acted Richard III at a benefit, and so great was his success that the managers brought him out in other leading parts: Othello, Shylock, Sir Edward Mortimer, and Hamlet. However, he did

not continue long in these roles. When the first excitement over his achievement died down, his elder brother Junius, who was in the management of the theatre, San Francisco Hall, again cast him for parts in comedy, farce, and burlesque. "You have had a wonderful success for a young man," said Junius, "but you have much to learn." [4] Three times, it is said, the young actor went from star parts back to utility roles without making a protest. One of his hits as a utility man was scored as "Dandy Cox" in a Negro farce produced by the Chapman family. Another was his impersonation of Plume, a local celebrity. A more important comic hit was scored when he played Shakespeare's Petruchio for the first time.

Such training was of incalculable value to the young actor. It developed his confidence, his range, and his sensitivity to audience response. Booth testified to the efficacy of his early training in a letter to his daughter written in 1873. He said: "When I was learning to act tragedy, I had frequently to perform comic parts, in order to acquire a certain ease of manner that my serious parts might not appear stilted. . . ." [5] Later on, in a letter of advice to a young actor, he wrote:

A frequent change of role, and of the lighter sort . . . is the best training requisite for a mastery of the actor's art.

I had seven years' apprenticeship at it, during which most of my labor was in the field of comedy,—"walking gentlemen," burlesque, and low comedy parts,—the while my soul was yearning for high tragedy. I did my best with all that I was cast for, however, and the unpleasant experience did me a world of good. Had I followed my own bent, I would have been, long ago, a "crushed tragedian." [6]

After Booth's apprenticeship in California, he returned to the East and immediately scored an enduring triumph. Although his art was not yet fully developed, he was successful enough to be hailed as "the hope of the living drama." An interesting picture of his qualities at this time is given by William Winter, who writes:

Those who saw him at that time saw a young man of extraordinary grace, robust yet refined vigor, and a spirit ardent with the fire of genius. In the form of his acting there were defects . . . but it was felt that in the soul of Booth's acting there was spontaneous passion, imaginative power, —the nameless beauty which thrills, entices, and enables, and which is the inseparable attribute of inspiration. [7]

From the time of Booth's eastern debut in 1856, until his death in

1893, he remained a star of the first magnitude. At the peak of his career, after Forrest had passed his prime, he was universally acknowledged to be America's greatest tragic actor.

The major premise in Booth's artistic creed was his belief that art should interpret, exalt, ennoble. He felt, like Sir Joshua Reynolds (who had influenced the Kembles), that art should appear natural and illusionistic but not by copying all the literal details of life or by exalting the drab and the commonplace. Art should reveal the higher reality, the universal essence of people and problems. It should achieve naturalness by interpreting and elevating nature.

To achieve his high ideal in acting, Booth utilized all his physical and mental endowments. Edwin Forrest had been criticized for relying on the physical and omitting the spiritual. James Murdoch was accused of over-intellectualizing his roles. But Booth, it was claimed, had the ideal combination of mind, voice, and body. Winter said he was endowed with "profound and intense power equally of emotion and of intellect." [8]

There can be no doubt but that Booth was richly endowed by nature. His voice had superb quality, range, and carrying power. Towse thought that his tones lacked "the organ-like volume of Salvini's" but that Booth's voice was "a rich and beautiful instrument upon which he played with great skill." [9] Henry Austin Clapp describes his delivery in these words: "Faultless pronunciation, an enunciation distinct, clean, and clear, without formalism or apparent effort, an exquisite feeling for the sweetness of words, and a delicate sense of their relation to one another, unite to give his delivery exemplary distinction, and to make it a model and a standard." [10]

The revelation of mood and meaning which Booth could achieve through the tone of his voice alone is shown by the success of his acting in Germany. In 1883 he fulfilled a sensationally successful engagement at the Residenz Theatre in Berlin. He spoke his lines in English while the supporting cast used their native German. In spite of this, Oscar Welten in the *Taglishe Berliner Rundschau* wrote: "Booth is the best Hamlet I have ever seen. . . . You can understand . . . perfectly, although you may not know a single word that he utters." [11]

Booth was a man of average height, endowed with agility and excellent coordination. He was always praised for the eloquence of his movements. His slim build and graceful manner made him the ideal Hamlet but were a handicap to him in roles like Macbeth and Lear.

Towse believes that such characters require "massive grandeur in emotion" based on rugged physique and that Booth's firm intellectual grasp of the roles could not compensate for the advantage which physically powerful actors like Forrest and Davenport possessed in the crises of emotion.

When it came to intellectual and spiritual grasp, Booth was never equalled. His power to illuminate his characters through imaginative, poetic insight was his chief glory. Strang called him "the foremost poet of his profession," [12] and Winter declares: "the distinctive quality that illuminated his acting was the personal one of poetic individuality." [13]

The revealing, spiritual quality of Booth's acting was felt by everyone, but it was hard to analyze and describe. Henry C. Pedder, writing in *The Manhattan* magazine for April 1884, comes close to an acceptable explanation when he says:

In the portrayal of human passion it is possible to be at times strong and terrible and yet human. And in this essential human quality Mr. Booth never fails. There are times when the heroes and heroines of Shakespeare cry aloud in their pain . . . yet we never seem to lose the sense of a harmonizing unity which is always present, and which, when adequately interpreted, strikes the keynote to the deep, mysterious undertone of life.

Booth's penetrating, spiritual insight, Pedder thinks, always struck the keynote and thus was able to illuminate "the darkness of the moment by the calm beauty of a comprehensive consciousness." Winter says, "Poetry in acting cannot be carried further. . . ." [14]

Booth's style of acting was shaped by his natural gifts: a beautiful voice, a graceful though not a powerful physique, and a penetrating, poetic mind. The result was acting which excelled in consistency and lack of mannerism. His art was smooth, even of texture, and marvelously relaxed. It never depended for its effect upon tricks or explosions. Nat Goodwin, who specialized in burlesquing famous people, was once asked why he never tried an imitation of Edwin Booth. He replied: ". . . what's there to hang a caricature on? His art's round like a ball. . . . You can't be funny by exaggerating something that is not in the first place a little overdone. . . . No, I won't tackle Booth. I couldn't be funny caricaturing perfection." [15] George William Curtis, the editor of *Harper's Magazine,* had the same impression of Booth's art. In reviewing a performance of *Hamlet,* Curtis wrote: "His playing throughout has an exquisite tone, like an old picture. . . . It is not any

particular scene, or passage, or look, or movement, that conveys the impression; it is the consistency of every part with every other. . . ." [16]

The beauty and perfection of Booth's playing were the result, not only of great natural talent, but also of careful preparation and life-long study. He was a keen observer of nature and copied many effects from actual life. For example, in preparing for the mad scenes of *Hamlet* and *King Lear,* he visited hospitals and asylums all over the country and carefully studied the behavior of the patients. However, consistent to his artistic ideals, he did not literally reproduce the behavior he witnessed. Rather, he selected the ideas and elements which suited his purpose and incorporated only these into his characterizations.

His art was never static. He studied his parts as long as he played them, tirelessly probing for deeper meanings and more effective expression. He scrutinized the texts of Shakespeare and tested every possible interpretation of the lines. He studied all the commentaries, and personally consulted the best Shakespearean scholars. Observers noted that his Macbeth changed with the years, becoming more robust and massive as the actor grew more mature. His Lear mellowed and strengthened as the actor passed through the ordeal of personal suffering. His portraits of Richelieu and Iago gained in profundity from season to season. His Hamlet, always one of his best roles, grew and developed until it became his masterpiece. Clapp, in praising Booth's tireless improvement of his roles, says: ". . . through his shifting ideals, as they were embodied from year to year, the spectator could discern the extraordinary variety of treatment which Shakespeare's creations, because of their many sided humanness, will permit." [17]

Shylock was a character which challenged Booth all of his life. He acted the role during his first season in California and played it successfully many times after that. He portrayed Shylock "sometimes as a fierce money-catching old clothes dealer. . . . Sometimes as a majestic Hebrew financier and lawgiver; sometimes . . . in the just mean between the two extremes. . . ." [18] Yet Booth was never satisfied. As late as 1885, only eight years before his death, he was still studying the part. Writing to Harold H. Furness, he complains:

Shylock haunts me like a nightmare: I can't mount the animal—for such I consider Shylock to be.

I made an effort to get at him through G. F. Cooke's notes on his own acting of the part, but was surprised to find out how he was influenced by

tradition. . . . My effort was a vain one. I will try again before the "call boy" summons me to work.[19]

Two years later Booth again wrote to Furness, announcing joyfully:

Hold on! The Jew came to me last evening, just as I was leaving Pittsburgh and stayed with me all night, on the sleeping car, whence sleep was banished, and I think I've got him by the beard, or nose, I don't know which; but I'll hang on to him a while, and see what he'll do for me. I'll have his pound of flesh if I can get it off his old bones.[20]

Evidently Booth did hang on until he achieved a remarkable characterization, for at a late date the judicious Towse writes that Booth's skillful blend of prejudice, hate, avarice, dignity, craft, and abject defeat created a "perfect picture, finished to the nails." "One is inclined to apply to it," continues Towse, "the certificate given to old Macklin's 'This is the Jew that Shakespeare drew.' " [21]

As a means of gaining truth and conviction in his performances, Booth tried to "think himself" into his roles. He attempted, imaginatively, to *become* the characters so he could better understand how they felt. On nights when he could not sleep, he let the moods of his roles "flood through his mind." Before a performance, he tried to avoid distractions which might break his mood. One night in the "Tubal scene" of *The Merchant of Venice,* the actress playing Jessica watched the scene from the wings where Booth could see her. When the scene was over, Booth asked her never to do it again, explaining: "I go into that scene with a clear picture of Jessica. My own flesh and blood has betrayed me. . . . I am deserted. . . . I am hopeless—alone. I charge my voice with Shylock's agony, and then look up and see you—my daughter—standing before me, come back to me. My picture breaks up! I lose my scene!" [22]

Booth was, to some extent, a temperamental actor and at times depended too much on thinking himself into the proper mood of his role. If he could not summon the necessary emotion, his acting could be cold and formal; when thoroughly aroused, he could enthrall his audience with the beauty and fire of his performance.[23] However, it should not be assumed that Booth habitually "let himself go." There is abundant evidence to show that he had learned to exercise a critical, artistic control over his emotions at all times. "When I am enrapt in a character I am impersonating," he once said, "there seems to be another and a distinct individuality, another me, sitting in judgment on myself." [24]

It is sometimes said that Booth was indifferent to the quality of his supporting players and to the *mise en scène* in which he appeared. It is also said that he deliberately surrounded himself with inferior actors so that his own genius would shine more brilliantly. There is little evidence to substantiate these claims. During his career Booth acted with all the leading stars—Salvini, the Italian; Irving, the Englishman; Cushman, Janauschek, Modjeska, Barrett, and Murdoch—and he always welcomed comparison with them. When he built his own theatre and organized his own company, he surrounded himself with the best talent available. He dazzled New York with a series of sumptuously mounted and historically accurate Shakespearean revivals. As a manager and stage director, he spent endless hours planning, rehearsing, and supervising every element of his productions. Katherine Goodale, who toured with him in 1886–87, tells how he scrutinized every detail of her costumes and make-up, suggesting changes and improvements, and—on one occasion—making her completely re-do her make-up as one of the apparitions in *Macbeth*.

During the many years of his life when he was a traveling star, Booth was forced to accept whatever support was provided for him. Often both the scenery and the players were wretchedly poor, and then he had to carry the play by his own virtuoso efforts. If the support happened to be good, he took full advantage and responded eloquently to the actors around him. He could "listen" well, and he could respond to any emergency or challenge. Many stories relate how supporting players improvised new business or gave surprise readings to their lines just to see how skillfully Booth could meet the situation.

Among the great players of the nineteenth century, Booth was the finest artist; he was also one of the most versatile. It should be remembered that in his apprentice days, he made several hits in farce and burlesque; he acted the comedy roles of Petruchio and Benedick many times and kept them in his repertory almost to the end of his career; [25] he played Romeo, Don Caesar, and several other romantic heroes. But it was in the field of tragedy that his real versatility was displayed. He acted with striking success heroes and villains of every age and every temperament. In this field, says Strang, his art "was magnificently full and comprehensive. It encompassed the mental enigma of the intellectual Hamlet and the brutal animalism of the jealousy-mad Othello; it exemplified the very essence of evil in the diamond-like brilliancy of Iago, and the fullness of pitiable pathos in the . . . physically and men-

tally warped Bertuccio." [26] William Winter confirms this judgment when he says: "Booth can pass with ease from the boisterous levity of Petruchio to the height of Hamlet's sublime delirium. . . . Othello, the Moor, Iago, the Venetian, Richelieu, the French priest, and Don Caesar, the Spanish gallant—emblems of a great variety of human nature and experience—are all, as he presents them, entirely distinct individuals." [27] Booth's greatest creation, Hamlet, tended to obscure the numerous other characters which he could act with equal skill. Yet the discriminating critics were well aware of his versatility. Otis Skinner remarks: "With such gentleness as his it was singular that his greatest effects should have been made in parts of sinister and diabolic character—Iago, Richard, Bertuccio, Macbeth, Pescara, Shylock. . . ." [28] Katherine Goodale records how shocked she was when she saw Booth act Sir Giles Overreach for the first time and realized that her idol could create a horrifying portrait of "a monster without one redeeming trait." Booth himself enjoyed playing the villains. During long runs of *Othello*, he alternated between Iago and the title role, and confessed that he much preferred Iago. Skinner relates how Booth remarked to him one evening: "This fellow (Benedick in *Much Ado About Nothing*) is a lover . . . I loathe the whole pack of them. Always did. Even as a youngster I loved the villains." [29]

The art of Edwin Booth can be summarized as follows: Acting, to him, was not entertainment. It was the revelation of the beauty and wisdom contained in great dramatic poems. To interpret these masterpieces worthily, he tirelessly cultivated his talents. He realized that his physique was limited but that his voice was richly expressive and that his poetic temperament was capable of illuminating many roles. He built his technique upon these strengths, and was able to act a wide variety of parts with great distinction.

He learned from nature, but he never believed in a literal transcription of life. He repudiated extravagant displays of passion and theatrical trickery. He studied his parts continually, and sought to identify himself with his characters without ever losing control of his emotions. His playing, at its best, was harmonious, unmannered, and "round as a ball." "When he made his final bow," wrote Towse, speaking for a host of admirers, "the curtain—so far as the American stage was concerned—fell also upon the legitimate drama." [30]

JAMES E. MURDOCH

In the winter of 1830, Edwin Forrest was playing a star engagement in Augusta, Georgia, under the management of Vincent DeCamp. One morning at a rehearsal of *Damon and Pythias,* Forrest became so disgusted with the wretched performance of the actor playing Pythias that he stopped the rehearsal and refused to continue until a better actor could be found. DeCamp protested that the present Pythias was the best his company could offer. "No," said Forrest decisively, "he is not. You have a man named Murdoch in your company whom I once saw act in Philadelphia. Give the part to him." [31] This was the beginning of James E. Murdoch's rise to eminence in his profession.

The name of James Murdoch is not often linked with that of Edwin Booth, and yet they were leaders in their profession during the same years and held the same artistic ideals. Murdoch was twenty-two years older than Booth, yet each reached the zenith of his acting career in the third quarter of the nineteenth century. In 1853 they acted together in San Francisco. In 1856, while Booth was winning New York, Murdoch was conquering London. In the ensuing years, their paths crossed many times. Both men died in 1893 within a month of each other.

Murdoch was a far less gifted actor than Booth, and his name does not retain the luster of his younger colleague's. Yet Murdoch was the more influential of the two in shaping the style of American acting. Whereas Booth wrote no treatise on the art of the stage, and left no successors or disciples, Murdoch recorded his theories in three different books; [32] he became an eminent teacher of elocution; his methods and beliefs influenced the course of dramatic instruction throughout the whole United States.

Murdoch was born in Philadelphia in 1811, the son of a bookbinder and paper-ruler—a profession which young Murdoch was expected to follow. But early in his life he joined a local dramatic group and began the study of elocution under two popular instructors: Lemuel G. White, who had been the teacher of Edwin Forrest, and Dr. James Rush, the author of an influential book on elocution. In 1829, Murdoch forsook the book-binding business, much to his father's disappointment, and made his debut at the Arch Street Theatre in Philadelphia. Shortly thereafter, he joined the first of several dramatic

troupes which were to guide him during his apprenticeship. He worked steadily, studied diligently, and rose in his profession. In 1842 he retired from the stage for three years to lecture, to teach, and to write a book on vocal culture. He returned to the stage in 1845 and during the next fifteen years he established a national reputation as a versatile player who could perform excellently in a wide variety of parts. During this period, he starred for 110 consecutive nights at the Haymarket Theatre in London. When the Civil War began, Murdoch abandoned the professional stage and devoted his talents to entertaining Union troops in camps and hospitals. Following the war, he made a farewell tour of the principal cities, then retired to his farm in Ohio. His retirement was not absolute, for he reappeared on at least two occasions. However, more of his time between 1865 and 1893 (the year of his death) was devoted to writing and teaching than to acting.

Murdoch shared with Booth a noble conception of the art of acting. He believed the true actor possessed a creative capacity as great as any other artist. To be sure, fidelity to the poet's image must be uppermost in the actor's mind, and he is not free to distort or to improvise according to his own whim. Yet, to understand and grasp the poet's vision requires a "receptive power" which, Murdoch declares, "is by no means the passive and servile thing which a superficial criticism would make it . . ." and "it demands an assimilating and cooperative soul, a positive genius to develop it." [33]

Besides the "receptive faculty" the actor must have a genuine expressive faculty, for he must project the poet's image and convince the spectator of its truth and beauty. Murdoch believed that such a task requires a creativeness which is equal to the dramatist's.

In projecting a "vivid impress" of the poet's conception, an actor must keep his portrait true to nature. Like Booth, Murdoch believed that truth to nature is not to be found in harsh reality but rather in an idealized rendering of it. "The exaggerating attempts . . . to make everything in dramatic representation seem as real as possible," says Murdoch, "proceed upon the assumption that nature is found only in the actual and real, while the natural in expression lies ever nearest to the ideal." [34]

The confusing of individuality with human nature is another misconception to be avoided. Murdoch believed that too many actors cultivate mannerisms which are natural only to themselves, and in so doing destroy the illusion of dramatic character. An actor who exploits

his own idiosyncrasies under the mistaken notion that he is being natural "appropriates both the stage and Shakespeare to himself, and swallows them up in the inordinate self-esteem of the individual." [35] Murdoch cautions his fellow actors to remember that the plays of Shakespeare mirror the universal truths of nature, and if an actor is to communicate them, he must universalize his impersonations in such a way that he reaches the hearts of all his spectators.

In preparing a role, Murdoch believed—like the rest of the versatile tragedians—that careful study and sound scholarship were necessary. He also recommended the cultivation of the imagination. Without specifically naming the imaginative process, Murdoch states that an actor should "pass out of self consciousness" and should "take on the fresh and deep impression" of the poet's thought. In preparing a role, an actor must put himself "under the influence of a poetic spirit"; in so doing, "he loses self in the picturing of the mind," and by means of such "mental workings" a convincing portrayal emerges. The process of cultivating the imagination is further described when Murdoch states that an aspirant training for the stage "must study the profoundest forms of thought, the noblest moods of sentiment, the most vivid emotions of the soul, and dwell upon them until their full power and value are deeply felt, and their intensity glows into expression." [36]

It is interesting to note that Murdoch's belief in imagination seems to be the same as that which characterized the influential teachings of S. S. Curry some two generations later. Both men believed that imagination can be cultivated, and that when it is strong enough it can stimulate the voice and the body to effective expression. Murdoch, however, eventually adopted a system of voice cultivation which prescribed precise rules for vocal expression. In Curry's opinion, he thus cut off the inspiration of the imagination and substituted a system of dead mechanics.

Although an actor should cultivate a vivid, glowing imagination, he should not forget his own identity and try to become the character he represents. Murdoch believed that complete absorption in a role destroys the critical detachment which is necessary for the finest acting. Two other pitfalls which an actor should avoid are the extremes of either monotony or ranting. The impulse to strut and roar and posture is one of the "prominent vices" of the stage, says Murdoch. The other is sermonizing. An actor who seeks to avoid excess often becomes "a mere elocutionist and declaimer." "Words, words, words," says Mur-

doch, "form the sum and substance of his performance . . ." and "such a counterfeit presentation of a passion . . . falls down to the monotonous delivery of a sermonizing lecture or the recitation of a school boy's task." [37] The ideal player, Murdoch believed, sought a careful and honest revelation of the poet's vision through balance and proportion in his acting.

Despite his belief in balance, Murdoch had a definite bias toward the importance of vocal expression in dramatic art. He firmly believed that gesture and movement were decidedly inferior as means of expression. Early in his discussion of acting he says: "To . . . personal bearing, modes of action and gesture—I shall only refer in a passing way; such being the mere physical attributes of the performers, and of less importance to the public than the more intellectual qualities of voice and speech." [38] On rare occasions, Murdoch praised the effect of pantomime and physical action, as when he commended Garrick for having a body which was capable of "answering readily to the manifestations of fancy or will." [39] In general, Murdoch was so personally engrossed in the study and teaching of elocution, and he so despised the "pantomimic ranters" with whom he was often surrounded, that it is not surprising for him to have written:

The only way by which the reader or actor can reach the sympathies and affections of the human heart is through the magnetic power of the voice. When that delicate organism, which produces the broad effects and nice distinctions in kind and degree of expressive vocality, is subjected to true feeling and good taste and judgment, then may Shakespeare's creations be transformed from the dead letter of the printed page to that stage of action where they first drew breath and looked and moved as living things.[40]

In his own acting, Murdoch tried conscientiously to illustrate the validity of his theories. He studied his roles carefully and cultivated his own powers of imagination. He attempted, creatively, to idealize and universalize the characters he played and thus to avoid the literalness of commonplace reality. He practiced a critical self-possession even in scenes of violent passion, and he shunned both rant and verbosity. Above all, he cultivated the expressive powers of his voice and developed an elocution which, at its best, was a delight to the listener.[41] Alfred Ayres ranked him fourth in achievement after Forrest, Cushman, and Edwin Booth. Indeed, says Ayres, "If versatility would make greatness, he would rightfully have been counted great." [42]

Like Booth and the other versatile tragedians, Murdoch acted successfully in comedy, tragedy, and romance. The great tragic roles—such as Hamlet, Macbeth, and Othello—were all popular features of his repertory. His portrayal of romantic characters like Claude Melnotte in *The Lady of Lyons* was widely acclaimed. In the roles of artificial comedy, Murdoch was even more successful. Many critics affirmed that he had no peer in such parts as Young Mirabel in *The Inconstant,* Charles Surface in *The School for Scandal,* Rover in *Wild Oats,* Don Felix in *The Wonder,* and Vapid in *The Dramatist.* He acted Benedick and Petruchio with great credit, but he was more praised in roles where he could use his gift for artificial comedy.

All of Murdoch's acting, from farce to tragedy, was characterized by sincerity, intellectuality, imagination, and finesse. Early in his career, *The Spirit of the Times,* New York, praised his portrayal of Hamlet in these words:

The pervading quality of the performance was grace and propriety of conception and delivery: relieved by electric flashes on passages of a more elevated character. All our contemporaries concur in acknowledgement of his manly bearing, the beauty of his voice, and his admirable reading. . . . A performance freer from rant, more entirely with good discretion throughout was never presented.[43]

More than thirty-five years later, when Murdoch was seventy-one years old, Otis Skinner saw him play the same role and he wrote:

No longer able to look the Prince of Denmark, he yet contrived to convey in his bearing much grace and courtliness, and his reading was a delight. In watching his Hamlet from the wings, I found myself shutting my eyes . . . leaving my ear to drink in the clarity and music of his elocution.[44]

Murdoch earned high rank among nineteenth-century players for the distinction and versatility of his acting. He also won renown as a pioneer in the teaching of elocution. His long activity and wide influence in this sphere deserve additional comment.

Murdoch acquired a lively interest in the study of elocution from his first teacher, Lemuel G. White. Shortly thereafter he came under the influence of Dr. James Rush and eventually became a devoted disciple of the Rush theories of vocal instruction.

In 1827, Rush had published a work entitled *The Philosophy of the Voice.* It was a ponderous book, long, complicated, and full of scien-

tific terminology. Many people found it incomprehensible. A few, like Murdoch, saw beneath the verbiage an exciting new approach to the art of elocution. The young actor studied the text avidly and discussed its principles with the author. The theories it advanced fitted his own predilection and practice. He came to believe that it was "the most complete system ever offered to the student of elocution." A burning ambition rose in him "to see these principles universally recognized and accepted in their integrity." The fulfillment of this ambition accounts for his temporary retirement from acting in 1842 and for his subsequent interest in teaching and writing.[45]

The Philosophy of the Voice presented a theory and a method which, Murdoch felt, had never before been successfully outlined. Among the contributions of the book were a scientific terminology for speech instruction, and a system of notating speech sounds. The need for such a system was keenly felt by many actors. Elocution teachers and dramatic coaches were accustomed to describing the effects they wanted in general terms like "fervent expression," "modulation," "tone of feeling," etc. Such vague instruction led generally to unsatisfactory results. Rush declared:

> We seem not to be aware that no describable perceptions are associated with such terms until required to illustrate them with some definite discriminations of vocal sounds. . . . The studious inquirer has long wanted a language for the meaning of the voice he has always felt. . . . The few and indeterminate designations of the modes of the voice in reading, compared to the number and accuracy of the terms in music, imply the different manner in which ease has been cultivated.[46]

Rush, building on the earlier work of John Walker and Thomas Sheridan, developed a comprehensive system of nomenclature and notation which defined and labeled every speech sound. The system employed the musical staff to indicate pitch, and symbols to represent each syllable, its duration in time, and the direction and variation of its pitch. Additional symbols represented metrical pauses, heavy and light accents, and a variety of other vocal effects. Also, an extensive descriptive vocabulary was used preceding each selection, so that directions like the following were found: "Moderate movement. Natural Quality. Middle Pitch. Gentle Force. Waves and Intervals of a Second and Third" [47] or, "Slowest Movement. Low Pitch, Slightly Aspirated. Suppressed Force. Median waves. The Refrain here is Semitonic." [48]

Rush also advanced a "theory of correspondence" between the inner feeling of the performer and the vocal sign. This theory, which Murdoch admits was not entirely new but was scientifically explored by Rush for the first time, was based on observable physical phenomena. Thoughts, sentiments, passions—said Rush—affect the muscles of the body, among them the vocal muscles. Thus, in natural speaking the tone of the voice is automatically altered to correspond to the inner feelings. Murdoch asserts that:

. . . the great fundamental principle of Dr. Rush's philosophy of spoken language, and overlooked in anything like scientific detail . . . in former systems, was that *every state of mind* had its corresponding vocal sign in *some of the varied forms of pitch, force, time, and quality.* These vocal signs he observed and recorded, not only . . . with reference to their individual form and character, *but classified them on the principle of this natural relation to the mental phenomena of which they are the audible* indication.[49]

Rush's system was not intended to constitute an arbitrary, iron-clad scheme. The "scoring" of a speech or a poem according to this system was simply a means of stimulating and inspiring the student. "The principles which the notations illustrate," says Murdoch, "are positive, but the notation itself only suggestive of the means of attaining the desired end of natural effect in the utterance of premeditated language." [50] Also, the notations were to serve the purpose of giving the student "command, through the practice it affords, over the different vocal movements it indicates." [51]

Murdoch firmly believed that the Rush system of elocution was the only "true method." S. S. Curry, and other teachers of a later generation, found the system hopelessly mechanical and productive of pedantic, artificial expression. However, before the system was abandoned, it exerted wide influence throughout the country. Murdoch used it to train many actors who played with him or sought formal instruction from him. His text book was used for years in American schools and colleges. Some of the terms he employed and techniques he advocated still appear in manuals of dramatic instruction. Many of his pupils gained prominence in the field of education and profoundly influenced the development of speech training in American universities. Among the most noted of his students were Robert I. Fulton, who became Professor of Elocution and Oratory in the Ohio Wesleyan University,

Interior of the Park Theatre, New York, as painted by John Searle in 1822. Courtesy of the New York Historical Society, New York City.

Edwin Forrest at the age of twenty.
Portrait by Samuel Lawrence.

Mary Ann Duff.
From the Harvard Theatre Collection.

(*left*) Exterior of the Park Theatre, New York, in 1799. This theatre was the leading playhouse in New York for almost fifty years.

John McCullough.

Fanny Janauschek in 1894. From the
Ross Theatre Collection, University of
California Library at Berkeley.

Mary Anderson.
Photograph by Bradley and Rulofson.

Edwin Booth as **Richelieu in Bulwer-**Lytton's play. From the Ross Theatre Collection.

Charlotte Cushman.
(top) From the Harvard Theatre Collection. *(bottom)* From the Hoblitzelle Theatre Arts Library.

Edwin Booth. Portrait by John Singer Sargent. Courtesy of the
Walter Hampden Memorial Library at The Players, New York
City.

(right) Anna Cora Mowatt as Rosalind in *As You Like It*. From the Harvard Theatre Collection.

Lawrence Barrett as Count Lanciotto in Boker's *Francesca da Rimini*. From the Ross Theatre Collection.

(right) James E. Murdoch in Kotzebue's *The Stranger*. From the Ross Theatre Collection.

Mrs. Leslie Carter. From the Theatre
Collection, University of California Library at Berkeley.

Fanny Davenport.
Photograph by Sarony.

Clara Morris, "Queen of Spasms."
From the Ross Theatre Collection.

Thomas C. Trueblood, who became Professor of Elocution and Oratory in the University of Michigan, S. S. Hamill, who became Professor of Rhetoric, English Literature, and Elocution first at Illinois Wesleyan University and later at Illinois College, and Professor John R. Scott, who became head of speech instruction at the University of Missouri.

James E. Murdoch, as actor, teacher, and writer, demonstrated an impressive range of talents and, like Edwin Booth and the other versatile tragedians of his day, enriched the offerings of the American Theatre.

EDWARD L. DAVENPORT

Edwin Forrest is said to have called E. L. Davenport "the best actor on the American stage." [52] Lewis Strang described him as "entitled to rank next to Edwin Booth, Charlotte Cushman, Edwin Forrest, and William Warren, as the most brilliant product of the stage in the United States." [53]

This gifted player, whose very versatility tended to obscure his brilliance, was born in Boston in 1815 and twenty years later made his professional debut in Providence, Rhode Island. He served a distinguished apprenticeship in theatres up and down the east coast for more than ten years until, in 1846, he became the leading man of Anna Cora Mowatt, who had made her sensational debut only the year before. In 1847, Davenport accompanied Mrs. Mowatt to England and remained there for seven years. During the first few of these years, Davenport remained with Mrs. Mowatt—much to the satisfaction of that talented lady, who praised him in these words:

His moral character, his unassuming and gentleman-like manners, his wonderful versatility and indisputable talents, caused him to be selected as the person who was to travel with us during my second year on the stage. Upon his selection, every succeeding month and year gave us new cause for congratulation. The prominent position he has since won upon the English stage, and the honors he has received from fastidious English audiences, are just reward of intrinsic and *unostentatious* merit.[54]

Mrs. Mowatt might also have mentioned the fact that he *looked* like a leading man. He possessed an unusually distinguished face, a graceful walk and carriage, and a voice which was soft and musical but capable of great range and power. All his photographs, both as a young man

and as an old one, show him to be handsome, aristocratic, and manly.

In January, 1851, while he was still in England, Davenport was chosen to support the eminent English tragedian, William Charles Macready, in a series of farewell appearances and won high honor for himself. Shortly afterwards, he acted with James H. Hackett, who was then performing as a star.

Davenport returned to the United States in 1854 and made his reappearance at the Broadway Theatre in New York. During the ensuing months and years, he acted everything from Bill Sykes to Hamlet and from Sir Lucius O'Trigger to Othello. On a single evening he is known to have presented three acts of *Hamlet,* one act of *Black-Eyed Susan,* and finally a farce in which he impersonated a stage-struck Yankee.

On several occasions during his career, Davenport tried his hand at managing a theatre but he was never very successful. Although he possessed both energy and taste, he also possessed the sort of liberality which made him generous to everyone but himself. In casting a play, he first took care that all members of the company were satisfied with their parts and then, if there was anything left, he assigned it to himself. Often he succeeded in making these minor studies noteworthy, but his constant minimizing of his own ability had a deteriorating effect on his reputation. However, he scored many triumphs during the years of his maturity. His career culminated in the famous production of *Julius Caesar* at Booth's Theatre in 1875–76, in which Davenport played Brutus, Lawrence Barrett played Cassius, and Frank C. Bangs played Marc Antony.

It was during the long run of this play that Davenport demonstrated once again the consideration and thoughtful kindness for others which always endeared him to his fellow actors. He was suffering so painfully from rheumatism in one of his hands that he could not bear anyone to touch it and yet, it is said, he concealed his suffering with genial gaiety and had a good word and a pleasant smile for everyone around him. "His kind and amiable disposition," wrote one of his fellow actors, "endeared him to his associates, while his great abilities as an actor won their unbounded admiration." [55] Another actor wrote: "In all the relations of life, he was a gentleman, courteous in every sense to those with whom he came in contact, walking the earth as if he loved it, and ever ready to extend the right hand of fellowship to anyone who sought his aid. . . ." [56]

The season of 1876–77 was Davenport's last. During that year he

acted many roles, among them Richard III, Edgar in *King Lear,* and a sturdy blacksmith in *Dan'l Bruce*—again demonstrating the wide versatility he possessed. He died on September 1, 1877, but his name was not soon forgotten. His beautiful daughter, the talented Fanny Davenport, achieved great fame as an actress of the emotionalistic school.

Davenport's acting was always praised for its smoothness and polish. He studied his roles carefully before enacting them, with the result that every detail of characterization and every aspect of motivation were revealed in his performances. In his hands a role had symmetry and balance from first to last, and was always presented with grace and repose. He didn't aim to be sensational or to win the applause of his audience. All his effects were governed by good taste. His elocution was always exemplary. H. D. Stone summarizes his excellences in these words:

He does not seek to take his auditors by storm; he is content with *winning* them. In his impersonations, calm judgment controls his impulses; his action and declamation are never measured and gauged by popular applause, but regulated by his own correct taste. He appears utterly unconscious of the presence of his audience. . . . His conception of character, matured in his closet, is produced upon the stage as he was learned to understand it. He leaves nothing to chance-thought. Of course, like every man of genius, he is not insensible or unaided by the inspiration of the hour. In reviewing any one of his delineations one is struck with its harmony. None of its local lights and shades will be found to have been exaggerated, but the various parts appear so duly balanced that the impression left upon the mind is precisely that produced by a well-drawn, well grouped, and well colored picture.[57]

On certain occasions during his career, Davenport was criticized for lacking fire. One critic said that his Hamlet was "tame" and "never excited any real emotion." Clara Morris, who saw him in his last years on the stage, said that his followers "delighted in the beautiful precision and distinctness of his reading" of the part of Hamlet, but, she said, "He always seemed to me a Hamlet cut in crystal—so clear and pure, so cold and hard he was." [58] Other critics disagree with these estimates and praise Davenport for the power and fire he could display when he felt it was appropriate. One of his most memorable roles was that of Sir Giles Overreach in *A New Way to Pay Old Debts*—a character which, early in his career, he had seen acted by the elder Booth. Dav-

enport performed the part off and on during his whole career and is said to have been peerless in the role. His performance had force, intensity of passion, subtlety, malignancy, and furnished a "terrible picture of the grasping, avaricious father" whose final collapse was played with an intensity which was "almost fearful." Mrs. John Drew, a notable actress herself and the mother of a whole line of actors, declared that Davenport, as Sir Giles, "surpassed even the Elder Booth, and to those who remember that great actor nothing can be said beyond that." [59]

Davenport was universally praised for his great versatility, but this gift was, to some degree, a handicap. Because he seemed to be good in everything, nothing stood out as memorable—at least in the mind of the general public. Clara Morris explained the apparent contradiction by saying that Davenport

. . . was wonderfully versatile, but though versatility is a requisite for any really good actor, yet for some mysterious reason it never meets with great success outside a foreign theatre. The American public demands specialists —one man to devote himself solely to tragedy, another to romantic drama and duels, another to dress-suit satire. One woman to tears, another to laughter, and woe betide the star who, able to act both comedy and tragedy, ventures to do so; there will be no packed house to bear witness to the appreciation felt for such skill and variety of talent.[60]

The hallmark of Booth, Murdoch, Barrett, and many lesser players was versatility, yet their merits received greater acclaim than Davenport's—despite the opinion of Clara Morris. But perhaps within a wide range of parts they specialized to a degree—and certainly, also, they were less self-effacing than Davenport.

Whatever the reasons, E. L. Davenport never received the rank and the acclaim which seem rightfully to belong to him. Yet the record of his achievement is proof that he thoroughly merits the high praise given him by his discerning followers.

LAWRENCE BARRETT

Perhaps the least gifted but certainly the most persevering of this group was Lawrence Barrett. His great success in the theatre is a testament to the efficacy of consuming ambition, unremitting industry, and stubborn intelligence. He began his career ignorant and penniless,

without education or influence, and possessed of only the meagerest physical and vocal equipment. Yet he became an outstanding actor, the leading scholar of the American stage, and a man whose "lasting influence on the theatre of this country was far beyond that of Davenport and nearly equal to that of Booth." [61]

Barrett was born in Paterson, New Jersey, April 4, 1838, the son of ignorant Irish immigrants. At the age of ten he ran away from home. At the age of fourteen he became call boy at the Metropolitan Theatre in Detroit. Fired with ambition to become an actor, he began his theatrical education by studying the only book he possessed—a battered copy of Webster's Dictionary. He practically memorized the dictionary, and he literally memorized the plays of Shakespeare as soon as he could lay his hands on them. He plagued the manager to give him bit parts, and whenever he received one, performed with an awkward intensity which was ridiculed by the rest of the company. But he persisted, and with no encouragement except his own ambition and effort, he developed slowly and fumblingly. After two years he secured a humble place in a Pittsburgh stock company. He went from here to New York—where he almost starved to death before any manager would give him a chance. Finally, in 1857, at the age of nineteen, he obtained an engagement at Burton's old Chambers Street Theatre and was successful enough to win a permanent position. With passionate zeal and single-minded intensity, he studied dramatic literature, disciplined his mind and body, exercised his voice, and pushed his claims with every friend and every manager. He rose slowly but surely, fiercely proud of his accomplishments, and keenly jealous of those who were more talented or successful than himself. He eventually became a leading man, then a star, and—as a climax to his career—arranged the famous partnership with Edwin Booth, during which, as manager and co-star of the combination, he achieved the prestige of equal billing with America's greatest tragedian. His career ended on March 18, 1891, when he insisted upon filling an acting engagement even though he was suffering from pneumonia. He collapsed during the performance and died the next day.

Barrett was a man of medium height and slight physique. His principal physical grace was "the curve in his back," of which, says Otis Skinner, he was "quite vain." [62] His features were not handsome, but his deep-set, burning eyes gave his face an intensity which reminded Skinner of a monk. The voice of the actor was not naturally full and

rich, but assiduous effort gave it strength and flexibility. By the time Barrett had reached his prime, his voice was described as an instrument "of unusual range . . . compelling and powerful" in its effect.[63]

The lack of schooling and cultural training in his early life gave Barrett a deep reverence for scholarship. As soon as he gained access to books, he became a diligent student and soon acquired a reputation for wide reading and sound learning. Like Booth, Murdoch, and Davenport, he studied his roles thoroughly, acquainting himself with all the history and commentary associated with them. No part was ever undertaken without intensive and painstaking research, a research which included study of the broad backgrounds of the drama as well as scrutiny of the individual role. So widely and thoroughly did Barrett venture in the realms of scholarship, that before he died he was credited with being an authority on the history of the stage, an expert in every branch of English literature, and "pre-eminently the scholar of the American theatre."

Barrett's zeal for improvement and his arduous self-training could not compensate, however, for limited endowments. His acting never achieved the poise, the grace, and the naturalness of a great artist. It was always studied and somewhat artificial. Otis Skinner, who acted with Barrett many times, thought he was "one of the most mannered men the American stage ever produced," [64] and wondered where in the world he had ever acquired such a style. Another critic said he performed like a scientist, solely with his brain, revealing a character "with the watchful precision of a botanist at work on a delicate flower." [65] Because the mechanism of his art was always apparent, he rarely seemed spontaneous and he never assumed "the convincing dash of a master."

Barrett's elocution was the most artificial element in his acting. In the actor's anxiety to perfect himself, he practiced his elocution assiduously, but always in the direction of precision and elegance. The result was pedantic enunciation and a monotonous, deliberate reading of the blank verse. Alfred Ayres says: "He was a chanter, a sing-songer; his mind was always more occupied with the tones he was making than with the thoughts he was speaking." [66] Barrett, incidentally, was unconscious of the way he sounded. The jibes of the critics offended him, and he is said to have remarked stiffly: "It would not become me to say that they are wrong; I will say this however: if my elocution is as bad as they say it is . . . I am not conscious of it." [67]

In addition, Barrett lacked a warm, attractive stage personality. He commanded respect and admiration but he very rarely inspired affection. Audiences were not charmed and warmed by his personality as they were by actors like Booth and McCullough. Without a popular play and strong support, Barrett could not draw large crowds to a theatre. In the season of 1871–72, for example, he starred in *Man O'Airlie* for over four weeks at Booth's Theatre, with a resultant loss to the management of $8,500. Barrett was angered when the play was withdrawn, and even more angry when Edwin Booth tried tactfully and sympathetically to point out his deficiencies.[68]

But the acting of Lawrence Barrett was not without its excellence. All his roles were illuminated by two virtues: intelligence of conception, and earnestness of purpose. The actor's studious analysis of his characters always resulted in a coherent and logical delineation which revealed appreciation of the dramatist's purpose and a firm grasp of his design. Intelligent treatment of this sort was recognized by Barrett's audiences and appreciated by them. Also, they never failed to perceive the earnestness in his work. The actor was passionately devoted to his profession and fiercely ambitious for fame and fortune. In pursuance of his goals, he acted with a sincerity and an intensity which raised many a performance from mediocrity to success. Alfred Ayres wrote: "His position as a player was due mainly to his ability to be in earnest, a faculty that often blinds the millions to every shortcoming. . . ." [69]

Barrett's acting, although mannered and formal, was not without its moments of excitement. When a scene demanded passionate display he was capable of rising to the challenge and thrilling an audience with vehemence and force of feeling. Sometimes these displays sounded calculated; at other times they appeared to be the natural overflow of powerful emotions. Otis Skinner tells us that despite the artificiality of his style, on occasions "There was a tempestuous, torrential character . . . in many of his parts that swept his audiences into enthusiasm" and that sometimes he displayed a "high pitch of nervous intensity" that caused him to "shoot through his parts like a race horse." [70]

During his career, Barrett acted all the great Shakespearean roles such as Hamlet, Macbeth, Othello, etc., and in these he was considered more than adequate. With Booth he played "seconds," appearing as Horatio, Macduff, Iago, etc., and was highly successful. Perhaps his outstanding characterization was that of the "lean and hungry" Cassius in *Julius Caesar*. Barrett's looks and temperament exactly fitted this

role. Many spectators felt that the tense, ambitious Cassius had actually come to life when the tense, ambitious Barrett strode onto the stage. The actor's skill at presenting "stinging, biting . . . passion, . . . anger suppressed but struggling for an outlet" [71] found ample scope in the part of Cassius, and won high critical acclaim for the performer.

Barrett's acting was always overshadowed by the peerless art of Edwin Booth,[72] but Barrett contributed to the American theatre in other ways. He demonstrated superior ability as a manager and promoter: he had a sharp sense of business, he cared about details, and he was a tireless worker. During his lifetime, he not only promoted himself, but he also promoted the cause of good drama throughout the United States. He hated what was cheap and sensational on the stage, and tried to maintain the popularity of the classic repertory. He encouraged new playwrights and sponsored the first presentation or the revival of many plays which he considered to have literary and dramatic merit. His revival of Boker's *Francesca da Rimini* was noteworthy, and he could take credit for many other successful presentations such as *Yorick's Love, Pendragon,* and *Ganelon.*

One of his most valuable contributions to the theatre was his creation and management of the Booth-Barrett combination in the 1880's. By this time, Edwin Booth, worn out physically and emotionally, was in the closing years of his career. The great tragedian had been battling personal tragedy and business disasters for more than thirty years, and now was too tired to care about fame or reputation. His acting had become empty and mechanical. The form was there but the fire was gone. Barrett realized that the fire was not quenched but merely smouldering and, under favorable circumstances, could flare up again—much to the profit of anyone who stoked it. He proposed to stoke it himself, as a service to American drama and to himself, and so he arranged a partnership between himself and Booth—in which he assumed the complete responsibility of business and artistic management, while Booth had no obligations or worries except his own acting. Barrett became, as Clara Morris has described it, the "agent, manager, stage-manager, friend, co-worker, and dramatic guardian angel" of Edwin Booth, and "all he asked of him in return was to act." [73] The results were epochal. Booth responded with a splendid revival of his old-time genius; Barrett reaped high honor and profit for himself; and American audiences enjoyed an Indian summer of great drama greatly acted, the like of which is rarely seen.

For his services in this undertaking, and for his many other contributions to the well-being and high standing of the American theatre, Lawrence Barrett well deserves the tribute written by William B. Laffan: ". . . Mr. Barrett has done more than anyone else in America to present the higher drama under conditions of artistic completeness, and to stimulate the literary and artistic development of a stage impressed with his own character and taste." [74]

There were other capable actors, more limited in talent and less eminent in position than Booth, Murdoch, Davenport, or Barrett, who played the same roles and demonstrated to a lesser degree the same range of versatility. Among the actors who belong in this group are several who made noteworthy contributions to the American stage.

GEORGE C. VANDENHOFF

Son of an eminent English actor of the Kemble school, George C. Vandenhoff made his American debut in 1842 and remained in this country, except for occasional visits to Great Britain, until his death in 1884. Vandenhoff's first role in the United States was Hamlet and in the part he was praised for grace and dignity, for correctness of delivery, and for the poetic elegance of his style. In the other parts he played, such as Richard III, Hotspur, Marc Antony, Mercutio, Macbeth, Benedick, and Claude Melnotte, these same excellences were extolled, and, at the same time, a certain deficiency of passion and lack of fire were noted. Evidently, refinement and polish were his forte while strength and power were somewhat lacking. His feeling for refinement and his disappointment at what he considered to be a decline in taste for good drama led him to withdraw from regular stage appearances in the middle years of the 1850's, after which he devoted his life to teaching elocution and to reading Shakespeare in public. One of his pupils was Mary Anderson who took ten lessons from him, the only instruction in dramatic art she ever received. But Vandenhoff returned to the stage on occasions; one of his last appearances was in 1874 when he played Macbeth to Charlotte Cushman's Lady Macbeth in Miss Cushman's farewell appearance in New York City.

EDWIN ADAMS

Edwin Adams (1834–1877), a native-born American, is remembered as a light comedian, but he had sufficient scope to warrant his inclusion here. It is true that Adams played romantic comedy with dash and brilliance, but early in his career his emotional power was noted and encouraged. Mrs. John E. Owens, wife of the famous comedian, records that in 1855, two years after Adams' debut, he made a hit as Edward Mapleton in *The Merchant and His Clerks* and in the portrayal he "developed such force and emotional power that Mr. Owens advised him to devote attention to tragedy, feeling sure that his talent was great for that line of drama." [75] Apparently Adams took this advice, because in 1860 he played Hamlet and three years later he was the leading man in H. L. Bateman's company where he acted all the top roles in tragedy and romance. In 1869 when Booth's Theatre opened in New York, Adams played Mercutio to Edwin Booth's Romeo. He remained in the company as a leading man, acting such roles as Iago to Booth's Othello, Rover in *Wild Oats,* Claude Melnotte in *The Lady of Lyons,* and many of the chief roles in Shakespearean tragedy. He was efficient and capable as a tragedian but his greatest strength seemed to lie in romance and comedy. He created the role of Enoch Arden in a play based on Tennyson's poem, and was considered such a perfect embodiment of the character that other actors hesitated to attempt the part. He excelled as Mercutio, and was the first portrayer of Robert Landry in *The Dead Heart*. William Winter says that "next to E. L. Davenport, he was the best Mercutio I have ever seen." [76] Clara Morris goes farther and declares that as a portrayer of Mercutio "no greater ever strode than . . . Edwin Adams." [77]

Adams, unlike the greatest of the tragedians, was not a careful scholar nor a skillful analyst of motives and character. However, he had a dramatic instinct which was unerring and a vitality and charm which "thrilled the feelings and fired the imagination" of his audience. His voice, too, enhanced his appeal. All of his contemporaries praised it as "superb," as "rich, soulful, lovely," or as "one of the most melodious and sympathetic ever heard."

Evidently Adams' joyous charm, his winning vitality, and his engaging manliness were an intrinsic part of his personality. He was liked

and admired as much off the stage as on. Joseph Jefferson says that "As a man he was loving and beloved. . . ." [78] And William Winter, lamenting his early death at the age of forty-three, writes that "He was one of those rare men who refresh mankind by spontaneous, shining exposition of the loveliness which is an inherent element of human nature." [79]

CHARLES W. COULDOCK

Charles W. Couldock (1815–1898) was another Englishman who became identified with the American stage and who during more than sixty years of acting contributed many well-loved portraits to our theatrical gallery. The actor was brought to America by Charlotte Cushman in 1849 and made his United States debut as leading man in her production of *The Stranger* on October 8 at the Park Theatre in New York. He was an immediate success and continued as a star for many years. He played heroes and villains in both comedy and tragedy but was best, perhaps, in romantic melodramas like *The Willow Corpse, The Chimney Corner,* and *Hazel Kirke*. He is not remembered for the great roles of tragedy—although William Winter lists him as one who could play Hamlet in an efficient and thoroughly satisfactory manner—but he is remembered for having given brilliant life to such roles as Abel Murcott in the original United States production of *Our American Cousin* and Dunstan Kirke in the original New York production of *Hazel Kirke*. William Winter calls him one of the "shining names" which "brightly spangled" the last half of the nineteenth century.

JOSEPH HAWORTH

Joseph Haworth (1855–1903), who was born and reared in Cleveland, Ohio, made his debut there and served his early apprenticeship in John Ellsler's Cleveland company. As a young man he acted with Edwin Booth, John McCullough, Lawrence Barrett, and many other great players. From them he learned to know and love the Shakespearean repertory and he eventually played the great roles of Hamlet, Othello, Richard III, etc. His Shakespearean characters were always soundly conceived, carefully worked out, and performed with skill and effectiveness. When he became a star, he followed the trend of the times

and appeared less often in Shakespeare and more frequently in the romantic drama and melodrama of the late nineteenth century. He was admired for his force, his technical control, and his theatrical effectiveness in such plays as *The Christian, The Bells, Ruy Blas,* and *Paul Kauvar.* He died at the age of forty-eight and is remembered as one of the very good actors of his time but not as a great one.

Following are some other actors of lesser stature whose names are associated with the versatile tragedians.

John Howard Payne (1791–1852) is best known as the author or adapter of over sixty plays. He was hailed as the "American Roscius" when he made his debut as a child prodigy in 1809 although he was seventeen years old at the time. For the next five years he acted such roles as Hamlet, Romeo, Petruchio, Edgar in *King Lear,* and a variety of romantic heroes, but after 1813, when he went to England, his active career as a player virtually ended. His principal occupations for the rest of his life were playwriting and government service.

Peter Richings (1797–1871), born and reared in England, spent his entire professional life in the United States as an actor and a manager. His style in such roles as King Claudius in *Hamlet,* Henry Bertram in *Guy Mannering,* and Sikes in *Oliver Twist* was considered artificial but effective.

William Wheatley (1816–1876), son of the famous comedienne Sarah Ross Wheatley but best known as a manager and as the producer of *The Black Crook,* was an actor of repute who played such roles as Hamlet and Romeo but was far more successful in showy, romantic parts like Claude Melnotte in *The Lady of Lyons* or in stuffy comic roles like Captain Absolute in *The Rivals.*

Charles Barron (1843–1918), for many years the leading man at the Boston Museum, was famous for his portrayal of Bill Sikes as well as for many other characterizations among the more than five hundred parts he played during his lifetime. His great versatility in both classic and modern roles earned him the admiration of his fellow players, one of whom declared: "I never knew a man who could play so many parts so well, and play them so easily." [80]

STEELE MACKAYE, DISCIPLE OF
FRANÇOIS DELSARTE

James Morrison Steele MacKaye, eccentric genius and jack-of-all-arts, can hardly be said to have been a "master" of any single activity but he succeeded, to a degree, in every theatrical activity he tried. Among his talents were: scene designing, stage lighting, the invention of stage machinery, directing, managing, teaching, acting, and playwriting. Perhaps he is best remembered as a dramatist, for he wrote or adapted or collaborated in the writing of thirty plays, of which the best known is *Hazel Kirke*. However, it is his contribution to American acting which concerns us here. This contribution is more indirect than direct. That is, his introduction to America of the Delsarte theories of expression and his establishment of the first dramatic school in the United States, which later became the American Academy of Dramatic Arts, exerted more influence on the development of American acting than did his own professional appearances on the stage.

MacKaye, who was born in Buffalo, New York, in 1842, evidenced talent and artistic temperament at a very early age. His father, an affluent and influential attorney, encouraged the artistic ambitions of his son, sending him to Paris at the age of sixteen to study painting and placing "unlimited funds at his disposal." But neither painting nor an unrestricted bank account were sufficient to hold the interest of the restless, volatile young man. Within a year he returned to the United States, and shortly after the outbreak of the Civil War, he joined the Union forces. It was in the Army, of all places, that he first demonstrated his theatrical talents. During the month of August, 1862, in the barracks of the Seventh New York Regiment, then stationed in Baltimore, Maryland, he played five Shakespearean roles: Othello, Antonio, Hamlet, Cassius, and Shylock. He was supported by a cast of fellow soldiers.

After the war, he deserted his newly found love of acting and tried his hand at a variety of enterprises, all of which proved unsuccessful. He eventually returned to Paris and began the serious study of singing and acting with François Delsarte. He became Delsarte's best student, avidly absorbing the master's teaching and brilliantly demonstrating his principles. Then, with characteristic enthusiasm, MacKaye returned to the United States eager to reform the American stage

through an application of the system he had just discovered. He became the high priest and chief representative of the Delsarte principles in this country. He lectured on them, he taught them to other actors who sought his guidance, and he made them the basis for the dramatic school he established in connection with the Lyceum Theatre in 1884. It was this school which was later to evolve into the American Academy of Dramatic Arts under the leadership of Franklin H. Sargent.

MacKaye's professional debut as an actor occurred in New York in January of 1872 when he performed the leading role in a play written by himself and Francis Durivage entitled *Monaldi*. The supporting cast of this production was composed of MacKaye's pupils to whom he had been imparting the principles of Delsartism. Fired anew with a zeal for acting and, apparently, desiring additional instruction in the art, MacKaye returned to Paris later in 1872 and placed himself under the tutelage of François Régnier, Director of the Théâtre Français. He appeared as Hamlet in the Paris Conservatoire late in 1872, acting the role in French. The following spring he played the part in London, acting it in English—the first American ever to perform the role on the British stage. This seems to be the high point of MacKaye's career in acting, for shortly thereafter his enthusiasms were directed elsewhere. During the rest of his life he occasionally assumed roles in his own plays or appeared in benefit performances for other actors. But he did not develop his talents as a tragedian or as an exponent of Shakespearean drama. In the twenty years between his return from England in 1874 and his death in 1894, he made brief appearances in only sixteen different plays, eleven of which were his own dramas. The "wayward genius," described by William Winter as "impetuous, capricious, volatile, prone to extravagant fancies and bold experiments," [81] directed his restless energies into playwriting, teaching, theatrical management, the rebuilding of playhouses, the invention of stage machinery, and into grandiose schemes such as those for a "Spectatorium" to embellish the Chicago World's Fair of the 1890's.

MacKaye's achievements as an actor were not sufficient to exert much influence on the development of American acting. But his teaching of the Delsarte principles of expression both to private pupils and to the classes he established exerted considerable influence—some of it good, much of it bad.

What were the main principles of Delsarte which MacKaye found so stimulating? They were chiefly concerned with action and gesture

as a means of expression and not with speech. "The text is only a label," writes the Abbe Delaumosne, one of Delsarte's disciples. "The sense lies not in speech but in inflection and in gesture. Nature institutes a movement, speech names the movement. . . . Speech is only the title of that which gesture has announced; speech comes only to confirm what is already understood by the auditors." [82] With such a belief in the primacy of movement, Delsarte proceeded to establish a "science of movement." He declared that man's fundamental nature has three aspects: physical, mental, and moral. These aspects are conditioned and modified by man's normal, concentric, or eccentric states of being. The normal state is the calm state of the individual; the concentric inclines him toward concentration and inversion, while the eccentric state impels him toward expansion and extroversion. The fundamental aspects of man's nature, modified by his state of being, have a special apparatus for their expression in which each organ of the body participates. Every thought, sentiment, emotion, or sensation arising from man's triple nature is reflected and expressed in a characteristic way through his physical body.

On the basis of this general theory, Delsarte proceeded to examine the reactions and movements of each physical organ and to analyze their roles in the expression of thought and feeling. The movements of the head, the torso, and the limbs are all classified and described according to their meaning and significance. The result is a series of charts where, for instance, one can see illustrated the position of the eye in exaltation, aversion, astonishment, and every other emotional state. The same careful classification of response is given to the arms, the legs, the hands, and each expressive part of the body.

It may be surprising to many readers to learn that this theory of expression, which later became so mechanized and distorted, was designed to produce greater sincerity and naturalness in acting. MacKaye introduced the system to America believing that it would render an actor more life-like and would eliminate the posturing and artificiality too often observed on the stage. Indeed, Delsarte had evolved his system as a revolt against the teachings of the Paris Conservatoire which he found to produce a conventionalized and unnatural style of performance. The purpose of Delsarte's research was to discover natural physical movements, the responses of real people in real situations. To this end, he studied anatomy and physiology, he visited hospitals and dissecting rooms, he spent endless hours observing people in all walks

of life, and he scrutinized the masterpieces of painting and sculpture in the Paris galleries. The aim of the system which resulted from his research was the elimination of the artificial and mechanical in movement and the substitution of the real and the true as nature revealed them.

When MacKaye applied Delsarte's principles in his own acting, he impressed his audiences as being sincere, natural, and free from artificiality. The reviews of his performances all praise him for quiet intensity, for the absence of rant, for movement and gesture which were simple and "true to nature." MacKaye transmitted Delsarte's aims and methods, with embellishments of his own, to his classes and to his private pupils. Many of them found the instruction rewarding and productive of greater sincerity and naturalness in their own acting. Perhaps the outstanding example of the success of MacKaye's teaching was the popular tragedian, John McCullough, whose early style of performing, as has been noted in a previous chapter, was patterned after the heroic, muscular school of Edwin Forrest. In 1877, after twenty years on the stage, he took some lessons from Steele MacKaye and the results were notable. The period of his finest acting ensued. The critics now praised him for "tempered emotion," for "discipline and control," for "more repose, more dignity, more grace." McCullough was generous in crediting his improvement to Steele MacKaye, for he reported to A. C. Wheeler: ". . . that teacher, MacKaye, has taught me more in three months than I could have learned otherwise in twenty years, and I don't care who knows it." [83]

The Delsarte principles benefited many performers, but these principles were easily distorted and misapplied. Unhappily there was as much misapplication as there was sound teaching, so that today the principles are remembered for the grotesqueries they spawned rather than for the good they did. Delsarte's science of movement became a system of gymnastics. (MacKaye abetted this perversion by adding "harmonic gymnastics" to the Delsarte exercises.) Delsarte's system of gestures became elaborate pantomimes accompanied by music and recitations. His aim to reproduce the truth of nature became a mechanical distortion of nature which was so absurd as to discredit the art of elocution for several decades. American acting was influenced for the worse in many cases.

Perhaps the best effects of MacKaye's teaching, aside from his assistance to certain actors like John McCullough, was the stimulation

given to three students who eventually became prominent teachers of expression and acting. These were Samuel S. Curry, who became the author of many books and the head of the Curry School of Expression; Dr. Charles W. Emerson, a pupil of a pupil of MacKaye's, who became head of the Emerson College of Oratory; and Franklin H. Sargent, a pupil and co-worker of MacKaye's, who became President of the American Academy of Dramatic Arts. These men freely acknowledged their indebtedness to MacKaye and to the stimulation they received from the Delsarte principles. But these principles, in their hands, were altered, refined, and expanded according to their own research and experience and thus evolved into quite different approaches to acting than the one created by Delsarte.

In general, these leaders rejected the practice of teaching attitudes and gestures or of specifying particular vocal devices for the revelation of emotion. They felt that life-like creation of expression can only develop from within. Thus they emphasized the cultivation of imagination and sensitivity, and they sought to develop not only the intellectual and physical faculties and functions, but "the powers of personality itself—the inner and deeper natures . . . the temperamental and imaginative, instinctive, and conceptively original powers of feeling." [84]

The teachings of these three leaders, and of other responsible students of MacKaye, were absorbed by several generations of students and performers, many of whom became teachers themselves in American universities and in professional schools of dramatics. Thus the original inspiration of the Delsarte principles, as transmitted by MacKaye in his classroom rather than in his own performances, came to exert a widespread but indirect influence on the development of American acting.

[NOTES ON THE SETTING]

Later Nineteenth Century

BY THE MIDDLE OF THE NINETEENTH CENTURY THE colorful cultural backdrop before which Edwin Forrest and his colleagues had made their entrance in 1820 had shifted to reveal a new and altered landscape before which the American actor played his part.

The most notable feature of the new landscape was its astonishing increase in size. The territory of the United States had grown enormously. The Louisiana Purchase had been made in 1803, three years before Forrest was born, and Florida had been acquired a year before Forrest made his debut as an actor. During the succeeding years, while Forrest was climbing to stardom, the Texas and Oregon territories were annexed, and then—following the War with Mexico—a vast western empire was acquired, later to be carved into the states of California, Nevada, Utah, Colorado, Arizona, and New Mexico. By 1850, some form of dramatic activity stretched from the Atlantic seaboard across the wilderness for three thousand miles to California.

In mid-century, this enormous territory was being opened to settlement, to trade, and to theatrical enterprise by the rapid development of the railroads. As early as 1854 several lines had crossed the Mississippi, and in 1869 the first transcontinental line, joining New York with San Francisco, was completed. Now the stars and traveling companies—instead of bumping over hazardous roads in wagons and stagecoaches, as their predecessors had done—could move from town to town both quickly and comfortably.

Within this greatly expanded country population was growing and

industry was booming. In 1820, when Forrest made his debut, there were over nine and one half million inhabitants in the United States. Thirty-six years later, when Edwin Booth made his first appearance in New York City, the population had grown to thirty million and large numbers of these citizens were congregated in cities where they could be easily lured into the playhouses. New York City, in 1850, with a population of over 600,000, boasted seven legitmate theatres and the Astor Place Opera House plus many halls and gardens devoted to concerts, vaudeville, and minstrel shows. Boston and Philadelphia each had several excellent theatres as did many other cities in the East and South. New Orleans was a thriving theatrical town, Chicago and Cincinnati were building playhouses, and in San Francisco Thomas Maguire opened the Jenny Lind Theatre with the enthusiastic support of a population of 50,000. Almost every village, hamlet, and town had some kind of a playhouse. In 1850, there were more than fifty stock companies opening in American cities, and by 1880, according to William Winter,[1] there were in the United States and Canada about 3,500 towns in which plays were regularly given. Distributed in these towns were approximately 5,000 playhouses supplied by more than 250 companies and stars drawn from no less than 5,000 professional players.

The country, as a whole, was vigorous and prosperous. There were recurring financial panics and depressions which slowed down all business, including show business, but the set-backs were temporary. Even the growing tensions which were to culminate in the Civil War did not seriously impede the steady progress toward greater wealth and leisure—both of which were of major importance to show business. The Puritan prejudice against the theatre as a center of sin and depravity was not dead by any means, but the prejudice was weakening. When ladies of virtue and social position, like Mrs. Anna Cora Mowatt, became actresses and conducted themselves with exemplary propriety, thousands of citizens decided that the theatre might not be so sinful after all.

A significant portion of the growing population of the country were immigrants speaking a babel of tongues. Often they crowded into the cities in such great numbers that it was profitable to open foreign language theatres for their entertainment. New York City had two German theatres by 1866 and later on a Yiddish, an Italian, and a Chinese theatre. New Orleans had French theatres, and San Francisco

was soon to have both a Chinese and an Italian theatre. But the real influence of the many-tongued population showed itself in the tremendous growth of the "popular" theatre. The polyglot population began to give enthusiastic support to minstrelsy, vaudeville, burlesque, the circus, and every form of variety entertainment which could be enjoyed without an understanding of any language. During the second half of the nineteenth century, these forms of popular theatre gained immense appeal.

In the legitimate playhouses, Shakespeare was still standard fare, and so were the plays of Goldsmith, Sheridan, and other writers of "old comedy." The reigning contemporary playwrights were all foreign, and they were turning out romantic tragedies and sentimental melodramas with great appeal to American audiences. Native playwriting was still suffering from prejudice and an inferiority complex, and American dramatists were still copying foreign models—even though Anna Cora Mowatt had written a sparkling comedy of social satire called *Fashion,* and George Henry Boker had produced what was perhaps the best American romantic tragedy with his drama, *Francesca da Rimini.* Other Americans had written Yankee plays or comedies of life-in-the-big-city or farces, but the slapstick, rough-and-tumble farces—which for years had been played as afterpieces following the main drama of the evening—were now being eliminated.

In mid-century, the metropolitan theatres which presented the plays of the time had become elaborate structures with ornate lobbies, upholstered seats, and every form of luxury known to the period. Often they were of immense size. New York's Bowery Theatre, rebuilt in 1845, seated 4,000, and even P. T. Barnum's "Lecture Room" was remodeled in 1849 to hold 3,000. The shape of these theatres had not changed since the debut of Edwin Forrest. Proscenium doors were disappearing and the forestage was diminishing in depth, but the picture frame stage still faced an auditorium with boxes and galleries suspended in a horseshoe curve above a pit or orchestra floor. Both stage and auditorium were lighted by gas.

As yet, most of the scenery which surrounded the players on the stage was composed of elaborately painted wings and drops. But now there was occasionally seen the exciting new "box" type setting introduced by Dion Boucicault. This energetic, versatile Irishman is credited with introducing the interior setting composed of three walls and a ceiling which gave the illusion of an actual room. Moreover, the

floor was carpeted, the doors and windows were the "working" type —not painted on canvas—and the furniture and properties were numerous and practical. Such scenery earned Boucicault the title of "the upholsterer of the stage," and it was the type of realistic setting which, with increasing refinement, has dominated the American stage ever since—varied and transformed only occasionally by the art of the "New Stagecraft" introduced in the twentieth century by Gordon Craig and Adolphe Appia. In the middle of the nineteenth century, the realistic box setting was a novelty.

Boucicault is credited with another innovation which was to have far-reaching effects upon the American theatre, that is, his introduction of the "combination" or road company. Until about 1860, the only actor who traveled was the star. He journeyed from town to town acting with one of the resident companies in each city. He chose the plays he wished to give and the resident company provided the complete supporting cast as well as all the other elements of the production. On the whole it was a good system because it encouraged strong resident companies in each city and it provided immense and varied experience for the members of these companies. About 1860, Boucicault saw the economic advantages of organizing a cast to perform a single popular play and then dispatching the entire company on a tour of the nation. The local community was now asked to supply only the playhouse and the facilities but no supporting actors. The system, proving profitable to the manager or impresario, quickly gained in popularity and soon began to destroy the venerable institution of the resident company.

However, in mid-century and for twenty years thereafter, the resident companies were strong and prosperous and the actor dominated the theatrical scene. These were the so-called "palmy days" when the star player was king. He evolved his own style, worked out his own characterizations, designed his own make-up and costumes, and performed in the manner which *he* felt was effective. The actors of the supporting cast had the same independence to a lesser degree, because there was no director or régisseur to tell them what to do. The company manager or the stage manager rarely if ever ventured to give advice to the player. It was not until the advent of such men as Augustin Daly and David Belasco, at the end of the century, that the concept of the modern director emerged. In the palmy days the star actor was supreme.

In 1860, who were the players who thus dominated the theatrical scene? Edwin Forrest, John McCullough, and other actors of the heroic school were still active and popular. Forrest did not retire until 1872, the year of his death. But he had formidable rivals. Booth was the new sensation of the tragic drama; Murdoch and Davenport were established favorites; Barrett was beginning his rise to prominence. Mary Ann Duff, the first great classic actress, was dead, but Charlotte Cushman was still acting her superb tragic roles and was to continue for another fifteen years. Two other classic actresses, who were to adopt the United States as their homeland, were flourishing in Europe: Helena Modjeska was the leading actress in Poland and not due to make her American debut until 1877; Fanny Janauschek, a star in Germany, would appear in the United States in 1866. Of the actresses of the emotionalistic school, Laura Keene and Matilda Heron were enjoying great popularity; Anna Cora Mowatt had made her sensation and was now retired; Clara Morris, Fanny Davenport, and other actresses of the emotionalistic school had not yet begun their careers and neither had the great ladies of the personality school —with the exception of Clara Fisher, who had ended her reign as a child prodigy and was now playing adult roles with charm and effectiveness. Great comic performers were flourishing more vigorously than perhaps at any other time in the history of American drama. Such superb character comedians as William Warren, Henry Placide, John Gilbert, and Mrs. John Drew were at the height of their powers, and they were surrounded by a host of other players almost as good. Comic specialists like Joseph Jefferson III and John T. Raymond had already made names for themselves and so had other unforgettable characters like Francis Chanfrau, E. A. Sothern, and George Holland. In addition to the legitimate theatres playing the standard repertory of tragedy and comedy, melodrama and farce, there were hundreds of halls, saloons, tents, and playhouses where the public was enjoying vaudeville, minstrelsy, burlesque, circus, and productions of *Uncle Tom's Cabin*. It was, indeed, a luxuriant and prosperous time for American acting, and it was due to last for many more years. The Civil War was to provide a temporary setback, and the tragedy at Ford's Theatre in Washington was to force Edwin Booth into retirement for several months. But neither war nor the assassination of a President were to impede seriously the progress of the theatre or the development of the colorful careers of American players.

IV

THE SCHOOL OF EMOTIONALISM

DURING THE SECOND HALF OF THE NINETEENTH CENTURY, WHILE the actresses of the classic school were demonstrating their art in the great roles of the standard drama, another group of actresses was winning popular acclaim as purveyors of emotionalism. Developing their style through different methods, and usually exercising their appeal in tearful domestic melodramas adapted from French or German dramatists, these actresses constitute a group which can be called the school of emotionalism. This kind of acting was developed almost exclusively by female performers for the simple reason that emotionalistic roles were not often written for men. It would have been unthinkable for a male, in the American theatre with its Puritan, Anglo-Saxon background, to exhibit the kind of emotionalistic behavior which seemed probable and acceptable when coming from a lady in distress. The actresses who specialized in playing the lady in distress and who were the most notable exponents of the emotionalistic school included, among the early representatives, Anna Cora Mowatt, Laura Keene, and Matilda Heron; among the later the most famous were Clara Morris, Fanny Davenport, and Mrs. Leslie Carter.

As a manner of performing, emotionalistic acting could be recognized by three dominant characteristics.

First of all, the actress of this school actually experienced the feelings and passions of her role and surrendered herself to these emotions. She did not simulate but actively participated in the agonies of the mimicked character.

Secondly, she cultivated a lush, overt display of the passions she

was feeling. Her performance was marked by sobs, tears, screams, shudders, heavings, writhings, pantings, growlings, tremblings, and all manner of physical manifestations. Sometimes these reactions were reproduced fully and realistically. This was the case with Clara Morris and the later representatives of the school. Sometimes the reactions were subdued and sentimentalized, this being the case with Laura Keene and the early representatives of the school.

The third major characteristic of the emotionalistic school was neglect of technique. In surrendering to emotion and cultivating lavish, overt expression, the emotionalistic actress disregarded discipline and control. Her elocution, gestures, movement, and performance of stage business were likely to be impromptu, unstudied, and haphazard. She relied on inspiration rather than art.

Every actor and actress will recognize that emotion is an indispensable ingredient of acting, and almost all players will testify that every performer who is worth his make-up feels the emotions of his role to some degree, although players differ greatly in the amount of feeling they experience and in the length of time it takes them to summon this feeling. The actress of the classic school certainly experienced the emotions of her roles to a greater or lesser degree, but at the same time she exercised artful discipline and control over her own emotional output. In contrast, the emotionalistic player abandoned control and surrendered herself entirely to the emotions of the part.

In any performance, the emotion of a role must be communicated by voice, gesture, movement, and facial expression. The actress of the classic school selects those details which best suggest the emotions of the situation and suppresses others. Only the most significant physical manifestations are projected and these in a conscious pattern for, as George Henry Lewes has written, "the internal workings must be legible in the external symbols; and these external symbols must also have a certain grace and proportion to affect us aesthetically." [1] The emotionalistic player, in contrast, exercises little selectivity but includes in her performance the maximum number of "external symbols."

No actor performs without some technique. But whereas the actress of the classic school uses it as a means of refining and controlling her emotional output, the emotionalistic player considers it of minor importance and relies, instead, upon uncontrolled feeling to gain her effects.

In addition to these three dominant traits, certain correlaries are significant.

Apparently, youth, beauty, and personal magnetism are absolutely essential in successful emotionalistic acting. The careers of members of this school indicate that youth is necessary to insure the actress an abundance of fresh and vigorous emotion, for with advancing age the well springs of passion appear to dry up. Beauty and magnetism are needed to charm the eye and touch the heart of the spectator so that he suspends his critical faculties while he revels in the personal spell of the player. It is true, of course, that these qualities are helpful in every style of acting. They can always be utilized on the stage to good advantage. However, those performers who earned a lasting reputation as great players did not rely on youth, beauty, and magnetism alone but developed powers which were independent of these— powers which served them well into old age and won them plaudits long after they had passed their physical prime. Among the actresses of the classic school, Mary Ann Duff, Charlotte Cushman, Helena Modjeska, and Fanny Janauschek are outstanding examples of players who succeeded greatly long after their youth was gone. On the other hand, it will be seen that the actresses of the emotionalistic school usually sank into disfavor and obscurity when they lost their youth and beauty.

Emotionalistic acting also needs a certain kind of play for its fullest development. All the actresses who gained fame in the emotionalistic school utilized dramas which are characterized by abundant sentiment, melodramatic action, and contrived emotional crises. The plays of Kotzebue, Bulwer-Lytton, Dion Boucicault, Bronson Howard, Augustin Daly, and David Belasco are all examples of this kind of drama. Such fervid works as Sardou's *Fédora* and *La Tosca,* which were unusually popular in the late nineteenth century, typify the vehicles in which the emotionalistic actresses were notably successful. When they attempted to act in plays of a different type—for example, the plays of Shakespeare or, later on, the dramas of Ibsen and Chekhov— they were notably unsuccessful. The careers of a few exponents of this school are surveyed below.

MRS. MOWATT (ANNA CORA OGDEN MOWATT RICHIE)

In May, 1845, Mrs. Anna Cora Mowatt suddenly decided to become an actress, and three weeks later her debut became the sensation of the New York season. For nine years she illumined the dramatic heavens, and then she withdrew as suddenly and as unexpectedly as she had appeared. Her career is significant because it marks the beginning in the American theatre of the school of emotionalism. Mrs. Mowatt was the first of a long line of actresses who achieved success primarily through personal charm and emotional exhibitionism.

Anna Cora Mowatt was an unusual and remarkable woman. Born into a household of twelve children, the daughter of well-to-do and socially prominent parents, she showed signs of precocity at an early age. When she was ten she had read the whole of Shakespeare's plays many times over. At the age of fifteen she married a wealthy New York lawyer. At the age of seventeen she published an epic poem, and when the critics condemned it as worthless, she refuted the critics in an effective verse satire. At eighteen she was threatened with consumption and went abroad for fifteen months to recover her health. While she was recuperating she found energy to write magazine articles, visit the theatre, take lessons in Italian, and compose a play in blank verse. When she was twenty-one, her husband lost his fortune, whereupon she launched a successful career as a public reader after only two weeks of training. When her health forced her to abandon the platform, she retired to her study and wrote magazine articles, novels, a life of Goethe, a life of Madame D'Arblay, and books on House-keeping, Cookery, Embroidery, Etiquette, and Marriage. When she was twenty-five, a friend suggested that she try playwriting. The result was her famous comedy *Fashion,* which was submitted to the Park Theatre and was produced immediately with outstanding success. A few weeks later, because her husband had suffered additional financial reverses, she decided to become an actress. She allowed herself three weeks of preparation and one rehearsal. On June 13, 1845, she made a triumphal debut at the Park Theatre, New York, as Pauline in *The Lady of Lyons.* She shocked her genteel friends, but delighted the playgoing public. Her acting career, once started, prospered enormously. During her first year on the stage she appeared in all the

principal cities of the United States, acting for more than two hundred nights in such roles as Lady Teazle, Mrs. Haller, Lucy Ashton, Katherine, Julia, and Juliet. In view of this prodigious activity and phenomenal success, Laurence Hutton declares: "In the history of the stage in all countries there is no single instance of a mere novice playing so many important parts so many nights, before so many different audiences, and winning so much and such merited praise, as did this lady during the first twelve months of her career as an actress." [2]

For nine years Mrs. Mowatt performed successfully and prosperously in Great Britain and the United States. Then, in June, 1854, when her appeal was still great and her charms unimpaired, she suddenly withdrew from public life and never appeared on the stage again. However, her busy private life continued until her death in 1870.

Mrs. Mowatt's great success, achieved without training or apprenticeship, seems to refute the belief that good acting is the result of careful preparation and long practice. The home theatricals, in which Mrs. Mowatt had participated since the age of five, and her brief career as a public reader, gave her a modicum of experience, but these activities cannot be considered adequate preparation for an acting career. To what can her quick success be attributed, and how praiseworthy was her style of acting?

There can be no question but that Mrs. Mowatt was a remarkably gifted person. She had unusual intelligence, keen aesthetic perception, thorough education, wide cultural experience, an excellent speaking voice, and beauty of face and figure—all of which are invaluable endowments for any actress. In addition, Mrs. Mowatt had an emotional sensitivity which enabled her to "abandon herself to a role," to "live the part," and this ability, added to her other endowments, was sufficient to win her success on the stage for nine prosperous years.

Edgar Allan Poe was a warm admirer of Mrs. Mowatt's acting (although he was a harsh critic of her dramaturgy). He describes her physical charms in these words:

Her figure is slight—even fragile—but eminently graceful. Her face is a remarkably fine one, and of that precise character best adapted to the stage. The forehead is the least prepossessing feature, although it is by no means an unintellectual one. The eyes are gray, brilliant and expressive, without being full. The nose is well formed, with the Roman curve, and strongly indicative of energy; this quality is also shown in the quality of

the chin. The mouth is somewhat large, with brilliant and even teeth, and flexible lips, capable of the most effective variations of expression. A more radiantly beautiful smile we never remember having seen. Mrs. Mowatt has also the personal advantage of a profusion of rich auburn hair.[3]

In analyzing Mrs. Mowatt's acting, Poe singles out certain qualities for special commendation. He praises her ease and self-possession, her graceful movement, her richness of voice, and her distinctness of utterance. But, says Poe, "the greatest charm of the . . . acting . . . is its naturalness. She moves, looks, and speaks with a well-controlled impulsiveness as different as can be conceived from the customary rant and cant—the hack conventionality of the stage." [4] In amplifying his praise of Mrs. Mowatt's "well-controlled impulsiveness," Poe notes that she is able to make her bosom heave, her cheek grow pale, her limbs tremble, and her eyes fill with "nature's own tear" when she is called upon to portray feelings which are generous, noble, or unaffectedly passionate. Poe feels that this "freshness of the heart" and this "well of deep feeling" from which she draws so naturally, are gifts which distinguish her from the usual actress of the day and which enable her "effectively and unimpededly" to "lay bare to the audience the movements of her own passionate heart." [5] Poe was obviously much impressed by the emotionalistic aspects of Mrs. Mowatt's acting.

Other critics besides Poe were struck by the natural emotional quality of Mrs. Mowatt's portrayals. One English reviewer, in commenting on her performance in her own play *Armand,* said: "There seems no acting, but the direct and spontaneous expression of individual character." [6] Other critics mention her lack of exaggeration, her ability to enter into the spirit of a part, her gift for balancing "sensitivity and mirth," and the sincere appeal of her "poetic fervor."

Mrs. Mowatt comported herself gracefully and confidently on the stage—as she did in life—but she was never able to simulate emotions which she did not feel. As Poe observed, she was an impulsive, emotional actress, and she needed both a warm heart and a warm head to achieve her effects. She could not arouse an audience unless she herself were deeply stirred. Describing her very first appearance on the stage, she writes: "I gave myself up to the part, and acted with all the *abandon* and intensity of which I was capable." [7] On many other occasions she affirmed that she had to lose herself in a role before she could act effectively.

It is clear that the appeal of Mrs. Mowatt's acting came from her

ability to arouse emotions in herself and, at the same time, to communicate these to an audience in a manner which seemed natural and graceful. Her lack of rant, and her personal beauty, charm, and refinement added to her appeal. Despite these abilities, it is unlikely that she ever mastered the subtle physical and vocal skills of the seasoned professional, or the technical facility to appear convincing when her own inspiration was at low ebb. Joseph Jefferson, always a perceptive critic, makes the following comment on her style:

I am of the opinion that "once an amateur, always an amateur." There are many good actors that have this peculiar, raw quality who have been on the stage for years; and it is because they began their careers by acting leading characters. Mrs. Mowatt and James H. Hackett were examples of many in our profession who have committed this fatal error. No matter how bold and dashing they may appear, there is a shyness and uncertainty about everything they do. It exhibits itself in the casting of the eyes down upon the stage in an embarrassed way just after they have made a point. This is very disastrous. When a strong effect is made the eye, the pose, the very feeling, should be, for an instant only, a picture, till the public digest it. If it is disturbed by some unmeaning movement the strength is lost, and the audience will at once discover that they are not looking at a master. This characteristic of the amateur may wear off in some instances, but I do not remember any.[8]

Mrs. Mowatt recognized that there were at least two schools of acting, which she described in somewhat extreme terms as follows: "The actor of the one school totally loses his own individuality and abandons himself to all the absorbing emotions that belong to the character he interprets. His tears are real, his laughter real, as real to himself as to the audience." [9] In contrast to this school stands the actor who "exercises perfect command over the emotions of the audience . . . but not a pulse in his own frame beats more rapidly than its wont." [10] Mrs. Mowatt was perfectly aware that she belonged to the first school, and furthermore she declared that this type of acting could not be called "the highest school of art." At the end of her discussion of acting she writes:

No amount of study or discipline could have enabled me to belong to the grand and passionless school. I never succeeded in stirring the hearts of others unless I was deeply affected myself. The putting off of self-consciousness was, with me, the first imperative element of success. Yet I agree with those who maintain that the highest school of art is that in

which the actor, Prospero-like, rises or stills tempestuous waves by the magical force of his will—produces and controls, without sharing, the emotions of the audience.[11]

Although Mrs. Mowatt's stage career was meteor-like in both its brilliance and brevity, she nevertheless exerted a strong influence on the theatre of her day. In one respect, her influence was unfortunate. Her quick success set a false standard and encouraged countless amateurs to try their luck in a profession for which they had no qualifications except an ardent desire and a pretty face. Laurence Hutton notes that "There have been *debutantes* enough in New York since the *debut* of Mrs. Mowatt to fill to overflowing the auditorium of any single city theatre . . . but the great majority, dispirited and disheartened, have gone back to the private life from which they sprung, without song, without honor, and without tears, except the many tears they have shed themselves." [12]

Mrs. Mowatt's acting, whose chief appeal was feminine charm and emotionalism, undoubtedly confirmed a trend which became a major style in American acting. Feminine emotionalism of some kind and in some degree can be found in all periods of acting from the time the first female actress, Mrs. Coleman, performed on an English public stage in 1656, until the present day. However, Mrs. Mowatt is the first American actress of stature to use feminine emotionalism as her principal method and appeal. Undoubtedly the force of her example and the effect of her success influenced many other actresses to adopt her style. This aspect of her influence cannot be called beneficial. However, other aspects of her influence were entirely praiseworthy. The sincerity and naturalness which she displayed in her emotionalism encouraged many players to develop these qualities in their own acting. Furthermore, Mrs. Mowatt's very presence on the stage, whatever her style of performance, did great service to the profession of acting and helped to weaken the Puritan hostility toward the American theatre. Being a well known woman of wealth, education, and social position, Mrs. Mowatt's decision to go on the stage invoked the wrath of countless puritanical people. Yet for nine years she conducted herself with all the virtue, dignity, and graciousness of a born lady, and when she retired thousands of people throughout the nation had revised their opinions of the sinfulness of the theatre. As Arthur Hobson Quinn remarks, Mrs. Mowatt "took into the profession her high heart, her

utter refinement, her keen sense of social values, and her infinite capacity for effort, and her effect was a real and a great one. . . . Her career as related in the steady sparkle of her Autobiography makes any compatriot who reads it thankful that she has lived." [13]

LAURA KEENE

Another woman of strong will and varied abilities, who made her American debut just two years before Mrs. Mowatt quit the stage, was the imperious beauty, Laura Keene. Like Mrs. Mowatt, Laura Keene had boundless energy, abiding self-confidence, and enough ability to demonstrate competence in several fields. She was a charming and graceful actress, a successful manager, a respected business woman, and an able enough student of aesthetics to lecture occasionally on the fine arts and to edit, for a brief time, a magazine devoted to the fine arts. Though she made no lasting impression on the American theatre and though her popularity and success declined long before she quit the stage, her name is associated with the careers of many great stars of the American theatre, her acting was a worthy example of feminine charm and emotionalism, and her name is forever linked with American history because she was the star of the play being presented in Ford's Theatre the night Abraham Lincoln was assassinated, and she was the one who recognized John Wilkes Booth as he made his escape and who, it is said, held the dying President's head in her lap until he was carried from the theatre.

Laura Keene was born in England sometime between 1820 and 1830 and received her early theatrical training in Madame Vestris' London company. It is thought that she acquired two traits from Madame Vestris: (1) A taste for lavish stage ornamentation, and (2) a haughty and imperious manner in directing a company. Both of these traits were prominent in Miss Keene's management of her own theatre.

Miss Keene was "discovered" in 1852 when James W. Wallack visited England in search of a leading lady for his theatre. Struck by her beauty and talent, Wallack engaged her at once. She accompanied him to the United States where she made a brilliant debut on September 21, 1852. Henceforth her theatrical career was exclusively Ameri-

can, and her name must be included in the history of American, not British, acting.

During the season of 1852–53 at Wallack's Theatre, Laura Keene acted such roles as Lady Teazle, Lydia Languish, Lady Gay Spanker, Beatrice, Portia, and Rosalind, and was greatly admired for her looks, her gentility, and her deft comic touch. Though slight of figure, she had a fine carriage and admirable grace in all her movements. Her large expressive eyes were set in a face of "exquisite pallor" and topped by a mass of auburn hair. In addition, Odell says she had "temperament and magnetism" and, to the audiences at Wallack's, was "irresistible." [14]

Her acting at the time—and throughout her entire career—was marked by delicate taste and feminine charm. She did not so much draw details of character as suggest them, so that Kate Reignolds declared that her acting "was not photography or labored art, but a water color sketch, full of light and grace." [15]

After one highly successful season at Wallack's, Miss Keene departed abruptly without even giving notice to Mr. Wallack. She spent the next two years acting in Baltimore and San Francisco, and also in Australia where her touring partner was the young Edwin Booth. She returned to New York in 1855 and opened a theatre of her own called "Laura Keene's Varieties." The following year she moved into a new theatre built for her by John Trimble and called "Laura Keene's New Theatre." She remained there as manager and leading lady until 1863. Finally tiring of her managerial chores, she relinquished her theatre and became a traveling star. But her career began to decline and her health began to fail. She tried theatrical management again, she gave public lectures, she edited a magazine, but though her courage and sense of humor were unimpaired, her health and talent were not. After several years of declining fortune, she died of consumption on November 4, 1873.

The years from 1856 to 1863 were the most successful in the career of Laura Keene. Before evaluating her acting as another example of the school of emotionalism, it is interesting to note her activity as a manager and her influence as a tutor of other players.

As manager of her own theatre, she delighted New York with a series of comedies and extravaganzas which were elaborately mounted and which reflected the feminine grace and poetic tastes of the producer. The entire scene of one of her plays, for example, was com-

posed of the finest white lace to be found on the market and cost Miss Keene several hundreds of dollars. Other scenes in other plays were praised for their novelty, ingenuity, or splendor.

Miss Keene, as manager, not only designed and painted scenery; she also made costumes, trained actors, directed publicity, wrote or adapted scripts, and tried to encourage native Americans to write for the stage. At one time she offered a prize of $1,000 for the best American play submitted to her.

Miss Keene presided over all these activities with the imperious manners of a dictator; her word was law, and no opinion but her own was tolerated. Even her husband and business manager, John Lutz, if on the stage during rehearsal, was brushed away by a wave of the hand, according to the testimony of Frank Mordaunt.[16] Miss Keene's haughty temper often resulted in tiffs and quarrels with her actors, who called her "the Duchess," but underneath her dictatorial manner she was loyal and kind hearted, and won the respect and admiration of her fellow workers. Joseph Jefferson, who acted for some time in her New York company, recognized her basic charity and goodness of heart and affirmed that he "never heard her speak ill of anyone but herself." [17]

An indication of Miss Keene's high repute as a manager and worth as a person is found in the distinguished company of players she attracted to her theatre. Joseph Jefferson, E. A. Sothern, Kate Reignolds, Dion Boucicault, Agnes Robertson, John T. Raymond, Charles M. Walcot, Stuart Robson, W. J. Florence, and Charles W. Cauldock—all of these acted under the aegis of Laura Keene and many of them graduated to stardom from her theatre. It may be true that Miss Keene, as a manager, often presided over warring elements in her company, and it also may be true, as Odell says,[18] that her theatre lacked policy or "idea"—an audience never knowing what to expect of any announced new play—still, from 1856 to 1863, Miss Keene's energy and talents made her theatre one of the most popular and successful in New York.

Laura Keene not only managed and directed the multifarious details of her company; she also played all the leading feminine roles. The beautiful face, graceful figure, and musical voice which had won her great applause during her first season at Wallack's, were unimpaired in the years from 1856 to 1863. These endowments served her well in roles which ranged from high comedy to emotional melodrama. William Winter admired her versatility, pointing out that she did equally

well as the cruel selfish beauty in *The Marble Heart* and as the simple, artless maiden in *The Heir-At-Law,* and he noted, with approval, one of the pecularities of her acting, "a swift, gliding movement, which was remarkably effective." Winter was not so enthusiastic, however, about another of her mannerisms—"the singular expedient," he called it, "of rapidly and continuously blinking her eyes" by way of expressing emotion.[19] Joseph Jefferson praised her for "the rare power of varying her manner" from "the rustic walk of a milkmaid" to "the dignified grace of a queen," [20] and John Creahan, her worshipful biographer, declared she was "a master of high classic comedy" and "equally great in pastoral, spiritual, romantic, pathetic, poetic, and the emotional school of acting." [21] Other critics felt that her charming, sprightly portrayal of Florence Trenchard in *Our American Cousin* represented her best comic style. Certainly this play, which she introduced to America, was her most successful production and will be long remembered not only because of the parts played in it by Miss Keene and Joseph Jefferson but because of the stardom it gave to E. A. Sothern for his creation of the role of Lord Dundreary.

Although Laura Keene began her American career by successfully acting a variety of parts, including roles in Shakespearean drama and in "Old Comedy," she soon limited her range by specializing in plays where personal charm and emotional display were the primary attractions. The character of the plays, which she produced with increasing frequency, is indicated by their titles. *Mary's Birthday, Two Loves and a Life, Birds of Prey, The Elves,* or *The Statue Bride, Blanche of Brandywine, Old Heads and Young Hearts, The Wife's Secret, Plot and Passion, Rachel the Reaper, Camille,* and *Judith of Geneva*— these are only a few samples of the kind of dramas in which Miss Keene was the star. William Winter dubbed such plays "ultra-emotional drama of the hydrostatic order" [22] and deprecated the fact that Miss Keene blighted her talents by identifying herself with this kind of drama.

There is no record of how keenly Miss Keene felt the passions she portrayed or how extravagantly she may have embroidered the emotional fabric of her roles. It is clear, however, that her feminine charm and emotionalism were the primary attractions in her acting. It is also clear that after a brilliant beginning as a versatile actress she limited her talents largely to emotional and sentimental histrionics and subsequently lost her hold on the public. As William Winter said in

1915, ". . . it is scarcely possible, even at this long distance from the time of her feverish exploits and melancholy end, to think of her without a certain sense of regretful disappointment." [23] She died before she reached the age of fifty,[24] leaving the memory of talents which never fully matured but also leaving a record of activity, energy, and versatility which made her, for a time, an outstanding woman of the theatre.

MATILDA HERON

As early exponents of the emotionalistic school, Mrs. Mowatt and Laura Keene emphasized feminine charm and sentiment in their acting. They occasionally indulged in exhibitions of tears, rage, and hysteria, but such exhibitions were not their stock in trade. Moreover, the roles they played and the tastes of the time caused them to subdue and to idealize, in some degree, their emotional pyrotechnics. They were content to suggest the overt responses of emotion and to suppress ugly details. Their successors, however, shunned idealization and exploited other traits of the emotionalistic school. With the rise of such performers as Matilda Heron, Clara Morris, and Mrs. Leslie Carter, primary emphasis was placed on extravagant displays of the more violent feelings. Moreover, the representation of these feelings became realistic and naturalistic. Instead of refining or sentimentalizing their emotional exhibitions, the later actresses reproduced the overt manifestations of passion in detail and with clinical accuracy. By these means they shocked and fascinated their audiences and won notoriety for themselves.

The first influential actress of this branch of the emotionalistic school was Matilda Heron. Her contribution to American acting is represented in her single outstanding role: Camille. This is the role which brought her fame and fortune. In this role she most effectively displayed her naturalistic, emotional style of acting. This is the role which influenced many other actresses to join the school of emotionalism. And this is the role which was remembered at the time of her death: on her coffin was engraved the single word "Camille."

Miss Heron, Irish by birth but American by adoption, had gained a name for herself before she discovered *Camille*. Her career had begun in traditional fashion. She had been trained in an elegant style of elocution by Peter Richings. She had made her debut, February 17,

1851, in the standard role of Bianca in *Fazio*. She had played other standard roles such as Juliet, Parthenia, and Mrs. Haller and had been highly successful. She had traveled to San Francisco and made a great hit in that city. Then in 1854 she went to Paris and saw Mme. Doche act in Dumas' *La Dame aux Camélias*. The American actress was fascinated. She returned to the play night after night and memorized every detail of the production. She bought a copy of the play and made her own translation. By the time she returned to the United States, she was ready to act the Matilda Heron version of *Camille*. This she did in New Orleans in 1855, but the results were unsensational. It was not until two years later, when she staged her production at Wallack's Theatre in New York, that the furor began. She and *Camille* became the rage. Her picture appeared in all the journals; she was pursued, serenaded, and lionized. Poems were dedicated to her, and music was written in her honor. Her *Camille* ran for one hundred nights at Wallack's and was repeated with phenomenal success all over the United States. Before she sank into obscurity, the play netted her at least $100,000.

Matilda Heron was not the first Camille America had seen, but she was by far the most sensational. The play she had adapted from Dumas afforded her wide scope for the display of both emotionalism and naturalism. Her *Camille* was written in a far more realistic style than the standard drama of the period. It did not deal with courtly or poetical figures but with more familiar human beings. The passions exhibited were not noble or exalted; they were the visceral emotions of sexual love and physical suffering. Miss Heron developed on her own a style of acting compatible with this type of drama. Helen Ormsbee said: ". . . from neither Cushman nor Forrest, nor from the many inferior copies of them, could Matilda Heron have got her naturalistic method. She must have thought it out herself." [25]

The naturalism of Miss Heron's acting had several characteristics new enough in the mid-nineteenth century to cause excited comment. Miss Heron did not make her entrance with her face to the galleries and wait for a "reception"; she walked in naturally and ignored the audience. She did not raise her voice or project her words perceptibly, but spoke in what seemed to be a commonplace, conversational tone. On occasions, she even dared to turn her back to the audience. She utilized a multitude of realistic details. She made no attempt to idealize or refine her character; she did not even select and arrange her

effects, but included commonplace business of every sort, no matter how awkward or distracting it appeared. And finally, she portrayed physical and clinical reactions which were rarely if ever exhibited on the stage of that period. Many of her scenes were called repulsive and revolting. Her death-bed scene was considered especially painful. But all of the "disgusting minutiae" added to the fascination of the play and attracted thousands of spectators.

Miss Heron was impulsive and sentimental by nature, given to such foibles as writing on the wall of her St. Louis hotel room, in immense crayon letters: "Easter Sunday. God bless St. Louis! Matilda Heron." [26] On the stage she had an animal vitality and a wildness of passion which she displayed freely and extravagantly. She projected all the passions and agonies of a woman's heart with a vivid sense of reality. Her emotionalism was the realistic passion of the boudoir and the sickroom unrefined by poetry or idealism.

Although she exhibited limited imagination or intellect, Miss Heron's stage personality had an irresistible magnetism which could hypnotize an audience. As long as her magnetism was potent, she retained her hold on the public, but when her youth and animal vitality waned she apparently did not have sufficient art to sustain her and so sank rapidly into disfavor and obscurity. She will be remembered not only because of the sensational success of her *Camille* but because she developed a style of acting which influenced American actresses for many years to come. Her attraction as a performer is aptly summarized by William Winter when he says: ". . . if she was not a great artist, she certainly was a very remarkable example of elemental power. She had a wildness of emotion, a vitality in embodiment and many indefinable magnetic qualities . . . no spectator of her acting ever—till her powers were on the wane—missed the sense of an original, vigorous, brilliant, and startling personality." [27]

CLARA MORRIS

In the first volume of her reminiscences, Clara Morris asks the question: "What could *you* do to make yourself cry seven times a week for nine or ten months a year?" And then she wonders: ". . . did I ever do anything else? For it seems to me I have cried steadily through all the years of my dramatic life. Tears gentle, regretful; tears petulant,

fretful; tears stormy, passionate; tears slow, despairing; with a light patter, now and then, of my own particular brand. . . ." [28] It was precisely this ability—to weep all kinds of tears at every single performance for season after season—that distinguished the acting of Clara Morris. She was the Mistress of the *Ductus Lachrimalis,* the Queen of the Streaming Eye. She wept her way to stardom; she maintained her position by weeping; and her unending rain of tears earned her the large fortune which, dissipated too soon, brought forth new showers of tears from both the actress and her sentimental public. The kingdom of Robert Bruce is said to have been founded on a spider's web. The dramatic empire of Clara Morris was founded on a drop of water.

Miss Morris's career in emotionalistic acting was longer and more varied than the careers of her predecessors. Laura Keene, Matilda Heron, and Mrs. Mowatt, the early representatives of the emotionalistic school, all enjoyed a relatively brief popularity; Matilda Heron succeeded brilliantly in only a single role. Clara Morris, in contrast, played many parts and her career lasted for more than thirty years. She is the outstanding representative of a later group of emotionalistic actresses which included Fanny Davenport and Mrs. Leslie Carter, all of whom practiced the style of acting described in the careers of their predecessors—with emphasis, however, on a fervid naturalistic display of emotion rather than on a suggested or sentimentalized display.

Miss Morris's affiliation with the theatre began in 1862 when, at the age of fourteen she became a ballet girl for John Ellsler, manager of the Cleveland Academy of Music. The only theatrical instruction she ever received was a lesson in make-up, given her by an older actress of the company. The rest of her knowledge was gained by observation, and by playing every kind of part, large or small, comic or tragic, in Ellsler's company. While still in her teens she acted Gertrude to the Hamlet of Edwin Booth, and Emilia to the Othello of E. L. Davenport. Her apprenticeship lasted seven years, and ended when she became leading lady at Woods Theatre in Cincinnati. But she remained in Cincinnati for only one season. The encouragement she received from critics and friends led her to apply for a position in Augustin Daly's New York company. Daly engaged her, at a nominal salary, with the idea of making a comedienne of her. "Your forte is comedy, pure and simple," he told her after studying her face.[29] But Clara Morris never acted comedy for Mr. Daly. When Agnes Ethel refused

the feminine lead in a play called *Man and Wife,* Miss Morris was given the part. It was an emotional role in a domestic drama, and the young actress from the West played it with triumphant success. Henceforth, she became a specialist in domestic emotionalism. Parts in comedy or high tragedy were abandoned for the tearful heroines of contemporary French melodrama. She played so many of these roles, and she identified herself so completely with them that when, later on, she tried to extend her range and play Lady Macbeth or Evadne or Jane Shore, she was criticized for converting these heroines into "incongruous women of the present day."

Typical of the plays with which Miss Morris became identified, and in which she scored her triumphs, were *L'Article 47, Alixe,* and *Miss Multon,* all of them adaptations from the French. In the first of these, the heroine, Cora, is the mistress of a young Frenchman, who shoots her in a fit of passion, leaving a hideous scar on her face. He then marries a "pure" woman and Cora devotes her life to winning him back and plotting revenge. *Alixe* is the spectacle of a young girl tortured almost to madness by the loss of her lover, then rent with double anguish by the discovery that her rival is her own sister, and finally driven to suicide by the discovery of her mother's past dishonor. *Miss Multon* is a version of *East Lynne,* in which a wife abandons her children for a lover then, repenting, returns in disguise to become their governess, is finally discovered, and dies with her children sobbing around her.

In such plays as these, Miss Morris won the title of "Queen of Spasms." She was always the "soiled dove," the woman who dies a heartrending death after several acts of sinning and suffering. In her ability to portray the required emotions, Miss Morris was unmatched. No actress could equal her flashes of scorn, her overpowering grief, or her tumultuous passion. At times she was feverish and cat-like; at other times she was a human volcano "lighting up the stage with blazes of emotional lightning." But more successful yet was her portrayal of the inner struggles which manifest themselves in the quivering lip, the heaving breast, and especially the streaming eye. Miss Morris's power to manufacture stage tears was phenomenal. She could weep any time the dramatic situation demanded it. The tears were real, too, not simulated by trickery or illusion. They flowed whenever the actress turned her thoughts to sad or pitiable things. She tells us it was necessary for her to feel actual sadness before she could weep, but apparently she

was able to summon a tearful mood quite easily. If the role she played had lost its sadness through frequent repetition, she stimulated her emotions by imagining her own death, or by recalling a tragic book, poem, or incident from real life. "Thus," she tells us, "in *Alixe* it was not for my lost lover that I oftenest wept such racing tears, but for poor old *Tennessee's Partner* as he buried his worthless dead. . . . While in *Camille* many and many a night her tears fell fast over the memory of a certain mother's face as she told me of . . . returning from the burial of her only child. . . ." [30]

The sympathetic appeal of Miss Morris's tears was enhanced by the personal situation of the actress. When she was young, she had met with an accident which injured her spine and caused her considerable suffering for the rest of her life. In her public writings she also complained of her "chronic neuralgia" and the malaria which she never "got out of her bones." These ailments, and Miss Morris's courageous endurance of them, were well advertised to the public. Audiences knew she carried bottles of medicine with her on the stage and had a physician in attendance to minister to her between acts, so when the actress appeared to suffer torments as Alixe or Miss Multon or Camille, the audience suspected she actually was feeling great physical pain and enduring it for the sake of her performance. Miss Morris encouraged this belief by taking prolonged intermissions between each act of her plays. Sometimes these waits were as long as forty-five or fifty minutes each, and a performance lasted far, far into the night. During these waits, audiences imagined that the brave Miss Morris was backstage battling for strength enough to continue her acting. It is true that sometimes she was ill and was forced to rest and take treatment between the acts, but very often—according to Vivia Ogden, a fellow actress—she simply refused to hurry and frittered the time away while the audience waited with pity and admiration growing in their hearts.*

Even without such devices, Miss Morris could make an audience weep and suffer with her. Spectators experienced an immediate and strong empathic response to her acting; they identified themselves personally with her struggles. Few actresses have ever possessed so much personal magnetism. Sometimes the spell which Miss Morris exerted amounted to actual hypnotism. For example, in the mad scene of *L'Article 47* the actress would seat herself on a chair, put her elbow

* Despite her frail health, Miss Morris lived to the respectable age of 77.

on her knee, and play her scene gazing straight into the eyes of the spectators—with the result that invariably women in the audience would faint or become hysterical. Even the actors and actresses playing with Miss Morris felt the potency of her spell. The man who played Gaston to her Camille usually was weeping when he left the stage. Louis James, who played with her in *Miss Multon,* was so overcome by her mimic agony that he couldn't speak until she prompted him. Vivia Ogden, acting in the same play, burst into tears and could hardly control herself enough to continue the scene.[31]

Almost everyone felt the unusual magnetism of the Morris personality, but no one could explain it. Most of the critics agreed that her appeal defied analysis. In 1885, for example, "Nym Crinkle" (the dramatic critic, A. C. Wheeler) wrote: "I give it up. Critics have wrestled with that condition in and out of season—how she can play upon all sensibilities and sweep as with supernatural fingers the whole gamut of emotions passes critical knowledge." [32]

In stimulating the emotions of her spectators, Miss Morris was aided by a keen sensitivity to their moods and reactions. She detected the feelings of an audience and she played upon these feelings as a musician plays upon his instrument. In her *Life on the Stage* she declares: ". . . I possessed that curious sixth sense of the born actress, and as a doctor with the aid of his stethoscope can hear sounds of grim warning or of kindly promise . . . so an actress, with that stethoscopic sixth sense, detects even the *forming* emotions of her audience, feeling incipient dissatisfaction before it becomes open disapproval, or thrilling at the intense silence that ever precedes a burst of approbation." [33]

Like Matilda Heron, Clara Morris practiced a naturalistic type of acting. Her scar in *L'Article 47* was copied from a hideous disfigurement she saw on a woman who sat opposite her in a street car. Her simulation of death by heart disease in *Miss Multon* was copied from the horrors she watched when a physician friend of hers paid a sick patient to run up a long flight of stairs so that the actress could observe the actual symptoms of a heart attack. Incidentally, Miss Morris reproduced these symptoms so realistically in her performance that she alarmed several medical men who sat in the audience.

Miss Morris rendered other death scenes with equal realism. Her acting in *Camille* was criticized for including too much revolting detail. The poisoning scene in *The Sphinx,* another play adapted from the

French, was described by a contemporary critic as follows: ". . . anything more ghastly, terrible, and realistic than her death scene has not for a long time been seen upon the stage. . . . A visible shudder went through the audience, and horror was depicted upon every face. Mingled with this was a sensation of disgust. It is evident, however, that this scene is to prove the sensation here, as it was in Paris, that will crowd the theatre." [34]

Clara Morris's unique power to make the spectators feel the womanly emotions she displayed was her supreme dramatic talent, and it covered a multitude of deficiencies. She did not have a particularly beautiful face or graceful figure. In her middle years she was sometimes described as being stout and ugly. Her voice was ordinary and her elocution was faulty. She was frequently criticized for her nasal twang and her barbarous pronunciations. *The Spirit of the Times,* on December 18, 1880, went so far as to suggest that if she were planning to act in London she had only one chance of success. "Let her be advertized as an Indian star who speaks Choctaw, while the rest of the company speaks English . . . and the novelty may be a sensation."

Miss Morris was crude in her stage technique, too. Her gestures were monotonous, her movements were often careless and awkward and she had many irritating mannerisms. Yet she triumphed. In spite of all her sins and deficiencies, in spite of the melodramatic claptrap in her plays, she mesmerized both the public and the critics. She gave them a thrill. Her emotional pyrotechnics made them shudder and weep, and this power was enough to win her a large and devoted following.

It is clear that Miss Morris's acting was instinctive and intuitive. A few critics, especially in her early years, claimed that she was a careful artist who prepared her effects and exercised "the art that conceals art" but the evidence is against this point of view. We know that she never acted in rehearsals. "Only foreigners do that," she said contemptuously. Before each new play, Augustin Daly, her director, was in terrible suspense not knowing what she would do in performance. Often he begged her to give him some inkling of the way she planned to play a scene, but she always said it was impossible for her to act without an audience. In preparing the role of Cora in *L'Article 47,* Miss Morris tells us that she did not know how she was going to act the part until the night before the opening. After the final rehearsal, she was so worried that she retired to her own room, locked herself

in, and spent several hours devising a walk and a crouch for Cora, choosing a certain tone of voice, and determining where her climaxes should come.[35] With this last minute preparation, she was ready to act the part on the following day. Such a confession does not suggest careful artistry but rather an habitual reliance upon inspiration—an impression which is confirmed by the way her performances varied according to her moods and impulses.

One would expect that an actress who wept real tears and who, according to her own testimony, felt every emotion she portrayed, would have little control of herself while she was in the grip of these passions. Evidently this was not the case with Clara Morris. Her head was relatively cool even when her heart seemed to be breaking. In this trait she was not typical of the usual actress of the emotionalistic school who completely lost herself in the emotions of her role. In contrast, Miss Morris was able to maintain a particular state of mind which she describes as follows: "There are, when I am on the stage, three separate currents of thought in my mind; one in which I am keenly alive to Clara Morris, to all the details of the play, to the other actors and how they act and to the audience; another about the play and the character I represent; and, finally, the thought that really gives me the stimulus for acting. . . . As to really losing one's self in a part, that will not do: it is worse to be too sympathetic than to have too much art. I must cry in my emotional *roles* and feel enough to cry, but I must not allow myself to be so affected as to mumble my words, to redden my nose, or to become hysterical." [36]

Evidently Miss Morris could remain detached even in impassioned scenes. When Louis James was overcome by her agony in *Miss Multon* and couldn't force himself to speak, the actress—in the midst of her tears—muttered, "I say, what ails you. . . . Are you dumb?" [37] When Miss Morris and one of the child actors were performing a tearful scene in *Miss Multon,* the actress let the child weep for a while, then she leaned over, "her own face strained with tears, and agony in every line of it" and murmured: "Shut up now, and give me a show." [38] Often in a tense scene when the audience was dissolved in tears, Miss Morris would turn upstage and whisper something so spontaneous and witty that it was almost impossible for her fellow actors to keep a straight face. One of Miss Morris's hostile critics relates that in *Alixe* during the best scene with her mother, Miss Morris, as Alixe, "sawed one arm across the other as a sign to the leader of the orchestra to

start the music, and during one of her mother's most impassioned appeals, she walked to the wings and gave an order off stage!" The critic adds the horrified comment, "Fancy Alixe directing a fiddler and chatting with a stage-carpenter during one of the climaxes of her sufferings!" [39]

During the early years of Miss Morris's career, she enjoyed an immense popularity. Audiences had never seen anything like her opulent display of womanly emotions. Her ability to weep was the talk of the nation. Any faultiness in her stage technique was forgotten in the hypnotic spell she was able to cast. So long as her inspiration was strong and her emotions youthful and vigorous, she maintained a loyal following. As she grew older and stouter and failed to develop in versatility or artistry, and as public taste shifted away from the Sardou-type drama, the critics began to ridicule her methods. In the 1880's she was billed as "America's Greatest Living Actress." By 1902 the newspapers referred to her as "America's once famous actress." In 1876, her performance in *Miss Multon* received the following review in the *Spirit of the Times:* "Her great intensity was astonishingly effective, her pathos genuine and unaffected, and throughout she held her audience, so to speak, in the palm of her hand. . . . Her acting was superb. . . . Before such a rare manifestation of genius, criticism is perforce silent. Can we give greater praise? We have no fault to find. Not one blemish is to be discovered even by the most critical eye. . . ." [40] By 1888, the *Spirit of the Times* had lost its breathless admiration, and reviewed Miss Morris's *Renée de Moray* as follows: "She cries and makes her audience cry; she has long waits between the Acts and makes her audiences wait; she is the same Clara Morris and attracts the same admirers of stage hysteria and disease. It is as impossible to improve her by criticism as to reform the morphia habit by sensible advice. We can only wonder and pity and pass on." [41] And finally, the ultimate damnation was uttered in 1902 by Alan Dale who, after listening to a lecture by Clara Morris, wrote: "I not only found no symptoms of greatness, but though I tried hard, persistently, strenuously, I could not discover any one single peg upon which to hang the barren possibility of one solitary great moment." [42]

Ill health and, perhaps, waning popularity forced Miss Morris to retire from regular stage appearances in the 1890's. For several years thereafter, she was seen occasionally in vaudeville and revivals, and kept very much in the public eye by her lecture tours and her writing.

Three volumes of stage reminiscences came from her pen, and she was a regular contributor to the Sunday supplements with articles on such subjects as "Temptations of the Stage," "Why Men Don't Go to Church," and "If I Were a Girl Again." In 1903, 1909, and again in 1911 she received wide publicity because, according to the newspapers, the mortgage on her home was about to be foreclosed while the old actress was lying inside at death's door. Each time, Miss Morris's health revived, and each time the actors of New York came to her rescue with a splendid benefit. Miss Morris finally did lose her old home and went to live with relatives, but she did not die until 1925.

Probably the fairest estimate of the acting of this unusual woman can be found in an essay by John R. Towse, the noted dramatic critic of the New York *Evening Post*. In reviewing her career, Mr. Towse says:

It is by no means easy to define her place in any coldly critical category. She was, first and last, a natural born actress. If judged by her artistic equipment only, she could not establish a claim to any very high place in the ranks of her contemporaries. She was far behind many of them in artistic cunning, but she distanced all of them in flashes of convincing realism and in poignancy of natural emotion. She was often barely respectable as an elocutionist, she was habitually crude, and occasionally unrefined, in pose, gesture, and utterance; she had distressful mannerisms, she could not or did not attempt to modify or disguise her individual personality, her range was limited—she could not soar into the upper regions of tragedy—but, nevertheless, she showed, especially in emotional crises, a strong grasp of diversified characters within her own boundaries and illuminated them, at intervals, with such a blaze of vivid truthfulness that, for the moment, she seemed to be perfectly identified with them. . . . As she never really succeeded, or came very near to success, in any great part, she can never be called a great actress. . . . But she was great as a realist in the exaggerated, false, or morbid emotionalism of the current French plays of her period, and displayed high intelligence in a considerable range of English drama.[43]

FANNY DAVENPORT

When Agnes Ethel refused the leading role in Augustin Daly's production of *Man and Wife,* the part was entrusted to Clara Morris and her success in the role launched her career as the queen of domestic

emotionalism. However, there was another actress in the company who might have been given the role, and who might have proved equally successful in it. This was Fanny Davenport. She had been engaged by Daly in 1869, a year before Miss Morris joined the company, and had already established herself as a charming, vivacious comedienne. However, Daly feared she did not possess the emotional power for the lead in *Man and Wife* so, after some backstage finagling,[44] she was assigned the comedy role of Blanche and Clara Morris got the emotional role of Anne. Perhaps Daly was right in believing that Fanny Davenport could not play the role of Anne, yet before this actress ended her career she had metamorphosed from a sparking comedienne in such plays as *London Assurance, The Belle's Stratagem,* and *Merry Wives of Windsor,* to an emotional star in four melodramas by Victorien Sardou. Thus it is fair to say that in her early career Miss Davenport belonged to the personality school of Viola Allen, Julia Marlowe, and Ada Rehan, but during the last fifteen years of her acting she firmly established herself as a leader of the school of feminine emotionalism. It is as an exponent of this school that she is best remembered; ". . . when the name of Fanny Davenport is mentioned," says Mary Caroline Crawford, "it is of her Sardou period . . . that most of us think—such power and passion, such a wealth of artistic temperament did she display in these roles." [45]

Eminent and successful as was the career of Fanny Davenport, she set no styles in acting, established no school, and never achieved unanimous acclaim as a "great" actress; yet her solid success and her wide popularity deserve inclusion in the list of representative actresses of the school of emotionalism.

"Miss Fanny," christened Fanny Lily Gipsy Davenport, was the eldest child of the great American tragedian, E. L. Davenport, and literally grew up in the theatre and with a love for the theatre. As a child she appeared in many of her father's productions, and made her adult debut at the age of twelve, playing the role of Charles II of Spain in *Faint Heart Never Won Fair Lady.* The fact that she was always robust and big for her age enabled her, in her early career, to play boy's parts and parts beyond her years. Soon after her adult debut, she left her father's company and acted in Louisville and Philadelphia. In 1869 she attracted Augustin Daly's attention, and soon made her appearance in his Fifth Avenue Theatre as Lady Gay Spanker in *London Assurance.* Thereafter she acted a variety of roles

in Shakespeare, old comedies and new comedies, and, under Daly's tutelage, she established herself as an actress of charm, vitality, and sparkle. Her abundant physical endowments added to her appeal. William Winter, always appreciative of wholesome physical allure, described her as "a voluptuous beauty, radiant with youth and health, taut and trim of figure, having regular features, a fair complexion, golden hair, sparking hazel eyes, and a voice as naturally musical and cheery as the fresh, incessant rippling flow of a summer brook." [46]

Fanny Davenport's acting, before her Sardou period, was sprightly, high spirited, charming, and feminine. Her effectiveness was largely the result of her lavish physical endowments and captivating personality. John R. Towse says she was "a superb creature physically, in form and feature a thing of perfect beauty. . . . Her personal charms formed no small proportion of her theatrical assets." [47] In reviewing her roles, Towse always points out the defects of the actress's techniques, yet he always notes the compensating charm of her looks and personality. As Letitia Hardy in *The Belle's Stratagem,* for example, Towse says that Miss Davenport ruined the earlier scenes by grotesque exaggeration "but she was a bewitching vision." [48] As Peg Woffington in *Masks and Faces,* the actress was "In personal fascination . . . the equal, doubtless, of Peg herself. . . ." But "The tone of the comedy and the manners of the period she disregarded." [49] In *As You Like It,* "Fanny Davenport was a lovely Rosalind to the eye, was spirited, arch, gallant, and coquettish, but the poetic side of the character eluded her." [50] Brander Matthews, another perceptive critic, says that he remembers Fanny Davenport as the most satisfying Lady Teazle he ever saw, yet Matthews, too, adds the qualifying statement that "perhaps . . . her youth and her beauty, her high spirits and her enjoyment of life made me credit her performance with more merit than it had." [51]

During the first half of her adult career, Fanny Davenport relied upon beauty and personality for the success she achieved. During the last half, she forsook romantic and comic roles for more emotional and tragic parts, and became a leading actress of the emotionalistic school. Her developing dramatic power was first noted in 1873, when she played Madge, the tramp, in W. S. Gilbert's *Charity.* Augustin Daly, always ready to capitalize on the talents of his company, recognized Miss Davenport's new potentialities and, in 1876, wrote for her a play called *Pique.* In this drama Miss Davenport was asked to exhibit a considerable emotional range. She succeeded brilliantly, and

Pique ran for 238 consecutive performances. Shortly thereafter, Miss Davenport formed her own company and toured the United States as a star, accumulating a repertoire which included more and more emotional roles. In 1883 she secured the American rights to Sardou's *Fedora,* and from then until her death in 1898 she was strictly a devotee of "Sardoodledom." *Fedora* lasted for five seasons, and was followed by *La Tosca, Cleopatra,* and *Gismonda,* all of which were enormously successful.

In the emotional melodramatics of the Sardou drama, Miss Davenport used her imposing physique and her great vitality to good advantage. But instead of the coquetry and charm of her early acting she now displayed violent emotion—rage, jealousy, grief, hatred, and lust. That she succeeded in the portrayal of these passions is shown by the public reception of her plays and by the critical comments she received. The reviewers praised her "dramatic explosions," her "well-simulated frenzies," her "terrible struggles," and her "power and passion." Montrose Moses deplored her lack of "quietude and repression" and declared that she made her roles great "through exertion, not through unconscious inspiration." [52] At any rate, these emotional exertions captured the public fancy and earned rich financial rewards for Miss Davenport. She died a wealthy woman—albeit much too young—and will be remembered as a good, though not a great actress, who succeeded both as an exponent of the personality school and as a leader in the field of feminine emotionalism.

MRS. LESLIE CARTER

The school of feminine emotionalism found another prominent exponent in Mrs. Leslie Carter. This actress, whose career extended well into the contemporary period, can be considered as one of the last successful practitioners of this type of acting. Although feminine emotionalism of some kind will always be seen on the stage, the naturalistic exhibitionism practiced by Matilda Heron and Clara Morris was eventually obliterated by the demands of the Ibsen-Chekhov drama and by the ideals of acting, established in the United States by Minnie Maddern Fiske and in Europe by the Moscow Art Theatre. However, before the new ideals of acting gained dominance, Mrs. Carter triumphed in the field of feminine emotionalism and, although she eventually

changed her style to fit a new kind of drama and a changed public taste, she can be considered as a prominent representative of a vanishing school.

The emotional performances of Mrs. Carter attracted much notoriety; so did her private life and the plays in which she appeared. She was born Caroline Louise Dudley in Lexington, Kentucky, on June 10, 1862, and at the age of eighteen married the prominent and wealthy Leslie Carter. The marriage lasted nine years, ending in a divorce suit which was the sensation of the period. Left without a means of support, Mrs. Carter determined to try the stage. Since she had no experience or training, her only assets were (1) the publicity received from her divorce suit; (2) her determination; and (3) the beauty of her face and voice. David Belasco described her as "a pale, slender, red-haired girl with a pair of green eyes, gleaming under black brows, who alternately wept and smiled, whose gestures were full of unconscious grace, and whose voice vibrated with musical sweetness." [53]

After her appearances in two Broadway productions—*The Ugly Duckling* in 1890 and *Miss Helyett* in 1891—in which she did not achieve any particular distinction, Mrs. Carter retired for two years and placed herself under the tutelage of David Belasco. Her training during this period was unique. Belasco recruited a company whose sole purpose was to rehearse with Mrs. Carter. With only Belasco as critic and audience, the would-be actress prepared and acted forty roles ranging from Shakespeare to French melodrama, and from old comedy to modern farce. It is said that every one of the parts was studied, rehearsed, and acted as carefully and completely as though a crowded house was to see the performance. It is further said that Belasco used such teaching devices as dragging his protégé about the floor by the hair and kicking her in the spine so she could experience the sensations of physical suffering.[54]

Mrs. Carter emerged from this training in 1895 to act the leading role in Belasco's production of *The Heart of Maryland*. She was sensationally successful and played the role for three years. Then followed her triumphs in Belasco's *Zaza, Du Barry,* and *Adrea.* The first two plays received as much notoriety for their "lurid" and "immoral" subject matter as for the emotional pyrotechnics of Mrs. Carter's performances.

In 1906, Mrs. Carter defied the wishes of her tutor and manager, Mr. Belasco, and married an obscure actor named William L. Payne.

There ensued a sensational break between the actress and her manager, with charges and recriminations on both sides and with reams of publicity in the tabloids and Sunday supplements. Mrs. Carter never again acted for Belasco. Her career, however, continued for twenty-five years under other directors or under her own management. Although she flourished to a degree, her subsequent success was never so brilliant as it had been under Belasco. Her last stage appearances were in 1929, and she died eight years later at the age of seventy-five.

The bases for Mrs. Carter's success as an actress are clear. She had striking beauty: a mass of red hair "one shade hotter than Titian," an exquisitely pale complexion, soft blue eyes, and a slender, shapely figure; she had a mellifluous, musical voice, capable of great range and variety and trained for clarity and cadence; she had a fiery temperament to match her red hair; and, finally, she had the ability to lose herself in the emotions of her role and to involve an audience in the hysteria of her own feelings.

There is much evidence to illustrate the emotional nature of Mrs. Carter's acting. One scene in *The Heart of Maryland* required her to race up a flight of stairs and swing from the clapper of a bell to prevent its ringing. In rehearsal she tried running up the spiral stairs but found that the ascent made her dizzy. She refused to rehearse the scene, declaring that she could never do it except under the excitement of actual performance. This proved to be the case. Whenever there was an audience to stimulate her, Mrs. Carter could perform her gymnastics with admirable success, but without an audience she was unable to act.

The same situation prevailed in Mrs. Carter's performance of the sensational play *Zaza*. Her force and effectiveness, says Lewis Strang, came from a state of semi-hysteria. There was, he said, "an exciting spirit of gamble about Mrs. Carter's impersonation. One paid his money at the door, not knowing exactly what was coming to him in return for it. He might be favored with a wholly absorbing exhibition of hysterical theatrics; he might get merely a mildly interesting specimen of mechanical acting." [55]

On the opening night of *Zaza*, Mrs. Carter pulled all the emotional stops and gave a performance which stirred her audience with as much passion—almost—as she herself had been experiencing. Franklin E. Fyles describes this debauch in the following words: "Finally, the audience could no longer contain itself, and it burst into mad applause

and cheers, drowning the last words of the hysterical woman before them. As she fell back against the mantelpiece exhausted and trembling, the tears streaming down her face, . . . all over the house people rose, some standing on their chairs, waving handkerchiefs and programmes in fanatical irresponsibility." [56] Mrs. Carter was called upon for a speech, but, reports the New York *Herald* for January 10, 1899, she was "too overwrought for more than a mere expression of thanks."

This kind of exhibitionism characterized Mrs. Carter's acting in all her roles. Whenever she was able to throw herself into a state of semi-hysteria, she stirred and titillated her audiences; when the mood escaped her, she failed to make an impression. Thus it followed that her early performances in any role were generally her best; the longer she played a part the more mechanical it became because, with each repetition, she was less able to lose herself in the appropriate emotions.

William Winter despised the "lewdness and cheapness" of Mrs. Carter's roles, and he also ridiculed her reliance on physical and emotional exhibitionism. In commenting on her performance in *Du Barry,* Winter says: ". . . the method of Mrs. Carter . . . was to work herself into a state of violent excitement, to weep, vociferate, shriek, rant, become hoarse with passion, and finally to flop and beat the floor." [57] Although Winter disliked such a method, he nevertheless recognized the "executive force and skill" in Mrs. Carter's performances, and when she acted the role of Adrea in 1904, Winter had high praise for "the depth of tragical feeling" and the "power of dramatic expression" [58] which she revealed—to Winter—for the first time.

It is clear, therefore, that the main attraction of Mrs. Carter's acting, on which her fame largely rests, was her emotional pyrotechnics. In her early roles under Belasco these exhibitions won her great acclaim and gained her the reputation of having "shed tears over every square foot of all the older stages in America. . . ." [59] Besides her ability to emote, she had the assets mentioned previously: beauty of face and figure, clarity and purity of speech, and a large measure of feminine magnetism. However, these were used as adjuncts to her emotional exhibitionism and were always considered subsidiary to her main appeal. In her later years on the stage, after she broke with Belasco and after her youth and emotional powers had declined, she changed her style to fit her roles in such plays as Pinero's *The Gay Lord Quex* and

Maugham's *The Circle*. However, it is as a successful emotional actress in plays such as *Zaza* and *Du Barry* that Mrs. Carter earned her place as a successor to the vanishing tradition of Mowatt, Keene, Heron, Morris, and Davenport.

V

THE PERSONALITY SCHOOL

THE LADIES OF THE EMOTIONALISTIC SCHOOL ENJOYED WIDE POPULAR-
ity but they were not without rivals. Competing for public esteem was
a group of young players, mostly women, whose style of performance
was different and who appeared in plays that were a sharp contrast to
the fervid emotional dramas favored by Clara Morris and Mrs. Leslie
Carter. This group of performers, whose most prominent representatives at the end of the nineteenth century were Maude Adams, Julia
Marlowe, Viola Allen, and Ada Rehan, constituted a group which can
be termed the personality school. Its outstanding characteristic was the
appeal of the personality of the individual player. Personality, to be
sure, is an ingredient in the appeal of every performer. It flavors and,
in some degree, shapes each role which a player creates. At times, a
performer's personality, added to the dramatist's conception of a character, may effect a synthesis which creates a performance of memorable quality. Thus, Edwin Booth's personality helped to illuminate the
character of Hamlet and to shape his performance of that role into a
portrayal of unusual dimension. Charlotte Cushman's personality enabled her to complete and project the character of Queen Katherine as
few actresses have ever done. However, in neither case did the performer substitute himself or herself for the dramatic character. Booth's
Hamlet was Shakespeare's character plus Edwin Booth; Cushman's
Queen Katherine was the poet's ideal plus certain aspects of Charlotte
Cushman's personality.

In contrast to this kind of creative synthesis is the method of the
personality school: the substitution of the performer's personality for

the dramatic character, or the portrayal of dramatic characters which fit the performer's personality so exactly that performer and character are practically identical. In either case, the effect is the same: the basic appeal of the acting comes from the individual personality of the player.

The typical actress of the personality school based her acting on the appeal of personality and, moreover, on a particular kind of appeal: that of womanly loveliness and feminine virtue, unsullied by coarseness or passion. The actress of this school had usually undergone a thorough training and apprenticeship and, like the actress of the classic school, had performed a wide variety of roles in the standard drama, including parts in comedy and high tragedy. In her maturity, however, she confined herself to roles which were sweet, wholesome, and refined—like the actress herself. If she performed Shakespeare, it was not Lady Macbeth or Queen Katherine but Rosalind or Viola. If she acted in contemporary plays, they were not the social problem plays of Ibsen or the sexy melodramas of Sardou, but romantic and sentimental dramas like *The Christian, When Knighthood Was in Flower,* and *Peter Pan.* The great tragic roles of the old standard drama were avoided in favor of charming, romantic roles. The portrayal of strong passion was shunned in favor of sentiment and wholesome feeling. The actress aimed to charm her spectators with her feminine loveliness and to uplift and ennoble them by the moral appeal of her personal character and the wholesome effect of the role she was acting.

Typically, too, the actress of the personality school was assisted in her appeal by a lovely face and figure, by a rich or appealing voice, and by great competence in stage technique. She was, in short, a deft and artful performer with unusual personal magnetism who used the stage as a means of projecting her feminine charms to inspire her audience with a feeling of purity and optimism.

Although the personality school, as here defined, flourished most prominently at the turn of the nineteenth century, it was ably represented much earlier in the history of American acting. Two early and notable exponents of the style were Clara Fisher and Maggie Mitchell. They were worthy predecessors of the Adams-Marlowe-Allen-Rehan group, and illustrate the fact that the kind of acting whose chief appeal resides in the personality of the individual player can be found in every period of dramatic history. These two actresses will serve as the prototype of hundreds of other players of the same school who have en-

livened the theatrical scene but whose achievements are less worthy of review.

CLARA FISHER

Clara Fisher was the actress whom Noah Ludlow termed "the most fascinating woman on the stage or in private life that I remember to have ever met in the profession." [1] Singularly gifted both as an actress and a singer, Miss Fisher appears to have owed more success to her sparkling, vivacious personality than to her considerable histrionic ability. Some critics might group her with the classic actresses because of her range, her mastery of the techniques of her art, and her occasional appearance in such roles as Ophelia and Desdemona. Or she might be classed as a variety artist like Lotta Crabtree because of her gift at mimicry, her skill in entr'acte singing and dancing, and her direct, spontaneous appeal. Indeed, she was a clever, versatile performer whose long career and varied talents relate her to several styles and schools. Still, it was her fascinating personality which attracted most comment and which enlivened all her roles. Hence it is not unreasonable to consider her an early representative of the personality school.

Clara Fisher, like Mary Ann Duff and many other American actresses, was English born, but she adopted America as her home in 1827 when she was sixteen years old and spent the remaining seventy-one years of her life in the United States. She was already a star when she arrived in New York in 1827, for at the tender age of six she had appeared in a children's production at Drury Lane Theatre in which she had acted several characters, including Richard III. She was such a sensation that she became "the wonder of her times." Joseph Ireland declared that as a juvenile performer she "eclipsed all predecessors and has been surpassed by no successor." [2]

As a juvenile, Clara Fisher amazed her public by appearing to grasp the concept of her author and to understand the motives and psychology of the adult characters she played. Laurence Hutton records that when she acted with an adult cast she was never dwarfed by the contrast with them but, instead, made them appear to be entirely out of proportion.[3] However, it was as a young lady almost seventeen years old that Clara Fisher made her American debut, and the qualities which captivated her audience on this occasion—and which continued

to captivate them for many years—were her beauty of person and her irresistible buoyancy of personality. Ireland describes the physical charms which dazzled her first night audience in these words:

Though not possessing strict beauty of feature, she was . . . one of the most bewitching specimens of feminine creation that eyes have ever looked on. Her person, below the medium height and just reaching an agreeable plumpness, was exquisitely formed, her manners were sprightly and vivacious, yet perfectly natural and artless, her expression arch and intelligent, her cheeks dimpling with smiles. . . .[4]

During her early years on the American stage and, indeed, throughout most of her career, Clara Fisher impersonated a wide variety of characters, both male and female, but won greatest acclaim in those parts where her natural vivacity and charm were exploitable: rollicking boys and girls, saucy chambermaids, and coquettish belles. This type of character is well illustrated in the roles she performed oftenest, among which were Albina Mandeville in *The Will,* Letitia Hardy in *The Belle's Stratagem,* Maria in *The Actress of All Work,* Little Pickle in *The Spoiled Child,* and the Four Mowbrays in *Old and Young.* Miss Fisher was also a popular vocalist and often appeared in light opera or entertained her audience with entr'acte songs. Although her singing voice had limited range, she put over a song with resounding success by means of her varied facial expressions, her expressive gestures, and her amazing ability to act out the number while she was singing it. She was able to project her personality even in her singing.

Miss Fisher also parallels the later members of the personality school in the reputation she established for exemplary moral conduct. In her heyday she was the idol of the male population but she avoided temptation and maintained a spotless reputation. After she married the musician, James G. Maeder, she became a faithful wife and a devoted mother. James Murdoch called her "a lady of refined manners and irreproachable character" [5] and Charles Congdon, a journalist of the period, wrote that "those who talk foolishly about the immorality of the stage may be surprised and perhaps pained to learn that she was a good wife, a good mother, and a good woman altogether." [6]

Miss Fisher remained on the stage for many years, for she did not retire finally until 1880, but her appeal steadily diminished as she lost her youthful vivacity and allure. She eventually played classic parts and old lady roles in which her experience and technical skill were

great enough to make her successful. However, it was in the sprightly, youthful roles which fitted her sparkling, joyous personality that she made her greatest success and she deserves, therefore, to be called one of the earliest and brightest stars of the personality school.

MAGGIE MITCHELL

Another representative of this school, whose appeal was similar to that of Clara Fisher, was Margaret Julia Mitchell, beloved throughout the nation as Maggie Mitchell. Like Clara Fisher, Maggie began her career as a child and won acclaim for portraying three different male characters—Claude Melnotte, Richard III, and Young Norval—in a single evening. Also like Clara Fisher, Maggie captivated her audience with her sprightly dancing and, more importantly, with her elfin, roguish appeal—an appeal which was always presented in a wholesome, uplifting fashion. Her career extended from 1851 to 1891, and while it was not quite so long nor nearly so varied as Clara Fisher's, it was notable for its sustained success.

For most of her life, Maggie Mitchell specialized in roles which suited her wholesome vivacity and hoydenish charm. By far her most popular vehicle was a piece called *Fanchon the Cricket,* a dramatization of George Sand's story, *La Petite Fadette.* Maggie stumbled onto the play in 1861 and from then until the end of her career, Fanchon remained the most popular character in her repertory. Other plays like *Little Barefoot, The Pearl of Savoy, Mignon,* and *Jane Eyre* were presented with success but the public always demanded a return of *Fanchon the Cricket.* In all these vehicles, Maggie projected her own engaging personality. As Oral Coad and Edwin Mims remarked, "Her sketches were not careful studies, but pleasing improvisations," and the secret of their success was "naturalness and a seeming absence of art" [7] combined with youthful animation which she never lost even in her mature years. "She had," wrote Luther L. Holden, "the rare faculty of painting the picture of maidenly purity and nobility of soul most deftly; and her audience laughed when she laughed, and wept when she wept." [8] As a purveyor of personal charm for forty years, she is a colorful representative of a style of acting which has been seen in every age of the American theatre but which flourished as a school after Maggie Mitchell left the stage.

A SISTERHOOD OF SWEETNESS AND LIGHT

The actresses who made the personality school a dominant force in the American theatre at the turn of the nineteenth century were four outstanding performers: Maude Adams, Julia Marlowe, Viola Allen, and Ada Rehan. This quartet of charming and virtuous ladies form a "sisterhood of sweetness and light." In contrast to the ablest players of other schools, their achievement was not the greatest. For example, none of them attained the stature of Charlotte Cushman and none of them possessed the elemental emotional power of Clara Morris. Yet all of them won great popularity and acclaim; all of them were admired for their personal refinement and uplifting influence; and all of them provided superior examples of the kind of acting characteristic of the personality school.

The Misses Adams, Marlowe, and Allen were born within six years of each other and made their adult debuts within six years of each other. Maude Adams and Viola Allen were children of theatrical parents and both of them practically grew up in the theatre. Julia Marlowe, who was born in England and came to America when she was four, began her theatrical career at eleven, playing children's roles in musical shows. The first two ladies learned their art through practical experience, while Miss Marlowe, in addition to practical experience, had a three-year course of training with a retired actress, Miss Ada Dow, who took the girl into her home and administered a thorough, old-fashioned course in how to prepare and how to act the great feminine roles of the standard drama.

Miss Marlowe made her adult debut as Parthenia in the old-fashioned tragedy of *Ingomar*. For the ensuing nine years she acted nothing but classical roles. Then, bowing to popular taste, she appeared in modern romantic comedies and played in them for six years. Returning to the classics, she began starring in Shakespearean drama with E. H. Sothern, and from 1914 until her retirement in 1924, she and Sothern became famous as the leading exponents of Shakespearean drama in the United States.

Miss Allen, like Julia Marlowe, received her initial training in the classics. Her second adult role was Desdemona, which she played to the Othello of John McCullough. She also supported McCullough in *Virginius, The Gladiator,* and *Richard III.* She continued her theatrical education by playing engagements with Lawrence Barrett and Tom-

maso Salvini, after which she acted for two seasons in "Old Comedy" with Joseph Jefferson, W. J. Florence, and Mrs. John Drew. Such early and thorough experience in the standard drama of the mid-nineteenth century gave Miss Allen's style an elevated, poetic quality which she never lost. It enabled her in later life to succeed admirably in romantic drama but handicapped her in the performance of modern comedy.

In the training they received, the Misses Marlowe and Allen represent the survival of the classic repertory in the American theatre, but Miss Adams, who exceeded both of them in popularity, was identified almost exclusively with contemporary drama. She began her career acting modern roles and scored her greatest triumphs in the plays of James M. Barrie. Whereas we remember Miss Marlowe for her Rosalind and Miss Allen for her Viola, we remember Maude Adams for her Lady Babbie and Peter Pan.

None of the sisterhood of sweetness and light can be called great in her art. Adams, Allen, and Marlowe were accomplished actresses who served their professions with integrity and devotion, but all three were limited to roles which suited their own personalities. They could claim a modest versatility, but when they attempted the greatest tragic roles or the greatest comic roles, either they failed completely or they achieved only a moderate success.

Within their own range they were remarkably effective. They triumphed through the potency of their individual charms and through the appeal of their admirable womanhood. Personality and character were the secrets of their success, a success which illustrates, as one critic has remarked, how manner and temperament can eclipse the claims of genius.

Maude Adams, the most popular of the three, was the top money-making star in the entire United States. During her most active years, the public paid over a million and one half dollars to see her in Chicago and Boston, while almost twice as much was spent in New York City. She was, at the peak of her career, "the most conspicuous figure upon the English speaking stage, the most notable woman in a nation of a hundred million people. . . ." [9] And yet she could not claim either dramatic genius of the first order or great beauty of face and figure. She was merely "a little home-like woman, with gentle intimate graces, a fanciful, elfin humor, retiring, shy, and unworldly" but whenever she appeared, the theatres were packed—not only with seasoned

playgoers—but with thousands of people who never entered a play-house except to see Maude Adams.

The attraction of Miss Adams was the irresistible appeal of joyful-ness, of goodness, of optimism, and of eternal youth. She symbolized all that was fine and pure and hopeful. Her acting filled the spectator with a clean, sweet sense of happiness and well being. The spectator identified himself keenly and joyfully with Miss Adams' creations and the experience seemed to satisfy his hunger for better things. The affec-tionate relationship between actress and spectator which Miss Adams created in her portrayal of Lady Babbie is typical of her unique ap-peal. Lewis Strang writes:

Babbie was to us some dear friend, a cherished companion, whom we loved very much, whom we wished always with us, whose happiness was our greatest pleasure, whose sorrows awoke in us keenest sympthy; a friend whom we felt that we could trust to the end of time, who never dis-appointed nor wounded us, who never fell from our ideal, who returned sentiment for sentiment, who inspired us to look up and seek beyond, whose sympathy was rich, full, and complete, whose influence was en-nobling, purifying, and broadening.[10]

Miss Adams avoided roles which portrayed the seamy side of life, and she very rarely attempted parts which included the fierce, ele-mental passions of hate, jealousy, anger, or sex. When she played Juliet, she was admired for the convincing sweetness of her portrayal, but her performance lacked the depth and strength of high tragedy. William Winter said she presented "A balcony scene without passion, a parting scene without delirium of grief, and a potion scene without power." [11] It was in the realm of sentiment, of wholesome ideals and heart-warming charm that she excelled. Her appeal in this field was unique. Rarely has the power of an actress been described in such evangelistic terms as are used in the following summary of Miss Adams' influence: "She is building hope in the hearts of the despair-ing, courage in the souls of the conquered, and reviving beauty and joy and love in the lives of those whom misery and sin have crushed." [12]

The appeal of Viola Allen was also one of wholesomeness and up-lift. This actress had a refined, ladylike charm which added a touch of nobility to all the roles she played. She was unusually competent in her art, studious in her approach to any role, and well grounded in

the techniques of her profession. Her appeal was not directly to the hearts of her audience, like that of Maude Adams, but she touched the minds of her spectators, she pleased the critics with her well-rounded performances, and she satisfied the moral aspirations of a large segment of the public. She played many Shakespearean roles, and was greatly admired as Viola. But perhaps her most successful play was a piece called *The Christian* which, although universally acknowledged to be an "uncommonly bad drama," nevertheless drew audiences for two full seasons because of the uplifting nature of its message and the wholesome charm of its star.

Julia Marlowe, the third member of the sisterhood of sweetness and light, was perhaps the most versatile of the group. She played almost all the heroines of Shakespeare, including Cleopatra and Lady Macbeth, and she even attempted the role of Prince Hal. However, her success in the latter parts was negligible, whereas her achievement in such roles as Rosalind, Viola, and Juliet was admired and praised in both England and America. The latter roles suited Miss Marlowe exactly, for she was the epitome of womanly virtue and feminine loveliness—the foremost romantic actress of her time. She was careful and studious like Miss Allen, but possessed more warmth and personal magnetism. Arthur Symons, the English poet and critic, called her "warm and engaging" and said that "she fills and gladdens you with a sense of the single human being she is representing." [13] She did not, however, equal Maude Adams in arousing fervent loyalty and adoration. In an Adams performance, the spectator identified himself completely with her joyous, heart-warming youthfulness, whereas in a Marlowe performance, the spectator was content to sit back and enjoy the spectacle of winsome, lovely womanhood. Miss Marlowe always evoked such comments as "admirable, graceful, and sweet," "a beautiful, appealing, and poetic portrayal of a sweet character," "the very quintessence of femininity," "an enthralling influence of sweet and lovely womanhood."

An important element in Miss Marlowe's appeal, in addition to grace of person, was beauty of voice and delivery. Her tones were varied and flexible. Sometimes they were rich and satin-like or tender and appealing; at other times they could be hard and impervious or sharp and pitiless. In reading her lines, Miss Marlowe was always distinct and fluent and, according to Winter, she showed a fine discrimination for the meaning of words and a nice ability to "make her

speeches seem the utterance of thoughts prompted by words addressed to her. . . ." [14] Even higher praise was given her elocution by Arthur Symons who declared that there was no actor on the British stage who could speak English or English verse as beautifully and effectively as could Julia Marlowe and her partner Edward Sothern.[15]

Critics of an older generation who watched Miss Marlowe in her Shakespearean roles felt that she was always worthy but never great. She did not equal the famous Shakespearean performers of the mid-nineteenth century, but in an era when modern comedy had supplanted the standard repertory, she was welcomed and lauded for maintaining the Shakespearean tradition. Through long and devoted effort and, perhaps, for lack of competition, she won universal recognition as the foremost Shakespearean actress of her time. William Winter said: "She was not a Siddons, a Cushman, or a Faucit, but she is a superb actress. The sum of her influence has been distinctly and strongly helpful. . . ." [16]

For the first time in the history of American acting, uplifting influence became a major element in the appeal of popular stage performers. Audiences were attracted by the individual virtues of these ladies and by their reputations as moral leaders. Miss Allen was widely known for her activity as a Sunday School teacher. She refused to include any but virtuous characters in her repertory and made her greatest success as the noble heroine of *The Christian*. Miss Marlowe, too, specialized in virtuous roles and guarded her productions against coarseness or profanity. In the romantic play, *When Knighthood Was in Flower,* she refused absolutely to say the word "damn" on the stage even though the script called for it. Like Miss Allen, she maintained a spotless personal reputation and identified herself with many worthy philanthropies.

Maude Adams also set an example of purity and goodness in her personal life. She was a shy and reticent person who, in her heyday, never submitted to a press interview and never mingled in the world of fashion. On one occasion a certain magazine offered her $35,000 for a single article of biographical interest, but she refused the offer on the ground that her private views were of no consequence and should not be imposed on the public. She was a woman who guarded her integrity and her high ideals, who felt deep sympathy for all human suffering, and who dreamed of a world where beauty and goodness and happiness might be shared by all mankind. These aspirations, well

illustrated in the roles Miss Adams acted, inspired and ennobled the many thousands of people who flocked to see her. David Gray epitomized her influence when he wrote: ". . . Maude Adams must be accepted as an evolution-working personality, luminous with sweetness and light, even more than an artist; as a public influence even more than an actress. . . . The main current of her force is ethical rather than aesthetic." [17]

Maude Adams, Julia Marlowe, and Viola Allen were not great creative performers nor pioneers in any branch of theatrical art, but their admirable talents and their high moral influence, projected through charming personalities, give them high rank as exponents of the personality school.

Ada Rehan began her career a few years before her "sisters" and retired while they were still in their prime, yet Miss Rehan is closely related to them in the style and appeal of her acting and in the influence she exerted. Like them, Miss Rehan's range of parts was limited; she excelled in roles which suited her own personality; feminine charm and personal magnetism were strong elements in her appeal; and she was admired for her industry, her virtue, and her wholesome influence.

Ada Rehan was not a native American. She was born in Limerick, Ireland, April 22, 1860, but when she was five years old her family moved to Brooklyn, and there she grew up and went to school. Except for professional trips abroad, she lived her whole life in the United States, and died in New York City on January 8, 1916.

She received a sound, practical training in her profession. Her elder sisters had gone on the stage, so it was natural for Ada to consider a career in the theatre. She made her debut in Newark, New Jersey, at the age of thirteen, and two years later, through her sister's influence, she secured a place in Mrs. Drew's famous stock company at the Arch Street Theatre in Philadelphia.[18] She played stock there and in other eastern theatres for the next four years, and received a well-rounded training in the standard repertory of tragedy and old comedy. Like so many other young actresses of the period, she was called upon to support various traveling stars in their local appearances, and thus she had the opportunity of playing Ophelia to the Hamlet of Edwin Booth, and Virginia in John McCullough's production of *Virginius*. But Miss Rehan's career was not to be in tragedy; she was destined to shine for twenty years as the bright star of Augustin Daly's company, and to make her reputation as America's representative comedienne in cer-

tain Shakespearean roles and in the comedies and melodramas which Daly adapted from contemporary German playwrights.

Augustin Daly first took note of the acting of Ada Rehan in 1877. He observed her several times thereafter, and in 1879 engaged her as a permanent member of his own company. Miss Rehan became his leading lady and remained in this position until Daly's death in 1899. During this time she played over two hundred parts and played them all with a skill, a charm, and a magnetism which placed her in the front rank of American comediennes.

The two outstanding qualities of Miss Rehan's acting were vivacious humor and womanly charm. All the reviews of her acting laud these qualities in an amazing variety of phrases. Miss Rehan was always "sweetly reckless," "ardently impetuous," or "piquantly alluring." In all her roles she displayed "kindly vivacity," "ingenuous glee," "demure archness," "bewitching reserve," or "roguish charm." Whatever the female she portrayed, a basic womanliness and feminine appeal shone through. In her acting of Katherine in *The Taming of the Shrew,* "the crown of the assumption was woman-like charm." [19] As Valentine in *The Railroad of Love,* the outstanding trait was "tantalizing, delicious feminine caprice." [20] The chief beauty of her Julia in *Two Gentlemen of Verona* was "womanlike loveliness and grace." [21] And, as the leading lady in Tennyson's *The Foresters,* "the crowning excellence of her art was its expression of essential womanhood." [22]

Miss Rehan's looks, voice, and temperament enabled her to project and enhance her two outstanding qualities of vivacious humor and womanly charm. William Winter, a fervent admirer, says her physical beauty was "of the kind that appears in portraits of women by Romney and Gainsborough—ample, opulant, and bewitching." [23] She was tall and generously proportioned, with gray-blue eyes and a mass of brown hair. Many of her admirers considered her goddess-like in beauty, while others felt that it was her charm and vitality and not the perfection of her features which created the illusion of beauty. Walter Prichard Eaton says she was "not conventionally beautiful but arch, piquant, incessantly alive, with great feminine charm. . . ." [24] A study of her photographs reveals a face which a modern critic would call fresh, wholesome, and pleasing—but certainly not beautiful in the way Lillian Russell was beautiful.

As to the beauty of her voice, there was no disagreement. Everyone praised it for roundness, fullness, richness, and clarity, and many

critics were struck by what they termed its "caressing" quality. Otis Skinner said that Miss Rehan's voice "melted and caressed as it drawled," [25] and George Bernard Shaw, who witnessed her London performance in 1895, said: "When she is at her best, the music of her voice melts in the caress of the emotion it expresses." [26]

Another accomplishment on which there was little disagreement, was the clarity and grace of Miss Rehan's elocution. William Winter spoke of the "delicious purity" of her articulation and believed that her delivery of English verse was "the most melodious" then heard upon the stage. Even the London critics praised her "distinct enunciation" and the "perfect delivery" of her lines. A minority opinion was expressed by John R. Towse, who declared that: "Her delivery of verse, whether blank or rhymed, was always curiously monotonous and inexpressive." [27] The majority of critics and playgoers, however, agreed with George Bernard Shaw who, after witnessing her performance of Helena in *A Midsummer Night's Dream,* described her elocution in admiring terms, as follows: "Her treatment of Shakespearean verse is delightful after the mechanical intoning of Sarah Bernhardt. She gives us beauty of tone, grace of measure, delicacy of articulation: in short, all the technical qualities of verse music, along with the rich feeling and fine intelligence without which those technical qualities would soon become monotonous." [28] Evidently Miss Rehan's elocution made a lasting impression on Shaw because several years after her death he still classed her and Forbes Robertson as "the best speakers you could find on the stage." [29]

But perhaps the outstanding appeal of Miss Rehan's acting was the personal magnetism she exerted. Her exuberance and wholesome animal spirits coupled with her innate sweetness and tenderness were strong enough to captivate her audiences. Miss Rehan possessed the fortunate and somewhat rare power to impress her rich, warm personality on a single visitor chatting in her dressing room or, with equal force, on a thousand spectators sitting in a darkened auditorium. Undoubtedly her success on the stage was as much attributable to this personal magnetism as to her theatrical technique.

In the techniques of her art Miss Rehan was accomplished. Her training in stock and her association with the mature stars of the classic repertory gave her skill and assurance and taught her a style which perfectly suited the parts she acted. It was a deft, artificial style in which graceful movement and gesture, artful timing, and fluent,

musical delivery were so combined as to give the effect of spontaneity and naturalness. Augustin Daly, who monopolized Miss Rehan's talents for twenty years, capitalized on this style. The plays he chose for his star were not the modern, realistic dramas of Ibsen, then beginning to reshape the theatre. Rather, they were old comedies like *The School for Scandal* and *The Belle's Strategem,* or carefully selected and adapted comedies of Shakespeare, like *The Taming of the Shrew, Twelfth Night,* and *As You Like It,* or, most often, they were farces and melodramas borrowed from German dramatists and reworked by Mr. Daly. The following plays are examples of this latter group: *Red Letter Nights,* in which Miss Rehan played an amiable but mischievous girl; *The Transit of Leo,* in which the leading lady must alternate between "piquant playfulness" and "rueful self-censure"; *The Two Escutcheons,* which offered Miss Rehan another "arch and gay" part; and *The Countess Gucki,* which is described as "a fabric of comic complexities and playful colloquy." [30]

In all of these plays Miss Rehan was able to exploit her vivacious humor and womanly charm. She was also able to use her sprightly, artificial style of acting. As she was absolute mistress of this style, it won her great applause and wide popularity. But continued repetition of the same kind of role in the same style of acting eventually arrested Miss Rehan's growth as an actress and limited her range of accomplishment. George Bernard Shaw, in 1895, warned Miss Rehan that if she persisted in playing only the light, artificial roles which Daly selected, her style would become increasingly rhetorical and unreal. Shaw urged her to leave Daly's management, to espouse young ideas, and to seek plays with real women's parts in them. But Shaw's advice went unheeded. Miss Rehan remained faithful to Daly, acting in the plays he chose for her until his death. Then the situation, foreseen by Shaw, came to pass. Miss Rehan was unable to adapt her style to the demands of twentieth century realism. The years, too, had taken their toll, and Miss Rehan's youthful buoyance and charm were no longer strong enough to captivate her audiences. In the season of 1903–4, when Miss Rehan toured with Otis Skinner in a repertory of three of her best roles, Skinner sadly records: "From the opening rehearsal it was evident that the exquisite comedienne with whom I had the happiest memories of five years' association, was no more." [31]

In 1905, at the age of forty-five when she should have been in her prime, Miss Rehan made her final appearance on the stage. She died

eleven years later. As an actress she had provided wholesome pleasure for thousands of playgoers; she had brought to life a whole gallery of sprightly, charming, attractive women shaping them into likenesses of her own radiant personality; but certain of her techniques, suitable for poetic plays and artificial comedy, were not flexible enough to meet the needs of the new naturalistic drama. Her style became rhetorical and unreal as the years passed; and so, to the regret of many playgoers, Miss Rehan's appeal vanished with her youth and with the outmoded repertory of the Daly company.

VI

THE COMIC STAGE

THE SECOND HALF OF THE NINETEENTH CENTURY MIGHT BE CALLED the golden age of comic acting in America. During this period there flourished a host of players who were prodigal both in number and in comic genius. Their enormous versatility, their unending variety, and their astonishing achievements are enough to dazzle an admirer who studies their careers a full hundred years after their great performances. They can honestly be called comedians without peer, consummate artists, and the greatest comic performers in the history of the American stage. In order to understand the unique kind of acting they achieved in their time, one must glance at the type of comic acting which is seen today.

Many of the comedians of the twentieth century fall, roughly, into two classes. There are the clowns and gagsters, like Bob Hope, Jack Benny, and Red Skelton, and there are the sophisticates like Noel Coward and Cary Grant. The first group includes the men who have created a unique stage personality for themselves and who exploit it largely through verbal gags, and absurd situations which lead to gags. Bob Hope, for example, is always the exuberant, ingratiating smart alec, rolling his eyes and delivering rapid-fire wise cracks; Jack Benny is always the egregious tightwad bragging about himself and exchanging insults with his colleagues; Danny Kaye (with rare exceptions) is always the irrepressible clown, singing, dancing, cavorting, and double-talking his way in and out of scrapes. In cinema, television, or living theatre, the roles played by these comedians are always the same, and the programs are always tailored to fit the players. Bob Hope, Jack

Benny, Danny Kaye, and their fellows are enormously successful because the public enjoys the characters they have created for themselves, and the players behind the characters are expert in manipulating themselves through an endless succession of situations.

The sophisticated comedians seen on the recent American stage are a somewhat different breed. They are not clowns, gagsters, and entertainers like the Hopes and the Bennys. They are charming, polished, urbane drawing-room heroes with a dash of romantic appeal. They appear on stage, screen, and television in sprightly comedies like *Mary, Mary* or *The Moon is Blue*. Generally they do not vary their roles but play their attractive and clever selves over and over again.

The great decades of the nineteenth century had clowns and sophisticates, but it had, in addition, a group of expert actors whom I shall call character comedians. These gifted players were quite different from the clowns and sophisticates because they could change their personalities with their roles; they could produce uproarious laughter through careful portrayal of character; and they could and did create rich galleries of unique comic portraits.

To understand the kind of character acting they developed and the versatility they achieved, one should recall the extensive comic repertory of the period. First of all, there were the comedies of Shakespeare, which were part of the standard repertory and which offered such challenging roles as Bottom, Dogberry, Falstaff, Malvolio, Sir Andrew Aguecheek, etc. Secondly, there was so-called "old comedy," best represented by the plays of Goldsmith, Sheridan, and Farquhar, and offering such popular parts as Sir Peter Teazle, Sir Anthony Absolute, Bob Acres, Sir Lucius O'Trigger, Tony Lumpkin, and a galaxy of other characters which no comedian could resist. A third group of plays, which furnished some of the most popular vehicles of the century, were the dramas and adaptations of recent or contemporary playwrights. A few of the best known examples are Boucicault's adaptation of *Rip Van Winkle*, which provided Joseph Jefferson with his greatest role; Morris Barnett's *The Serious Family*, which included the character of Aminidab Sleek; Tom Taylor's *Our American Cousin*, which included the roles of Asa Trenchard and Lord Dundreary; and George Coleman's *The Heir-at-Law*, which featured the popular characters, Dr. Pangloss and Zekiel Homespun. A final group of plays, providing further tests for the skill of the comedians, were the farces which generally appeared as after-

pieces to the main drama of the evening. Representative examples are the lively inventions of J. Madison Morton such as *Slasher and Crasher, Betsey Baker,* and *Poor Pillocoddy.* A character comedian in the mid-decades of the nineteenth century customarily played a major role in the main drama of the evening; then, very likely, he performed comic songs or turns in the "olio" which separated the main drama from the farce; and, finally, he cavorted for an additional hour in the afterpiece or farce.

It is difficult for a modern playgoer to visualize the kind of character acting demanded by the repertory of the nineteenth century and developed by the great comedians of that period. It is rarely seen today. The two illustrations which come most readily to mind are foreign actors: Alec Guiness, in such a film as *Kind Hearts and Coronets,* and Fernandel in *The Sheep Has Five Legs.* In these films the leading actor did not play himself; each created several different characters and the comic effect resulted from the uniqueness of the portraits. In separate films, also, Guiness and Fernandel are successful in creating distinct and different characterizations, an example being Guiness's markedly different personalities in *The Swan* and *The Ladykillers.*

The mid-decades of the nineteenth century are illustrious for the surprising number of superlative character comedians who flourished at the time. Heading this illustrious company are four great names: Henry Placide, William E. Burton, John Gilbert, and William Warren. Let us look at the kind of comic acting they practiced.

HENRY PLACIDE

Henry Placide, the first of the great comedians to make his debut, was called "almost a faultless actor," [1] and "the best comedian the United States has yet produced." [2] He had every personal requisite for success —a handsome, expressive face, a supple figure of medium height, a clear, melodious voice, a spirited, vivacious personality, and an alert, inquiring mind which savored all the peculiarities and eccentricities of human nature. Born into a family of actors and acrobats, he became one of the troupe at an early age and subsequently underwent a long and intensive apprenticeship. The results were rare and wonderful: he emerged as an actor whose range of roles was extraordinary. He could play every variety of comic part from broad farce to exquisite high

comedy, and was unequalled in three kinds of roles: middle-aged gentlemen, drunken servants, and simple country lads. In addition, his French ancestry and knowledge of the French language gave him an immense advantage in parts requiring a Gallic background. During his twenty years at the Park Theatre in New York he acted more than five hundred roles and was the first portrayer of over two hundred of them.

In all his acting, Placide was the discriminating artist, analyzing his characters and seeking to present their traits and eccentricities with exactness, precision, and rich humor. He never relied on grimace or buffoonery and never distorted a role to gain comic advantage. His power to slough off his own personality and become the character of the play was so great that spectators could not believe they were seeing the same actor play, in succession, the foppish dandy, the stupid country dolt, and the doddering old grandfather. Except for his voice, the purity and clarity of which were always recognizable, Placide's disguises were perfect; so much so that he was never the subject of imitation or impersonation. From role to role there were no uniformities of mannerism or style on which to base an imitation. Placide's achievements in the creation of comic characters earned him the ultimate praise from Edwin Forrest. When that great tragedian was performing in Europe, he was asked to name the best American actor and he unhesitatingly replied, "Henry Placide is unquestionably the best general actor on the American boards, and I doubt whether his equal can be found in England." [3]

WILLIAM E. BURTON

The loyal American fans of William E. Burton, however, would contest this verdict. In the minds of thousands of theatregoers, Placide was great but Burton was "the funniest man who ever lived." [4] The very sound of his voice off stage could send an audience into an uproar, and in the famous drunk scene from The Toodles he could hold his spectators convulsed for a full fifty minutes without speaking a line. He could also make them weep, mingling laughter and tears in miraculous combination. No comedian, perhaps, has ever exercised such complete command over the responses of his audience.

Burton, who was English born, had learned his style from the great

British comedian, Liston, and therefore was more broad and exaggerated in his effects than was Placide. A few critics found him unnecessarily coarse at times. All critics and spectators, however, agreed that he was a born comedian who was original in his conceptions, painstaking in building his characters, and masterful at by-play, grimace, and mimetic effect. He had a rather heavy figure, a broad genial face, and a voice of extraordinary flexibility. Some of his funniest effects came from his voice and face. Both were protean: he could vary his tones from the boyish squeak of the terrified adolescent to the roar of the enraged sea captain, while his face was a huge map on which was outlined every degree and kind of comic emotion. Joseph Jefferson, in praising Burton's mastery of facial expression, declares that the comedian's entrance as Van Dunder in a play called *The Dutch Governor* was a picture "so full of genius that it stamped itself indelibly on the mind . . . ," and then Jefferson describes the actor's appearance as follows: "The great stupid face was a blank. The heavy cheeks hung down stolidly on each side of a half-opened mouth; the large, expressionless eyes seemed to look hopelessly for some gleam of intelligence. There he stood, the incarnation of pompous ignorance, with an open letter in his hand. The audience swayed with laughter; for, though he had not said a word, they knew he had just received an important state document and couldn't read it." [5]

Like the other great comedians of his time, Burton was marvelously versatile and creative. He could embody with exquisite humor a sharply conceived character like Shakespeare's Bottom, or he could take a sketchily written part in a modern farce and could so build it, shape it, and embellish it that it became a full-length masterpiece. He never distorted the dramatist's conception, but he always succeeded in adding additional magic which was unmistakably Burtonian. The roles for which he was nationally famous illustrate his versatility. He habitually performed the parts of Timothy Toodles in *The Toodles* and Aminidab Sleek in *The Serious Family* on the same bill, and a spectator, unfamiliar with his genius, could hardly recognize that the person who had acted the jolly, effusive Toodles was, a few moments later, personating the sanctimonious, lugubrious Sleek. Incidentally, these two portrayals were so popular that for years, at Burton's Chambers Street Theatre in New York, Tuesday and Friday nights were regularly set aside for the performance of these plays—and this was in

an era, it will be remembered, before the long run had been established.

Burton's other most popular role was that of Captain Cuttle in a stage version of Dickens' *Dombey and Son,* a role which Odell calls "one of the famous things of the stage." [6] However, the great comedian did not confine himself to three roles, great as was the public clamor for a constant repetition of them. He created almost two hundred unforgettable portraits, many of them Shakespearean, and doubtless would have equalled the number of parts played by his great contemporaries had not an untimely death ended his career.

During the years from 1848 to 1856, Burton's Theatre in New York became a nationally famous institution; it was also a training school for an astonishing number of the great comedians of the century. Besides Burton himself, the company boasted Henry Placide, and the following notable performers who will be discussed later: William Rufus Blake, John Brougham, George Holland, Charles Fisher, and Lester Wallack.

Two great comedians who challenged the supremacy of Burton and Placide but who never performed in their company, were John Gilbert and William Warren. Both rank in the top quartet of all-time American comic geniuses.

JOHN GILBERT

John Gilbert, who made his debut five years after the advent of Placide and Burton, was noted for the polish, grace, dignity, and exquisite finish of his style. He was a master technician who modelled his acting after the style of the English genius, Farren, and who became so expert that no matter how painstaking his preparation of a role, the final effect appeared spontaneous and unrehearsed. In his early years he was criticized for being somewhat formal and cold, but in later life he developed a warmth and tenderness which made his portrayal of Old Dornton in *The Road to Ruin* one of his best parts. He portrayed a great number of old men but each was individual and distinct for he was another actor gifted with the supreme power to submerge his own personality and to transform himself into the character conceived by the dramatist. His range was prodigious, and the perfection of his por-

traiture was the subject of boundless praise. John R. Towse says that his acting of Sir Anthony Absolute "has never been equalled anywhere in the last half century. . . ." [7] William Winter believes that he gave "the best performance of Caliban that ever was seen in America," [8] while Brander Matthews declares, ". . . I have never seen, nor has anyone else in the past half-century, any rendering of Sir Peter Teazle comparable with John Gilbert's." [9] These are only three out of the 1,150 parts he performed during his lifetime and in all of these parts, as William Winter writes, he was "sometimes a great actor . . . always a correct one." [10]

WILLIAM WARREN

William Warren, the final member of the top quartet of comic geniuses, is considered by many critics to have been the greatest of them all. In view of the encomiums I have already cited for Placide, Burton, and Gilbert, it is difficult to contend that another actor could be greater than they. But Warren's claims are strong, and certainly he is a peer of the greatest if, indeed, he does not surpass them.

Warren's career on the stage covered more than fifty years, for he made his debut in 1832 and retired in 1883. The final thirty-six of these years were spent at one theatre, the Boston Museum. Except for a single starring tour in 1864–65, the world had to travel to Boston to see Mr. Warren; he disliked touring and preferred to let others come to him. But even though he remained in one city, in one theatre, and with one stock company, he became a national institution admired equally as much by fellow players as by an adoring public.

Warren was a meticulous student, a penetrating observer, and a genuine lover of his fellow men. He surveyed with a sympathetic eye the thousands of human beings around him, and from them he learned the infinite complexity and drollery of human thought and behavior. Warren drew on his vast storehouse of observation and intuition for each character he played; when finally presented, each creation was "complete, uniform, and fulfilled to its absolute possibilities," [11] and each was suffused with a delicious, genial humor which lacked any trace of sarcasm or satire. Whenever he stepped on the stage—or even before, when his voice was heard off stage—a thrill of joy went through the audience. And this thrill was felt by the players on the

stage as well as by the spectators. Mary Shaw, who acted with him many times, declares: "He was so wonderful an actor that simply his standing on the stage seemed to fill and overflow the whole scene . . . I have played with most of the great actors and actresses that have lived during my time, but few of them had the power to affect me personally in the scene, to make me struggle to resist the artistic appeal, which is intended for the audience. But Mr. Warren captured my feelings to such an extent that I found it difficult to hold my place in the scene." [12] H. S. Barnabee, a light opera star who acted with Warren on occasions, pays additional homage when he says: "Talk of your emotional actors! Why, he could and did, nightly, draw tears and laughter in the same breath. To observe his finesse and gradations in marking the many phases of complicated character was a priceless lesson in the art of acting." [13]

Warren's versatility as a portrayer of comic types was practically limitless. He seemed able to create complete and unique portraits out of every part assigned to him. The critics said he was the best Touchstone of his period and incomparable as Dogberry or Polonius or Autolycus or Sir Andrew Aguecheek. He was practically unrivalled in roles from the plays of Sheridan and Goldsmith, and was equally fine in contemporary comic roles such as Triplet, Jesse Rural, and Dr. Pangloss. Another of his strong points was dialect acting—and he was at home in all of them: French, Scotch, Irish, Yorkshire, and Yankee. At the same time, he was said to be unapproachable in farce and low comedy, being able to produce uncontrollable laughter in these parts. A contemporary admirer summarizes his versatility and artistry in these words: "He gave us finished to the finger-tips, to the last intonation, to the last detail of costume, to the last queer turn of dialect, not only an infinite variety of types, but an infinite variety in those types. . . ." [14] During his professional life Warren's powers did not decline: he performed 13,500 times in almost six hundred different roles. Joseph Jefferson said, ". . . it is safe to conclude that this versatile comedian studied and created more parts than any other actor of his day," [15] and Lewis Strang declares, ". . . he was, beyond a reasonable doubt, the greatest comedian that the American Theatre has produced." [16]

Placide, Burton, Gilbert, and Warren form a quartet whose comic genius was without peer. But so vital was the American theatre in

their day, and so rich was the array of talent, that this quartet of actors was challenged by nine other comedians whose talent was close to theirs. Of these nine, William J. Florence, William Rufus Blake, and Henry J. Finn belong at the top.

Blake was a portly man with a heavy face and figure, and yet he managed to convey meaning and humor with telling effect. He infused each of his parts with rare spirit, richness of color, and poetic fervor, and was as powerful in roles demanding tender pathos as in those requiring eccentric humor.

William J. (Billy) Florence likewise had versatility and range. He began his career playing serious roles, such as Laertes and MacDuff; then for ten years he specialized in Irish peasant types; finally he broadened his repertory to include most of the roles featured by his great contemporaries. He acted Bob Brierly in *The Ticket of Leave Man* more than 1,500 times, and after creating the role of Bardwell Slote in *The Almighty Dollar,* he played it more than 2,500 times. His portraits were all vivid, consistent, and lifelike—with the actor's own personality entirely effaced. When he died, it was said that he had reigned as a star for forty years without a single failure.

Henry J. Finn, who met an untimely death in 1840, is almost entirely forgotten by historians of the stage, and yet he was considered by many to be "the most versatile comic genius of his day." [17] He began his career as a tragedian and never completely abandoned serious roles. Wemyss reports that as late in his career as 1836 Finn played an engagement which began with the popular comic roles of Lord Ogilby and Paul Pry, continued through such eccentric characters as Dr. Pangloss, Billy Black, Philip Garbois and Beau Chatterley, and ended with—Richard III! However, despite his hankering for tragic roles, it was in the characters of eccentric comedy that Finn was inimitable. His dry, brilliant, sharply etched portrayals led managers and critics to regard him as one of the brightest stars in the theatrical galaxy. Ludlow records that in the role of Philip Garbois, Finn was "pre-eminently superior to any person I have seen attempt it," [18] while Wemyss declares: "his Lord Ogilby . . . his Paul Schack, his Beau Chatterley have never been equalled on the American stage." [19]

Ranking slightly below the overall level of Florence, Blake, and Finn were Charles Fisher, John Sleeper Clarke, John E. Owens, James H. Hackett, William P. Davidge, and Charles Burke. Burke died at the early age of thirty-two, but his grace and wit were remembered for

years by his contemporaries. The others all lived to respectable ages and were famous for certain specialties as well as for a worthy versatility. Fisher's sparkle, precision, and courtly grace made him brilliant in such parts as Malvolio, Dandy Dinmont, and Sir Peter Teazle. Owens, who brilliantly carried on the tradition of the Yankee comedian, made a "tangible reality" and a national institution out of Solon Shingle in *The People's Lawyer,* and scored hits as Caleb Plummer in *The Cricket on the Hearth* and as Dr. Pangloss in *The Heir-at-Law.* John Sleeper Clarke, who won a distinguished place on the English stage as well as in the United States, suffused many parts with his own exuberant comic temperament, but was perhaps best known for his role of Major Wellington de Boots in *Everybody's Friend,* which he acted at least 1,000 times in America and many times in England. James H. Hackett, the father of James K. Hackett, was considered the greatest Falstaff of his period as well as one of the best dialect actors of his time. Two of his specialties, which won him renown in America and which were eventually accepted in England, were Yankee roles such as that of Solomon Swap in *Jonathan in England* (Hackett's own adaptation of George Colman's comedy, *Who Wants a Guinea?*) and western frontier heroes such as Colonel Nimrod Wildfire in *The Lion of the West.* William P. Davidge, who was born and trained in England, adopted America as his home and acted here during the last thirty-eight years of his life in a wide variety of comic roles ranging from Sir Toby Belch in *Twelfth Night* to Dick Deadeye in *H.M.S. Pinafore.* He brought to all his roles "a robust humor which could be dry, saturnine, unctuous, or Bacchic at will." [20] Still other names which deserve listing on the roster of gifted character comedians are Daniel E. Setchell, Mark Smith, and James H. Stoddart.

Along with this group of versatile male performers should be mentioned several women: Mrs. Hughes, who usually acted with William E. Burton, Mrs. John Drew, Mrs. G. H. Gilbert, and Mrs. Sarah Ross Wheatley. All of these ladies were known for their brilliant portrayal of such notable comic characters as Mrs. Malaprop, Lady Teazle, Lucretia McTab, and Lady Creamly, and in many ways their art paralleled that of the great male performers.

DION BOUCICAULT

In a somewhat different category, yet still deserving mention in the ranks of the character comedians, was that tireless and multi-talented Irishman, Dion Boucicault. Although he was thirty-three years old when he arrived in the United States in 1853, the "Ubiquitous Boucicault" immediately became a dominating influence on the stage of the United States, and during the remaining thirty-seven years of his life he left his stamp on every department of the American theatre. He died in the United States in 1890.

Born in Dublin in about 1820, he became stage struck at an early age and eventually found his way to London where, says William Winter, he "haunted theatres and wrote plays." [21] In 1841, after serving as an actor in the English provincial theatres, he established a name for himself by producing the highly popular success, *London Assurance.* From then until the year of his death, he never ceased his multifarious activities in the theatre.

One of his principal activities was acting. As a performer he exhibited the same cleverness and skill which he showed in constructing his plays. He did not attempt the varied comic roles of the great comedians like Warren or Burton or Gilbert; rather, he exploited the characters of his own plays, such as Mantalini in his play *Smike,* or Wah-no-tee in *The Octoroon,* or Nana Sahib in *Jessie Brown,* and in these he demonstrated commendable versatility. However, it was as a "lovable Irish" character in his plays based on Irish life that he achieved his greatest success. As William Winter wrote, ". . . his rightful fame is that of an author of romantic Irish plays and an actor of romantic eccentric Irish parts." [22] Three such roles are especially notable: Myles-na-Coppaleen in *The Colleen Bawn,* Daddy O'Dowd in the play of the same name, and Conn, the Shaughraun, in *The Shaughraun.* In all these parts Boucicault mingled tears and laughter, sentiment and shrewdness, in such a whimsical, engaging manner that his audiences were captivated. As Conn, the Shaughraun, Boucicault is said to have "interpreted to the life the generous, hearty, irresponsible, and none too sober wanderer, ever ready to help others but with little of an eye to his concerns." [23]

In all of his acting, Boucicault was primarily the clever technician who could simulate emotion and manipulate the responses of his audi-

ence. His long and intimate knowledge of the stage had taught him all the tricks and artifices of the actor's profession; his canny sense of public taste enabled him to utilize his technique at the right times with the desired effects. As a dramatist, he was an imitator and adaptor; it is said that he borrowed the plots of every play he ever wrote. Likewise as an actor he imitated the successful characterizations he saw created by other players and adopted the effects he found useful in his own roles. Thus his portrait of Conn, the Shaughraun, says William Winter, "was, in spirit and drift, an Irish copy of Jefferson's Rip Van Winkle. . . ." [24] But, derivative as his plays and acting may have been, Boucicault always added original, inventive touches of his own which, during most of his life, exactly suited the public taste and won for Boucicault immense popularity. He was always the shrewd opportunist, utilizing and exploiting every whim and fashion and trend of his time.

Boucicault's influence on American acting came not only from his own style of performance but even more so from his other activities in the theatre. Some of his contributions—like the introduction of fireproof scenery, the sponsorship of the first copyright law for the protection of American playwrights, and the innovation of road or combination companies—had little or no effect on the style or technique of acting. But some of Boucicault's other activities exerted considerable influence. For example, he directed innumerable productions and coached hundreds of actors and thus spread his own concepts of effective performance. He promoted the use of box settings which enclosed realistic furnishings, and these settings undoubtedly influenced the style of the actors who appeared in them. But Boucicault's most important contribution to style in acting was the result of his playwriting. For fifty years he supplied the theatres of both America and Great Britain with more than one hundred and thirty of the most popular plays of the century, and these dramas exerted an enormous influence on the actors who performed them.

Boucicault always said that a play was not written—it was rewritten. With him this process occurred in the heat of rehearsal when the actors themselves suggested lines, business, characterizations, and even whole scenes or episodes. In the process of development, the play was shaped to suit the ability of the players and to furnish them a happy vehicle for the display of their talents. In the finished product, plots and incidents were contrived and artificial; sentiments and language

were ornate and high-flown; characterizations and psychology were simple and obvious. Yet these plays provided a field day for the actors. The melodramatic situations afforded the player a wonderful opportunity to display passion and vehemence. The picturesque quality of many of the roles offered a chance for vivid characterization. The ornateness of the speeches challenged a performer's skill at reading. In short, in Boucicault's plays the actor discovered "media for the exercise of virtuosité, opportunities for technical display." [25]

Plays of the Boucicault variety inevitably demanded a special skill and a special style of the actor. He couldn't move and speak as he did in ordinary life—because the situations and language were not those of ordinary life. At the same time, he could not assume the classic manner of tragedy because the plays were not tragic or poetic. The actor had to assume a grace or a courtliness or a charm which was exaggerated enough to match the material yet deft enough to hide the exaggeration. His style had to suit the mood and situation of the play and yet be pleasing and convincing in its artificiality. To be sure, many other plays of the period demanded the same style of acting, but the prolific Boucicault must be counted the chief representative of this kind of playwriting. It must not be forgotten that he was a clever, versatile actor and thus deserves mention with the other notable comedians of the nineteenth century; the influence on style of acting exerted by his innumerable plays must also be remembered.

The comedians I have so far discussed were all distinguished for range and versatility. The great reputations they achieved came from their power to transform their own personalities into the likeness of a dramatic character and then to win laughter through projecting the foibles and eccentricities of that character. Unlike the Hopes, Bennys, and Skeltons of today, they did not play themselves or a single character closely related to themselves; they were able to play any comic personality they chose to portray.

Allied with these versatile character comedians during the great decades of the nineteenth century was another group of superlative comic actors who based their fame on the creation of a single part or a single line of parts. They were similar to the comedians of today in that they generally played a single role or line of roles in which they infused the richness of their own personalities; they were unlike their modern counterparts in that the roles they played were within the

framework of a drama and not presented as independent, vaudeville-type entertainment. These single-role comedians often challenged the popularity of the versatile comedians; they well deserve the fame they have won in the history of American acting. Prominent among the single role comedians were such talented players as the following:

William B. Wood, whose career began at the end of the eighteenth century and thus antedated the activity of the other great comedians of the nineteenth century. He was famous for his co-managership of the Chestnut Street Theatre, Philadelphia, in its palmiest days, but his admirable playing of a single line of roles, the elegant, artificial, characters of "old" comedy, was equally famous and entitled him to be listed by William Winter as one of the "serene luminaries" of the early American theatre.

John T. Raymond, who so injected his own buoyant personality into the role of Colonel Mulbery Sellers in *The Gilded Age* that he made it internationally famous;

E. A. Sothern, who immortalized the eccentric Lord Dundreary in *Our American Cousin;*

Dan Marble, one of the first and best of the Yankee comedians;

Francis S. Chanfrau, whose dashing portrayal of Mose the Fireboy started a national craze and who played the frontiersman, Kit, the Arkansas traveller, equally well;

James Lewis, who made priceless portraits out of the fussy old men who were his specialty;

Barney Williams, who won the hearts of both British and American audiences with his portrayal of the Irish peasant boy;

George Holland, who was the greatest jokester of his time and who converted every part he played into a vehicle for his own gags and slapstick;

Stuart Robson, whose drolly innocent appearance, squeaky, unpredictable voice, and eccentric movements dominated every role he undertook and titillated audiences for over fifty years;

John Brougham, who had a fair measure of versatility but whose breezy, genial Irish personality infused all his roles and whose fame at making impromptu curtain speeches was as great as his popularity as an actor;

George "Yankee" Hill, Dan Marble, Joshua Silsbee, and Denman Thompson, and a whole host of skillful interpreters of the stage Yankee who carried the fame of Jonathan Ploughboy and other Yan-

kee types to every corner of the country and to England as well, where James H. Hackett's pioneering in similar roles had paved the way for later American comedians.

There were also many skillful actors who specialized in light, romantic comedy. Two of the best of these were Lester Wallack and John Drew. Their charm, dash, and sophistication could easily challenge the mantinee idols of today. All these single role performers were popular and successful. But by far the greatest of them, whose fame surpassed and outlasted the others, was Joseph Jefferson, the immortal Rip Van Winkle.

There are some who might protest the classification of Jefferson as a one role actor, and they will point to the other parts he played before and after he developed his famous characterization of Rip. It is true that he was the original Asa Trenchard in *Our American Cousin* and that he was applauded in such other roles as Caleb Plummer, Dr. Pangloss, and Bob Acres. It is also true that some critics professed to find a distinct creation in each of these portrayals. However, the best of the critics reached a different conclusion. They agreed that Jefferson was a one role comedian, and that every part he played was a variation of his single great creation, Rip Van Winkle. John R. Towse writes, "In parts so diverse as Caleb Plummer, Pangloss, and Bob Acres, the basic individualities were identical. . . . They were all unmistakably the same man in different guises." [26] Henry Austin Clapp calls Rip Van Winkle "the sole and single product" [27] of Jefferson's life, while Lewis Strang declares: "As played by Mr. Jefferson, Bob Acres is not Bob Acres, Caleb Plummer is not Caleb Plummer, Dr. Pangloss is not Dr. Pangloss; but each and every one of them is Rip Van Winkle, absolutely and entirely." [28]

But, what a wonderful creation Rip Van Winkle turned out to be! As finally perfected by Jefferson, this portrait was a masterpiece which warmed the hearts and tickled the risibilities of several generations of playgoers throughout the entire United States. The public did not want him to play a different role; the artistry which Jefferson lavished on this part was considered by the public to be ample recompense for the actor's lack of versatility.

It is not surprising that Joseph Jefferson succeeded so brilliantly in the theatre. He sprang from a long line of successful actors. His great grandfather had gone on the stage under David Garrick's patronage.

His grandfather, the elder Joseph Jefferson, came to the United States in 1795 and made a name for himself. His father, too, was an actor, so it was natural that young Joseph should grow up in the theatre. He made his debut at the age of four, and seventy-one years later, only a year before his death, he gave his final performance as Rip.

Jefferson established himself as a popular comedian very early in his career, but he was not satisfied with the roles he played. He began searching for a character where, as he says in his *Autobiography,* "humor would be so closely allied with pathos that smiles and tears should mingle with each other." [29] He found such a character in Washington Irving's Rip Van Winkle—and he decided to make the character his own even before it was embodied in a play. It was not until 1865, when Jefferson was thirty-six years old, that Dion Boucicault dramatized Irving's story and Jefferson produced it at the Adelphi Theatre in London. The play was shoddy, and the character of Rip was sketchily drawn, but Jefferson's interpretation won hearty approval. Thereafter, for the rest of his life, Jefferson continued to shape and to develop the role of Rip. As he finally played the part, the character was more his own creation than it was the dramatist's. Into the part Jefferson poured all the warmth of his own personality and all the artistry of his many years of acting.

As a man, Jefferson was beloved throughout the whole country for his kindliness, his broad sympathies, his tolerance, his whimsical humor, and his love of the world and the people in it. To him, life was rich and enjoyable; his fellow men, with all their follies, were delightful and lovable; existence was an experience to be savored and enjoyed. These attitudes of the actor, and the captivating personality which embodied them, shone through all of Jefferson's acting and were particularly apparent in his characterization of Rip. This portrayal was notable for ease and naturalness, for the absence of tricks or bombast or the striving for effect. The character had a kindliness, a spirituality, and a humor which were projected so deftly and effortlessly that they seemed inseparable from the actor (and, in reality, they were inseparable). Every moment was filled with expressive action and by-play, and every line was nursed for the tears or laughter inherent in it. Yet the performance had a simplicity and repose which were enchanting. Jefferson's artistry and personal fascination were so consummate that Clara Morris declared he was a "poet of comedy," [30] and Lewis Strang, echoing the unanimous sentiments of his fellow critics, wrote:

"Jefferson's Rip Van Winkle is a wonderful thing, a unique achievement, an astonishing exhibition of virtuosity, a creation impossible to anyone but Joseph Jefferson." [31]

It is an interesting speculation to ask: who was the greater actor—Joseph Jefferson or a performer like William Warren, William Burton, John Gilbert, or Henry Placide? Whose achievement is most noteworthy—the actor who produces a single perfect creation or the versatile player who creates a whole gallery of convincing portraits? Perhaps such a question, provocative as it may be, is impertinent and irrelevant. Both kinds of performers can be ranked as first rate and, in actual fact, the crown of greatness has willingly been awarded to many of the actors whose achievements have been limited. And yet a modern critic or playgoer cannot escape the force of the conclusion reached by Henry Austin Clapp when he wrote: "Mr. Jefferson can point . . . to one work of supreme distinction, the sole and single product of his life, the masterpiece of our stage,—the figure of the immortal Rip. Our Warren, like another Rubens, could conduct you through a vast gallery, crowded with noble canvases, of which at least a hundred glow with the beauty and the truth of life, every one bearing his firm signature." [32]

In view of the number and brilliance of comic actors during the nineteenth century, one is compelled to echo the remark made by Lawrence Barrett (in other circumstances) when he said that to the playgoer of today "the splendor of this company . . . seems unreal." [33]

Phineas T. Barnum once said that "show business has all phases and grades of dignity from the exhibition of a monkey to the exposition of that highest art in music and the drama. . . ." [34] The "highest art" in show business was represented when Edwin Booth or Charlotte Cushman or William Warren performed in one of the plays of Shakespeare. But as Barnum shrewdly realized, show business also included the exhibition of a monkey—and ten thousand little variety acts, burlesque skits, minstrel shows, animal exhibitions, and circus performances. These forms of "popular theatre" were the common theatrical activities which, like Whitman's leaves of grass, "bathed the globe" during the nineteenth century. And from these vigorous and lusty forms arose a type of performance and a technique of acting which was a stimulating force in the theatre as a whole.

Like television, radio, and the motion pictures of today, the popular

theatre of the nineteenth century provided much of the entertainment for the masses. Vaudeville, minstrelsy, burlesque, the circus, and comedies of the Harrigan-Hoyt variety attracted an astonishing number of spectators. Barnum's American Museum, which featured the piously named "Lecture Room" where "concerts" and "variety acts" were presented, drew the tremendous total of 37,560,000 admissions in the years from 1841 to 1865. New York City alone, in 1869, boasted a total of six hundred "concert saloons." In 1846, Christy's Minstrels, having established themselves at Mechanics Hall in New York, began a series of shows which ran continuously for ten years, reaching a total of at least 2,792 performances. In 1869, Olive Logan, speaking before the women's suffrage convention, declared that out of sixteen theatres existing in New York City, fourteen were given over to burlesque or spectacle and only two were offering legitimate drama.

The growth and great drawing power of the popular theatre were due, in the main, to the rapid growth of cities and to the polyglot population which poured into these cities. At the close of the American Revolution, only five urban centers in the nation boasted a population of 8,000 or more. By 1850, there were 141 cities of this size and by the end of the century there were more than five hundred. In 1790, only New York and Philadelphia had populations of 20,000 or more; by 1880, sixty-five cities had reached or surpassed this figure. By 1900, thirty-two per cent of the population of the nation lived in cities —compared to three per cent in 1800.

Into these cities flowed a constantly increasing flood of immigrants. Before 1840, immigrants arrived at the rate of about 60,000 per year. In 1840, the influx was tripled, and in the 1850's it was quadrupled. In every decade thereafter, from 1850 through the 1870's, more than 2,000,000 aliens arrived. In the 1880's, more than 5,000,000 poured in. By 1890, Chicago's foreign born numbered as many as the entire population had totaled ten years earlier. In New York City there were as many Italians as in Naples, as many Germans as in Hamburg, twice as many Irish as in Dublin, and two and a half times as many Jews as in Warsaw.

The cosmopolitan population of American cities created a colorful, carnival-like scene. Dion Boucicault, who arrived in the United States in 1853, described New York City in these words:

It was not a city. It was a theatre. It was a huge fair. Bunting of all nationalities and of no nationality were flaunting over the streets. Poles of liberty accentuated the "rights of man." Bands of music preceded processions of ragged boys bearing flags and tattered banners. Irish was spoken at the wharves, German in the saloons, French in the restaurants.[35]

Such a city, composed of so many nationalities speaking so many languages, could not be expected to support the standard repertory of the English-speaking theatre exclusively. The polyglot crowds failed to understand its language and intentions. Their frustration is illustrated by the riot which broke out in a Rochester, New York, theatre when Edwin Booth, who had been advertized as "Herr" Edwin Booth, began to speak in English and not in German. Patrons who knew only a foreign language could not appreciate long plays in English. But these same patrons flocked to the popular theatre. Spectacle, vaudeville, burlesque, and minstrelsy were received with immense enthusiasm. Such entertainment offered something to please everyone—and it could be understood and enjoyed by everyone.

The cultivated English speaking portion of the population who enjoyed legitimate drama made little effort to alter the taste of the masses or to encourage the production of standard plays. In fact, when the craze for public lectures arose in the 1840's, cultivated people deserted the playhouse and flocked to the lecture rooms. It was considered fashionable as well as educational to hear the great orators and preachers of the day, who could command a larger audience than a celebrated actor. And so the less sophisticated portion of the population and the large foreign speaking elements were left to dictate the taste in dramatic entertainment with the result that the popular theatres grew and flourished and developed a technique of presentation which was distinctive and stimulating.

In the early years of the nineteenth century, vaudeville, burlesque, and minstrelsy were appendages of legitimate drama. A classical play was usually embellished with entr'acte specialties and a farcical afterpiece. For example, a certain performance of *Richelieu* with Edwin Forrest was "enlivened by a 'grand pas de deux' and a 'national descriptive melange' between acts" [36] and ended with a farce entitled *The Double Bedded Room*. As the century advanced, the "specialties" drew away from legitimate drama and emerged as a distinctive type of entertainment housed in theatres of their own.

VAUDEVILLE

The variety show or vaudeville was perhaps the first type to achieve independence. A kind of variety show, revealing most of the elements of vaudeville, is as old as public entertainment itself. Since the beginning of recorded history there have been gatherings where the singer, the reciter, the dancer, and the mimic have performed their bits. For many centuries professional entertainers performed their tricks in inns, beer halls, and public squares. So the entr'acte specialties in the American theatre of the nineteenth century were nothing new. But during the century they broke away from legitimate drama and set up shop in public museums—like Barnum's—and in saloons, beer halls, and concert halls. By the middle of the century they had grown so popular that every city of any size had regular theatres devoted to variety programs. In New York City one house was renamed the "New Theatre of Mirth and Variety" and presented on a single bill such numbers as "Elboleros, Cachuchas, Scotch flings and Strathspeys," plus a selection of "the most astonishing feats of gymnastics and contortions ever presented in this country," and an act described as "the Flying Cord by the unequalled Mr. Ruggles." [37] Clearly this was the type of popular entertainment which was to culminate in the great vaudeville circuits of the early twentieth century.

MINSTREL SHOWS

Vaudeville soon had a powerful competitor in Negro Minstrelsy, a type of entertainment which rose suddenly and took the country by storm. Before 1830 American audiences had seen the forerunners of Negro Minstrelsy. Many actors had blacked up for specific occasions and appeared between the acts of legitimate plays. Very often Negro songs had been sung by circus clowns from the backs of horses. However, it was Thomas D. Rice, in 1830, who began the real vogue for minstrel entertainment when he invented his famous song and jig in imitation of an old Negro named "Jim Crow." It was, to the nineteenth-century audience, an appealing representation, and Rice instantly became a star. He traveled all over the United States and Europe, playing to packed houses wherever he went. Carl Wittke says:

"He was the first blackface performer, who was not only the main actor, but the entire act." [38]

It was not until 1843 that the first complete minstrel show was invented, that is, a show composed entirely of the singing and dancing and "gagging" of a blackface company. The first performance was the inspiration of Dan Emmett and three other actors who styled themselves "The Virginia Minstrels." In costumes that later became traditional, they serenaded the audience with music from a violin, a banjo, a tambourine, and bones.

At about the same time there was organized the "Christy Minstrels," the most famous troupe in the history of blackface entertainment. This organization gave to the show the traditional form for which it became noted: the "first part" with the performers in a semicircle, the interlocutor in the center, and with the endmen with bones and tambourine at the extreme ends; and the "second part" with its stump speech, its "olio" of variety acts, and its "hoe-down" dance at the end.

For many decades minstrelsy was phenomenally successful. Every city had its resident companies, and traveling groups toured the country from Maine to the gold fields of California. In the urban centers the craze was so great that three performances a day—morning, afternoon, and evening—had to be given.

As an indication of the appeal of American minstrel shows, it is interesting to note that in Europe they became almost as popular as they were in the United States. Foreign audiences, entirely unacquainted with American plantation traditions, were strangely moved by the shuffling dances of the blackface artists, by their homely humor, their quaint costumes, and especially their rhythmic, melodious songs—best represented in the haunting music of Stephen Foster. The great novelist, William Makepeace Thackeray, after witnessing a minstrel performance, wrote:

I heard a humorous balladist not long ago, a humorist with wool on his head and an ultra-Ethiopian complexion, who performed a negro ballad that I confess moistened these spectacles of mine in a most unexpected manner. They have gazed at thousands of tragedy queens dying on the stage and expiring to appropriate blank verse, and I have never wanted to wipe them. They have looked, be it said, at many scores of clergymen without being dimmed, and behold, a vagabond with a corked face and a

banjo sings a little song, strikes a wild note, which sets the heart thrilling with happy pity.[39]

BURLESQUE

Still another offering of the popular theatre which developed during the nineteenth century and attained great popularity was burlesque. This poor but saucy relative of legitimate drama was originally what its name implies: a take-off or travesty on a serious play. John Poole is said to have started the vogue for it when, in 1811, he produced a burlesque of *Hamlet*. Very soon, however, young ladies, scantily clad and waving shapely limbs, began to invade burlesque. At first the effect upon the audience was shattering. One witness records that the first time a group of dancers appeared on the stage in ballet skirts and tights, "the women in the audience screamed aloud and the greater part left the theatre; the men remained, for the most part, roaring and sobbing with ecstasy. . . ." [40] Pioneers in the introduction and exploitation of "leg art," the art which finally became identified with burlesque, were Mlle. Hutin, who appeared at the Thalia Theatre in New York in 1827; Adah Isaacs Mencken, who starred in *Mazeppa* during the 1860's; and Lydia Thompson, who toured the country with her "British Blonds" in 1868. Miss Thompson is credited with being "the progenitress of American burlesque." However, M. B. Leavitt, an American theatrical manager, gave to this kind of entertainment the typical form it maintained during its prosperous days. He modeled the opening of his program—an act made up of songs, choruses and gags —from the minstrel show. He took the second part—an assorted array of talents and specialties called the "olio"—from vaudeville. The third part, the afterpiece or burlesque, was a development of the minstrel show walk-around: a grand finale by the entire company.

THE CIRCUS

The circus in America was less sensational in its origin and appeal than was burlesque. Still it became a flourishing and well-loved feature of the American popular theatre.

During colonial days little menageries and bands of itinerant acrobats had flourished in the United States. They traveled from town to

town, delighting the country folks who never saw any other kind of theatre. In the nineteenth century these little shows began absorbing riding acts from the popular equestrian drama and variety acts from the theatres and museums. Eventually the acrobats and the menageries, with their attendant attractions, began to combine, and finally there emerged the dazzling tent theatricals of Barnum and Bailey's "Greatest Show on Earth."

HARRIGAN AND HOYT

The popular theatre had strong influence in shaping modern musical comedy and revue. But even before these later types emerged it produced a unique and wonderful form of farce—the comedies of Edward Harrigan and Charles Hoyt.

Harrigan and his partner Tony Hart began their theatrical careers as variety artists. They specialized in sketches of city life, presenting humorously and faithfully a wide variety of familiar American characters. In these skits Harrigan acted the male role and Hart impersonated the female, but the authorship of the skits was almost entirely the work of Harrigan. Arthur Hobson Quinn tells us that there is a record of over eighty vaudeville sketches composed by Harrigan between 1870 and 1879. These sketches "take in politics, baseball, life insurance, the army and militia, and deal with the Negro, and the Irish, German, Italian, and other immigrant types." [41]

It was from these vaudeville acts that the full-length plays of Harrigan emerged. The process was a gradual one. In their first form the sketches were popular songs ridiculing some well-known personage or type. The song led to the duet and the duet to the dialogue. Under the inspiration of audience response the dialogue was elaborated and lengthened. New incidents were improvised from performance to performance, and eventually enough material was created for a full length play. Just when the first of these was born is not known, although one of the earliest and most enduring is the comedy *Old Lavender,* first produced in 1877 and expanded in 1878.

Out of the skits on Irish and German immigrant types grew the most famous Harrigan plays—the "Mulligan Guard" series. The first of these, *The Mulligan Guard Ball,* was produced in 1879 and ran for one hundred nights. It was followed with great success by seven or

eight other plays all recounting the adventures of a group of Irish and German immigrants, the Mulligans and the Lochmullers, and their Negro and Italian friends. These plays, which were remarkably free from coarseness or lewdness, were glorious mixtures of wild burlesque, lilting songs, dancing and military drills, outrageous puns, breathtaking spectacle, and—above all—knockdown, dragout, slambang farce. They were so popular in their time that, together with other comedies from the facile pen of their author, at least twenty-three of them achieved runs of more than one hundred performances each on Broadway, "phenomenal displays of longevity in those days." [42]

Ned Harrigan and Tony Hart (whom E. J. Kahn, Jr., calls "The Merry Partners") were the perfect team for presenting the plays which Harrigan developed out of his early vaudeville skits. Hart, younger than his partner by ten years, had the round, angelic face of an "Irish Apollo" and could act feminine roles as well as masculine parts with persuasive conviction and compelling charm. Nat C. Goodwin, a fellow comedian, said: "He sang like a nightingale, danced like a fairy, and acted like a master comedian," [43] and Mrs. Fiske thought he had "a smile that would coax the birds off the trees." [44] Harrigan, the older partner, was a "stocky, serene" man with an appealing Irish face and such versatile talents that he successfully wrote his own plays, acted every kind of part in them, produced, financed, and directed them in a theatre he ran himself with a company he recruited and trained himself.

Equally as important as the "Merry Partners" in the success of Harrigan's comedies was the audience which viewed and helped to shape them. This audience was largely composed of the immigrant types represented in the plays. Harrigan drew his inspiration directly from them. He tirelessly haunted the parks, wharves, saloons, and tenements where they congregated, observing their habits, listening to their conversation, taking notes on their eccentricities and even buying the clothes off their backs in order to obtain absolutely authentic costumes for his plays. "I have sought above all to make my plays like pages from actual life," [45] he declared. Late in his career he expressed regret at the passing of these types, saying that if his plays had lost their appeal it was because other waves of immigration had pushed the Mulligans and the Lochmullers out of the picture.

Another colorful figure who contributed to the tradition of the popular theatre in America was Charles Hoyt. His plays were related

to the comics of Edward Harrigan because, like the Harrigan plays, they were close to the vaudeville tradition. Songs were interspersed throughout, low comedy "gagging" was plentiful, and the actors were given ample opportunity for comic improvisation. In the first scene of Hoyt's *A Texas Steer,* for example, the action stops while four cowboys sing a quartet. At the end of each act of the play there are gags and tableaux suggested for use in the curtain calls. Hoyt often sat in the audience to note the reactions of his neighbors and to gather ideas for improving his shows. "He capitalized the 'movements' of his day," says Montrose Moses, treating them "with a newspaper deftness which was closely akin to the way contemporaneousness thrusts its way into musical comedy." [46] Indeed, our modern musical comedy is directly descended from the vaudeville-Harrigan-Hoyt tradition.

When one surveys the motley and sprightly offerings of the popular theatre—burlesque, vaudeville, minstrelsy, circus, and the Harrigan-Hoyt comics—two interesting conclusions emerge: (1) These types are intimately related; and (2) in all of them the technique of presentation is similar.

The close relationship of the types is evident. The circus borrowed blackface entertainment from minstrelsy, horseback performances from the equestrian drama, and variety acts from vaudeville. Minstrelsy borrowed its street parade from the circus and its "olio" from vaudeville. In its later development it became almost indistinguishable from vaudeville. Burlesque patterned its show after minstrelsy and introduced song and dance numbers from vaudeville. Vaudeville adopted blackface numbers from minstrelsy, leg shows from burlesque, and acrobatics and animal acts from the circus. In fact, all the types of popular theatre are basically a series of specialties strung together in a characteristic way. Each lays emphasis on a slightly different specialty, but each aims to satisfy the tastes of a polyglot audience by providing novel and varied entertainment which is easily understood.

In each form of popular entertainment the technique of presentation is very similar. The appeal of the actor has to be *immediate* and *direct.* There is no chance for slow build up of atmosphere and revelation of character as in legitimate drama. The appeal, says Caroline Caffin, "is personal and unashamed. It looks its audience straight in the face and says, in effect, 'Look at ME! I am going to astonish you!'

It makes no claim to aloofness or impersonality, but comes right to the footlights and faces the crowd and tells it 'All for your delight WE are . . . here.' " [47]

Moreover, the popular actor aims to achieve a feeling of fellowship with his audience. In the early days of the music hall, when the performers drank beer and swapped stories with the customers, it was easy to establish this relationship. When footlights intervened between spectator and player such friendly contact was virtually destroyed. Still, vaudeville, burlesque, and minstrel performers tried to attain some cameraderie by speaking directly to individuals in the audience, by arguing with the orchestra leader, by relating bits of local gossip, and often by crossing the footlights and parading in the aisles of the theatre.

The most important means of achieving immediate fellowship with an audience is strong, attractive personality. Somehow or other the performer must be able to impress an audience, immediately, with a likable, appealing presence. His ability to do this is equally as important as his skill in any specialty. The popular performer is thus frankly presentational in his method; he appeals to the audience always in his own guise.

Neither the performer or his specialty must ever appear "highbrow." "It is the first law of the cult of vaudeville," says Caffin, "that Highbrow Stuff Never Pays." [48] The spectator in the popular theatre wants to feel at home. He wants the sentiment, the humor, and the language to be familiar to him; he doesn't wish to exert an effort at comprehension or to feel that the entertainment is over his head.

The popular performer must not only be "lowbrow" and "folksy," he must at all times be instantly intelligible. His speech must appear completely unstudied and effortless, and yet must be understood by everyone in the house. The success of his brief number depends on every line striking fire. The popular audience is not interested in poetry or rhetoric; it simply wants to be entertained.

To maintain interest in any individual act and in the program as a whole, speed of performance is essential. Gags must come in rapid fire order. Song and dance numbers must blend smoothly and quickly. The pace of the whole show must be sprightly and exhilarating.

Other prime requisites for the popular performer are *adaptability* and *spontaneity*—the talent for *improvisation*. The sketches in vaudeville, minstrelsy, burlesque, etc., like much of the business in a Harri-

gan play, were not rigidly set. They were generally intended for spur-of-the-moment elaboration during the inspiration of performance. This was especially true of minstrelsy. Carl Wittke, historian of the blackface art, writes:

. . . a minstrel with a speech of a dozen lines probably never made it twice in exactly the same way,—a good minstrel was always improvising, and adding little comic bits on the spur of the moment while the show was in full progress, quite as much for the amusement of his fellow members in the company as for the audience. The endman's chatter with the interlocutor usually varied to a greater or less degree from night to night, and many stories and jokes about the local community were introduced with real skill. Some companies actually sent advance agents ahead to pick up bits of local news to be used in their show for the peculiar delight of their special audience.[49]

This type of improvisation was also popular—and necessary—in vaudeville, circus, and burlesque. In the latter, a high degree of skill seemed to be required, for early burlesque was very sketchily prepared. The actors were seldom given scripts. Instead, situations were outlined to them and they were expected to create and improvise as they went along. This tradition persisted through the heyday of burlesque and still persists in the remnants of burlesque which have survived in the theatre of the twentieth century. In 1965, the sixty-nine year old Steve Mills, a veteran performer appearing in Ann Corio's *This Was Burlesque,* said: "Every audience is a challenge. You find the first thing that hits, then you have to know how to keep it rolling, and you have to know when to stop. Things happen. You ad-lib. You bring it up, keep it revolving." [50]

Thus a successful actor in the popular theatre needed diverse abilities. He had to possess an attractive personality and the ability to project it quickly and directly. He had to establish a feeling of fellowship with his audience and be instantly intelligible—but never labored or highbrow. He had to perform with easy speed and to possess skill at improvisation. The total effect, as Walter Prichard Eaton wrote, had to be one of "unforced, jovial intimacy between audience and stage, of spontaneous fooling, of impromptu jest. . . ." [51]

The American stage was enriched by the training and the opportunities offered by the popular theatre. Thousands of performers, of every level of competence, served their apprenticeship there. Some of them became variety stars who delighted audiences for many years and

who never forsook the variety stage. Others graduated to the legitimate theatre and became leading players in the standard drama. Still others appeared in legitimate plays often written especially for them, but always remained the variety artist with all the appeals necessary for that kind of performer.

CHARLOTTE CRABTREE

One of the most famous of the latter group, who epitomized all the skills and endowments of the variety artist, was the sensationally successful Charlotte Crabtree, affectionately known and better remembered as "Lotta." Her career and style of acting will serve as a representative example of the countless performers who were produced by the popular theatre and who exhibited the essential characteristics of the variety artist: personal magnetism, congeniality, deftness, naturalness, articulateness, and skill at improvisation.

Lotta began her dramatic training in California at the age of six when she became the pupil of the notorious Lola Montez, who taught her to dance, to sing ballads, and to ride horseback. Presently the child also learned to play the banjo, and with these skills—plus her captivating looks and personality—she launched a career which was to make her a national favorite. She first became the darling of the California mining camps, which she trouped for ten years under the shrewd and tireless supervision of her mother. In 1864, she left the golden state and began her rapid and complete conquest of the rest of the nation. The reasons for her success, achieved so early and maintained so long, are vividly summarized by Constance Rourke in this description of Lotta's appeal:

If an exacting public wanted diversity, in the small person of Miss Lotta that quality was oddly comprised. She was both sturdy and delicate, full of rowdy caprice and quaintly aloof. Her voice was developing into a flexible soprano with a mezzo range. All her life she was to speak and sing with a smothered fire that seemed at variance with the light content of her words. Her clear tones, which made every syllable carry into the furthest corner of an audience hall, suggested greater force and more ample meaning than anything she had to say. . . . But it was her dancing, well caught within pantomime and impersonation, which aroused the special heady enthusiasm which was to envelop her for years. Jigs, flings, wild polkas, breakdowns, the whole range of soft-shoe dancing. . . . Her

dancing was light as gossamer when she wished it to be, or boldly hoy-denish.[52]

In 1867, at the age of twenty, she appeared in New York as the star of a play written especially for her by the talented John Brougham. This was a dramatization of Dickens' *Old Curiosity Shop* called *Little Nell and the Marchioness*. It was a great success and ran for six weeks. Later it proved a smash hit whenever it was presented in the United States. Thereafter, and for the rest of her life, Lotta appeared either in burlesque or extravaganza or in light, flimsy vehicles which had been written especially for her and which enabled her to exploit her sprightly charms and captivating skills. The nature of these tailor-made vehicles is evident in the titles of three of them: *Nan the Good for Nothing, Pet of the Petticoats,* and *The Little Detective*.

In acting such comic frivolities, Lotta never attempted a charac-terization and never tried to conceal her own personality. As John R. Towse observed, she appeared in many parts but "played them all exactly the same way. She never developed or suggested any real dramatic force or adaptability." [53] She was the eternal variety artist, joyously presenting herself to an audience directly and frankly, with-out artifice or disguise, and cloaking her performance in a youthful innocence which concealed the sometimes raciness of her material. Constance Rourke confirms this conclusion in the statement that "Whatever Lotta became, however often she was to command plays of her own, she remained essentially a variety actress, with the vivacious original turns, the irrepressible humor, the unaccountable mode of the lighter theatre flowing through her chosen parts." [54]

Lotta needed no other appeals. The public adored her just as she was and, until the day she retired in 1891, never tired of her. One critic said: "The charm of Lotta's acting penetrated every heart; she defied convention; she was not measurable by rule or line. The secret of her charm was hidden as the scent of the rose. . . . Lotta was incom-parable and inimitable." [55] Even distinguished players of the legitimate drama paid high tribute to Lotta's appeal. The great classic actress, Helena Modjeska, said that her individuality covered all the sins of the commonplace characters she portrayed; that she "infused life" into every part; and that "her realism was simply wonderful." [56] Otis Skinner praised her in these words: "The figure of a child, eyes that held a world of laughter, set in a dimpled roguish face, crowned by a fluff of curling bronze hair, a voice that sang and feet that danced,

fingers that tripped nimbly over banjo strings, spirits that never flagged; that was Lotta . . . the embodiment of joy and thoughtlessness." [57]

Lotta epitomizes the endowments and style of the successful variety artist. Many other examples could be cited from every specialty within the realm of the popular theatre. Negro minstrelsy produced such notable performers as Lew Dockstader and the team of James McIntyre and Thomas Heath. Modern burlesque began with the success of Adah Isaacs Mencken and Lydia Thompson, produced comedians like Lew Fields and Joe Weber, and as late as the twentieth century produced a star like Fanny Brice. Vaudeville and the musical comedy stage gave us performers like Eddie Foy and the beautiful Lillian Russell. And so on, ad infinitum.

Many other notable players, later identified with the legitimate stage, received their early training in the popular theatre and testify to its effectiveness as a school for actors. Chauncey Olcott began his career in the ranks of the blackface artist. Francis Wilson was a circus performer and a minstrel before he became a legitimate star. David Warfield was hired by Belasco directly from a Weber and Fields burlesque. Fred Stone, Raymond Hitchcock, De Wolf Hopper, Nat Goodwin, Otis Skinner, and George M. Cohan all played in vaudeville or minstrel shows. Even such great stars as Joseph Jefferson, Edwin Booth, and Edwin Forrest appeared in the ranks of vaudeville, burlesque, or minstrelsy at some time in their careers.

The influence of the technique of the popular theatre was felt in the legitimate theatre quite early. Audiences became accustomed to entertainment which was varied, which moved swiftly, and which appealed to the eye. In the legitimate theatre they became restless during long speeches and wordy dialogue. In 1870 Joseph Jefferson noticed this and remarked about it. Later, when he made his acting version of *The Rivals,* he acknowledged the popular trend by condensing the play and cutting much of the dialogue. Other managers did the same thing. They speeded up the action and the dialogue in their productions and embellished them with eye-filling costumes and scenery. For several decades American plays, in contrast to the British, were notable for the swiftness of their pace. Today even British productions have succumbed to the speeding-up process begun many years ago by the American popular theatre.

After the vogue for burlesque, vaudeville, and minstrelsy passed,

their influence was clearly observable in the Broadway revues and musical comedies of the 1920's and 1930's. These productions utilized the old structure and the old techniques. In form they were a series of sketches and specialties, interspersed with songs and spiced with novelty and variety. They were geared to a lightning-like speed and tried to have something happening every instant. The star performers were still expected to be deft, natural, and articulate, as well as skillful at improvisation. During this period influences from the popular theatre were also recognizable in such productions as William Saroyan's *The Time of Your Life,* John Howard Lawson's *Processional,* and the Federal Theatre's *Living Newspaper* because all of them borrowed their techniques largely from vaudeville rather than from legitimate drama. Today the influence of the popular theatre is less discernible in sophisticated musical plays like *South Pacific, My Fair Lady,* and *Hello, Dolly.* Yet the speed, color, and variety of these productions still remind us that they are descendants of an older genre of popular theatre.

The American comic theatre of the nineteenth century was a rich and lusty creation. With its roots deep in the fun loving, polyglot character of America, it achieved a glorious popularity and revealed the magic of theatre to countless thousands of citizens old and new. It also shaped the development of several forms of native drama and created a recognizable technique of acting, the influence of which is still discernible.

[NOTES ON THE SETTING]

The Transition

 THE YEARS SURROUNDING THE TURN OF THE CENTURY can rightfully be called a period of transition. The old order of theatrical affairs was passing; the new world of the twentieth century theatre was not yet born. The background, the traditions, the ideals, and the practices which had produced the supreme tragic art of Edwin Booth and the consummate comic achievement of William Warren had weakened and changed until these ideals and practices no longer exerted the inspiration and motivation necessary for creative theatre.

The tempo of life in America had increased and was destined to accelerate at a faster and faster rate as the century advanced. Population continued to multiply and immigrants poured in by the hundreds of thousands. Cities increased in number and size. Rapid transportation reached every village and hamlet in the nation. Industrialization proceeded with giant strides. Inventions of miraculous ingenuity and influence poured from workshops and laboratories. One of these, the motion picture, eventually was to diminish and to supplant much of the activity of the legitimate stage. The automobile began to transform the landscape of every town and countryside and to alter the lives of every citizen, young and old. Social troubles, labor troubles, and political troubles agitated the nation and produced an era of "muckraking" and reform.

In such a changing, complex, burgeoning society, the theatre was not keeping pace—except in one respect which most critics deplored.

Big business invaded show business. Tycoons and speculators began to apply industrial methods to theatrical production. Dramatists wrote plays to appeal to the largest number of customers; productions were turned out on an assembly line basis; the road was organized into a tight monopoly by the infamous Theatrical Syndicate which gained control of the playhouses throughout the nation and dictated which actors should play in which dramas in which cities. Under this system, show business was more prosperous but the overall quality of production was poorer than ever before.

In almost every respect the theatre had become sterile and stereotyped. Playhouses retained the shape and the defects they had exhibited since the eighteenth century. There were thousands of them throughout the United States and promoters continued to build them at a rapid rate. But they were all slightly modified versions of the Restoration playhouse. The proscenium doors and boxes had been eliminated but all other traditional features were there: a picture-frame stage with tiers of boxes and galleries facing it in a horseshoe curve, a lower or "orchestra" floor, poor sight lines, cramped leg space, inadequate lobbies, and poorly ventilated dressing rooms. The inflexible form of stage and auditorium limited directors to a single style of "peep-hole" drama.

The mounting of the play was equally stereotyped. The tradition of flat, two-dimensional scenery consisting of wings, drops, and borders with all décor for both interior and exterior scenes painted on, still lingered in the theatre, particularly in playhouses outside of New York. Such scenery alternated with the carefully realistic settings introduced by Boucicault and perfected by Belasco, in which every object called for in the play was tangible and authentic. If a New York City street scene were needed, real store fronts were erected with actual merchandise in the windows. The street itself was furnished with lamp posts, fire hydrants, sidewalks, garbage cans, gutters, and push carts containing actual vegetables.

The lighting of such settings was sometimes imaginative and suggestive of the mood of the play. Belasco tried to introduce both realism and imagination in the lighting of his productions. In too many plays, however, the illumination was flat, uniform, and uninteresting —as might be expected when its source was a set of footlights in front and a row of border lights overhead, relieved now and then by a spotlight focussed on the leading player.

A survey of the hundred or more plays which reached Broadway every year during this period reveals an astonishing number of flimsy, stereotyped dramas. There were dozens of farce comedies and sentimental comedies; there were melodramas of all kinds, including the domestic melodrama of tears imported from France; there were endless romantic costume plays laid in exotic lands and faraway times. Each one of these popular plays was given as long a run on Broadway as the public would sustain, then it was sent on tour to every village, hamlet and town which boasted a playhouse—and most of them did. When the "road" was exhausted, the play was then released for production by the hundreds of stock companies throughout the nation— companies which now were second rate imitators of Broadway rather than the independent repertory companies they once had been. Now and then a theatre was enlivened by a poetic play or a play of social significance or a play which probed the problems of the individual in a complex society. Also, the plays of Shakespeare or of the old standard repertory were occasionally revived. Julia Marlowe and E. H. Sothern, for example, did their best to create and maintain an interest in Shakespeare. But in the main, the regular dramatic fare of the nation consisted of slick entertainment, easily digested and quickly forgotten. It was the same kind of entertainment which dominates the television screens of today.

With such plays, such scenery, and such playhouses, it was inevitable that much of the acting would be routine and stereotyped. Several schools or styles of acting were popular. There was the Personality School of such sweet and lovely ladies as Maude Adams, Viola Allen, Julia Marlowe, and Ada Rehan. These ladies played in sentimental comedies or historical romances and impressed their audiences with their wholesome charm, their feminine appeal, and their technical competence. There was the Emotionalistic School represented in the acting of Fanny Davenport and Mrs. Leslie Carter. These ladies played the overwrought, hysterical heroines of Victorien Sardou, roles like Fedora and Tosca, and thrilled their audiences by substituting emotional pyrotechnics for acting. There were the actors of the transition, conscientious performers often trained in the classic repertory but now pulled in the direction of the romantic costume drama. In many cases they tried to keep alive the traditions of the classic school but too often the influences of the time led them to specialize in dashing, strenuous roles reminiscent of the heroic school

of Forrest and McCullough. There was also the slick, mechanical school, which is found in every period of the theatre, and which is represented by the actor who has mastered the external techniques of speaking, moving, and performing stage business, who can indicate an emotion without ever feeling it or projecting it, and who performs his roles with a competence which is appropriate to the superficial dramas in which he appears. Finally, there was the beginning of the school pioneered by Minnie Maddern Fiske, destined to be not only an influence in the theatrical renaissance of the twentieth century but also a dominant force in the style of acting of the contemporary stage.

VII

COMEDIANS OF THE TRANSITION

THE GREAT TRADITION OF COMIC ACTING, SO BRILLIANTLY ESTAB-
lished early in the nineteenth century by such players as Henry Placide, William Wood, and Henry J. Finn and so marvelously enriched
later on by geniuses like William Warren, William J. Florence, and
Joseph Jefferson, was carried on for a number of years at the end of
the century by a corps of younger comedians who were reared in the
shadow of their towering predecessors. For a time, the younger group
acted the same roles and fulfilled the same ideals. But as the repertory
altered and as theatre practice changed to meet the shifting public
taste, so did the style and quality of the acting undergo a change.

The comedians of the mid-nineteenth century were challenged by a
repertory of unusual complexity and variety. They acted the great
comic roles found in Shakespeare and in the traditional comedies of
Sheridan, Goldsmith, and Farquhar—playing Bottom, Falstaff, and
Dogberry as well as Sir Peter Teazle, Tony Lumpkin, and Bob Acres.
In addition, they performed a rich variety of comic roles in the ephem-
eral melodramas, farces, and comedies of their own time. Their roles
were constantly changing because the production changed almost every
night. But they were able to return to these roles at regular intervals
because the popular offerings of both the classic and contemporary
repertories were repeated several times during a season and in succeeding seasons. This meant that the same audience viewed the
same plays year after year and judged the performances of the
actors not on the basis of novelty and surprise but on the basis
of the quality and effectiveness of the acting. An audience which

knew *The Rivals* by heart concentrated its attention not on the developments of the plot but on the skill and inventiveness of the actors who performed Bob Acres and Sir Lucius O'Trigger. An audience which had watched William Warren play the same role a dozen times could judge the variations in his performances and the growth of his characterizations. Such an audience provided an actor with a motive for continuous development. Also, the variety of the repertory challenged the player to increase his versatility and to perfect his techniques. The great comedians of the mid-nineteenth century met these challenges brilliantly.

As the century waned, the repertory changed. Shakespearean comedies and old English comedies were performed less frequently. The farcical afterpiece disappeared. The backbone of the repertory became contemporary comedies—romantic, melodramatic, and sentimental. The cheapening of the repertory was speeded up by the growing commercialism of the theatre. During most of the nineteenth century, theatrical business was controlled by actors and actor-managers. They were interested in financial success, to be sure, but at the same time they loved and respected the art of the drama; they believed it should nourish the heart and the soul of a man and not merely divert and entertain him. Often they sacrificed monetary gain for artistic principle. And so the theatre-going public was nourished and sustained by a consistently rich and healthful dramatic fare. But at the end of the nineteenth century the businessman, whose sole motive was profit, invaded the theatre. He cared nothing for art or public enlightenment: actors were commodities to be peddled to the public; audiences were customers to be exploited for their dollars. William Winter described the situation in these terms: "Fine actors were visible, and here and there splendid things were being done. . . . But actors, and men truly comprehensive of, and sympathetic with, actors no longer controlled the Theatre: that institution had passed almost entirely into the hands of the so-called 'business man'—the speculative huckster and the rampant vulgarian. . . ." [1] The hucksters and vulgarians cared nothing for the great comedies of Shakespeare or Goldsmith or Sheridan. They fed the public any shoddy farce or cheap comedy which could attract an audience. Thus the range and the variety of the roles as well as the depth and complexity of the roles offered to the comedian steadily decreased.

Moreover, the long run continued to gain in popularity. A success-

ful play now held the boards as long as it could attract an audience. The repertory idea, as a general policy, faded and vanished. In general, audiences attended the same play only once, then looked for something new and different at another theatre. Thus an actor was not subjected to the repeated scrutiny of the same patrons but played to a different house each night. If there was a falling off in his performance or an enriching of it, few patrons were able to perceive the change.

Under these conditions it is little wonder that the nature of comic acting changed and that the overall quality of comic acting diminished. Yet the players who met the demands of the new repertory and of the changed conditions were often of the highest caliber and in many cases might have equalled their illustrious predecessors had they been faced with as stern a challenge.

E. M. HOLLAND

One of the best of the group of younger comedians was Edmund Milton Holland (1848–1913), son of the great clown and gagster, George Holland. "E. M.," as the son was generally billed, began his adult career in 1866 just four years before his father died. The two men acted together in Wallack's company during the season of 1867–68, thus illustrating the overlapping relationship of two theatrical eras.

The younger Holland began in humble parts and developed slowly but steadily. For several years, unwilling to trade on his father's popularity and afraid of blemishing so illustrious a theatrical name as Holland, he was known simply as "E. Milton." But when he had achieved a measure of experience and success, he assumed his rightful identity.

In his early career, young Holland played a great variety of roles, many of them parts which the older comedians had made famous. But in his mature years he appeared almost exclusively in the roles provided by contemporary plays and often played one of these roles for an entire season. Examples of the parts in which he excelled are: Pitticus Green in *Hazel Kirke,* Lot Bowman in *Saints and Sinners,* Captain Redwood in *Jim the Penman,* Uncle Gregory in *A Pair of Spectacles,* Colonel Moberly in *Alabama,* and Colonel Carter in *Colonel Carter of Cartersville.* Such roles do not offer either the range nor the complexity of the roles performed by earlier comedians.

The demands placed on an actor in the days of the great character comedians as compared to the demands placed on later comedians is vividly illustrated if we compare the parts played by William Warren in the middle of the century to the parts played by E. M. Holland at the end of the century. During the season of 1850–51, Warren appeared at least 265 times in at least fifty-seven different plays performing at least fifty-eight different roles. His characterizations ranged from the comic singer in two musical spectacles through the roles of Dr. Ollapod in *The Poor Gentlemen* and Mr. Marmaduke Mouser in *Betsy Baker* to Polonius in *Hamlet,* Dogberry in *Much Ado About Nothing,* and Jacques in *As You Like It.* Forty-five years later, in the season of 1895–96, E. M. Holland spent the entire year playing only three roles, two of them characters from contemporary comedies: Hooper in *The Man with a Past,* Jenkins Hanby in *The Social Highwayman,* and Fag in *The Rivals.*

Within the limits of the changed comic repertory, Holland was a gifted player who enriched the roles assigned to him. His thorough apprenticeship, served in the company of accomplished older players, gave him a mastery of comic techniques. He attended to detail in acting a part but did not overelaborate a character. He could be dry and subtle, droll and humorous, but his effects were never labored or strained. He scored his comic "points" sharply and tellingly but did not overdo them or repeat them. Lewis Strang says that "his method was clean-cut and precise. . . . His powers of suggestion were apparently unlimited, and his font of humour unfailing." [2]

Apparently Holland, like the great character comedians who preceded him, could submerge his own personality and create the illusion of a completely different individuality. To accomplish this, he sometimes relied on gait, gesture, and facial expression. He relied even more on assuming the unique psychology of a dramatic character and then allowing action to flow from this identification. William Winter says he was able to "make the *condition* of a personality as positive and effective as the most brilliant stroke of its *action.* . . ." [3] Lewis Strang felt that Holland's ability to efface his own personality was so remarkable that a spectator would be at first puzzled and in the end defeated if he tried to figure out what kind of a man Holland really was, or even what Holland looked like, after seeing him perform a dozen of his best known roles.

Holland's gift as a character comedian inspired several critics to

write that he would take the place of such great character actors as William Warren and John Gilbert. He never did. Although he was as successful as any comedian of his time, the roles he played and the audiences he entertained never demanded the greatness of a Warren or a Gilbert, so the performer was never able to prove the extent of his own talent.

MAY IRWIN

May Irwin (1862–1938) is a later representative of the great comediennes who early in the nineteenth century played such roles as Mrs. Malaprop and Mistress Quickly. These comic ladies began their careers in resident stock companies and slowly climbed from the drudgery of playing "utility ladies" to the challenge of acting comic or heavy "old women." Their entire careers were spent in the resident companies, and their comic talents were displayed in the classic and popular plays of the standard repertory. But when May Irwin made her debut, the old theatrical order was changing and her career was typical of the altered traditions.

Although she was born in Canada, Miss Irwin made her debut, in 1875, as a variety artist in Buffalo, New York, where she scored a hit singing duets with her younger sister. Thus encouraged, the two little girls toured the variety houses of such cities as Cleveland, St. Louis, and Cincinnati with a repertory of comic and sentimental songs. One of their most popular numbers was "Sweet Genevieve." Even at this early age—May was 13—she was able to create laughter by her sparkling good nature and her chubby figure. After two years of successful touring, the girls were dazzled by an offer from Tony Pastor to appear in his famous New York variety theatre. They jumped at the offer, and succeeded so well that they remained at Pastor's for seven years. It was here that May developed an expert comic technique by appearing in a rich variety of vaudeville turns, improvised burlesques, dramatic sketches, and musical numbers. Her skills and her appeal eventually attracted the attention of Augustin Daly, then head of one of the most flourishing companies in New York. May became a comic actress in Daly's troupe, where she played such parts as Susan in *A Night Off* and Betsey in *Nancy & Co.* But her love of variety and the greater financial rewards of the variety stage eventually proved too great. After four years with Daly, she

returned to her first love and during the remainder of her career, which was a long and successful one, she played farce and burlesque, comedy and vaudeville with a number of companies all over the United States. One of her biggest hits, in which she played her first starring role, was a variety piece by John J. McNally entitled *The Widow Jones*. Another of her contributions was to popularize ragtime, a type of singing she learned from the Negro servants in the hotel where she stayed. She even appeared in an early motion picture, during the course of which she shocked the clergy of the time by reproducing the "kiss episode" from *The Widow Jones*.

Although her career was different from that of an early comedienne like Mrs. Drew, May Irwin's ability to create mirth and laughter was the same endowment which characterized her predecessors. She was a gifted fun-maker, with infectious high spirits and with the ability to enjoy her own humor. She also had a remarkable ability to communicate her sense of fun to her delighted audiences. She was always described as "jolly and stout . . . the image of wholesomeness" [4] or as "a female Falstaff" with a "jolly, rotund figure and with a face that reflects the gaiety of nations . . . the personification of humour and careless mirth. . . ." [5] When she appeared on the stage, every person in the audience sensed her warmth and kindliness and they quickly accepted her as a personal friend. She did not try to transform her individuality and assume the identity of a dramatic character, as did earlier comediennes. Rather, she always exploited her own personality in sketches and roles written expressly for her and thus she is more closely related to the single-role comedians of the mid-nineteenth century who followed the same practice. But Miss Irwin's skills, experience, and natural endowments were great enough to win her a secure place on the American stage for more than thirty-five years, and she is rightfully remembered as a worthy successor to the comic artists of earlier years.

OTHER COMEDIANS OF THE LATER PERIOD

There are many other comedians who might be mentioned here, because the living theatre at the turn of the nineteenth century was prolific and popular. Hundreds of comedies were produced each year in cities and towns from coast to coast and these productions offered em-

ployment to hundreds of actors. Most of these were second-rate, run-of-the-mill, and represented the commercialism which dominated the stage of this period. A comedian did not have the stimulus to growth and development which was enjoyed by actors a few decades earlier. Thus, although there were hundreds of performers, there were not many giants. And so a brief mention of a few representative performers is sufficient for the record.

Among the popular comedians who demonstrated both talent and skill were the following.

Nat C. Goodwin (1857–1919) was a light comedian whose first substantial success was gained at Tony Pastor's Theatre and who subsequently played comic parts which ranged from Gilbert and Sullivan to William Shakespeare. Throughout his career he retained the appeal and the skills of a vaudeville performer and built a reputation as one of America's favorite comedians—and yet he never ceased to yearn for a career in serious, emotional drama.

Francis Wilson (1854–1935), the first President of Actors Equity Association, made his debut as a song-and-dance artist and divided his subsequent career between comic opera and the legitimate stage. As a comedian he was a great "mugger" who loved to "ham up" a role with as many gags as he could conceive and who would do anything for a laugh. Yet he was a thoughtful performer who wrote three books and who declared that the prime requisites for success in acting are personality and sensibility and then said that if one will add to these two qualities "aptitude and enthusiasm, radiant enthusiasm, and then crown all with industry, one will find himself perfectly equipped for the art of acting." [6]

Fritz Williams (1865–1930) made his first appearance on any stage as an infant in the arms of the great William Warren. He saw or performed with many of the best comedians of the nineteenth century (his parents were professional actors) and at the height of his career he shared honors with E. M. Holland as a comic star in the 1898 production of Alexander Bisson's farce, *On and Off*. Williams' best effects were achieved in comic parts which bordered on the eccentric and, although his acting was "remarkable for its brilliancy, vivacity, and unflagging spirit . . . there was very little of the broad sympathy of full-blooded humour in evidence, but a great deal of the biting quality that is inherent in wit." [7]

Sol Smith Russell (1848–1902), bearer of an illustrious name from

the annals of early American theatrical history, was a younger comedian who succeeded admirably in certain kinds of roles. His specialty
was the awkward, eccentric character with the heart of gold who is
found—or supposedly is found—in almost every phase of American
life. Russell acted all his characters in much the same style. They each
had a pronounced individuality of manner which varied little from
role to role. But the awkward absurdity of the style was appealing and
so was the quaint pathos which was added to the portrayals. Audiences returned to enjoy Russell's performances so many times that he
was able to act a single role in a single play, *Edgewood Folks,* for
five years before the public tired of it.

Roland Reed (1856–1901), like Russell, belongs in the group of
single-role comedians. He played many of the parts made famous by
the earlier company of comedians—such as Dr. Ollapod in *The Poor
Gentleman,* Dr. Pangloss in *The Heir-at-Law,* and Bob Acres in *The
Rivals*—and he played them in a broad, jolly style with a sure sense
of the ridiculous. However, he had little or no gift for impersonation
but shaped and adapted each character to fit his own personality. "He
won success on the stage," says Lewis Strang, "by remaining distinctly himself. . . . He is never anything but Roland Reed." [8]

William H. Crane (1845–1928) was another popular comedian of
the younger group who always played himself no matter what his role.
His versatility was limited, but his control of those characters which
fitted his own personality was sure and convincing. His humor was
broad and genial, without spite or malice, and his open, direct appeal
was enhanced by the traits of shrewdness, good sense, and generosity
of spirit. Thus he was the perfect embodiment of such characters as
David Harum, Colonel M. T. Elevator in *Our Boarding House,* and
Senator Hannibal Rivers in *The Senator.* He was characterized in
1901 as "one of the greatest favorites on the American stage." [9]

James A. Herne (1839–1901) was a more versatile actor than
Crane and might be listed under a category other than "comedians."
He played both serious and romantic parts and was a successful leading man for many years. And yet in the history of American acting he
is remembered most vividly for his effective portrayal of comic roles
in his own plays. It must be remembered that Herne was a dramatist
—and perhaps better remembered as a dramatist than as an actor—
because he pioneered in the movement to free American playwriting
from the contrivances and artificialities of nineteenth-century melo-

drama and he helped to establish a true-to-life drama where real characters struggle with real problems. In pursuing his artistic ideals, and in emphasizing character as a basis for dramatic action, he popularized the types of people found in the rural areas of America. Two of his most effective creations are Nathaniel Berry, "Uncle Nat," of *Shore Acres* and Captain Marble of *Sag Harbor*. The dramatist himself played these roles, and played them so well that he created memorable portraits. He made Captain Marble "a perfect representation of gentleness and kindliness, a man, too, bubbling over with humour, and with a heart that inspired kindly sympathy." [10] Uncle Nat was an equally effective portrayal. Although he was closely related to Captain Marble, when the part was played by Herne the character emerged as a man with an individuality of his own. Herne's success in these two comic parts relates him to a long line of American comedians who have portrayed rural types; it also enables one to think of Herne as a successor, in some respects, to the great comedians of earlier years.

VIII

HEIRS OF THE CLASSIC
AND HEROIC SCHOOLS

THE FINAL YEARS OF THE NINETEENTH CENTURY WERE YEARS OF transition and change. The traditions of comic acting were altered by the influences discussed in the previous chapter: the displacement of the old repertory system by the long run, the cheapening of the quality of the plays produced, and the domination of theatrical affairs by "commercial vulgarians." These same influences, in addition to significant other developments, naturally affected the acting of serious drama. The players who can be considered the heirs of Booth, Davenport, Cushman, and Janauschek reflected the changed situation in many ways. A survey of the careers of four representative figures of the transitional period—David Belasco, Richard Mansfield, E. H. Sothern, and Otis Skinner—will reveal and clarify the conflicts and new directions observable in the art of acting at the turn of the century.

DAVID BELASCO

When Edwin Booth played in San Francisco in 1876, his acting was watched with scrupulous care by a keen-eyed, idolatrous young man named David Belasco. There was no spectator, on the stage or off, who felt greater awe for Booth's art; none whose ambition and vision were more inspired by it. Although Booth was completely unaware of his young worshipper with the "clutching eye," he might have been greatly affected to know that here was a man who was to influence the

next era of the American theatre, who was, in fact, to be a dominant figure in the period of transition between the great days of the nineteenth century and the new theatre of the twentieth.

Belasco is not generally remembered as an actor. His contributions in the fields of directing, playwriting, and stagecraft are better known. Yet he belongs in the history of American acting because acting was an important part of his early career, and because his later career in directing, playwriting, and stagecraft exerted considerable influence on the styles of performance of his time.

The man who became a leader in the New York theatre at the turn of the century was born in San Francisco in 1853, just a year after Booth had arrived in the city to serve a brilliant apprenticeship. From his early childhood, Belasco was attracted to the theatre. At the age of five, while his parents were residing in Victoria, B. C., he appeared on the stage with Julia Dean and again with Edwin Forrest. When he was eleven he played the Duke of York to Charles Kean's Richard III. At the age of twelve, back in San Francisco, he wrote his first play. Four years later he appeared at Maguire's Opera House as a newsboy in Augustin Daly's *Under the Gaslight*.

Belasco worked laboriously and eagerly at every theatrical job which came his way. He was copyist, call boy, errand boy, and boy-of-all-trades at several theatres. When he was old enough, he traveled up and down the coast as a vagabond player. Between 1871 and 1880 he acted over 170 roles. Unfortunately we know very little about his style of performing during this period.

In 1876 he became assistant stage manager, and later stage manager, at San Francisco's newest theatre, Baldwin's Academy of Music. He continued to hold this position, with a few interruptions, until 1882. It was a job which gave wide scope to his talents. He not only directed the plays which were produced in the theatre, he wrote some of them and adapted many more. Whenever there was an opportunity, he acted in them. During these years he had the opportunity of seeing and studying most of the leading performers of the American stage, players like Forrest, McCullough, Booth, Barrett, and Clara Morris. During this period he also served briefly as a secretary to the active and prolific Dion Boucicault.

Thus qualified in background and experience, Belasco left San Francisco in 1882 to assume his first New York position, that of stage manager of the Madison Square Theatre. The young man from Cali-

fornia arrived in New York at a propitious time. The old order was on the verge of dissolution. For the moment, the independent manager, such as Augustin Daly, and the star actor, such as Edwin Booth, still controlled the theatre. By 1902, when Belasco established his own playhouse, the old order had almost entirely vanished. The great stars of the nineteenth century were dead or retired; the independent manager or actor-manager had been replaced by businessmen whose primary interest was making money.

David Belasco was one of the men who assumed a role of leadership in this changing world of the theatre. Almost alone among the "commercial vulgarians," says Winter, he was an artist. He sought to carry on the old tradition of independent management. He tried to maintain the theatre as a temple of art and public service. He contributed to styles in acting, in playwriting, and in stagecraft. He helped to establish the concept of the master director or régisseur. Until the day of his death, in 1931, he continued the active production of plays and during most of his career was acknowledged to be one of the most important figures in American theatrical life.

The kind of plays which Belasco presented exerted considerable influence on the actors who performed them. Belasco himself wrote or re-wrote almost all of the dramas he produced. He was the author of a long list of original plays and the revisor of a great many more. A piece submitted to him by another dramatist was sure to undergo extensive alteration. Every Belasco play seemed to have a distinctive form and substance. Perhaps their most significant characteristic was their suitability for acting. Belasco searched for situations which were effective and dramatic, characters that were vivid and picturesque, dialogue which had snap and sparkle. His method of composition furthered his aim. He gathered ideas, jotted them down on slips of paper, then pinned the slips on a series of screens—each screen representing an act of the play-to-be. The slips—representing ideas, situations, or bits of dialogue—were transferred from screen to screen until the most effective setting was found for them. Then the sequence of situations was acted out by Belasco himself. Every bit of the play was tested in an improvised performance. A secretary sat by and recorded the results. This method resulted in dramas which usually lacked literary merit, but they were perfect vehicles for the actors.

The appeal of Belasco's dramas was directly to the heart. He aimed to arouse and indulge all the popular sentimentalities of the American

people. "The theatre of ideas is of secondary consideration to him," says Montrose Moses, ". . . his problem is always how 'to get it across' —into the hearts of his audience." [1] Belasco himself freely admitted this. He wrote: ". . . the complete play is impressive and fulfills its purpose only to the extent that it carries an audience back to its own experiences. If my productions have an appealing quality, it is because I have kept this important fact constantly in mind and have tried, while concealing the mechanism of my scenes, to tug at the hearts of my audience." [2] Such drama inevitably produced a style of acting which was sentimental and appealing—like the performances of the personality school—or it was highly emotionalistic—like the performances of Mrs. Leslie Carter.

Belasco's stage settings, the famous "Belasco realism," also exerted an influence on the style of acting of his productions. He began his career when the scenery for most plays consisted of backdrops, wings, and borders, on which were painted a pretense of reality. Early in his career he began to question the effectiveness of this kind of scenery, for he noted how eagerly an audience responded to real touches and how much these seemed to add to the illusion of the play. In one of his first productions in San Francisco, he experimented with using a flock of real sheep, and in his own drama, *Hearts of Oak,* he introduced a real cat, a real baby, and real food on the table. The public was delighted with all these effects. Belasco continued to supply more and more of them. He determined to bridge the gap between the life he saw around him and the artificial representation of it portrayed on the stage.

At the zenith of his career he came as close to his ideal, perhaps, as it is possible to come. His settings were marvels of solid walls, illusionistic lighting, and authentic properties. "I will allow nothing to be built out of canvas stretched on frames," he said. "Everything must be real." [3] And so the play *Du Barry* displayed furniture and ornaments actually owned and used by Mme. Du Barry. *The Darling of the Gods* used brocades, swords, and trappings imported from Japan. *The Easiest Way* exhibited rugs, furniture, and wall paper which had been removed in toto from a cheap theatrical boarding house in New York City. Such authentic settings influenced a performer to increase the realism of his movements, gestures, delivery, and reactions.

Furthermore, the lighting was designed to heighten the reality of the scenery. Belasco was a pioneer in this field. As early as 1877 he had

experimented with locomotive headlights, and had used colored silks as a medium for changing the hue of stage illumination. Later in his New York theatre he maintained a lighting laboratory and spent large sums on experimentation. He did away with footlights because they were unnatural, and he evolved a system of diffused lighting from above which better simulated the light of the sun. For *Rose of the Rancho* he spent a huge sum to create a realistic sunset, and then rejected it because it lacked the quality of a California sunset.

It is interesting to note that Belasco's realism was not always intended for the eye of the spectator. Sometimes its sole purpose was to aid the actor in identifying himself with the mood of the play and with the character he was representing. For example, if the actor were supposed to make his entrance from a stairway, Belasco built the stairway complete, whether the audience could see it or not. He believed it helped the actor get the spirit of his entrance.

In *The Return of Peter Grimm* there was supposed to be a horticultural garden offstage. Although no one in the audience could see it, Belasco created a garden backstage using real fruit trees and bulbs with their scientific names attached to each. In his *The Concert,* the letters which his actors handled were genuine copies of letters by Mozart and other famous composers, although no one in the audience would have known if they had been blank pages.

On occasions, Belasco was criticized for focussing too much attention on setting, lights, and properties, and for distracting attention from the actors and from the play. The evidence seems to show that if this happened now and then, the occurrences were rare and did not truly represent Belasco's aim. His ideal was to produce an environment which, although scrupulously realistic, would strengthen the play and aid the players. When this ideal was realized, the acting inevitably was affected. Realistic settings encouraged realistic performances. By transmitting mood and atmosphere to the audience and to the player as well, the settings heightened the illusion of actuality. Thus atmosphere and scenery were important factors in Belasco's theory of good acting.

Belasco influenced American acting not only through his playwriting and stagecraft, but also through his teaching and training of players. He believed that acting can be taught. It is not, he felt, an art which is entirely God-given; it is the result of certain innate qualities which have been developed through competent training. Belasco's list

of the five "all important factors" for good acting includes: ability, imagination, industry, patience, and loyalty. A person with these qualifications should be put through a rigorous course of training, said Belasco. He felt that most young American actors are hopelessly ignorant. They know little about their own art and nothing about the other fields of learning which might aid them on the stage. Since America, unlike France, has no national academy to stimulate acting and to set standards, the young player has little encouragement to develop himself. To remedy this, Belasco advocated training which included elocution, dancing, and fencing. In addition, he recommended that the young actor should learn literature, languages, current history, and composition. Finally, the young actor should be taught to observe— keenly and unceasingly. He should be alert to every living thing around him. "The great storehouse to which all dramatists must go is Life," writes Belasco. "Life must be studied constantly and minutely." [4]

Belasco demonstrated the power of good teaching by himself producing several outstanding performers. He took the novice, Mrs. Leslie Carter, and made her one of America's leading emotionalistic players. He hired David Warfield from a Weber and Fields burlesque show and made him a highly successful character actor. He perceived great potentialities in Blanche Bates and Frances Starr when they were only awkward young girls and through his training they became popular leading actresses. These successful performers are evidence of his faith that acting can be taught.

Still another development in the era of transition is illustrated by the career of David Belasco. During most of the nineteenth century, the actor dominated the world of the theatre. He was often playwright and more often manager. He always had the privilege of interpreting his roles as he saw fit. There was no such thing as a director, in the modern sense of the term. With the advent of such men as Augustin Daly and David Belasco, the régisseur or master director makes his appearance. The actor no longer creates independently. He works along the lines laid down by the director. The actor no longer evolves a style and a manner of performance to which the rest of the play must conform but is told by the director what style to adopt for the good of the play. David Belasco was one of the first of these modern directors or régisseurs. The plays he produced were interpreted through his eyes and his mind. He planned the scenery, the lighting, the costuming; he

trained the actors and fitted them, like pieces, into the large mosaic of the play. The actors were not puppets, but neither were they the independent creators which they had been earlier in the century.

In retrospect, it is clear that David Belasco was an influential figure. In several fields he helped bridge the gap between the old order of the nineteenth century and the new theatrical world of the twentieth century. In playwriting, he supplied the romantic, sentimental dramas which, after the demise of the classic repertory, helped to prepare the public for the plays of Ibsen, Shaw, and Chekhov. In the field of directing, he emerged as a régisseur in the modern sense and established practices and procedures which are still followed by directors of today. In scenery and lighting, he helped to destroy the artificial attempts at realism of the nineteenth century and to establish a three-dimensional realism which was a useful link between the old style of mounting a play and the new stagecraft inspired by Adolphe Appia and Gordon Craig. In acting, consistent with his other contributions and influenced by them, he championed a contemporary naturalism which exploited personality and emotion and which is still found, to a degree, on many American stages.

RICHARD MANSFIELD

During the last dozen years of the nineteenth century, it was popular for wags and dramatic critics to declare: "There are good actors, bad actors, and Richard Mansfield." The witticism is revealing because it suggests the controversy and the perplexity which were aroused by the career of one of America's most individual and most exciting actors, Richard Mansfield. During his career on the stage, this actor was lauded and ridiculed, he was adored and hated, he was admired and scorned. Some critics called him the most versatile actor in the world; other critics, equally reputable, declared that he had no versatility at all but submerged every character he played in his own powerful personality and peculiar mannerisms. In retrospect, it is clear that he was not only a controversial performer but a most exciting one.

One essential key to understanding the art of Mansfield was his dominating personality. He was intense, egotistical, and independent to the point of lawlessness. His chosen friends found him a marvel of wit, charm, magnetism, and courtesy. His managers and sometimes his

fellow actors found him a demon of temperament and conceit. He was that unique individual who was born to be a star and who *had* to be the star of every situation both on the stage and off or suffer a complete eclipse of personality. For example, as a schoolboy he could lead a footrace but he could not cooperate on a team; as a host he was perfect, but as a guest he was fidgety and uncomfortable; as the star of a production he was the absolute dictator of every detail or he was nothing. John R. Towse declared that Mansfield's outstanding characteristics were "strong individuality, burning ambition, intense egoism, and high artistic instinct." [5]

Mansfield's critics, both friendly and hostile, agreed on one point: that he was an immensely gifted man. He sang beautifully, he danced well, he painted pleasingly, he wrote plays and composed poetry, he was brilliant intellectually, and he was an excellent athlete—all these in addition to his premier position on the American stage. Given these varied talents and his dominating personality, it is little wonder that both Mansfield's acting and his personal life aroused controversy and perplexity as well as admiration and acclaim.

Mansfield's parentage and upbringing were far from ordinary. He was born in Berlin, May 24, 1854, of an English father and a German mother. His father, a London wine merchant by profession, died when Richard was five years old and appears to have had little influence on the life of the boy. But his mother, a noted grand opera singer named Erminia Rudersdorff, profoundly influenced his life and career. She bequeathed to her son artistic temperament and talent; she trained his voice; she developed his sensibilities; she sent him to excellent schools in England and on the continent; she introduced him to the world of art and culture; and finally, she brought him with her to America where, in 1872, she settled in Boston to become a singing teacher. With such a background it was natural for Richard to seek a career in the arts. He first tried painting and, at about the same time, he joined an amateur dramatic group. After five years in America, he went to London but here his painting brought him nothing and to support himself he was forced to become an entertainer. He presented songs and skits at private parties and in public music halls. He eventually secured a role on the stage, his first part being that of Sir Joseph Porter in a touring production of *H.M.S. Pinafore*. He played small roles in other operas and occasionally in plays. When his mother died in 1882, he returned to America where he continued to play

inconspicuous roles in various musical and dramatic productions. His great opportunity came when A. M. Palmer offered him a part which J. H. Stoddart had refused, that of Baron Chevrial in a play entitled *A Parisien Romance*. Mansfield, a young man of twenty-eight, created a vivid and startling portrait of a doddering old lecher—a portrait which audiences found both fascinating and horrible. The impersonation was sensationally successful and Mansfield found himself suddenly famous. He continued to play the Baron for several months. Then, with characteristic ego, he launched himself as a star—but was soon forced to return to lesser status. For two years he performed in a variety of productions with moderate success. Then in 1886 he scored another hit as the charming, eccentric prince in a play entitled *Prince Karl*. After this success, Mansfield became his own manager and the star of his own productions. He remained so for the rest of his life.

Mansfield's acting career flourished for the next twenty years. Each season he added a new character to his repertory. He alternated long runs of his popular plays with repertory seasons which featured the most appealing characters from his past successes. During this period he was considered to be America's foremost actor. His prestige and leadership in the United States were comparable to that achieved by Henry Irving in England. Among the roles which won him most renown, in addition to Baron Chevrial and Prince Karl, were Dr. Jekyll and Mr. Hyde, Richard III, Beau Brummell, Shylock, Rev. Arthur Dimmesdale in *The Scarlet Letter*, Captain Bluntschli in *Arms and the Man*, Cyrano de Bergerac, Henry V, Monsieur Beaucaire, Ivan the Terrible, and Peer Gynt. Mansfield's last stage appearance was on March 23, 1907, when he overtaxed himself by playing Peer Gynt at a matinee and Baron Chevrial in the evening. The next day, exhausted from tension and overwork, he was forced to cancel subsequent appearances. Five months later, on August 30, 1907, he died at his home in New London, Connecticut.

Mansfield's vivid personality dominated a body of less than average height but more than average strength. Walter Prichard Eaton describes his physical appearance as follows: "Mansfield's stature was below the normal height, a difficulty which he triumphantly overcame by pose and fire, as well as high heels. He always wore his scant hair cropped, displaying a broad and high forehead. His eyes were brown,

his jaw aggressive, his neck large, his shoulders broad, and his whole figure athletic and sturdy." [6]

Eaton also points out, as do all the students of Mansfield's acting, the extraordinary protean nature of his face and body. They could assume, with apparent ease, any shape or appearance or expression he wished to impose upon them. His face in particular was marvelously plastic, and even without the aid of heavy makeup could take on the outline and expression of the character Mansfield was playing.

The unusual flexibility of face and body helped to make Mansfield an expert mimic. In fact, excellence at mimicry became one of his outstanding gifts as a performer and often was mistaken for profound characterization.

Also contributing to Mansfield's success was his magnificent voice. It had richness of quality, flexibility of range, and seemingly limitless reserves of power. Moreover, the actor could use it in long and taxing roles, such as Peer Gynt, without tiring or coarsening it. He always declared that he owed his unusual vocal strength to the method of voice production which his operatic mother had taught him.

In spite of his remarkable voice and body, Mansfield nevertheless was frequently criticized for the way he used them. John R. Towse, always a judicious critic, says that "his manner on stage and off, was apt to be stiff, precise, and angular." [7] Other critics deplored his spasmodic gestures and stiff, jerky walk. Of his voice, Towse wrote: it "was deep, resonant, and musical—few actors have been gifted with a finer organ—but he never learned to take full advantage of it, adopting a falling inflection ending upon the same note at every period, which soon wearied the ear and was especially fatal in the delivery of blank verse." [8] Other critics concurred in this opinion and even William Winter, who was inclined to admire and defend Mansfield's acting on most counts, admitted that he was not "scrupulously heedful . . . in the speaking of blank verse . . . of the niceties of elocution." [9]

In the projection of emotion Mansfield had certain strengths and definite weaknesses. He excelled in portraying the melodramatic horrors of Dr. Jekyll and Mr. Hyde or of Ivan the Terrible. He won universal acclaim for the romantic force and passion he gave to Cyrano de Bergerac. Evidently he could grasp and project the simple, violent, baser emotions which are characteristic of melodrama. However, he was less successful in portraying the more complex emotions of his

Shakespearean characters—Richard III, Henry V, Brutus, and Shylock. Discriminating viewers felt that, with few exceptions, he could not touch either the depths or the heights of great tragic emotion and though he often simulated these emotions there was no "informing soul" behind the simulation. In reviewing Mansfield's Shakespearean performances, Towse continually complains of the shallowness and lack of sincerity which Mansfield manifested in scenes of passion. "The loftier heights of tragic emotion he could not scale," Towse declares flatly.[10] In this connection it is significant to note that Mansfield's list of Shakespearean characters is limited and that, ambitious and egotistical as he was, he never attempted such roles as Hamlet, Othello, or King Lear.

Mansfield's success at transformation—that is, at suppressing his own individuality and projecting the illusion of a created personality —depended on the role he was playing and upon the spectator who was observing him. In such eccentric, bizarre characterizations as Baron Chevrial or Dr. Jekyll and Mr. Hyde, the actor created convincing portraits for most spectators. In picturesque, off-beat, romantic young men such as Prince Karl, Monsieur Beaucaire, or Cyrano he was equally successful. Also, he was universally praised for Captain Bluntschli in Shaw's *Arms and the Man* because Mansfield was able to identify himself perfectly with the "stolid imperturbability," the "deliberate speech," and the "quizzical manner" of the character.[11]

Evidently whenever there was an element of the superficially eccentric, the out-of-the-ordinary, or the bizarre in a character, Mansfield's extraordinary powers of mimicry came into play and he was able to construct an artfully convincing portrait for all his audience. However, when he played Richard III or Henry V or even Shylock—out-of-the-ordinary as these characters are—the discriminating viewer felt that Mansfield failed to identify himself with the character and, instead, substituted too much of the Mansfield personality and too many of the Mansfield mannerisms. Opinion, of course, differed. There were those who marvelled at his versatility and felt that he created in each role a unique and sharply differentiated character. Others felt that his strong individuality infused and dominated every role so that his only convincing creations were those where the actor's personal eccentricities fitted the eccentricities of the dramatic character.

But the outstanding success of Mansfield's acting, on which every-

one agreed, came from a certain "electric" quality. His acting "gave off sparks, it was strangely exciting," says Eaton.[12] Spectators were absorbed and their attention was riveted. There was never a dull moment no matter how awkward the movements of the actor or how monotonous his utterance. A personal force and magnetism, akin to the hypnotic power of Clara Morris in her prime, vivified all his performances and made Mansfield the most talked-about actor of his time. Towse declared that "Few actors could be more interesting and attractive than he when at his best, still fewer more exasperating when he was at his worst," [13] and William Winter summarized his qualities in these words: "He was one of the most extraordinary, versatile, and, above all, interesting actors that have ever graced our stage." [14]

Mansfield had a passionate dedication to his career and to the art of the theatre. His major productions were lavishly mounted and prepared with scrupulous attention to every detail. And each detail was supervised by the intense, high-strung star whose explosions, when things went wrong, were the terror of managers and fellow performers. Once the production was prepared, however, and once the actor was ready to perform, he lost himself in the role he was playing. An incident which occurred in 1894 during his production of *Scenes and Incidents from the Life of Napoleon Bonaparte* illustrates his power of absorption and concentration. Shortly before the curtain rose, Mansfield had exploded in fury when a stage hand had accidently dropped a broom against his dressing room door. But during the performance, when Mansfield was waiting in the wings to begin the crucial scene at Waterloo, a supernumerary stumbled over a stack of rifles and sent them clattering to the floor. The cast was petrified, expecting a titanic outburst. But Mansfield did not move or blink an eye. He appeared not even to have heard the noise—so absorbed was he in the thoughts and feelings of his imaginary situation.

In many ways, Mansfield represented and hastened the transition from one theatrical era to another. He was close to the tradition of repertory; he produced and acted fine plays (including Shakespeare) in the grand manner; and he, the star performer, was the dominating force and the center of attraction in all his productions. At the same time, Mansfield anticipated the changed theatre of the twentieth century and made his contributions to the new order: he acted far fewer roles than his great predecessors, and his seasons of repertory were secondary to the long runs of his hit plays; he produced two plays of

G. B. Shaw and performed them in a manner which suited their sa-
tiric, modern content; he was the first to produce Ibsen's *Peer Gynt*
in the United States and contributed to the growing recognition of the
great Norwegian.

Can Mansfield be grouped with such notable performers as Booth,
Davenport, Barrett, and Murdoch? In a sense, he represents the vanishing tradition of which they were the great representatives. But his
background and achievement do not measure up to theirs. He did not
undergo the long, varied, and intense apprenticeship which gave
Booth and Davenport experience in hundreds of roles representing
every form of spoken drama from broad farce to high tragedy. During
Mansfield's apprenticeship he acted only twenty-six different parts,
many of them minor roles in operettas. After his first major achievement as Baron Chevrial in 1884, his career continued for twenty-two
years and during this period he acted twenty-seven additional roles—
slightly more than one per year. This record contrasts sharply with
the achievements of a Booth or a Davenport. For example, in his
prime Edwin Booth's active repertory included twenty-five of the
greatest roles in poetic drama, to say nothing of the numberless other
roles he had acted or could act.

Of the twenty-seven roles which Mansfield performed after 1884,
only four were Shakespearean characters: Richard III, Henry V,
Marcus Brutus, and Shylock. These cannot be called the most profound or complex of Shakespeare's creations. Neither can Mansfield's
embodiment of them be called his most successful performances. The
versatile tragedians of an earlier period performed these four roles
plus a score of others, including the most demanding parts in all of
dramatic literature: Hamlet, Macbeth, Othello, King Lear, Coriolanus,
Sir Edward Mortimer, Richelieu, etc. In these complex, demanding
roles the versatile tragedians achieved their greatest triumphs and they
continued to act these roles until the end of their careers.

Mansfield, of course, was a product of his times. As has been noted,
the taste for the great roles of the poetic drama was vanishing; the
varied repertory of the old stock companies was giving way to the long
runs of popular successes; the emphasis on plays concerned with contemporary problems or manners was creating a restrained, unpoetic
style of acting. Richard Mansfield was pulled in two directions—toward the vanishing traditions of the old century and toward the
emerging practices of the new. With his strong individuality and

marked dramatic talents, he contributed to the traditions of both centuries.

E. H. SOTHERN

Edward Hugh Sothern, another representative of the transitional period, did not move toward the theatre of Shaw and Ibsen during the early years of the twentieth century as did Richard Mansfield. Instead, he returned to the traditions of an earlier period by establishing himself, first, as a leading representative of contemporary comedy, then as an exponent of romantic drama, and finally as a tragedian and a Shakespearean specialist. His career falls into three distinct phases.

The first phase in Sothern's development was his apprenticeship in comedy. Born in New Orleans on December 6, 1859, the son of the comedian who immortalized the character of Lord Dundreary, he was hopefully but unsuccessfully trained for a career in painting. After this ambition was abandoned, Sothern gravitated to the theatre and, at the age of 19, made his stage debut in the company of his famous father. His first appearance, in a one-line part, was a dismal failure, but with the persistence, energy, and earnestness which marked his whole career, he plugged along in minor roles and slowly acquired skill and poise. After seven years of apprenticeship, he became leading man at Daniel Frohman's Lyceum Theatre in New York. Here he established himself as a light comedian of charm and adroitness who was justly described as a player "of unusual finesse, of much subtilty, of splendid sincerity, of great personal charm. . . ." [15] His typical roles in this period were Jack Hammerton in *The Highest Bidder* and Lord Chumley in a play of that name.

Still under the aegis of Frohman, with whom he remained for fourteen years, Sothern next began to appear in the dashing, romantic roles of cloak-and-sword drama. He possessed all the necessary physical endowments for success in such roles. Although he was only average in height, he had a manly, handsome face, fine brown eyes, a lithe, expressive body, and an overall air of distinction. He became the near-perfect embodiment of such heroes as François Villon, D'Artagnon, and the Prisoner of Zenda. Walter Prichard Eaton nostalgically writes that "Those who saw Sothern act in . . . *The Prisoner of Zenda,* will most fondly remember him as the dashing, charming, alluring symbol of that pseudo-romance which had such a brief but beau-

tiful Indian summer before the realistic new century set in. Better than any other player on either continent, Sothern embodied its humor and gaiety, its chivalric love, its delicate grace, its wistfulness." [16] At this point in his career, William Winter summarized Sothern's artistic achievement as "the development and practical perfection of a distinct, authoritative, crisp style, not unique, but neat, expert in mechanism, and felicitous in assumption of nonchalant, lackadaisical demeanor." [17]

Even at this stage of Sothern's career, successful as it was, judicious critics noted a certain lack of emotional sweep, a faultiness in clarity and cadence of delivery, and a deficiency in spiritual and intellectual grasp. These were flaws which were to keep Sothern from the highest achievement in the third stage of his career.

The third stage began late in 1899 when Sothern appeared as the hero of Hauptmann's poetic tragedy *The Sunken Bell*. It was not a great performance, but it astonished the public by its excellence and, even more, by the fact that so different a role should be undertaken by an actor who previously had been identified exclusively with parts in light comedy and romance. Sothern's followers noted that the actor's elocution had improved and his emotional responses were stronger and truer.

The "new" Sothern, who first emerged in *The Sunken Bell,* was fully revealed in 1900 when the actor performed Hamlet for the first time. During the rest of his career he devoted himself with dogged perseverance and earnest studiousness to developing himself as a tragedian and as a specialist in Shakespearean drama. Before he retired in 1927 he had achieved his goals. He was considered to be the best tragedian since the great days of the nineteenth century and, together with his partner and wife, Julia Marlowe, the leading Shakespearean actor in America.

Sothern played a large number of Shakespearean roles. They included: Romeo, Hamlet, Macbeth, Antony, Shylock, Malvolio, Petruchio, and Benedict. To all of his performances the actor brought earnest studiousness, honest artistic standards, a never-ending zeal for self-improvement, and great capacity for hard work. The results were uniformly sound and praiseworthy. With rare exceptions, however, the critics agreed that his performances could not be called great.

The excellence of Sothern's acting could be found in the care with which he analyzed his characters and the skill with which he executed

Viola Allen in a scene from Caine's *The Eternal City*.
From the Theatre Collection, University of California
Library at Berkeley.

Julia Marlowe.
Photograph by Falk.

Maude Adams in 1904. From the Theatre Collection, University of California Library at Berkeley.

(right) Henry Placide. From the
Harvard Theatre Collection.

Ada Rehan as Beatrice in *Much Ado
about Nothing*. Photograph by Dupont.

(right) Joseph Jefferson as Rip Van
Winkle. From the Ross Theatre Collection, University of California Library at Berkeley.

(left) Dion Boucicault as Myles-na-Coppaleen in his own play, *The Colleen Bawn.* From the Harvard Theatre Collection.

A scene from Thompson and Ryer's *The Old Homestead.*
Photograph by Houseworth.

(left) Thomas D. Rice as Jim Crow.
From the Harvard Theatre Collection.

Lotta Crabtree.
Photograph by Sarony.

(left) Lydia Thompson as Robinson
Crusoe. A British beauty, she introduced burlesque to the American stage.

E. H. Sothern and Julia Marlowe
as Romeo and Juliet.

Richard Mansfield.
Photograph by Elite.

Otis Skinner as Hajj in *Kismet*. From the collection of Cornelia Otis Skinner.

William Gillette as Sherlock Holmes.
Photograph by White.

Minnie Maddern Fiske in her prime.

Mrs. Fiske as Tess in Stoddard's adaptation of *Tess of the D'Urbervilles*.

his conceptions. He was a patient and thorough student and, with each year on the stage, he became a surer technician. In his early appearances he was awkward and mannered and his voice lacked both power and flexibility. But as his career advanced, he grew in confidence and in the ability to execute his effects with vigor and precision. His voice and delivery, too, steadily improved in the direction of control, power, and variety of utterance. When he performed the roles of Romeo, Hamlet, and Malvolio in London, Arthur Symons was so impressed that he wrote a pamphlet entitled *Great Acting in English,* in which he declared that the only great performances of Shakespeare to be found anywhere in the English speaking world were the performances of E. H. Sothern and Julia Marlowe. Symons said that Sothern's Romeo "has an exquisite passion, young and extravagant as a lover's, and is alive." [18] Symons called Sothern's Hamlet "majestical" and exclaimed, "How magnificently he interprets, in the crucifixion of his own soul, the main riddles of the universe!" [19] And finally, Symons' highest praise went to Sothern's portrayal of Malvolio. "It is an elaborate travesty," wrote Symons, "done in a disguise like the solemn dandy's head of Disraeli." Sothern "acts with his eyelids, which move while all the rest of his face is motionless; with his pursed, reticent mouth, with his prim and pompous gestures; with that self-consciousness which brings all Malvolio's troubles upon him. It is a fantastic, tragically comic thing, done with rare calculation, and it has its formal, almost cruel share in the immense gaiety of the piece." [20]

Such fulsome praise was not echoed by the critics who knew Sothern best. After studying his performances for many years, they agreed that Malvolio was his finest Shakespearean portrayal, but they found deficiencies in his acting of the great tragic roles. For all his excellences, they agreed that Sothern lacked "the great ground-swell of passionate emotion," [21] the magic of supreme poetic utterance, and the penetrating spiritual insight which produces truly great acting. William Winter summarizes the general consensus when he writes:

. . . while it cannot justly be said that this actor has provided any splendid, inspiring example, or made upon the theatre and the public mind an impression destined to endure, it can justly be declared that he has exhibited energy and zeal, a high order of talent, much force of character, and that, as a whole, he has exerted a beneficent influence. He . . . largely dominates the dramatic field in America, partly because of his abilities, and partly because of the dearth, which seems to increase, of dramatic genius

and artistic competition. The sum-total of his achievement is substantial and admirable, and he has richly deserved the public gratitude and esteem.[22]

OTIS SKINNER

In 1939, Otis Skinner, then eighty-one years old, published a book entitled *The Last Tragedian*. Readers unacquainted with the volume assumed that it was an autobiography. It was not. The book is a tribute to Edwin Booth. However, if one surveys the career of Otis Skinner, the author, one is inclined to say that he and not Booth should be considered "the last tragedian," or at least the last of the old guard. Skinner outlived Booth by almost fifty years. Skinner did not possess the consummate genius of the older actor, but Skinner was an outstanding performer who played classic roles well into the twentieth century. Trained in the old traditions, possessed of a versatility akin to that of his great predecessors, he was a man who helped to link the contemporary stage with the theatre of the previous century. If he was not *the* last, certainly he was *one* of the last of the versatile performers of the old school.

Otis Skinner served a rich and vigorous apprenticeship. Born in 1858, the son of a Universalist clergyman, he made his professional debut in 1877 as a member of the resident stock company of the Philadelphia Museum. During his first season he acted ninety-two characters of every age, color, and description. "There was no kind of part I did not play," he writes, "even sex was no bar, for I was sometimes clapped into skirts for nigger wenches and coarse old hags. I scowled as villains, stormed as heavy fathers, dashed about in light comedy, squirmed in character parts, grimaced in comics, and tottered as the Pantaloon in pantomime." [23]

Skinner continued this kind of apprenticeship for several more years, acting with many of the ablest veterans of the nineteenth century. He was a member of the Walnut Street Theatre, Philadelphia, for a season. He supported Edwin Booth for ten weeks. He played "seconds" in Lawrence Barrett's company for three years. He acted with John McCullough, Fanny Janauschek, and Mary Anderson on various occasions. He joined Augustin Daly's famous troupe and for five years played with such performers as Mrs. Gilbert, May Irwin, John Drew, and Ada Rehan. For two seasons he was Helena Mod-

jeska's leading man, acting the roles of Henry VIII, Orlando, Shylock, Macbeth, and Sir Edward Mortimer. In the season of 1895–96, he filled an emergency engagement in Chicago where he played Hamlet for two weeks. His success on this occasion was triumphant. During his appearances, "The house held audiences that had not been duplicated since Edwin Booth and Lawrence Barrett were the stars." [24]

As a result of such extensive experience, Skinner acquired a knowledge and technique of acting which served him admirably for all of his life. He never ceased to be grateful for this apprenticeship. Writing many years later, after the old order had vanished, he expressed his appreciation in these words:

I am glad I was able to be in . . . before the old system quite passed away; glad that my novitiate was one of hard knocks that compelled me to swallow my technique in great gulps; glad of the vast experience that gave me every sort of character—in two years I had played over 140 parts; glad of that compulsion of quick study and performance which renders the body supple and the mind obedient; and glad that my dramatic kindergarten was placed among men and women filled with the knowledge of their trade, and with honor for their calling—residents of a true Bohemia since changed for an estate of greater respectability and social recognition and less art.[25]

The success which Otis Skinner achieved, and which was sustained through a career lasting almost sixty years, was based not only on thorough training but on ample endowments of body, voice, and mind. He had a well knit, athletic build which enabled him to wear Elizabethan tights or Roman togas or, indeed, any manner of costume with handsome effect. His face was strong, masculine, and appealing; his voice was resonant and flexible; his temperament was magnetic. He was a scholarly man, too, even though his formal education had been slight. Amy Leslie called him a person "of deep poetic thought" with a "fine hardy brain," [26] and this description must be reliable because the several books which came from his pen show perception, sensitivity, and scholarly competence.

With such endowments, there is little wonder that Otis Skinner was an ideal romantic hero. He played many such parts, acting them with convincing dash and authentic appeal. But he was more than a matinee idol. He was also a skillful comedian, an able delineator of character roles, and a fine tragedian. In surveying his accomplishments, Lewis

Strang exclaims, "Here is versatility to an unusual degree, and versatility, moreover, that has been tested, that is real and genuine." [27]

During the early years of his career, Skinner played the varied and ever changing roles which were characteristic of the versatile actors of the nineteenth century. But the influences of an era of transition overtook him. At the height of his career he succumbed to the long run. He played Colonel Bridau in *The Honor of the Family* for two and a half years; he played Hajj in *Kismet* for three years. He succumbed also to the changed public taste in drama. Instead of roles in Shakespeare or in "old comedy" or in Restoration tragedy—the roles in which he had learned his art—he played mostly in quaint, sentimental comedies or in romantic costume dramas. The list of these is long but among the most popular, in addition to *Kismet* and *The Honor of the Family,* were such favorites as *His Grace de Grammont, Prince Otto, Mister Antonio,* and *Blood and Sand.* Unlike Richard Mansfield, who recognized the growing importance of Ibsen and Shaw, Skinner remained an exponent of the kind of drama which has already been described as "that pseudo-romance which had such a brief but beautiful Indian summer before the realistic new century set in." [28]

Whether Skinner acted his romantic costume parts or the roles of Shylock, Falstaff, Charles Surface, and Petruccio—to which he occasionally returned—in all his acting he demonstrated the skill and authority of his "classic" nineteenth century training. He knew how to make an effective entrance; he knew how to listen and still hold attention; he knew how to control his efforts for the maximum effect in crucial scenes; he knew how to keep a cool head while arousing tears and thrills in his audience; he recognized that "it is a collaboration between actor and audience that makes for cohesion and unity" [29] and he developed this collaboration for maximum response; finally, he knew the range and versatility of the human voice and he used his voice to communicate the heartbreak of tragedy, the rapier sting of satire, and the healthful mirth of comedy. Writing in 1900, Lewis Strang praised Skinner for his versatility, for his magnetic appeal, and for his artistic honesty, but he criticised the actor because he felt that Skinner lacked strong dramatic instinct. "His art is not intuitive," wrote Strang, "and the effects he produces are the results of hard study and painstaking effort." [30] Thirty years later, John Mason Brown analyzed Skinner's acting and found it mature and impressive with few of the weaknesses Strang had observed. Brown wrote: "It is a veteran's method,

sure in its devices, conscious of its 'points' and certain in making them.
. . . It is character acting enlarged beyond the ordinary; bold, romantic, mellow but high-tensioned. It admits no moments of loafing and is
never more active than when someone else is speaking. . . . See his fine
Falstaff . . . and you understand just what 'the great tradition' can
mean in poise, in manner and authority. . . ." [31]

During an era of transition, Skinner carried on many of the great
traditions of nineteenth century acting. In his autobiography, written
in 1924, he declares with justifiable pride: "In taking an inventory of
my professional experience, I find that I have played in all 325 parts;
have appeared in sixteen plays of Shakespeare, acting therein, at various times, thirty-eight parts, and I have produced under my direction
thirty-three plays." [32] Skinner lived until 1942 and continued to prove
the effectiveness of his training and his style of acting even when they
were used in the new theatre of the twentieth century.

ROMANTIC HEROES

The romantic costume plays, which formed so large a part of the later
repertory of Otis Skinner, were attractive to many other players.
Actors who might have developed varied skills under different circumstances became specialists in romance and confined themselves largely
to one kind of role. There have always been romantic heroes on the
American stage and love for the kind of play in which they appear.
The late nineteenth and early twentieth centuries are notable for the
unusual popularity of this kind of drama, and the players who developed a style of acting appropriate to the romantic costume plays are
first cousins—albeit more suave and sophisticated cousins—of Edwin
Forrest and the members of the heroic muscular school.

An outstanding example of an actor who specialized in romantic
roles was James O'Neill (1847–1920), father of Eugene O'Neill. He
began his career as a versatile player who acted many parts and who
showed promise of becoming a worthy successor to Booth, Davenport,
and Barrett. But presently he was cast as the Count of Monte Cristo
in the famous play of the same name by Alexandre Dumas. His fate
was sealed. His success in the part was so great and the monetary
returns were so enormous that he continued to play the role year
after year. He occasionally tried other parts but, like a drunkard to his

bottle, he kept returning to Monte Cristo. Gradually his ambition for self-development declined; his versatility withered away, and he became solely identified with one role. At the end of his life he regretted the abasing of his talents and the atrophy of his reputation, but it was too late. As an actor, he is remembered solely as the dashing, romantic hero of *Monte Cristo.*

William Faversham (1868–1940) was called in his prime "a matinee girl's ideal" and the "hero of a thousand matinees." He deserved the titles because he was a handsome fellow, tall, muscular, vigorous, and healthy, who kept himself in superb physical condition by careful diet and strenuous exercise. Although he was born in London and served a brief apprenticeship on the stage there, he came to the United States in 1887 and built his career in this country, eventually becoming an American citizen. He played many roles during his lifetime including such Shakespearean heroes as Romeo and Marc Antony. However, he won his greatest popularity as the vigorous, masculine, romantic hero of such plays as *Under the Red Robe, Lord and Lady Algy, The Squaw Man,* and *The Prince and the Pauper.* Lewis Strang says he was "at his best in characters requiring buoyancy and vivacity of spirits and rapid, energetic action—action, moreover, that is open, and above board without subtilty or ingenuousness." [33] His last role, however, was an ironic contrast to the handsome heroes he had embodied so well in the early years of the twentieth century: he ended his career by playing Jeeter Lester in that shabby modern play, *Tobacco Road.*

James K. Hackett (1869–1926), son of the fine comedian James H. Hackett, was another matinee idol who provided Faversham with keen competition in romantic roles. Like Faversham, he was tall, handsome, and athletic. He excelled in swimming and fencing and was proud of his reputation as a football player at New York City College. He made his stage debut in 1892 and soon thereafter was playing Shakespearean roles for Augustin Daly. He later joined Daniel Frohman's company where he became the leading romantic actor, causing palpitation of the heart in thousands of ladies who watched him as *The Prisoner of Zenda* or as *Rupert of Hentzlau.* In these roles his shapely, muscular legs were a noticeable asset. One critic wrote that "Mr. Hackett's brilliant, quivering, scintillant legs in 'Don Caesar' are really the best thing he has ever done." [34] Toward the end of his career, after many years of performing in romantic costume drama, he

returned to Shakespearean roles but found that the "picturesque artificiality" of his romantic style limited his accomplishment in the great roles of Macbeth or Othello.

John B. Mason (1857–1919) belongs in a somewhat different group from O'Neill, Faversham, and Hackett. Like them, he excelled in romantic roles but he was even more successful in the performance of classic and modern comedy. His career is typical of many actors of the transition. Before the turn of the century he was the leading man at the Boston Museum. He joined the company in 1879 while William Warren was still active, and during his first few seasons there played romantic juveniles and light comedy parts. Also he was given considerable experience in old comedies such as *The School for Scandal,* the revival of which was a feature of each season at the Boston Museum. When he became leading man of the company in 1888, he was cast for such romantic roles as Captain Vere in *Bells of Haslemere,* Lt. Kerchival West in *Shenandoah,* Eliot Grey in *Rosedale,* and Lord Travers in *Hazel Kirke.* He brought to these parts so much "grace, dash, . . . masculine charm . . . sincerity and . . . mastery of technique" that he lent "conviction and force to the wildest melodrama." [35]

After Mason left the Museum company in 1890, his star went into partial eclipse. But in 1898 he re-established his reputation as a superior actor by making an outstanding success of the uncongenial role of Horatio Drake in Viola Allen's famous production of *The Christian.* Following this achievement, he became the leading man of Daniel Frohman's Lyceum Theatre Stock Company. Here he made the transition to roles in the comedies of Arthur Wing Pinero and Henry Arthur Jones and won the accolade from Lewis Strang of being "the finest modern comedy actor in the country." Strang contends that in the roles of modern comedy Mason "displayed an art so delicate, so subtle, so natural, so human, that it has seemed the realism of nature instead of the realism of art." [36]

Mason can be counted among the romantic heroes of the transitional period because he mastered such roles early in his career. He can also be counted among the comedians of the twentieth century because when the vogue for the romantic drama passed, he cultivated his other talents and won a new reputation as a skillful performer in modern comedy.

There are many other popular players who earned reputations as

romantic heroes. The list is too long for detailed discussion. However, one additional name—that of William Gillette (1855–1937)—deserves mention because he specialized in a particular kind of romantic role, he was the author of several enormously popular plays, and he propounded a particular theory of the art of acting.

Gillette, who was the son of a United States Senator and a friend of Mark Twain, ran away from home in order to pursue his dramatic ambitions. After a short apprenticeship in the stock company of Ben De Bar, he made his New York debut, 1877, in a two-line role in *The Gilded Age.* He trained himself carefully and developed steadily as an actor. He was aided by good looks and a compelling personality. One description called him "tall, slender, studious looking . . . a man of wit, charm and great vanity." [37] In 1881, he appeared in the first play from his own pen, a character study called *The Professor,* and made a decided hit. Thereafter he wrote or adapted or collaborated in the writing of some twenty plays, of which the most famous and popular are *Secret Service* and *Sherlock Holmes.* Both of these are colorful, suspenseful melodramas, and in both of them Gillette played the firm-jawed, resourceful, imperturbable hero. Instead of performing his heroics with cape and sword as O'Neill, Faversham, and Hackett usually did, Gillette used a pistol, a magnifying glass, and native cunning. His manner was so effortless, and his crisp, staccato delivery of lines seemed to be so spontaneous, that he projected "the illusion of great naturalness." [38] He created such a vividly convincing image of the fictitious character, Sherlock Holmes, and he so impressed this image on American and English audiences, that for several generations of playgoers Gillette *was* Sherlock Holmes. Even today when elderly playgoers visualize the imaginary detective they unconsciously recall the firm jaw, the hawk nose, the keen eye, and the authoritative manner of William Gillette.

In all of his roles Gillette exploited his own strong personality. In fact, he chose only those parts which perfectly suited his own personality. He believed that successful acting is the projection of the actor's own individuality through the medium of a dramatic character. Gillette declares: "In all the history of the stage no performer has yet been able to simulate or make use of a personality not his own. . . . The actors of recent times who have been universally acknowledged to be great have invariably been so because of their successful use of their own strong and compelling personalities in the roles which they made

famous." [39] Gillette was aware that many of his fellow actors disagreed with him, but he nevertheless held strongly to his belief in the importance of personality in performance.

Gillette was also an advocate of the "Illusions of the First Time in Acting." The increasing realism of the plays of his time, and of his own plays, their "closeness to life" as Gillette termed it, demanded that the performer abandon the exaggerated gesture, the unnatural stride, and the elocutionary delivery which, Gillette implied, suited some plays of the nineteenth century. Instead, the performer must cultivate verisimilitude and produce the illusion of actual life. Each time the actor performed a role, said Gillette, he must listen as though hearing the lines for the first time and respond as though formulating his replies for the first time. In every bit of action and stage business he must create the impression of spontaneity. Finally, the spirit of the whole play must be so alive and fresh that:

Each successive audience before which it is given must feel—not think or reason about, but *feel*—that it is witnessing, not one of a thousand weary repetitions, but a life episode that is being lived just across the magic barrier of the footlights. That is to say, the whole must have that indescribable life-spirit or effect which produces the Illusion of Happening for the First Time." [40]

In all his activities in the theatre—in playwriting, acting, and theorizing—Gillette helped to reshape the acting of the nineteenth century and advance it toward the psychological naturalism of the twentieth. He also used his own strong, manly personality to create vivid portraits of a special kind of romantic hero.

IX

MRS. MINNIE MADDERN FISKE

MINNIE MADDERN FISKE'S ROLE AS A PIONEER IN THE AMERICAN theatre is often overlooked. Although she is rarely given credit for being an innovator, her career marks a clean break with the traditions of the nineteenth century and the emergence of those ideals which dominate the stage of our own time. She was a champion of the works of Henrik Ibsen and encouraged plays which, like his, discussed modern problems in a truthful, realistic manner. She deprecated the star system and tried to develop a company of players in which the individual was subordinate to the ensemble, and in which all elements of the production served the design of the dramatist. She advocated a simple, natural style of acting based upon psychological truthfulness and freedom from theatrical trickery. Above all, she demanded that the intellect of an actor control his emotions and direct both his conception and his performance. Clara Morris represented the triumph of emotion over intellect. Mrs. Fiske, in sharp contrast, addressed the minds of her spectators before she tried to touch their hearts. She was the most intellectual actress of her day, and played a significant part in shaping the stage history of the twentieth century.

It is important to remember that Mrs. Fiske did not emerge at the end of one era and, through a brilliant new theory and practice, convert her contemporaries and inaugurate an entirely new era of acting. Mrs. Fiske's career extended from 1870 until 1931, and thus she served her theatrical apprenticeship and reached stardom during a period when many other styles of acting were vigorous and flourishing. Her contemporaries in the late nineteenth century and the early years

of the twentieth were classical performers like Helena Modjeska, who acted until 1907, or emotionalistic actresses like Mrs. Leslie Carter, who acted until 1929, or players of the personality school like Maude Adams and Julia Marlowe, who acted until 1918 and 1924, or actors of the transition, like Sothern, Skinner, and Gillette, whose careers extended well into the twentieth century. Mrs. Fiske's theory and practice in the theatre were not typical of the generally accepted theory and practice during most of her career. Not until her last years and in the years which followed did her style and her methods become a dominant influence.

A few characteristics sharply differentiate her school from those which preceded it and which were or are contemporary with it:

1. Emphasis on psychological truthfulness in the portrayal of a character;
2. Concentration on inner feeling with simplified, repressed external action;
3. Cultivation of a simple, true-to-contemporary-life manner of moving and speaking;
4. Fidelity to the design of the play with all performers and effects subordinate to the over-all purpose of the dramatist.

The follower of this school believes that his head should guide his heart in preparing a role. He aims to grasp the psychological truth which motivates the dramatist's character and to build his portrayal according to the logic of this psychological truth. In contrast, the emotionalistic actress grasped her characters intuitively and subordinated psychological truthfulness to emotional display, while the player of the personality school achieved psychological truthfulness only if the logic of the dramatic character fit his or her own personal psychology. The player of the modern school is closest in method to the performer of the classic school who also sought to grasp his roles intellectually and to understand the motives which shaped the actions of a dramatic character but who worked without the assistance of modern psychological insights.

Emphasis on psychological truthfulness in the portrayal of a role leads the performer of the modern school to concentrate on inner feeling; the expression of this inner feeling takes the form of a simplified, restrained external action. In contrast, the player of the classical school, acting the great tragic roles of the standard drama of the nineteenth century and performing them in large, dimly lighted theatres,

used broad movements, bold gestures, and strong facial expression. The emotionalistic actress, performing in sentimental melodrama, surrendered herself to her passions and cultivated extravagant overt display. But the player of the modern school usually performs realistic plays dealing with social problems or contemporary manners, and in these plays a restrained, suggestive style is used, the effectiveness of which is made possible by the small, artfully lighted theatres in which he performs. Even when he acts a Shakespearean role, the modern player tends to eschew both exhibitionism and broad, bold action, relying, instead, as in all his performances, on the cumulative force of subtle, simple effects consistently built up during the whole course of the performance.

His concentration on inner feeling and his restrained expression of this feeling often leads to a neglect of adequate elocution. His speech is not cadenced and poeticized to fit blank verse or declamatory prose; it is the speech of everyday life with its broken rhythms and more limited, less varied range. In fact, the performer of the modern school is sometimes criticized for his slovenly, unintelligible speech and is urged to cultivate greater clarity and precision of delivery.

The ideals of contemporary stagecraft have helped to shape another characteristic of the style of the modern player. The star of the play is no longer the main element of the production but only one of the many elements, all of which must blend into a harmonious whole. At certain periods in the history of American acting a leading player has been able to carry a production despite shoddy scenery, shabby costumes, and a careless third-rate supporting company. But the ideal of the modern school is a production where every element of acting and stagecraft are uniformly excellent and all are coordinated to fulfill the overall design of the dramatist. Thus, the leading player of the modern stage must be part of the ensemble. He or she cannot dazzle like a comet in the night sky—unless the play calls for such a comet. The dazzle of the portrayal must fit into the constellation conceived by the dramatist, and the performance must shine or flicker or fade according to the demands of the play. The ideal of harmonious ensemble acting blended with the other elements of a production to achieve a vivid embodiment of the dramatist's conception is not a new ideal, to be sure. It has been respected and observed, at times, by players and managers of every school of acting. However, it is only in the modern

school that this ideal has been universally accepted and has become a dominant force in American dramatic production.

Many influences, both direct and indirect, have been responsible for the establishment of the modern school of psychological naturalism in the United States. The most powerful foreign influence came from Russia where, at the turn of the century, the Moscow Art Theatre began applying the theories of Stanislavsky and Meyerhold in the production of a new kind of play by Anton Chekhov and other realistic dramatists. The Russian example, and particularly Stanislavsky's system of training actors, became a major force in the classrooms and theatres of this country later in the century. However, before the theories of the Moscow Art Theatre gained currency in America, Minnie Maddern Fiske was teaching similar principles and applying them in her productions. She began her adult career as an actress in 1882, her ideals and methods reached maturity as early as 1897, and she organized her Manhattan Theatre Company in 1904 as a repertory company to demonstrate her theories of acting and play production. The Moscow Art Theatre was not founded until 1898, and the first Stanislavsky-trained player to perform in the United States, Alla Nazimova, did not appear in this country until 1905. So Mrs. Fiske can rightfully be called a pioneer in the establishment of the modern school of psychological naturalism.

Minnie Maddern was the daughter of theatrical parents who began her career as a babe in arms. Throughout her infancy and youth she was in steady demand as a child actress and thus had acquired extensive experience by the time she made her adult debut in 1882 at the Park Theatre, New York. The part she played on this occasion was that of Chip in a comedy-melodrama called *Fogg's Ferry*. Her backers had hoped she would become another Maggie Mitchell or Lotta Crabtree, but in this she disappointed them. She could neither sing nor dance, but she nevertheless exerted a youthful charm which won favorable comment. *Music & Drama,* for May 20, 1882, said: "Magnetic she certainly is; for everybody was pleased with her, although she did nothing extraordinarily pleasing," while the New York *Mirror* declared: "She possesses a native grace, freshness, and a quaint mischievous sense of humor all her own. . . . There is no art about Minnie Maddern. She is perfectly natural. The ebullition of animal spirits, the charm of youth; these are the materials she employs. . . . She is a ray

of dancing sunshine." [1] Other comments on her early appearances mention her wealth of bright red hair—which gave distinction to an otherwise plain face—her slight figure, and her clear, dry voice, "predominantly a head voice," which was considered staccato and unmusical by many listeners.

These early reviews presage many of the comments made on Mrs. Fiske's mature style. When she became a star she continued to be praised for the strong attractiveness of her personality and for the simple naturalness of her manner. In the course of the years, she did not become physically beautiful, nor did her voice develop outstanding richness and range, but she did cultivate her mind and perfect her technique. It became customary to regard her as the most intellectual actress on the American stage.

Evidently Mrs. Fiske was intellectual and analytical by nature. Her approach to any role was careful and studious. Before acting a character, she tried to understand both his mind and his heart, and to know the reason or impulse which prompted his words and actions. Lewis Strang says: "She goes straight to the source of all vital action and all enduring achievement—the infinite power of mind. Mentally she comprehends . . . the full scope of the drama, and the fact that she does comprehend so much makes possible the conviction, the positive appeal, the truth, and the suggestive power manifest in her acting." [2]

Some actors grasp a character instinctively or by intuitive leaps. Mrs. Fiske dissected her characters element by element, scrutinized each component, then assembled the bits as one assembles a mosaic. For the finished creation, she included only those elements which fulfilled the overall design. Anything confusing or superfluous was eliminated. When her character emerged, each detail counted; every gesture and tone had significance. She developed a gift for revealing her characters in deft, subtle strokes. The New York *News,* in reviewing her performance in Ibsen's *Doll's House,* said:

One of the marked features of her acting is the care she gives to detail. She is not given to bold, sketchy portrayals. . . . If she makes an entrance in street costume, she suggests her mood by the manner in which she doffs her gloves, wrap, and bonnet. . . . Her characters are not commonplace or lackadaisical because of these details: they are strongly drawn, intensely interesting and well sustained; the detail introduced by her furnishes the proper tone effect and enhances the vividness of the picture.

Mrs. Fiske's acting was not intuitive and impulsive, like Clara Morris's. Whereas the portrayer of Alixe and Miss Multon depended upon the stimulus of an audience and the inspiration of the moment to evoke startling effects, the impersonator of Becky Sharp and Salvation Nell planned every gesture and inflection of her role with painstaking care. Her acting appeared spontaneous and natural but Lewis Strang discovered, after watching her act the same role several nights in succession, that her effects were "as fixed, as determined, and as certain as the perfect engine, smooth running and positive in its action. . . ." [4] Mrs. Fiske confirmed this impression in a conversation with Alexander Woollcott when she declared, "Any one may achieve on some rare occasion an outburst of genuine feeling, a gesture of imperishable beauty, a ringing accent of truth; but your scientific actor knows how he did it. He can repeat it again and again and again. He can be depended on." [5]

Clara Morris was a triumphant "first nighter"; the excitement and challenge of an opening inspired her best efforts. Mrs. Fiske, on the other hand, was a wretched "first nighter"; she was not at her best until her effects had been perfected in numerous performances. Both Miss Morris and Mrs. Fiske declared that they believed in maintaining a cool-headed control no matter how impassioned the scene, but Miss Morris's acting indicated that she valued the passion more than the control, while Mrs. Fiske's acting illustrated her own dictum that an actor must first of all "have the mechanism of his character at his fingertips" and after that he should try to "fill it in with soul." [6] She also said, "The eternal and immeasurable accident of the theatre which you call genius, that is a matter of soul. But with every genius I have seen—Janauschek, Duse, Irving, Terry—there was always the last word in technical proficiency." [7]

Of course Mrs. Fiske's technique did not suddenly emerge, full blown, like Venus rising from the waves. The deftness of her artistry was the result of long practice and experience. The actress grew and developed as the years went by, apparently reaching her prime in her performance as Tess of the D'Urbervilles. The following review from the Boston *Transcript* for March 5, 1897, is typical of the high praise she received for Tess: "Her mental capacity to analyze a character to its core has never been more evident. Her temperamental capacity to embody and reveal it has gained new force. . . . The execution was worthy of the conception. Her play of feature, in significance, power,

and swiftness of transition, is comparable to La Duse's herself. Her voice reflects the mood of the moment. . . . Her gestures reveal and emphasize. She knows the worth of repose, reserve, silence. She has attained a human verity that makes the stock theatrical devices pale and hollow."

Mrs. Fiske's greatest asset, her intellectual strength, was also a weakness, for it opened her to the charge of "coldness." It was said that she was all head and no heart. Her characters were presented with incisive acumen and skill but, according to many of her critics, she omitted the warm, human appeal which Clara Morris was able to project so effectively. The reviewer of the New York *Transcript* declared that she could analyze and dissect but could not synthesize or vivify. On the other hand, many observers asserted that she could be deeply human and passionate whenever the occasion justified it, while Alan Dale of the New York *World* felt that her "chill, intellectual" interpretations had a fascination which far exceeded the appeal of an ordinary "human" interpretation. Mrs. Fiske herself was sensitive to the criticism that she was too cold and analytical. At a press interview in 1901, she said: "Don't emphasize my mentality, please. If my intellectual proclivities are hurled at the public much more they will begin to believe that I have no feeling to spur emotional expression, although I sometimes think I overstudy a part, that I analyze too much." [8]

Mrs. Fiske's temperament and artistic method created a style of acting which was quiet and repressed, yet, at its best it was charged with vital intensity. The actress avoided noise, display, and theatrical trickery. She suggested rather than exhibited the emotions of her characters and often gained powerful effects by so doing. Strang says she was marvelous at exhibiting "the inherent force of suppression," [9] while the Milwaukee *Sentinel* declared: "Her most powerful effects are gained by the suggestion of intense repressed force. She is one of the few who can project not only words, but thoughts over the footlights and make the audience grasp a mental process without the aid of a spoken line." [10] Alexander Woollcott, who considered Mrs. Fiske's portrayal of Lona in Ibsen's *The Pillars of Society* to be the finest acting he had ever seen, described her performance as "the outgiving of a dynamic being, an inspirational, communicable emanation, a transcendent expression of the spirit." [11]

One of Mrs. Fiske's most successful scenes in *Salvation Nell* was a scene lasting ten minutes during which she sat on the floor, almost

motionless, holding her drunken lover's head in her lap without uttering a word. Even though hurried activity was going on around her, she riveted the attention of the audience on her own silent agony. After watching this scene in performance, the distinguished actress-singer, Mary Garden, is said to have exclaimed, "Ah, to be able to *do nothing* like that!" [12] George Arliss, a fellow actor, said: "Her great moments come in flashes—in silences, in exclamations, or in brief utterances." [13]

Apparently all observers were not as acute as Mr. Arliss or as the reviewer of the Milwaukee *Sentinel*. Some of them complained that Mrs. Fiske repressed so much that an average spectator could not follow her. Because she omitted the customary gestures, movements, and expressions, the spectators couldn't divine what the actress was up to. Most of them were accustomed to acting in which a player had an easily recognizable way of expressing the cardinal emotions. The trouble with the "new school" of Mrs. Fiske, according to its critics, was that the player concentrated on feeling correctly and deeply the emotions belonging to a situation and then trusted to the "happy chance of nature" to put the desired expression on his face. The Boston *Herald* accused Mrs. Fiske of doing this. In the issue of July 22, 1896, occurs the following criticism:

Those who remember Minnie Maddern in that dire failure, "Hester Crewe," recall moments when she walked to and fro, expecting the audience to see the working of her mind, which they did not understand at all. That was simply because she refused to train her face and to make certain that the emotion she wished to express was there. She was content, instead, to feel certain that she was experiencing the right feeling and would doubtless have considered it the loss of, or the stupidity of, the public that could not understand.

Mrs. Fiske was further criticized for the unintelligibility of her delivery. Early in her career, she developed a rapid tempo and a clipped enunciation which baffled many listeners. They complained that she crowded her words together, dropped the terminal sounds, and rushed headlong through her speeches without regard to clarity or emphasis. Charles M. Bregg asserted, "it isn't artistic to speak in quick, staccato passages which completely obscure the sounds of words," and then he declares: "As if to add to this amazing defect, Mrs. Fiske has recently acquired the habit of talking with her back to the audience." [14]

Such irritation over Mrs. Fiske's delivery * was not shared by Alfred Ayres. He, of all people, admired fine elocution and bewailed its disappearance from the American stage, yet he found Mrs. Fiske's delivery to be entirely admirable. He claimed it was her chief asset and had won her foremost rank among American actresses. Her elocution, he said, was happily free of the sing-song, the chanting, and the "conjuring with tones" that marred the speaking of so many players. "The distinctive characteristic of her elocution," he wrote, "is its simplicity, its exceeding naturalness, its freedom from any apparent effort to be effective. With her the thought and nothing but the thought determines." [15]

It is interesting to note that in the latter part of her career, Mrs. Fiske began to insist on the importance of voice and speech in the practice of acting. In one of her conversations with Alexander Woollcott, published in 1917, she declared that her first admonition to an inspiring actor would be this: "Dear child . . . consider your voice. It is the beginning and the end of acting. Train that until it responds to your thought and purpose with absolute precision. Go at once . . . to some master of the voice, and, if need be, spend a whole year with him studying the art of speech. Learn it now, and practice it all your days in the theatre." [16] When Woollcott questioned this dictum and asked about the value of imagination in acting, Mrs. Fiske told him it is

---

* In 1910, Franklin P. Adams wrote some amusing verses that accurately characterized Mrs. Fiske's voice and manner of speaking. They read, in part:

> Staccato, hurried, nervous, brisk,
>   Cascading, intermittent, choppy.
> The brittle voice of Mrs. Fiske
>   Shall serve me now as copy.

> Time was, when first that voice I heard,
>   Despite my close and tense endeavor,
> When many an important word
>   Was lost and gone forever
> Though unlike the others at the play,
> I never whispered: "Wha'd she say?"

> Some words she runs togetherso;
>   Some others are distinctly stated
> Somecometoofast and s o m e   t o o   s l o w
>   And some are syncopated,
> And yet no voice—I am sincere—
> Exists that I prefer to hear.

only by means of a perfectly trained voice that an actor can communicate the inspiration of his imagination. She then somewhat qualified her original assertion by explaining that "If I put the voice first, it is a little because that is something he can easily develop . . . he is likely to forget its importance and if we put it first, he will remember it longer." [17] Mrs. Fiske also admitted that her early style of elocution, "staccato . . . nervous . . . intermittent, choppy," was no part of her theory of acting but was "simply slovenliness," after which she confessed that: "For years I had no appreciation whatever of the importance of careful speech. Only of recent years, after some preliminary lessons given to me by Victor Maurel, have I learned to use my voice." [18] Evidently, then, Mrs. Fiske improved her manner of delivering lines in the later years of her career, and yet her elocution continued to be a subject of debate and analysis among her critics.

One trait of Mrs. Fiske's acting, on which all observers agreed, was its naturalness. In her very first roles she was praised for being simple, charming, and *true to life.* During all of her subsequent career she was admired for the "unstudied" realism of her style. Clara Morris had been praised for naturalness, too, but hers was a different kind from Mrs. Fiske's. Miss Morris displayed raw emotionalism, untouched by poetic elevation. Her strong physical displays heightened the effect of the late nineteenth century French drama, a drama which seemed realistic compared to the earlier melodrama of Victor Hugo, Sheridan Knowles, and Bulwer-Lytton, but which appeared sensational and artificial beside the plays of Henrik Ibsen. Mrs. Fiske acted the realistic plays of Ibsen in a simple, repressed style, and this manner seemed far more true to life than that of Clara Morris or any other actress of the time.

An outstanding example of the Fiske realism, both in acting and staging was found in her production of *Salvation Nell.* This play, produced in 1908, depicted a Salvation Army lass working among the barrooms and tenements of the New York slums. The sordid side of life was revealed so faithfully and daringly in the acting, situations, and setting, that the country was shocked. A Chicago newspaper expressed the general reaction in these terms: "Here is a frankness that sets aside the conventional code of theatrical propriety in characterizing fallen women and drunken brutes; audacity that makes a veritable panorama of debauchery and poverty."

The realism of Mrs. Fiske's acting was based on ideals which are

distinctly modern. The plays she produced had to pass the test of truthfulness and reality. Of every situation she asked the questions: "Is it true? Do people do this?" She said she could not interpret a character or read a line unless both were convincing and life-like. "I've tried to play 'Frou-Frou,' " she once told a reporter, "but unsuccessfully, because in analysis the fabric of the character failed; I felt as if I were speaking lies." [19] George Arliss tells us that her constant warning to her fellow actors was, "Keep it true—keep it true." [20]

In preparing a role, Mrs. Fiske first of all analyzed her part thoroughly and discovered the psychological and emotional make-up of the character. She then worked slowly and carefully to identify herself imaginatively with the personality she had conceived. Concerning her method she once said: "For months before I attempt even to rehearse a part, and many weeks before I begin to study the words assigned to me to say, I am imagining myself to be the character to be assumed. Eating, reading, walking up and down the stairs even, I am Becky or Tess as the case may be." [21] On one occasion, in preparing the role of Hedda Gabler, she locked her cousin, Emily Stevens, out in the cold while she recreated a scene between Hedda and Lovborg, and later, when Emily expressed astonishment over the fact that the scene was not in the play—having been imaginatively conjured up by Mrs. Fiske, the older actress answered: "Ibsen shows us only the last hours. To portray them I must know everything that has gone before. . . . I must know all that Hedda ever was. When I do, the role will play itself." [22] On another occasion she said that modern acting, such as hers, aimed "to penetrate deeper and deeper into human consciousness." [23]

Whether Mrs. Fiske ever succeeded in penetrating into the human consciousness of her characters and creating the illusion of separate personalities, is a matter of sharp dispute. For each observer who said she did, another observer declares she did not. Many reviews praise her for displaying versatility in a wide range of parts, while just as many claim she was always herself and never acted any role but that of Minnie Maddern Fiske. John R. Towse wrote: "In all her 'creations' she has presented her own identity without any substantial modification of speech, gesture, look, or manner." [24] On the other hand, Walter Prichard Eaton said "her sympathy with every part she plays seems so great" that in each different role he felt "strongly the sense of true impersonation." [25] The truth of the matter seems to be that Mrs.

Fiske's vivid personality and individual style were apparent in all her creations. She did act a variety of roles and each one of them was built around a different conception, and yet in her embodiment of these different conceptions her own personality and style were always apparent. Those spectators who grasped the differing conceptions felt that Mrs. Fiske was versatile; those who observed only the style of rendering the conceptions claimed that her roles were undifferentiated. Probably neither observer was entirely right and neither was entirely wrong. Mrs. Fiske herself came close to explaining the puzzle when she said, "Indeed, the greatest actors have, in a sense, always played themselves. When I remember Duse . . . I cannot think of her variations. I think only of the essential thing, the style, the quality, that was Duse." [26]

Mrs. Fiske exerted strong influence on the stage, not only as an actress, but also as a manager and a stage director. As a manager she fought the theatrical syndicate, encouraging other actors and managers to be independent, and helped to loosen the stranglehold of the syndicate's monopoly. As a stage director she adopted many of the practices of the modern régisseur. She tried to develop expert ensemble playing in which small parts were as well acted as the large parts, and in which each actor served the overall design of the play. She believed in giving special attention to the weaker sections of the play so that the whole drama would be strengthened. She announced that the aim of a production should be "perfect harmony . . . one on a par with the performance of a well balanced orchestra." [27] As the leading actress she did not care whether her own part had two lines or many hundreds, and she willingly subordinated herself when she felt that a scene demanded it. George Arliss reports that when he acted with her in the cast of *Leah Kleschna,* "Our greatest difficulty . . . was to prevent her effacing herself." [28] In order to realize better her artistic ideal of expert ensemble playing, Mrs. Fiske organized her Manhattan Company as a permanent troupe, and in its heyday the company was declared, somewhat extravagantly, to be "in every respect equal to the ensemble of the Comédie-Française." [29]

In directing her actors, Mrs. Fiske worked tirelessly to develop their awareness of psychological truth. She demanded that her players have a reason for every movement they made and for every speech they uttered. In rehearsals she carefully explained the circumstances of each scene, the state of mind of each character, and then the company

worked out the business which seemed logical and appropriate for the scene. Once the action and the details were decided on, they were rehearsed until they fitted perfectly into the smooth flow of the drama. Mrs. Fiske's advice to her company was: "Take plenty of time. Don't hurry. Tremendous situations, wonderful emotions, great events do not rush. They are like the mills of the Gods, grinding slowly but exceedingly small." [30] That Mrs. Fiske practiced what she preached is indicated by the testimony of Beatrice Sturges who, after watching her direct a rehearsal, wrote: "Nothing is too small for the eye and the attention of Mrs. Fiske—whether it be the gesture of an actor, a detail in stage setting or lighting, a tone of voice, or a strain of music—and it is her watchful care and artistic sense that have made her company a model one to see." [31] Mrs. Fiske even worried about how the ushers in the front of the house performed their tasks. The morning after a strenuous opening night in Kansas City, a newspaper reporter visited the Shubert Theatre and was astonished to find Mrs. Fiske busy drilling a squad of ushers. In answer to his startled question she replied, ". . . I find that I can neglect nothing. I have to give much thought to the details of establishing the correct relationship between the stage and the auditorium." [32]

Mrs. Fiske's artistic ideals and her style of acting were necessary correlaries of the kind of plays she preferred to produce. Her tastes and convictions led her to one kind of drama and, in turn, the successful staging of this genre inevitably influenced her methods and her style. While Clara Morris, Fanny Davenport, and Mrs. Leslie Carter were titillating their audiences with the emotional dramas of such playwrights as Sardou, Dumas, Feuillet, Daly, and Belasco, Mrs. Fiske was introducing the United States to Ibsen's *Doll's House, Hedda Gabler, Pillars of Soceity, Rosmersholm,* etc., and praising these plays not only for their substance and truth but also for their drawing power. "Our finest plays," she said, "have always, with one exception, been the ones that made the most money." [33] At the same time, Mrs. Fiske was searching for plays which portrayed the lives and problems of ordinary American citizens. In her speech to the Harvard Ethical Society in 1905 she indicated her dramatic preferences when she said: "Today we live in a practical age. . . . From great general principles the drama is coming down to specific incidents in life, and there are arising masters of the craft who can make the details of existence, even the homely or sinister details, suggestive and instructive. From

grand reaches and highly colored and heroic figures, we have been brought to the basis of everyday problems. . . . I confess that my own interest is more definitely enlisted by the modern drama." [34] Some years later, in a speech prepared for the Society of American Dramatists and Composers, she reiterated her beliefs when she said: "I am one with the modern American theatre in its fresh themes from our daily lives, freshly treated." [35] Mrs. Fiske's search for dramas of this kind was rewarded only occasionally when she found such plays as *Salvation Nell* by Edward Sheldon, or *Mrs. Bumstead-Leigh,* by Harry James Smith. At other times she was forced to act in foreign importations like Sardou's *Divorçons* or Meilhac and Halevy's *Frou-Frou,* while two of her most successful vehicles were the plays based on Hardy's *Tess of the D'Urbervilles* and Thackeray's *Vanity Fair*. Still, her preference for the dramas of Ibsen, and for their American counterparts, was strong, and this preference had a profound influence on the style of her productions and her own style of acting. These, in turn, had a significant influence on the American theatre of the twentieth century.

While she was alive, critics found it hard to estimate the stature of Mrs. Fiske. Some declared that she was a great actress who could vivify a dramatization of the telephone directory, while others believed that her achievements were in no way extraordinary. The very diversity of opinion she created indicates the vividness of her personality, and, perhaps, the originality of her methods. The least that can be said of her is that she was an accomplished actress with a strong personality who occasionally achieved moments of greatness; that she illustrated in both her acting and directing many ideals and techniques which are still dominant; and that, as a player, manager, and régisseur, she was a pioneer who helped to establish a modern style of acting which has exerted considerable influence on the stage history of our time. Many of the players who have followed her, and whose performances can be seen today on the stages, in the movie houses, and on the television screens of the nation, are largely inheritors and adaptors of a style of acting perfected many years ago by Mrs. Fiske.

[NOTS O N A NEW SETTING]

The Twentieth Century

 IN GENERAL, THE AMERICAN THEATRE AT THE ONSET OF the twentieth century was sterile, stereotyped, and commercialized, despite the efforts of such a pioneer as Mrs. Fiske. It clung to traditions and practices which had produced great theatre in the nineteenth century but which failed to provide inspiration and creativity for the twentieth. The time had come for rejuvenation and change. Every other aspect of American life was feeling the burgeoning influences of the new century. Now the legitimate theatre was to undergo a renaissance in playwriting, architecture, stagecraft, acting, and public enthusiasm. It was to be transformed into a revitalized force in American life. But it was also, alas, to meet such competition from the motion picture—and eventually from radio and television—that its new enthusiasm and creativity were to flower for a brief period only.

The influences which transformed the American theatre in the early years of the twentieth century were varied, and they came both from Europe and from the United States itself. The most powerful of these influences emanated from four great European dramatists: Henrik Ibsen, August Strindberg, Anton Chekhov, and George Bernard Shaw. These giants revolutionized the writing of plays. They discarded every stale convention of nineteenth-century dramaturgy and opened up unexplored fields of subject matter and technique. They taught their contemporaries new ways to construct a play, new truthfulness in character portrayal, new realism in action and dialogue, and new

approaches to the problems of modern society. They freed their fellow dramatists from the clichés of melodrama and sentimentality, and introduced a whole new world of formerly forbidden subject matter dealing with social, economic, and moral problems. Their influence penetrated every nation of the western world and had profound effect upon American playwriting.

These pioneer playwrights—Ibsen, Strindberg, Chekhov, and Shaw —were writing startling new realistic plays long before there were directors and audiences to appreciate them. If the influence of these dramatists was to be felt, their plays had to be produced and understood. In every country, there was a response to this need. Starting in Paris with the Théâtre Libre of André Antoine, the idea of free theatres to introduce new playwrights and to experiment with new methods of production spread from country to country like a chain reaction.

Antoine opened his theatre in the spring of 1887 and for ten years presented to private audiences the revolutionary new works of dramatists who could not get a hearing elsewhere. It is interesting to note that while Antoine was introducing the problem plays of Ibsen, Strindberg, and Tolstoi to French audiences, the biggest hits on the American stage were those marvelously contrived and wholly artificial melodramas, *Hazel Kirke* and *Shenandoah*.

Other countries soon followed the lead of André Antoine. In Germany, the Freie Buhne, under the direction of Otto Brahm, opened with a performance of Ibsen's then-shocking drama, *Ghosts,* and within a month produced the first play of Gerhart Hauptmann, the dramatist who was to dominate German playwriting for a generation. In London, J. T. Grien launched the Independent Theatre Society with a production of *Ghosts* and soon thereafter presented a play entitled *Widowers' Houses* by a new playwright named George Bernard Shaw. In Moscow, seven years later, Constantin Stanislavsky and Vladimir Nemirovich-Danchenko founded the Moscow Art Theatre, which nurtured the playwriting of Tolstoi, Chekhov, and Gorky, and which evolved a method of acting soon to exert a noticeable influence on American performers. At about the same time, the Irish Literary Theatre was founded by William Butler Yeats and Lady Gregory for the purpose of inspiring the writing of Irish poetic drama. The results of the movement were the establishment of the Abbey Theatre Company and the encouragement of several gifted Irish playwrights.

The impulse toward revitalization of the theatre next reshaped the

architecture of the playhouse and the art of stagecraft. Toward the end of the nineteenth century, Richard Wagner built his first festival theatre in Bayreuth, which rejected the pit, boxes, and galleries of the Restoration theatre and, instead, placed all the seats on a single floor which sloped up sharply from the stage. Shortly after the turn of the century, Max Littmann, Europe's leading theatre architect, copied this plan for the Munich Art Theatre. From these two buildings spread the influences which eventually transformed the playhouses of Germany and America—and other western nations—into auditoriums which, as Sheldon Cheney writes, were "so democratic that practically every spectator could see the stage." [1]

The revolution in stagecraft was even more startling. It was fomented principally by two men: Gordon Craig, an Englishman, and Adolphe Appia, a Swiss. They rejected not only the two-dimensional reality of nineteenth-century scenery and lighting, but also the detailed, authentic realism of David Belasco. Instead they advocated a noble simplicity which related the three-dimensional actor to the surrounding three-dimensional scenery by means of "living light," light which changed from moment to moment as the mood and action of the play changed from scene to scene. Neither Appia nor Craig believed that the setting should be an end in itself, designed to create a spectacle and to delight the eye of the spectator. They believed, instead, that the scenery and lighting were means to an end: through simplification, suggestion, and synthesis they helped to reveal the truth and beauty of the drama. The "New Stagecraft," as the movement founded by Appia and Craig was called—inspired innovations in lighting, stage machinery, and every aspect of scene design. The movement also inspired a brilliant corps of American designers—Norman Bel Geddes, Robert Edmund Jones, Cleon Throckmorton, Lee Simonson, Donald Oenslager, and Jo Mielziner—who were to give to the American theatre the finest stagecraft it has ever enjoyed.

The influences emanating from Europe were important in revitalizing the theatre in the United States. But also many American men and women were reacting independently to the need for change and reform and were making independent contributions. Mrs. Fiske evolved a theory and style of acting which paralleled the Stanislavsky method and which antedated it by several years. A group of wealthy New Yorkers established and financed the New Theatre in New York City in the hopes that it would become a national repertory company. The

project failed, but it contributed to the movement toward reform and rejuvenation.

Many other American influences shaped and stimulated the theatrical renaissance. In 1910, the Drama League of America was founded with the aim of establishing study groups all over the nation where citizens could develop an appreciation for good drama and through which they could exert pressure for better plays and productions. The universities, led by Professor George Pierce Baker of Harvard, began to accept the study of theatre arts as a discipline in their curricula. Professor Baker's class in playwriting, English 47, encouraged the work of such dramatists as Eugene O'Neill, S. N. Behrman, Sidney Howard, Philip Barry, and Percy MacKaye, while Professor Baker's 47 Workshop, which produced the student-written plays, provided training and inspiration for a host of American theatrical leaders including Winthrop Ames, Sam Hume, Irving Pichel, Theresa Helburn, John Mason Brown, Kenneth Macgowan, Osgood Perkins, Lee Simonson, and many others. Percy MacKaye, the son of Steele MacKaye, led the movement to establish civic theatres throughout the nation where large numbers of citizens could join together in creative theatrical enterprises. MacKaye's fervent essays on the subject of community drama, as well as the impressive pageant plays which he wrote and produced, stimulated activity in many communities. But even more successful was the movement to establish Little Theatres throughout the nation. In Europe the "free" threatres provided a show place for the work of the new dramatists whose plays were rejected by the censors and the commercial producers. In America, the Little Theatres became the outlet for these plays, and they also provided a laboratory and training ground for directors, actors, designers, and technicians of all kinds. The Little Theatre movement, begun in 1912 in Boston, Chicago, and New York, spread with astonishing rapidity and soon blanketed the nation with earnest, energetic producing units. In the 1920's Kenneth Macgowan found that there were literally thousands of active Little Theatres in the country. Four of the earliest of these, all launched in 1915, deserve special mention because they made unusual contributions to the theatrical renaissance in America.

Stuart Walker's Portmanteau Theatre toured the country for several years bringing new plays imaginatively mounted to thousands of children and adults. The Neighborhood Playhouse, of New York City, organized the community of the lower East Side into a theatrical

group that produced dozens of plays, dance festivals, revues, concerts, and even motion pictures—and continues to exert an influence on the American theatre through the surviving Neighborhood School of the Theatre. The Washington Square Players of New York, during the four years of its active life, introduced such new dramatists as Philip Moeller and Zoe Atkins; gave the designer, Lee Simonson, his first opportunity; provided training and experience for such talented players as Roland Young, Katharine Cornell, Frank Conroy, and Glenn Hunter; and furnished the inspiration for the establishment, in 1919, of one of America's primary producing organizations, the famed Theatre Guild.

Perhaps best remembered of these four influential organizations is the Provincetown Players. This group gained immortality by giving Eugene O'Neill his first hearing and by nurturing him until he was firmly established as America's most important playwright. The organization—representing young writers and artists who were stirred by the intellectual ferment of the early twentieth century—was founded in Provincetown, Massachusets, but after two seasons there moved to Macdougal Street in Greenwich Village. Here the group helped to train and inspire a large number of talented people. Among the individuals who claimed membership in the organization were Floyd Dell, Edna St. Vincent Millay, Lawrence Langer, Jasper Deeter, Walter Houston, Cleon Throckmorton, and many others. However, Eugene O'Neill, America's first playwright of worldwide importance—remains the greatest name associated with the Provincetown Players.

In addition to the organized groups in towns and cities, there were individual pioneers—sometimes inspired by the example of the groups and sometimes completely independent—whose names stand out as leaders in the theatrical renaissance. Sam Hume is one of these. A native Californian, he studied with Gordon Craig in Italy, then returned to the United States to help introduce the New Stagecraft to America and to introduce, also, Craig's radical new ideas on the purpose and possibilities of theatrical art. Another pioneer was Sheldon Cheney, also a Californian, who founded the magazine *Theatre Arts* in 1916 and made it the leading theatrical publication for many years, one which helped to raise the artistic and intellectual standards of the entire American theatre. Still other representative pioneers were Frederic McConnell, who built the Cleveland Playhouse into a great non-

commercial theatre, and Gilmor Brown, who guided the Pasadena Community Playhouse to prosperity and to worldwide recognition.

For a few brief years the American theatrical renaissance bloomed and flourished. The influences from abroad and the groups and individuals at home combined to revitalize and reshape every aspect of the living theatre. When the renaissance had spent its force, all the outmoded traditions and practices of the nineteenth century had been swept away, and in their place were new inspiration, new ideals, new concepts, and a new technology. Playwrights now probed every problem of the individual and society, creating new form and structure for their works and experimenting with every kind of technique which might truthfully and dramatically communicate their ideas. Architects redesigned the playhouse giving it new beauty, new comfort, and a flexibility of shape which enabled directors to experiment with many different modes of presentation. Designers invented new machines and techniques, and with them created visual beauty which aided the director and strengthened the impact of the play. Audiences were awakened to the significance of drama as a means of interpreting modern life, and which could, at the same time, provide both entertainment and satisfying aesthetic experience.

Even more powerful influences in re-shaping the total world of the theatre in the twentieth century were the motion picture, radio, and television—those mechanical marvels so typical of the inventive genius of the new century. The early twentieth century not only saw the living stage revitalized, it saw the creation of a fabulous new kind of popular theatre.

ORIGIN AND DEVELOPMENT OF THE MOTION PICTURE

On April 14, 1894, in a phonograph parlor located at 1155 Broadway, New York City, occurred an event which had a profound effect upon the theatre and, indeed, upon the world in general. On that date Thomas A. Edison's "kinetoscope" was first offered to public view. It was a peephole box containing a spool of pictures photographed on George Eastman's new flexible film. When a spectator dropped a coin in a slot, turned a crank, and glued his eyes to the peephole, the spool of pictures revolved and created the illusion of motion. Thus the first

moving pictures came to America and opened a fabulous new era in public entertainment.

Edison's invention was the culmination of a series of discoveries which had begun centuries before. As far back as the time of ancient Egypt, men had noticed the phenomenon of the persistence of vision, that is, the phenomenon of the "after image." They discovered that if a series of pictures is passed before the eye, the image of one picture lingers on the retina of the eye and seems to merge with the image of the succeeding picture. If the pictures represent a sequence of motion and if they pass before the eye at a considerable speed, the illusion of continuous motion is created. Centuries after this phenomenon was first noted, Leonardo da Vinci discovered the principle of the "camera obscura" and, following this, curious men in several countries tinkered with machines which combined a series of photographs with a device for rotating them to create the illusion of motion. In the nineteenth century several such devices were invented. In England, in 1833, one of these devices was called "The Wheel of Life." It comprised a hollow cylinder with pictures pasted inside which could be viewed through slits in the upper part of the cylinder. As the device revolved, the viewers saw a succession of images which seemed to be in motion. Other inventions of a similar nature were called, variously, an "auto-scope," a "motorscope," a "vibroscope," etc., but were regarded as toys rather than steps in the evolution of an important invention.

Pioneers in many parts of the world contributed improvements to the existing devices. The final step in the creation of the motion picture is generally credited to Thomas A. Edison who, in an effort to provide a visual accompaniment to his phonograph, experimented with pictures recorded in spirals on a cylinder. These first efforts were unsatisfactory, but when flexible photographic film was placed on the market by George Eastman, Edison found the material he needed and proceeded to build his first peephole moving picture machine, the kinetoscope. Later, the principle of the magic lantern was applied to the peephole pictures of the kinetoscope and when Thomas Armat's successful projector was finally combined with Edison's kinetoscope, a new machine, the vitascope, was born. It was capable of projecting a series of photographs or moving pictures to a whole group of people assembled as an audience. The vitascope made its appearance just two years after the debut of the kinetoscope and entranced an audience

which had assembled to see a vaudeville show at Koster and Bial's Music Hall in New York City.

With the invention of the kinetoscope and the vitascope, the dazzling, incredible career of motion pictures was launched. Here was a new form of popular theatre with a kind of magic and a style of acting destined to win the devotion of millions of people—and destined, also, to inflict an almost mortal injury on the legitimate stage. Here was a new medium of mass entertainment capable of attracting audiences on a scale undreamed of in the nineteenth century and destined to flourish prodigiously for fifty years—until it received from a younger competitor, television, the same kind of grievous injury the legitimate stage had suffered. But before the movies faced the competition of television, they achieved a success and an artistic individuality which added richly to the history of American acting.

During the nineteenth century, as we have seen, the popular theatre consisted of the sprightly, motley offerings of vaudeville, burlesque, minstrelsy, circus, and related entertainments. They developed in the fast growing cities of America and were nourished by the polyglot populations who, speaking a babel of tongues, were unable to understand clearly or to appreciate fully the offerings of legitimate drama. Such audiences nevertheless needed the relaxation and recreation which theatre can give. Vaudeville and its fellow entertainments reached, at the most, a modest ten to twenty per cent of the population. A less expensive, more available, and even more understandable form of theatre was needed for the remaining eighty per cent. The motion picture came as a boon and a salvation to this gigantic group.

Once invented, vitascope booths began to appear in penny arcades throughout the nation. They stimulated curiosity, they attracted attention, and soon they became so popular that the other attractions of the arcade were abandoned and the whole establishment was turned into a vitascope parlor. The booths or parlors were located in the most congested areas of the big cities and were open continuously from early morning until late at night. For the small sum of ten cents anyone could purchase admission and could lose himself in the marvel of pictures which moved—and which soon began to tell stories, to report news events, and to depict the exotic beauties of foreign lands. These pictures on the screen did not require a knowledge of the English language in order to be understood. They were silent and communicated their meaning through visual representation which everyone could

grasp. If occasionally there was a subtitle in English it did not detract from the visual enjoyment and might even be an advantage because it could be used by the growing immigrant population as a simple aid to learning the language. The admission price of ten cents was not excessive but, to make the appeal of the movies even wider, this price was soon dropped to five cents.

In 1905, John P. Harris and Harry Davis remodeled a storeroom in McKeesport, Pennsylvania, installed ninety-two seats and a piano, and announced their theatre as a "nickelodeon," admission to which was only five cents. Their first attraction was *The Great Train Robbery,* produced in 1903 by an Edison cameraman, and later credited with establishing the art of narration on the screen. So popular was the nickelodeon and so fascinating was a story picture like *The Great Train Robbery* that similar movie houses showing similar thrillers sprang up everywhere. Within four years there were at least 8,000 nickelodeons in the United States.

One influential factor in the shaping of film fare has already been implied: the majority of the audience was polyglot, poorly educated, and working-class. Another, equally influential factor was the canny, small businessman promoter, who perceived the possibilities of the new medium and who devoted his life to establishing and building the motion picture industry. In general, the stars, managers, and directors of the stage were not interested. Leaders in the fields of art and entertainment, captains of finance, and the educated classes in general all ignored the new invention. Most of them thought it was cheap and tawdry, unworthy of their attention. They saw it as a passing fad which offered no real threat to the established theatre and no real opportunity for financial exploitation. As late as 1915, Daniel Frohman, a leading producer of legitimate plays, declared: "As for the motion picture being a menace to the theatre . . . that is manifestly impossible. . . . As long as civilization endures, the stage will form one of its chief sources of amusement. . . ." [2]

The men who perceived the potential of the movies and who risked their careers to exploit it were a strange but remarkable group. For example, one of them was a cowboy, Thomas Tally, whose imagination was so aroused when he saw his first motion picture that he sold his horse and invested the money in a vitascope booth. He pioneered in building public confidence and educating his audiences to the wonders of the motion picture. Even more influential were men like Carl

Laemmle, Adolph Zukor, Marcus Loew, and William Fox, who forsook their positions in business to gamble on careers in the motion picture. Carl Laemmle, for example, was a Bavarian immigrant who worked many years in a Wisconsin clothing store, scrimping and hoarding in order to amass enough money to start his own establishment. When he had made his stake, he traveled to Chicago in search of a suitable location. In the course of roaming the city, he ran across one of the new vitascope booths. Fascinated, he watched a steady queue of customers come and go in what seemed a never-ending stream. When he inquired into the finances of the operation, he discovered that a man could make as much money from the movies in one month as he had been able to save during twenty years of labor in the clothing business. He immediately abandoned his plan to open a store and, instead, began a career which made him a leader in the motion picture industry.

The movie industry, from the very start of its career, grew and flourished without the leadership of people experienced in the ways of the legitimate theatre. A few of the early actors, directors, and producers had some stage experience but, in general, the founders of the movie industry were true pioneers. They came without preconceived notions or past experience in the field of entertainment and they worked with a brand new medium. Also, it should be pointed out, their aim was a practical one, namely, to make as much money as possible by giving the public the kind of entertainment that pleased it most. Such conditions for development offered decided advantages—and serious disadvantages. Producers and directors were not hampered by a commitment to traditional ideas and practices but often they were uncommitted to artistic ideals either.

POPULARITY OF SILENT MOVIES

There quickly developed an enormous demand for motion pictures. Millions of ordinary people, hungry for entertainment and escape, flocked to the films. Vitascope booths flourished and became nickelodeons. Nickelodeons multiplied and became movie theatres. Movie theatres waxed rich and became Palaces of the Cinema. In 1914, the Strand Theatre in New York, boasting 3,300 seats and an orchestra of thirty pieces, opened its doors and welcomed an audience of 40,000

during a single week. At the same time, D. W. Griffith's masterpiece, *The Birth of a Nation,* was sweeping the country, playing to audiences which paid as much as two dollars for admission. Between 1915 and 1929, this picture earned $18,000,000 and many subsequent films were similarly lucrative. By 1916, there were 28,000 movie theatres in the United States.

During the early years of the motion picture, the legitimate theatre continued to hold an audience and so did vaudeville, burlesque, and the circus. But as more and more movie palaces opened, and as film idols like Douglas Fairbanks, Mary Pickford, and Charles Chaplin produced better and better films, the living theatre started to feel the competition. Instead of growing with the nation, it began to decline and shrink—but it was unaware of how great the shrinkage was destined to be.

RADIO AND TALKING PICTURES

In the early 1920's, the motion picture industry experienced its first serious competition. Radio broadcasting became widespread and popular. There had been broadcasting as early as 1909 when a pioneer station in San Jose, California, station SJN, began to transmit regular programs of spoken announcements and phonograph music. However, it was not until after 1920 that broadcasting began to flourish on a grand scale. It grew fantastically and soon blanketed the nation with a network of stations transmitting an infinite variety of programs in hectic, round-the-clock fashion. It is estimated that by 1939, there were at least 43,000,000 radio sets in operation.

In the mid-1920's, the movies began to feel this competition. Film fans deserted the neighborhood cinema in order to listen to their favorite broadcasts. In alarm, the movies offered door prizes, vaudeville acts, live orchestras, and all manner of enticements. But the public remained at home, enchanted with the free entertainment offered in its own living rooms. Then Warner Brothers, one of the major film producers in Hollywood, introduced talking pictures in the fall of 1927, and the film industry quickly recovered its audience.

Talking pictures became enormously popular. They also dealt the coup de grace to vaudeville, which had been declining for some time, and caused further shrinkage in the legitimate theatre. The drawing

power of talking pictures continued well into the years of the great depression. Even during this time of financial panic, when other forms of entertainment collapsed, the motion pictures continued to attract customers. Eventually the movies felt the effect of the depression—but not for long. Toward the end of the 1930's, war in Europe and the preparation for war by the United States created a new boom in Hollywood. With movie production suspended in most foreign countries, the demand for American films increased. With almost every citizen employed in the armed forces or in war production everyone had money and everyone, servicemen and civilians alike, felt the need for entertainment. American movies prospered fantastically, turning out over four hundred films per year—some of them in color, an innovation which had appeared in the late 1930's. In 1947, motion pictures attracted an estimated weekly audience of 90,000,000 people.

TELEVISION

The movie boom ended with the advent of television—and motion pictures began to suffer the same fate it had dealt the legitimate theatre. Experimentation with television, which had begun before the Second World War, was suspended during the conflict, but as early as 1945— with the war barely ended—television sets began to appear in the United States. By 1948, there were forty-eight T.V. stations in twenty-five cities sending programs to more than 700,000 receiving sets. A year later, there were seventy stations and 2,000,000 sets in operation —and the numbers continued to increase by leaps and bounds. By 1958, the sending stations totaled 512 and the receiving sets, 50,-000,000. A year later the television industry claimed that eighty-five per cent of the people of the United States were watching television.

The impact on the movies of this tremendous growth was cataclysmic. Spectators by the millions deserted the cinema and stayed home to watch "the big eye." Customers who for years had regularly attended the movies once or twice a week stopped abruptly. From an estimated weekly attendance of 90,000,000 in 1947, the figure dropped to 28,000,000 in 1957. In 1947, gross receipts had been $1,565,000,000; in 1956, they shrank to $1,185,100,000. In 1945 there had been 20,355 movie theatres in the United States. Ten years later, 6,000 of them had closed. In panic, film producers tried to stem the

tide. They introduced wide screens, three-dimensional effects, stereophonic sound systems, and epic spectacles—in the hope of luring customers back to the movie houses. But the enticement of free motion pictures—however old or distorted on a T.V. screen—and the lure of occasional "live" programs—however cheap or heavily burdened with commercials—were far too great to be resisted. The shrinkage of movie audiences went on and continues to do so. Patronage decreases year by year and so does the number of films produced in Hollywood. In 1941, the number reached an all-time high of 497. In 1959 only 224 films were made.

Television had a different effect upon radio. It altered the kind of programs produced and virtually destroyed the national networks, but it did not eliminate the medium. Instead, the coming of national television gave a tremendous boost to local radio stations specializing in recorded music, in local news and sports, and particularly local advertising. In 1962, home viewers were likely to watch the national network television programs but they listened to the local, independent radio station. Since 1948, the first big year for television, the number of AM and FM radio stations has more than doubled. Now there are over 3,000 of them broadcasting programs to at least 90,000,000 home receiving sets and 40,000,000 car sets.

THE DECLINE OF THE LEGITIMATE
PROFESSIONAL THEATRE

The early years of the twentieth century were years of international ferment and rejuvenation for the living stage. For a time, as was noted above, the American theatre was more vital and creative than it had been in many decades. Then, in the midst of prosperity came competition, and shortly thereafter came nation-wide financial depression. During the 1920's the popularity of the motion pictures and radio caused the closing of hundreds of theatres and stock companies throughout the nation, although the Broadway stage continued to prosper. At the end of the decade, the financial panic and ensuing depression speeded the decline which had already begun. Many more theatres closed, production on Broadway shrank alarmingly, and hundreds of actors were thrown out of work. The legitimate, professional theatre suffered a reversal of fortune from which it has never recovered.

The disastrous years of the 1930's were relieved by several significant developments in dramatic affairs, the two most important of which were the establishment of the Federal Theatre by the national government and the organization of the Group Theatre by a band of dedicated young actors and directors.

The first of these developments, the Federal Theatre, provides an unusual chapter in the annals of the American stage. It is the only example of a Federal program devoted solely to the theatre. The project was not motivated by concern for the arts but, rather, by concern for the unemployed artists of the theatre. It was launched in 1935 as a division of the gigantic make-work program of the Works Progress Administration, and was an ambitious undertaking which aimed to give employment to as many theatre workers as possible. The nation was organized into regions and producing units were established in each region. Within a year there were active groups operating in thirty-one states and the District of Columbia, employing more than 12,000 actors, directors, writers, technicians, and theatre people of all kinds. The undertaking was harried by many troubles: red-tape, confusion, quarreling, hurt feelings, and charges of subversion. Yet the project, under the overall direction of Mrs. Hallie Flanagan, managed to grow and flourish and to accomplish its major objective. During the four years of its existence, before it was abolished by Congress on the charge of subversion, it provided employment and creative opportunities for thousands of theatrical workers. Among its productions were not only hundreds of regular stage plays but also pageants, ballets, musical comedies, operas, puppet shows, radio plays, vaudeville, revues, and even a circus. No definable style of acting developed from all this activity, but hundreds of performers were enabled to practice their art and develop their technique through the opportunities offered by the project. At least two of these actors, Orson Welles and John Houseman, used their start in the Federal Theatre to launch their own Mercury Theatre which, for a time, provided some original and exciting productions.

Another significant development of the 1930's, the establishment of the Group Theatre, exerted far more influence on American acting than did the Federal Theatre. In fact, the Group Theatre and its individual members became the principal promoters of the Stanislavsky method of acting in the United States.

The idea of gathering together a company of young actors and di-

rectors who could help each other to achieve artistic maturity within a common set of ideals was the brain child of Harold Clurman, an apprentice actor and a play-reader for the Theatre Guild. He propounded his ideas to his fellow workers so persuasively that by the summer of 1931 he had gathered a group of twenty-eight actors and three directors to form a summer colony at Brookfield Center, Connecticut. The colony drew its principal inspiration from the ideals of Stanislavsky and the Moscow Art Theatre, ideals which had been introduced to the United States by the writings of Stanislavsky, by the visit of the Moscow Art Theatre in 1923, and by two noted teachers of the Stanislavsky method, Richard Boleslavsky and Maria Ouspenskaya. The influence which the Stanislavsky-inspired Group Theatre was later to exert on the American stage is indicated by the names found on its original roster. The directors included, besides Clurman himself, Lee Strasberg and Cheryl Crawford. The actors included Elia Kazan, Stella Adler, Clifford Odets, Franchot Tone, Morris Carnovsky, and J. Edward Bromberg. Most of them later became noted exponents or teachers of "Method" acting.

After a summer of study, self-analysis, and rehearsal at Brookfield Center, the Group opened its first production in New York City in September, 1931. The play was Paul Green's *The House of Connelly* and it achieved a run of ninety-one performances after receiving excellent reviews. Then followed three more productions, two of which were failures and one, a moderate success. The financial position of the Group was precarious until it presented Sidney Kingsley's *Men in White,* which proved to be a smashing success. From then until the end of the decade, the Group continued to produce plays and to achieve success in a variety of ways. It discovered that Clifford Odets, one of its apprentice actors, was a gifted playwright and helped him launch his career. It gave a hearing to other serious young playwrights like Paul Green, Irwin Shaw, and William Saroyan. It provided the training which made first-rate actors or directors out of several of its people. And it spread the gospel of Stanislavsky's principles until his method became a major force in American acting. Although the Group ceased its operations in 1941, after ten years of activity, its influence is still felt in the teaching and directing of such men as Kazan, Strasberg, and Clurman.

During the great depression and despite the contributions of the Federal Theatre and the Group Theatre, all the inherent weaknesses

and ills of the professional stage were exposed and magnified and the competition from movies and radio was intensified. The effect, which has continued to the present day, is vividly illustrated by the sharp decline in the number of plays produced on Broadway. In the season of 1927–28, there were 280 new productions staged. Twelve years later this number had shrunk to eighty. By 1948–49, it was down to seventy, and by 1963–64 it was only fifty-seven, including musicals and revivals of the classics.

Competition from the mechanical media of entertainment is the main reason for this decline, but there are other important causes which stem from long-standing weaknesses. One of these is the concentration for many decades of professional theatre activity in New York City. Instead of many centers of drama drawing inspiration and nourishment from the varied regions of the United States, there has been, during much of our history, only one center to which all theatre workers have had to gravitate. Plays and performances have had to meet the tastes of a single metropolitan audience and if they did they were then sent on tour to cities all over the United States. Theatrical activity thus has had a narrow base so that when the New York stage suffered so did all the other stages in the nation.

The peculiar economics of professional play production is a factor which discourages experimentation and expansion in New York City and elsewhere. There is little or no public subsidy for professional theatre activity such as there is for playgrounds, beaches, zoos, and baseball parks. Private investors must risk their money to produce a play on Broadway, and they are usually chary of doing so when the chance for profit is small. The cost of staging a play, renting a playhouse, and meeting the demands of the fragmentized theatrical unions is so staggering that only smash hits can return a profit. The play with a moderate appeal which might enjoy a moderate run cannot hope to pay its way. Thus, fewer and fewer professional plays are presented.

Broadway playwrights complain that the fate of their work is in the hands of a few supercilious professional critics. Playgoers themselves are not allowed to judge the merits of a production but must accept the verdict of a dozen men who arbitrarily mete out life or death sentences to each theatrical offering. Is it any wonder, asks the playwright, that professional play production is a discouraging enterprise?

The professional actor has for many years faced an equally unpromising situation. Only Hollywood or New York has offered him much

chance for employment and often an appearance on Broadway has been the best entree to Hollywood. Thus many players have flocked to Broadway where they have found no stock companies or repertory companies to give them experience. Only a handful of plays which promise to be smash hits have been in production. If the novice were lucky enough to secure a part in one of these, he has found himself performing a single small part in a single play for many months or even years. If he wished to get broadening experience he has had to join an acting class or find some other substitute for active participation in living theatre. The obstacles to the achievement of versatility and distinction in acting have been formidable.

The melancholy state of the professional theatre is undeniable. Yet hopeful developments are observable and these offer real promise for the future. For example, because the cost of presenting a play on Broadway is so extortionate, producers who wish to try out experimental or unorthodox plays or who have meager budgets now present these plays *off* Broadway in little theatres or makeshift theatres of various kinds where often rents and production costs are relatively low. In the season of 1956–57, there were 75 productions of this type. In the season of 1962–63, the number had grown to 117, if productions of the ANTA Matinee Theatre, the Equity Library Theatre, etc., are included. Many of these Off Broadway productions have offered the kind of original, exciting experimentation which is so necessary if the theatre is to grow and advance, and Off Broadway can point with pride to the development of such creative talents as Edward Albee, Arthur Kopit, and Jose Quintero—to name only three. But, alas, the disease of higher and higher costs has begun to afflict Off Broadway activity as well. Stella Holt, a persistent producer of Off Broadway shows, reports that a production which she staged for $500 in 1953 would today cost her $15,000. "Such economics are murderous," she adds.[3] As a result of these increasing costs, some Off Broadway productions have fled to attics and coffeehouses and to the remotest areas of greater New York, thus creating the phenomenon of "Off Off Broadway" activity.

The continuing growth of summer theatres is another encouraging situation of the present day. Such theatres are firmly established on the east and west coasts and in many cities and vacation colonies in between. Besides offering summer employment to established actors, they provide experience for hundreds of novice players and a stage

where new plays can be tested in actual production. They range in emphasis from musical comedy to Shakespeare and offer astonishing variety both in scope and quality. Some of these summer theatres are attempting year-around operations and a few of them are succeeding.

A third hopeful development and one of the most exciting is the revival of interest in community-sponsored repertory theatres. In the early years of the twentieth century, the community theatre movement produced such notable centers as the Dallas Theatre, the Pasadena Playhouse, and the Cleveland Playhouse. The latter, setting a pace for the rest of the nation, "has been overflowing with good productions" for fifty years.[4] After the initial outburst of enthusiasm which produced these playhouses, interest in community theatre declined. It has been vigorously revived in the past few years by the establishment and growth of repertory theatres in widely separated sections of the country. *Life* magazine for February 28, 1964, reports that "Community theatre is growing so explosively that it is almost impossible to tell where Broadway . . . ends and Main Street begins. New drama groups are popping up all over, in superbly equipped theatres as well as makeshift ones. More and more of these companies are using professional actors and directors." On the east coast can be found such repertory theatres as the Charles Playhouse of Boston, the Arena Stage of Washington, D.C., with a handsome total of 11,000 subscribers, the McCarter Theatre of Princeton University, and the much publicized repertory theatre of New York's Lincoln Center. The middle west can boast of not only the famous old Cleveland Playhouse, but of Milwaukee's Fred Miller Theatre; of the Association of Producing Artists, which moved from New York to the University of Michigan; and of Minneapolis' Tyrone Guthrie Theatre which, like some of the other repertory theatres, serves both as a community theatre and also as a laboratory in dramatic art for graduate students of the University of Minnesota. The southern section of the country shows vigorous interest with such centers as Memphis' Front Street Theatre, Houston's Alley Theatre, Oklahoma City's Mummer's Theatre, and Dallas' Theatre Center Group, while the west coast is proud of the Seattle Center Playhouse, the Theatre Group at U.C.L.A., and San Francisco's famous Actors' Workshop.

This list is by no means exhaustive because there are dozens of other repertory groups which are thriving or beginning to thrive or hoping to thrive. The Ford Foundation has been the angel for many

of them, having donated $7,000,000 to various repertory theatres in the four years between 1960 and 1964. Help also has come from other foundations and donors, from local governmental agencies, and from loyal subscribers. With adequate support and with the enthusiastic participation of both professional and non-professional artists, the repertory theatres have been so successful that a report in *Time* magazine for February 14, 1964, declares: "Broadway shows are having difficulty finding understudies . . . almost every serious young actor who can walk or crawl has gone off to a repertory company." Certainly here is a development which offers hope that the old, old dream of an American theatre decentralized from Broadway, dispersed over the length and breadth of the land, and drawing inspiration and character from the proudly different regions of the country may, at long last, be on the verge of reality.

Equally encouraging, and often intimately associated with the repertory companies, are the college and university theatres of the nation. Beginning with the pioneer course instituted by George Pierce Baker at Harvard, curricula in theatre have been established in more than three hundred institutions throughout the nation. They offer courses in dramatic history and literature, in playwriting, acting, and every art and craft of the theatre. They encourage the production of new and original plays and they keep alive the classic drama of all nations. Every year they stage hundreds of productions of all kinds which often combine the best professional talent, engaged as "artists in residence," with the most promising university students. Such productions give inspiration and practical experience to neophyte actors and technicians and they introduce dramatic literature to thousands of students and townspeople. They are often housed in the newest and finest theatres of the land. Centers of the performing arts, with a playhouse or playhouses as the heart and center of the complex, are rising on an astonishing number of campuses. For example, the University of California at Berkeley, which has never in its long history had a playhouse or a theatre building, is now spending $7,000,000 for an edifice which will contain a large theatre seating two thousand and a smaller one of great flexibility seating five hundred. Included in the complex are workshops, rehearsal rooms, dressing rooms, storage rooms, broadcast studios, offices, and all the other adjuncts of a major theatrical center. The newest and most experimental features of playhouse architecture are represented in the Berkeley complex, and the same can be said for

the numerous other college and university theatres being built all over the nation. In these theatres, also, the newest and most experimental techniques of play production are being tried and tested. In view of this outpouring of enthusiasm, creative energy, and money on the campuses of the United States, many observers believe that the major responsibility for preserving and adding to the great cultural heritage of dramatic art rests jointly with the regional repertory companies and with the colleges and universities of the nation.

X

THE ACTOR IN THE
NEW THEATRE

THE EVENTS AND DEVELOPMENTS WHICH RE-SHAPED THE AMERICAN theatre of the twentieth century had a striking effect upon the actor and upon his manner of performance. That most revolutionary development, the motion picture, produced a unique style of acting, particularly in silent films, as well as a group of gifted performers who perfected and illustrated the possibilities of the cinematic style.

STYLE OF ACTING IN EARLY MOVIES

In early silent films, two distinct kinds of presentation are evident. One represents the transplanting of stage techniques to the screen. Films of this kind are simply stage plays photographed, like the 1964 production of *Hamlet,* starring Richard Burton, which was photographed on the stage of the Lunt-Fontanne Theatre in New York, then shown in movie houses throughout the nation. An earlier example, less sophisticated but more illustrative of the photographed stage play, is the classic film *Queen Elizabeth,* a four-reel tragedy starring Sarah Bernhardt which was made in France and first shown in the United States in 1912. Throughout this film the camera remains in one position—as though it were a spectator facing a proscenium arch—and all the performers move in and out of the frame. Entrances are made from the back or sides of the setting, and then the actor moves to the center of the picture—just as he would move to the center of the stage

in legitimate drama. When a scene terminates, there is no fade-out, no dissolve, and no blending with the ensuing action; the scene simply ends, as though a curtain has been dropped. The camera angle never changes and, of course, there are no closeups. Subtitles are freely used and there is much lip movement as the actor stands and recites his lines, unheard by the audience. The scenes are all interiors and the actors are crowded into the setting, grouped always within a single frame. Movement is subdued, much of the performance is static, and when gestures are made they seem artificial and stagy. *Queen Elizabeth* is simply a stage play recorded on film, without imagination and without awareness of the possibilities of the new medium. This style of presentation disappeared when the pioneers of the motion picture began to discover how to use their cameras and how to direct their actors in performances which pleased the eye and stirred the heart of the spectator.

In the first movies which developed in the direction of true cinematic art, pantomime is the principal means of communication. It is crude, exaggerated, and obvious. If a character wishes to tell another character that he is about to leave a room, he points at himself, then at the door, then at himself again. Eventually he strides to the door, measures its outline, examines its knob, then swings it open with a flourish. No one in the audience, however dim his wit or however poor his command of the English language, can mistake the intention of such an action. But crude pantomime of this sort did not persist. Slowly but surely movie makers discovered the uses of pantomime for comic or emotional effects rather than for simple communication of ideas. As they learned their craft, they found that the intimacy of the camera allowed for pantomime which was even more subtle than stage pantomime. They also discovered the immense advantage of a camera which follows the action rather than remaining stationary. In so early a film as *The Great Train Robbery,* produced in 1903, one can see the beginnings of those techniques which are unique to the motion picture and have no connection with stage plays. In this film, the camera changes position constantly, following the action through a wide variety of indoor and outdoor scenes. The characters of the story do not make entrances into a peephole setting; the camera finds them and follows them into action. Scenes often fade out or blend with succeeding scenes. The whole story is clearly told through visual action and there is no need for subtitles. The movement and gestures

of the characters often seem exaggerated but they are subtler than the pantomime in many earlier films.

The motion pictures and the enthusiastic men who produced them progressed and developed with astonishing rapidity. Several of the young directors who began working with the new medium turned out to be men of talent and imagination. By the time that one of these, D. W. Griffith, produced *The Birth of a Nation* in 1912, cinematic art had already discovered its real potential and had established its basic techniques. This film demonstrated magnificent use of devices unique to the motion picture, such as montage, the closeup, fade-outs and dissolves, angle shots, and many other techniques. These, with improvements and refinements, became the basis for the subsequent development of motion pictures.

The style of acting which evolved in motion pictures was shaped by the conditions of motion picture production. These conditions, markedly different from those which surround the performance of the stage actor, create the significant differences between acting for the screen and acting for the stage. Style in motion picture acting can be understood only if these differences are perceived. It should be remembered that stage and screen performers have much in common. The same endowments of body and mind, personality and sensitivity, are important to both—although they may be used in different ways. Many of the same techniques of assimilating character and projecting emotion are used by both—but in different degrees and for different effects. The fact that stage technique is not alien to the movies is shown by the numerous players who learn their art on the legitimate stage and then perform successfully in the motion pictures. Yet there are some significant differences in acting for the stage and acting for the screen which are clearly revealed if we compare the conditions which surround the stage actor with those which surrounded the actor in the silent films before the introduction of sound.

The stage actor performs in a theatre before a live audience; the screen actor performs in a studio or out of doors before a camera and a director. This is an obvious and easily recognized difference—but the consequences are tremendous. A stage actor is confined in space and can be viewed by any one spectator from only a limited range of angles. He must project his voice, his facial expressions, and his movements to the entire audience, from the business executive in the first

row of the orchestra, to the student in the last row of the gallery. He must orient his acting in one direction and he must enlarge it so that words, expressions, and movements will carry a considerable distance. If he is performing in a playhouse seating two or three thousand people, his effects must be exaggerated if they are to be effective. In contrast, the film actor is not confined to a single space but may roam the world at will—with the camera following him from any distance and at any angle. The film actor *must not* project his gestures or expressions; the camera will do it for him because it can catch and enlarge the smallest movement or the most subtle change of expression. The camera, with its omnipotent eye, can search out tiny details or minute objects and give them enormous significance. Thus the screen actor can perform with maximum realism; no action or reaction need be faked or simulated. Furthermore, he must perform with restraint and complete naturalness for any exaggeration or artificiality will be enormously enlarged by the camera.

The presence of a live audience has great influence on the stage actor. It stimulates him to develop his personal magnetism and to find a way of projecting it to the spectators. It challenges him, night after night, to establish a rapport with the ever-changing audience he faces. Personal appeal and sensitivity are vital elements in the success of his art. The screen actor, on the other hand, faces only his director and the camera. He performs in isolation for one man and a machine. His personal magnetism can rarely be projected to an audience as a living influence. It may be captured, in part, on film, but more likely it is an effect created by the director through montage and skillful editing, and enhanced by colorful publicity. The stage actor varies his performances to win the response of varying audiences; he is a free agent while the curtain is up and performs his role as his training and inspiration dictate. If the director of the play dislikes the performance, he must wait until the play is over before giving instructions. The film actor has no such freedom. He is almost a puppet in the hands of the director and must shape every movement and expression and gesture to suit the demands of his single spectator. As Mortimer Adler writes, "the actors are technicians to be used by the director for the sake of the work being made. It is his art, not theirs, which must dominate." [1]

The director's artistic dominance is established in many ways. A motion picture is not photographed as a continuous whole but is made in bits and pieces. Final scenes may be shot early and opening scenes

may be photographed late, with the intervening scenes recorded in a jumbled sequence which only the director may understand. The actor may know the script as a whole but may be unaware of the position or purpose of individual scenes. He is thus completely dependent on the word of his director and must follow, often blindly, the suggestions given to him.

In the final editing or piecing together of the film, the director, again, is the controlling artist. He can create any effect he desires by joining scenes together in certain sequences. He can make an actor appear effective and powerful or awkward and dull. Many stars of the cinema have been created through ingenious directing and editing; many successful careers have been sustained by artful cutting. The style or effectiveness of any movie actor owes much to the director; it is often, in fact, the creation of the director and not the performer.

The standard method of making films in bits and pieces has another effect on the technique of the performer. He must be able to summon a mood or an emotion instantly, sustain it a few moments for a particular scene, then shift to an unrelated emotion for a succeeding scene. The stage actor, following a coherent script, can develop his emotion logically and gradually as the play develops. He can "warm up" to the big scenes and fit them into a unified pattern of response. In contrast, the movie actor must perform on demand, without warm-up, and in a jumbled sequence which follows no emotional logic. Thus he must be an expert at instant emotional response—or at least the director and editor of the film must arrange the scenes so that the actor *appears* to be projecting the desired emotions.

The differing conditions of performance faced by stage and screen actors produce another result which is both obvious and significant. The stage actor, repeating his performance *in toto* night after night for differing audiences will vary noticeably in style and effectiveness. Some nights his inspiration and vitality will be high; on other nights he may feel tired and depressed. Even on the nights when his inspiration and energy are equally high, his performances will differ because he cannot hope to reproduce, night after night, precisely the same tones, gestures, expressions, and effects. As Lawrence Barrett remarked many years ago, the stage actor is forever carving "statues of snow."

The situation of the screen actor is completely different. He performs only for a director and a camera, and he repeats a scene over and over again. Innumerable shots are taken from which the director fi-

nally chooses one which he feels represents the best performance of the particular scene. When this performance is included in the finished picture, it is fixed and unchangeable—a statue in marble—which will remain exactly the same as long as the physical substance of the film endures. The viewing public sees and studies only the unchanging, best single performance of any screen actor in any film.

The biggest difference between silent films and the stage is, of course, the silence. On the stage, voice and delivery are of paramount importance; they are major tools of the actor's art. Without them, half the actor's effectiveness is lost. In the silent film, however, the actor has no voice; delivery is of no consequence. The movie actor's appeal is purely visual. He must rely upon his facial expressions, his gestures, and his movements to communicate the narration as well as the thought and emotion which accompany it. The camera provides such an intimate view of the performer and is so capable of enlarging even fleeting expressions that no exaggeration is needed. In fact, precisely the opposite—subtlety and suppression—are desirable. As Iris Barry writes, "There is an intimacy between the cinema audience and the film actor as great as between any two persons talking face to face." [2]

The absence of sound and the need for subtle but expressive pantomime created an admirable style of acting in the silent movies. It ranged from the hilarious slapstick of the Keystone comedies, through the graceful acrobatics of Douglas Fairbanks, to the expressive art of Charles Chaplin. The best way to study the acting of the silent films is to survey the style and achievements of a few outstanding performers. Four pioneers who deserve mention for their notable contributions to film acting are Mary Pickford, Douglas Fairbanks, William S. Hart, and Charles Chaplin.

Mary Pickford, who earned the title not only of "America's Sweetheart" but "the World's Sweetheart," has been identified with motion pictures for a large part of their history. Born Gladys Mary Smith in Toronto, Canada, in 1893, she was attracted to the stage at an early age. When she was only five years old she made her debut with the Valentine Stock Company of Toronto and after four years of apprenticeship reached stardom—this at the age of nine—in a play called *The Fatal Wedding*. She continued to play leading roles both in Canada and the United States in such formidable favorites as *East Lynne* and *Uncle Tom's Cabin*. Then, in 1907, David Belasco engaged

her to create the part of Betty Warren in his production of *The Warrens of Virginia*. At the same time he persuaded her to drop the label of Gladys Smith and adopt a name which had more glamor and appeal.

During all these early years, Miss Pickford, née Smith, enchanted her audience with her elfin, appealing charm. She was a petite youngster with huge, expressive eyes and a mass of golden curls. She could be lively and tomboyish; she could be wistful and tremulous. Her sensitivity to changing moods and her ability to portray them in an unaffected, poignant fashion won the hearts of her theatre audiences—just as they captivated her movie audiences a short time later.

Soon after *The Warrens of Virginia*, Miss Pickford made her first motion picture under the direction of D. W. Griffith at the Biograph Studio—and her career as America's Sweetheart was launched. She returned to the legitimate stage once, to perform a leading role for David Belasco, but after that she concentrated on film acting and achieved a success which may never be duplicated in motion pictures. In three years her salary rose from $40 per week to $2,000 per week plus fifty per cent of the profits of her films. In 1916, when the Mary Pickford Film Corporation was organized, her salary again jumped—to $10,000 per week plus fifty per cent of the net profits. At the time, it was said that she "was receiving the largest salary ever paid to any woman in the world." [3]

During this period, Miss Pickford made films in rapid succession and each film increased her popularity. Such pictures as *Tess of the Storm Country, The Little Princess, The Poor Little Rich Girl, Rebecca of Sunnybrook Farm,* and *The Little American* won overwhelming acclaim for the actress and endeared her to millions of people throughout the entire world. In all these films she played essentially the same character and used the same appeals which had proved successful on the stage. She was always the wholesome child, alternately hoydenish and wistful, who won love and created happiness wherever she went. Like Maude Adams in her prime, Miss Pickford gave her audiences a clean, sweet sense of hope and enjoyment. She fulfilled their dreams of goodness and success. As Elinor Hughes wrote in 1932, she acts "in the sort of plays that appeal to young and old alike —the Cinderella theme predominating, to be sure, but filled with humor, pathos, and plenty of excitement." [4]

To project her appeal, Miss Pickford adapted the style of perform-

ing which she had learned on the stage to the requirements of the camera—and quickly became a master of film acting. Her sensitive, expressive face and eyes perfectly mirrored the emotions of the moment. Her movements and gestures, shy and natural as a child's, communicated meaning without the need of subtitles. In her early films —as in most early films—her pantomime was sometimes obvious and exaggerated, but, as the film art developed, Miss Pickford's pantomime became increasingly refined and subtle.

In the early 1920's, after playing children's roles all of her life, Miss Pickford decided to experiment with adult roles to see if her public would accept them. She produced a series of films which included *Rosita, Dorothy Vernon of Haddon Hall,* and *Little Lord Fauntleroy,* in the last of which she played both the mother and the son. These films fell far short of the popularity of her former pictures, so she returned to little girl roles—but only temporarily. Late in the 1920's, talking pictures made their debut and took the country by storm. Miss Pickford decided to cut off her curls, to abandon children's roles for good, and to make her talking debut in the adult role of *Coquette*—a play made famous on the stage by Helen Hayes. The picture won Miss Pickford an Academy Award as the best motion picture actress of the year 1928–29, but it did not attract the popular following which Miss Pickford had come to expect. Following *Coquette* she made a few more films and then quietly retired from the screen to devote herself to civic and business enterprises and to the management of the large fortune she had accumulated. She is still a powerful figure in Hollywood but is best remembered as the sensitive child with the golden curls who mastered the techniques of film acting when the medium was new and who was able to project so appealing an image that she became "the World's Sweetheart."

Closely associated with Mary Pickford in the public mind is another pioneer film idol, Douglas Fairbanks. For fifteen years, from 1920 to 1935, he was the husband of "the World's Sweetheart" and during these years the two celebrities represented the dream marriage of filmdom. They were the unofficial King and Queen of Hollywood, and their mansion, Pickfair, was visited by notable men and women from all over the world. Like Mary Pickford, Douglas Fairbanks earned his distinction by creating a film personality and a style of acting which were unique and inimitable.

Fairbanks, born in Denver, Colorado, in 1883, won a reputation on the stage before he experimented with film acting. An active, restless, exuberant boy, he was educated at Jarvis Military Academy and the East Denver High School, then attended college at the Colorado School of Mines. He also took dramatic lessons from a local teacher who introduced him to the actor Frederick Warde. Encouraged by Warde, Fairbanks abandoned his college education and traveled to the east coast. In the fall of 1900, at the age of seventeen, he made his debut with a road company in Richmond, Virginia, performing the role of a lackey in a play entitled *The Duke's Jester*. A few minor parts followed, and then the restless young man left the stage to try his luck at various odd jobs and to take a vagabond tour of Europe. He returned to the stage in 1902, joining Minnie Dupree's company in *The Rose of Plymouth Town*. He continued to act, with increasing popularity and success, and he developed an exuberant, athletic manner of performance which Miss Dupree described, unflatteringly, as "a bad case of St. Vitus dance." But the public liked his happy athleticism and by 1909 he was playing a starring part for William A. Brady in a play called *A Gentleman from Mississippi*. The play and its star were so successful that they enjoyed a run of two years. During the period from 1910 to 1915, Fairbanks was "an established Broadway success, never exciting great critical acclaim but sure of his public and himself." [5]

In 1915, the Hollywood producers persuaded more than sixty popular actors and actresses to leave their Broadway billets and join the rapidly growing movie colony in Hollywood. Few of them remained for long, but Douglas Fairbanks, who was lured with a salary of $2,000 per week, proved to be a smash hit. His high spirits and exuberant athleticism "brought to the camera an instinctive, natural grace that proved to be the best of silent movie acting," says Arthur Knight. "Within the year, he was among the most popular of all screen players, ranking with Charles Chaplin, Mary Pickford, and William S. Hart; within the decade his buoyant, healthy personality and flashing grin had become familiar—and loved—throughout the world." [6]

During the first six years of his movie career, Fairbanks played the part of a healthy, optimistic young American who overcame obstacles with a leap and a grin, who exposed the evils of sham and pretense, and who preached the gospel of confidence and success at a time when America needed just such a tonic. The optimism of films like

The Americano (1916), *He Comes Up Smiling* (1918), and *Knickerbocker Buckeroo* (1919) was reinforced by a series of eight inspirational books written by Fairbanks and bearing such titles as *Laugh and Live, Making Life Worthwhile, Profiting by Experience,* and *Whistle and Hoe—Sing as We Go.* Fairbanks emerged as a popular hero, says Alistair Cooke, who "stood for the film industry's total respectability . . . a positive ideal worthy of any small fry's devoted emulation." [7]

Fairbanks' early films and the style of acting he demonstrated in them did more than entertain and inspire. They showed the visual rhythm and pictorial effectiveness which distinguished the motion picture from the legitimate stage. Louis Delluc, a French critic who stumbled onto the early Fairbanks films long after they were withdrawn from general circulation, hailed them as "something not of the theatre, something which is simple, direct, sincere, with a vital rhythm . . . in fact a true moving picture." [8]

In 1920, Fairbanks produced his first costume picture, *The Mark of Zorro,* and scored an even greater success than he had with his red-blooded-young-American films. The exotic settings, the romantic costumes, and the deeds of daring found in this film were perfectly suited to Fairbanks' temperament and style. He enjoyed the milieu so enormously that henceforth, with the exception of a film called *The Nut* (produced in 1921), he devoted himself exclusively to costume pictures and will be forever remembered as the dashing hero of such spectacular romances as *The Three Musketeers, Robin Hood, The Thief of Bagdad,* and *The Black Pirate.* In these films, so vividly remembered by all moviegoers and especially by spectators who were children when they first saw them, Fairbanks was not only the star actor; he assisted with the writing; he outlined the action; he set the tone, the pace, and the style of the entire production. Everything about the picture, says Knight, "was designed to follow the almost balletic trajectory of his own lithe figure and broad-gestured acting." [9]

There has never been any style of acting quite like Fairbanks'. Heroes galore have graced the stage; heroes who could wield a sword, ride a horse, and rescue a maiden with dash and style. But Fairbanks exceeded them all in grace, inventiveness, and dazzling dexterity. He was a superb athlete with a body so marvelously trained that it responded to any demand instantly and beautifully. His acrobatics had an effortless, instinctive grace which reminded many spectators of

ballet rather than athletics. His physical feats delighted the viewer with their rhythm and fluidity—and also with their ingenuity. The most unexpected and inventive exploits were continuously developing in a Fairbanks film. Everything from a simple entrance to a daring escape was performed in so clever and surprising a fashion that the spectator was forever gasping in astonishment and pleasure. Says Alistair Cooke:

Fairbanks' glory, the mystery of his visual fascination, is that he could throw all the textbook tricks on the makeshift apparatus of life. He appears to the moviegoer to be a sort of Ariel, leaping where he has a mind without any of the natural checks of gravity. . . . To Fairbanks the limb of a tree suggests a hocks-off; a narrow lane with high walls is a risky, but workable, set of parallel bars; a spear is a pole to vault with . . . it is that virtuoso use of the landscape as a natural gymnasium whose equipment is invisible to the ordinary man, the use of his own body as a crazy but disciplined bow on something that turns into a handy fiddle, that made him an enchanting image. . . .[10]

Enhancing his superb athleticism was Fairbanks' captivating grin, always ready to disarm and delight, and his radiant personality, always a happy concomitant of his physical dexterity. The glow of Fairbanks' exuberant optimism and wholesomeness was strongly projected from the silent celluloid to the hearts of all his spectators, and the world seemed brave and new because it had such a person in it. As his old friend and associate, Charles Chaplin, has said, "The spirit of his pictures, their optimism and infallibility, were very much to the American taste, and indeed to the taste of the whole world. He had extraordinary magnetism and charm and a genuine boyish enthusiasm which he conveyed to the public." [11]

Fairbanks' spell remained potent and his popularity dazzling until the advent of talking pictures. Then, although he made a few successful talking films, his star began to decline. He continued to write, to direct, and occasionally to act, and he continued to live the same vigorous, athletic life he had always enjoyed. His death in 1939 was a shock to the world. It came without warning while he slept, and removed him from the screen before decrepitude could destroy his image as the wholesome, unconquerable hero of a thousand wonderful adventures.

A third idol of the silent films was the original Western Hero of the

movies, William S. Hart. He never achieved the same world celebrity as Mary Pickford or Douglas Fairbanks but he earned immense popularity and established a style of acting which exerted an influence on dozens of his fellow performers.

Although his pre-cinema career has been forgotten, it is interesting to know that Hart was a successful stage actor for twenty-five years before he appeared on the screen and during much of that period he was a popular leading man. Born in Newburgh, New York, in 1872, he made his stage debut seventeen years later and soon was performing important roles in Shakespearean repertory with Lawrence Barrett. Subsequently he acted with Helena Modjeska, playing such parts as Duval to her Camille, Benedick to her Beatrice, and Marc Antony to her Cleopatra. He was the original Messala in the first stage version of *Ben Hur,* he made a notable character of Cash Hawkins in *The Squaw Man,* and beginning in 1907 he played the title role of *The Virginian* for two years. It was not until 1914 that he joined the exodus to Hollywood, by which time he had already perfected the character of the strong, silent hero in western romances. He continued to play these roles in the movies and although he had numerous competitors, he quickly outdistanced them to become the model of the firm-jawed, clear-eyed, square-dealing, hard-riding, straight-shooting western hero. The image he created has influenced western heroes ever since. Also, his suppressed style of under-playing his roles set a new fashion in movie acting. When Hart began his film career many actors continued to use broad gestures and exaggerated movement and facial expression before the camera. Hart perceived the power-to-enlarge inherent in the camera and he demanded the right to underplay his roles, that is, to suppress the over-emphatic pantomime used by other players. His first film made for the Triangle Corporation was a great disappointment to the producers. They told Hart that his acting would be considered wooden, that he did not exaggerate enough, and that the public would feel that he wasn't acting at all. The Triangle people, fearful of losing money, sold Hart's first film to another releasing organization. The film proved to be a great success and Hart's style of acting was vindicated. On the basis of this experience, it is said that Hart "was one of the first, if not the first, to prove that screen acting should be natural, and not a series of exaggerated movements." [12]

The actor of the silent screen who did most to establish cinema as

an art and who perfected a comic character which won the hearts of the whole world is Charles Spencer Chaplin—the immortal "Charlie" of the toothbrush mustache, the baggy pants, the jaunty derby hat, and the willowy cane. He became the foremost artist of the silent screen and firmly established his claim as one of the greatest comedians of all time.

Although generally considered to be an American actor because almost his entire film career has been pursued in the United States, Chaplin is English by birth and has never changed his citizenship. He was born in London in 1889 of theatrical parents, and made his stage debut at the age of five when, on the spur of the moment, he substituted for his mother in a variety act because her voice had failed her. "That night," says Chaplin, "was my first appearance on the stage and my mother's last." [13]

At the age of twelve and a half, Chaplin began regular stage appearances when he successfully acted the role of a newsboy in a play entitled *Jim, the Romance of a Cockney*. His first American appearance was with a traveling English company in a variety sketch entitled *The Wow-wows*. Evidently Chaplin's comic talents attracted notice because, when he returned to the United States in the fall of 1912 on his second visit, the Keystone Film Company offered him $150 per week. After completing his engagement in vaudeville, Chaplin accepted the offer and traveled to Hollywood to begin a film career which was to be meteoric. Within two years his salary jumped to $10,000 a week plus a yearly bonus of $150,000. The comedies he produced in a single year were sold by his studio to the British empire for $670,000—and the British distributors, in turn, made a handsome profit on the deal. This sensational rise to fame and fortune illustrates not only Chaplin's genius as a comedian but also the explosive popularity of the movies in the early years of the twentieth century.

The character of Charlie the Tramp, which Chaplin was to immortalize, appeared in the second movie he made, a ten minute film without plot and without distinction except for the character which Chaplin introduced on the spur of the moment. Chaplin had been standing by in Mack Sennett's studio watching the filming of a comedy when Sennett suddenly ordered him to put on a comic make-up and introduce a few gags into the scene. Chaplin records that "I had no idea what make-up to put on. . . . However, on the way to the wardrobe I thought I would dress in baggy pants, big shoes, a cane and a

derby hat. I wanted everything a contradiction: the pants baggy, the coat tight, the hat small and the shoes large. . . . I had no idea of the character. But the moment I dressed, the clothes and the make-up made me feel the person I was. I began to know him, and by the time I walked onto the stage he was fully born." [14] Chaplin was not aware of the enormous potential of the character he had created—suddenly and full-grown—but he was soon to discover its possibilities, and he was to spend his life elaborating the character and adding depth and dimension to the first rough sketch.

Once created, the character of Charlie the Tramp, began to weave an irresistible spell. Audiences took an instant liking to the funny little man who, as Robert Payne observes, "does all the absurd and wonderful things which people do when they think they are alone and not being watched." [15] At first the antics of the little clown—his ingenious battles with an exasperating world—were enjoyed as pure slapstick. Spectators both young and old roared with laughter at Charlie's inventive clowning and did not bother to analyze its unusual appeal. It was much later that critics recognized in Charlie the Tramp, an epitome of the human condition in all its ridiculous poignancy and pathetic bravery. The little man in the baggy trousers wears a tragi-comic mask which is somehow the mask of all of us.

During his first year in the movies, Chaplin made thirty-five films for the Keystone Company. He then accepted an offer from the Essanay Studios and during the following fourteen months produced an average of one picture per month. His fame grew by leaps and bounds and, as it did so, his films increased in length and elaborateness. In 1917 he signed a contract with First National Pictures and through them he released such classics as *Shoulder Arms, The Kid,* and *The Pilgrim.* A year later he became an independent producer and soon thereafter joined Mary Pickford, Douglas Fairbanks, and D. W. Griffith to establish the United Artists Corporation, a company founded to distribute the productions of the "Big Four."

As the years passed, and as both Chaplin and the public developed a fuller appreciation of the Tramp, more and more was expected of each film, and so fewer and fewer pictures issued from the Chaplin Studio. Instead of slap-dash filming of almost impromptu scripts, now each picture became an elaborate and carefully worked-out production. Each one represented the creative genius of a single individual—Charles Chaplin. He wrote his own scenarios; he composed the musi-

cal accompaniment; he produced the film; he directed the film; and of course he performed the leading role. He became a perfectionist who agonized over every detail of a production and shot thousands of feet of film before he obtained the effects he wanted. In *Modern Times,* for example, he exposed 215,000 feet of film to get the 8,000 feet which were finally used in the picture.

The character of the little tramp who now appears in these carefully wrought films is a fully and marvelously developed portrait— unforgettable in such pictures as *The Gold Rush, City Lights,* and *Modern Times.* The Tramp appears, thinly disguised, as *The Great Dictator* in 1940—another unforgettable film. In *Monsieur Verdoux* (1947), the Tramp wears a disguise so sophisticated as to make the character almost unrecognizable. This film disappointed the public and enraged many critics yet it is considered by some to be a masterpiece. In Chaplin's latest films, *Limelight* (1953) and *The King in New York* (1957), the classic character of the little tramp is almost entirely abandoned.

Chaplin was not immune to the crisis in Hollywood caused by the introduction of talking motion pictures. Hollywood capitulated to the new Frankenstein of sound but for many years Chaplin refused to do so. He had discovered and exploited the immense advantages of the silent film and had demonstrated the artistic capabilities of true cinema. He felt that to adopt spoken dialogue was to destroy the uniqueness of motion pictures and to make them merely a mechanical imitation of the stage. He was willing to introduce synchronized music and special sound effects and demonstrated how such additions could enhance a silent picture without destroying its essential character. A classic example of his ingenious use of sound is the whistle scene in *City Lights.* In this sequence, Charlie's frantic little whistles, when he tries to conceal the fact that he has swallowed a policeman's whistle, is an uproarious addition to the pantomime of the scene. It was not until the end of his picture-making career that Chaplin finally surrendered to the overwhelming demand for spoken dialogue and introduced it into his last films.

The perfection of Chaplin's comic style is difficult to describe—but it can be studied by anyone who takes the time to attend a re-run of his films. He is a master of pantomime from the tiniest gesture to the wildest slapstick, and from the most fleeting expression to the most violent pandemonium. Moreover, every one of his movements, ges-

tures, and expressions has meaning and conveys with exquisite timing and clarity the precise emotion or idea Chaplin has in mind. Belly-laughs or tears, pathos or satire—Chaplin communicates them all without clumsiness or strain and with magnificent humor. The range of his inventiveness is limitless. His manipulation of people and things is endlessly surprising but always comically logical for the given situation. And all of this superb clowning seems to result from the natural reactions of a dramatic character which has universal human appeal. Charlie, the tramp, is a tragi-comic Everyman forever portraying the human dilemma in a crazy world. Chaplin's supreme achievement is to join a marvelous technique of performance to a significant, enduring character. The uniqueness and importance of his creation is ably summarized by Robert Payne when he writes:

> In time Chaplin will be forgotten, but Charlie will remain. He will have a place in the cosmography of the imagination which every generation maps afresh, but in every thousand years only a few new legends are permitted to enter. He will live in the world inhabited by Alexander the Great, Napoleon, and the Borgias, with Robin Hood, King Arthur and the Wandering Jew as his companions; Punch, Pierrot and Harlequin will be his accomplices in mischief. . . . It is even possible that his place is at the very centre of the fabulous island, since of all the heroes he is most like ourselves once we have removed our false beards, ear-trumpets and magnifying spectacles and show ourselves more naked than we care to be. . . . The elements have been so mixed in him that the recreative activities of latter-day actors will hardly be able to change him. For all the foreseeable future he will walk down the brightly lit roads of the mind, swinging his cane and dexterously picking up cigarette butts, flaunting his absurdly human dignity in the face of the world's importunity, a pirate nailing his flag to the mast, but instead of crossed bones and a skull the flag shows a pair of battered boots and a polished derby, those signs of human dignity and waywardness.[16]

Many other capable performers contributed to the growth of the movies and to the development of film acting. Often these players—like Chaplin, Hart, Pickford, and Fairbanks—served an apprenticeship in the legitimate theatre before turning to the screen. But as the movie industry grew, many new performers were trained and developed within the film studios themselves and became stars without any experience on the legitimate stage.

ACTING IN TALKING PICTURES

The introduction of the talkies in 1927 caused a major revolution in the film industry. Production became vastly more complicated and expensive; acting now demanded voice as well as looks and pantomime. For a while, the new dimension of sound arrested the development of cinema technique, and movies again resembled photographed stage plays—just as they had done in their earliest infancy. Instead of communication through rhythm, pantomime, and significant movement of the body, communication now depended on the spoken word. In place of a roving camera which achieved its effects through free and fluid movement, there was substituted a static machine which recorded set conversations. Much of this conversation was affected and unnatural. Movie actors, anxious to maintain their jobs, flocked to teachers of elocution and often acquired an "elegant" delivery which was stilted and unconvincing. It took time for actors to realize that if they had reasonably pleasant and flexible voices they need only to follow the usual patterns of conversation and to use the natural tones of normal speech to produce acceptable delivery. Projection of volume and exaggeration of articulation—so necessary for effectiveness in large legitimate theatres—were wholly unnecessary before a microphone which magnified every tone and every syllable. Directors also needed time and experience to realize that the techniques they had learned in silent films were still valid—and that a good movie still depended on visual excitement. Sounds and spoken words, they discovered, were merely additional means of reinforcing the dramatic impact of the pictures, and were to be used as counterpoint is used in music—to repeat and vary, to expand and emphasize the thought and emotion of the scenario.

Many actors and directors of the silent screen made the transition to sound with notable success. Directors like Lewis Milestone and Cecil B. DeMille, who were veterans of the old order, became skillful users of film-with-sound. Players like Greta Garbo and Zazu Pitts startled their fans when they opened their mouths but proved to be equally capable—and sometimes more effective—as talking stars than as silent performers. Some popular players failed to make the adjustment because their voices were squeaky or monotonous or incompatible with the image they had created in the silent films. The

romantic hero, John Gilbert, is a notable casualty of the era of sound. Yet, after much stress and strain and after several false starts, Hollywood mastered the use of sound and learned that the basic differences between film acting and stage acting—which had long been accepted in silent pictures—were unchanged. The camera was still free and mobile, unconfined to an area enclosed by a proscenium arch. The film actor was still subject to the relentlessly intimate scrutiny of this camera, which recorded every nuance and enlarged every expression, discouraging exaggeration or artificiality and encouraging a subtle simplicity and realism to match the natural world which surounded the actor. In addition, the film actor still performed without a live audience; he was subject only to the imperious dictates of the camera and the director and was asked to perform a role not as a unified whole but, as in silent films, in bits and pieces which made emotional sense only when the tiny individual scenes were properly pieced together. The necessity to speak did not alter the player's working conditions. Speech was an additional tool which, when properly used, enhanced the art of cinema without destroying its unique character.

Many players utilized the new opportunities of talking pictures to achieve performances of genuine artistry. The noted teacher of legitimate stars and artistic director of the Actors' Studio in New York, Lee Strasberg, declares that "with the rise of sound movies, the role of the individual actor increased. Greta Garbo, Emil Jannings, Harry Baur, Bette Davis, Paul Muni, Luise Rainer, Spencer Tracy, Sylvia Sidney, Humphrey Bogart, Katharine Hepburn, Sir Lawrence Olivier, Marlon Brando and others created authentic acting performances which could have held their own on the stage."[17]

In the new era of sound, actors began to move freely from stage to screen and back again. Players who mastered one set of techniques found they could ajust to the other set without great difficulty because the traditional skills and endowments of the actor were required in both. The legitimate stage once more became a training ground for movie performers and provided Hollywood with many experienced actors. In turn, the movie producers began regularly to send their players back to the living stage for refreshment and stimulus. The roster of performers who list or have listed themselves truthfully as stars of both stage and screen is a long one and includes such notable names as Lionel, Ethel, and John Barrymore, Helen Hayes, Frederic March, Tallulah Bankhead, Shirley Booth, Marlon Brando, Ruth

Chatterton, Lillian and Dorothy Gish, Katharine Hepburn, Ed Wynn, and many others.

ACTING IN RADIO AND TELEVISION

For a time, radio—another mechanical marvel of the twentieth century—developed a unique but limited technique of performance which was different from either the legitimate stage or the motion picture. The silent film was visual entertainment and communicated thought and emotion through sight alone. Radio relies wholly upon sound and requires a type of performance based exclusively on the power and expressiveness of the human voice. In a radio play, no movement, gesture, or physical expression can be seen. They exist only in the mind of the listener. They are created by him imaginatively from the sounds he hears. The radio gives him many clues and suggestions: doors are slammed, papers rattled, shots fired, and lips smacked—but the human voice is the principal medium of communication. In the early 1920's, the marvelous flexibility and infinite variability of the human voice were recognized and cultivated once more. Actors discovered anew that emotion could be stirred, attitudes and states of mind could be revealed by nuances of tone and variation in vocal quality. Comedians returned to the verbal gags which had been a mainstay of vaudeville but had died with the movies. Performers who excelled in vocal expressiveness, either comic or serious, became stars of radio and commanded a popularity as great as the following of the film idols. To be sure, radio never duplicated the pageantry, the spectacle, or the visual excitement of the films—but it had an inherent advantage which the movies never offered. It was free and it was mobile. A broadcast could be listened to—without charge—in one's home or one's car, in public or in private, on land or at sea. The sales slogan of those who manufactured receiving sets soon changed from "A Radio in Every Home" to "A Radio in Every Room," and presently the ubiquitous device was found in every automobile and almost every purse and pocket.

But the heyday of radio acting was brief. As soon as television invaded the living room, radio acting all but disappeared. The national radio network programs which had commanded an audience of millions were transferred to television. Soap operas, comic serials, and adaptations of standard plays deserted radio, and the hundreds of per-

formers who had learned to act with voice alone while remaining stationary before a microphone now had to adjust to the techniques of television, that is to say, to the techniques of the talking picture. The radio performers who remain today and who are employed by the hundreds of local radio stations, which appeared after the demise of the national networks, can hardly be called actors. They are disc jockeys, sports-casters, news-casters, and hucksters, and their style of performing is that of the public speaker or the circus barker.

Television itself has had no significant effect on style or technique in acting because T.V. acting is the same as motion picture acting. Almost all the dramatic programs shown on television are filmed in a studio under exactly the same conditions as any other movie. The few live dramatic shows offer little variation in style or technique, and the daily re-runs of old motion pictures are exactly that: re-runs of old motion pictures. The stars of stage and screen appear frequently on television but they use the same style they have developed for use in talking pictures.

The popular theatre of the nineteenth century—vaudeville, minstrelsy, burlesque, circus, and Tom shows—offered a rich variety of entertainment; it also developed a lively, joyous, direct, performer-to-audience kind of acting which is still seen in revues and night clubs. The popular theatre of the twentieth century—movies, radio, and television—is less varied than its predecessor but it, too, particularly in silent motion pictures, developed a unique style of communication which reached a fine art in the performances of actors like Douglas Fairbanks and Charles Chaplin. The best performers in present day television and cinema still retain many of the skills of the early days, combining them with the subtle vocal skills demanded by the talkies. The popular theatre of this century reaches an enormously larger audience than any form of theatre in previous centuries and, faulty though television, radio, and cinema may be much of the time, they promise to remain the major forms of theatre for many years to come.

ACTING IN THE LIVING THEATRE BETWEEN TWO WORLD WARS

During the years of the prosperous twenties and the depressed thirties, and despite the overpowering competition of the movies and radio,

American players of the living stage continued to contribute memorable performances.

John Barrymore carried on the traditions of the classic school of acting by playing the roles of Hamlet and Richard III early in his career. His older brother, Lionel, and his sister, Ethel, also performed a variety of serious and romantic parts before they, like John, migrated to Hollywood and became identified with a single type of role. Margaret Anglin, who also performed in the traditions of the classic school, began her career in Bronson Howard's famous melodrama, *Shenandoah;* but she eventually became America's outstanding exponent of the great roles of Greek tragedy—Medea, Antigone, and Electra—which she played with sweep and power and respect for the beauties of Greek verse. Nance O'Neil also is remembered for the controlled emotional intensity she brought to classic roles like Lady Macbeth and to modern parts like Hedda Gabler and Mrs. Phelps in *The Silver Cord.* Alice Brady, another gifted actress of the 1930's, is known to younger theatre fans only as the scatter-brained, garrulous, middle-aged comedienne of many movies whereas, in truth, she was a versatile performer who played both comedy and tragedy effectively and who contributed a superb portrait of the Electra-like Lavinia in Eugene O'Neill's original production of *Mourning Becomes Electra.* Pauline Lord, a contemporary of Miss Brady, contributed several memorable dramatic portraits, foremost among which were her roles in *Anna Christie, They Knew What They Wanted,* and *Ethan Frome.* Equally notable was Laurette Taylor, whose long career stretched from the sensationally successful *Peg O' My Heart* in 1912 to the much lauded portrait of Amanda Wingfield in the 1945 production of *The Glass Menagerie.* Jane Cowl, like Laurette Taylor, began her career by playing the sweet, romantic roles of *Smilin' Through* and *Lilac Time,* but she also succeeded in the classic roles of Juliet, Rosalind, and Cleopatra. Less versatile was the colorful Jeanne Eagels, who is described as being "explosive, mercurial, neurotic, loyal, generous and sweet" [18] and who utilized all these qualities to make a fascinating portrait of her single great role, that of Sadie Thompson in *Rain.* Among the comediennes, Grace George is remembered for the dainty, mirthful charm mixed with wistfulness which she brought to such comedies as *The New York Idea* and *Divorçons,* and Mary Boland is remembered for the saucy, romantic roles of her early career as well as for the robust, garrulous comedy of her later years. These players,

and many others, maintained the high standards of American acting in the period between the First and Second World Wars, and prompted Lee Strasberg to write, "After World War I, American actors created outstanding performances that could by all right be called great. . . ." [19]

CONTEMPORARY ACTING

In the American theatre of the 1960's, what is the state of acting on the living stage and who are the notable players of the present day? The diminshed activity of the professional theatre of our time is, inevitably, reflected in the dimished number of eminent performers and in the quality of their performances. There are fewer notable players in America and there are fewer notable performances on our stages. The legitimate theatre, television, and cinema offer some opportunity for gifted actors to appear in challenging roles, but not enough to alter the general impression of decreased quantity and diminished quality. The contributions of the new festival companies, of the civic centers of performing arts, and of the university theatres are too recent to evaluate properly. It is hoped that they represent a new renaissance in the living theatre, but the number of new performers which may be developed, the new styles of acting which may emerge, and the quality of both remain a promise and a hope.

The established corps of contemporary actors represent many of the styles which have flourished in the past history of American acting. The heroic school of Edwin Forrest reappears in the acting of some of the muscular heroes of western drama and in some of the costume epics seen on stage and screen. The personality school has many successful exponents, particularly among actresses. Such eminent and greatly admired performers as Lynn Fontanne, Katharine Hepburn, and Tallulah Bankhead belong in this group because, with rare exceptions, they substitute their own unique individualities for the dramatic character they are playing or they portray those characters which exactly suit their own individualities. Their manner of performing is related to the style of earlier actresses like Maude Adams, Ada Rehan, and Viola Allen, although the contemporary group differs from their predecessors by basing their appeal on more varied attractions than womanly loveliness and feminine virtue. The personality school is also well represented in the cinema and television where practically all

roles are cast strictly to fit the personality of the individual player.

Three contemporary actresses who in many respects can claim kinship to the classic school are Judith Anderson, Helen Hayes, and Katharine Cornell. These eminent women have performed roles of high seriousness in a variety of plays both modern and classic. Miss Anderson is noted for her powerful performances in Greek tragedy, Helen Hayes for such parts as Mary of Scotland, Queen Victoria, and Harriet Beecher Stowe, while Katharine Cornell will be remembered for her portrayal of Shaw's St. Joan, Shakespeare's Juliet, and Besier's Elizabeth Barrett of Wimpole Street. No contemporary actress seems to have the range or the power of Charlotte Cushman or Helen Modjeska, but Anderson, Hayes, and Cornell have given to their careers an integrity, a devotion, and a standard which resemble the ideals of the classic school.

It is difficult to find male performers today who have fulfilled the ideals of the classic school. The only versatile tragedians who perform in the contemporary American theatre are English by birth, by training, and, generally, by citizenship. Sir Lawrence Olivier, Sir John Gielgud, Sir Ralph Richardson, as well as Maurice Evans, Michael Redgrave, and Richard Burton all belong to the British tradition. Christopher Plummer is Canadian born and trained. They are all versatile, gifted players, worthy of the standards established by Edwin Booth and E. L. Davenport but, alas, they are not American. Three successful native actors, Alfred Lunt, Orson Welles, and Frederic March, who might be considered exponents of the classic style have rarely or never attempted the great roles of classic tragedy. Orson Welles has acted a few Shakespearean parts successfully, including Macbeth and Othello, but he is largely identified with so-called character roles in which, more often than not, he plays Orson Welles. Alfred Lunt has specialized in comedy during much of his career, including the role of Shakespeare's Petruchio. Even when he could have named his own parts, his serious roles have not been Hamlet or Lear or Macbeth but less challenging parts in modern plays such as Sherwood's *There Shall Be No Night* and Duerrenmatt's *The Visit*. Frederic March, perhaps the most versatile of the three, has portrayed a wide variety of characters with skill and conviction but his ability has never been tested in the greatest roles of the classic school. Other gifted American performers, like Morris Carnovsky and Jason Robards, Jr., have largely devoted themselves to roles in contemporary plays although with the

establishment of the Shakespearean festivals in Stratford, Connecticut, and Stratford, Ontario, they have met the challenge of a limited number of Shakespearean characters. Carnovsky gained fame as a member of the Group Theatre in the 1930's. Since then he has successfully played such parts as Shylock and Claudius. Jason Robards, Jr., vividly remembered for his acting in O'Neill's *The Iceman Cometh, Long Day's Journey into Night,* and *Hughie,* has also appeared in Shakespearean roles with the Stratford, Ontario, company and in 1959 he starred in *Macbeth.* It is true, of course, that the plays of the classic repertory are rarely given today in the American commercial theatre (although they are frequently done in England) so that American players have little opportunity to test themselves in the great roles. Whatever the reasons, few contemporary American actors have measured up to the high standards set by the best American tragedians of the 19th century.

One school of the past which has few adherents among contemporary players is the school of emotionalism. The lack of representation is not due so much to a dearth of talent as to a change in playwriting and public taste. No Queen of Spasms has appeared to carry on the tradition of Clara Morris because contemporary plays do not include this type of emotionalistic display, and the public will not tolerate them except when they are deliberately burlesqued. Modern ideals of acting which emphasize truthfulness, restraint, and balance have almost completely eliminated the tears and hysteria of the old "hydrostatic" order.

The style of acting most frequently seen and acclaimed on the contemporary American stage is the school of psychological naturalism, or the Stanislavsky method of acting. The two are identical in aim and similiar in the means of achieving the aim. The school of psychological naturalism, whose chief exponent and teacher was Minnie Maddern Fiske, emphasized psychological truthfulness in the portrayal of a role, concentration on inner feeling with repressed overt responses, cultivation of a simple true-to-contemporary-life manner of moving and speaking (which often led to careless delivery), and fidelity to the over-all design of the play. The close relationship of these ideals to the Stanislavsky method is illustrated by the statements of Lee Strasberg, leading teacher of "Method" acting in the United States. He writes that when an actor takes the stage "His appearance . . . is not the beginning, but is a continuation of the given circumstances that

have previously taken place." Moreover, the actor must "create the impression of being private in public" and must train his senses "so that he is able to see, hear, touch, taste, smell, and relate to the many objects which compose his imaginary situation." He must also "delve beneath the lines to find the meaning or sub-text of a play . . . to find the 'kernel' or core of a part. . . ." [20] Thus, the Method actor, as did Mrs. Fiske, seeks the basic motivation of a character and concentrates on inner truthfulness. He, like Mrs. Fiske, is not interested in surface response or external display but, rather, in re-creating the soul of a dramatic character and letting the imaginary character direct his movements and expressions. The Method actor feels perfectly at home following Mrs. Fiske's practice, cited in Chapter IX, of re-creating a character as he or she must have been before the action of the play begins and then acting out imaginary scenes from this pre-play existence.

The Actors Studio of New York, under the artistic direction of Lee Strasberg, and the Neighborhood Playhouse School of the Theatre, directed for many years by Sanford Meisner, have been two of the nation's leading centers for the teaching of Method acting. In addition, ideals similar to those of Stanislavsky and closely related to those of Mrs. Fiske are taught by the American Academy of Dramatic Arts, the oldest professional school of acting in the United States. The late Aristide D'Angelo, for many years the authority on acting at the Academy, said that the ideal of the school "has always been to work from within: to build the idea, the concept, the truth of the character and scene—and let the form of expression follow naturally." Mr. D'Angelo also stated that the "Academy ideal and Stanislavsky's ideal are much the same, but Stanislavsky formalized the method of responding while the Academy has not." [21]

The latter statement names the principal difference between the Stanislavsky school of acting and Mrs. Fiske's school or the Academy style. Stanislavsky organized his principles and evolved a detailed method of teaching them. He wrote several treatises on acting to expound his theories and techniques. He developed exercises and methods for achieving the aims he sought. His exercises and methods changed with the years, and sometimes a later practice seems contradictory to an earlier one, but his aim was always the same, namely, to find a "grammar of acting" or, as Strasberg describes it, "to achieve that level of inspiration, or of living on the stage, which great actors

had found accidentally and sporadically. . . . Stanislavsky tried to find means to stimulate and develop the actor's essential requirements: his concentration, his belief, and his imagination. He did not seek to fabricate inspiration, but to create the proper foundation for its appearance." [22]

It is Stanislavsky's clarification and formalization of the means of liberating an actor's creativity which have made his method so sought-after and which have caused many contemporary actors and theatre-goers to forget that similar ideals were held by many great performers in the past and are particularly close both to the aim and the method of Mrs. Fiske's school of psychological naturalism.

Most of the notable young actors in modern America have been trained in the Stanislavsky method or in the style of psychological naturalism or in some related school, and they all represent similar aims and ideals. Their achievements in many cases have been outstanding. Actresses like Kim Stanley, Julie Harris, Uta Hagen, Shirley Booth, and Maureen Stapleton have contributed moving, authentic portraits of the troubled heroines of contemporary drama. Eli Wallach and Marlon Brando have achieved equal success in male roles. It is too early to evaluate their total contribution, and it is too early to chart their further development. Performers of the past have always been judged, eventually, by their success in the great comic or tragic roles of Shakespeare, Sophocles, Schiller, Goethe, Molière, Sheridan, and others. The younger players of today have little opportunity to test their ability in these roles and without the perspective of time it is hard to judge whether parts in contemporary plays offer a comparable challenge.

It is probable that the younger players in the United States are as gifted as any generation of actors in the past. It is also probable that there exists a great reservoir of talent which will be developed only if the living theatre prospers and offers increased opportunities to the coming generation of players and playwrights. Certainly the fabulous history of American acting, which began so many years ago, is not about to end. The ranks of notable players stretching back to Mary Ann Duff and Edwin Forrest will be filled with talented new actors, perhaps inspired and trained in civic or university theatres, and they will add new styles, new insights, and new achievements to the colorful and continuing pageant of American acting.

NOTES

GENERAL INTRODUCTION

1 Lewis C. Strang, *Players and Plays of the Last Quarter Century,* Vol. I (Boston, 1903), p. 156.

2 Katherine Goodale, *Behind the Scenes with Edwin Booth* (Boston & New York, 1931), p. 232.

3 See Lawrence Barrett, *Charlotte Cushman—A Lecture* (New York: The Dunlap Society, 1889), p. 14.

4 William Winter, *The Life and Art of Edwin Booth* (New York and London, 1893), p. 223.

5 Henry Austin Clapp, *Reminiscences of a Dramatic Critic* (Boston & New York, 1902), p. 215.

6 Lily B. Campbell, "The Rise of a Theory of Stage Presentation in England During the Eighteenth Century," *PMLA,* XXXII (1917), p. 164. [I am indebted to Miss Campbell's excellent article for much of my material on English styles of acting in the eighteenth century.]

7 Ibid., p. 165.

8 Ibid., p. 188.

9 Margaret G. Mayorga, *A Short History of the American Drama* (New York, 1934), p. 54.

I. THE HEROIC SCHOOL

1 Lawrence Barrett, *Edwin Forrest* (Boston, 1881), p. 4.

2 James E. Murdoch, *The Stage* (Philadelphia, 1880), p. 281.

3 James Rees, *The Life of Edwin Forrest* (Philadelphia, 1874), p. 55.

4 Barrett, op. cit., p. 46.

5 W. R. Alger, *Life of Edwin Forrest,* Vol. I (Philadelphia, 1877), p. 142.

6 Quoted in several biographies, among them Montrose Moses, *The Fabulous Forrest* (Boston, 1929), p. 74.

7 Richard Moody, *Edwin Forrest* (New York, 1960), p. 399.

8 Alger, op. cit., Vol. I, p. 178.

9 Moody, op. cit., p. 68.

10 Rees, op. cit., p. 226.

11 Gabriel Harrison, *Edwin Forrest, The Actor and the Man* (Brooklyn, 1889), p. 37.

12 Ibid., p. 37.

13 Alger, op. cit., Vol. I, p. 477.

14 Ibid., p. 477.

15 Rees, op. cit., p. 200.

16 Alger, op. cit., Vol. II, p. 649.

17 Barrett, op. cit., p. 125.

18 Moody, op. cit., p. 396.

19 Moses, op. cit., p. 326.

20 Murdoch, op. cit., p. 295.

21 Harrison, op. cit., p. 133.

22 Quoted in Moses, op. cit., pp. 338–339.

23 Moody, op. cit., p. 405.

24 Barrett, op. cit., p. 156.

25 Alger, op. cit., p. 643.

26 Susie C. Clark, *John McCullough* (Boston, 1905), pp. 31–32. See also William Winter, *Other Days* (New York, 1908), p. 212.

27 See Leander Richardson, "John McCullough—of the Palmy Days," *Vanity Fair* (March, 1916).

28 Joseph I. C. Clarke, *My Life and Memories* (New York, 1925), p. 266.

29 Clark, op. cit., p. 33.

30 Clarke, op. cit., p. 266.

31 Winter, *Other Days,* p. 214.

32 *The San Francisco Chronicle,* August 27, 1877.

33 Clarke, op. cit., p. 267.

34 See Percy MacKaye, *Epoch, The Life of Steele MacKaye,* Vol. I (New York, 1927), pp. 270–271.

35 Alfred Ayres, "America's Greater Players No. 4—Murdoch, McCullough and Rush," *The Theatre* (March, 1902), p. 22.

36 When praised for being "second only to Booth," McCullough said with great sincerity, "I will always gladly be second to Edwin." See Winter, op. cit., pp. 205–206.

37 Ibid., p. 204.

38 Ibid., p. 224.

39 Ibid., p. 224.

40 William Winter, *The Wallet of Time,* Vol. I (New York, 1913), pp. 264–268.

41 Ibid., p. 264.

42 Quoted in Clark, op. cit., p. 89.

43 From an unidentified newspaper clipping in the Players Collection, New York Public Library.

44 Walter M. Leman, *Memories of an Old Actor* (San Francisco, 1886), p. 37.

45 Alfred Ayres, *Acting and Actors—Elocution and Elocutionists* (New York, 1899), p. 235.

46 Winter, *Other Days,* p. 44.

47 Robert L. Sherman, *Actors and Authors* (Chicago, 1951), p. 179.

48 Francis C. Wemyss, *Twenty-Six Years of the Life of an Actor and Manager* (New York, 1847), p. 191.

49 Barrett, op. cit., p. 46.

50 Alger, op. cit., p. 643.

II. THE CLASSIC SCHOOL: THE LADIES

1 Lewis C. Strang, *Players and Plays of the Last Quarter Century,* Vol. I (Boston, 1903), p. 129.

2 Joseph N. Ireland, *Mrs. Duff* (Boston, 1882), p. 146.

3 Ibid., pp. 1–2.

4 Ibid., p. 21.

5 William W. Clapp, Jr., *A Record of the Boston Stage* (Boston, 1853), p. 116.

6 John Smith Kendall, "The American Siddons," *The Louisiana Historical Quarterly,* XXVIII (July, 1945), 925.

7 Ibid., p. 55.

8 Horace Greeley, *Recollections of a Busy Life* (New York, 1868), p. 203.

9 Noah M. Ludlow, *Dramatic Life as I Found It* (St. Louis, 1880), pp. 463–464.

10 New York *Mirror,* May 5, 1827, quoted in Joseph N. Ireland, *Records of the New York Stage from 1750 to 1860,* I (New York, 1866), 419.

11 See Ireland, op. cit., p. 42.

12 Strang, op. cit., p. 194.

13 Boston *Herald,* June 18, 1889.

14 Edward Robins, *Twelve Great Actresses* (New York, 1900), p. 359.

15 Lawrence Barrett, *Charlotte Cushman—A Lecture* (New York, 1889), p. 17.

16 See Appendix to Barrett, *Charlotte Cushman,* pp. 37–44.

17 *Spirit of the Times,* New York, November 14, 1874.

18 George Vandenhoff, *Dramatic Reminiscences; or, Actors and Actresses in England and America* (London, 1860), p. 184. The masculine strain in Miss Cushman's nature was sometimes the subject of ridicule by the press. In a jocular mood, *The Spirit of the Times* for August 6, 1870, said: "She discovered the circulation of the blood by squeezing a young man's hand a good many years ago. His name was Harvey—hence the erroneous idea that Harvey made the discovery. Chemically considered, Miss Cushman is a success. She possesses ferruginous properties, which made her an exceedingly difficult woman to borrow money from."

19 *Spirit of the Times,* New York, October 31, 1874.

20 William Winter, *Other Days* (New York, 1908), pp. 152–153.

21 Strang, op. cit., p. 98.

22 Brander Matthews and Laurence Hutton, *Actors and Actresses of Great Britain and the United States—Macready and Forrest and Their Contemporaries* (New York, 1886), pp. 146–147.

23 Alfred Ayres, "America's Greater Players No. 2—Charlotte Cushman," *The Theatre,* II (January, 1902), 19.

24 *The Theatre* (April, 1905).

25 Henry P. Goddard, "Some Actresses I Have Known," *The Theatre Magazine,* VI (August, 1906), 206.

26 See letter in the handwriting of Charlotte Cushman addressed to Mr. J. B. Wright, Esq., and dated from New York, September 30, 1851, in the Robinson Locke collection of dramatic scrapbooks, Volume 139, New York Public Library.

27 Letter reproduced in the Chicago *Record* for January 10, 1909.

28 *Spirit of the Times,* New York, November 14, 1874.

29 James E. Murdoch, *The Stage* (Philadelphia, 1880), p. 240.

30 Winter, op. cit., pp. 158–159.

31 *Spirit of the Times,* New York, November 16, 1860.

32 S. R. Elliott, "A Group of Notable Women No. 2—Glimpses of Charlotte Cushman," *The Delineator,* LIX (February, 1902), 274.

33 Letter reprinted in the *Spirit of the Times,* New York, July 4, 1846.

34 Ibid., pp. 91–92.

35 John B. Clapp and Edwin F. Edgett, *Players of the Present,* Vol. II (New York, 1900), p. 172.

36 Philip Hale, "Mme. Janauschek," in McKay and Wingate, *Famous American Actors of Today,* Vol. I (New York, 1896), p. 22.

37 Walter Prichard Eaton, "Helena Modjeska," *Dictionary of American Biography,* Vol. XIII (New York, 1934), p. 73.

38 William Winter, *The Wallet of Time,* Vol. I (New York, 1913), p. 367.

39 See Helena Modjeska, *Memories and Impressions* (New York, 1910), p. 109.

40 John R. Towse, *Sixty Years of the Theater* (New York, 1916), p. 210.

41 Ibid., p. 211.

42 Hale, op. cit., p. 22.

43 Ibid., p. 211.

44 Otis Skinner, *Footlights and Spotlights* (Indianapolis, 1924), p. 62.

45 Towse, op. cit., p. 212.

46 Skinner, op. cit., p. 63.

47 Ibid., p. 125.

48 Ibid.

49 Modjeska, op. cit., p. 500.

50 Winter, op. cit., p. 360. Winter also notes another aspect of her style worth recording. He says, "Her movements, always graceful, were sometimes electric in their rapidity and long sinuous reach." Ibid., p. 370.

51 John Creahan, *The Life of Laura Keene* (Philadelphia, 1897), p. 122.

52 Eaton, op. cit., p. 73.

53 Skinner, op. cit., pp. 199–200.

54 Lewis C. Strang, *Famous Actresses of the Day in America* (Boston, 1899), p. 309.

55 Ibid., p. 320.

56 Skinner, op. cit., p. 221.

57 Modjeska, op. cit., pp. 129–130.

58 Winter, op. cit., p. 367.

59 Mary Anderson, *A Few Memories* (New York, 1895), pp. 44–45.

60 *The Spirit of the Times,* New York, November 17, 1877.

61 Anderson, op. cit., p. 197.

62 William Winter, *Stage Life of Mary Anderson* (New York, 1886), pp. 29–30.

63 Anderson, op. cit., pp. 85, 97.

64 Towse, op. cit., pp. 216–217.

65 Anderson, op. cit., p. 119.

66 Towse, op. cit., p. 217.

67 Miss Anderson's only reappearances on the stage were for five charity performances given in England during the First World War.

68 Towse, op. cit., p. 215. Henry Austin Clapp, noted as a judicious critic, makes the following comparison between Mary Anderson and Charlotte Cushman: "Miss Anderson, perhaps the most celebrated of our home-born actresses, bore about the same relation to Charlotte Cushman as a march of Sousa to a symphony of Beethoven." See Clapp, *Reminiscences of a Dramatic Critic* (Boston, 1902), p. 83. On the other hand, William Winter, in 1892, reversed his earlier judgment of Miss Anderson and argued that her art was the kind which needed special insight, and when this insight was applied her acting revealed all the elements of greatness. See William Winter, *Shadows of the Stage* (New York, 1892), pp. 97–102.

III. THE CLASSIC SCHOOL: THE GENTLEMEN

1 Lewis C. Strang, *Players and Plays of the Last Quarter Century,* Vol. I (Boston, 1903), p. 129.

2 Katherine Goodale, *Behind the Scenes with Edwin Booth* (Boston, 1931), pp. 59–60.

3 William R. Alger, *Life of Edwin Forrest,* Vol. I (Philadelphia, 1877), p. 142.

4 Stanley Kimmel, *The Mad Booths of Maryland* (Indianapolis, 1940), p. 312.

5 Edwina Booth Grossmann, *Edwin Booth* (New York, 1894), p. 35.

6 Ibid., p. 277.

7 William Winter, *The Life and Art of Edwin Booth* (New York, 1893), p. 3.

8 Ibid., p. 224.

9 John R. Towse, *Sixty Years of the Theater* (New York, 1916), p. 181.

10 Quoted in Strang, op. cit., p. 179. The critics as a whole agreed that Booth excelled in voice and delivery. One dissenting observer was Alfred Ayres who declared that Booth's reading "was exceedingly faulty. Never, probably, has there been another actor, with a great reputation, that misplaced his emphasis as often as did Edwin Booth." (Alfred Ayres in *The Theatre,* New York, Feb. 12, 1902, p. 19.) Ayres ranked Edwin Forrest as the greatest American player and Charlotte Cushman as the second greatest.

11 Kimmel, op cit., p. 309.

12 Strang, op. cit., p. 156.

13 Winter, op. cit., p. 223.

14 Ibid., p. 129.

15 Goodale, *Behind the Scenes with Edwin Booth,* p. 75.

16 Asia Booth Clarke, *The Elder and the Younger Booth* (Boston, 1882), p. 160.

17 Henry Austin Clapp, *Reminiscences of a Dramatic Critic* (Boston and New York, 1902), pp. 134–135.

18 Ibid., p. 135.

19 Grossman, op. cit., p. 263.

20 Ibid., p. 268.

21 Towse, op. cit., p. 190.

22 Goodale, op. cit., p. 84.

23 Walt Whitman was not a Booth enthusiast. He said that Booth "never made me forget everything else and follow him, as the greatest fellows, when they let themselves go, always do." See Gamaliel Bradford, *As God Made Them* (Boston, 1929), p. 178. In this opinion, Whitman differed from the vast majority of the critics. In the final years of Booth's life, he was criticized with increasing frequency for carelessness and coldness. Otis Skinner says that the years "had dug devitalizing claws into his strength, his spirit, and his ambition." See Otis Skinner, *Footlights and Spotlights* (Indianapolis, 1924), p. 171.

24 Winter, op. cit., p. 111.

25 Although Booth played these parts with success for many years, comedy was not his forte. Clapp notes: "Like his father, and all his father's other sons, he had small gift in mirth. It was therefore of interest to note that his Petruchio, Benedict, and Don Caesar de Bazan were almost sufficient, by virtue of his vivacity, fire, and mental alertness, and, in the case of the last two characters, by the elegance and distinction of his manners and speech." See Clapp, op. cit., p. 138.

26 Strang, op. cit., p. 156.

27 William Winter, *Edwin Booth in Twelve Dramatic Characters* (Boston, 1872), p. 50.

28 Skinner, op. cit., p. 171.

29 Ibid., p. 172.

30 Towse, op. cit., p. 194.

31 From J. Bunting's biographical sketch of Murdoch, found in the introduction to James E. Murdoch's *The Stage* (Philadelphia, 1880), p. 17.

32 *Analytic Elocution* (New York, 1884); *A Plea for Spoken Language* (New York, 1883); *The Stage* (Philadelphia, 1880).

33 Murdoch, *The Stage,* p. 27.

34 *Ibid.,* p. 37.

35 Ibid., p. 32.

36 Ibid., p. 252.

37 Ibid., pp. 30–31.

38 Ibid., p. 42.

39 Ibid., p. 74.

40 Ibid., p. 114.

41 At its worst it was mechanical and pedantic. In his zeal for faultless de-

livery, Murdoch was often guilty of being overly precise and refined. Alfred Ayres in *The Theatre* magazine for March, 1902, says: "With the adherents of the Murdoch school voice and tone are not everything, but they come so close to being everything that they destroy any tendency there might otherwise be to be natural."

42 Ayres, in the magazine article quoted in the preceding note.

43 *Spirit of the Times,* New York, Oct. 25, 1845. Quoted in Odell, *Annals of the New York Stage,* Vol. V, p. 169.

44 Skinner, op. cit., p. 121.

45 Thomas C. Trueblood, a student of Murdoch's and one of the pioneer teachers of speech in the Middle West, has written of Murdoch: "He was the greatest reader of his time and had incomparably the finest voice I ever listened to. It was of wide range, powerful, a clear ringing baritone. He was not only a great reader, but an inspiring teacher, for he taught from the scientific standpoint and led one to find the way." See "A Chapter on the Organization of College Courses in Public Speaking," *The Quarterly Journal of Speech Education,* February, 1926, Vol. XII, pp. 2–3.

46 Murdoch, *A Plea for Spoken Language,* p. 77.

47 Murdoch, *Analytic Elocution,* p. 357.

48 Ibid., p. 360.

49 Murdoch, *A Plea for Spoken Language,* pp. 73–74.

50 Ibid., p. 84.

51 Ibid., p. 83.

52 Edwin F. Edgett, *Edward Loomis Davenport* (New York, 1901), p. 105.

53 Strang, op. cit., pp. 129–30.

54 Anna Cora Mowatt, *Autobiography of an Actress* (Boston, 1854), pp. 253–54.

55 Unidentified newspaper clipping in Vol. 146 of the Robinson Locke collection, New York Public Library.

56 Henry Edwards in Matthews and Hutton, *Actors and Actresses of Great Britain and the United States,* Vol. IV (New York, 1886), pp. 128–29.

57 H. D. Stone in Matthews and Hutton, op. cit., p. 136.

58 Clara Morris, *Life on the Stage* (New York, 1901), p. 185.

59 Mrs. John Drew, *Autobiographical Sketch* (London, 1900), p. 113.

60 Morris, op. cit., p. 185.

61 Strang, op. cit., p. 144.

62 Skinner, op. cit., p. 110.

63 Ibid.

64 Ibid., p. 109.

65 See *Le Chat Noir* for July 26, 1889.

66 Alfred Ayres, "America's Greater Players, No. 5," *The Theatre,* April 1902.

67 Ibid.

68 See the correspondence between Booth and Barrett in Otis Skinner's *The Last Tragedian* (New York, 1939), pp. 158–181.

69 Ayres, op. cit.

70 Skinner, *Footlights and Spotlights,* p. 111.

71 Strang, op. cit., p. 153.

72 Barrett resented Booth's superiority. In the bitter letter written to Booth on January 1, 1873, which caused a seven year break in the friendship of the two men, Barrett wrote: "When you offer me your own inferiors as my equals I reply that if *you* really stand at the head of my profession then *you* only are my compeer—I own no rivals save such as *you* allow, and when Time, the great connector of all things gives his judgment, I may not after all be so very far behind your illustrious self, whom I care now as little to see or hear from as I was once anxious and delighted." See Skinner, *The Last Tragedian,* pp. 180–181.

73 Clara Morris, op. cit., p. 221.

74 William M. Laffan in Matthews and Hutton, *Actors and Actresses of Great Britain and the United States,* Vol. V (New York, 1886), p. 42.

75 Mrs. John E. Owens, *Memories of John E. Owens* (Baltimore, 1892), p. 73.

76 William Winter, *Vagrant Memories* (New York, 1915), p. 139.

77 Clara Morris, *Life on the Stage* (New York, 1902), p. 195.

78 Joseph Jefferson, *Autobiography* (London, 1889), p. 323.

79 Winter, op. cit., pp. 142–43.

80 Melbourne MacDowell as quoted by Lewis C. Strang, *Famous Actors of the Day in America,* First Series (Boston, 1900), p. 244.

81 William Winter, *The Life of David Belasco* (New York, 1918), Vol. I, p. 274.

82 Edgar S. Werner, ed., *The Delsarte System of Oratory* (New York, 1893), p. 127.

83 Percy MacKaye, *Epoch, The Life of Steele MacKay,* Vol. I (New York, 1927), p. 271.

84 *Annual Catalogue,* The American Academy of Dramatic Arts, 1939–40, p. 9.

NOTES ON THE SETTING

1 William Winter, *The Wallet of Time,* Vol. I (New York, 1913), p. 23.

IV. THE SCHOOL OF EMOTIONALISM

1 George Henry Lewes, *On Actors and the Art of Acting* (New York, 1878), p. 91.

2 Laurence Hutton, *Curiosities of the American Stage* (New York, 1891), p. 67.

3 From *The Broadway Journal,* July 19, 1845, reproduced in *The Complete Works of Edgar Allen Poe,* Virginia Edition, XII (New York, 1902), p. 187.

4 Ibid., p. 188.

5 Ibid., p. 191.

6 Quoted in Anna Cora Mowatt, *Autobiography of an Actress* (Boston, 1854), p. 300.

7 Ibid., p. 221.

8 Joseph Jefferson, *Autobiography* (New York, 1889), pp. 138–139.

9 Mowatt, op. cit., p. 241.

10 Ibid., p. 242.

11 Ibid., p. 244.

12 Hutton, op. cit., pp. 64–65.

13 Arthur Hobson Quinn, *History of the American Drama from the Beginning to the Civil War,* 2nd ed. (New York, 1943), p. 319.

14 G. C. D. Odell, *Some Theatrical Stock Companies of New York* (An essay issued by The Brander Matthews Dramatic Museum, Columbia University, to accompany its exhibition, "Two Centuries of the New York Theatre," March–October, 1951), p. 9.

15 Catherine M. Reignolds-Winslow, *Yesterday with Actors* (Boston, 1887), p. 67.

16 See John Creahan, *Life of Laura Keene* (Philadelphia, 1897), p. 138.

17 Jefferson, op. cit., p. 206.

18 Odell, op. cit., p. 13.

19 William Winter, *Vagrant Memories* (New York, 1915), p. 56.

20 Jefferson, op. cit., p. 206.

21 Creahan, op. cit., p. 101.

22 Winter, op. cit., p. 57.

23 Ibid., p. 59.

24 According to her daughter. See Creahan, op. cit., p. 15.

25 Helen Ormsbee, *Backstage with Actors* (New York, 1938), p. 150.

26 Reignolds-Winslow, op. cit., p. 110.

27 William Winter, New York *Tribune,* March 12, 1877.

28 Clara Morris, *Life on the Stage* (New York, 1901), pp. 141 and 317.

29 Ibid., p. 257.

30 Ibid., pp. 316–317.

31 According to an anecdote, Sarah Bernhardt once attended a performance of Miss Morris in *Camille.* For a long time the French actress was uninterested, but at a certain point in the play she sat up and exclaimed, "Mon dieu! that woman is not acting, she is suffering." From an unidentified clipping in the Robinson Locke collection of dramatic scrapbooks, Volume 351, New York Public Library.

32 New York *World,* September 25, 1885.

33 Morris, op. cit., p. 69.

34 From an unidentified review in the Robinson Locke collection of dramatic scrapbooks, Volume 351, New York Public Library, concerning the premier of Octave Feuillet's *The Sphinx,* done at the Union Square Theatre, September 21, 1874. This same scene was described in less complimentary fashion by the critic of the New York *Mail* who wrote, on September 22, 1874, as follows: ". . . the last convulsions of death are simulated on the stage. Miss Morris chews soap, turns the whites of her eyes up and the corners of her mouth down, smears white powder and red paint over her cheeks and chin, angles her wrists and stiffens her back. Such is the pleasing spectacle presented to a horrified audience as the final tableau of this moral drama. . . ."

35 Morris, op. cit., p. 340.

36 Brander Matthews and Laurence Hutton, *Actors and Actresses of Great Britain and the United States—The Present Time* (New York, 1886), p. 224.

37 Lewis Strang, *Players and Plays of the Last Quarter Century,* Vol. II (Boston, 1903), p. 237.

38 Vivia Ogden, "Childish Recollections of Clara Morris," *The Theatre,* Vol. II (June, 1902), p. 17.

39 *Spirit of the Times,* New York, November 6, 1880.

40 Ibid., November 25, 1876.

41 Ibid., April 7, 1888.

42 Alan Dale, "Why the Ex-Tragedienne Should Be Muzzled," New York *American,* April 27, 1902.

43 John R. Towse, *Sixty Years of the Theater* (New York, 1916), pp. 150–151.

44 See Morris, op. cit., p. 285.

45 Mary Caroline Crawford, *Romance of the American Theatre* (Boston, 1925), p. 339.

46 William Winter, *Vagrant Memories* (New York, 1915), p. 229.

47 Towse, op. cit., pp. 125–126.

48 Ibid., p. 129.

49 Ibid., p. 130.

50 Ibid., p. 133.

51 Brander Matthews, *These Many Years* (New York, 1917), p. 349.

52 Montrose Moses, *Famous Actor Families in America* (New York, 1906), p. 253.

53 Quoted in an obituary notice appearing in *Newsweek,* Vol. X (November 22, 1937), p. 6.

54 See Franklin E. Fyles, "Mrs. Leslie Carter—A Study," *Leslie's Magazine,* Vol. LIII (April, 1902), p. 658.

55 Lewis Strang, *Famous Actresses of the Day in America,* Second Series (Boston, 1902), p. 201.

56 Fyles, op. cit., p. 658.

57 William Winter, *The Wallet of Time,* Vol. II (New York, 1913), p. 327.

58 Ibid., p. 332.

59 Heywood Broun, "On the New York Stage," *Collier's,* Vol. LXVIII (November 26, 1921), p. 24.

V. THE PERSONALITY SCHOOL

1 Noah M. Ludlow, *Dramatic Life as I Found It* (St. Louis, 1880), p. 375.

2 Brander Matthews and Laurence Hutton, *Actors and Actresses of Great Britain and the United States—Kean and Booth; and Their Contemporaries* (New York, 1886), p. 262.

3 Laurence Hutton, *Curiosities of the American Stage* (New York, 1891), p. 237.

4 Matthews and Hutton, op. cit., p. 263.

5 James E. Murdoch, *The Stage* (Philadelphia, 1880), p. 235.

6 Matthews and Hutton, op. cit., p. 272.

7 Oral S. Coad and Edwin Mims, *The American Stage* (New Haven, 1929), p. 191.

8 Luther L. Holden, "Maggie Mitchell" in McKay and Wingate's *Famous American Actors of Today*, Vol. II (New York, 1896), pp. 319–320.

9 David Gray, "Maude Adams A Public Influence," *Hampton's Magazine*, Vol. XXVI (June, 1911), p. 725.

10 Lewis Strang, *Famous Actresses of the Day* (Boston, 1902), Second Series, p. 55.

11 New York *Tribune*, May 9, 1899.

12 Gray, op. cit., p. 737.

13 Arthur Symons, *Great Acting in English* (London, 1907), p. 13.

14 William Winter, *Vagrant Memories* (New York, 1915), p. 469.

15 Symons, op. cit., p. 7. Symons also declared that Marlowe and Sothern alone in the English speaking world were giving great performances of Shakespeare's plays.

16 Winter, op. cit., p. 473.

17 Gray, op. cit., pp. 725–726.

18 Miss Rehan's family name was Crehan, but on the occasion of her debut at the Arch Street Theatre she was erroneously billed as Rehan, a name which Mrs. Drew persuaded her to keep because her debut had been so successful.

19 William Winter, *Ada Rehan* (New York, 1891–1898), p. 36.

20 Ibid., p. 45.

21 Ibid., p. 102.

22 Ibid., p. 133.

23 Ibid., p. 153.

24 Walter Prichard Eaton, "Ada Rehan," *Dictionary of American Biography*, Vol. XV (New York, 1935), p. 472.

25 Otis Skinner, *Footlights and Spotlights* (Indianapolis, 1924), p. 138.

26 George Bernard Shaw, *Dramatic Opinions and Essays*, Vol. I (New York, 1906), p. 174.

27 John R. Towse, *Sixty Years of the Theater* (New York, 1916), pp. 356–357.

28 Shaw, op. cit., pp. 173–174.

29 Bernard Shaw, *To a Young Actress* (New York, 1960), p. 16.

30 Winter, *Ada Rehan*, p. 141.

31 Otis Skinner, op. cit., p. 270.

VI. THE COMIC STAGE

1 New York *Mirror*, June 20, 1829, quoted in Brander Matthews and Laurence Hutton, *Actors and Actresses of Great Britain and the United States— Kean and Booth; and Their Contemporaries* (New York, 1886), p. 153.

2 G. C. D. Odell, *Some Theatrical Stock Companies of New York* (An essay issued by The Brander Matthews Dramatic Museum, Columbia University,

to accompany its exhibition, "Two Centuries of the New York Theatre," March–October, 1951), p. 8.

3 Henry Dickinson Stone, *Personal Recollections of the Drama or Theatrical Reminiscences* (Albany, New York, 1873), p. 13.

4 Laurence Hutton, *Plays and Players* (New York, 1875), p. 236.

5 Joseph Jefferson, *Autobiography* (New York, 1889), pp. 100–101.

6 Odell, op. cit., p. 6.

7 John R. Towse, *Sixty Years of the Theater* (New York, 1916), pp. 99–100.

8 William Winter, *The Wallet of Time,* I (New York, 1913), p. 158.

9 Brander Matthews, *These Many Years* (New York, 1917), p. 349.

10 Winter, op. cit., p. 157.

11 Catherine M. Reignolds-Winslow, *Yesterday with Actors* (Boston, 1887), pp. 127–128.

12 Mary Shaw, "The Boston Museum and Daly's Theatre," *The Saturday Evening Post* (May 20, 1911).

13 Henry Clay Barnabee, *Reminiscences* (Boston, 1913), pp. 178–179.

14 Lewis Strang, *Players and Plays of the Last Quarter Century,* I (Boston, 1903), 281.

15 Jefferson, op. cit., p. 403.

16 Strang, op. cit., p. 267.

17 William Winter, *Other Days* (New York, 1908), p. 44.

18 Noah M. Ludlow, *Dramatic Life as I Found It* (St. Louis, 1880), p. 427.

19 Francis C. Wemyss, *Twenty-Six Years of the Life of an Actor and Manager* (New York, 1847), p. 271.

20 Towse, op. cit., p. 124.

21 Winter, *Other Days,* p. 125.

22 Ibid., p. 129.

23 Arthur H. Quinn, *A History of the American Drama from the Beginning to the Civil War, Second Edition* (New York, 1951), p. 384.

24 Winter, *Other Days,* p. 145.

25 Vance Thompson, "Dion Boucicault," in McKay and Wingate's *Famous American Actors of Today* (New York, 1896), p. 84.

26 Towse, op. cit., p. 229.

27 Henry Austin Clapp, *Reminiscences of a Dramatic Critic* (Boston and New York), p. 64.

28 Strang, op. cit., p. 269.

29 Jefferson, op. cit., p. 223.

30 Clara Morris, *Life on the Stage* (New York, 1901), p. 198.

31 Strang, op. cit., p. 268. For those who are interested in the story of Jefferson's career and in a discussion of his artistic principles and practices, his famous *Autobiography* is still absorbing reading.

32 Clapp, op. cit., pp. 64–65.

33 Lawrence Barrett, *Edwin Forrest* (Boston, 1881), p. 46.

34 Phineas T. Barnum, *Life of P. T. Barnum* (Buffalo, 1888), p. 37.

35 Townsend Walsh, *The Career of Dion Boucicault* (New York, 1915), pp. 50–51.

36 Foster R. Dulles, *America Learns to Play* (New York, 1940), p. 112.

37 Ibid., p. 119.

38 Carl Wittke, *Tambo and Bones* (Durham, North Carolina, 1930), p. 20.

39 Marjorie Barstow Greenbie, *American Saga* (New York, 1939), pp. 278–279.

40 Dulles, op. cit., p. 116.

41 Arthur Hobson Quinn, *A History of the American Drama from the Civil War to the Present Day* (New York, 1927), p. 84.

42 E. J. Kahn, Jr., *The Merry Partners, The Age and Stage of Harrigan and Hart* (New York, 1955), p. 14.

43 Ibid., p. 9.

44 Ibid., p. 10.

45 Ibid., p. 38.

46 Montrose J. Moses, *Representative American Dramas, National and Local* (Boston, 1926), p. 4.

47 Caroline Caffin, *Vaudeville* (New York, 1914), p. 10.

48 Ibid., p. 19.

49 Wittke, op. cit., pp. 159–160.

50 "The Talk of the Town," *The New Yorker,* Vol. XLI (April 17, 1965), p. 39.

51 Walter Prichard Eaton, *The Actor's Heritage* (Boston, 1924), p. 214.

52 Constance Rourke, *Troupers of the Gold Coast or the Rise of Lotta Crabtree* (New York, 1928), pp. 155–156.

53 John R. Towse, *Sixty Years of the Theater* (New York, 1916), p. 89.

54 Rourke, op. cit., p. 154.

55 Deshler Welch, "Lotta Crabtree," in McKay and Wingate's *Famous American Actors of Today* (New York, 1896), p. 326.

56 Helena Modjeska, *Memories and Impressions* (New York, 1910), pp. 374–375.

57 Otis Skinner, *Footlights and Spotlights* (Indianapolis, 1924), p. 65.

VII. COMEDIANS OF THE TRANSITION

1 William Winter, *The Life of David Belasco,* Vol. II (New York, 1918), p. 428.

2 Lewis Strang, *Famous Actors of the Day in America,* First Series (Boston, 1900), p. 59.

3 William Winter, *The Wallet of Time,* Vol. II (New York, 1913), p. 536.

4 Daniel Blum, *Great Stars of the American Stage* (New York, 1952), Profile 22.

5 Lewis Strang, *Famous Actresses of the Day in America* (Boston, 1899), p. 174.

6 Francis Wilson, *Life of Himself* (Boston, 1924), p. 370.

7 Lewis Strang, *Famous Actors of the Day in America,* Second Series (Boston, 1902), p. 77.

8 Strang, *Famous Actors,* First Series, pp. 297–98.

9 A. D. Storms, *The Players Blue Book* (Worcester, Mass.), p. 30.

10 Strang, *Famous Actors,* Second Series, p. 185.

VIII. HEIRS OF THE CLASSIC AND HEROIC SCHOOLS

1 Montrose J. Moses, "Belasco: Stage Realist," *The Independent* (May 29, 1916), p. 336.

2 David Belasco, *The Theatre Through Its Stage Door* (New York, 1919), p. 229.

3 Ibid., p. 61.

4 David Belasco, "What I Am Trying to Do," *The World's Work* (July, 1912), p. 299.

5 John R. Towse, *Sixty Years of the Theater* (New York, 1916), p. 318.

6 Walter Prichard Eaton in *Dictionary of American Biography,* Vol. 12, p. 260.

7 Towse, op. cit., p. 319.

8 Ibid.

9 William Winter, *The Life and Art of Richard Mansfield,* Vol. II (New York, 1910), p. 145.

10 Towse, op. cit., p. 339.

11 Towse's phrases. See his *Sixty Years of the Theater,* p. 333.

12 Eaton, op. cit., pp. 260–261.

13 Towse, op. cit., p. 334.

14 Winter, op. cit., p. 251.

15 Lewis C. Strang, *Famous Actors of the Day in America,* Second Series (Boston, 1902), p. 12.

16 Walter Prichard Eaton in *Dictionary of American Biography,* Vol. 17, p. 402.

17 William Winter, *Vagrant Memories* (New York, 1915), pp. 433–434.

18 Arthur Symons, *Great Acting in English* (London, 1907), p. 6.

19 Ibid., p. 6.

20 Ibid., p. 8.

21 Winter, *Vagrant Memories,* p. 438.

22 Ibid., pp. 445–446.

23 Otis Skinner, *Footlights and Spotlights* (Indianapolis, 1924), p. 42.

24 Lewis C. Strang, *Famous Actors of the Day in America,* First Series (Boston, 1900), p. 276.

25 Skinner, op. cit., p. 80.

26 Amy Leslie, *Some Players* (New York, 1906), p. 26.

27 Strang, *Famous Actors,* First Series, p. 261.

28 Eaton, op. cit., p. 402.

29 Otis Skinner, "Kindling the Divine Spark," *Theatre Arts Monthly* (Sept., 1938), p. 670.

30 Strang, *Famous Actors,* First Series, p. 260.

31 John Mason Brown, *Upstage* (New York, 1930), pp. 100–102.

32 Skinner, *Footlights and Spotlights,* pp. 353–354.

33 Strang, *Famous Actors,* First Series, p. 95.

34 Daniel Blum, *Great Stars of the American Stage* (New York, 1952), Profile 8.

35 Strang, *Famous Actors,* First Series, pp. 110–111.

36 Strang, *Famous Actors,* Second Series, pp. 64–65.

37 Blum, op. cit., Profile 10.

38 Ibid.

39 William H. Gillette, *The Illusion of the First Time in Acting* (New York, 1915), p. 46.

40 Ibid., p. 43.

IX. MRS. MINNIE MADDERN FISKE

1 See clipping in the Robinson Locke collection of dramatic scrapbooks, Volume 202, New York Public Library.

2 Lewis Strang, *Players and Plays of the Last Quarter Century,* Vol. II (Boston, 1903), pp. 297–298.

3 New York *News,* March 23, 1896.

4 Strang, op. cit., p. 300.

5 Alexander Woollcott, *Mrs. Fiske, Her Views on Actors, Acting and the Problems of Production* (New York, 1917), p. 79.

6 Beatrice Sturges, "Mrs. Fiske: Actress Manager," *Public Opinion,* XXXVIII (May 20, 1905), p. 777.

7 Woollcott, op. cit., p. 76.

8 From an unidentified clipping in the Robinson Locke collection of dramatic scrapbooks, Volume 203, New York Public Library.

9 Lewis Strang, *Famous Actresses of the Day in America* (Boston, 1899), p. 67.

10 Milwaukee *Sentinel,* October 7, 1906.

11 Woollcott, op. cit., p. 228.

12 Archie Binns, *Mrs. Fiske and the American Theatre* (New York, 1955), p. 204.

13 George Arliss, *Up the Years from Bloomsbury* (New York, 1927), p. 215.

14 Pittsburg *Gazette,* November 17, 1903.

15 New York *Mirror,* June 4, 1898.

16 Woollcott, op. cit., p. 82.

17 Ibid., pp. 84–85.

18 Ibid., p. 95.

19 From an unidentified clipping in the Robinson Locke collection of dramatic scrapbooks, Volume 203, New York Public Library.

20 Arliss, op. cit., p. 215.

21 From an interview reported in the Brooklyn *Eagle* for August 13, 1899.

22 Binns, op. cit., p. 139.

23 Minnie Maddern Fiske, "Ethics of the Drama," an address delivered to the Harvard Ethical Society, printed in the Boston *Transcript,* December 13, 1905.

24 John R. Towse, *Sixty Years of the Theater* (New York, 1916), p. 413.

25 Walter Prichard Eaton, "Mrs. Fiske and Her Influence on the American Stage," *Century Magazine,* LXXXI (April, 1911), p. 867.

26 Woollcott, op. cit., p. 160.

27 Fiske, "Ethics of the Drama," Boston *Transcript,* December 13, 1905.

28 Arliss, op. cit., p. 215.

29 Amy Leslie in the New York *Mirror,* November 17, 1906.

30 Toledo *Blade,* November 2, 1898.

31 Sturges, op. cit., p. 778.

32 Binns, op. cit., p. 175.

33 Woollcott, op. cit., p. 117.

34 Fiske, "Ethics of the Drama," Boston *Transcript,* December 13, 1905.

35 Binns, op. cit., p. 251.

NOTES ON A NEW SETTING

1 Sheldon Cheney, *The Theatre* (Tudor Edition, New York, 1949), p. 428.

2 Daniel Frohman, "Do Motion Pictures Mean the Death of the Drama," *The Theatre,* Vol. XXII (December, 1915), p. 310.

3 Henry Hewes, "The American Theatre '64, Its Problems and Promise," *The Saturday Review,* Vol. XLVII (February 22, 1964), p. 29.

4 "Regional Theatre," *Life,* Vol. 56 (February 28, 1964), p. 9.

X. THE ACTOR IN THE NEW THEATRE

1 Mortimer J. Adler, *Art and Prudence* (New York and Toronto, 1937), p. 485.

2 Iris Barry, *Let's Go To The Movies* (New York, 1936), p. 17.

3 Elinor Hughes, *Famous Stars of Filmdom (Women)* (Boston, 1931), p. 270.

4 Ibid., p. 273.

5 Alistair Cooke, *Douglas Fairbanks—The Making of a Screen Character* (The Museum of Modern Art, New York, 1940), p. 13.

6 Arthur Knight, "Douglas Fairbanks," *Dictionary of American Biography,* Vol. XXII (New York, 1958), p. 172.

7 Cooke, op. cit., p. 31.

8 Ibid., pp. 29–30.

9 Knight, op. cit., p. 173.

10 Cooke, op. cit., pp. 24–25.

11 Charles Chaplin, *My Autobiography* (New York, 1964), p. 199.

12 Inez and Helen Klumph, *Screen Acting* (New York, 1922), p. 103.

13 Chaplin, op. cit., p. 21.

14 Ibid., p. 144.

15 Robert Payne, *The Great Charlie* (London, 1952), p. 33.

16 Ibid., p. 278.

17 Lee Strasberg, "Acting," *The Encyclopaedia Britannica,* Vol. I (Chicago, 1960), p. 132.

18 Daniel Blum, *Great Stars of the American Stage* (New York, 1952), Profile 80.

19 Strasberg, op. cit., p. 132.

20 Ibid., p. 131.

21 Statements from a private conversation held with Mr. D'Angelo at the Academy in New York in September, 1939.

22 Strasberg, op. cit., p. 131.

INDEX

acting, Belasco's five factors for, 205; classic, 41-103, 281; comic, 155-85, 191-99; contemporary, 280-84; emotionalistic, 110-39; English, 9-10; heroic, 19-40, 219-23; modern, 224-37, 280-84; in movies, 259-74; of the new theatre, 259-84; 19th-century, 3-4, 105-9; personality as basis for, 140-54, 189; post-Revolutionary, 16-18; psychological naturalism in, 224-37; in radio and television, 277-78; schools of, 2-3; stage vs. screen, 259-64; style in, 6-13; transitional at turn of the century, 187-90, 200-22; 20th-century, 239-58, 280-84

Actors Equity Association, 197

Actors' Studio, 11, 283

Adams, Edwin, 63, 96-97

Adams, Franklin P., quoted, 232n

Adams, Maude, 7, 140, 145-50

Addams, Augustus A., 20, 37-39

Adler, Mortimer, quoted, 262

Adler, Stella, 253

Albee, Edward, 255

Alger, W. R., quoted, 21, 23, 27, 29, 39

Allen, Viola, 140, 145-50, 221

American Academy of Dramatic Arts, 99, 100, 103, 283

Ames, Winthrop, 242

Anderson, Judith, 281

Anderson, Mary, 7, 63-70, 216

Anglin, Margaret, 279

Antoine, André, 240

Appia, Adolphe, 108, 206, 241

Arena Stage, 256

Arliss, George, quoted, 231, 234, 235

Armat, Thomas, 245

L'Article 47, 126-29

Atkins, Zoe, 243

Ayres, Alfred, quoted, 34, 38, 50, 51, 83, 92, 93, 232

Badeau, Adam, quoted, 51

Baker, George Pierce, 242, 257

Bangs, Frank C., 88

Bankhead, Tallulah, 276, 280

Barnabee, H. S., quoted, 162

Barnett, Morris, 156

Barnum, Phineas T., 107, 171-72; 177

Barrett, Lawrence, career and personality, 90-95; mentioned, 33, 71, 88, 109, 145, 216, 270; quoted, 20, 21, 29, 38, 51, 171, 263

Barrie, James M., 146

Barron, Charles, 98

Barry, Iris, quoted, 264

Barry, Philip, 242

Barrymore, Ethel, 276, 279

Barrymore, John, 276, 279

Barrymore, Lionel, 276, 279

Barton, Mr., 48

Bateman, H. L., 96

Bates, Blanche, 205

Behrman, S. N., 242

Bel Geddes, Norman, 241

Belasco, David, career and personality, 200-6; and Mrs. Carter, 136-38; influence on American acting of, 205-6; and Mary Pickford, 264-65; mentioned, 2, 108, 184; as a playwright, 112, 202-3; quoted, 136; stagecraft of, 188, 203-4, 241; as a teacher, 11

Benny, Jack, 155

Bernhardt, Sarah, 152, 259

Birth of a Nation, The, 249, 261

Bisson, Alexander, 197

blackface. *See* minstrel shows

Blake, William Rufus, 160, 163

Bogart, Humphrey, 276

Baker, George Henry, 107

Boland, Mary, 279

Boleslavsky, Richard, 253

Booth, Edwin, career and personality, 71-79, 140; Forrest's comment on,

Kahn, E. J. Jr., quoted, 178
Kaye, Danny, 155-56
Kazan, Elia, 253
Kean, Charles, 201
Kean, Edmund, American tours of, 10; influence on Forrest, 21-22, 42; and Mary Duff, 45, 47
Keene, Laura, 109, 118-22
Kemble, Fanny, 45
Kemble, John Philip, 10
Keystone Film Company, 271-72
kinetoscope, 244-45
Kingsley, Sidney, 253
Kirby, J. Hudson, 37-39
Knight, Arthur, quoted, 267, 268
Knowles, Sheridan, 11; quoted, 55
Kopit, Arthur, 255
Kotzebue, August, 11, 16, 112

Lady of Lyons, The, 113
Laemmle, Carl, 248
Laffan, William B., quoted, 95
Langer, Lawrence, 243
Last Tragedian, The, 216
Lawson, John Howard, 185
Leavitt, M. B., 176
lectures, public craze for, 173
Leslie, Amy, quoted, 217
Lewes, George Henry, quoted, 111
Lewis, James, 168
lighting, Belasco's pioneering in, 203-4; revolution in, 241; at turn of the century, 188
Lincoln, Abraham, 118
Liston (comedian), 159
Little Theatre movement, 242
Littmann, Max, 241
Loew, Marcus, 248
Logan, Olive, 172
"Lotta" (Charlotte Crabtree), 142, 182-84
Ludlow, Noah M., quoted, 46, 142, 163
Lunt, Alfred, 281
Lutz, John, 120

Macauley, Barney, 64-65
MacDowell, Melbourne, 39-40
Macgowan, Kenneth, 242
MacKaye, James Morrison Steele, 33, 99-103, 242
MacKaye, Percy, 242
Macklin, Charles, 9

Macready, William Charles, 48-49, 88
Maeder, James G., 48, 143
Maguire, Thomas, quoted, 33
Mansfield, Richard, 206-13, 218
Marble, Dan, 168
March, Frederic, 276, 281
Marlowe, Julia, 140, 145-50, 189, 214
Mason, John B., 221
Matthews, Brander, quoted, 134, 161
Maurel, Victor, 233
McConnell, Frederic, 243
McCullough, John E., career and personality, 30-37; as Delsarte disciple, 103; encouraged Mary Anderson, 64-65; mentioned, 109, 150, 216
McIntyre, James, 184
McNally, John J., 196
Meisner, Sanford, 283
Mencken, Adah Isaacs, 176, 184
Mercury Theatre, 252
Metamora, 23-24
Method acting, 283-84
Meyerhold, V. E., 227
Mielziner, Jo, 241
Milestone, Lewis, 275
Millay, Edna St. Vincent, 243
Mills, Steve, quoted, 181
Mims, Edwin, quoted, 144
minstrel shows, 172-76, 179-82, 184
Miss Multon, 126-28, 130-31
Mitchell, Maggie, 144
Modern Times, 273
Modjeska, Helena, 57-63, 109, 216-17, 270; quoted, 183
Moeller, Philip, 243
Montez, Lola, 182
Moody, Richard, quoted, 29
Mordaunt, Frank, 120
Morrell, T. H., quoted, 25
Morris, Clara, career and personality, 124-32; Mrs. Fiske compared with, 224, 229, 233; mentioned, 109, 211; quoted, 89, 90, 94, 170
Morton, J. Madison, 157
Moscow Art Theatre, 135, 227, 240, 253
Moses, Montrose, quoted, 27, 135, 178, 203
motion pictures, acting in silent, 259-74; acting in talking, 275-77; origin and development of, 244-50